LAW OF THE STUDENT PRESS
4TH EDITION

STUDENT PRESS LAW CENTER
ARLINGTON, VIRGINIA

Law of the Student Press
Written by Frank D. LoMonte, Adam Goldstein and Michael Hiestand
Fourth Edition, September 2013

Published in the United States of America by the Student Press Law Center.

Design by Norman Mallard and Elizabeth White
Cover photographs by, clockwise from left: SHFwire photo by Matt Wettengel, Sheila De Guzman (Louisiana State University's *Daily Reveille*), Brianna Paciorka (Louisiana State University's *Daily Reveille*), Becca Clemmons (University of Kentucky's *Kentucky Kernal*)

Printing by United Book Press, Inc., Baltimore, Md.

The first edition of this book was published in 1985 (with an addendum added in 1988) by the Student Press Law Center. The second edition was published in 1994, with several reprints in succeeding years. The third edition was published in 2008.

Additional copies of this book are available by contacting the Student Press Law Center at the address below:

Student Press Law Center
1101 Wilson Blvd., Suite 1100
Arlington, VA 22209-2275

(703) 807-1904
E-mail: splc@splc.org
On the Web: www.splc.org

Library of Congress Catalog Card Number: 2013952251

ISBN 978-0-9910167-0-9

Contents

CHAPTER 9
ONLINE STUDENT MEDIA 135

CHAPTER 10
BROADCAST STUDENT MEDIA 153

CHAPTER 11

CHAPTER 12

CHAPTER 13

Foreword

The title of this book, *Law of the Student Press*, keeps faith with a tradition dating back to 1984, when a slender volume not much bigger than a brochure first was published, but the title is increasingly an incomplete description. With the student media mirroring – and at times outdistancing – the professional media's move toward digital delivery, "press" is a stand-in for the gathering and sharing of information and ideas across all platforms. And with students providing remarkably sophisticated coverage of stories of national significance, the concept of "student" press soon may fade into anachronism as well. One thing that will never change, however, is the need for all journalists to inform themselves about their legal rights and responsibilities to confidently do their most courageous work. Providing that foundational legal knowledge – and helping journalists recognize when it's time to seek professional advice – is the objective of this book.

Law of the Student Press originated as the idea of two then-SPLC directors, Marc Abrams and Michael Simpson, who recognized the need for a centralized body of research collecting the cases and statutes that define the rights and responsibilities of high school and college journalists. The book was substantially expanded and reissued in 1994 and again in 2008, each time updated to capture a generational wave of change – in 1994, the aftermath of the Supreme Court's devastating 1988 ruling in *Hazelwood School District v. Kuhlmeier*, which so greatly altered the landscape for student publishing, and in 2008, the widespread migration of publishing to the Internet. Reflecting the rapid pace of change – when the third edition was published in 2008, the word "Twitter" did not appear in it – this 2013 edition greatly increases the emphasis on non-print methods of delivering content. It incorporates dozens of new rulings and enactments addressing the authority of government regulators to reach into students' off-campus social media lives, recognizing that the line between "media" and "social media" is blurring almost to the point of nonexistence. And it includes greatly expanded information for student broadcasters about frequent topics of uncertainty, including the use of licensed music online and over the air.

The Student Press Law Center is an advocate for the rights of the student media to publish free from censorship, and this book unmistakably reflects that advocacy position. It is intended in no small part to instruct students and educators in both the legal and the tactical considerations that apply when (as so often occurs) they are confronted with an order to refrain from broadcasting or publishing legitimate editorial content. The scholarship behind the legal research, however, is untainted by the Center's policy agenda. Where the law disfavors student rights, we prominently acknowledge it, without shading. Indeed, we believe it is vital that the public understand where the law's protection of speech is deficient, because pressure for reform will come only through understanding.

A compilation of this breadth requires many contributors. Longtime SPLC attorneys Mike Hiestand and Mark Goodman are primarily responsible for building this body of research, and their passion for meaningful student journalism as a force for good animates every page. SPLC Attorney Advocate Adam Goldstein lent countless hours to the research, writing and editing of this update. SPLC Publications Fellow Sara Gregory had primary responsibility for the layout and design of this edition, as well as contributing a sharp proofreading eye.

One of the most gratifying aspects of working in the field of student speech rights is the extraordinary eagerness of people to donate their time and talent for little or no reward, other than the knowledge that they have helped young people learn. SPLC volunteers, interns and staff members have given generously of their time and talent over the last two decades to assembling the research that resulted in this publication. We give our warmest thanks to these contributors: Elizabeth White, Brian Schraum, Michael Beder, Dori Goldstein, Jeanette Jones, Robert Kiel, Monica Dias, Joseph Tomain, Kathleen Kirby, Dineen Pashoukos Wasylik, Matt Gibson, Marla Hackett, Laura Merritt, Sarah Baxter, Susan Burgess, Ryan Dietrich, Mark Fiore, Jon Goldberg, Sean Kane, Norman Mallard, Alison Warden, Malissa Wilson, Rick Peltz, Karen Graziano, Meghan Gourley, Signe Brunstad, Tracy Sisser, Sunjha Hattin, Nia McDonald, Laura

Petelle, Sara Rose, Sam Wilder and Jennifer Kiel, and to the law firms of Frost Brown Todd LLC and Wiley Rein LLP.

As a nonprofit organization, the SPLC relies on the generosity of philanthropic benefactors to make it possible to offer free legal services and training to students and teachers who cannot afford to pay. We are indebted to our perennial contributors whose loyalty keeps the SPLC vibrant as a center of legal research and scholarship in support of the student media:

Ethics & Excellence in Journalism Foundation
McCormick Foundation
Yellow Chair Foundation
Journalism Education Association
American Society of News Editors
College Media Association
National Scholastic Press Association /Associated Collegiate Press

The law of the student press can be confusing and at times intimidating, but it is our hope that you come away from this book neither confused nor intimidated, but empowered. It is, in fact, exceedingly uncommon for student journalists to encounter serious legal difficulty because of what they have reported. To the contrary, the law more often will function as the friend of the student journalist – opening the door to information that would otherwise be off-limits, and protecting legitimate expression against censorship or retaliation. Knowing the law will put a journalist (whether student or full-time professional) in the best position to protect her rights and to recognize risks and opportunities.

Finally, we dedicate this edition of *Law of the Student Press* to the memory of Richard Goehler of Frost Brown Todd LLC, one of the SPLC's most trusted attorney volunteers and a longtime member of our Board of Directors, who died March 20, 2011. Dick Goehler's optimistic spirit enlivened the work of the SPLC, and his memory is a daily inspiration and reminder of our duty to (in his favored phrase) "play like a champion" each day in service to the betterment of young lives.

Frank D. LoMonte
Executive Director
Student Press Law Center
September 2013

About the Student Press Law Center

In 1973, the Robert F. Kennedy Memorial created a national "Commission of Inquiry into High School Journalism" to examine the problems student journalists were facing. After holding hearings around the country, conducting extensive research and tabulating a national survey, the Commission published its report in 1974 in a book called *Captive Voices*. Among the recommendations of the Commission was the following:

> "A national center advocating First Amendment guarantees for youth journalists should be established.... The center should circulate information on rights of free expression, receive and refer complaints to local advocates, and generally make every effort to encourage a consciousness and use of those rights among youth journalists."

As a result of that recommendation, the Kennedy Memorial and the Reporters Committee for Freedom of the Press launched the Student Press Law Center in December 1974. Since that time, the SPLC has become an independent, not-for-profit corporation that provides free legal information and assistance to high-school and college journalists and advisers around the nation.

The institutional vision of the SPLC is set forth in its 2010-2015 Strategic Plan, which provides: The Student Press Law Center will use the law to help students of all ages meaningfully participate in civic life and learn essential skills, ethics and values through the vehicle of journalism. The SPLC will: (1) Create greater awareness of, and protection for, the rights of students to gather and distribute news and commentary, (2) Provide training and opportunities for students to use their voices to influence public policy, (3) Educate the entire education community about the responsible use of technology to share ideas, and (4) Improve students' access to essential documents and meetings, and teach them to put the knowledge gained to productive use. Drawing on its expertise in the realms of law, journalism and education, the SPLC works as an advocate in four interlocking policy areas: freedom of expression, government transparency, civic engagement, and digital citizenship.

Many student journalists and their advisers know the SPLC through its educational media, including: the SPLC Report, a magazine published three times a year; its website (www.splc.org); its PowerPoint classroom presentations; its online First Amendment and student press law quizzes; the SPLC "Virtual Lawyer," which matches student journalists with the legal resources they need; its monthly podcast and LegalAlert newsletter, or its dozens of other topical print and online publications.

Many also know the SPLC as a source of legal guidance, a place to turn for answers to questions on subjects relating to censorship, libel, access to government records and meetings, copyright and other media-law topics. In recent years, approximately 2,500 student journalists or advisers have contacted the Center's media law attorneys annually by telephone or through the Center's website to obtain free legal assistance. Hundreds of others contact the Center each year for research help or to obtain the Center's public comment on issues affecting America's student media, which are regularly reported by local and national news media organizations. While censorship remains the fundamental concern of the Center, its mission includes teaching the creative and responsible use of legal tools in the pursuit of substantive journalism.

The SPLC also maintains a nationwide Attorney Referral Network of volunteer media-law attorneys to assist students in obtaining local pro bono legal representation when the need arises. Additionally, the SPLC legal staff speaks to thousands of student journalists and teachers each year at national and regional student media conventions, monitors litigation and legislative efforts across the country, and files friend-of-the-court briefs before state supreme courts, federal courts of appeals and the United States Supreme Court in important press-law cases. Although the SPLC's core concern is the welfare of student journalism, the Center can and does intercede in other student speech cases in which larger First Amendment protections are at stake — including, in recent years, cases testing the boundaries of government control over online speech.

The SPLC is run by an executive director and a corporate board of directors composed of media professionals, journalism educators, attorneys, civic and community leaders, and a youth representative. The Center's staff is assisted by two advisory councils, made up of prominent media attorneys and of journalism educators from high schools and colleges nationwide.

Student interns play an important role in the work of the Center. They serve as reporters and editors for the SPLC Report and website, and assist with the research that goes into the Center's educational publications. Interns serve for a full semester or summer, and are overseen by the Center's publication fellow or legal staff.

For more information about becoming a partner with the Student Press Law Center, visit us at:
www.splc.org/give

The Student Press Law Center offers various individual and organizational memberships, which help support the work of the SPLC. Members receive special publications and benefits that keep them up to date on the legal issues affecting the student media. However, membership is not required to utilize SPLC services, including obtaining free legal help.

For more information about becoming a partner with the Student Press Law Center, visit us at: www.splc.org/give

As with any not-for-profit organization, the Student Press Law Center is dependent on the contributions of individuals, which include many teachers and students, and organizations — such as the McCormick Foundation, Gannett Foundation, Journalism Education Association, College Media Advisers, Associated Collegiate Press, National Scholastic Press Association, American Society of News Editors, Ethics and Excellence in Journalism Foundation, Park Foundation and many others — that share the Center's goal of creating an appreciation among young people that they possess important free-press rights and encouraging a national climate of respect for the First Amendment freedoms of all Americans. All contributions, which are tax-deductible, make the Center's day-to-day efforts possible. In 2006, the SPLC successfully completed "Tomorrow's Voices," its first endowment campaign, aided by the generous assistance of the Knight Foundation.

If you have questions about the Student Press Law Center, or about your rights as a student journalist or publication adviser, you can contact the SPLC at:

Mailing address:
Student Press Law Center
1101 Wilson Blvd.
Suite 1100
Arlington, VA 22209

Telephone:
(703) 807-1904

Web site:
www.splc.org

The American Court System and Legal Citations

M ost anyone who has had a civics or American government course has seen, and perhaps been forced to memorize, the flow chart "how a bill becomes a law." While it is true that federal statutes are made by congressional enactment and presidential approval, and that state statutes result from legislative enactment and gubernatorial approval, that does not account for the entire body of "the law."

"Common law," or judge-made law, consists of legal principles that judges have set down over time in published rulings. Although not enacted by any legislative body, common law can be decisive in the outcome of a legal dispute; cases can be dismissed, property can change hands, and damages can be awarded based on common-law principles not found in any statute book. That is why the chapters that follow will focus heavily on examining judicial opinions.

The Federal Court System Hierarchy

U.S. Supreme Court
(1)

Court of Appeals
(13)

District Courts
(94)

The courts of this country are divided into two groups: state and federal. Generally, federal courts hear claims based on alleged violations of federal statutes or the United States Constitution. State courts hear cases involving state statutes or common (court-made) law or a state's constitution. For example, a First Amendment claim charging public school officials with censorship is typically brought in federal court because the First Amendment is part of the United States Constitution. A lawsuit accusing campus police officials of violating a state's open records law or claiming that a principal has violated a state's student free expression law will typically be brought in state court. It is possible for a federal court to hear a state law claim (and vice versa) but usually that happens only when state and federal law questions are both part of one case.

Federal and state courts are divided into trial courts, which hear the case initially, and one or more levels of appellate courts. While the specific names of state courts vary, all federal trial courts are called *district courts*. There are 94 federal districts in the country, at least one in each state. No district overlaps two states. Each federal district court has jurisdiction to hear cases within its geographic area. Someone who loses his case can appeal from a federal district court to a *circuit court of appeals*. There are thirteen of these around the country. All but one have jurisdiction over district courts within the geographic boundaries of their circuit.

THE FEDERAL CIRCUIT COURT SYSTEM

There are 11 numbered geographically divided circuits, one District of Columbia circuit and a federal circuit, which hears only specific types of cases and appeals from district courts in cases where the federal government is a defendant.

FIRST CIRCUIT: Maine, Massachusetts, New Hampshire, Puerto Rico, Rhode Island
SECOND CIRCUIT: Connecticut, New York, Vermont
THIRD CIRCUIT: Delaware, New Jersey, Pennsylvania, Virgin Islands
FOURTH CIRCUIT: Maryland, North Carolina, South Carolina, West Virginia, Virginia
FIFTH CIRCUIT: Louisiana, Mississippi, Texas
SIXTH CIRCUIT: Kentucky, Michigan, Ohio, Tennessee
SEVENTH CIRCUIT: Illinois, Indiana, Wisconsin
EIGHTH CIRCUIT: Arkansas, Iowa, Minnesota, Missouri, Nebraska, North Dakota, South Dakota
NINTH CIRCUIT: Alaska, Arizona, California, Guam, Hawaii, Idaho, Montana, Nevada, Northern Mariana Islands, Oregon, Washington
TENTH CIRCUIT: Colorado, Kansas, New Mexico, Oklahoma, Utah, Wyoming
ELEVENTH CIRCUIT: Alabama, Florida, Georgia

Parties to a lawsuit decided by a federal court of appeals can ask the United States Supreme Court to review their case. However, the Supreme Court typically can choose the cases it wants to consider. There is no appeal beyond the U.S. Supreme Court.

Decisions of a federal court of appeals must be followed by all of the district courts located within that circuit. District courts outside that circuit, however, are not bound by such decisions. Further, one district court does not have to follow the rulings of any other district court. A court is bound only by the decisions of higher courts that have direct jurisdiction over it. This is the concept of *precedent*. Because it is the highest court in the country, all courts must follow precedent established by the United States Supreme Court. When one court must follow the rulings of another court, it is called mandatory, or binding, precedent. Note, however, that state courts do not have to follow the rulings of federal courts on matters solely based on state law, and vice versa. For example, while the U.S. Supreme Court significantly reduced the amount of First Amendment protection available to most high school student journalists in its *Hazelwood* decision (see **Chapter 5**) — a ruling based only on federal law — a state court may, nevertheless, find that high school journalists in its state remain protected by state law.

Cases that are not mandatory precedent may nonetheless be persuasive to a court. For example, although the federal District Court for the Northern District of California (which is located in the Ninth Circuit) is not bound by a ruling from the First Circuit on a particular point of law, it may still find the logic in the decision persuasive and choose to adopt it. If that occurs, it is said that the court has *adopted* the precedent. When discussing student press law, it is important to remember that precedent that may be mandatory in one federal circuit or state may not be mandatory in another.

If a court refuses to follow precedent or misinterprets the law, its decision may be reversed by a higher court. A court has the option, rarely exercised, to reverse its own precedent, although usually such precedent is *distinguished*, meaning that the court decides that the facts in the present case are so different from the facts in the past case that the court need not reach the same conclusion. Courts can be very creative in finding differences between fact situations that will allow them to distinguish the case in front of them from what might seem, to everyone else, to be binding precedent.

A QUICK GUIDE TO LEGAL CITATIONS

Throughout this book, the text will provide citations to published opinions, which courts issue to explain the basis for their rulings. The legal system has established a uniform system of citing opinions, such as in an attorney's legal brief that relies on the reasoning of a prior court opinion. This uniform citation system allows anyone interested in locating the cited case to find it readily in reference books or using on-line legal research services.

These citations are not difficult to understand.

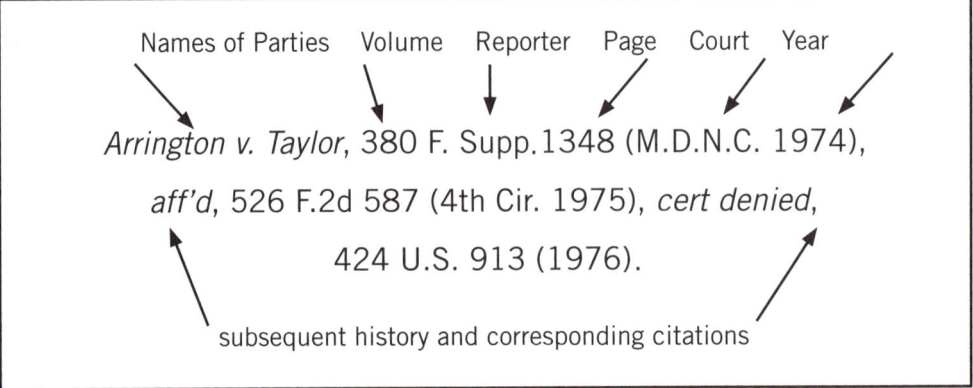

Names of Parties   Volume   Reporter   Page   Court   Year

Arrington v. Taylor, 380 F. Supp.1348 (M.D.N.C. 1974),

aff'd, 526 F.2d 587 (4th Cir. 1975), *cert denied*,

424 U.S. 913 (1976).

subsequent history and corresponding citations

In the case above, a University of North Carolina student named Robert Arrington sued University Chancellor Ferebee Taylor. The person who is suing is usually called the *plaintiff* and the person being sued the *defendant*. There can be more than one plaintiff and defendant, but usually only the last name of the first person in each party will be given in the citation. For trial court decisions, the first name listed is the plaintiff. But when cases are appealed, the names can reverse order depending on who asked the appellate court to hear the case. The person who brings the case to a higher court is known as the "appellant," and the opposing party is the "appellee."

The *Arrington* case was first reported in volume 380 of the Federal Supplement, beginning on page 1348. The Federal Supplement is a set of books that publish the decisions of federal district courts. The parenthetical indicates that the first court to hear the case was the district court for the Middle District of North Carolina ("M.D.N.C."). The judge in that court handed down his decision in 1974. In 1975, the U.S. Court of Appeals for the Fourth Circuit decided the case. Its decision can be found beginning on page 587 of volume 526 of the second series of a set of books called the Federal Reporter. Note that F. Supp. and F. Supp. 2d are the abbreviations for Federal Supplement and F., F.2d or F.3d are the citation forms for the Federal Reporter. There are currently two series of the Federal Supplement and three series of the Federal Reporter; *Arrington* was reported in the second series, thus the "2d" in the citation. This citation also tells you that the Fourth Circuit affirmed (agreed with) the decision of the Middle District of North Carolina. Had it decided differently, the citation would read *rev'd*, short for "reversed," or "*vacated*." The case was then taken to the Supreme Court, which refused to consider it. That is the meaning of *cert. denied* (certiorari denied). A petition for certiorari is a request for the Supreme Court to hear a case. Had the Court taken the case, the Supreme Court citation would have said either "*aff'd*," "*rev'd*," or "*vacated*" depending on the Court's decision. A decision by the U.S. Supreme Court takes the form [volume] U.S. [page number] (date). For example, *Hazelwood School District v. Kuhlmeier*, 484 U.S. 260 (1988). "U.S." stands for the set of books called the United States Reports. Supreme Court cases can also be found under citations reading "L. Ed." (Lawyers Edition U.S. Supreme Court Reports) or "S. Ct." (United States Supreme Court Reporter).

Occasionally you will find a citation to a statute. Federal laws are cited in much the same way as court decisions, and appear in the United States Code. For example, the federal Freedom of Information Act can be found at 5 U.S.C. Sec. 552 (volume 5 of the United States Code, section 552).

State court decisions can be found in a number of places. Many states publish their own case reporters, or contract out to have a reporter published for the state court system. The National Reporter System, however, is the easiest way to find most cases from state courts and is used for state cases in this book wherever possible. Example: *Metter v. Los Angeles Examiner*, 95 P.2d 670 (Cal. App. 1939). This case is found in the Pacific Reporter, Second Series, beginning on page 670 of volume 95. It is a 1939 case from the California Court of Appeals. National Reporter System citations include Pacific (P.), Atlantic (A.), Southern (So.), Southeastern (S.E.), Southwestern (S.W.), Northeastern (N.E.), and Northwestern (N.W.) reporters. Because the system was established before our current ideas of geography formed, these abbreviations may seem strange to you; Tennessee is in the Southwestern Reporter, for example, while Kansas is in the Pacific Reporter. A cite to "Med. L. Rptr." refers to the Media Law Reporter, published by a private publishing service, The Bureau of National Affairs, Inc. (BNA), Washington, D.C.

Court opinions or lawyer's briefs sometimes quote from scholarly legal publications such as university law journals (*e.g.*, the *Harvard Law Review*) or Restatements, which are authoritative compilations of common-law principles updated periodically by leading scholars. Citations to these publications are similar to court case citations. Citations to state statutes vary by the state, but are generally fairly easy to decipher.

While legal citations may look confusing, they tend to follow a standard pattern: [volume number] [source] [page number]

Plaintiff: The person who sues in a civil lawsuit
Defendant: The person being sued or defending against a legal proceeding
Appellant: the party (either the original plaintiff or defendant) who asks a court to hear an appeal. The other party to the appeal is the "appellee."

Where a citation is trying to point the reader to a specific sentence or passage in a court ruling, rather than the ruling as a whole, the decision will be "pinpoint" cited with an additional page number. For example, "436 So.2d 1300, 1303" means that the case begins on page 1300 of Southern 2d, volume 436, and that the specific portion being cited can be found on page 1303. If a citation is to the same case as the previous footnote, but with a different page number, the format 436 So.2d at 1304 or *Id.* at 1304 is used. When used alone, the abbreviation "*Id.*" means that the cite is identical to the one preceding it.

If you would like to read some of the cases and statutes cited in this book, check online at one of the many legal resource sites that are available, or visit a library that has legal materials (for example, a law school library, a large public library, or a local courthouse library) and ask the librarian for guidance.

Court decisions are either "reported" (published) or "unreported." Sometimes only reported decisions may be cited as a precedent before another court, depending on the jurisdiction.

CHAPTER 1

Introduction

Congress shall make no law respecting an establishment of religion, or prohibiting the free exercise thereof; or abridging the freedom of speech, or of the press; or the right of the people peaceably to assemble, and to petition the government for a redress of grievances.

— The First Amendment to the United States Constitution

The rights to speak, publish, worship, assemble and petition are fundamental to our democracy; without these foundational rights, the other privileges secured by the Constitution would become meaningless and unenforceable. But for many young Americans, the promise of the First Amendment has a hollow ring. At thousands of high schools and colleges from one coast to the other, the ability of students to speak and publish freely simply does not exist. Critical thinking that questions school policies is discouraged under threat of punishment.

Students who live under a regime of censorship are being taught that freedom of speech and government accountability are disposable values that must give way to "making the school look good." The lessons these students learn about the First Amendment — lessons they will carry with them into their adult lives — are that people with power get to control what is said about them, and that viewpoints should be suppressed by the government if they challenge prevailing beliefs. This is not only bad preparation for journalism; it is bad preparation for citizenship.

In the past three terms, the U.S. Supreme Court has told us — again and again — that the government may never punish people for the content of their speech. As interpreted by the Roberts Court, the Constitution protects even speech that is highly disturbing (videos of dogfights),[1] that has detrimental effects on some audience members (ultraviolent video games),[2] that is brazenly false (lying about having won military honors)[3] or that is grossly offensive to basic human decency (anti-gay hate banners outside military funerals).[4] This First Amendment absolutism — "Congress shall make no law" truly means "no law" — only makes it more anomalous that millions of Americans are still denied a seat at the grown-up table of citizenship: Students in public schools and colleges. Anomalously, they are the only American demographic whose legally protected rights have actually worsened in the last 40 years.

When 18-year-old newspaper editor Krystal Myers sought to blow the whistle on heavy-handed religious indoctrination by teachers at her rural Tennessee public high school, the superintendent ordered her not to publish her opinion column, saying that the article might provoke "passionate conversations."[5] How schools reached the point where "passionate conversations" are something to be feared and punished – rather than being a central part of the educational experience – is the story of a generation of "*Hazelwood* justice."

Twenty-five years ago, the Supreme Court decided *Hazelwood School District v. Kuhlmeier*, a case that stripped away constitutional protection for students who use a "curricular" means of communication (in that case, a high school newspaper). A generation's worth of legalized *Hazelwood* censorship has damaged the learning environment in schools, discouraged young people from meaningfully engaging in civic life, and obstructed the public's access to truthful information. As the director of the University of Arizona's journalism program told a law-school symposium reflecting on the legacy of *Hazelwood*, "We are raising a nation of sheep. I don't think it's extreme to say that we risk democracy."[6]

Because of *Hazelwood*, a Tennessee high school was emboldened to fire its yearbook adviser for "allowing" his students to publish the profile of a gay student under the headline, "It's

OK to be gay." A Virginia high school confiscated its student newspaper — and removed the adviser — for a column documenting the inadequacies of the school's handicapped-inaccessible facilities. An Indiana high school forbade a student from publishing a story bringing to light pervasive hazing among track-and-field athletes. And the list goes on.[7]

More disturbing than any judicial misapplication of *Hazelwood* is the pervasive mentality that it has fostered in schools. When the *Hazelwood* ruling is set side by side with the earlier Supreme Court precedent that it modified, *Tinker v. Des Moines Independent Community School District*,[8] the directional choice they offer is stark. *Tinker* comes from a place of optimism and trust of young learners. It acknowledges that freedom is always "hazardous," yet concludes, "our Constitution says we must take this risk."[9] Left unchecked, Justice Abe Fortas wrote, administrators will turn schools into "enclaves of totalitarianism," treating their students as "closed-circuit recipients of only that which the State chooses to communicate."[10] *Hazelwood* comes from a place of suspicion and fear. Inadequately supervised, Justice Byron White wrote, students will use the right of free expression to advocate "alcohol or drug use, irresponsible sex" or other behavior violating "the shared values of a civilized social order."[11] The primary objective for educators, *Hazelwood* tells us, is to get through a day without controversy and preserve the school's reputation.

As difficult as it may be for some adults to believe, the views and perspectives of young people do have value. Student journalists can translate the language of their peers into words the larger society can understand; their work provides a window for the adult world into the thoughts of young people, even if those thoughts are at times uncomfortable to confront. Student journalists provide the fresh insights and perspectives that advance our collective understanding of issues affecting young people.

Although online publishing has expanded opportunities for young people to express themselves outside of school, the availability of these unofficial channels in no way lessens the urgency of opposing needless censorship, because censorship no longer stops at the schoolhouse gate. As described in Chapter 9 (Online Media), some school administrators are urging the courts – at times successfully – to expand school disciplinary authority to reach students' personal, off-campus speech, arguing that any website discussing school matters has the potential to be "disruptive" by provoking discussion at school. This new generation of speech cases – some might call it "Censorship 2.0" – continues to apply the decades-old case law that evolved when newspapers were the only outlet for student expression. So, regardless of the form in which news is delivered in generations to come, the law of the student "press" remains greatly relevant to young people's lives.

In a 2011 speech to students at George Washington University, then-Secretary of State Hillary Clinton hailed the power of online media to bring about positive social change. She highlighted the bravery of young people in Syria, who used a Facebook group to expose the beating of children by their teachers.[12] This uplifting story underscores the ability of the Internet to empower previously unheard voices, allowing all citizens – even the youngest – to be heard on topics of public concern. But the story becomes somewhat less inspiring in view of the fact that the Syrian students' Facebook page would, in many United States jurisdictions today, be regarded as a punishable disciplinary offense.[13] Incongruously, the ubiquity of online publishing that has freed journalists and activists elsewhere to share their messages with less government interference is having the opposite effect on students in the United States, who may not be safe from the censor's grasp anytime and anywhere they write about their schools.

There is reason for optimism that more enlightened days lie ahead. Each World Press Freedom Day concludes with a declaration that sets forth the consensus of the attendees challenging UNESCO and its member states to commit to improving conditions for journalists. In 2011, World Press Freedom Day was headquartered for the first time in the United States, in our nation's capital. The Washington Declaration explicitly recognizes the problem of excessive censorship of students' online speech. By enacting the declaration, UNESCO member states commit to "take prompt and effective action to assure the safety of journalists, bloggers, and all those, including students and youth, who express themselves on digital media platforms from intimidation, threats, physical attacks, and attempts against their lives."[14]

Closer to home, the nation's leading journalism education organizations are speaking out as one to declare that 25 years of *Hazelwood* is one generation too many. In a resolution unanimously adopted by the board of directors of the Association for Educators in Journalism and Mass Communication ("AEJMC") and by the Journalism Education Association ("JEA"), the nation's two largest journalism teaching groups, representing those at the college and K-12 levels, declared: "no legitimate pedagogical purpose is served by the censorship of student journalism even if it reflects unflatteringly on school policies and programs, candidly discusses sensitive social and political issues, or voices opinions challenging to majority views on matters of public concern. The censorship of such speech is detrimental to effective learning and teaching, and it cannot be justified by reference to 'pedagogical concerns.'"[15]

There is growing recognition, as well, that the public is more reliant than ever before on student news-gatherers to fulfill the foundational information needs of their communities. With the economic devastation that has cost professional newsrooms thousands of full-time jobs, unpaid students are being called on to fill the gap. A coalition of journalism philanthropies (including the Knight Foundation, McCormick Foundation, and Ethics & Excellence in Journalism Foundation) called in 2012 for the nation's journalism colleges to reconfigure themselves as "teaching hospitals" for news, putting students to work not in the confines of the classroom but out on local streets, gathering and sharing the information that once was provided by salaried professionals.[16] The consensus is clear that censorship of student journalism is incompatible with fundamental civic and educational imperatives. The law will, in time, inevitably catch up.

The Student Press Law Center, and countless journalists and journalism educators, are committed to helping students become responsible, professional journalists. We know that the work of journalism can teach students to think and to write better than coursework alone, and can nourish the intellectual curiosity that best prepares young people to participate meaningfully in the civic life of the community and the nation. We are persuaded by years of experience and the lessons of history that the only way to teach these lessons is to give students the freedom to speak and publish (in all forums, including online) without limitation from school officials. We think it no coincidence that those student media that consistently win awards for the quality and impact of their work are also the ones that are the most free.

Given the space to innovate, student journalists are creating astonishing work that at times surpasses that of professionals. The staff of *Verde* magazine at Palo Alto High School produced a searing narrative of underage drinking and date rape among students in their affluent, high-achieving district – a package recognized as "sophisticated and revealing" by *The San Jose Mercury News* – that ignited a communitywide dialogue about how sexual assault happens even in "good schools" and among "good kids."[17] Students in Prof. Mark Arax's journalism class at Fresno State University lifted the lid on a "nest of nepotism" at a local charter school where politically connected employees drew public paychecks for no-show jobs, provoking a grand jury investigation that led to revocation of the school's charter.[18] Prof. Dave Armstrong's students at Emory University broke the story of the "double life" of the powerful Georgia Senate majority leader who worked as a tout for an illegal sports gambling operation run by business associates with shady pasts.[19]

This book was created as a tool to help students produce good journalism. Those who understand the legal protections and the constraints that control their work will be best able to focus on the substance of gathering and disseminating information. Because students' free press rights are often distinct from those of their counterparts in the commercial media,

Garrison Keillor
(humorist/radio personality)
Phil Knight
(founder, Nike)
Nicholas Kristof
(author/columnist)
David Letterman
(entertainer)
Richard Linklater
(movie director)
Garry Marshall
(TV producer)
Aaron McGruder
(cartoonist)
Arthur Miller
(playwright)
Bill Moyers
(professional journalist)
Brent Musburger
(sportscaster)
Conan O'Brien
(entertainer)
Bill O'Reilly
(TV personality)
Ernie Pyle
(war correspondent)
Dan Rather
(professional journalist)
Harry Shearer
(actor)
Liz Smith
(columnist)
Potter Stewart
(Supreme Court justice)
Gary Trudeau
(cartoonist)
Kurt Vonnegut
(novelist)
E.B. White
(novelist)
Roy Wilkins
(NAACP leader)
Woodrow Wilson
(U.S. President)

other press-law books seldom provide answers to the questions they ask.

Any student journalist – from a staff member at the largest-circulation collegiate daily to a home-based blogger – can use this book as a resource. For simplicity, the terms "publication," "press" and "newspaper" are routinely used as a stand-in for all forms of media. The legal principles described in this book relate to all forms of journalistic expression; if the method of delivery makes a difference, that distinction is noted. Finally, student journalists and their advisers should remember that the law, like this book, is only a tool. It can provide guidance and protection or direction and constraints. But it cannot produce a news story, or even tell you exactly how to produce one. Nor does knowledge of the law substitute for sound editorial judgment. Students learn to make editorial judgments best when – with the assistance of a well-trained adviser – they reach the ultimate decisions for themselves. The Student Press Law Center hopes that this book will guide students and advisers alike in making responsible and informed judgments.

ENDNOTES

1   *United States v. Stevens*, 130 S. Ct. 1577 (2010).
2   *Brown v. Ent'mt Merchants Ass'n*, 131 S. Ct. 2729 (2011).
3   *United States v. Alvarez*, 132 S. Ct. 2537 (2012).
4   *Snyder v. Phelps*, 131 S. Ct. 1207 (2011).
5   Nick Glunt, "Tenn. school censors student's atheism editorial, says it would be distracting," SPLC *News Flash*, Feb. 24, 2012, *available at* http://www.splc.org/news/newsflash.asp?id=2339.
6   Victoria Ekstrand, "Hazelwood's Sheep," UNC Center for Media Law and Policy blog, Nov. 9, 2012, *available at* http://medialaw.unc.edu/2012/11/Hazelwoods-sheep/ (last viewed April 22, 2013).
7   An inventory of *Hazelwood*-based censorship of all forms of student speech is available online at www.cureHazelwood.org.
8   393 U.S. 503 (1969).
9   *Id.* at 508.
10 *Id.* at 51.
11 *Hazelwood*, 484 U.S. at 272.
12 Remarks of Secretary of State Clinton, "Internet Rights and Wrongs: Choices & Challenges in a Networked World," delivered Feb. 11, 2011, George Washington University, Washington, D.C., *available at* http://www.state.gov/secretary/rm/2011/02/156619.htm (last viewed Aug. 30, 2013).
13 *See, e.g., Bell v. Itawamba County Sch. Bd.*, 859 F.Supp.2d 834 (N.D. Miss. 2012) (dismissing student's First Amendment claim challenging suspension for off-campus YouTube rap-music video in which he warned that coaches at his school were engaging in sexually inappropriate conduct with female students, because student's lyrics used violent imagery that coaches perceived as threatening).
14 UNESCO, "The Washington Declaration," May 3, 2011, *available at* http://www.unesco.org/new/fileadmin/MULTIMEDIA/HQ/CI/CI/pdf/WPFD/WPFD2011/Washington%20Declaration%202011.pdf (last viewed Aug. 30, 2013).
15 *AEJMC Resolution: 25th Anniversary of Hazelwood v. Kuhlmeier*, April 2, 2013, *available at* http://www.aejmc.org/home/2013/04/resolution-one-2013/ (last viewed Aug. 30, 2013).
16 Eric Newton, "How Journalism Education Can, and Should, Blow Up the System," PBS MediaShift blog, May 23, 2012, *available at* http://www.pbs.org/mediashift/2012/05/how-journalism-education-can-and-should-blow-up-the-system144 (last viewed Aug. 30, 2013).
17 Lisie Sabbag, "You can't tell me I wasn't raped," *Verde Magazine* (April 2013) at 15, *available at* http://issuu.com/verdemagazine/docs/verdeedition14issue5 (last viewed Aug. 30, 2013).
18 Alan Wileman & Sam Cosby, "Troubled New Millennium charter school keeps getting second chances," *The Fresno Bee*, Sept. 16, 2012, *available at* http://www.fresnobee.com/2012/09/16/2994236/troubled-charter-keeps-getting.html (last viewed Aug. 30, 2013).
19 David Michaels, "Playing the Odds: The Rise of Sen. Chip Rogers," *The News Enterprise*, May 25, 2012, *available at* http://newsenterprise.emory.edu/playing-the-odds-the-rise-of-sen-chip-rogers (last viewed Aug. 30, 2013).

CHAPTER 2

Freedom of Expression
Cornerstone of a Free Society

One of the greatest historians of the American Constitution, Pulitzer prize-winning journalist Anthony Lewis, titled his 2007 book about the First Amendment, "Freedom for the Thought That We Hate." Lewis was quoting from a famous passage in a Supreme Court opinion by Justice Oliver Wendell Holmes: "if there is any principle of the Constitution that more imperatively calls for attachment than any other it is the principle of free thought — not free thought for those who agree with us but freedom for the thought that we hate."[1] That is a stirring passage, but it's worth remembering that Justice Holmes was on the losing side of that argument. In that case, *United States v. Schwimmer*, a majority of the Supreme Court found no constitutional problem with requiring new immigrants to swear a loyalty oath pledging to fight to defend the United States, even if war violated their religious beliefs. History proved Justice Holmes to be right. Seventeen years later, the Court overturned its own ruling.[2]

The First Amendment does not exist to protect popular, majority views. Those need no defending. As Justice Holmes knew, and as Anthony Lewis so well explained, the First Amendment ensures that people with views that might be considered "edgy" or challenging cannot be restrained from speaking out — even if the majority of those listening find the speech unpleasant to hear. Those with the benefit of the vantage point of the 21st century, where as of this publication the United States was in its second term with an African-American president and where the Supreme Court just overturned a federal law prohibiting same-sex couples from marrying[3], realize that "fringe" ideas often very quickly make their way into the mainstream — if they have a chance to be aired and debated.

Still, support for First Amendment values can be fragile. For example, a 2008 national survey conducted by New England Survey Research Associates and commissioned by the First Amendment Center found that 29 percent of those surveyed said the press has too much freedom in America. Only 15 percent could identify freedom of the press as a right guaranteed by the First Amendment.[4]

Another survey, conducted by the McCormick Tribune Freedom Museum in 2006, found that Americans actually knew more about "The Simpsons" TV show than the First Amendment. The study found that over half of those surveyed could name two or more members of the Simpsons family. At the same time, only 28 percent of them could name more than one of the five freedoms protected by the First Amendment. And just one in 1,000 people surveyed (.1 percent) was able to name all five freedoms guaranteed under the First Amendment.[5]

Any lack of enthusiasm for First Amendment freedoms generally, or freedom of the press specifically, may actually be a reflection of the complacency that Americans feel in these firmly established rights. People whose right to speak or vote was only recently won, or whose rights feel insecure, tend to cling to those freedoms more tightly and exercise them more avidly. United States law continues to give citizens a greater degree of liberty to speak out on a wide range of issues than in almost any other country in the world. That liberty is primarily embodied in the First Amendment to our Constitution.

"Congress shall make no law ... abridging the freedom of speech, or of the press," says the relevant portion of the First Amendment.

MARKETPLACE OF IDEAS

Several theories attempt to explain why it is important to protect the right of free speech and a free press in a democracy. The most powerful justification, articulated by 17th

---

Did You Know? A 2008 national survey found that 39 percent of Americans thought the press has too much freedom.
Source: First Amendment Center, *State of the First Amendment 2008*

52 percent of Americans could name at least two members of "The Simpsons" TV show family.
28 percent of Americans could name more than one of the five freedoms guaranteed to them by the First Amendment.
Source: McCormick Tribune Foundation (2006)

There must be freedom not only "for those who agree with us, but freedom for the thought that we hate."
— Justice Oliver Wendell Holmes (1929)

The process of "free, robust, uninhibited communication in the public marketplace of ideas" provides a means for determining the value of different ideas.
— *Whitney v. California* (1927)

century philosopher John Milton and by Justice Holmes, among others, is that free expression is the "protector of truth." The process of "free, robust, uninhibited communication in the public marketplace of ideas" provides a means for determining the value of different ideas.[6] Each person, this theory holds, should be free to state his or her own opinion and to criticize the opinions of others. Some ideas will be rejected outright, others will be compromised, and still others will be tested and either succeed or fail. The American legal system is built on the theory that out of this "marketplace of ideas" we have the best chance of finding workable solutions to problems. An uncensored media can expose citizens to differing and competing viewpoints on all aspects of society: government, morality, religion, lifestyles, science, sex and any other topic that is a subject of debate.

The fundamental principle behind the concept of free expression is that all ideas and voices, no matter how objectionable they may be to the general population, have the right to be heard. That is why in our society Neo-Nazi skinheads and civil rights activists alike enjoy the right to hand out leaflets and march down city streets.[7] That may also explain why true freedom of speech is not popular with many citizens. The Supreme Court, however, has made it clear that the majority cannot trample on the rights of individuals, even – and perhaps especially – those holding extreme views disfavored by the mainstream:

Immediately following the terrorist attacks of September 11, 2001, support for the First Amendment among Americans plunged dramatically, though it later rebounded.

> "The very purpose of a Bill of Rights was to withdraw certain subjects from the vicissitudes of political controversy, to place them beyond the reach of majorities and officials and to establish them as legal principles to be applied by the courts. One's right to life, liberty and property, to free press, freedom of worship and assembly, and other fundamental rights may not be submitted to vote; they depend on the outcome of no elections."[8]

Public attitudes about free expression can swing rapidly. When there is a perceived threat to the nation's safety, regard for constitutional rights often diminishes. In the year prior to the September 11, 2001, terrorist attacks that struck New York City and Washington, D.C., 22 percent of those responding to the First Amendment Center's annual "State of the First Amendment" survey indicated they felt the First Amendment went too far in the rights that it protects. In the year after the attacks, that number more than doubled, reaching 49 percent. By 2007, attitudes had calmed down, and only 25 percent of those surveyed said the First Amendment went too far.[9] But the public's willingness to compromise First Amendment values spiked again in 2013, when the same survey was conducted right after a lethal bombing at the Boston Marathon that claimed three lives; in that year, 34 percent of Americans surveyed said that the First Amendment goes too far in the rights that it guarantees.[10] While public opinion fluctuates, the First Amendment remains constant, preserving even the ability to debate the scope of the First Amendment itself.

SOCIETY'S WATCHDOG; CONSCIENCE

A second rationale for free expression and press freedom is its importance in ensuring that citizens can prevent the abuses of government power. Without protections for freedom of expression, some government officials undoubtedly would try to increase their influence and control by stifling dissent and censoring critical voices among the people. Press freedom is a vital means for assuring that a government "of" and "for" the people remains that way.

It is often said that a free press is the watchdog of a free society; the news media serve the people by guarding against a potentially corrupt government. For example, *The Washington Post's* dogged reporting of the Watergate affair may not have been solely responsible for the downfall of the Nixon White House, but it undoubtedly played a major role in uncovering the crimes that occurred there.

In a related vein, more idealistic advocates of the First Amendment claim that the primary responsibility of the media is to bring about needed social change. As the "conscience of society" the media should ferret out and publicize social problems and injustices to improve the plight of the underprivileged. It can hardly be doubted that media attention played a pivotal role in changing society's attitudes about civil rights for African-Americans and about the Vietnam War.

OTHER THEORIES

But abuse of power by government officials is not the only free expression threat to the citizens of a democracy. There is also the very real danger of the "tyranny of the majority." In the words of columnist and author Nat Hentoff: "[W]hen it comes to the rights and liberties of individual dissenters, a democratic majority can be as repressive as a king."[11]

Thomas Jefferson offered his own opinion on why freedom of speech is so important in a democracy. He said by allowing the people to criticize the government openly, necessary reforms could be affected without the bloodshed of an armed rebellion. Three years before he died, Jefferson told a French correspondent, "This formidable censor of the public functionaries, by arraigning them at the tribunal of public opinion, produces reform peaceably, which otherwise must be done by revolution."[12]

Finally, both judges and scholars have recognized the importance of free expression to individuals, independent of any benefit it may provide to society as a whole. Under this theory, the ability to speak freely is a fundamental component of human development — it makes better people. A person's sense of self-worth and understanding grows from being able to express himself, even if others believe what he says is wrong.

THE ARGUMENT FOR STUDENT PRESS FREEDOM

The arguments for the right of free expression by students are no less compelling, though the obstacles, in terms of public support and understanding, appear even more daunting. For example, just over half of Americans polled in 2007 said that public school students should not be allowed to report on controversial issues in their student newspapers without the approval of school authorities.[13] Even more alarming: 37 percent of those surveyed agreed that the same restrictions should hold true for student journalists at public colleges,[14] where statistics compiled by the U.S. Department of Education showed that 99 percent of enrolled students in fall 2010 were 18 years of age or older and more than 60 percent were over 21 years old.[15]

Sadly, too many young people today remain woefully uninformed about the most important issues that directly affect their lives — from drug use to AIDS, from college financial aid to mounting government budget deficits, from American energy policy to U.S. foreign policy and military action overseas. Students have a unique perspective on such issues and a big — and on some issues, the biggest — stake in their outcome, and the student press should be free to ensure that their voices are heard.

An independent student media is, increasingly, the public's only source of unbiased information about what is going on inside of schools and colleges. The economic decline of much of traditional corporate-owned professional news organizations — accelerated by a lingering global recession that began in 2007 — has been devastating to news coverage. As the Project for Excellence in Journalism reported during the depths of that recession, "between 2001-2009, approximately 1/3 of newsroom jobs in U.S. newspapers vanished."[16] As a result, the depth of coverage of educational institutions has greatly suffered. The Brookings Institution, a Washington, D.C., think-tank, sounded the alarm in a December 2009 study that found mainstream print, broadcast and online news

58 percent of Americans polled in 2007 said that public school students should not be allowed to report on controversial issues in their student newspapers without the approval of school authorities.

37 percent said the same restrictions should apply to college student journalists.
Source: First Amendment Center, *State of the First Amendment 2007*

operations devoted only 1.4 percent of their airtime and space to education news, much of it superficial and crisis-driven, such as coverage of school violence.[17] The authors warned that citizens would be unable to participate intelligently in the debate over critical education policy issues when given so little information. They specifically cited student news media as a valuable alternative source of news for readers of all ages: "Some school officials discourage student reporters from asking difficult questions or raising controversial issues. In fact, student journalism of this kind should be encouraged. Student newspapers often lead the media to important education stories."[18]

The ability of public employees, including schoolteachers, to "blow the whistle" on ineffective or wasteful programs has been greatly eroded by Supreme Court rulings that give government employers the power to regulate what employees say when speaking in the course of their employment.[19] Since mainstream professional news organizations no longer have the staffing to provide day-to-day coverage of how schools are functioning, and since employees within the school no longer have the assurance that they may speak out about shortcomings in their schools and keep their jobs, it is fair to ask the question: If the student media is not allowed to tell the public when schools are falling short and are in need of improvement, just who will?

CIVICS EDUCATION

Schools are where most students are first exposed to the fundamentals of democracy, including values embodied in the Constitution. What is a student to believe when taught about the First Amendment in a social studies classroom, only to have free expression in a student newspaper or yearbook suppressed by school officials? In the words of former *New York Times* editor Tom Wicker:

> All too many of these high school editors and reporters may well conclude, from hard experience, that freedom of the press is as bad a joke as the ones school boards would like for them to print in place of news and opinion; and holding that cynical view they are far more likely to become doctors, engineers, or politicians than reporters. If they do become reporters, having felt the knife so early, they are not likely to stick their necks out in the name of the First Amendment.[20]

The lack of meaningful civics education in schools is increasingly being recognized as an urgent national priority. In a September 2011 report, the nonprofit Campaign for the Civic Mission of Schools, co-chaired by retired Supreme Court Justice Sandra Day O'Connor, decried the "staggering" consequences for American democracy when civics is taught in a "minimal or superficial" way in schools.[21] The report, "Guardian of Democracy," recommended revitalizing schools' approach to civics education by (among other recommendations) emphasizing "civic skills" that include "news comprehension," promoting classroom discussion of political issues important in young people's lives, and giving students genuine input into school governance. And the report specifically mentioned student media as an example of the "engaging and empowering civic activities" that all schools should offer.[22]

Students with no understanding or appreciation of the First Amendment grow into citizens with no respect for the First Amendment. In fact, a 2007 survey, conducted by the John S. and James L. Knight Foundation, found that nearly three-fourths of high school students surveyed "don't care much" about the First Amendment or take it for granted.[23]

The student press plays a role in the school environment not unlike the role its commercial counterparts play in the larger community: to convey valuable information about the workings of the schools and to provide a forum for members of the school community to voice their opinions about issues of concern.

FREE PRESS IN AMERICA: A BRIEF HISTORY

It should come as no surprise that throughout history those in power — absolute rulers and elected officials alike — have used any means available to stifle the voices of dissent. One important reason the First Amendment was added to the United States Constitution was the shocking history of ruthless censorship practiced by the royal government in England. In fifteenth-century Britain, for example, it was a treasonable offense, punishable by death, to ridicule the king, call him a fool or even imagine his death. When the printing press was introduced into England in 1476, the Crown established a "licensing" requirement so that nothing could be published unless it had been read previously and approved by the royal authorities. Anyone caught with an "unlicensed" book could be jailed for life.

This heritage of intolerance for freedom of thought was transmitted to the American colonies by the early settlers. In 1650, the first reported public book burning in America occurred in Boston when Thomas Pynchon's *The Meritorious Price of Our Redemption* was torched in the marketplace. Pynchon incurred the wrath of government officials by propounding religious beliefs differing from those of the established religion.

It was also in Boston that the first American newspaper, *Publick Occurrences Both Foreign and Domestic*, was published in 1690 and immediately suppressed. The governor and his council shut down the paper after only one issue because its publisher, Benjamin Harris, had failed to obtain the necessary license and, incidentally, because the paper carried attacks on the English allies and the French king.

Perhaps the single most emotionally important event in the struggle for freedom of the press prior to the revolution, however, was the 1735 trial of John Peter Zenger. Zenger had angered the royal governor of New York by charging in his newspaper, *New York Weekly Journal*, that the governor's administration was guilty of incompetence, favoritism, interference with jury trials and rigging elections. The governor, William Cosby, had Zenger arrested and charged with "raising sedition." Under the law at that time, one was guilty of seditious libel if one published "criticism" of the government that tended to stir the people to rebellion. It was no defense that the charges against the government were actually true. Zenger's attorney, Andrew Hamilton, made a plea to the jury that every citizen in a free society had the inalienable right to complain about the government. Zenger could be found guilty, he argued, only if his charges against the government were false.

Ignoring the judge's instructions on the law, the jury found Zenger not guilty. The English Crown had been put on notice that the citizens of the struggling colonies would place a high premium on the right of the individual to criticize and complain about government. Indeed, a scant 40 years later the colonists would do more than just complain about the injustices of British rule: they would revolt.

After the American War for Independence, the new nation set out to establish a federal government, centralized but with limited powers. The Constitution of the United States, as adopted by the Constitutional Convention in 1787 and ratified by the states in 1788, contained no provision guaranteeing freedom of speech or freedom of the press. Many people, afraid of the powers to be held by the federal government, sought explicit protection of individual rights. Others, including Alexander Hamilton, felt that such protections were unnecessary since, under the Constitution, which spelled out the limited powers of the federal government, government officials had no authority to suppress speech.

To calm the fears of those who distrusted the new central government, the first Congress, meeting in 1789, adopted and submitted to the states a list of twelve amendments intended to safeguard individual liberties. Ten of the amendments, later to be called the Bill of Rights, were ratified by the states and on December 15, 1791, became a part of the Constitution. Despite its 220-plus-year history, the spirit and the letter of the First Amendment have not always been respected. Over the years, a number of laws have

Constitution Day recognizes the ratification of the U.S. Constitution. It is officially observed in the United States on September 17, the day the U.S. Constitutional Convention signed the Constitution in 1787.

The first ten amendments to the U.S. Constitution — later to be called the Bill of Rights — were ratified by the states on December 15, 1791.

The Espionage Act of 1917 and its Sedition Act amendment of 1918 made it a crime to "utter, print, write, or publish any disloyal, profane, scurrilous, or abusive language about the form of government of the United States, or the Constitution of the United States or the uniform of the Army or Navy of the United States."

been enacted that prohibited and punished certain kinds of speech.

In 1798, to cite one horrifying example, Congress passed the Alien and Sedition Acts, which prohibited the publication of "any false scandalous and malicious speech against the government of the United States." Punishment included up to two years in jail and a $2,000 fine. At least ten people were convicted under the law before it expired in 1801.[24]

Before the Civil War, many states enacted statutes that prohibited any person from saying or writing that slavery should be abolished. And many local laws in the South allowed postmasters to censor abolitionist literature.[25]

During the Civil War, President Abraham Lincoln closed the mails to "treasonable correspondence" and even ordered newspapers shut down and some editors jailed.[26] His justification was that the South's rebellion directly threatened the life of the nation, and he could not allow the press to incite armed uprising or cause desertions from the army if the country were to survive.

After President William McKinley was assassinated in 1901 by a self-proclaimed anarchist, Congress enacted an immigration law that forbade entry into the United States of any immigrant who opposed all organized government or belonged to a group that taught that doctrine. The rise of unions, in particular the Industrial Workers of the World, prompted a number of cities to pass laws prohibiting public speeches, the main tool for recruiting new members. One young logger was even arrested for reading the Declaration of Independence. The courts eventually struck down a number of these ordinances.[27]

Currently, the Supreme Court recognizes at least nine categories of "unprotected speech."

Fear induced by World War I led Congress to enact once again a law prohibiting "seditious" speech. The Espionage Act of 1917 and its Sedition Act amendment of 1918 made it a crime to "utter, print, write, or publish any disloyal, profane, scurrilous [vulgar], or abusive language about the form of government of the United States, or the Constitution of the United States or the uniform of the Army or Navy of the United States." In this atmosphere a number of pacifist ministers were attacked and imprisoned.[28]

Cases involving prosecutions under state and federal sedition laws eventually reached the Supreme Court, which was not very sympathetic to claims that such restraints on speech violated the First Amendment. In *Schenck v. United States*,[29] decided in 1919, for example, the Court upheld the conviction of a socialist under the Espionage Act for conspiring to publish a leaflet stating that the draft was unconstitutional and that those wishing to oppose the draft had a constitutional right to do so. The Court ruled that since the leaflet had been mailed to draftees during World War I, it obstructed the war effort and presented a "clear and present danger" to the country. In *Abrams v. United States*,[30] decided the same year, the Court upheld the 20-year sentences of three men for publishing and distributing (by throwing from the window of a building) leaflets urging workers in munitions factories to go on strike. And in *Gilbert v. Minnesota*, the Court upheld the conviction of a speaker for publicly opposing involvement in World War I.[31]

Today, these early 20th century cases seem like quaint historical artifacts. It seems they can best be explained as reactions to the fears of and threats to a country embroiled in a war for survival. More recent decisions from the nation's highest courts recognize the vital role that a free press and an informed public play — even during wartime — in curbing government abuses, and how difficult it should be for government to suppress speech.

Perhaps the high-water mark for First Amendment freedoms came in 1971, in the so-called Pentagon Papers case. In that case, the government would ask the courts, without success, to prohibit *The New York Times*, *The Washington Post* and the *Progressive* from publishing secret Pentagon documents describing U.S. involvement in Vietnam, on the rationale that publication threatened "national security."[32] The Supreme Court's ruling in the Pentagon Papers case emphasized that preventing the publication of controversial material — as opposed to punishing it afterward — is an especially noxious form of censorship that will almost never be tolerated, absent the most urgent national security justification.

Still, early rulings taking a narrow view of First Amendment rights are important to study because they demonstrate the fragility of free-speech rights, especially in times of national crisis. In recent years, civil-rights advocates and other critics have claimed that history is repeating itself and have raised warnings about government attempts to restrict civil liberties and expand government authority in the wake of the September 11, 2001, terrorist attacks.

UNPROTECTED SPEECH

While the debate over the scope of civil liberties in America will no doubt continue, one thing is clear: The First Amendment is not absolute. Even though the words of the amendment are unambiguous — "Congress shall make no law…" — the Supreme Court has declared that Congress can make laws that prohibit and punish certain kinds of expression.

Currently, the Court recognizes at least nine categories of "unprotected speech" — expression that the government can lawfully prohibit or punish to some extent. Most of these categories are more fully defined in later chapters of this book, but briefly stated they are: (1) obscenity; (2) defamation; (3) expression that is intended and likely to incite imminent lawless action (for example, instigating a riot); (4) fighting words (personally abusive language addressed to a specific person likely to provoke a violent reaction); (5) unwarranted invasions of privacy; (6) deceptive or misleading advertisements or those for illegal products or services; (7) clear and immediate threats to national security (for example, publishing information about troop movements during wartime); (8) copyright violations; (9) expression on high school grounds that causes a material and substantial disruption, is indecent or vulgar, or advocates illegal drug use.

Some of these forms of expression, such as libel and invasions of privacy, can be punished only after publication, not restrained beforehand. A few, such as copyright violations and obscenity, may be subject to prior restraints.

In addition to carving out these "exceptions" to the First Amendment, the Supreme Court has declared that the government can regulate the "time, place and manner" of expression as long as its regulations are reasonable. This means, for example, that the government can limit a protest demonstration on government property to a certain time of day and location. And while a public high school student has the right to distribute material to his classmates on school grounds, an administrator can reasonably regulate when, where and how such distribution occurs. (See Chapter 8 Independent Media for more information on time, place and manner distribution regulations.)

STATE ACTION DOCTRINE

An essential concept in the field of constitutional law is the notion of "state action." The First Amendment (and the rest of the Bill of Rights) generally protects individuals only from action taken by the government or government officials and not from action taken by private persons. For example, it is a violation of the First Amendment for a police officer to confiscate a protester's sign on a public sidewalk, but it is not a violation of the First Amendment for some irate passer-by to seize the sign (though of course it might be an illegal theft or assault). In short, the First Amendment is a limitation on the power of the government to censor or punish expression.

Today it is clear that for purposes of the First Amendment, "government" means not only the federal government, but also state, local and county governments, including the boards of public schools and colleges and the administrators who work under them. That was not always the case. It is apparent from the literal language of the First Amendment ("Congress

The government can regulate the "time, place and manner" of expression as long as its regulations are reasonable and content-neutral.

The First Amendment generally protects individuals only from action taken by the government or government officials and not from action taken by private persons.

shall make no law abridging . . .") that the framers of the Constitution intended to limit the power of the federal government and not the various state governments. In fact, one of the 12 amendments submitted to the states in 1789, but never ratified, provided that "no state shall violate the equal rights of conscience, or of the freedom of the press...."

Until 1925 the Supreme Court had interpreted the First Amendment to prohibit censorship only by the federal government and not the states, but in *Gitlow v. New York*, the Court declared that the First Amendment, by way of the Fourteenth Amendment, also limits the powers of state and local governments.[33]

It is important to note, however, that while public schools are subject to the limits placed upon state action by the First and Fourteenth Amendments, these limitations do not apply to private institutions. The courts have not found state action involved in the acts of private colleges and high schools, because the private school is not acting on the government's behalf. (See Chapter 7 for a further discussion of the rights of private school student media.) Throughout this book, it is important to remember the distinction between public and private institutions wherever a right is premised upon protection from state action rather than upon some other privilege or immunity.

SUMMARY

The 19th century educator Horace Mann, widely referred to as "The Father of American Education," wrote way back in 1845 that: "The great moral attribute of self-government cannot be born and matured in a day; and, if school children are not trained to it, we only prepare ourselves for disappointment if we expect it from grown men."[34]

The thing is: the First Amendment is not a given. It is written on paper, not stone. It is an idea. And history (both distant and recent) suggests it is an idea that can disappear tomorrow if enough of those whom it was intended to protect don't understand it, don't believe in it and don't care enough to defend it.

Congress shall make no law respecting an establishment of religion, or prohibiting the free exercise thereof; or abridging the freedom of speech, or of the press, or the right of the people peaceably to assemble, and to petition the Government for a redress of grievances.

As veteran journalist and former Freedom Forum First Amendment ombudsman Paul McMasters once noted: The First Amendment is just forty-five words, but it embraces "five of the most fundamental freedoms to which any human or nation can aspire. It is a remarkable compact between a government and a people, unique in all the world, unique in all of history ... [recognizing as it does] that a human being achieves his and her greatest promise and potential when allowed to think and believe and speak freely; and that a nation achieves its full promise and potential only when it allows its individual citizens to enjoy that freedom."[35]

If our democracy is to flourish, if our idea of freedom is to survive, our next generation needs to hear and understand those forty-five extraordinary words. And they must experience them as more than just words on a page.

ENDNOTES

1   *United States v. Schwimmer*, 279 U.S. 644, 654-55 (1929) (Holmes, J., dissenting).
2   *Giouard v. United States*, 328 U.S. 51 (1946).
3   *United States v. Windsor*, No. 12-307, ___ U.S. ___ (June 26 ,2013).
4   State of the First Amendment 2008, First Amendment Center (Nashville, Tenn.), survey conducted July-August 2008 and released on September 11, 2008, *available at* http://www.firstamendmentcenter.org/madison/wp-content/uploads/2011/03/SOFA2008survey.pdf (last viewed Aug. 28, 2013).
5   "Characters from 'The Simpsons' more well known to Americans than their First Amendment freedoms,survey finds," McCormick Foundation Press Release, March 1, 2006, *available at*: http://www.prnewswire.com/news-releases-test/characters-from-the-simpsons-more-well-known-to-americans-than-

their-first-amendment-freedoms-survey-finds-55189462.html (last visited July 2, 2013).

6   *Whitney v. California*, 274 U.S. 357, 375-77 (1927).
7   In *National Socialist Party v. Skokie*, 432 U.S. 43 (1977), the U.S. Supreme Court upheld the right of the Nazi party to march through downtown Skokie, Ill., despite the potential to alarm that city's large population of Holocaust survivors.
8   *West Virginia State Bd. of Educ. v. Barnette*, 319 U.S. 624, 638 (1943).
9   'State of the First Amendment Survey, The First Amendment Center (Nashville, Tenn.), survey conducted August 2007 and released on Sept. 11, 2007, *available at* http://www.firstamendmentcenter.org/madison/wp-content/uploads/2011/03/SOFA2007results.pdf (last viewed Aug. 28, 2013).
10 State of the First Amendment Survey, The First Amendment Center (Nashville, Tenn.), survey conducted May 2008 and released on July 16, 2013, *available at* http://www.newseum.org/news/2013/07/state-of-the-first-amendment-2013.pdf (last viewed Aug. 28, 2013).
11 One of the most readable histories of the First Amendment is found in Nat Hentoff's book, *The First Freedom — The Tumultuous History of Free Speech in America* (Delacorte Press 1980). Much of the information in this chapter was gleaned from that work.
12 *Hentoff* at 87.
13 State of the First Amendment 2007 at 5.
14 *Id.*
15 Digest of Education Statistics, National Center for Education Statistics, Table 200, *available at* http://nces.ed.gov/programs/digest/d11/tables/dt11_200.asp (last visited June 2, 2013).
16 *See* Dorie Clark, "Career Advice for Aspiring Journalists," Forbes, June 1, 2013 (summarizing Project's May 2011 "state of the media" report).
17 E.J. Dionne, Jr., Darrell M. West and Grover J. "Russ" Whitehurst, "Invisible: 1.4 Percent Coverage for Education is Not Enough," The Brookings Institution, December 2, 2009, *available at* http://www.brookings.edu/research/reports/2009/12/02-education-news-west (last visited June 2, 2013).
18 *Id.* at 3.
19 In *Garcetti v. Ceballos*, 570 U.S. 410 (2006), the Supreme Court decided that a prosecutor had no First Amendment protection against punishment for a memo he circulated within his agency that exposed irregularities in a pending criminal case. As a result of the *Garcetti* ruling and subsequent lower-court cases applying it, it is uncertain that a school employee would have any constitutional protection for speaking out about inadequacies in school programs, if she became aware of those inadequacies as a result of her professional responsibilities.
20 *Captive Voices: The Report of the Commission of Inquiry Into High School Journalism*, at 136, Schocken Books (1974).
21 Campaign for the Civic Mission of Schools, "Guardian of Democracy: The Civic Mission of Schools," Sept. 15, 2011, *available at* http://civicmission.s3.amazonaws.com/118/f0/5/171/1/Guardian-of-Democracy-report.pdf (last viewed July 11, 2013).
22 *Id.* at 19.
23 Future of the First Amendment 2007, John S. and James L. Knight Foundation (Miami, Fla.), survey conducted April-June 2007 and released on September 17, 2007, Key Finding 2, *available at* http://www.firstamendmentfuture.org (last viewed July 11, 2013).
24 *Hentoff* at 79-81.
25 *Id.* at 89-90.
26 James Morton Smith, *Freedom's Fetters* (Cornell University Press 1956).
27 *Hentoff* at 107. And *see* Russell Nye, *Fettered Freedom* (Michigan State University Press, rev. ed., 1964).
28 *Hentoff* at 110-11.
29 *Schenck v. United States*, 249 U.S. 47 (1919).
30 *Abrams v. United States*, 250 U.S. 616 (1919).
31 *Gilbert v. Minnesota*, 254 U.S. 325 (1920).
32 *New York Times Co. v. United States*, 403 U.S. 713 (1971).
33 *Gitlow v. New York*, 268 U.S. 652 (1925). Ratified in 1868, immediately following the Civil War, the Fourteenth Amendment reads: "No State shall make or enforce any law which shall abridge the privileges or immunities of citizens of the United States; nor shall any State deprive any person of life, liberty, or property, without due process of law; nor deny to any person within its jurisdiction the equal protection of the laws." In *Gitlow*, the Supreme Court said that freedom of speech was one of the "liberties" included in the protection of the Fourteenth Amendment, thus no state could deprive a citizen of that freedom. Therefore, the First Amendment is applied to the states through the Fourteenth Amendment. The First Amendment protects individuals from censorship not only by federal and state officials but also by local, county and city government officials, including public school administrators, since the government employs them.
34 Horace Mann, "Report for 1845," Annual Reports of the Secretary of the Board of Education of Massachusetts for the Years 1845-1848, Lee and Shepard Publishers, Boston, Mass. (1891), at 37.
35 Paul McMasters, "Disarming truth by restricting student speech," Quill & Scroll, February-March, 1996, at 13.

CHAPTER 3

Ethical Journalism

"Journalists must decide for themselves, rather than having others decide for them, what information they will distribute, and what form that information will take."
— Doing Ethics in Journalism (1997)[1]

The law sets the standard for what journalists can do, but professional ethics set the standard for what journalists *should* do. The two should never be confused. There are times when the law and ethics will pull in different directions, and perhaps put a journalist in the dilemma of choosing which duty to obey. At those times, ethical principles may counsel that the journalist carry out a professional obligation even at the risk of legal peril.

This book is about the law. It does not pretend to be a book about ethics. The two are related, but they are not the same. Lyle Denniston, longtime Supreme Court correspondent for *The Boston Globe*, has observed that if journalists paid more attention to ethical concerns, they might be able to spend less time working with lawyers. The law tells journalists what they may or may not do. Ethics, on the other hand, are more concerned with helping journalists decide what they ought to do as moral human beings and professionals. For example, while there is no law against journalists accepting gifts from those they report on, almost every newsroom has a strict policy prohibiting its staff from accepting anything of value (because of the ethical imperative to avoid conflicts of interest). Conversely, while a judge might legally compel a reporter to reveal the identity of a source to whom the reporter promised confidentiality, journalistic ethics typically demand that the reporter disobey the court order, thereby breaking the law, and face the legal consequences.

> The law tells journalists what they may or may not do. Ethics, on the other hand, are more concerned with helping journalists decide what they ought to do as moral human beings and professionals.

When journalists need the answer to a legal question (for example, "Does the law allow me to print the name of a rape victim?"), a lawyer — and specifically a lawyer with media law experience — can be an invaluable resource. When journalists need the answer to an ethical question ("*Should* I print the name of a rape victim, given that there is no law against it?"), lawyers cannot furnish the final answer. Not because lawyers are unethical, but because they are not journalists. Lawyers have a professional obligation to protect the media they represent. That is much different from the duty of journalists, which is to insure that their readers receive complete and accurate information.

Of course, journalists do not — and should not — broadcast anything and everything they have a constitutionally protected right to say. Too many ethical debates end with reporters explaining their decision to publish controversial or unpleasant material by simply invoking their First Amendment right to do so. Such an argument tends to give the First Amendment, and the press, a bad reputation. It fails to explain that in our system of government, where the press is charged with acting as a public watchdog and protector, journalists sometimes have an ethical duty to engage in aggressive, confrontational newsgathering, and to publish information that some might find unpleasant or consider nobody else's business. In other cases, although less common, journalists may determine that the harm in publishing certain information may outweigh the public interest in reporting it, even though publication would be within the protection of the First Amendment. This is simply to say that the right to publish something does not mean that a journalist has a duty to publish it, or that it even should be published; those decisions are where a journalist's professional judgment takes over.

Journalism is referred to, for good reason, as a "profession," alongside such professions as medicine, law and accounting. While journalism does not require the same level of formal education and licensure as those professions, it shares two fundamental traits that separate a profession from merely "a job." First, the customer is paying for the honesty and independence of the professional's judgment, even if that judgment requires telling the customer an unwelcome truth. And second, the professional is expected to put the customer's interests ahead of self-interest if those interests tug in different directions. Journalists who adhere to these imperatives — who put aside self-interest and who provide the audience their honest and independent judgment — are worthy of the title "professional."

Journalism is unique among professions in that a journalist's obedience to the standards of the industry is not policed by a government agency (the way a state medical licensing board oversees the conduct of doctors), or by a private licensing body (the way a state bar association regulates lawyers). Journalists occupy a trusted position in which only they and their employers determine whether their actions satisfy, or fall short of, ethical standards. Journalism is an honorable profession, but if journalists are ever to convince the public of that, they must be able to explain why their editorial decisions are right, not just that they have the right to make them.

This book should help you answer the legal questions. For the ethical ones, we have included a list of other sources, including some of the excellent resources created by the nonprofit Poynter Institute. In addition, we have included codes of ethics from both scholastic and professional journalism organizations in our Appendix. Even the best ethical codes, however, are not "one-size-fits-all" absolutes. It is important to adhere to ethical standards, but it is more important to understand the reasons behind those standards, so that the journalist acts ethically based on a well-developed sense of right and wrong, not based on a memorized platitude.

> Ethical codes were never intended to be enforced against journalists by courts or other parties outside the newsroom.

It is also important to note that ethical codes are simply guides for journalists. While editors may punish (or even fire) a reporter who they determine has violated the newsroom's ethics policy, codes such as the Society of Professional Journalists or Associated Collegiate Press ethics codes were never intended to be enforced against journalists by courts or other parties outside the newsroom. Their language is — and was meant to be — aspirational, not legal or punitive in tone.[2]

As former Executive Director of the Society of Professional Journalists Ira Perry once said, "The Society's Code is purely voluntary. While we encourage our members to follow its principles, we recognize that there are few situations that can be reduced to black and white statements of fact."[3]

From time to time, journalists have faced threats from outside enforcers who attempt to use perceived lapses in professional judgment as grounds (or perhaps, pretexts) for punishment. In New Mexico, college administrators briefly shuttered a student newspaper and announced plans to cancel the entire journalism program after branding the newspaper's sex issue "offensive and not appropriate."[4] In Missouri, two college editors were threatened with disciplinary sanctions, potentially including expulsion from school, after an April Fool's Day parody edition that prominently included a sex-themed pun offensive to many readers.[5]

Because ethical principles are ultimately a matter of conscience and of professional judgment, they are not "laws" for which violators can or should be prosecuted. It is foolish and dangerous for school authorities to use ethical codes as a pretext for punishing aggressive newsgathering or controversial speech. Ultimately, ethical judgments are matters of conscience, and students learn the lessons of conscience best when schools allow them to make the ultimate decisions for themselves.

ENDNOTES

1   *See* Jay Black, Bob Steele and Ralph D. Barney, Doing Ethics in Journalism (Allyn & Bacon, 3d ed. 1997) (a project of the Society of Professional Journalists), page 18.

2   For example, in 1987 the Society of Professional Journalists deleted from its code of ethics a clause requiring journalists to "actively censure" code violators.

3   *See* Mike Hiestand, "Don't let ethics codes become law," *It's the Law*, ACP Trends, November 1998 (*available at*: http://www.studentpress.org/acp/trends/~law1198college.html (last visited July 29, 2013).

4   Sara Tirrito, "New Mexico college administrators reinstate staff, return confiscated papers," SPLC *News Flash*, March 27, 2013 (*available at*: http://www.splc.org/news/newsflash.asp?id=2553&year=2013.

5   Nick Glunt, "Mizzou changes course, opts not to pursue discipline of editors behind April Fools' edition," SPLC *News Flash*, April 12, 2012, *available at* http://www.splc.org/news/newsflash.asp?id=2366.

FOR MORE INFORMATION

Additional Sources for Information on Journalism Ethics:

1. The American Society of News Editors High School Journalism Project includes more than two dozen lesson plans focused on journalism ethics specifically geared to student media.
www.hsj.org

2. Indiana School of Journalism's Journalism Ethics Cases Online features over 100 ethical case studies for class and newsroom discussion.
http://journalism.indiana.edu/resources/ethics/

3. The Poynter Institute's Web site includes hundreds of articles, online discussions, sample ethical guidelines, ethics tip sheets, an Ask the Expert feature, a comprehensive ethics bibliography and much more.
www.poynter.org

4. The Ethics Section of the Society of Professional Journalists website includes reporter resources, ethics teaching tools, news of the latest ethical controversies involving journalists, a discussion of the SPJ and other media ethics codes, an ethics hotline and ethics case studies.
www.spj.org/ethics.asp

5. Journalism Ethics Cases Online: A project of Indiana University's School of Journalism, this site provides students, teachers, researchers, professional journalists and others with over 100 case studies that explore various ethical issues in journalism.
http://journalism.indiana.edu/resources/ethics/

The American Society of Newspaper Editors has compiled a list of codes of ethics adopted by various journalism organizations and news media outlets at: **www.asne.org/ideas/codes/codes.htm**

CHAPTER 4

Through the Schoolhouse Gate
Tinker Sets the Standard

It is fair to say that the men who ratified the Bill of Rights never anticipated that the First Amendment would play such an important role in public education (or that public education would play such an important role in American life). But since the late 1960s, the courts have made clear that the Constitution protects the right of public high school and college students to express themselves on school grounds. The debate, for more than half a century now, has been how far that protection goes.

Even before pacifists, union organizers and communists took their free speech cases to the Supreme Court in the 1920s and 1930s, high school students were going to court claiming the First Amendment protected them. However, these early efforts to win the right of free speech were failures. In 1859, for example, a Vermont court declared that a high school student could be paddled for ridiculing a teacher off-campus.[1] In 1908, a Wisconsin court upheld the suspension of two high school students for submitting a poem to a local newspaper that ridiculed school officials.[2] In 1915, a California court allowed a school board to expel a high school student for making disrespectful remarks about school authorities at a school assembly.[3] In 1924, a Michigan court declared that a high school student's airing in the public press of a grievance against school officials justified his expulsion.[4]

As the courts began to interpret the First Amendment more expansively in the last half of the 20th century, students eventually benefited from the trend. By the mid-1970s, public school students were regarded as having free expression rights similar to those of adults outside of school.

These protections were the result of the application of the First Amendment to the states through the Fourteenth Amendment. "The Fourteenth Amendment, as now applied to the States, protects the citizen against the State itself and all of its creatures — Boards of Education not excepted," the Supreme Court said.[5] "That they are educating the young for citizenship is reason for scrupulous protection of Constitutional freedoms of the individual, if we are not to strangle the free mind at its source and teach youth to discount important principles of our government as mere platitudes."[6]

Both the Supreme Court and virtually every lower court confronted with the issue have now recognized that public high school and college students are entitled to some First Amendment protection.

The first Supreme Court case directly involving student free expression rights was *Minersville School District v. Gobitis*,[7] decided in 1940. In *Gobitis*, the Court held that a public school district could expel a student for refusing to recite the Pledge of Allegiance. In a remarkable change of heart, the Court reversed itself only three years later and overturned *Gobitis*. In *West Virginia State Board of Education v. Barnette*,[8] the Court ruled that elementary and secondary public school students have the right under the First Amendment to refuse to say the Pledge. The Court reasoned that compelling school children to participate in the flag ceremony infringed their rights because it coerced them to accept and affirm political beliefs and ideas with which they might not agree. Writing for the majority of the Court, Justice Robert H. Jackson offered stirring support for freedom of thought:

> If there is any fixed star in our constitutional constellation, it is that no official, high or petty, can prescribe what shall be orthodox in politics, nationalism, religion, or other matters of opinion or force citizens to confess by word or act their faith therein.[9]

Since the late 1960s, American courts have recognized that the Constitution protects the right of public high school and college students to express themselves on school grounds.

Barnette is important because it is the first case in which the Supreme Court unquestionably recognized that the First Amendment does, in fact, protect public school students. But the true landmark in defining students' free expression rights did not come for another quarter-century. It was not until the 1969 decision in *Tinker v. Des Moines Independent Community School District*[10] that the Court clarified just how far student First Amendment protection would extend. While the Barnette decision held that school officials could not force students to swear an oath of allegiance to the government, the Court in *Tinker* faced the more difficult question of whether school administrators could stifle a student's own expression. In a decision that would have a dramatic impact on every public school in America, the Court held that school administrators' authority over students' speech while in school was limited. Students have the right under the First Amendment to express themselves peacefully on school grounds, the Court said.

The case was brought by three students from Des Moines, Iowa: Mary Beth Tinker, a 13-year-old junior high student, her 15-year-old brother, John, and Christopher Eckhardt, 16. John and Christopher both were in high school. The three students, their parents and several other families decided in December 1965 to speak out against the war in Vietnam by wearing black armbands during the holiday season and by fasting on December 16 and New Year's Eve. School officials learned of the planned protest and quickly adopted a policy prohibiting any student from wearing an armband to school. Mary Beth, John and Christopher wore their black armbands to school despite the policy and were consequently suspended and sent home.

The students then sued the school district claiming a violation of their free expression rights under the First Amendment. The lower courts upheld the suspensions, but the Supreme Court ruled in favor of the students. After reaffirming the authority of school officials to control student conduct in the schools, the Court declared that public school students — including those in junior high schools — have the First Amendment right to express themselves at school, free from administrative censorship, so long as their speech does not cause a "substantial disruption of or material interference with school activities" or intrude upon the rights of others.[11]

Writing for the seven-member majority of the Court in *Tinker*, Justice Abe Fortas declared:

> First Amendment rights, applied in the light of the special characteristics of the school environment, are available to teachers and students. It can hardly be argued that either students or teachers shed their constitutional rights to freedom of speech or expression at the schoolhouse gate.[12]

Fortas warned administrators that they could not run the schools so that student expression is suppressed. Students, he wrote, have the constitutional right to voice even unpopular opinions at school:

> In our system, state-operated schools may not be enclaves of totalitarianism. School officials do not possess absolute authority over their students. Students in school as well as out of school are 'persons' under our Constitution. They are possessed of fundamental rights which the State must respect, just as they themselves must respect their obligations to the State. In our system, students may not be regarded as closed-circuit recipients of only that which the State chooses to communicate. They may not be confined to the expression of those sentiments that are officially approved. In the absence of a specific showing of constitutionally valid reasons to regulate their speech, students are entitled to freedom of expression of their views.[13]

Tinker is undoubtedly the most important student First Amendment case in the nation's history. In the decades following the ruling, courts around the country began to apply its holding to a wide variety of student free expression issues at elementary and secondary schools as well as colleges and universities. Even today, a firm grasp of the standard used by the Supreme Court in *Tinker* is vital to an understanding of the law of the student press.

The full text of the *Tinker* decision is available at: **www.splc.org/tinkercase**

DEFINING THE TINKER STANDARD

In the *Tinker* case, the Supreme Court outlined the limits of a public school official's power to restrict student expression. In the words of the Court, student speech that "materially disrupts classwork or involves substantial disorder or invasion of the rights of others is ... not immunized by the constitutional guarantee of freedom of speech."[14] The burden is on school officials to show that they have met the *Tinker* standard before they can censor.[15]

Student expression may not be censored merely because the school officials dislike its content or because it offers harsh criticism of them or of school policies.[16] In fact, courts have said that criticism is to be protected and fostered.[17]

The *Tinker* Standard: Student expression is constitutionally protected unless it materially and substantially disrupts normal school activities or invades the rights of others.

Determining whether some particular student expression, be it a protest armband or a student newspaper column, will result in "material and substantial disruption" or "invasion of the rights of others" is thus the key question. Court rulings since 1969 have demonstrated that although the *Tinker* standard is subject to some interpretation, it is not as nebulous as it may seem.

One thing that is clear is that school officials must present factual support for their claim that the *Tinker* standard has been met based on the circumstances at the time they censored.[18] According to the *Tinker* decision itself, school officials need not wait until a disruption actually occurs before they can limit student expression. But they must make a "reasonable forecast" of disruption.[19] They cannot base their claim on "undifferentiated fear or apprehension of disturbance" or "a mere desire to avoid the discomfort and unpleasantness that always accompany an unpopular viewpoint."[20] While *Tinker* does not require certainty of disruption,[21] it does require "a specific and significant fear of disruption, not just some remote apprehension of disturbance."[22] Nor is it enough for school officials to show that students intended to disrupt school activities with their expression unless additional evidence indicates their plan has a reasonable likelihood of success.[23] In short, to justify suppression, an administrator needs demonstrable *facts*.

Under *Tinker*, student expression may not be censored merely because school officials dislike its content or because it provokes controversy or debate.

Whether certain expression is potentially disruptive will frequently depend on the environment or atmosphere at the school, not the specific expression used. For example, as one might expect, expressive activity is much less likely to be found disruptive on a college or university campus than at a junior or senior high school.

Also, school officials must typically offer compelling evidence of imminent or immediate physical disruption for it to be considered "material and substantial." Past experience in the school as well as current events that might influence students' behavior would be relevant in showing the reasonableness of the prediction of disruption.

Of course, the best evidence that a particular publication is disruptive is proof that the publication or other expressive activity has actually caused some type of significant disorder such as a student walkout, fighting or damage to school property. The opposite is also true: school officials hardly can claim that a publication is disruptive if it already has been distributed and has caused no disturbance.[24]

In *Scoville v. Board of Education*,[25] two Illinois high school students were expelled for distributing their underground paper, *Grass High*. The paper urged students "not to accept in the future, for delivery to parents, any 'propaganda' issued by the school and to destroy it if accepted." The federal Seventh Circuit Court of Appeals ordered the students reinstated, rejecting the administrators' argument that they could reasonably forecast a disruption; the evidence showed that no disruption actually occurred as a result of the paper's distribution. A similar result was reached in the case of *Shanley v. Northeast Independent School District*,[26] where five Texas high school students were suspended for distributing their underground paper, *The Awakening*. School officials objected to an article on birth control and an editorial advocating reform of marijuana laws. The court was not persuaded by the assistant principal's testimony that the "attitude of the school had somehow changed" because of the paper.[27] Since no disruption had actually occurred, the court ordered the students readmitted.

By contrast, another federal appeals court upheld a forecast of disruption even when no disruption occurred. In *Boucher v. School Board*,[28] a Wisconsin high school student was expelled after he distributed an underground newspaper at school that included an article with instructions and encouragement for hacking into the school's computer system. Even though there was no evidence that students actually used the article to gain unauthorized access to the school's network, the court concluded that the prediction of such an event was reasonably foreseeable and thus the requirements of *Tinker* were satisfied. "It is a call to action detrimental to the tangible interests of the school," the court said.[29]

One situation where courts have been more willing to accept a forecast of substantial disruption as reasonable, even when no disruption actually occurred, is when the student expression is seen as threatening school violence. In *Lavine v. Blaine School District*,[30] for example, the federal Ninth Circuit Court of Appeals concluded that school officials reasonably forecast substantial disruption before temporarily expelling a student who distributed a poem at school that described a school shooting from the shooter's perspective.[31] But once the school determined no threat existed, the court said it could not maintain negative documentation of the incident in student's file. See more discussion of this topic later in this chapter.

As most courts have defined it, the "material and substantial disruption" standard requires some sort of physical disturbance, such as a walkout, a riot, or destruction of school property.

School officials will have a difficult time arguing that their censorship was justified under *Tinker* when the only disruption that occurs is a minor one. "[S]tudent expression may not be suppressed simply because it gives rise to some slight, easily overlooked disruption, including but not limited to 'a showing of mild curiosity' by other students, 'discussion and comment' among students, or even some 'hostile remarks' or 'discussion outside of the classrooms' by other students."[32] The same holds true if the disruption was a reaction to the censorship itself (for example, a student protest demanding that confiscated newspapers be released).

There is some authority to support the notion that even if the expression of an unpopular viewpoint by a student were likely to provoke a violent or disruptive reaction by other students, school authorities have an obligation to protect the student and punish the attackers rather than suppress the unpopular speech. For example, in a Rhode Island case, a male high school student wanted to bring another male student as his date to the prom to express his views in support of gay rights, but the school prohibited his date, fearing a violent reaction from other students.[33] One fight at school had already occurred over the matter. The court supported the student.

> [E]ven a legitimate interest in school discipline does not outweigh a student's right to peacefully express his views in an appropriate time, place and manner. To rule otherwise would completely subvert free speech in the schools by granting other students a "heckler's veto," allowing them to decide through prohibited and violent methods what speech will be heard. The First Amendment does not tolerate mob rule by unruly school children.[34]

Similarly, in *Sullivan v. Houston Independent School District*,[35] high school administrators argued that an underground student newspaper was disruptive because some students read copies during class. The court ruled that such evidence did not constitute a substantial disruption. Teachers can, of course, prohibit the reading of newspapers during class and punish students who disobey such a rule, but that is not a sufficient reason to ban distribution of a paper in the first place.[36]

By contrast, another court found that even though "no serious or substantial disruption stemmed directly" from students' distribution of materials, school officials could still lawfully censor such speech when other circumstances might prompt a reasonable forecast of disruption.[37]

One federal court of appeals has offered a compelling statement of where the balance between school officials' authority and students' rights should lie.

> [W]e do not agree that the precedential value of the *Tinker* decision is nullified whenever a school system is confronted with disruptive activities or the possibility of them. Rather we believe that the Supreme Court has declared a constitutional right which school authorities must nurture and protect, not extinguish, unless they find the circumstances allow them no practical alternative. As to the existence of such circumstances, they are the judges, and if within the range where reasonable minds may differ, their decisions will govern. But there must be some inquiry, and establishment of substantial fact, to buttress the determination.[38]

Perhaps the most authoritative example of how the Supreme Court intended to define the substantial disruption standard is seen in two cases that were decided three years before *Tinker*, but which the Court cited with approval.[39] Both cases involved prohibitions in Mississippi schools against the wearing of "freedom buttons" that advocated equal rights for African-Americans. In one school, the buttons were peacefully worn and only caused "mild curiosity" and some discussion.[40] The court found that the prohibition of the buttons at this school violated the students' First Amendment rights. But a similar restriction at another school was allowed. At that school, the buttons were forced on students and thrown through windows, a situation the school and the court saw as a substantial disruption of the school environment.[41]

INVASION OF THE RIGHTS OF OTHERS: THE SECOND PART OF THE *TINKER* STANDARD

The "material and substantial disruption" language of the *Tinker* standard is what has been most mentioned in court decisions, but a few rulings have attempted to define the vague "invasion of the rights of others" phrase as well. For example, most courts have suggested that at high schools, libelous material could be censored under *Tinker*, if only because libel is generally considered to be without First Amendment protection even when it occurs outside of school.[42] (See Chapter 12 for more explanation of the law of libel.) But one federal court of appeals has indicated that school officials who censor material claiming it is libelous or an unwarranted invasion of privacy will satisfy the "invasion of the rights of others" language of the *Tinker* standard only if they can show that the school will be held legally responsible for the material in question.[43] This is unlikely in most cases involving independent student publications or those at public colleges and universities. (See Chapter 16 on liability.) Of course, a school could also try to argue that the distribution of the libelous material was "substantially disruptive," even if it could not prove that the school would be held legally responsible.

In one case a court delved into the "invasion of the rights of others" language and used it to justify censoring material that the school admitted would not have resulted in any

Under the "heckler's veto" doctrine, school authorities should have an obligation to protect an unpopular student speaker engaging in lawful speech and punish his attackers rather than suppress the unpopular speaker.

"[W]e believe that the Supreme Court has declared a constitutional right which school authorities must nurture and protect, not extinguish, unless they find the circumstances allow them no practical alternative."
— *Butts v. Dallas Independent School District*

The meaning of the second prong of *Tinker* — student speech that would "invade the rights of others" — remains unclear but almost certainly includes legally "unprotected speech" such as libel, invasion of privacy and copyright violations.

kind of visible disruption. In *Trachtman v. Anker*,[44] the staff of *The Stuyvesant Voice* at Stuyvesant High School in New York City sought to distribute a survey to fellow students asking questions about their sexual attitudes, preferences, knowledge and experience. Among other things, the survey inquired about contraception, homosexuality and masturbation. When the principal denied permission to distribute the survey, the students sued. At the trial, school officials presented the affidavits of four expert psychologists and psychiatrists who swore that if distributed, the questionnaire would cause "significant emotional harm" to some students even though it was voluntary and anonymous. Despite affidavits from the students' own experts that no harm would result, a divided court upheld the censorship. The majority opinion said that the administrators had presented sufficient evidence that distribution of the questionnaire would cause a substantial "psychological disruption" and "invade the rights of other students by subjecting them to psychological pressures which may engender significant emotional harm."[45]

But even the majority decision in *Trachtman* indicated that the suppression of the survey would not have been upheld solely on the basis of the school officials' unsupported claim that it was potentially disruptive. They were required to prove, through expert testimony, that they had a reasonable belief that actual harm to students would occur. The court also made a point to distinguish the distribution of a survey that asked questions of students from the distribution of a publication that gave information about sexuality. The First Amendment, the court said, would have more likely protected the latter.[46]

In a more recent case, the U.S. Court of Appeals for the Ninth Circuit relied on the "rights of others" language from *Tinker* to allow a California high school to prohibit a student from wearing a T-shirt to school that contained an anti-gay message.[47] "As *Tinker* clearly states, students have the right to 'be secure and to be let alone,'" the two judges in the Ninth Circuit majority said. "Being secure involves not only freedom from physical assaults but from psychological attacks that cause young people to question their self-worth and their rightful place in society."[48] But the controversial ruling, perceived by some as an opening to a much broader array of censorship in the schools, was vacated by the U.S. Supreme Court on procedural grounds without a substantive ruling on the "invasion of the rights of others" question it raised. Thus, it remains that "[t]he precise scope of *Tinker*'s 'interference with the rights of others' language is unclear."[49]

DISRUPTION IS SOMETIMES FOUND

There are cases where courts have found student expression disruptive enough to justify censorship under the *Tinker* standard.

In *Dodd v. Rambis*,[50] students at an Indiana high school were suspended after they distributed leaflets announcing the plan for a student walkout the following day to protest the school's disciplinary policies. In upholding the suspensions, the court found that the following facts justified the school's forecast of substantial disruption: First, 54 students had engaged in a walkout at the school one day before the leaflets were distributed that materially disrupted several classes. Second, two school administrators testified that there was a general atmosphere of excitement at the school the previous day, with "noisy and rowdy" passing periods and an increase in tardiness by students. Third, the principal anticipated that the second walkout would likely be larger and would prompt an even greater disruption than the previous one.[51]

In *Quarterman v. Byrd*,[52] a North Carolina high school student was suspended for distributing – without the prior permission of the school administration – an underground paper that contained this statement:

> We have to be prepared to fight in the halls and in the classrooms, out in the streets because the schools belong to the people. If we have to – we'll burn the buildings of our schools down to show these pigs that we

want an education that won't brainwash us into being racist. And that we want an education that will teach us to know the real truth about things we need to know, so we can better serve the people!!![53]

The federal Fourth Circuit Court of Appeals reinstated the student because the school prior review policy under which he was disciplined was unconstitutional. But the Court did suggest that the statement was "inflammatory" and "potentially disruptive," implying that the school might have satisfied the *Tinker* standard if its policy had been adequate.[54]

In *Smith v. Mount Pleasant Public Schools*, a federal court in Michigan upheld a school's punishment of a student who delivered a speech in the school cafeteria that criticized the school's tardy policy and referred to one administrator as a "skank" and a "tramp" who had cheated on her husband and another as confused about his sexuality.[55] Noting the extreme disrespect of the references to the administrators and the fact that demonstrably upset students complained about having to listen to the speech, the court said the school's punishment was consistent with *Tinker*.[56]

In *Karp v. Becken*,[57] an Arizona high school student claimed his First Amendment rights were infringed when school officials confiscated signs he was distributing to other students supporting a fired English teacher at the school. The court upheld the school's response as a reasonable forecast of a substantial disruption, noting that the incident accompanied a planned walkout over the teacher's dismissal that student athletes at the school had pledged to prevent and that had already resulted in the presence of news media crews at the school and a pulled fire alarm.[58]

In *Frasca v. Andrews*,[59] a high school principal seized the copies of a school-sponsored student newspaper and refused to allow it to be distributed. The principal objected to two letters printed in the paper. One, which was purportedly from the school's lacrosse team, criticized the newspaper's sports editor for lack of sports coverage and threatened to "kick your greasy ass" if a formal apology was not made.[60] An editorial response to the letter referred to the lacrosse team members as "hotheaded, egotistical, 'Pissed Off' jocks."[61] The second letter criticized the conduct of the student government vice president and accused him of changing his grades through the school's computer system and failing to attend meetings he was supposed to run.[62] School officials raised concerns that the first letter might not, in fact, have been written by the entire lacrosse team, some of whom might object to it. They testified that team members might react violently to the words used to describe them and that a physical confrontation could result. They also said that they believed the accusations against the student government officer were false even though the newspaper's editors said they could support them. The court found the school's justification for censorship sufficient under *Tinker*, in part because the letters were published in the last issue of the newspaper for the school year and neither the lacrosse team members nor the student government vice president would have an opportunity to respond.[63]

GROWING CONCERN ABOUT SCHOOL VIOLENCE

As mentioned earlier in this chapter, there is one context where school officials' forecast of substantial disruption has been given greater deference by the courts in recent years. When school officials raise reasonable concerns about student expression relating to physical violence, judges appear much quicker to accept their justification as satisfying the requirements of *Tinker*.

Incidents of school violence beginning in the late 1990s — most notably the 1999 shooting at Columbine High School in Colorado that resulted in 13 victims dead, at least 23 injured and the two student shooters committing suicide — appear to have dramatically changed the way many perceive American high schools. These concerns were amplified by the mass killing of 26 students and teachers at Sandy Hook Elementary

School in Newtown, Conn., in December 2012 — even though the gunman (who took his own life after the killing spree) was not a student. To many school administrators, statements that once would have been seen as flights of imagination, normal "teen angst" or students "blowing off steam" were now more likely to be perceived as a potential precursor to tragedy. And as a result, schools began cracking down on all forms of student speech that contained even a hint of a violent message or imagery.

When students contest punishment for speech perceived as hinting at violence, even if the actual likelihood of violence seems very farfetched, courts regularly side with the schools, relying on *Tinker*. In one memorable recent case, a federal appeals court even said that a school was justified in suspending a fifth-grader for a fanciful crayon drawing of a spaceman telepathically making the school explode.[64] Other examples include:

- A sixth-grade student reading a story he wrote describing graphic murders and sexual assaults of named students and teachers aloud to a class.[65]
- A junior high school student who wrote a letter to a former girlfriend, a copy of which was brought to school by a friend, in which he described the girl as a "bitch," "slut," "ass" and "whore" as well as expressing his wish to sodomize, rape and kill her.[66]
- A middle school student who used as his instant messaging icon from his home computer a drawing of a pistol firing a bullet into a person's head above the words "Kill Mr. VanderMolen," the name of his English teacher.[67]
- An 11th-grade student who brought a poem to school, which he asked his English teacher to critique, that described a first-person account of a school shooting.[68]
- A middle school student who accessed at school a Web site he created that included a page headlined "Why Should She Die?" filled with criticism of his algebra teacher and including his request that site visitors give him $20 to "help pay for the hitman."[69]
- A five-year-old kindergarten student, playing "cops and robbers" at recess, who pointed his finger at his friends and said, "I am going to shoot you."[70]

As these cases suggest, expression that encourages or even depicts violence is probably the least likely to be protected under *Tinker*. In fact, two federal appeals courts have concluded, relying on the Supreme Court's 2007 decision in *Morse v. Frederick*, discussed later in this chapter, that there is a special exception to First Amendment protection when student expression poses a direct threat to the physical safety of the school population. In the view of these courts, schools are not even obligated to demonstrate they have met the "substantial disruption" test of *Tinker*; all they need do is to show that a threat to school safety was made.[71]

"TRUE THREATS"

For the majority of courts that contend *Tinker* remains the appropriate censorship standard even for student expression that is deemed violent, a number have focused on the phrase "true threat" to determine when the speech is subject to punishment. A "true threat," as the Supreme Court has defined it, occurs when a speaker "directs a threat to a person or group of persons with the intent of placing the victim in fear of bodily harm or death."[72] In applying this true threat standard to student speech at school, courts have disagreed over one important question: from whose viewpoint should the statement be interpreted? Some courts have said the threat should be assessed from the perspective of a reasonable recipient of the message and how they would assess the alleged threat.[73] Others have said the question is whether a reasonable person, standing in the shoes of the speaker, should have anticipated his expression would be perceived by others as a serious threat to cause harm. As most agree, applying either standard would reach the same conclusion in the vast majority of cases.[74] The true threat standard is an objective one focused primarily on two things: (1) the reaction of a reasonable person and (2) evidence of at least some intent by the speaker to communicate the message.[75] When student expression constitutes a "true threat," it appears school officials will have an easy time justifying their acts of censorship or post-publication punishment. The "true threat" standard is an extremely high bar. Merely discussing violence in a journalistic or artistic context almost never can rise to the level of a "true threat." On occasion, however, courts have found that a student's writing about violence was so specifically directed at a known target that it posed a realistic threat and went beyond the protection of the First Amendment. For instance, a federal appeals court ruled that a Minnesota high-school student crossed the "true threat" line when he submitting a series of essays with increasingly vivid violence (including references to the Columbine school massacre) to his English teacher, culminating in an essay that depicted "in gruesome detail" a character modeled on the student writer murdering a character modeled on the teacher and then taking his own life.[76]

SATISFYING THE *TINKER* STANDARD AT COLLEGES

Some First Amendment advocates question whether *Tinker* — which, after all, represents a step down from the rights that adults in the "real world" enjoy — has any place on a college campus at all. It has, however, become relatively common for courts to rely on *Tinker* when deciding cases brought by college students.[77]

Courts very rarely find materially disruptive expression on a college or university campus, but a few cases do exist. For example, in the 1969 *Norton v. Discipline Committee of East Tennessee State University*,[78] one of the earliest cases to apply *Tinker*, the court permitted university officials to discipline students and stop distribution of leaflets that the court believed advocated disruptive activity. The leaflets included questions such as, "Have [students at the school] precipitated a revolution like the French students [or] seized buildings and raised havoc until they got what they were entitled to like other American students" and contained phrases such as "stand up and fight" and "assault the bastions of administrative tyranny."[79] The court emphasized that the mood of campus unrest exemplified by demonstrations at other colleges at the time justified the administrators' fear of a substantial disruption.

In another case involving a Vietnam War protest, University of Southern Mississippi officials confiscated leaflets falsely announcing that classes scheduled for the two days before final exams had been canceled because of violence on other campuses. The court upheld the suspensions of the students involved, noting that the leaflets would likely disrupt the academic process and interfere with the rights of others by making unsuspecting students miss class.[80]

The Sixth Circuit Court of Appeals also affirmed the 1967 expulsion of several Tennessee college students, in part for disrupting meetings on campus and in part for distributing leaflets calling for a boycott of class registration. They were disciplined for "conduct obstructing the educational functions of the University."[81]

These decisions, as their facts suggest, are the exceptions rather than the rule. In no case since the turbulent times of the early 1970s has a court found content in a college student publication to justify a school's claim of material and substantial disruption of school activities.

LIMITATIONS BEYOND *TINKER*

For many years after the *Tinker* ruling, the standard created by the Supreme Court in that case was seen as the exclusive, all-encompassing measure for determining the constitutionality of administrative censorship of student expression. Speech would be protected unless school officials could demonstrate that a student's words or images would create a substantial disruption of school activities or an invasion of the rights of others (or that the speech would be unprotected even if conveyed by an adult outside of school, such as libel or obscenity). But over time, some courts questioned whether *Tinker* was intended to be the sole limitation on student speech.

In 1986, in the case *Bethel School District v. Fraser*, the Supreme Court upheld a school's punishment of a student for giving a speech at a school assembly that contained "an elaborate, graphic, and explicit sexual metaphor."[82] The First Amendment, the Court said, does not prohibit school officials from silencing or punishing student expression at school that is "vulgar," "lewd," "indecent" or "plainly offensive."[83]

For a time, many interpreted the confusing decision as an attempt to apply the *Tinker* standard. That belief was based on the Court's finding that the student's speech to a captive audience in a school-sponsored assembly was substantially disruptive. But more recently, the Supreme Court has said the *Bethel* case is not a substantial disruption case and that "the mode of analysis set forth in *Tinker* is not absolute."[84]

Just what can be considered vulgar, lewd, indecent or plainly offensive? These are inherently subjective terms and many have debated their definitions. Lower courts that have applied the *Bethel* ruling have tended to require evidence that school officials censored because of the form of expression (the particular words and images used) rather than any viewpoint the speech might be intending to convey.[85] Lewdness, vulgarity, and indecency normally connote sexual innuendo or profanity, and courts tend to interpret "highly offensive" as closely related.[86] The gratuitous use of "four-letter words" or extremely graphic sexual language used by students probably can be prohibited under *Bethel*; newsworthy references to sexuality probably cannot.

Two years later, in 1988, the Supreme Court once again cut back on the scope of *Tinker*'s protections when it allowed greater limitations on student speech that was "school-sponsored." That case, *Hazelwood School District v. Kuhlmeier*,[87] is discussed at length in the next chapter.

In 2007, the Supreme Court once again noted an exception to the strong First Amendment protection students were entitled to under *Tinker*. In *Morse v. Frederick*,[88] the Court was confronted with a case involving an Alaska high school student suspended from school for holding up a banner that read "Bong Hits 4 Jesus" as the 2002 Olympic Torch Relay passed through Juneau. Although the student, Joseph Frederick, argued he was off school grounds when he displayed his banner (he was across a public street from his school) and that his nonsensical banner created no disruption, the Supreme Court upheld the school's punishment of the speech. The Court classified the speech as being on-campus speech because of the unique factual circumstances — Frederick's display took place at a school-sanctioned event, under teacher supervision, in full view of the school and its student body — and found that it was reasonable to conclude that the banner conveyed a message of promoting illegal drug use.

The Court majority, over a strong dissent and with several concurring opinions, concluded that *Tinker* was not intended to be the sole limitation on non-school-sponsored student speech: "The 'special characteristics of the school environment,' and the governmental interest in stopping student drug abuse ... allow schools to restrict student expression that they reasonably regard as promoting illegal drug use."[89] The Court rejected the school's argument that under the Fraser case schools should be allowed to censor speech simply because school officials find it offensive or in conflict with the school's "educational mission." "[M]uch political and religious speech might be perceived as offensive to some," the Court said.[90]

Some have read the Court's majority opinion in *Morse* as suggesting that — in addition to restricting speech that promotes illegal drug use — courts could also cut back on *Tinker*'s protection in other contexts.[91] However, a concurring opinion, written by Justice Samuel Alito and joined by Justice Anthony Kennedy, when combined with the three dissenting justices who stood by the position that *Tinker* was still the standard school officials should be required to meet, suggests that at least five justices would require a narrow reading of the holding in Morse.

Morse, Justice Alito wrote, "goes no further than to hold that a public school may restrict speech that a reasonable observer would interpret as advocating illegal drug use. ... [I]t provides no support for any restriction of speech that can plausibly be interpreted as commenting on any political or social issue, including speech on issues such as 'the wisdom of the war on drugs or of legalizing marijuana for medicinal use.'"[92]

In other words, if Morse's banner had read "Legalize Marijuana" instead of "Bong Hits 4 Jesus," his punishment likely would have been rejected. The ability of students to comment in a non-disruptive way on important political and religious issues of the day —including the use of illegal drugs — remains protected after *Morse*.

As troubling as the *Morse* case was to some First Amendment advocates because of the exception it created to *Tinker*, the ruling may in fact turn out to diminish the ability of the lower courts to further carve away at *Tinker*'s protections. Again, as noted in Justice Alito's influential concurring opinion, "the opinion does not hold that the special characteristics of the public schools necessarily justify any other speech restrictions [than those already recognized by the Court in *Tinker*, *Bethel*, and *Hazelwood*]."[93]

SUMMARY

Since 1969, the courts have agreed that public school students are entitled to the free press and free expression protections of the First Amendment. However, in light of the special characteristics of the school environment, some student expression may be limited on campus in ways it could not be restricted outside of school. In 1969, the Supreme Court set the standard for when censorship by school officials would be permissible in *Tinker v. Des Moines Independent Community School District*. When school officials can make a reasonable forecast that material and substantial disruption of school activities will result from the student expression at issue or if they can show the speech invades the rights of others, they will be allowed to censor. But that forecast of disruption must be based on actual facts, not unfounded or speculative fears.

More recently, the Supreme Court has recognized exceptions to *Tinker*'s protections when student speech is pervasively lewd and vulgar or is reasonably perceived as advocating illegal drug use. And as the next chapter describes, some school-sponsored student expression also will be subject to a lesser level of First Amendment protection. But the *Tinker* standard remains the law of the land and will continue to guide decisions about whether school officials can legally censor student expression at school.

ENDNOTES

1   *Lander v. Seaver*, 32 Vt. 114 (1859).
2   *Slate v. Dist. Bd. of Sch. Dist. No. I*, 116 N.W. 232 (Wis. 1908).
3   *Wooster v. Sunderland*, 27 Cal. App. 51 (1915).
4   *Tanton v. McKenney*, 197 N.W. 510 (Mich. 1924).
5   *West Virginia State Bd. of Educ. v. Barnette*, 319 U.S. 624, 637 (1943).
6   *Id.*
7   310 U.S. 586 (1940).
8   319 U.S. 624 (1943).
9   *Id.* at 642.
10 393 U.S. 503 (1969).
11 *Id.* at 514.
12 *Id.* at 506.
13 *Id.* at 511.
14 393 U.S. 503, 513 (1969).
15 See, e.g., *Katz v. McAulay*, 438 F.2d 1058, 1060 (2d Cir. 1971) (citing *NAACP v. Alabama*, 357 U.S. 449 (1958)), *cert denied*, 405 U.S. 933; *Eisner v. Stamford Bd. of Educ.*, 440 F.2d 803, 810 (2d Cir. 1971); *Shanley v. Northeast Indep. Sch. Dist.*, 462 F.2d 960, 969 (5th Cir. 1972); *Scoville v. Bd. of Educ.*, 425 F.2d 10, 13 (7th Cir.), *cert denied*, 400 U.S. 826 (1970).

16 See *Shanley v. Northeast Indep. Sch. Dist.*, 462 F.2d 960, 972 n.10 (5th Cir. 1972).
17 *Butts v. Dallas Indep. Sch. Dist.*, 436 F.2d 728, 732 (5th Cir. 1971).
18 See, e.g., *Shanley*, 462 F.2d at 974; *Scoville*, 425 F.2d at 14; *Karp v. Becken*, 477 F.2d 171, 174 (9th Cir. 1973); *Vail v. Bd. of Educ.*, 354 F. Supp. 592, 600 (D.N.H. 1973), vacated on other grounds, 502 F.2d 1159 (1st Cir. 1973); *Rivera v. East Otero Sch. Dist.*, 721 F. Supp. 1189, 1193-94 (D. Colo. 1989).
19 *Tinker*, 393 U.S. at 514 (requiring "facts which might reasonably have led school authorities to forecast substantial disruption or material interference with school activities").
20 *Id.* at 508, 509. See also *Sypniewski v. Warren Hills Reg'l Bd. of Educ.*, 307 F.3d 243, 265 (3d Cir. 2002).
21 *Lowery v. Euverard*, 497 F.3d 584, 591-92 (6th Cir. 2007).
22 *Saxe v. State College Area Sch. Dist.*, 240 F.3d 200, 211 (3d Cir. 2001).
23 *Scoville*, 425 F.2d at 14.
24 See, e.g., *Thomas v. Bd. of Educ.*, 607 F.2d 1043, 1052 n. 17 (2d Cir. 1979), *cert denied*, 444 U.S. 1081 (1980).
25 *Scoville v. Bd. of Educ.*, 425 F.2d 10 (7th Cir.), *cert denied*, 400 U.S. 826 (1970).
26 *Shanley v. Northeast Indep. Sch. Dist.*, 462 F.2d 960 (5th Cir. 1972).
27 *Id.* at 974.
28 134 F.3d 821 (7th Cir. 1998).
29 *Id.* at 828.
30 257 F.3d 981 (9th Cir. 2001).
31 See also *Boim v. Fulton County Sch. Dist.*, 494 F.3d 978, 983 (11th Cir. 2007) (upholding school district's suspension of student for writing story about dream of shooting teacher and finding that student's writing "clearly caused and was reasonably likely to further cause a material and substantial disruption to the 'maintenance of order and decorum' within [the student's high school]").
32 *Holloman ex rel. Holloman v. Harland*, 370 F.3d 1252, 1271-72 (11th Cir. 2004) (citations omitted).
33 *Fricke v. Lynch*, 491 F. Supp. 381 (D.R.I. 1980).
34 *Id.* at 387. See also *Shanley*, 462 F.2d at 974; *Eisner v. Stamford Bd. of Educ.*, 440 F.2d 803, 809 n. 6 (2d Cir. 1971).
35 307 F. Supp. 1328 (S.D. Tex. 1969).
36 *Id.* at 1340. See also *Boyd County High School Gay Straight Alliance v. Bd. of Educ.*, 258 F. Supp. 2d 667, 689 (E.D. Ky. 2003).
37 *Dodd v. Rambis*, 535 F. Supp. 23, 29 (S.D. Ind. 1981).
38 *Butts v. Dallas Indep. Sch. Dist.*, 436 F.2d 728, 732 (5th Cir. 1971).
39 *Tinker*, 393 U.S. 503, 505 n. 1.
40 *Burnside v. Byars*, 363 F.2d 744, 748 (5th Cir. 1969).
41 *Blackwell v. Issaquena County Bd. of Educ.*, 363 F.2d 749, 751 (5th Cir. 1966).
42 See, e.g., *Draudt v. Wooster City School Dist. Bd. of Educ.*, 246 F. Supp. 2d 820, 832 (N.D. Ohio 2003) (rejecting First Amendment challenge to school officials' impoundment of student newspaper containing article that identified by name students who unlawfully drank alcohol underage, because "it is well established that defamatory expression falls outside the reach of the First Amendment"); see also *Nitzberg v. Parks*, 525 F.2d 378, 382 (4th Cir. 1975); *Frasca v. Andrews*, 463 F. Supp. 1043, 1052 (E.D.N.Y. 1979). Compare *Mazart v. State*, 441 N.Y.S.2d 600, 605 (N.Y. Ct. Cl. 1981) (public college cannot exercise prior review of school-sponsored publication for the purpose of censoring libel).
43 *Kuhlmeier v. Hazelwood Sch. Dist.*, 795 F.2d 1368, 1375-76 (8th Cir. 1986), rev'd on other grounds, 484 U.S. 260 (1988).
44 563 F.2d 512 (2d Cir. 1977), *cert denied*, 435 U.S. 925 (1978).
45 *Id.* at 516, 520.
46 *Id.* at 516 n. 2 and 520 (Gurfein, J., concurring).
47 *Harper v. Poway Unified Sch. Dist.*, 445 F.3d 1166, 1171 (9th Cir. 2006), vacated as moot, 127 S. Ct. 1484 (2007). The shirt read, "BE ASHAMED, OUR SCHOOL EMBRACED WHAT GOD HAS CONDEMNED" on the front and "HOMOSEXUALITY IS SHAMEFUL 'ROMANS 1:27'" on the back.
48 *Harper*, 445 F.3d at 1178.
49 *Saxe v. State College Area Sch. Dist.*, 240 F.3d 200, 217 (3d Cir. 2001) (citing *Slotterback v. Interboro Sch. Dist.*, 766 F. Supp. 280, 289 n. 8 (E.D. Pa. 1991); *Kuhlmeier v. Hazelwood Sch. Dist.*, 795 F.2d 1368, 1375 (8th Cir.), rev'd on other grounds, 484 U.S. 260 (1988)).
50 *Dodd v. Rambis*, 535 F. Supp. 23 (S.D. Ind. 1981).
51 *Id.* at 29.
52 453 F.2d 54 (4th Cir. 1971).
53 *Id.* at 55-56.
54 *Id.* at 57.
55 *Smith v. Mount Pleasant Pub. Sch.*, 285 F. Supp. 2d 987, 989 (E.D. Mich. 2003), reconsideration denied by, 298 F. Supp. 2d 636 (E.D. Mich. 2003).
56 *Smith*, 285 F. Supp. 2d at 997.
57 *Karp v. Becken*, 477 F.2d 171 (9th Cir. 1973).
58 *Id.* at 175-76.
59 463 F. Supp. 1043 (E.D.N.Y. 1979).
60 *Id.* at 1046.
61 *Id.*
62 *Id.*
63 *Id.* at 1051-52.
64 *Cuff v. Valley Cent. Sch. Dist.*, 677 F.3d 109 (2d Cir. 2012).
65 *D.F. v. Bd. of Educ.*, 386 F. Supp. 2d 119 (E.D.N.Y. 2005), aff'd, 108 Fed. Appx. 232 (2d Cir. 2006), *cert denied*, 127 S. Ct. 1170 (2007).

66 *Doe v. Pulaski County Special Sch. Dist.*, 306 F.3d 616 (8th Cir. 2002) (*en banc*).
67 *Wisniewski v. Bd. of Educ.*, 494 F.3d 34 (2d Cir. 2007), *cert denied*, 128 S. Ct. 1741 (2008).
68 *LaVine v. Blaine Sch. Dist.*, 257 F.3d 981 (9th Cir. 2001), *cert denied*, 536 U.S. 959 (2002).
69 *J.S. v. Bethlehem Area Sch. Dist.*, 807 A.2d 847 (Pa. 2002).
70 *S.G. ex rel. A.G. v. Sayreville Bd. of Educ.*, 333 F.3d 417 (3d Cir. 2003), *cert denied*, 540 U.S. 1104 (2004). This case, which received extensive national and international attention, was widely pointed to by critics as a glaring example of the growing irrationality of some zero tolerance policy enforcement. See, e.g., Dave Kopel, "Gunning for the Kiddies," National Review Online (Sept. 22, 2000) http://www. nationalreview.com/kopel/kopel092200.shtml (last visited June 21, 2013).
71 *Ponce v. Socorro Indep. Sch. Dist.*, 508 F.3d 765 (5th Cir. 2007); *Boim v. Fulton County Sch. Dist.*, 494 F.3d 978 (11th Cir. 2007). *But see Wisniewski v. Board of Educ.*, 494 F.3d 34 (2d Cir. 2007) (decided after *Morse* but concluding that *Tinker* is the standard that applied to censorship of student speech deemed to be violent), *cert denied*, 128 S. Ct. 1741 (2008).
72 *Virginia v. Black*, 538 U.S. 343, 344 (2003).
73 See, e.g., *Doe v. Pulaski County Special Sch. Dist.*, 306 F.3d 616, 622-23 (8th Cir. 2002) (*en banc*) (finding that relevant factors in determining a reasonable recipient's reaction include: 1) the reaction of those who heard the alleged threat; 2) whether the threat was conditional; 3) whether the person who made the alleged threat communicated it directly to the object of the threat; 4) whether the speaker had a history of making threats against the person purportedly threatened; and 5) whether the recipient had a reason to believe that the speaker had a propensity to engage in violence).
74 *Id.* at 623 ("The result will differ only in the extremely rare case when a recipient suffers from some unique sensitivity and that sensitivity is unknown to the speaker. Absent such a situation, a reasonably foreseeable response from the recipient and an actual reasonable response must, theoretically, be one and the same.").
75 *Id.* at 624 (But "[i]n determining whether a statement amounts to an unprotected threat, there is no requirement that the speaker intended to carry out the threat, nor is there any requirement that the speaker was capable of carrying out the purported threat of violence.").
76 *Riehm v. Engelking*, 538 F.3d 952, 964 (8th Cir. 2008).
77 See, e.g., *DeJohn v. Temple Univ.*, 537 F.3d 301, 317 (3d Cir. 2008) (citing *Tinker* but finding that a college's "harassment code" was unconstitutionally over-broad, because it penalized speaking with an intent to interfere with school even if no interference was actually likely to occur); see also *Ward v. Polite*, 667 F.3d 727, 733 (6th Cir. 2012) (citing *Tinker* and other high-school student-speech decisions in case involving college graduate student's claim she was expelled for espousing anti-gay religious views).
78 419 F.2d 195 (6th Cir. 1969), *cert denied*, 399 U.S. 906 (1970).
79 *Id.* at 197-98.
80 *Speake v. Grantham*, 317 F. Supp. 1253 (S.D. Miss. 1970), aff'd, 440 F.2d 1351 (5th Cir. 1971) (per curiam).
81 *Jones v. State Bd. of Educ.*, 279 F. Supp. 190, 204 (M.D. Tenn. 1968), aff'd, 407 F.2d 834 (6th Cir.), cert. granted, 396 U.S. 817 (1969), cert. dismissed, 397 U.S. 31 (1970). Note that *Jones* was a pre-*Tinker* case, in which the district court held (and the Sixth Circuit agreed) that the challenged disciplinary action was not the result of the content of the students' speech, but rather resulted from a laundry list of purportedly disruptive conduct, which ran a range from rock-throwing to refusing to wear shoes in the library to planting a worm in cafeteria food to being caught in bed with a person of the opposite sex.
82 478 U.S. 675, 678 (1986).
83 *Id.* at 685.
84 *Morse v. Frederick*, 127 S. Ct. 2618, 2627 (2007).
85 See, e.g., *Newsom v. Albemarle County Sch. Bd.*, 354 F.3d 249, 256 (4th Cir. 2003) ("When speech in school falls within the lewd, vulgar, and plainly offensive rubric, it can be said that *Fraser* limits the form and manner of speech, but does not address the content of the message.").
86 See, e.g., *Guiles v. Marineau*, 461 F.3d 320, 327-29 (2d Cir. 2006), *cert denied*, 127 S. Ct. 3054 (2007) (dismissing school's claim that high school student's T-shirt calling President George W. Bush, among other things, a "Crook," "Cocaine Addict," "AWOL, Draft Dodger" and a "Lying Drunk Driver" was not "lewd," "vulgar," "indecent," or "plainly offensive"). *But see Boroff v. Van Wert City Bd. of Educ.*, 220 F.3d 465, 471 (6th Cir. 2000) (upholding school's ban on T-shirts that featured the singer Marilyn Manson as vulgar and offensive, on ground that band promoted destructive conduct and demoralizing values that were contrary to the educational mission of the school, and that singer promoted drug use), *cert denied*, 532 U.S. 920 (2001).
87 484 U.S. 260 (1988).
88 127 S. Ct. 2618 (2007).
89 *Id.* at 2629.
90 *Id.*
91 See *Ponce v. Socorro Indep. Sch. Dist.*, 508 F.3d 765 (5th Cir. 2007); *Boim v. Fulton County Sch. Dist.*, 494 F.3d 978 (11th Cir. 2007). *But see Wisniewski v. Board of Educ.*, 494 F.3d 34 (2d Cir. 2007) (decided after *Morse* but concluding that *Tinker* is the standard that applied to censorship of student speech deemed to be violent), *cert denied*, 128 S. Ct. 1741 (2008).
92 Morse, 127 S. Ct. at 2636 (Alito, J., concurring).
93 *Id.* at 2637.

[Our decision in *Morse v. Frederick*] "provides no support for any restriction of speech that can plausibly be interpreted as commenting on any political or social issue...."
— *Morse v. Frederick* (Justice Samuel Alito, concurring) (2007)

CHAPTER 5

High School Press Freedom
The impact of *Hazelwood*

Although the *Tinker* case involved students who wore protest armbands to school, the Supreme Court's decision was quickly applied to the student press as well. Less than three months after *Tinker*, a federal court in New York decided a case, *Zucker v. Panitz*, involving censorship of a school-sponsored high school newspaper.[1] The principal of New Rochelle High School had ordered the school's student newspaper editor not to publish an advertisement that opposed the war in Vietnam. The editor and the student group that placed the ad contested the principal's order, and the court held that under the Supreme Court's recent ruling, the students' claim was a valid one. "The rationale of *Tinker* carries beyond the facts in that case," the court said.[2]

The *Zucker* decision directly confronted what in 1988 would become the central issue in the *Hazelwood School District v. Kuhlmeier* case: should censorship of a student newspaper be treated differently from censorship of a black armband because the student newspaper is school-sponsored? New Rochelle school officials argued that it should. In their argument before the court, they described the student newspaper as a "'beneficial educational device' developed as part of the curriculum and intended to inure primarily to the benefit of those who compile, edit and publish it."[3] Thus the school officials believed they had the authority to take steps they deemed appropriate to regulate the content of the publication. The students, on the other hand, argued that an important purpose of the newspaper was "to provide a forum for the dissemination of ideas and information by and to the students" of the high school.[4] They noted that the newspaper was published and sold outside of the journalism classroom and that it contained letters to the editor and many stories on substantive, controversial issues that students had selected.[5]

The court agreed with the students. It held that the newspaper was clearly "a forum for the dissemination of ideas."[6] After looking at the content of the publication, the court said, "The school paper appears to have been open to free expression of ideas in the news and editorial columns as well as in letters to the editor."[7] Thus the First Amendment protected the students' "nondisruptive" expression.[8]

The *Zucker* decision was the beginning of almost 19 years of agreement among the courts on student press rights. Even when a publication was school-sponsored or produced in relationship to a class, courts around the nation routinely said that students could not be censored unless school officials could demonstrate that they had met the *Tinker* standard.[9]

A common thread among some of these decisions was a reliance on what has come to be called "public forum analysis," a legal doctrine the courts have developed to evaluate the legality of government restrictions on expression on government-owned property such as at a civic auditorium or an airport, or in a government publication or broadcast.[10] Public forum analysis recognizes three kinds of government-owned property. The first is a traditional public forum, a place or other type of government-owned or sponsored property that by long tradition has been devoted to free expression such as a street or a park. The second kind of government property is the "designated" public forum (referred to by some courts as a "limited public forum"[11]). Such a forum has been opened by the government for expressive activity but only for certain groups or for expression on certain topics. Content- based restrictions on expression in either of these kinds of public forums are impermissible unless the government can demonstrate that its restrictions are "narrowly drawn" and serve a "compelling interest."[12] Thus, for example, if a city were to allow plays, speeches and meetings at a civic auditorium, that auditorium would be a designated public forum, and the city would violate the Constitution if it denied the auditorium's use for the performance of a play solely because city officials found the play offensive.[13]

One post-*Tinker* national study reported, "where a free, vigorous student press does exist, there is a healthy ferment of ideas and opinions, with no indication of disruption or negative side effects on the educational experience of the school." Source: *Captive Voices* (1974)

Public forum analysis: A legal doctrine the courts have developed to evaluate the legality of government restrictions on expression on government-owned property.

The final type is the "non-public" or "closed" forum, which is public property that has not by tradition or designation served as a location for free expression, such as a military base or a jail. In the non-public forum, the government can limit expression as long as its restrictions are "reasonable" and not simply an effort to silence a particular viewpoint.[14]

When confronted with cases involving censorship of a school-sponsored high school publication, some courts began to use this public forum analysis to determine the level of First Amendment protection to which students were entitled.

The 1977 *Gambino v. Fairfax County School Board*[15] decision was one of the most reasoned applications of the forum analysis to a student publication. The case began when the student editors of a school-sponsored newspaper in Virginia discovered through an informal survey that many students who were sexually active took no precautions to avoid pregnancy. In response, they prepared a news story that provided information about the forms of birth control available and their relative rates of effectiveness. The school principal balked, claiming the story would be in violation of a school policy that prohibited the teaching of sex education in the school. The students took their case to court, and both the federal district court and the Fourth Circuit Court of Appeals agreed that the First Amendment had been violated.

The school claimed that the student newspaper was merely an "in-house organ of the school system, funded and sponsored by the Board of Education"[16] and thus could not be considered a public forum. Most of the students on the newspaper staff were enrolled in a journalism class and received credit for their work. But after considering the board's general policy toward student publications, which allowed students to choose the topics they wished to include in their newspaper, and the articles that had been published in the newspaper in the past, the court agreed that the newspaper was a public forum for student expression. "The extent of state involvement in providing funding and facilities for the newspaper does not determine whether First Amendment rights are applicable," the court said.[17] "Accordingly, the general power of the Board to regulate course content does not apply."[18]

Not every court to confront censorship of school-sponsored student media in the years between 1969 and 1988 referenced forum analysis.[19] It appears some courts presumed that student-edited publications were, by their very nature, designated public forums for student expression. Either that or they considered public forum analysis inappropriate or unnecessary. But in all of those years, the courts that used forum analysis found every school-sponsored publication they examined to be a designated forum. And whether using forum analysis or not, the courts agreed that school officials must show either a "material and substantial disruption" or an "invasion of the rights of others" (the *Tinker* standard) if they were to satisfy the "compelling interest" test required of them in order to lawfully censor a student publication.[20]

In the years following *Tinker*, there was never an indication schools were suffering as a result of the burden the First Amendment placed on them. In fact, as one national study reported, "where a free, vigorous student press does exist, there is a healthy ferment of ideas and opinions, with no indication of disruption or negative side effects on the educational experience of the school."[21]

Nevertheless, when the Supreme Court was finally confronted with its first censorship case involving a school-sponsored high school publication, it chose to ignore the years of settled law and strike out in a new direction.

In the spring of 1983, students on the staff of the *Spectrum* newspaper at Hazelwood East High School near St. Louis, Mo., prepared a two-page center-spread of stories focusing on some of the problems faced by teenagers, including pregnancy, divorce and the plight of runaways.[22] The stories were scheduled for publication on May 13.

Spectrum was the official student newspaper at Hazelwood East and was produced almost entirely by students in the school's Journalism II class. The teacher for that class and faculty adviser to the newspaper, Robert Stergos, had approved the articles scheduled for publication, but two weeks before the issue was to be distributed, he resigned to take a job outside the school. A yearbook adviser from another school in the Hazelwood district, Howard Emerson, was brought in to advise the publication for the remainder of the school year.

Despite the confusion that surrounded the change in newspaper advisers, the censorship incident that prompted the lawsuit would probably never have occurred were it not for one unfortunate fact: *Spectrum* was subject to prior review by the school principal. Before he left, Stergos had begun the practice of submitting page proofs for the newspaper to Principal Robert Reynolds before the paper went to press. Emerson followed that same practice for the May 13 issue. As a result, Reynolds previewed the center-spread, and objected to two of the stories it contained. One, about teenage pregnancy, included the personal accounts of three unnamed Hazelwood East students who described their own experiences as pregnant teenagers. Another, about the impact of parents' divorce on children, contained quotes from students whose lives had been touched by divorce. Despite two trained publication advisers having given their approval to these stories — and without informing the students — Reynolds ordered the entire spread removed from *Spectrum*.

The newspaper staff first learned of the censorship after the publication returned from the printer two pages shorter than when they had sent it off. As one might expect, some students strongly objected to the principal's action, and three of the newspaper staff members, Cathy Kuhlmeier, Leslie Smart and Leanne Tippett, eventually took the school to court claiming their First Amendment rights had been infringed.

Principal Reynolds' comments about the censorship, reported in the media immediately after the incident occurred, indicated that he felt the stories were "too sensitive" and that the topic of divorce was simply inappropriate for inclusion in a high school newspaper. At trial, he testified he was concerned that the three girls in the pregnancy story might be identifiable even without their names, and that he objected to their discussion of the fact they were sexually active. He said he believed the students' parents should have been notified and given the opportunity to respond. In the divorce story, he objected to the use of quotes from one student, who, in describing how she felt about her parents' divorce, mentioned that her father was frequently away from home. Reynolds was not aware that, after he received the page proofs, the adviser and editors had already deleted the student's name from the story.

In a 1985 decision, a federal district court in Missouri upheld the school's censorship.[23] In stark contrast to earlier court decisions from around the country, the trial court said that because *Spectrum* was produced by a journalism class, it was not a forum entitled to strong First Amendment protection. Rather it was a part of the school's curriculum that school officials had the right to control as long as their censorship had a "reasonable basis."[24] The court concluded that the principal's concerns that the pregnant students could be identified and that the school might be perceived as endorsing their sexual activity as well as the lack of opportunity for response by the parents of the students quoted in the divorce article all were "reasonable" justifications for censorship.

The students appealed that decision, and, in July 1986, the Eighth Circuit Court of Appeals reversed the lower court's ruling and sided with the students.[25] The court of appeals' reasoning followed that used by other courts over the preceding 17 years. It found that although *Spectrum* was produced in relationship to a journalism class, it was more than a curricular exercise: it was a forum for student expression. As such, it could be censored only when school officials could show that they had met the "material and substantial disruption" or "invasion of the rights of others" requirements of the *Tinker* standard. The court said the school had not met that standard.

Hazelwood School District v. Kuhlmeier, 484 U.S. 260 (1988), was the first censorship case involving a school-sponsored student publication at an American high school to reach the Supreme Court.

The *Hazelwood Standard:* Censorship of school-sponsored student expression is constitutionally permitted only when school officials can show their actions are "reasonably related to legitimate pedagogical concerns."

Prior review: Reviewing material — reading only — before publication. Prior restraint: The act of censorship.

Despite the dozens of lower court decisions on student press rights from around the country, the Supreme Court had never taken the opportunity to define the First Amendment protections that student journalists working for a school-sponsored publication at the high school or the college level were entitled to. But on January 20, 1987, the Supreme Court accepted the school's request to review the case and heard oral argument on October 13 of that year. Thus the *Hazelwood* case provided the Court with the opportunity to focus on an important segment of the student press for the first time.

On January 13, 1988, the Supreme Court handed down its decision and by a five-to-three vote reversed the court of appeals and upheld the school's censorship.[26] The decision of the Court, written by Justice Byron White and joined by Justices William Rehnquist, John Paul Stevens, Sandra Day O'Connor and Anton Scalia, was in stark contrast to other rulings on student press rights. It began by reaffirming the holding of *Tinker* that students do not lose their constitutional rights to freedom of speech or expression at the schoolhouse gate. But the Court went on to say that the *Tinker* standard did not apply to the facts of this case.

"The question whether the First Amendment requires a school to tolerate particular student speech — the question that we addressed in *Tinker* — is different from the question whether the First Amendment requires a school affirmatively to promote particular student speech," the Court said.[27] The majority believed that school officials should have greater authority to control "school-sponsored publications, theatrical productions, and other expressive activities that students, parents, and members of the public might reasonably perceive to bear the imprimatur endorsement of the school."[28]

For these kinds of school-sponsored expression, the Court created a new standard for determining whether school officials' censorship is constitutional. Judges should uphold school censorship, the Court said, when officials can show it is "reasonably related to legitimate pedagogical educational concerns."[29] Only when the censorship has "no valid educational purpose" should a court act to protect student expression rights under the First Amendment, the Court said.[30]

But the Supreme Court made clear that this new standard did not automatically apply simply because Spectrum was school-sponsored. It was first necessary to determine if the newspaper had been opened as a designated public forum.[31] If it had, either "by policy or by practice,"[32] been opened as a forum for student expression where student editors had been given control over content, then the *Tinker* standard would still be used to determine whether Principal Reynolds' censorship was permissible.[33]

In the opinion of the Court majority, the school board's policies did not indicate an intention to open *Spectrum* as a public forum for student expression. Although a portion of the board policy said that "school sponsored student publications will not restrict free expression or diverse viewpoints within the rules of responsible journalism," another section of the policy stated that those publications were "developed within the adopted curriculum and its educational implications."[34] The Supreme Court read this as saying that the "school officials retained ultimate control over what constituted 'responsible journalism' in a school-sponsored newspaper."[35]

The Court also said that the practice at Hazelwood East High School had been for school officials to exercise complete editorial control over the student newspaper. Although the court of appeals believed adviser Stergos' testimony that the students determined the content of the publication, the Supreme Court, like the district court, did not. The Court said that Stergos was the "final authority" on almost every aspect of *Spectrum*, including its content. It also noted that Principal Reynolds exercised prior review over every issue of the publication, an indication the newspaper was not operating as a forum.[36]

Based on this examination of both the policy and practice at Hazelwood East High

School, the Supreme Court concluded that there was no intent by the school to establish *Spectrum* as a public forum for student expression. Thus the new censorship standard, not *Tinker*, applied.

Finally, the Court had to decide whether the school had met the newly created standard. Could school officials show that their censorship was "reasonably related to legitimate pedagogical concerns?" Could they show that removing the stories from *Spectrum* had a "valid educational purpose?" The majority opinion said that they could. The principal's concerns that the unnamed students interviewed for the pregnancy story might be identifiable, that the girls' boyfriends and parents had not been given the opportunity to consent or respond to their comments, that the girls' non-explicit description of their sexual histories might be inappropriate in a student newspaper that was distributed to 14-year-old freshmen, and that the father of the student initially named in the divorce article was not given the opportunity to respond to the comments critical of him all were reasonable justifications for the censorship, according to the Court.[37]

The dissenting opinion in the *Hazelwood* case, written by Justice William Brennan and joined by Justices Harry Blackmun and Thurgood Marshall, offered sharp criticism of the majority opinion, especially the Court's decision to effectively abandon much of the *Tinker* standard by distinguishing between "personal" and "school-sponsored" student speech. "The Court does not, for it cannot, purport to discern from our precedents the distinction it creates," the dissenting justices said.[38] They argued that even if there were not the long history of *Tinker*'s application to student free expression cases, there was no independent justification for giving school officials "'greater control' over school-sponsored speech than the *Tinker* test would permit."[39]

"The case before us aptly illustrates how readily school officials (and courts) can camouflage viewpoint discrimination as the 'mere' protection of students from sensitive topics," the dissent said, claiming that the true motivation for the censorship appeared to be the school's belief that the pregnancy story might be read as advocating "irresponsible sex."[40] If school officials were truly concerned that the information published might be mistakenly attributed to the school, they could easily enough have required the newspaper to publish a disclaimer or they could have simply announced an official school response and explained why the students' perspective was wrong, the opinion said.[41]

The dissenting opinion concluded that the ruling of the court took from high school students much of the First Amendment protection that *Tinker* said they were entitled to. "The young men and women of Hazelwood East expected a civics lesson, but not the one the Court teaches them today."[42]

THE PROBLEM OF PRIOR REVIEW

Prior review of student publications by school administrators has long been one of the most troublesome forms of censorship high school student media confront. On its face, a principal's demand to see all content of a student publication before it goes to press may seem like an innocent request. But in reality, many media advisers consider it an affront to their role and an impediment to the creation of true journalism. As most journalism professionals would agree, a student publication cannot remain an independent source of news or serve as a watchdog for the school community when a school administrator is shaping its content before it goes to press. In fact, it may become difficult for student media to come out on time when the staff is forced to delay printing or broadcast to give a principal the opportunity for detailed content review.

Unfortunately, the Supreme Court in *Hazelwood* said that high school officials could exercise prior review — reading only — of school-sponsored publications without written guidelines,[43] and they may be able to do so even if the publication is operating as a public forum[44] unless school policy or state law prohibits it.

The full text of the *Hazelwood* decision is available at: **www.splc.org/ hazelwoodcase**

A copy of the censored pages from the Hazelwood East High School *Spectrum* newspaper is available at: **www. splc.org/spectrum**

But that does not mean the practice is wise. In fact, the Journalism Education Association has specifically condemned the practice of administrative prior review. Student journalists and advisers who are confronting demands for prior review should use this statement from professional journalism educators to persuade their school that prior review is a mistake and seek alternatives.

It is also important to understand that the authority to read content before it goes to press or air is not the same as the authority to demand changes, to punish for content decisions, or otherwise censor disfavored material. Before school officials take that step, they must meet the requisite legal standard (typically *Tinker* or *Hazelwood*), described in this and the preceding chapter. Moreover, it is likely that imposing prior review because of a dispute over specific, lawful editorial content is itself a First Amendment violation, because the First Amendment bans not only the restraint of lawful editorial content, but also after-the-fact retaliation meant to send a message that disfavored content will not be tolerated in the future.

MAKING SENSE OF HAZELWOOD

Although the Supreme Court was dealing with a student newspaper in the *Hazelwood* case, any school-sponsored high school student media could be affected by the decision. Students who staff yearbooks and magazines as well as Web publications and television or radio programs all should understand where they fit under the First Amendment analysis presented by the Court.

Clearly the decision in *Hazelwood* reflected an intention by the Supreme Court to give school officials significant leeway in determining what is educationally appropriate for publication in many school-sponsored student media. But the Court left open the possibility that student publications at schools that had operated differently than the newspaper at Hazelwood East might still be considered public forums for student expression, even though they are school-sponsored.

And even when the *Hazelwood* standard does apply to a student publication, it still requires school officials to legally justify any act of censorship. The standard may provide less First Amendment protection than the *Tinker* standard, but it still places some limitation on school officials' ability to censor.

The best way for high school student journalists, their advisers and school officials to determine whether any particular act of censorship is allowed under the First Amendment is to follow a step-by-step analysis similar to what the Supreme Court used in *Hazelwood* (as many post-*Hazelwood* cases have done). The chart on the next page can be used as a guide for navigating this course.

Forum status is determined for each student news medium by examining the policies and the practice of how the medium has operated.

(1) Is the student media school-sponsored? The *Hazelwood* standard applies only to those forms of student expression to which the school has lent its name and resources.[45] Non-school sponsored student expression such as the wearing of armbands or the distribution of "underground" newspapers is still entitled to the protections of *Tinker*.[46] (See Chapter 8.) Some students and advisers working on an official school publication that receives no direct funding from their administration but instead pays their printing bills from advertising and sales revenue or other outside funding have asked if their financial set-up might allow them to avoid the limitations of *Hazelwood*. In fact, if the publication is produced in relationship to a class, it will probably remain school-sponsored under the *Hazelwood* analysis no matter who pays the bills.

But one court rejected a school's far-reaching attempt to argue that essentially all on- campus student expression was school-sponsored and thus should be covered by *Hazelwood*. In *Westfield High School L.I.F.E. Club v. City of Westfield*,[47] a federal district court in Massachusetts rejected a school's punishment of members of a Christian student group that met at school after they distributed candy canes with religious messages to

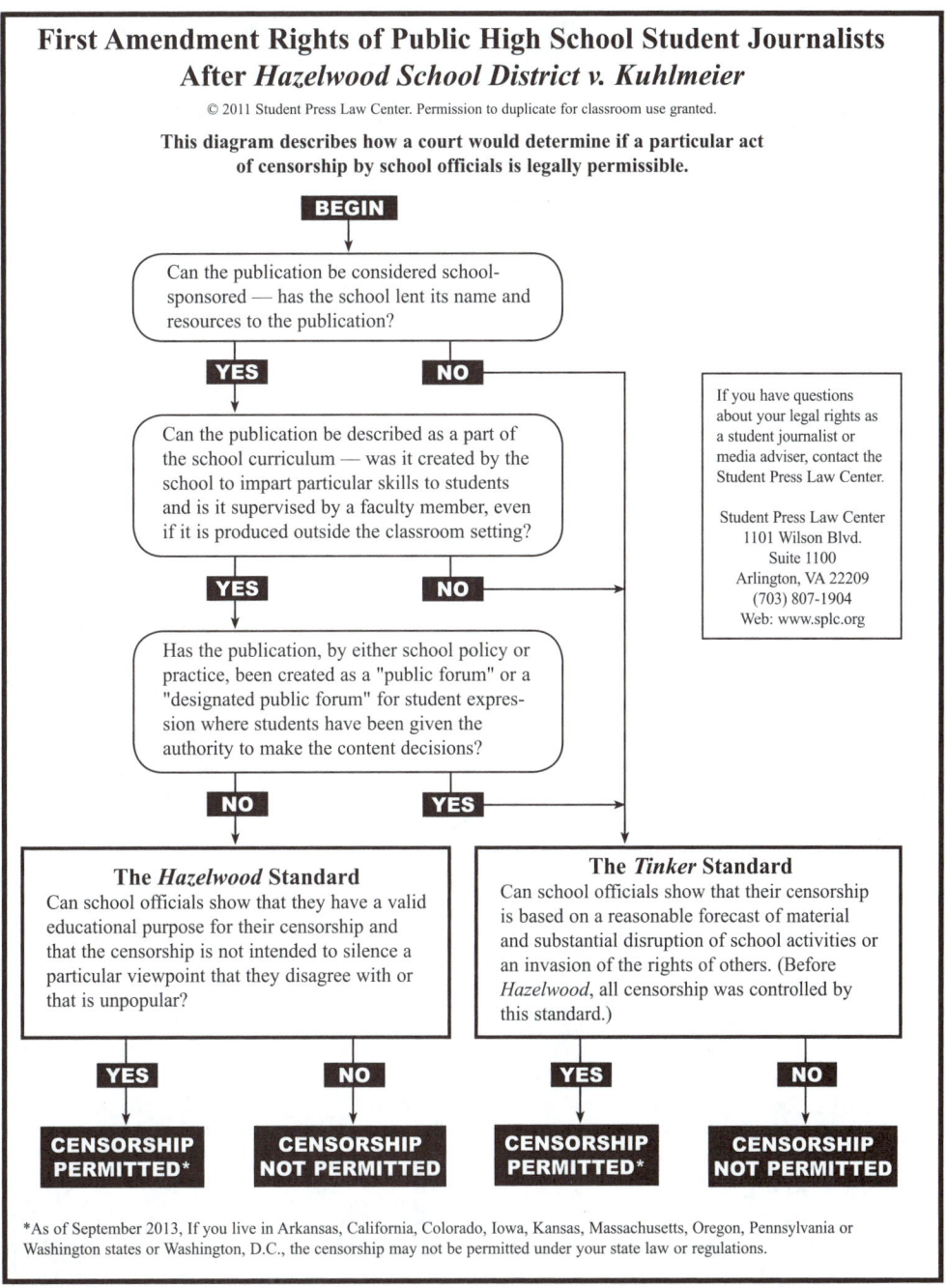

First Amendment Rights of Public High School Student Journalists
After *Hazelwood School District v. Kuhlmeier*

© 2011 Student Press Law Center. Permission to duplicate for classroom use granted.

This diagram describes how a court would determine if a particular act of censorship by school officials is legally permissible.

BEGIN

Can the publication be considered school-sponsored — has the school lent its name and resources to the publication?

YES **NO**

Can the publication be described as a part of the school curriculum — was it created by the school to impart particular skills to students and is it supervised by a faculty member, even if it is produced outside the classroom setting?

YES **NO**

If you have questions about your legal rights as a student journalist or media adviser, contact the Student Press Law Center.

Student Press Law Center
1101 Wilson Blvd.
Suite 1100
Arlington, VA 22209
(703) 807-1904
Web: www.splc.org

Has the publication, by either school policy or practice, been created as a "public forum" or a "designated public forum" for student expression where students have been given the authority to make the content decisions?

NO **YES**

The *Hazelwood* Standard
Can school officials show that they have a valid educational purpose for their censorship and that the censorship is not intended to silence a particular viewpoint that they disagree with or that is unpopular?

The *Tinker* Standard
Can school officials show that their censorship is based on a reasonable forecast of material and substantial disruption of school activities or an invasion of the rights of others. (Before *Hazelwood*, all censorship was controlled by this standard.)

YES **NO** **YES** **NO**

CENSORSHIP PERMITTED* **CENSORSHIP NOT PERMITTED** **CENSORSHIP PERMITTED*** **CENSORSHIP NOT PERMITTED**

*As of September 2013, If you live in Arkansas, California, Colorado, Iowa, Kansas, Massachusetts, Oregon, Pennsylvania or Washington states or Washington, D.C., the censorship may not be permitted under your state law or regulations.

other students. The school argued that the group was school-sponsored because it used school facilities for meetings, had a faculty adviser and appeared in student activities announcements and the yearbook. The court strongly disagreed.

"To adopt the defendants' definition of 'school-sponsored' would devoid that term of any helpful meaning, as nearly every student group activity happening to occur on school grounds can, in some tenuous sense, be described as using school facilities and as designed to impart some sort of knowledge upon its members," the court said. "Rather, for expressive activity to be school-sponsored, the school needs to take affirmative steps in promoting the particular speech."[48]

But if student media is school-sponsored, then the next question must be asked.

(2) Can the publication fairly be characterized as part of the school curriculum? The Supreme Court indicated that when a student newspaper was "curricular," school officials were more justified in their concern that "members of the public might reasonably perceive it to bear the imprimatur of the school" and thus had a valid reason for controlling it.[49] The Supreme Court suggested that those student media supervised by a faculty member and created by the school to impart particular skills to students would be considered part of the school curriculum, even if they were not produced in a traditional classroom setting.[50] But not necessarily all school-sponsored student publications will be considered "curricular." And, as explained in a moment, even some curricular student media might still be able to avoid *Hazelwood*.

Hazelwood does not apply to: (1) student expression that is not school-sponsored (for example, underground student newspapers, off-campus student websites) or (2) student expression that occurs in a traditional or designated public forum. For these, *Tinker*'s more protective standard remains the law.

At least two federal courts have confronted this curriculum question since *Hazelwood*. In a 1989 case, a New York high school fired a student newspaper adviser after the paper published an editorial column disapproving of the effort then underway to make the Rev. Martin Luther King Jr.'s birthday a national holiday.[51] The court said that because the publication was produced after school and not for course credit, student journalists' rights were "less limitable" than those of the students at Hazelwood East.[52] And a federal district court in Connecticut ruled in March 1989 that a school-sponsored literary magazine may not be "characterized as part of the school's curriculum," and thus censored under the *Hazelwood* standard, if its history and method of operation show it was more an independent student endeavor than a school activity designed by school authorities.[53]

Journalism educators have successfully pushed for many years to move more high school publications into the classroom and away from the extra-curricular activity tradition because of the benefits that come with having scheduled time for training and production. Ironically, those student journalists who receive no classroom instruction may be able to argue that they have stronger free press protections as a result.

So if student media can be described as independent of the school's curriculum, *Tinker* will still set the standard for administrative censorship. But if it is curricular, the next question must be answered.

(3) Has the publication, by either school policy or practice, been opened as a public forum for student expression? Even curricular, school-sponsored student media still may be entitled to strong First Amendment protection and exempt from *Hazelwood*'s limitations if they have been designated a "public forum" for student expression. A public forum is created when school officials have "by policy or by practice" opened student media "for indiscriminate use by the general public" or by some segment of the public, such as students.[54] In the context of a student publication, that segment of the public would be the student staff.

In the *Hazelwood* case, the Court said that it believed that both the policy and practice at Hazelwood East High School reflected school officials' intent to exercise complete control over the student newspaper's content. That finding prompted the Court to say a forum did not exist. Nevertheless, student publications at other schools with different policies and different practices relating to editorial control might be public forums. Where student editors have been given final authority over content decisions in their publications or where a school policy explicitly describes a student publication as a public forum, the *Tinker* standard will still apply. How the school actually allows the publication to operate may be more important than self-serving statements the school makes about its forum status.[55]

Several post-*Hazelwood* cases have indicated how important this forum/non-forum distinction can be. In *Planned Parenthood of Southern Nevada v. Clark County School District*,[56] a federal court of appeals upheld the authority of school officials to reject pregnancy-related advertising in school publications, but only after the court had determined that the publications in question had not been opened as public forums. "We must first resolve whether the school newspapers, yearbooks and athletic programs are forums for public expression" with regard to their advertising, the court said.[57] The court noted that the school's policies gave principals broad discretion to reject certain kinds of advertising, and so the publications at issue had not been opened up as public forums to advertisers.

In the Connecticut case mentioned on the previous page involving a school's effort to control the content of a student literary magazine, the court agreed that the forum question was an important one. "Fair ground for litigation exists as to the literary magazine's status ... as a 'public forum' never validly closed by school authorities."[58] Because this case was settled out of court, there was never a final ruling on whether the magazine was in fact a forum for student expression. But the court suggested it very well might have been.

More recently, at least two federal courts, applying the analysis of Hazelwood, have found school-sponsored student newspapers were operating as public forums. In *Draudt v. Wooster City School District*,[59] officials at Wooster High School in Ohio confiscated the entire press run of an edition of the *Blade* student newspaper in 2003. The issue included an article about the school's policy regarding punishment of students caught drinking that indicated the school had given preferential treatment to athletes. Newspaper staff members went to court requesting an injunction to prohibit the school from continuing to censor the paper. The students claimed that their publication was a public forum. The court agreed.

Citing to a college censorship case, the court said that two questions were relevant to determining the forum status of the newspaper: (1) whether the school intended to create a limited public forum and (2) the context within which the forum was found.[60] As for determining the school's intent, the court said it looked at a number of overlapping factors including: whether the students produced the newspaper as part of the high school curriculum; whether students received credit and grades for their work on the publication; whether there was a faculty adviser; whether the school deviated from its policy of producing the paper as part of the educational curriculum; the degree of control the administration and faculty adviser exercised; applicable written policy statements of the administration or school board; the school's practice with respect to the forum, and the nature of a student newspaper and its compatibility with expressive activity.[61]

In this case, although the newspaper was produced in relation to a class for which students received grades and credit and there was a faculty adviser overseeing the production (all factors arguing against public forum status), the court noted that the newspaper regularly printed guest columns from teachers and community members, distributed almost three-quarters of its press run outside the school in community businesses, was minimally controlled by the administration or adviser (no prior review by the principal), was subject to school policies that referenced free speech and included in its masthead a statement that it was a public forum (all factors in support of the public forum status).

Most important to this court was the actual practice of how the publication operated. "'Actual practice speaks louder than words' in determining whether the government intended to create a limited public forum."[62] Given that both the newspaper adviser and principal stated that the student editors determined the content of the publication, the public forum status became obvious. "A student newspaper, by its very nature, exists for expressive activity," the court said.[63] The *Blade* was a public forum.

In 2004, a federal district court in Michigan followed the reasoning of the *Draudt* decision and once again found a school-sponsored student newspaper was operating as a public forum. The case, *Dean v. Utica Community Schools*,[64] involved an effort by students at Utica High School to publish a story in their student newspaper, the *Arrow*, about a lawsuit filed against their school district. Community members who lived adjacent to the school bus parking lot and garage claimed that breathing diesel exhaust from idling buses had damaged their health and sought compensation from the school. Student Katy Dean interviewed the family that had filed the lawsuit, researched the science behind their claims and wrote a news story about the situation. When Dean attempted to get comment and response from school officials, they refused to provide any information for the story. As the story — and an accompanying editorial and editorial cartoon — was about to go to press, school officials told the adviser it could not be published.

When Dean contested the censorship, the court followed closely the analysis and reasoning of the *Draudt* decision and reached the same conclusion: that the Arrow was a public forum. The court noted that although the newspaper was produced in relationship to a class with a faculty adviser, students were allowed to take the class for credit more than once, the *Arrow* published letters and guest columns from anyone, a community newspaper published articles from it regularly, the paper was not subject to prior review by the administration, students were required to sell advertising to support the paper's printing costs, and no policy existed indicating that the paper was not a public forum. And the all-important practice only reinforced the forum status. The adviser testified that for at least 25 years, the school administration had never interfered with students' authority to make their own content decisions.[65]

The fact remains that as a result of *Hazelwood*, the long-held presumption that student publications, even if school-sponsored, are by their very nature public forums for student expression is no longer the law.[66] Rather forum status is to be determined for each individual student news medium at each school by examining the relevant policies and the practice of how the publication has operated. At those schools where student editors have been given the authority to make final decisions about what will be included in their publication or where a school policy reflects an intent to give students that authority, public forum status will still be found and schools will still have to meet the more protective *Tinker* standard before they can legally censor.[67]

Thus in the post-*Hazelwood* world, it is more important than ever that student journalists and their advisers know what policies their school has adopted relating to student media or student expression and how the publication or other student media organization has operated in the past. The language of those polices (whether they give editorial control to students or keep it in the hands of school officials) and the amount of freedom that students have traditionally operated under can determine whether *Hazelwood* or *Tinker* sets the standard for what school officials will be allowed to censor.

THE QUESTION OF VIEWPOINT DISCRIMINATION

A number of courts have said that there is another important requirement that school officials must meet before they can censor, one that significantly narrows the scope of *Hazelwood*. Traditionally, even in a non-public forum, the Supreme Court has required government officials' censorship to be "viewpoint neutral."[68] In other words, the government must demonstrate that it did not censor simply because it disagreed with a particular view that was being expressed or in an effort to silence one view on a subject but not an opposing view.

According to at least three federal appeals courts, that same limitation applies to school officials censoring nonforum publications under *Hazelwood*.[69] But other courts have disagreed,[70] saying as long as the school's justification for censorship is educationally reasonable, censoring particular viewpoints will be allowed. Until the U.S. Supreme Court rules on this issue, there will not be a definitive answer to this question.[71]

But where the courts do recognize a limit on viewpoint discrimination, that restriction is an important protection for student journalists whose publications are subject to the limited First Amendment protections of the *Hazelwood* decision. For example, the court concluded in the *Dean* case, mentioned above, that the school's censorship of a story about a lawsuit against the school was also impermissible because it was based on the viewpoints contained in the article.[72] With a limitation on viewpoint discrimination, courts would have a difficult time censoring editorials or columns simply because they disagreed with the views they expressed.

The restriction on viewpoint discrimination demonstrates again that even after *Hazelwood*, high school journalists have legal tools that enable them to contest school censorship.

APPLYING THE *HAZELWOOD* STANDARD

Even if a student media organization is school-sponsored, a part of the school's curriculum, and has not been opened as a public forum, students still might have grounds for contesting school censorship. Contrary to the perception of many, *Hazelwood* does not stand for the proposition that school officials can censor anything they dislike. The "valid educational purpose" standard of *Hazelwood* continues to provide some First Amendment protection for students that school officials cannot ignore.

Just what will be considered a "valid educational purpose" that would allow a school to censor? Given the fact that national organizations of journalism educators routinely reject administrative censorship of high school journalists as educationally unsound, one might think that schools could never meet the requirements of *Hazelwood*. (Some of these statements in support of student press freedom are reprinted in the Appendix.) However, the Supreme Court has indicated otherwise.

The *Hazelwood* Court gave some examples in its decision of what might fit within the standard it had created: material that is "ungrammatical, poorly written, inadequately researched, biased or prejudiced, vulgar or profane, or unsuitable for immature audiences;" potentially sensitive topics, such as "the existence of Santa Claus in an elementary school setting," "the particulars of teenage sexual activity in a high school setting," "speech that might reasonably be perceived to advocate drug or alcohol use, irresponsible sex, or conduct otherwise inconsistent with the 'shared values of a civilized social order;'" and material that would "associate the school with anything other than neutrality on matters of political controversy."[73]

These examples suggest that school officials might be allowed to censor a great number of things simply because they disapprove of them. The Court said schools could require student media to meet standards "higher than those demanded by some newspaper publishers ... in the 'real' world."[74]

Among the reasons courts have found sufficient to justify censorship under the *Hazelwood* standard are: a lack of "civility" by a student who gave a student government campaign speech that harshly criticized an assistant principal at the school;[75] a school district's concern about maintaining neutrality on the controversial issue of abortion when enacting a policy against abortion or pregnancy counseling ads in school publications,[76] a school's belief that a parent, not the student, selected the content of a poster the child brought to school to satisfy a class assignment,[77] and a school's conclusion that a student distributing condoms with his student government campaign material was encouraging teenage sexual activity.[78]

But other courts have emphasized that the *Hazelwood* standard does not give school officials unlimited censorship authority. In the *Dean v. Utica* case mentioned above, a federal district court in Michigan rejected a school's censorship of the student newspaper story about a lawsuit filed against the school. Ultimately, the court noted that the publication was operating as a public forum. But the judge indicated that even if he had ruled that the newspaper was not a public forum, the school's censorship of Dean's article still would have been unlawful because it was also "unreasonable" under *Hazelwood*.[79]

As justification for prohibiting the article, the school claimed that it was improperly researched (including reliance on background material attributed, correctly, to *USA Today*), biased and prejudicial, contained pseudonyms, and alleged that the school's actions endangered the community, which the school claimed was untrue.[80] The court rejected these claims, finding that the school's "stated pedagogical concerns are not supported by the evidence in the record and that the school's complete removal of Dean's article was not reasonably related to any stated pedagogical concern."[81]

First, the court noted that Dean's article did not raise privacy concerns (the lawsuit was a matter of public record) or include sexual material, as was at issue in the *Hazelwood* case. As to the accusation of unfairness, the court noted that Dean attempted to include comments from all of the relevant school officials, yet every one of them failed to respond (which her story mentioned). Dean did include in her story conflicting views on the health effects of breathing diesel exhaust. Thus the court said the school could hardly argue that she was unfair in her treatment of them. In fact, the court noted that, based on expert testimony from a professional journalist and a journalism professor, there was no indication that Dean's article was of any lesser quality than those in "professional" newspapers.[82]

As to the objection to pseudonyms, the court noted that the real names of the people suing the school were included in the final version of the story. However, the court noted that the school offered no evidence to explain why the use of pseudonyms in the story would have been inappropriate. And the court held that the accusation of inaccuracy was unjustified as well.

"The issue is not whether the allegations in the underlying lawsuit were ever accurate or meritorious," the court said. "Katy Dean had a right to publish an article concerning one side of a lawsuit so long as it accurately reported that side...." The school's disagreement with the claims in the lawsuit was not evidence of its inaccuracy.[83]

The *Dean* decision is perhaps the clearest declaration of the risks faced by school officials who try to extend *Hazelwood* too far. But it is not the only case to do so. For example, in *Desilets v. Clearview Regional Board of Education*,[84] the New Jersey Supreme Court rejected school officials' justifications for censoring reviews of R-rated movies from a junior high school student newspaper under the *Hazelwood* standard as "equivocal and inconsistent."[85] The court noted that there was nothing offensive in the reviews, that R-rated movies were discussed in class by teachers, that such reviews were available in the school library and that the student newspaper had, in fact, reviewed such movies in the past.[86]

Thus, just because school officials say they have met the *Hazelwood* standard does not mean they are correct. As the *Desilets* court noted, "The curtailment of cherished First Amendment rights mandates careful analysis of the reasons given for the censorship in light of the facts of each case to determine if there is any valid educational purpose to support the censorship."[87]

HAZELWOOD HORROR STORIES

One result of the *Hazelwood* decision has been a sharp rise in censorship incidents reported to the Student Press Law Center. Requests for assistance received by the SPLC from student journalists and their advisers seeking legal help had risen about 330 percent in the nearly two decades following the Supreme Court's decision.[88] Although the decision requires that school officials who choose to censor must provide a valid educational reason for their censorship, calls to the SPLC show that some administrators have apparently interpreted the decision as providing them with a license to censor anything they choose. For example:

• An Illinois principal confiscated all copies of the student newspaper and ordered it reprinted without an editorial that criticized the administration's failure to strictly enforce disciplinary rules, leading to what the student editors decried as an "I can do as I please and not get caught" disregard for school conduct codes. The school justified the censorship in reliance on a *Hazelwood* publications policy permitting removal of material "inconsistent with the District's educational mission."[89]

• Another Illinois school blocked publication of a story about the arrest of the school superintendent for drunk driving. "The focus of a school newspaper is to be positive, to build pride in a school," the principal told a local newspaper. "I would not want to see the student newspaper used as a forum that would be critical of students or staff."[90]

• In Tennessee, a principal seized all 1,800 copies of a student newspaper over objections to articles about birth control and body art. The birth control article contained information — provided by a local physician — about the failure rates for various birth control methods. The article also quoted the physician telling students that under state law they did not need parental permission to get birth control.[91]

• In Washington state, a principal forced the student paper to pull an article about a controversial high school coach. The paper reported that, in a letter to the student journalists, the principal said, "a student newspaper is not an appropriate vehicle for airing concerns, complaints or criticisms about District staff." She also cited the *Hazelwood* decision, which, she claimed, says a school "need not tolerate" student speech that is "inconsistent" with the "basic educational mission, even though the government could not censor similar speech outside the school."[92]

In a press release, the district superintendent said the high school "acted in accordance with the legal principles set forth by the United States Supreme Court that permitted the administration to exercise editorial direction of articles in the school newspaper. ... The administration felt that the interests of the student population would not be served by certain content of the articles."

• In Indiana, a principal censored a story that painstakingly detailed how the girls' tennis coach had improperly pocketed more than $1,000 that team members had paid for court time. All agreed the story was accurate. The editor later learned that school administrators had used his story as a bargaining chip, threatening the coach that they would allow the story to run if he did not resign.[93]

• In Alaska, a principal censored a junior high school student newspaper editorial that complained about unnamed teachers who regularly smoked in a room next door to an occupied classroom, which the student wrote, made students "sick from the smoke coming into our room." At the time, smoking was prohibited in the school. The principal told the editor the story could not run because it would be an embarrassment. Two local, commercial papers subsequently picked up the story.[94]

• In Ohio, a superintendent censored an advertisement submitted to the student newspaper by a local school board candidate. After the ad was censored, the student editor wrote an editorial criticizing the superintendent's act of censorship. "The fundamental truth of the First Amendment is that all ideas have a right to be heard," the editor wrote. School officials censored the editorial as well.[95]

• In Florida, students literally had to cut an article out of their high school newspaper after their principal objected to the piece, which described the "achievement gap" in state test scores between white and minority students. Students opted to physically remove the article from each copy of the paper rather than wait for the issue to be reprinted.

The article reported that 69 percent of white students passed the reading portion of Florida's Comprehensive Assessment Test, while only 16 percent of the black students passed. The students received the information, which is public record, from the school.

Between 1988 and 2003, calls to the Student Press Law Center from those seeking legal help rose from 588 calls per year to 2,360, an increase of over 300 percent.

But a district spokeswoman said the principal felt the article would make black students feel inferior. She also said "students have other means to seek the information on their own."[96]

• In Texas, a student newspaper randomly asked students what one thing they would change about their school. One student jokingly replied, "the principal." After the quote ran, the principal required all issues to be submitted to him for review before being printed. The newspaper's faculty adviser (who was later fired by the principal) complained to the school board that any story that the principal thought "made the school look bad" was censored, including a student editorial on the importance of the First Amendment. The principal said at a school board meeting, however, that he had not actually censored the newspaper — it had been his wife.[97]

POST-*HAZELWOOD* SUCCESSES

Hazelwood does not give administrators an unlimited license to censor. Several courts, applying *Hazelwood*, have held censorship unconstitutional after finding that school officials failed to provide a reasonable educational justification.

Not all schools have reacted to *Hazelwood* by taking content control from students. A growing number of school districts have recognized the importance of press freedom to journalism education and have either adopted or reaffirmed their support for student press freedom. They recognized that the Supreme Court's ruling does not require any school to censor.

• Several weeks after the *Hazelwood* decision, the school superintendent in Baltimore County, Md., sent a memo to principals throughout the district that said, "we have no desire to take advantage of the expanded authority the Supreme Court has granted us. ... We do not want to chill criticism of school personnel, school board policies, school administration or the superintendent of schools."[98]

• In the fall of 1990 some community members objected to the fact that a high school newspaper at Kirkwood High School in Missouri published an advertisement for Planned Parenthood. School officials eventually received 300 phone calls and 121 letters regarding the issue. But despite the pressure, the school principal, superintendent and school board members unanimously supported the right of student editors to determine their publication's content.[99]

• In May 1994, the Dade County, Fla., School Board reaffirmed its decade-old policy protecting the press freedom of students working on school-sponsored publications throughout one of the largest school districts in the country. The board also amended its policy to explicitly prohibit school administrators from demanding prior review of student publications.[100]

Student journalists and advisers are not the only ones who think censorship is a bad idea. See what some principals say as well. **www.splc. org/advisers**

• In March 2001, the First Amendment Center and the Association for Supervision and Curriculum Development launched the First Amendment Schools program, designed to educate the public about the importance of First Amendment freedoms. Among other elements, First Amendment Schools commit to encouraging freedom of expression and a free student press. By the end of 2007, the program was directly working with 17 Project Schools, from California to New York, and almost 100 schools had officially adopted the program's philosophy.[101]

• In October 2007, school officials in Georgia publicly defended a student paper's right to run a controversial opinion column that called homosexuality a "reproductive error" and compared it to Down Syndrome. Although some students were upset that the paper was allowed to publish the piece, the principal at Carlton J. Kell High School said she was "standing by" her decision that the article did not violate the district's policy for student media. A Cobb County School District spokesman explained that students, not school officials, control what the paper publishes.

Said the spokesman, "Whether the content is popular or not, it's not up to us to decide what runs as long as it's not disruptive."[102]

THE (VERY) LIMITED PUBLIC FORUM

After Hazelwood, many students and advisers sought "public forum" status for their student publications to try to qualify for a higher degree of censorship protection.

Because a student news outlet cannot be thrown open to unlimited use by the whole world, it has become commonplace to refer to student publications as "limited" public forums, meaning they are limited to one category of users (the students in that school). However, as the term "limited public forum" has been interpreted in recent court rulings, the term has become practically meaningless.

Recall that in the middle tier of forums — a "designated" public forum — the government's ability to regulate the content of speech is extremely limited. Only where a compelling justification exists, and the restriction is narrowly designed so as not to limit more speech than necessary, will a regulation be upheld as constitutionally permissible. While the terms "designated public forum" and "limited public forum" once appeared to be more-or-less synonyms, courts have begun treating a "limited" public forum as an entirely new type of government property. Under this view, the government has a free hand to "limit" the subjects that can be discussed in a "limited" forum — with no greater protection for the speaker than if no forum existed at all.

The case best illustrating this view, one that directly and negatively affected the rights of student journalists, originated at a New York high school in 2005.[103] The principal of Ithaca High School ordered student editors of *The Tattler* newspaper to remove an editorial cartoon that used stick figures in sexual poses to mock the school's sex-education program. Administrators called the drawing "lewd" and said it would undermine compliance with the school's abstinence-based teachings. Robert Ochshorn, editor of *The Tattler*, challenged the censorship in court, arguing that the newspaper operated as a "public forum" and should have received a high degree of First Amendment protection.[104] Federal courts, however, disagreed.

Even though the paper historically had operated without administrative involvement, and was governed by a school-approved policy calling *The Tattler* "a forum for student views and opinion," the Second Circuit decided that the paper was only a "limited" forum. The court noted that the paper's adviser exercised prior review and on a few occasions had removed articles, and that the paper was not thrown open for "indiscriminate use by the general public."[105] Because the paper was just a "limited" forum, the court concluded, the school could restrict what students published "in a way that is viewpoint-neutral and reasonable in light of the forum's established purpose,"[106] including removing an objectionable cartoon.

The *Ochshorn* ruling, while binding only in the states governed by the Second Circuit (New York, Connecticut, Vermont), is a warning to all student media that the mere label of "forum" will not reliably convey any heightened level of First Amendment protection. Those seeking to insulate student media against censorship would be better-advised to seek laws or policies that spell out exactly the grounds on which administrators may alter or withhold students' work.

PROTECTION BEYOND THE FIRST AMENDMENT: STATE LAW

Within days of the *Hazelwood* decision, the scholastic journalism community began to look for ways to avoid the harm that many anticipated the ruling would do to high school student media. Attention soon focused on the fact that in 1971, the California legislature enacted a law protecting the free press rights of high school students.[107] The law begins by saying, "Students of the public schools shall have the right to exercise freedom of speech and of the press including ... the right of expression in official publications, whether or not such publications or other means of expression are supported financially by the school or by use of school facilities..."[108] Under the statute, student expression is not protected if it is obscene, libelous, or slanderous, or if it "so incites students as to create a clear and present danger of the commission of unlawful acts on school premises or the violation of lawful school regulations, or the substantial disruption of the orderly operation of the school."[109] The statute clearly reflects an intent by the legislature to make the protections of the *Tinker* decision the law of the state for even

The First Amendment provides a federal "floor" of free-speech protection, but any state can provide greater free speech protection under its own laws, rules or state constitution.

As of 2013, seven states had passed laws that guaranteed high school student journalists greater protection than that provided by the First Amendment: Arkansas, California, Colorado, Iowa, Kansas, Massachusetts and Oregon.

school-sponsored student expression.[110]

Until 1988, that additional legal protection for California students may have been redundant because of the protections of the First Amendment as the courts then interpreted it. But after the *Hazelwood* decision, this California law took on new significance. Because of the statute, "California public school students still enjoy substantial 'freedom of the press' despite the recent U.S. Supreme Court decision to the contrary," said State Superintendent of Public Instruction Bill Honig in a March 1988 press release.[111] Because states have the ability to create their own laws that give their residents more civil rights protection than exists in the federal Constitution, the U.S. Supreme Court has no ability to alter or limit the rights created in this California law.

A California court had the occasion to apply the student expression law just weeks after the *Hazelwood* case was decided.[112] Though the court ruled that the law allowed school officials to delete material from school-sponsored publications that they reasonably believed contained an actionable defamation,[113] the court nonetheless agreed that the statute "clearly confers editorial control of official student publications on the student editors alone, with very limited exceptions. The broad power to censor expression in school-sponsored publications for pedagogical purposes recognized in *Hazelwood* is not available to this state's educators."[114]

With California as an example, the drive began to create other *Hazelwood*-free zones. In July 1988, Massachusetts became the first state after *Hazelwood* to enact statutory protections for student expression.[115] The legislature made mandatory an existing law that had been optional for school boards. That law says that students' rights to free expression shall not be abridged except in situations where disruption or disorder within the school results,[116] again, a clear reference to the *Tinker* standard the court deviated from in *Hazelwood*. In 1989, Iowa enacted a student free press law,[117] followed by Colorado in 1990,[118] Kansas in 1992,[119] Arkansas in 1995[120] and Oregon in 2007.[121] These laws have different wording, but each provides students in those states with greater protections than they have under the First Amendment as defined by the Supreme Court in *Hazelwood*, and each uses *Tinker*'s "substantial disruption" standard as the primary limitation on student free press rights. By the end of 2012, some 30 state legislatures had considered bills similar to those passed in these seven states, and supporters of the legislation expected the effort to continue around the country for some time.[122] Pennsylvania, Washington and the District of Columbia have student free-expression regulations enacted by administrative agencies, not legislatures, that mirror the type of protection offered by anti-*Hazelwood* statutes.[123] These regulations are binding on all public schools in those jurisdictions, but because they are rules and not statutes, it is uncertain whether a censored student could pursue relief in state court, or would be limited to filing a complaint with the state school board to have the censorship decision overturned.

Courts have had only a handful of occasions to apply anti-*Hazelwood* statutes, but those cases have amply demonstrated the importance of such protection. An Iowa adviser successfully cleared his record of undeserved disciplinary sanctions imposed because his principal believed he failed to adequately censor his students' newspaper.[124] In Illinois, a Chicago State University adviser took advantage of that state's limited anti-*Hazelwood* statute, which benefits only college and not K-12 media, to win reinstatement after he was wrongfully discharged in a dispute over his students' aggressive coverage of college spending.[125]

STATE CONSTITUTIONS

State statutory protection for student press rights has received the most attention of the legal responses to *Hazelwood*, but several court cases have presented yet another alternative for legally contesting censorship: state constitutions. In New Jersey, Oregon and Washington state, student journalists who were censored went to court claiming that their rights under the free expression provisions in their state constitutions are broader than those under the First Amendment as defined by *Hazelwood*.[126] In New Jersey and Washington, courts said that the state constitutions do give students more free speech protections then they have under the federal Constitution as defined by *Hazelwood*.[127] "[I]nterpretations by federal courts of the United States Constitution only establish the floor for rights such as free speech and the individual states may grant broader protection under each of [their] constitutions than are granted under the Federal Constitution," the New Jersey court said.[128] These cases represent another front in the battle by students for press freedom after *Hazelwood*.

SUMMARY

Without question, the *Hazelwood* decision has made it much more difficult for high school student journalists working on school-sponsored publications to fight censorship. *Hazelwood*, however, does not entirely extinguish students' First Amendment rights, nor does it limit students' ability to pursue other sources of legal protection. The Supreme Court created two different standards for constitutional protection for high school publications. Determining which standard applies in a specific censorship situation will depend on whether the publication that has been censored is curricular or is a designated public forum for student expression. If a school has, by policy or by practice, given editorial control to the student media staff, school officials should be able to censor only when they can demonstrate the publication will cause a material and substantial disruption or an invasion of the rights of others. Even for those school-sponsored student publications that are not public forums, school officials still must show that they have a valid educational purpose for their censorship, and possibly, that they are not attempting to silence a particular viewpoint. And even when the First Amendment does not prevent school officials from censoring, state statutory or constitutional law may give students greater free press protections.

ENDNOTES

1 *Zucker v. Panitz*, 299 F. Supp. 102 (S.D.N.Y. 1969).
2 *Id.* at 105.
3 *Id.* at 103.
4 *Id.*
5 *Id.* at n. 1.
6 *Id.* at 105.
7 *Id.*
8 *Id.*
9 *See, e.g., Nicholson v. Bd. of Educ.*, 682 F.2d 858, 863 n. 3 (9th Cir. 1982); *Gambino v. Fairfax County Sch. Bd.*, 429 F. Supp. 731, 734 (E.D. Va.) (citing Fourth Circuit decisions that rely explicitly on *Tinker*), *aff'd*, 564 F.2d 157 (4th Cir. 1977) (per curiam); *Trachtman v. Anker*, 563 F.2d 512, 516 (2d Cir. 1977), *cert. denied*, 435 U.S. 925 (1978); *Reineke v. Cobb County Sch. Dist.*, 484 F. Supp. 1252, 1256-58 (N.D. Ga. 1980); *Frasca v. Andrews*, 463 F. Supp. 1043, 1049 (E.D.N.Y. 1979); *Bayer v. Kinzler*, 383 F. Supp. 1164, 1165-66 (E.D.N.Y. 1974), *aff'd*, 515 F.2d 504 (2d Cir. 1975).
10 Over time, courts have looked to public forum analysis to guide them in weighing the legality of government regulations over more than just geographic spaces or other physical, government property. For example, in its 1995 *Rosenberger* decision, the Supreme Court considered the student activity fund administered by University of Virginia school officials, which was at issue in the case, to be a "metaphysical" forum to which forum analysis was applicable, just as forum analysis would be applicable if access were denied to a school's mail system. *Rosenberger v. Rector & Visitors of the Univ. of Va.*, 515 U.S. 819, 830 (1995) ("The SAF is a forum more in a metaphysical sense than in a spatial or geographic sense, but the same principles are applicable.") (citing *Perry Educ. Ass'n v. Perry Local Educators' Ass'n*, 460 U.S. 37, 46-47 (1983) (forum analysis of school mail system)).
11 A debate exists among the courts as to whether the phrase "limited public forum" is in fact a fourth category of public forum or a different name for a non-public forum or subcategory of a designated public forum. *See, e.g., Summum v. Pleasant Grove City*, 499 F.3d 1170, 1173-74 (10th Cir. 2007), *cert. granted*, 128 S. Ct. 1737 (2008). But the preferred term for the middle level public forum is clearly a "designated public forum."
12 *Perry Educ. Ass'n*, 460 U.S. at 45.
13 *See, e.g., National Socialist White People's Party v. Ringers*, 473 F.2d 1010 (4th Cir. 1973) (school board could not prevent Nazis from renting public school auditorium without evidence of a threat to property or order).
14 *Perry Educ. Ass'n*, 460 U.S. at 46; *Cornelius v. NAACP Legal Defense & Educ. Fund*, 473 U.S. 788, 806 (1985).

15 *Gambino v. Fairfax County Sch. Bd.*, 429 F. Supp. 731 (E.D. Va.), *aff'd*, 564 F.2d 157 (4th Cir. 1977) (per curiam).
16 *Gambino*, 564 F.2d at 157.
17 *Gambino*, 429 F. Supp. at 734.
18 *Gambino*, 564 F.2d at 158.
19 *See, e.g., Bayer*, 383 F. Supp. at 1164; *Schiff v. Williams*, 519 F.2d 257 (5th Cir. 1975); *Joyner v. Whiting*, 477 F.2d 456 (4th Cir. 1973); *Stanton v. Brunswick Sch. Dept.*, 577 F. Supp. 1560 (D. Me. 1984); *Reineke*, 484 F. Supp. at 1252; *Korn v. Elkins*, 317 F. Supp. 138 (D. Md. 1970); *Panarella v. Birenbaum*, 327 N.Y.S.2d 755 (N.Y. App. Div. 1971), *aff'd*, 296 N.E.2d 238 (N.Y. 1973).
20 *See, e.g., Nicholson v. Bd. of Educ.*, 682 F.2d 858, 863 n. 3 (9th Cir. 1982); *Gambino*, 429 F. Supp. at 736 (citing Fourth Circuit decisions that rely explicitly on *Tinker*); *Trachtman*, 563 F.2d at 516; *Reineke*, 484 F. Supp. at 1256-58; *Frasca*, 463 F. Supp. at 1049; *Bayer*, 383 F. Supp. at 1165-66.
21 *Captive Voices, The Report of the Commission of Inquiry into High School Journalism*, at 49 (J. Nelson ed., Shocken Books 1974).
22 The facts of *Hazelwood* related here are taken from the three court rulings in the case. *Hazelwood Sch. Dist. v. Kuhlmeier*, 484 U.S. 260 (1988), rev'g, 795 F.2d 1368 (8th Cir. 1986), rev'g, 607 F. Supp. 1450 (E.D. Mo. 1985). An earlier decision in the case, reported at 596 F. Supp. 1422 (E.D. Mo. 1984), denied the students' request for injunctive relief.
23 *Kuhlmeier v. Hazelwood Sch. Dist.*, 607 F. Supp. 1450 (E.D. Mo. 1985).
24 *Id.* at 1466 (quoting *Frasca*, 463 F. Supp. at 1052).
25 *Kuhlmeier v. Hazelwood Sch. Dist.*, 795 F.2d 1368 (8th Cir. 1986).
26 *Hazelwood Sch. Dist. v. Kuhlmeier*, 484 U.S. 260 (1988). Because of the retirement of Justice Lewis Powell Jr. in 1987, there were only eight sitting justices on the Supreme Court at the time the *Hazelwood* case was argued. Thus if one additional justice had sided with the dissenters, the court would have been equally split, four to four. In the event of a tie, the court of appeals' decision, which in this case favored the students, would have stood as the final ruling in the case.
27 *Id.* at 270-71.
28 *Id.* at 271.
29 *Id.* at 273.
30 *Id.*
31 *Id.* at 267.
32 *Id.*
33 *Id.* at 270 (because the student newspaper at Hazelwood East was found not to be a public forum, it was the new reasonableness standard, "rather than our decision in *Tinker*, that governs this case").
34 *Id.* at 269.
35 *Id.*
36 *Id.*
37 *Id.* at 274-75.
38 *Id.* at 281 (Brennan, J., dissenting).
39 *Id.* at 282.
40 *Id.* at 288.
41 *Id.* at 289.
42 *Id.* at 291.
43 Hazelwood, 484 U.S. at 273 n. 6.
44 *Lueneburg v. Everett Sch. Dist.*, No. C05-2070RSM, 2007 WL 2069859 (W.D. Wash. July 13, 2007) (finding that policy allowing principal to exercise prior review over student newspaper that may have been operating as a public forum was not an impermissible "prior restraint"). The best way a publication operating as a public forum can protect itself against administrative prior review is to seek a school policy explicitly prohibiting it.
45 *Hazelwood*, 484 U.S. at 272-73.
46 *Id.* at 271.
47 *Westfield High Sch. L.I.F.E. Club v. City of Westfield*, 249 F. Supp. 2d 98 (D. Mass. 2003).
48 *Id.* at 117-118.
49 *Hazelwood*, 484 U.S. at 271.
50 *Id.*
51 *Romano v. Harrington*, 725 F. Supp. 687 (E.D.N.Y. 1989).
52 *Id.* at 690. *But see Desilets v. Clearview Reg'l Bd. of Educ.*, 630 A.2d 333, 338 (N.J. Super. A.D. 1993) ("[t]he *Hazelwood* Court did not limit its holding to classroom activities only, and its emphasis on 'curricular' activities must be read in light of the very broad definition which it gave that term"), *aff'd*, 647 A.2d 150 (N.J. 1994).
53 *Lodestar v. Bd. of Educ.*, No. B-88-257, slip op. at 9-10 (D. Conn. March 10, 1989) (unpublished).
54 *Hazelwood*, 484 U.S. at 267 (citing *Perry Educ. Ass'n v. Perry Local Educators Assn.*, 460 U.S. 37, 46 n.7, 47 (1983)).
55 *See, e.g., Child Evangelism Fellowship v. Montgomery County Pub. Sch.*, 457 F.3d 376, 383 (4th Cir. 2006); *Draudt v. Wooster City Sch. Dist.*, 246 F. Supp. 2d 820, 829 (N.D. Ohio 2003) and *Dean v. Utica Community Sch.*, 345 F. Supp. 2d 799, 809 (E.D. Mich. 2004) (both cases noting that "'[a]ctual practice speaks louder than words' in determining whether the government intended to create a limited public forum") (citing *Kincaid v. Gibson*, 236 F.3d 342, 351 (6th Cir. 2001) (other citations omitted)).
56 Planned Parenthood of Southern Nevada v. Clark County Sch. Dist., 941 F.2d 817 (9th Cir. 1991) (en banc).
57 *Id.* at 821. This case focused on the status of the publications as public forums for the community, not the student editors.
58 Lodestar, No. B-88-257, slip op. at 10.
59 Draudt, 246 F. Supp. 2d 820.

60 *Id.* at 827 (citing *Kincaid v. Gibson*, 236 F.3d 342, 349 (6th Cir. 2001) (en banc)).

61 *Id.* at 827.

62 *Id.* at 829 (citing *Kincaid*, 236 F.3d at 351) (other citations omitted).

63 *Id.*

64 *Dean v. Utica Community Sch.*, 345 F. Supp. 2d 799 (E.D. Mich. 2004).

65 *Id.* at 809.

66 Courts examining the issues "must assume that school-sponsored publications are nonpublic and that unless the schools affirmatively intend to open a forum," the limitations of *Hazelwood* will apply. *Planned Parenthood of Southern Nevada v. Clark County Sch. Dist.*, 941 F.2d 817, 819 (9th Cir. 1991) (en banc).

67 In another case involving censorship of a school-sponsored high school newspaper, a court found, on a motion for summary judgment, that there were "genuine issues of material fact with respect to whether school officials clearly intended to create a nonpublic forum, or whether the [newspaper] was intended to operate as a limited public forum." *Lueneburg v. Everett Sch. Dist.*, No. C05-2070RSM, 2007 WL 2069859 at 11 (W.D. Wash. July 13, 2007).

68 *Cornelius v. NAACP Legal Defense & Educ. Fund*, 473 U.S. 788, 806 (1985) (citing *Perry Educ. Ass'n v. Perry Local Educators' Ass'n*, 460 U.S. 37, 49 (1983)).

69 *Planned Parenthood of Southern Nevada v. Clark County Sch. Dist.*, 941 F.2d 817, 829 (9th Cir. 1991) (en banc); *Searcy v. Harris*, 888 F.2d 1314, 1319 n. 7 (11th Cir. 1989); *Peck v. Baldwinsville Central Sch. Dist.*, 426 F.3d 617, 633 (2d Cir. 2005). The federal Fourth Circuit Court of Appeals appears to have reached the same conclusion for in-school speech, although without specifically referencing *Hazelwood*. *Child Evangelism Fellowship v. Montgomery County Pub. Sch.*, 457 F.3d 376, 383 (4th Cir. 2006). The Sixth Circuit appears to have reached this conclusion in the context of college student speech. *Kincaid v. Gibson*, 191 F.3d 719, 727 (6th Cir. 1999), vacated on other grounds, 236 F.3d 342 (6th Cir. 2001) (en banc), and district courts within the Sixth Circuit have applied that conclusion to high schools as well. *Hansen v. Ann Arbor Pub. Sch.*, 293 F. Supp. 2d 780, 797 (E.D. Mich. 2003); *Dean v. Utica Community Sch.*, 345 F. Supp. 2d 799, 813 (E.D. Mich. 2004).

70 *Fleming v. Jefferson County Sch. Dist.*, 298 F.3d 918, 926-28 (10th Cir. 2002), *cert. denied*, 537 U.S. 1110 (2003); *Muller v. Jefferson Lighthouse Sch.*, 98 F.3d 1530, 1542 (7th Cir. 1996), *cert. denied*, 520 U.S. 1156 (1997). *See also Ward v. Hickey*, 996 F.2d 448, 452 (1st Cir. 1993). (*Ward* was a teacher speech case and may not relate to *Hazelwood*'s application to student speech.) An en banc panel of the federal Third Circuit Court of Appeals appears equally divided on the issue, *C.H. v. Oliva*, 226 F.3d 198 (3d Cir. 2000), and the Fifth Circuit has avoided the issue, *Chiras v. Miller*, 432 F.3d 606 (5th Cir. 2005).

71 Many Court-watchers were hoping the Supreme Court would clarify the law regarding viewpoint discrimination in a public forum when the Court agreed to hear the case of *Pleasant Grove City v. Summum*, 499 F.3d 1170, 1173-74 (10th Cir. 2007), *cert. granted*, 128 S. Ct. 1737 (2008). The case involved a small religious sect's request to place a marker in a municipal park alongside an existing monument to the biblical Ten Commandments. But the Court did not decide the viewpoint discrimination question. Instead, it ruled that the choice of historical markers is "government speech" and not the speech of the individual providers of the markers, and therefore no speaker's First Amendment rights were implicated. *Pleasant Grove City v. Summum*, 129 S. Ct. 1125, 1134 (2009).

72 *Dean*, 345 F. Supp. 2d at 813 (E.D. Mich. 2004).

73 *Hazelwood*, 484 U.S. at 272.

74 *Id.*

75 *Poling v. Murphy*, 872 F.2d 757 (6th Cir. 1989), *cert. denied*, 493 U.S. 1021 (1990).

76 *Planned Parenthood of Southern Nevada v. Clark County Sch. Dist.*, 941 F.2d 817 (9th Cir. 1991) (en banc).

77 *Peck v. Baldwinsville Central Sch. Dist.*, 426 F.3d 617 (2d Cir. 2005), *cert. denied*, 547 U.S. 1097 (2006).

78 *Henerey v. City of St. Charles*, 200 F.3d 1128 (8th Cir. 1999).

79 *Dean*, 345 F. Supp. 2d at 806.

80 *Id.* at 809, n. 4.

81 *Id.* at 809.

82 *Id.* at 810-812.

83 *Id.* at 812.

84 *Desilets v. Clearview Reg'l Bd. of Educ.*, 137 N.J. 585 (N.J. 1994).

85 *Id.* at 593.

86 *Id.*

87 *Desilets v. Clearview Reg'l Bd. of Educ.*, 630 A.2d 333, 338 (N.J. Super. A.D. 1993) (ruling that "[f]or the [school officials] in the instant matter to say that censorship here was justified by pedagogical concerns does not make it so"), *aff'd*, 647 A.2d 150 (N.J. 1994).

88 The Student Press Law Center legal staff received 548 requests for legal help in 1988. By 2003, that number had risen to 2,360. "Calls to SPLC legal help hotline jump in 2003," Student Press Law Center *Report*, Winter 2004-05, p. 3.

89 "Editor files grievance after Ill. school censors pro-discipline editorial," SPLC *News Flash*, March 9, 2012, *available* at http://www.splc.org/news/newsflash.asp?id=2346.

90 "Principal silences article on drunk driving arrest of school superintendent," Student Press Law Center Report, Fall 1992, p. 17.

91 "Principal censors newspaper over articles on birth control, tattoos," SPLC *News Flash*, Nov. 29, 2005, Press release, office office of Superintendent Thomas E. Bailey, November 29, 2005, *available* at http://www.splc.org/pdf/oakpressrelease.pdf.

92 "Washington state high school journalists see article censored on eve of legislature's vote," SPLC *News Flash*, March 12, 2007, available at http://www.splc.org/newsflash.asp?id=1469&year=2007.

93 See *Death by Cheeseburger: High School Journalism in the 1990's and Beyond*, Freedom Forum

(Washington, D.C. 1994), p. 113-15.

94 "Principal censors anti-smoking editorial," Student Press Law Center *Report*, Winter 1992-93, p. 9.

95 "Superintendent first nixes ad, then censors student's editorial," Student Press Law Center *Report*, Winter 1993-94, at 16. When told that the *Hazelwood* decision required that he provide a valid educational reason for his censorship, the superintendent replied, "That's your interpretation. We have our own." *Id.*

96 "Florida high school newspapers passed out with a hole," SPLC *News Flash*, Oct. 27, 2006, *available* at http://www.splc.org/newsflash.asp?id=1359&year=2006.

97 "Principal fires adviser for allowing criticism," Student Press Law Center *Report*, Fall 1992, p. 13.

98 "Baltimore County school system says it won't censor," YNS Special Report, February 1988, p. 5.

99 See *Death by Cheeseburger*, p. 122-24.

100 "New Dade County policy adopted," Student Press Law Center *Report*, Fall 1994, p. 5.

101 "A different path," Student Press Law Center *Report*, Winter 2007-08, at 26.

102 "School officials in Ga. 'standing by' decision to run controversial column," SPLC *News Flash*, Oct. 3, 2007, *available* at http://www.splc.org/newsflash.asp?id=1620&year=2007.

103 *See R.O. v. Ithaca City Sch. Dist.*, 645 F.3D 533 (2d Cir. 2011)

104 *Id.* at 537.

105 *Id.* at 540.

106 *Id.*

107 CAL. EDUC. CODE SEC. 48907 (1993) (formerly CAL. EDUC. CODE SEC. 10611).

108 *Id.*

109 *Id.*

110 See *Bright v. Los Angeles Unified Sch. Dist.*, 556 P.2d 1090, 1095 (Cal. 1976). Additionally, California enacted a law in 1992 that provides high school students with free expression protections even stronger than those of the *Tinker* decision. CAL. EDUC. CODE SEC. 48950 (West 1993).

111 News Release, California State Department of Education, March 18, 1988.

112 *Leeb v. Delong*, 243 Cal. Rptr. 494 (Cal. Dist. Ct. App. 1988).

113 *Id.* at 502. Over the years, the California statute has been effectively used in a number of other cases and controversies to strike down censorship that might otherwise have gone unchecked. *See, e.g., Smith v. Novato Unified Sch. Dist.*, 59 Cal. Rptr. 3d 508 (Calif. App. 2007), *cert. denied*, 128 S.Ct. 1256 (2008); "Settlement reached in East Bakersfield High School case," SPLC *News Flash*, Nov. 17, 2006, *available* at http://www.splc.org/newsflash.asp?id=1374&year=2006.

114 Leeb, 243 Cal. Rptr. at 497 (footnote omitted).

115 MASS. GENERAL LAWS ANN. ch. 71, Sec. 82.

116 *Id.*

117 IOWA CODE ANN. SEC. 280.22.

118 COLO. REV. STAT. ANN. Sec. 22-1-120.

119 KANS. STAT. ANN. SECS. 72.1504 to 1506.

120 ARK. STAT. ANN. SECS. 6-18-1201 to 1204.

121 ORE. REV. STAT. SEC. 336.477 (2007).

122 "In Oregon, a new law protects students," Student Press Law Center *Report*, Fall 2007, p. 27.

123 See 22 PA. CODE SECTION 12.9; WASH. ADMIN. CODE SEC. 392-40-215; D.C. MUNI. REG. RULE 5-E2401.

124 *Lange v. Diercks*, 808 N.W.2d 754 (Iowa App. 2011).

125 *Moore v. Watson*, 838 F.Supp.2d 735 (N.D. Ill. 2012).

126 *Desilets v. Clearview Reg'l Bd. of Educ.*, No. C-23-90 (N.J. Super. Ct. Law Div. May 7, 1991), *aff'd* on other grounds, 630 A.2d 333 (N.J. Super. A.D. 1993), *aff'd*, No. A-133-93 (N.J. Sept. 22, 1994); *Lueneburg v. Everett Sch. Dist.*, No. C05-2070RSM, 2007 WL 2069859 (W.D. Wash. July 13, 2007). A similar claim was raised in Oregon in the case *Barcik v. Kubiaczyk*, 873 P.2d 456 (Or. Ct. App. 1994), *rev'd as moot*, 321 Or. 174, 895 P.2d 765 (Or. 1995). The subsequent enactment of the student free expression statute in Oregon described above, which includes a reference to the state constitution, indicates a combination of state law protections for the rights of student journalists.

127 *Desilets*, No. C-23-90 (N.J. Super. Ct. Law Div. May 7, 1991); *Lueneburg*, slip op. at 14 ("we are not persuaded by defendant that plaintiffs do not have a private cause of action under the Washington State Constitution.").

128 *Desilets*, slip op. at 10-11. The New Jersey Superior Court, Appellate Division, and the New Jersey Supreme Court did not consider the state constitutional issue in this case because they were able to decide the case in favor of the student based on the First Amendment.

CHAPTER 6

College Press Freedom

Although the Supreme Court chipped away at the First Amendment protection of high school journalists in its 1988 decision *Hazelwood School District v. Kuhlmeier*, the freedom of college publications remains on firmer footing.

The Supreme Court has yet to directly address censorship of the content of school-sponsored student media at a public college or university. But it has touched on the issue once — in a 1995 case involving a college's financial support of a student publication[1] — and in a number of cases involving the First Amendment rights of college students generally.[2] In all of these cases, most of which are discussed later in this chapter, the Court has emphasized the important role it believes free speech plays on America's college and university campuses. Moreover, but for one notable exception,[3] dozens of college free expression and free press cases decided by lower courts give ample support to the notion that college officials — or those acting on their behalf — are prohibited from censoring student media in all but the most exceptional situations.

The Court's 1969 decision in *Tinker v. Des Moines Independent Community School District* and its progeny have been an important part of the development of college press law. In fact, until *Hazelwood*, many courts cited high school and college cases as if they were interchangeable. Thus the discussion in Chapter 4 of student press rights before *Hazelwood* is relevant here as well. But First Amendment protections for college students have had their own independent development, dating back more than four decades.

THE U.S. SUPREME COURT AND COLLEGE SPEECH RIGHTS

After the Supreme Court in *Tinker* adopted the "material and substantial disruption" test for the bounds of permissible censorship in the context of a high school, other courts soon began to apply the standard to limit censorship by school officials on public college and university campuses.[4] Then in 1972 and 1973, the Supreme Court handed down two decisions that confirmed the importance it placed on First Amendment protections for college students.

Healy and *Papish*

In *Healy v. James*,[5] the Court confronted a Connecticut state college's refusal to recognize a radical student group as an official student organization. The students claimed that the school's action was an infringement of their First Amendment rights.

In siding with the students, the Court noted, "The college classroom and its surrounding environs is peculiarly the 'marketplace of ideas.'"[6] Its own precedents, the Court said, "leave no room for the view that, because of the acknowledged need for order, First Amendment protections should apply with less force on college campuses than in the community at large. Quite to the contrary, 'the vigilant protection of constitutional freedoms is nowhere more vital than in the community of American schools.'"[7]

> "The college classroom and its surrounding environs is peculiarly the 'marketplace of ideas.'"
> — *Healy v. James* (1972)

A year later, in *Papish v. Board of Curators of the University of Missouri*,[8] the Court applied similar reasoning to a case involving censorship of a student journalist. Barbara *Papish* was a graduate journalism student at the University of Missouri who was expelled from school for distributing an independent newspaper called *The Free Press Underground*. The issue of the publication in question included on its cover a political cartoon that depicted policemen raping the Statue of Liberty and the Goddess of Justice with the caption " ... With Liberty and Justice for All." It also contained an article with the headline "Motherfucker Acquitted," which discussed the trial and acquittal on an assault charge of a man who was a member of the anarchist group called "Up Against the Wall, Motherfuckers."

In ordering that *Papish* be reinstated as a student at the university, the Court said "the First Amendment leaves no room for the operation of a dual standard in the academic community with respect to the content of speech."[9] "The mere dissemination of ideas — no matter how offensive to good taste — on a state university campus may not be shut off in the name alone of 'conventions of decency.'"[10]

These early cases seemed to leave little doubt that the Supreme Court would hold college and university officials to a high standard when they attempted to restrict student expression. Both the *Healy* and *Papish* decisions recognized *Tinker*'s "material and substantial disruption" test as the only legitimate justification for censorship of student expression that is otherwise constitutionally protected.[11]

And while lower courts handed down dozens of decisions over the next two decades that involved fights over college student First Amendment rights — cases that were almost always won by the students — the Supreme Court itself was largely silent.

Rosenberger and *Southworth*

Between the Court's 1973 ruling in *Papish* and 1995, the Court — though it had ample opportunity — handed down only a handful of decisions that implicated the First Amendment rights of college students, and none that directly addressed the free press rights of public college student media when facing administrative censorship.[12] In 1995, the Court answered a few questions when it announced its decision in *Rosenberger v. Rector and Visitors of the University of Virginia*.[13]

During the 1990-91 school year, Ronald Rosenberger, a junior at the University of Virginia, asked the school for $5,862 to subsidize the printing costs of his newspaper, *Wide Awake: A Christian Perspective at the University of Virginia*. The money would come from a student activities fund, which university officials administered and allocated pursuant to guidelines they established and that supported other student publications. The money for the fund came from mandatory student fees collected by the university.

Wide Awake, the student editors noted, offered "a Christian perspective on both personal and community issues, especially those relevant to college students at the University of Virginia." Founded in 1990, the paper included articles about racism, crisis pregnancy, stress, prayer, homosexuality, Christian missionary work, and eating disorders. It also included reviews of religious music and interviews with university professors. Each page of *Wide Awake*, and the end of each article or review, was marked by a cross. Most of the journal's advertisers were churches, centers for Christian study or Christian bookstores.[14] University officials denied Rosenberger's request because they found the publication violated school funding guidelines. Among other things, the guidelines forbade funding "religious activities" that "primarily promote[d] or manifest[ed] a particular belief in or about a deity or an ultimate reality." Funding a publication such as *Wide Awake*, the university argued, violated the Establishment Clause of the First Amendment that requires separation between church and state.

Rosenberger and other *Wide Awake* staff members argued that the university's actions violated the First Amendment's Free Speech Clause. In July 1991, they sued the university, claiming that school officials violated their First Amendment rights by denying *Wide Awake* funding that was available to student editors of secular publications.

Nearly four years later, in a 5-to-4 majority opinion written by Justice Anthony Kennedy, the Court sided with the students. It held that the university's denial of funding to *Wide Awake* because of its religious content amounted to unconstitutional viewpoint discrimination. The Court raised special concerns about university officials reviewing publications to determine whether the content qualified as "religious" and thus should not be eligible for funding. The Court said that if the university chose to promote or support student speech at all, it had to do so equally, without favoring the viewpoint of certain students over others. In this case, the Court said, the First Amendment required the University of Virginia to allow *Wide Awake* to obtain student activity fee funding on the same basis as other student publications. Though *Rosenberger* was, at the time, viewed by many as more of a religious speech case than a student speech case, the Court's decision was a strong rebuke to college officials who thought the Court might be weakening in its resolve to protect free speech on American college and university campuses following its earlier decision in *Hazelwood*.

In striking down the university's funding guidelines and ruling for the students, the Court made clear that it took seriously the First Amendment's protective role and the importance of free speech and open debate on campus. In his opinion, Justice Kennedy noted the important role universities had played throughout the world's history, "in places like Bologna, Oxford and Paris," as gathering places "for students to speak and to write and to learn."[15]

"Vital First Amendment speech principles are at stake here," Justice Kennedy continued. "The first danger to liberty lies in granting the State the power to examine publications to determine whether or not they are based on some ultimate idea and, if so, for the State to classify them. The second, and corollary, danger is to speech from the chilling of individual thought and expression. That danger is especially real in the University setting, where the State acts against a background and tradition of thought and experiment that is at the center of our intellectual and philosophic tradition."[16] The decision reinforces the conclusion reached by lower courts, described later in this chapter, that funding cannot be used as an indirect means of censoring.

Five years later, in 2000, the Court issued a decision in another First Amendment case with implications for some college student media organizations. And once again the Justices took the opportunity to come down on the side of encouraging campus speech. In *Board of Regents of University of Wisconsin System v. Southworth*, students at the University of Wisconsin challenged the university's imposition of a mandatory student activity fee.[17] The fee was used to support a variety of student groups, including some, the students claimed, whose stated missions and speech were at odds with their political and ideological beliefs.

At the time, it was estimated that approximately 70 percent of the nation's college and universities used student fees to fund campus groups, including student media,[18] and many feared a ruling that would force public colleges to revise, or even eliminate, their student fee programs. By allowing individual students to select the groups they wanted to fund or exclude entirely groups with political, ideological or religious objectives, such groups, including student media, could have lost funding or been prohibited from publishing editorials or endorsing candidates for office.

Nevertheless, the student plaintiffs argued that being forced to financially support groups that expressed ideas they found offensive violated their First Amendment rights.

The Court disagreed.

"The University of Wisconsin exacts the fee at issue for the sole purpose of facilitating the free and open exchange of ideas by, and among, its students," Justice Anthony Kennedy wrote on behalf of a unanimous Court.[19]

Such a goal — as long as the fee system was open to all students, regardless of their ideology — was a legitimate part of a public university's mission, the Court held.

> "Vital First Amendment speech principles are at stake here. The first danger to liberty lies in granting the State the power to examine publications to determine whether or not they are based on some ultimate idea and, if so, for the State to classify them. The second, and corollary, danger is to speech from the chilling of individual thought and expression. That danger is especially real in the University setting, where the State acts against a background and tradition of thought and experiment that is at the center of our intellectual and philosophic tradition."
> — *Rosenberger v. Rector and Visitors of the University of Virginia* (1995)

"The First Amendment," Kennedy continued, "permits a public university to charge its students an activity fee used to fund a program to facilitate extracurricular student speech if the program is viewpoint neutral."[20]

Prior to *Southworth*, at least five lower courts had rejected lawsuits filed by individual college students who objected to their mandatory student activity fees being used to fund newspapers that expressed editorial positions with which they disagreed.[21] In each of these cases, as in *Southworth*, the courts said it was permissible for a school to provide a forum through which students could express themselves as long as schools were not attempting to impose their views on the student editors.

Taken together, the Supreme Court's record protecting the free speech rights of college students and encouraging campus debate is reassuring. Yet to date, the Court still has not directly addressed the question most on the mind of a large part of the college student press community: to what degree does the First Amendment protect school-sponsored college media from censorship by public college officials and those acting on their behalf? It is, however, a question on which — for more than forty years — lower courts have provided considerable guidance.

Lower Courts and College Free Press Rights

From the time of the first college press censorship case, the rulings issued by lower courts have been remarkably uniform. Indeed, between 1967 and 2005, lower courts across the country consistently held that student editors were protected in determining the content of student media at a public college or university — regardless of whether the school provided financial or other support — and that censorship by college officials, or those acting on their behalf, was rarely permissible.[22]

BIRTH OF COLLEGE PRESS FREEDOM: THE *DICKEY* CASE

The first major court case to limit censorship of the college press arose even before the 1969 Supreme Court decision in *Tinker v. Des Moines Independent Community School District*. Gary Dickey was the student editor of the campus newspaper at Troy State University in Alabama. In the spring of 1967, Dickey wrote an editorial commenting on a widely publicized controversy at the University of Alabama. The president of that university had supported the right of students at his school to produce and distribute a publication that included commentary by radical activists of the time. The governor and state legislators criticized the university president for his tolerance. Dickey planned to publish his column in support of the Alabama president, but was told by his adviser and his own college's president that he could not do so. They offered in its place a story called "Raising Dogs in North Carolina."

Instead of running his editorial or the proffered feature story, Dickey left the space where his piece was to appear blank, except for the words "CENSORED." That summer, Dickey was suspended from school for his actions. He took his case to court, claiming university officials had violated his First Amendment rights.

In ordering that Dickey be allowed to return to school, the court essentially applied a standard that would soon be adopted by the Supreme Court in its *Tinker* decision:

> State school officials cannot infringe on their students' right of free and unrestricted expression as guaranteed by the Constitution of the United States where the exercise of such right does not "materially and substantially interfere with requirements of appropriate discipline in the operation of the school."[23]

1967-2005: Hands-Off

Dickey began what was effectively a 30-plus year winning streak for America's college student media when contesting administrative censorship. From 1967 until 2005, courts consistently held that student media at public colleges and universities were entitled to First Amendment protections that were generally equivalent to those enjoyed by their commercial counterparts. These courts, following *Dickey* (and later *Tinker*), held that school administrators could censor student media only if they could show, at a minimum, that the speech in question was legally unprotected (for instance, libelous or obscene) or if they could demonstrate that some significant and imminent physical disruption of the campus would result from the publication's content.

In *Bazaar v. Fortune*,[24] for example, the federal Fifth Circuit Court of Appeals declared that officials at the University of Mississippi could not prohibit publication in the student literary magazine of articles containing "earthy language" and a non-obscene depiction of an interracial love affair. The court explained why the school, which supported the literary magazine with facilities and funds and provided advisers through its English department, did not have the same power to control the publication's content as would a commercial publisher.

> The University here is clearly an arm of the state and this single fact will always distinguish it from the purely private publisher as far as censorship rights are concerned. It seems a well-established rule that once a [u]niversity recognizes a student activity that has elements of free expression, it can act to censor that expression only if it acts consistent with First Amendment constitutional guarantees.[25]

What the Fifth Circuit seemed to say is that when a public college or university creates a student publication and puts students in the position of editors, it is recognizing an "activity that has elements of free expression" and school officials are significantly limited in their ability to censor that publication.

Given this presumption of strong First Amendment protection for the college press, courts over the years have upheld the right of student journalists to publish many things. Included among these have been a four-letter reference to a university president,[26] a photograph of a burning American flag,[27] criticism of the governor and the state legislature,[28] editorials endorsing political candidates and ballot issues[29] and a scathing attack (termed "blasphemous" by the court) on the Roman Catholic church.[30] The courts have agreed that unless college or university officials can demonstrate that the material they object to has met the substantial disruption requirement of *Tinker*, the First Amendment prohibits censorship.[31]

INDIRECT CENSORSHIP

As the First Amendment's protections for public college student media seemed to become increasingly certain over the years, censorship-minded college officials likewise became increasingly clever in their attempts to disguise their censorship as something else. As the years went by, fewer censorship incidents involved an outright ban on a particular article or editorial. Rather, a growing number of cases dealt with more subtle, indirect forms of content control. But whatever the method, courts have ruled such censorship is as unconstitutional as direct censorship.

Withdrawal of Financial Support

As discussed above, the U.S. Supreme Court has handed down only one decision directly involving school-sponsored college student media. That case — *Rosenberger*

"The University here is clearly an arm of the state and this single fact will always distinguish it from the purely private publisher as far as censorship rights are concerned. It seems a well-established rule that once a [u]niversity recognizes a student activity that has elements of free expression, it can act to censor that expression only if it acts consistent with First Amendment constitutional guarantees."
— *Bazaar v. Fortune* (1973)

— struck down a public college's attempt to eliminate school funding of a student publication based on the publication's religious content.[32] *Rosenberger* made a point that bears repeating: Neither school officials nor those acting on their behalf can use their financial control over a student publication as a tool to dictate content or favor a particular viewpoint. Censorship through the "power of the purse" is still censorship and lower courts have consistently struck down attempts to use such power to control or manipulate what their student media publish.

In *Joyner v. Whiting*,[33] for example, the student newspaper at North Carolina Central University published an editorial that urged students to resist efforts to integrate their historically black college. The president of the university attempted to withhold student activity fee funding to the paper because he said that it did not meet "standard journalistic criteria" and did not reflect "the full spectrum of views on this campus."[34] When the university's attorney told him that the Constitution would not permit such a content-based hold on money, the president terminated the newspaper's funding entirely. The editor of the newspaper and the president of the student government association filed a lawsuit against the president, and the federal Fourth Circuit Court of Appeals agreed that the students' First Amendment rights had been infringed.

Citing the Supreme Court's decision in *Healy v. James*, the court noted that the strong procampus speech principles of that case had been "extensively applied to strike down every form of censorship of student publications at state-supported institutions."[35]

"Censorship of constitutionally-protected expression," the court held, "cannot be imposed at a college or university by suspending editors, suppressing circulation, requiring imprimatur [approval] of controversial articles, excising repugnant material, withdrawing financial support, or asserting any other form of censorial oversight based on the institution's power of the purse."[36]

Note, however, that the First Amendment will not limit a school's ability to reduce or eliminate funding for student media if its decision to do so is not related to the publication's past or anticipated content.[37] Thus the motivation of school officials in reducing funding is frequently the key issue in these kinds of censorship cases.

In *Stanley v. Magrath*,[38] for example, the University of Minnesota attempted to alter the funding mechanism for the student newspaper by allowing students to request a refund of the portion of their student activity fee that went to support the paper. The change was prompted by the board of regents' displeasure over a finals week "humor issue" of the paper that included, among other things, an "interview" with Jesus on the cross that the court said "would offend anyone of good taste, whether with or without religion."[39] The federal Eighth Circuit Court of Appeals ruled that the university's action violated the First Amendment and established a two-part test for determining when actions taken by a school against a student publication will be considered unconstitutional censorship: the publication must show (1) that the school's action was adverse – that it caused harm to the publication (the loss need not be major; any "measurable loss" is sufficient); and (2) that the decision by the school to take action was "substantially motivated by the content" of the publication.[40]

PROVING A MOTIVE TO CENSOR

When school officials attempt to censor by cutting funds, denying equipment purchases, firing editors or advisers or some other indirect means, student journalists can have a more difficult time demonstrating that they have a First Amendment claim than in cases involving outright content censorship. The motivation of the censor is key; different kinds of evidence can be presented to show that the school's action was based primarily on an intention to control or punish the publication for its content.

For example, straightforward statements by school administrators or student government officials that they are cutting funds because they find the editorial stance of the student newspaper "too critical and one-sided" is clear evidence of unconstitutional motivation. However, even circumstantial evidence can be used to make a case. For example, an irate telephone call from a campus official complaining of news coverage and threatening to "do something," followed a month later by that administrator's announcement that the publication is being moved out of its current offices in the student union building and into a much smaller location on the outskirts of campus could be enough to persuade a court that the magazine was being punished based on its content, which the First Amendment does not allow.

Obviously, the more non-content-related justifications school officials can come up with for taking action against student media, the more difficult it will be for student journalists to contest those actions successfully. But a court should look not just to the explanations that school officials give, but to what circumstances indicate their motivations really were. If the court believes all of the school's "legitimate" reasons for taking action against the publication are merely a pretext, the school's action will be rejected.[41]

It is imperative that student media accurately record evidence that reveals such intent. For example, if a student government member takes time during a student senate meeting to launch a verbal attack against the newspaper for its recent story on election fraud — and, in the same breath, reminds the editor where her funding comes from — file away a copy of the minutes from that meeting, or better yet, an audio or video tape of the proceedings. If an administrator calls up the newsroom shouting about a "lousy editorial," be sure to write down a summary of the conversation immediately after she hangs up — signed, dated and tucked away in a "Censorship File."

Staff should be alerted of the importance of documenting all editorial criticism no matter how insignificant the comments might seem or how "rosy" the current relationship between student media and administration or student government might otherwise be. Such relationships can sour quickly. And though one nasty e-mail might not mean much by itself, it can prove significant when stacked up with a dozen others.

Also, administrators repeatedly use students' transitory status and lack of an institutional history to their advantage. To combat this, it is important that, once created, the "Censorship File" be carefully maintained and passed down to succeeding editors. The current editor might not need it, but his successor six years down the line will be grateful to have a pile of legal ammunition ready to go.

> Proving a motive to censor content is the key to winning a First Amendment case.

> At a public college, the First Amendment generally prohibits student government officials – as well as administrators – from censoring student media.

Censorship by Student Governments

Where once student publications and student governments joined forces to stand against school administrators,[42] today it is just as likely that a student government, often using its university-delegated authority to allocate student activity fees, will be the censor of student media.[43] The question of whether student governments are subject to the same First Amendment restraints as a school administration has rarely come before a court, but when it has, the courts have generally said that they are.

For example, when the Pikes Peak Community College student government cut off a $12,456 annual subsidy to the *Pikes Peak News*, three student journalists and their adviser filed suit, claiming an abridgment of their First Amendment rights. In a ruling on preliminary issues in the case, the Supreme Court of Colorado agreed that if the funding cut was based on the student senate's objection to the content of the *News*, the newspaper would have a valid First Amendment claim.[44] As the court noted, the college had "authority and control over the funds of Pikes Peak Community College, including activity funds," and college administrators approved the student senate's decision to cut funding for the paper.[45] The case was sent back for a trial, and the Colorado Court of Appeals ultimately agreed that the student senate's primary reason for cutting funds was the newspaper's failure to follow proscribed fiscal policies rather than displeasure with the content of the *News*.[46]

The federal Eighth Circuit Court of Appeals reached a similar conclusion in the 1988 case, *Gay and Lesbian Students Association v. Gohn*.[47] That case arose after the student senate at the University of Arkansas denied a request for money from a campus support group for gay and lesbian students. The group claimed the decision was based on at least some student senators' disagreement with the organization's views.[48] The court noted that the student senate had been "delegated the function of appropriating money from student service funds to student organizations" and that the university ultimately had the final say as to how the funds would be allocated.[49] Thus, the First Amendment prohibited the senate's actions, the court ruled.

In an earlier decision, the same court had suggested that a media board comprised of students, staff and outside journalism professionals that oversaw the operation of the University of Nebraska at Lincoln's student newspaper was similarly limited in its ability to censor. The court affirmed a trial court decision in *Sinn v. Daily Nebraskan*, which said that the university could not use a publications committee to control advertising decisions made by a student editor.[50]

More recently, however, the U.S. Court of Appeals for the Second Circuit ruled that student government officials at a public college, when overseeing and regulating student elections, were not "state actors," and therefore not subject to the First Amendment restrictions imposed on other government officials.[51] The case arose after editors of the *College Voice*, the student newspaper at the College of Staten Island, which is part of the City University of New York (CUNY) system, endorsed a slate of candidates in their special election issue. The issue was scheduled to be distributed two days before the elections, but student government officials — some of whom had not been endorsed by the newspaper — directed the printer to impound the issue. The next day, after an attorney for the *College Voice* contacted school officials, college president Marlene Springer intervened and directed college employees to retrieve the newspapers from the printer and distribute them on campus, which they did. Before the election ended, a student government elections committee, which was required by CUNY bylaws and administered by the college's student government, passed a motion "to postpone the election and to consider those ballots cast null and void as it is the committee's decision that the electoral process had been compromised [by the *College Voice* endorsements] beyond its ability to be fair to all candidates."[52] Five days later, after the elections had closed, President Springer announced that she would affirm the election committee's decision to nullify the election.

In 2007, the Second Circuit upheld a lower court ruling that dismissed all student government officials from the case. It rejected the student editors' argument that because the student government derived its existence and power to regulate student organizations from CUNY bylaws and college policy, student government officials should be considered state actors: "Assuming that state law or regulations gave the Student Government Defendants the power to act as they did, these laws and regulations certainly did not require the Defendants to do so."[53]

The court indicated that its ruling was limited to "the circumstances presented in this case," suggesting that student government officials might be considered state actors under a different set of facts.[54] It is difficult to reconcile this ruling with the Supreme Court decision in the *Southworth* case, mentioned earlier in this chapter, in which the Court accepted without discussion that funding decisions made by the student government could be attributable to the university.

Dismissal of Editors

Courts have also found that school officials cannot fire or reprimand student journalists because of disagreement over the viewpoints expressed in the articles they publish. In *Thonen v. Jenkins*,[55] the editor of the student newspaper at East Carolina University was expelled from school for publishing a letter-to-the-editor that referred to the university

> Public college officials are constitutionally prohibited from firing or reprimanding student journalists because of disagreement over the viewpoints expressed in material the students publish.

president with a four-letter word. The author of the letter was also expelled. A district court, upheld by the U.S. Court of Appeals for the Fourth Circuit, ordered them both reinstated. In similar cases the federal courts have declared unconstitutional the removal of student editors because they ignored administrative orders to submit copy for prior approval[56] and printed the word "censored" after the adviser canceled a critical editorial.[57]

One case, *Schiff v. Williams*,[58] is especially informative. In 1973, the president of Florida Atlantic University fired three student editors and used school employees to publish the paper. When the students sued to get their jobs back, the president justified the dismissals by claiming that, under the editors, the paper had deteriorated into a "smear sheet" that emphasized "vilification and rumor mongering," and published stories that were "incorrect and misleading."[59] He also claimed that the paper embarrassed and brought disrepute to the school because of its poor grammar, spelling and use of language. But the federal Fifth Circuit Court of Appeals reinstated the students, holding that even if the president's allegations were true, they were not the "special circumstances" that could lead to significant disruption and thus justify censorship.[60]

As with funding cuts, however, a student publication editor or staff member can be disciplined or removed for a reason unrelated to the content of the paper. For example, an editor could be fired for stealing newspaper funds or for failing to publish a newspaper at all. Once again, the motivation of the censor will be crucial to determining if there is a valid First Amendment claim.

Retaliation Against Student Media Advisers

One of the more troubling developments in recent years has been the increase in removals of student media advisers following censorship battles or controversies involving the campus press.[61]

As discussed more fully in Chapter 11, advisers — who are generally both champions of their students and school employees — can find themselves forced into a delicate balancing act. In many cases, traditional labor law can make for a tough legal battle for advisers challenging their removal. An interesting question arises, though, as to whether firing or non-renewing a supportive, and often beloved, student media adviser violates or "chills" the First Amendment rights of the student media staff by making them hesitant to publish or air stories that might provoke such retaliatory administrative acts. Thus far, attempts to challenge such acts have met with mixed results.

For example, on the same day they confiscated approximately 2,000 copies of the student yearbook in November 1994, and following frequent editorial battles with the student newspaper, school officials at Kentucky State University transferred Laura Cullen, the student media adviser, to a secretarial job in the school's housing office. Cullen had long defended her students' rights to publish stories and opinion pieces critical of the university. About three weeks later, after filing a grievance against the university, she was allowed to return to her advising position, but only after KSU administrators gave her a list of "specific expectations" regarding her job performance that, among other things, required that student media publish "more positive news."[62] A federal appeals court ultimately dismissed a lawsuit filed by Cullen as moot after the adviser voluntarily resigned to take another job before the case was completed.[63] A subsequent lawsuit filed by the editor of the yearbook, claiming the adviser's removal violated her First Amendment rights, was also dismissed after the judge found that no harm resulted from Cullen's "temporary transfer" because it was of limited duration.[64]

In 2004, Ron Johnson, a veteran student media adviser and former president of College Media Advisers, was fired as adviser to the *Collegian*, the student newspaper at Kansas State University, after student editors did not report on a multicultural event on campus, which upset campus minority groups and some administrators. Following their subsequent analysis of the newspaper's content, university administrators determined that the "overall quality" of the paper had gone down and blamed Johnson. After his removal, both Johnson and *Collegian* editors, Katie Lane and Sarah Rice, sued university officials.

A federal district court ruled that Johnson's dismissal was not a violation of the student editors' First Amendment rights because he was removed due to the "overall quality" of the paper and not because of specific stories.[65] The court also ruled that Johnson's own First Amendment rights were not violated because he did not have any control over the content of the paper.[66]

A court of appeals later threw out the district court ruling but also dismissed the students' claims as moot because the student editors had graduated.[67]

Student editors at Ocean County College's student newspaper, the *Viking News*, were more successful following their lawsuit against university administrators who had refused to renew the contract of their longtime adviser, Karen Bosley. The students claimed that Bosley's removal was the result of retaliation for several stories the newspaper wrote that were critical of the school's administration, including a number of stories the paper had run in 2000 criticizing the college president's $78,000 inauguration and his decision to change the college logo.[68]

In a July 2006 ruling, a federal district court issued a preliminary injunction reinstating Bosley.

"It is clear," the judge wrote, "that such a retaliatory removal would ... have an impermissibly chilling effect on the Paper's student editors' freedom of expression in future issues of the Paper, and inflict irreparable harm...."[69]

Other Forms of Censorship

The specific act of administrative censorship that may be encountered — and legally challenged — by student media at a public university is limited only by the imagination of the would-be censor(s).

Over the years, student journalists have called the Student Press Law Center for help after school or student government officials have, for example, raised the grade-point requirement for student editors in order to disqualify a particular incoming candidate, refused to fund trips to a national journalism convention, canceled an existing order for new computer equipment, moved the newspaper into less favorable office space, restricted after-hours access to the newsroom, threatened to fire a reporter from an unrelated, paid campus job — and even, on one occasion, taken away a student photographer's parking privileges after the student newspaper had published stories that had upset campus police officials. While these conflicts were usually resolved short of going to court, all of these actions — where students could show they were content-motivated — would be unlawful.

One case involving a somewhat unique form of censorship that did go to court was *Husain v. Springer*, discussed earlier. In that case, the *College Voice*, one of three student newspapers at the College of Staten Island in New York, published an election issue endorsing a particular campus group running candidates in the election, which the student government claimed violated election rules. College President Marline Springer nullified the election results five days later.

In ruling that Springer had violated the student editors' First Amendment rights when she canceled the election, the district court noted the dangers of indirect censorship. "It cannot be that University action taken as a direct result of the views printed in a student newspaper can escape First Amendment scrutiny simply because that action was directed toward the nullification of the goal that the students espoused rather than at the vehicle, the newspaper, in which that goal was promoted. The chill on expressive freedom is the same," District Court Judge Nina Gershon wrote.[70]

"It is clear," she concluded, "that 'constitutional violations may arise from the deterrent or "chilling" effect of governmental regulations that fall short of a direct prohibition against the exercise of First Amendment rights.'"[71]

THE EFFECT OF *HAZELWOOD* ON THE COLLEGE PRESS

On its face, the Supreme Court's 1988 decision in *Hazelwood School District v. Kuhlmeier* had no legal impact on the free press rights of college students. The decision upheld the authority of public high school administrators at Hazelwood East High School in suburban St. Louis, Mo., to censor stories concerning teen pregnancy and the effects of divorce on children from a school-sponsored student newspaper. All of the parties to *Hazelwood* were high school students and high school officials; the question of how much protection the First Amendment provided public college and university students was not before the Court.

In fact, in a footnote to its decision, the *Hazelwood* Court confirmed that it was required to define student First Amendment protections only in high schools, and declined to go further: "We need not now decide whether the same degree of deference [to censorship by school officials] is appropriate with respect to school-sponsored expressive activities at the college and university level."[72]

The Court — with those 26 words — effectively took a pass on the issue of *Hazelwood*'s application to student speech on America's public college and university campuses and, in doing so, began a fierce legal and academic debate that has continued for more than two decades.

The Supreme Court did not say that its decision in *Hazelwood* did not apply on public college campuses. Rather, the Court said it need not rule "now" on the issue. From this, one could infer that the Court might be willing to extend the *Hazelwood* ruling to college students. On the other hand, one could just as easily say that the Court purposely chose not to extend its ruling or had no interest in confronting an issue in the abstract without a particular set of facts directly before it and intended to give no foreshadowing of future rulings on college censorship.

Whatever reading one makes of *Hazelwood*'s college footnote, it continues to generate much controversy among both courts and court-watchers.

The First Amendment: High School vs. College

Prior to *Hazelwood*, a number of courts had given strong indications that a high school-based censorship standard such as *Hazelwood* would be inappropriate in a college and university setting. For example, at least one federal court of appeals has said that students' First Amendment rights "on college campuses are coextensive with those in the community at large."[73] In other cases as well, courts have attempted to distinguish between the free press rights of high school and college students.[74] As one court noted, "Few college students are minors, and colleges are traditionally places of virtually unlimited free expression."[75]

In the more than 25 years since *Hazelwood* was decided, relatively few cases involving the First Amendment rights of college students have squarely raised the question of *Hazelwood*'s applicability in the university setting. The closest the Supreme Court has come to providing additional guidance on the question came in the concurring opinion to its 2000 decision in *Board of Regents of Univ. of Wisconsin System v. Southworth*, discussed earlier.[76] There, Justice David Souter, joined by Justices John Paul Stevens and Stephen Breyer, cited *Hazelwood*, *Bethel Sch. Dist. No. 403 v. Fraser* and *Tinker* in noting that the Court's "cases dealing with the right of teaching institutions to limit

> "We need not now decide whether the same degree of deference [to censorship by school officials] is appropriate with respect to school-sponsored expressive activities at the college and university level."
>
> — *Hazelwood School District v. Kuhlmeier* (1988)

expressive freedom of students have been confined to high schools, whose students and their schools' relation to them are different and at least arguably distinguishable from their counterparts in college education."[77]

In the absence of firm guidance from the Supreme Court, lower courts are increasingly prone to rely on *Hazelwood* even when the speaker is an adult-aged college student, although the cases are infrequent and typically involve speech in a classroom setting. A 2006 survey identified 13 federal court of appeals cases that had addressed whether the "logic and reasoning" of *Hazelwood* was applicable in the university or college setting; of those, the authors found, seven applied *Hazelwood* "in some fashion" to speech on college campuses.[78]

An illustrative recent case involved a graduate student at Eastern Michigan University, who was kicked out of her academic program (preparing her to be a school counselor) after expressing religious-based qualms about an assignment that asked her to counsel a gay student, and asking to reassign the student to a more supportive counselor.[79] She challenged her dismissal as a violation of her First Amendment rights. College attorneys argued that the *Hazelwood* standard should extend to all "student" speech regardless of maturity level, and the appeals court agreed: "The key word is student. *Hazelwood* respects the latitude educational institutions—at any level—must have to further legitimate curricular objectives."[80] The Sixth Circuit thus became the fourth federal appeals court (out of 12 geographic circuits) to say that *Hazelwood* applies to the speech of students at every level. This increasing reliance on *Hazelwood* — particularly where the student is neither using a school-funded means of communication nor is speaking to a public audience in a way that might be confused for an official school message — has been widely criticized by legal commentators, yet it continues.[81]

Before *Hazelwood*, courts seldom explicitly used public forum analysis to determine what level of First Amendment protection college student publications were entitled to have.

Courts rarely have been forced to analyze *Hazelwood* in the setting of college media. Since college media commonly is produced outside of classroom time and under little-to-no supervision from an instructor, it bears scarce resemblance to the "curricular" speech that the Supreme Court dealt with in *Hazelwood*. Nor should the *Hazelwood* concern for the vulnerability of impressionable young listeners have relevance to a college audience.

The U.S. Court of Appeals for the First Circuit has indicated, though only in passing, that college media is so different from K-12 student media that the *Hazelwood* level of institutional control should not apply. In that case, decided the year after *Hazelwood* was handed down, the court rejected students' claims that a public university's decision to close down a student legal services office violated their First Amendment rights.[82] In doing so, the court distinguished the legal services office from student newspapers, which the court noted served as forums for student communication and had been given broad First Amendment protections. It referred to the new Supreme Court ruling and found that "*Hazelwood* … is not applicable to college newspapers."[83] While other early state and lower court cases also navigated around the edges of the issue, the question was largely left unanswered.[84]

Public Forum Analysis and the College Press

Chapter 5 discusses the concept that different levels of legal protection apply to speech in different types of forums. A forum may be a physical space, like a public park, or a conceptual space, like the pages of a newsletter. Prior to *Hazelwood*, courts seldom explicitly used public forum analysis to determine what level of First Amendment protection college student publications deserved. The language of most court decisions suggests something akin to forum analysis, but it appears these courts felt it went without saying that when college students were named as editors of a student publication, they were being given the authority to determine its content.

In the words of one federal court of appeals:

It may well be that a college need not establish a campus newspaper, or, if a paper has been established, the college may permanently discontinue publication for reasons wholly unrelated to the First Amendment. But if a college has a student newspaper, its publication cannot be suppressed because college officials dislike its editorial comment.[85]

The first post-*Hazelwood* case to directly raise the issue of whether a school-sponsored college newspaper should be considered a public forum for student expression was *Lueth v. St. Clair County Community College*.[86] In that case, the official student newspaper at the Michigan college published an advertisement for a nightclub across the border in Canada. The ad noted that the Canadian drinking age was two years lower than Michigan's, and that the club had dancers who were "totally nude," which was prohibited by law for clubs in Michigan. The dean of the college informed the editor of the paper, *The Erie Square Gazette*, that she could not publish the advertisement again, and the editor took the school to court.

To date, no court has found a student edited college publication to be a non-public or closed forum.

In evaluating the school's censorship, the court questioned the *Gazette*'s forum status.[87] To determine whether the paper was a public forum, and thus entitled to greater First Amendment protection, the court referred to *Hazelwood* to evaluate whether school authorities had "by policy or practice" opened the forum for student free expression.[88] The court found that "comparing the operation of the *Hazelwood* newspaper with that of the *Gazette* reveals significant differences between the two."[89]

The court noted one difference was that the *Gazette*, according to a college policy, was a student-administered activity. It was not a "laboratory situation" because it was not operated within a specific academic course and was not within the school's "adopted curriculum." Second, the court found the *Gazette* was entirely controlled by students, particularly the editor in chief, not by a faculty member or administrator. And third, the *Gazette* was distributed throughout the community and sought outside advertisers to financially support it.[90]

Crucial to the court's determination that the paper was a public forum was that the school's rules and regulations gave the editor authority to decide the paper's content, staffing and publication dates. These obligations had been attributed to the faculty adviser in *Hazelwood*. Finally, the court stated that it could not ignore the "unequivocal" language in the *Gazette*'s official rules and regulations, placing the paper's control in the students' hands.[91]

Like the court in *Lueth*, to date no court has found a student-edited college publication to be a non-public or a closed forum. In fact, most courts have suggested that presuming a college publication to be a closed forum would be extremely illogical. As one court noted:

> The university setting of college-age students being exposed to a wide range of intellectual experience creates a relatively mature marketplace for the interchange of ideas so that the free speech clause of the First Amendment[,] with its underlying assumption that there is positive social value in an open forum[,] seems particularly appropriate.[92]

Yet, even though *Lueth* ultimately fell in line with other court cases in upholding strong protections for the college press and rejecting the college's attempt to impose the high school-based *Hazelwood* standard on its campus, the case raised some troubling questions. Namely, was it appropriate to use public forum analysis in the context of a college student media censorship case? If so, the case raised the even more troubling question of whether a court would ever truly buy into the idea that it was appropriate for America's college campuses to be regulated under a *Hazelwood*-based standard that allowed school officials to censor student speech simply by declaring it, for example, "poorly written" or "inconsistent with the shared values of a civilized social order"? Those questions would not be directly addressed for another decade.

Kincaid v. Gibson: "*Hazelwood* has little application to this case."

Recognizing the problem, the first federal appeals court to hear a post-*Hazelwood* college student media censorship case said that forum analysis may not be the appropriate standard for college newspapers.

On November 28, 1994, administrators at Kentucky State University, following ongoing battles with the student newspaper and their removal the same day of the student media adviser, confiscated approximately 2,000 copies of the 1993-94 edition of the KSU student yearbook, *The Thorobred*. Prior to distribution, Betty Gibson, vice president for student affairs, reviewed the yearbook and in consultation with KSU President Mary Smith ordered that they be locked away in a closet, citing the yearbook's overall lack of quality. Specifically, Gibson objected to: (1) the color of the yearbook's cover (purple), which did not match the school's official colors (green and gold), (2) the yearbook's title "Destination Unknown," which she deemed "inappropriate," (3) a lack of captions under photographs and (4) the inclusion of what she felt were too many photographs depicting current events and celebrities. A year later, with the yearbook still locked away, Capri Coffer, editor of the 1993-94 edition of *The Thorobred* yearbook and a staff writer for the student newspaper, *The Thorobred News*, and Charles Kincaid, a student at KSU, filed a First Amendment lawsuit against Gibson, Smith and the individual members of the KSU Board of Regents.

The students' case had an exceptionally rocky beginning. Both the district court and later the initial appellate panel that heard the case, in a 2-1 ruling, sided with the university. Both courts cited *Hazelwood*; both found the yearbook to be a nonpublic forum and both concluded that university officials had acted "reasonably" in confiscating the yearbooks.[93]

Finally, in January 2001, after more than five years of litigation, the full Sixth Circuit U.S. Court of Appeals, in a 10-3 ruling, struck down the lower court rulings, finding that KSU had "no constitutionally valid reason" to confiscate the yearbook.[94]

Images from the censored Kentucky State University yearbook and the full text of the decision in *Kincaid v. Gibson* are available at: **www. splc.org/kincaid**

In rejecting the university's attempt to impose a *Hazelwood*-based "reasonableness" standard on *The Thorobred*, the court noted, among other things, that university students are generally young adults (Charles Kincaid, for example, was in his mid-30's while the case was going on) and found that "[t]he university environment is the quintessential 'marketplace of ideas,' which merits full, or indeed heightened, First Amendment protection."[95]

"*Hazelwood*," the court commented, "has little application to this case."[96]

While the court agreed that application of public forum analysis was appropriate in determining the forum status of *The Thorobred* yearbook at KSU,[97] it also understood the danger forum analysis posed and found that it may not be appropriate in all cases, particularly censorship cases involving public university student newspapers.[98]

Hosty v. Carter: "*Hazelwood* provides our starting point."

Despite the significant legal victory in *Kincaid* — and the hope of many in the student press community that the Sixth Circuit's strong support for college free speech would put the issue to rest — later that year, Illinois' Attorney General decided to take another shot, with another court, at bringing *Hazelwood* to America's college and university campuses.

In 2001, student journalists Margaret Hosty, Jeni Porche and Steven Barba sued Governors State University in Illinois after Patricia Carter, the university's dean of student affairs, ordered the newspaper's printer in October 2000 to hold future issues until a school official had approved the student newspaper's content. The paper, the *Innovator*, had published several news stories and editorials critical of the administration, and Carter's directive was issued despite a university policy that said the student newspaper staff "will determine content and format of their respective publications without censorship or advance approval."[99]

After the trial court refused to dismiss the students' case, Illinois Attorney General Jim Ryan, representing Carter, argued that the *Innovator* was a nonpublic forum and that *Hazelwood* was the appropriate legal standard. A unanimous three-judge panel of the U.S. Seventh Circuit Court Appeals, which initially heard the case, flatly rejected that argument.[100] The court found that *Hazelwood*'s rationale for limiting high school student press freedom was "not a good fit" for college students, whom it said should continue to receive "broad First Amendment rights" until the Supreme Court ruled otherwise.[101]

"The differences between a college and a high school are far greater than the obvious difference in curriculum and extracurricular activities," Circuit Judge Terence T. Evans wrote for the court. "The missions of each are distinct reflecting the unique needs of students of differing ages and maturity levels."[102]

"Treating these students like 15-year-old high school students and restricting their First Amendment rights by an unwise extension of *Hazelwood* would be an extreme step for us to take absent more direction from the Supreme Court," the court concluded.[103]

Two years later, however, a sharply divided en banc Seventh Circuit vacated the lower court rulings, officially opening the college door to *Hazelwood*-based censorship in that court's jurisdiction.

"*Hazelwood*," the court majority wrote, "provides our starting point."[104]

The sole issue before the en banc court was whether Carter's actions could be excused under the doctrine of qualified immunity, which allows government officials to escape liability if they can show that the law on a particular issue — in this case, ordering a printer to hold production of a college student newspaper until it was reviewed by university officials — was "unsettled." Nevertheless, while the court did not specifically reach the question of whether Carter's actions violated the First Amendment, the effect was the same. Even though the court said it would presume that the *Innovator* was a "designated public forum," the majority said that *Hazelwood*'s forum analysis determined the degree of First Amendment protection afforded student editors at public colleges and universities.

Finding "no sharp difference between high school and college papers"[105] the court pushed both the analysis and — where college student media were determined to be non-public forums — the censorship standard of *Hazelwood*, onto public and college university campuses.

For students attending a public college or university in Illinois, Indiana and Wisconsin, the states that fall within the Seventh Circuit U.S. Court of Appeals jurisdiction, *Hosty* is now the law. However, in 2007, Illinois passed a law in response to the ruling that effectively negates the impact of the decision on college student media in that state.[106]

Hosty is the first federal appeals court to conclude that forum analysis is necessary for determining the level of First Amendment protection afforded a public college student newspaper. As a practical matter, however, most college student newspapers still will be considered designated public forums and entitled to the strongest First Amendment protection because that is the way they have been operating for decades. Indeed, as mentioned earlier, no court (including the Seventh Circuit in *Hosty*) has found a student-edited, college newspaper to be a non-public or closed forum. Consequently, the decision's short-term impact may be limited. The danger of *Hosty*, however, is that

Images from the censored Governors State University newspaper, the *Innovator*, and the full text of the decision in *Hosty v. Carter* are available at: **www.splc.org/gsu**

it opens a door that legal scholars and other courts believed to be closed. Moreover, it is a door over which school officials — by slyly enacting new policies and enforcing new practices that alter a student publication's forum status — may have significant control.

The SPLC believes that traditional public forum analysis simply does not fit in the context of student-edited publications at public colleges and universities, a view shared by many commentators who have roundly criticized the *Hosty* ruling.[107] Many public college or university student newspapers were founded by students and are completely or largely financially independent of their school; almost all exist apart from the school's curriculum and are editorially independent. Still, there is little doubt that the post-*Hosty* world will present significant challenges to America's college student media, and not just for those within the Seventh Circuit. Indeed, within weeks of the decision being handed down, misguided school officials outside the Midwest had already pointed to *Hosty* to justify exercising additional control over their student media.[108] The fact remains, however, that *Hosty* is an anomaly. As the dissent in *Hosty* stated, "[n]o court, before or after *Hazelwood*, has held that a university may censor a student newspaper, and the only authorities to suggest otherwise are not directly on point."[109]

Consequently student journalists outside the Seventh Circuit retain the same strong protection from censorship that courts have recognized for decades,[110] and the SPLC is committed to helping students pursue college censorship cases more vigorously now than ever before. Student journalists must not back down or change their commitment to good journalism for fear of administrative censorship.[111]

State Laws Provide Protection

As noted earlier in this chapter, the impact of the *Hosty v. Carter* decision was limited in Illinois as a result of a law enacted by the state legislature specifically in response to the court ruling. As a matter of educational policy, the legislature determined that college student publications in the state should operate as public forums.[112] A student editor and newspaper adviser at Chicago State University successfully used the Illinois act when their college removed them from their positions over articles that the college media-relations director deemed overly negative.[113] But Illinois was not the only, or even the first, state to take up the issue of protecting college press freedom. As of 2013, two other states, California[114] and Oregon,[115] had enacted similar legislative protections in response to *Hosty*.

Prior Review of the College Press

When confronted with efforts by school officials to demand the right to review college student publications before distribution,[116] the courts have consistently rejected such efforts. The leading decision on the subject is *Antonelli v. Hammond*,[117] which involved the official, school-funded student newspaper at Fitchburg State College in Massachusetts. After the editor published an article by a member of the radical Black Panther organization that contained a number of four-letter words, the college president froze funding for the paper and set up a publications board to review each issue before it went to press. The federal district court said even if the system of prior review was only for identifying and suppressing legally obscene material (a context in which the courts have allowed some limited prior restraints), it was still a violation of the First Amendment because it gave no procedural safeguards to protect the student editor from arbitrary decisions.[118] Indeed, the court said it was "extremely doubtful" that any system of adequate procedural safeguards in a system of prior review of obscenity could be developed that would adequately protect student press freedom.[119]

A New York court agreed that the First Amendment would not tolerate prior review. "[A] policy of prior approval of items to be published in a student newspaper, even if directed only to restraining the publication of potentially libelous material" would run afoul of

Supreme Court decisions prohibiting prior restraint on expression, the court said.[120] Thus if prior review is not permissible in the context of obscenity or libel, neither of which has First Amendment protection, there seems little chance that prior review for other reasons would ever be permitted.

In another case, *Trujillo v. Love*,[121] the new faculty adviser to the Southern Colorado State College *Arrow* imposed a rule requiring the staff to obtain his approval prior to publishing any "controversial" material. He deleted an editorial cartoon critical of the college president, an editorial on campus problems and a column regarding the state attorney general's campaign then underway. The adviser eventually suspended the managing editor who had written the editorial and the column. The court found that the adviser's actions violated the First Amendment and ordered the student reinstated to her former position with back pay.

To date only one court decision, *Hosty v. Carter*, discussed above, has explicitly stated that prior review of a public college student publication might be lawful. In that case, a sharply divided court held that it was unclear — as of November 2000, when an official at Governors State University told the student newspaper's printer it would not pay his bill unless school officials first approved the newspaper — whether the First Amendment prohibited administrative prior review.[122]

CENSORSHIP BY THEFT

Beginning in the early 1990s, a growing number of college publications began to confront a crude but remarkably effective method of censorship: theft.[123] Dissenters have confiscated thousands of copies of "free" newspapers from distribution points and sometimes even destroyed or burned the publications in protest over their content. Thus the regular readers of the paper are denied a copy unless the publication takes the time and expense to reprint extra copies. Many members of the college press have been left wondering: can the people who take these newspapers get away with it?

Probably not. Criminal prosecution, civil lawsuits and campus judicial proceedings can all be tools in the arsenal for fighting newspaper theft.

The biggest limitation on pursuing criminal charges is that the ultimate decision to do so is out of a publication staff's hands. It is up to a prosecutor to decide if there is enough evidence that a crime has been committed to justify the filing of charges. The most frequent explanation given by police and prosecutors for not pursuing newspaper thieves is their belief that "you can't steal free newspapers." But there is a growing record of successful prosecutions for such stealing.

One of the first successful prosecutions occurred in February 1988 when four students at the University of Florida were charged with theft after they confiscated large quantities of a conservative campus newspaper, the *Florida Review*, which reported on dissension within the campus College Republicans. The students eventually pleaded "no contest" to the charges and were sentenced to six months probation and 25 hours of community service and were required to pay court costs.[124]

During the 1993-94 school year, two journalism students at Penn State University were charged with theft, receiving stolen property, and criminal conspiracy in the taking of a conservative campus newspaper that some called sexist. In exchange for the charges being dropped, the women agreed to enter into a "First Amendment rehabilitation program," which reportedly included a restitution payment of $3,000 to the newspaper.[125]

More recently, students in Texas and Kentucky were criminally charged and found guilty for their roles in newspaper thefts at their schools.[126] And in 2003, Berkeley Mayor Tom Bates pled guilty and was fined for his role in trashing 1,000 copies of the November 4, 2002, edition of University of California at Berkeley's student newspaper, which carried

Newspaper theft is a crime that has been successfully prosecuted. This is true even where the publications are distributed free of charge.

an editorial endorsement of his mayoral opponent.[127]

In addition to criminal prosecution, a growing number of schools — both public and private — have also started punishing student thieves for violating campus conduct codes.[128] Even a school that does not have an explicit policy prohibiting newspaper theft should have rules that can be used to punish thieves. Most colleges have policies that allow students to be punished through a campus judicial proceeding for committing a crime on campus. Newspaper theft should certainly fall within that prohibition. Some schools have also adopted free expression policies that make interfering with the expression rights of others a punishable offense.

Much more information on newspaper theft is available in the SPLC Newspaper Theft Forum at: www.splc.org/theft

To help prevent theft, some newspapers have added the phrase "take one" to their distribution boxes and published in their mastheads a phrase that indicates single copies are free, but additional copies have a price.

In direct response to "free" newspaper thefts, lawmakers in at least three states — California,[129] Colorado[130] and Maryland[131] — have enacted laws that specifically outlaw newspaper theft. For example, Maryland's law, the first in the country, makes the theft of free newspapers punishable by a fine of not more than $500 or imprisonment for not more than 60 days or both.[132] While existing theft laws in other states should apply to prohibit the stealing of free publications, newspaper theft laws provide law enforcement officials and prosecutors with extra legal ammunition to target newspaper thieves.

Student newspapers that have fallen victim to theft could also file a civil lawsuit for damages against those who have taken their publications. Although there is no record of such a case having been considered by a court, a newspaper that could show the loss of advertising dollars or the expense of reprinting a publication would seem to have a legitimate claim for damages.

Of course, if newspaper thieves are school officials or student government leaders at public schools or are part of an official law enforcement agency, the First Amendment would bar this form of censorship like it does other forms of state-sponsored censorship.[133]

SUMMARY

For more than four decades American courts have consistently ruled that public college officials, including student government officers or others acting on their behalf, may not exercise the power of a private publisher over student publications simply because they provide some financial support. They cannot tell students what to publish or demand prior approval of content; they cannot withdraw funding or discipline staff members for content-related reasons. While school authorities can regulate certain aspects of student media programs — for example, requiring that staff hiring policies do not discriminate on the basis of race[134] or ensuring that student media funds are being spent properly — such regulation cannot be based on the content of the publication or broadcast. While distinguishing permissible oversight from unconstitutional content-motivated control can sometimes be difficult, the message is clear: students who work on school-funded or school-sponsored publications enjoy the strong protection of the First Amendment.

While recent court decisions have raised concerns about whether the law protecting America's public college student media may be in flux, the Supreme Court has so far given no indication that it intends to back away from its long tradition of protecting free speech on college and university campuses. Unless that occurs, virtually all college administrators who interfere with the editorial freedom of student media do so at their peril.

You are the editor of *The Student Times*, the student-run newspaper at Central State University. The *Times* has a well-earned reputation as one of the top college student publications in the country. But its reputation for tough reporting and its willingness to take on thorny issues has created some enemies along the way.

For example, last month the *Times* published a story about the university president's purchase of a pair of adorable pug puppies for his family, which he named Bonnie and Clyde. Your reporters subsequently discovered that the purchase was made using university funds under a $4,000 budget line item marked "Miscellaneous Marketing Tools." The president defended his purchase, claiming that the cute, pint-sized snorting canines will assist him in wooing fundraisers (CSU's mascot, of course, is the "Tenacious Pugs"). Not surprisingly, he has taken a lot of public heat and it's clear he blames you. You've received two rather caustic e-mails from him about the paper's "yellow journalism" and a 1 a.m. rambling voicemail message telling you that you have no idea how the "real world" works and that "what comes around goes around." (You always thought the saying was "what goes around comes around," but no matter.)

You've also ticked off the student government president after an editorial last week criticizing her for proposing a ban on Italian dressing in campus food outlets after the Italian government refused to support America's latest foreign incursion. She came storming into the newsroom a couple days ago screaming at you and your managing editor for "making her look like a fool" and warning that you "don't want to make an enemy of me!"

Finally, members of the Alpha Bravo Charlie fraternity recently warned that there is "going to be trouble" if *Times* reporters keep nosing into rumors about a cow-tipping incident last month. The story, which came out in today's issue, provides details about last month's beer-induced, midnight outing to a nearby farm. Photos of the upended bovines and grinning fratboys showed up on an online social networking site, and you included some of the photos in your story.

The *Times* has a long history of editorial independence, but in the past 24 hours it has hit some pretty significant bumps on the free press road.

Specifically:

(1) Yesterday morning, the head of the campus maintenance department notified you that *Times* newsracks must be removed from inside all campus buildings. He said the memo from CSU's president ordering their removal states that the newsracks impede foot traffic and pose a safety risk. Given that more than half of your issues are picked up from those newsracks, which have been in place for as long as anyone can remember, you and your staff are extremely concerned about the impact this will have on circulation.

(2) Last night, at the monthly student government association meeting, it was announced that "because of declining enrollment," the SGA was slashing all student group budgets by 20 percent for the next school year. For the *Times*, which has traditionally had the largest budget allocation of any student group, that means a probable budget cut of about $20,000. (The glee club, which is the next biggest recipient of student fees, will only see their budget cut by about $10,000.) The *Times* is already feeling the pinch of a shrinking advertiser pool. A 20 percent budget cut is going to create some big problems for the newspaper and seriously test its ability to provide solid news coverage in the coming school year.

(3) This morning, one of your staff photographers came running into the newsroom to tell you that he just took a photo of a group of Alpha Bravo Charlie fraternity members going from rack to rack dumping issues of the *Times* into a wheelbarrow. When your photographer asked what they were doing, he said one of them responded, "Hey, they're free, aren't they? We're just helping the environment and making sure they get recycled."

You have called an emergency meeting with your editorial board this afternoon to determine how best to respond to the various problems. You will need to brief them on the newspaper's legal footing. What can you tell them?

ANSWER :
President's New Distribution Policy
You tell the editorial board that the president appears to be following through on his warning to even the score for your pugnacious reporting. While the president has authority to reasonably regulate campus buildings and the obligation to ensure that those inside the buildings are safe, it seems pretty clear here that he is taking unfair — and illegal — advantage of his power.

As a government official, he is clearly limited by the First Amendment, but the key to winning any legal case, you tell the board, will be showing that the president's new distribution policy has been motivated by the *Times*' reporting and not by legitimate safety concerns. Fortunately, it appears that you have considerable legal ammunition on your side.

First, the new distribution policy is coming after years of allowing the newspaper to distribute from within campus buildings. While there have been occasional complaints of old issues getting scattered and creating litter, there have been no recent official complaints or warnings that the newsracks have harmed anyone or created a safety risk. Moreover, while it may be that one or two newsracks are too close to fire exits, those issues can and should be addressed rack-by-rack. Banning all newsracks from all campus buildings would seem to be an unreasonable overreaction that poses a serious threat to campus free speech. You tell them that you also have your reporters looking into whether the ban is only on *Times* newsracks or on all of the various on and off-campus publications that are distributed in campus buildings. Targeting only *Times* newsracks would also be pretty clear evidence that something other than safety has motivated the president's new policy. In addition to questioning the reasonableness of the new distribution policy, you also let the board know about that you have carefully documented the president's reaction to the pug story. You have saved his emails and the voicemail he left, all of which show he is not a fan of the *Times* and its recent news coverage. Both are good evidence of a motive to retaliate against the newspaper for its content and would go a long way toward helping the *Times* win any First Amendment case against him should it come to that.

Budget Cuts
Unfortunately, there may not be a legal option here. Yes, the SGA president has made it clear that she's shaken by how you've dressed her down for what she believes is her patriotic stand against the oregano-laden vinaigrette. And yes, because the student government has been delegated the responsibility for allocating mandatory student fees collected by the university — a task that the university itself would otherwise be required to do — it's a pretty good bet that the SGA president would be subject to the limits imposed by the First Amendment, just like the university president himself. Further, her newsroom rant, witnessed by many on the *Times* staff, was carefully documented and certainly could be evidence of a content-based motive for attacking the paper. But all of that probably isn't enough. While it might make the SGA president happy to see the *Times* squirm, the cut was evenly leveled at all student groups. While the *Times* is taking a bigger hit as far as the dollar amount of money, its cut is proportional to those suffered by others. No one can dispute that the enrollment drop is having a ripple effect on the university system and that money is in short supply; the paper has covered stories about the enrollment situation for months. Like it or not, it appears that the SGA is simply doing what is fiscally required. The *Times* has no constitutional right to money that simply isn't there.

Newspaper Theft
Because the fraternity brothers are not government officials, you tell the board, you can't bring a First Amendment claim against them for dumping the *Times*. However, stealing or destroying campus newspapers — even those distributed for free — has been successfully prosecuted as a crime in many cases across the country. As the hefty monthly bill from your printer makes clear, just because the newspapers are distributed on an honor system, they aren't "free." Advertisers pay to have their ads seen by readers – something they wouldn't do if copies were regularly carted off in wheelbarrows. Students pay an activity fee with the expectation that a campus newspaper will be available to them

(essentially no different than any other pre-paid subscription service). Fortunately, your photographer caught the culprits red-handed and has incontrovertible evidence on his camera. Your first step should be to contact the local and/or campus law enforcement agency and file a police report. You've already printed out copies of legal documents showing other successful theft prosecutions from the Student Press Law Center's website to show to police if they balk about the newspaper being free. You tell the board that it may also be possible to file a civil lawsuit against the fraternity members to recoup all reasonable costs of reprinting the paper or refunding advertisers. You also suggest filing a complaint with the campus judicial system and calling on the university president to publicly denounce the theft. To help avoid any confusion in the future, you suggest to the board that now is the time to place notices on *Times* newsracks inviting students to "Take One Copy" and language in the newspaper's masthead indicating that "single copies of *The Student Times* are free, additional copies cost 25 cents each." Finally, such a blatant act of censorship — and the official response, or lack thereof to the theft — is news, and you've already assigned a reporter to work with the photographer in covering the issue for tomorrow's edition.

ENDNOTES

1   *Rosenberger v. Rector and Visitors of the Univ. of Virginia*, 515 U.S. 819 (1995).
2   *See, e.g., Healy v. James*, 408 U.S. 169 (1972); *Papish v. Bd. of Curators of the Univ. of Missouri*, 410 U.S. 667 (1973) (per curiam), *reh'g denied*, 411 U.S. 960 (1973); *Bd. of Regents of Univ. of Wisconsin Sys. v. Southworth*, 529 U.S. 217 (2000).
3   *Hosty v. Governors State Univ.*, 412 F.3d 731 (7th Cir. 2005) (en banc), *cert. denied*, 546 U.S. 1169 (2006).
4   *See, e.g., Antonelli v. Hammond*, 308 F. Supp. 1329 (D. Mass. 1970); *Trujillo v. Love*, 322 F. Supp. 1266 (D. Colo. 1971).
5   *Healy*, 408 U.S. at 169.
6   *Id.* at 180 (citing *Keyishian v. Bd. of Regents of the Univ. of New York*, 385 U.S. 589, 603 (1967) (emphasizing that the "Nation's future depends upon leaders trained through wide exposure to that robust exchange of ideas")).
7   *Id.*
8   *Papish v. Bd. of Curators of the Univ. of Missouri*, 410 U.S. 667 (1973) (per curiam), *reh'g denied*, 411 U.S. 960 (1973).
9   *Papish*, 410 U.S. at 671.
10 *Id.* at 670.
11 *Healy*, 408 U.S. at 189; *Papish*, 410 U.S. at 670 n. 6 ("Thus, in the absence of any disruption of campus order or interference with the rights of others, the sole issue was whether a state university could proscribe this form of expression").
12 *See, e.g., Bd. of Trustees of State Univ. of New York v. Fox*, 492 U.S. 469 (1989) (discussing First Amendment rights of college students to receive commercial speech on campus); *Widmar v. Vincent*, 454 U.S. 263 (1981) (concerning First Amendment right of religious student groups to use university facilities); *Zurcher v. Stanford Daily*, 436 U.S. 547 (1978) (addressing First and Fourth Amendment rights of student newspaper at private university following police search of newsroom).
13 *Rosenberger v. Rector and Visitors of the Univ. of Virginia*, 515 U.S. 819 (1995).
14 *Id.* at 826.
15 *Id.* at 836.
16 *Id.* at 835 (referencing *Healy v. James*, 408 U.S. 169, 180-181 (1972); *Keyishian v. Bd. of Regents of Univ. of State of N.Y.*, 385 U.S. 589, 603 (1967); *Sweezy v. New Hampshire*, 354 U.S. 234, 250 (1957)).
17 *Bd. of Regents of Univ. of Wisconsin Sys. v. Southworth*, 529 U.S. 217 (2000).
18 "Supreme Court upholds student fees," Student Press Law Center *Report*, Spring 2000, at 4 (citing to statistics provided by the National Association for Campus Activities).
19 *Southworth*, 529 U.S. at 229.
20 *Id.* at 221.
21 *Hays County Guardian v. Supple*, 969 F.2d 111 (5th Cir. 1992); *Kania v. Fordham*, 702 F.2d 475 (4th Cir. 1983); *Arrington v. Taylor*, 380 F. Supp. 1348 (M.D.N.C. 1974), *aff'd mem.*, 526 F.2d 587 (4th Cir. 1975), *cert. denied*, 424 U.S. 913 (1976); *Veed v. Schwartzkopf*, 353 F. Supp. 149 (D. Neb. 1973), *aff'd mem.*, 478 F.2d 1407 (8th Cir. 1973), *cert. denied*, 414 U.S. 1135 (1974); *Lace v. Univ. of Vermont*, 303 A.2d 475 (Vt. 1973).
22 *See, e.g., Kincaid v. Gibson*, 236 F.3d 342 (6th Cir. 2001); *Mississippi Gay Alliance v. Goudelock*, 536 F.2d 1073 (5th Cir. 1973), *cert. denied*, 430 U.S. 982 (1977); *Lueth v. St. Clair County Community College*, 732 F. Supp. 1410 (E.D. Mich. 1990); *Stanley v. Magrath*, 719 F.2d 279 (8th Cir. 1983); *Sinn v. Daily Nebraskan*, 638 F. Supp. 143, 148 (D. Neb. 1986), *aff'd*, 829 F.2d 662 (8th Cir. 1987); *Mazart v. State*, 441 N.Y.S.2d 600, 605 (N.Y. Ct. Cl. 1981); *Milliner v. Turner*, 436 So. 2d 1300 (La. Ct. App. 1983), *cert. denied*, 442 So.2d 453 (La. 1983); *Schiff v. Williams*, 519 F.2d 257 (5th Cir. 1975); *Joyner v. Whiting*, 477 F.2d 456, 460 (4th Cir. 1973); *Bazaar v. Fortune*, 476 F.2d 570 (5th Cir. 1973), *aff'd en banc with modification*, 489 F.2d 225 (5th Cir. 1973) (per curiam), *cert. denied*, 416 U.S. 995 (1974); *Panarella v. Birenbaum*, 32 N.Y.2d 108, 296 N.E.2d 238 (N.Y. 1973); *State*

Bd. for Community Colleges v. Olson, 687 P.2d 429 (Colo. 1984), *appeal after remand*, 759 P.2d 829 (Colo. Ct. App. 1988).

23 *Dickey v. Alabama State Bd. of Educ.*, 273 F. Supp. 613, 618 (M.D. Ala. 1967) (quoting *Burside v. Byars*, 363 F.2d 744 (5th Cir. 1966)), *vacated sub. nom., Troy State Univ. v. Dickey*, 402 F.2d 515 (5th Cir. 1968).

24 *Bazaar v. Fortune*, 476 F.2d 570 (5th Cir. 1973), *aff'd en banc with modification*, 489 F.2d 225 (5th Cir. 1973) (per curiam), *cert. denied*, 416 U.S. 995 (1974).

25 *Id.* at 574. See also *Antonelli v. Hammond*, 308 F. Supp. 1329, 1337 (D. Mass. 1970) ("The state is not necessarily the unrestrained master of what it creates and fosters.").

26 *Thonen v. Jenkins*, 491 F.2d 722 (4th Cir. 1973).

27 *Korn v. Elkins*, 317 F. Supp. 138 (D. Md. 1970).

28 *Dickey*, 273 F. Supp. at 618, *dismissed as moot*, 402 F.2d 515 (5th Cir. 1968).

29 E.g., *Rathbone v. Day*, No. 86-2420-S (Aug. 12, 1987); *Husain v. Springer*, 494 F.3d 108, 134-35 (2d Cir. 2007), *cert. denied*, 128 S.Ct. 1658 (2008).

30 *Panarella v. Birenbaum*, 32 N.Y.2d 108, 112, 296 N.E.2d 238, 239 (N.Y. 1973).

31 *See, e.g.*, Korn v. Elkins, 317 F. Supp. at 142 (citing "necessary to preserve order and discipline" language of Dickey); *Mazart v. State*, 441 N.Y.S.2d 600, 605 (N.Y. Ct. Cl. 1981); *Schiff v. Williams*, 519 F.2d 257, 260-61 (5th Cir. 1975) (citing to *Bazaar*, which used disruption language of *Tinker*); Panarella, 32 N.Y.2d at 118, 296 N.E.2d at 242; *Veed v. Schwartzkopf*, 353 F. Supp. 149, 152 (D. Neb. 1973), *aff'd without op.*, 478 F.2d 1407 (8th Cir. 1973), *cert. denied*, 414 U.S. 1135 (1974); *Antonelli v. Hammond*, 308 F. Supp. 1329, 1336 (D. Mass. 1970); *Joyner v. Whiting*, 477 F.2d 456, 461 (4th Cir. 1973).

32 *Rosenberger v. Rector and Visitors of the Univ. of Virginia*, 515 U.S. 819 (1995).

33 477 F.2d 456 (4th Cir. 1973).

34 *Id.* at 459.

35 *Id.* at 460.

36 *Id.* at 460 (footnotes omitted).

37 *Id.* ("[T]he college may permanently discontinue publication for reasons wholly unrelated to the First Amendment.").

38 *Stanley v. Magrath*, 719 F.2d 279 (8th Cir. 1983).

39 *Id.* at 280.

40 *Id.* at 282.

41 *See, e.g., id.* at 283.

42 *See, e.g., Joyner*, 477 F.2d at 456.

43 Examples of student government attempts to censor student media are now commonplace. *See, e.g.*, "Power of the purse," Student Press Law Center *Report*, Fall 2007, at 13; "Taking the Plunge," Student Press Law Center *Report*, Winter 2006-07, at 16; "Florida student paper struggles for autonomy from student government," Student Press Law Center *Report*, Spring 2005, at 22; "Student government vs. student newspaper," Student Press Law Center *Report*, Spring 2003, at 8.

44 *State Bd. for Community Colleges v. Olson*, 687 P.2d 429 (Colo. 1984), *appeal after remand*, 759 P.2d 829 (Colo. Ct. App. 1988).

45 *Id.* at 433 n.4.

46 *Olson v. State Bd. for Community Colleges*, 759 P.2d 829, 831 (Cal. Ct. App. 1988).

47 *Gay and Lesbian Students Ass'n v. Gohn*, 850 F.2d 361 (8th Cir. 1988).

48 During its funding debate, one student senator argued, "We cannot use state money to support a homosexual group. What if a group of students/arsonists wanted to start an arsonists club and start fires. Would you fund them? ... It's the same thing as funding homosexuals." *Id.* at 363.

49 *Id.* at 362, 365-66 (finding "state action was present in the [student senate's] funding decision" where university officials retained right to review and change the student government budget).

50 *Sinn v. Daily Nebraskan*, 638 F. Supp. 143, 148 (D. Neb. 1986), *aff'd*, 829 F.2d 662 (8th Cir. 1987).

51 *Husain v. Springer*, 494 F.3d 108, 134-35 (2d Cir. 2007), *cert. denied*, 128 S.Ct. 1658 (2008).

52 *Id.* at 117.

53 *Id.* at 135.

54 *Id.* In addition to the cases previously mentioned, other courts have found that student government officials at public colleges and universities do perform state functions, particularly when allocating mandatory student activity fees collected by the school. *See, e.g., Amidon v. Student Ass'n of the State Univ. of New York*, 399 F. Supp. 2d 136, 145 (N.D.N.Y. 2005) (finding that student government association "clearly acts in concert with the state to create a forum for the exercise of First Amendment rights"); *Alabama Student Party v. Student Gov't Ass'n of the Univ. of Alabama*, 867 F.2d 1344, 1345 (11th Cir. 1989) (noting that the district court determined that the student government association "was a state actor subject to the same constitutional restrictions as the University itself"); *Arrington v. Taylor*, 380 F. Supp. 1348, 1359 (M.D.N.C. 1974) (stating that the student government, which derives its authority from a state university, "is organized as and performs the functions of a governmental body"). *See also Smith v. City Univ. of New York*, 708 N.E.2d 983, 984 (N.Y. 1999) (finding that community college association charged with allocating student activity fees was a "public body" subject to state open records law because it performed a governmental function).

55 *Thonen v. Jenkins*, 491 F.2d 722 (4th Cir. 1973) (per curiam).

56 *Trujillo v. Love*, 322 F. Supp. 1266 (D. Colo. 1971).

57 *Dickey v. Alabama State Bd. of Educ.*, 273 F. Supp. 613, 618 (M.D. Ala. 1967), *dismissed as moot*, 402 F.2d 515 (5th Cir. 1968).

58 *Schiff v. Williams*, 519 F.2d 257 (5th Cir. 1975).

59 *Id.* at 259.

60 *Id.* at 261.

61 Many examples of controversies and cases involving administrative retaliation against student media

advisers — including a number of cases settled before a court's ruling — are available on the SPLC website (www.splc.org). "Fired Adviser Settles Claim with Fort Valley State U. for $192,000," SPLC *News Flash*, April 25, 2002, *available at* http://www.splc.org/newsflash.asp?id=416; "Adviser Gets $130,000 in Settlement with College," SPLC *News Flash*, Aug. 10, 2006, *available at* http://www.splc.org/newsflash_archives.asp?id=1309&year=2006; "Former Newspaper Adviser Sues Ind. University over Transfer," SPLC *News Flash*, Feb. 17, 2005, *available at* http://www.splc.org/newsflash_archives.asp?id=954&year=2005; "CMA Censures Oklahoma Baptist University After Adviser Contract Not Renewed," SPLC *News Flash*, Oct. 5, 2006, *available at* http://www.splc.org/newsflash_archives.asp?id=1346&year=2006; "Mo. College Newspaper Adviser Settles Suit over Firing," SPLC *News Flash*, Aug. 7, 2002, *available at* http://www.splc.org/newsflash.asp?id=464&year=2002.

62   *See Kincaid v. Gibson*, 191 F.3d 719, 724 (6th Cir. 1999), *rev'd en banc*, 236 F.3d 342 (6th Cir. 2001).

63   *Cullen v. Gibson*, No. 96-6116,1997 WL 547932 (6th Cir. Sept. 4, 1997) (unpublished opinion), *cert. denied*, 522 U.S. 1117 (1998).

64   *Kincaid v. Gibson*, Civ. No. 95-98 (E.D. Ky. Nov. 14, 1997).

65   *Lane v. Simon*, No. 04-4079-JAR, 2005 WL 1366521, *5 (D. Kan. Jun. 2, 2005), vacated and remanded, 495 F.3d 1182 (10th Cir. 2007), and vacated as moot, No. 04-4079-JAR, 2007 WL 4365433 (D. Kan. Dec. 7, 2007).

66   *Id.* at *4.

67   *Lane v. Simon*, 495 F.3d 1182 (10th Cir. 2007). The adviser did not appeal his case to the circuit court.

68   *Coppola v. Larson*, No. Civ. 06-2138(SRC), 2006 WL 2129471, *2 (D. N.J. July 26, 2006) (unpublished opinion).

69   *Id.* at *10. In 2007, both the students and adviser settled their cases with the college. The settlement included Bosley's permanent reinstatement, the creation of a Student Media Advisory Board, and the college's agreement to pay Bosley $90,000. "Students, Adviser Reach Agreements with College," Student Press Law Center *Report*, Fall 2007, at 7.

70   *Husain v. Springer*, 336 F. Supp.2d 207, 215 (E.D.N.Y. 2004), *vacated in part*, 494 F.3d 108 (2d Cir. 2007).

71   Husain, 336 F. Supp. 2d at 215.

72   *Hazelwood Sch. Dist. v. Kuhlmeier*, 484 U.S. 260, 273 n.7 (1988).

73   *Thonen v. Jenkins*, 491 F.2d 722, 723 (4th Cir. 1973) (per curiam) (citing *Healy v. James*, 408 U.S. 169 (1972)).

74   *See, e.g.*, *Nicholson v. Bd. of Educ.*, 682 F.2d 858, 863 n. 4 (9th Cir. 1982); *Quarterman v. Byrd*, 453 F.2d 54, 58 (4th Cir. 1971); *Schwartz v. Schuker*, 298 F. Supp. 238, 241-42 (E.D.N.Y. 1969).

75   *Bystrom v. Fridley High Sch.*, 822 F.2d 747, 750 (8th Cir. 1987), *on remand*, 686 F. Supp. 1387 (D. Minn. 1987), *aff'd without op.*, 855 F.2d 855 (8th Cir. 1988) (unpublished table decision).

76   *Bd. of Regents of Univ. of Wisconsin Sys. v. Southworth*, 529 U.S. 217 (2000).

77   *Id.* at 238 n.4 (Souter, J., concurring) (referencing *Hazelwood Sch. Dist. v. Kuhlmeier*, 484 U.S. 260, 262 (1988); *Bethel Sch. Dist. No. 403 v. Fraser*, 478 U.S. 675, 677 (1986); *Tinker v. Des Moines Indep. Community Sch. Dist.*, 393 U.S. 503, 504 (1969)) (citations omitted).

78   *See* Edward L. Carter & Kevin R. Kemper, *Applying Hazelwood to College Speech: Forum Doctrine and Government Speech in the U.S. Courts of Appeals*, 48 S. Tex. L. Rev. 157 (2006). The authors identified the seven cases applying the reasoning of *Hazelwood* as: *Hosty v. Carter*, 412 F.3d 731, 734-35 (7th Cir. 2005) (en banc) (applying *Hazelwood* to university-sponsored student newspaper); *Axson-Flynn v. Johnson*, 356 F.3d 1277, 1285-86 n. 6 (10th Cir. 2004) (applying *Hazelwood* to student classroom speech but specifically declining to "reach any analysis of university students' extracurricular speech"); *Brown v. Li*, 308 F.3d 939, 949-50, 956-57 (9th Cir. 2002) (upholding sanctions brought against student for his academic thesis, though the dissenting opinion raises significant questions regarding whether the decision can be cited to support the extension of *Hazelwood* to govern curricular college student speech); *Vega v. Miller*, 273 F.3d 460, 479 (2d Cir. 2001) (applying *Hazelwood* to college professor's classroom speech); *Vanderhurst v. Colorado Mountain College Dist.*, 208 F.3d 908, 914 (10th Cir. 2000) (presuming for purposes of appeal, without deciding, whether *Hazelwood* applied to college professor's classroom speech); *Cummins v. Campbell*, 44 F.3d 847, 853 (10th Cir. 1994) (citing *Hazelwood* in case addressing university's delay in allowing student group to show religious film on campus); *Bishop v. Aronov*, 926 F.2d 1066, 1074 (11th Cir. 1991) (applying *Hazelwood* to university professor's classroom speech). *Id.* at 170 n.78. The survey authors listed another five cases where they found the court had mentioned the issue, but "did not reach a determination of whether *Hazelwood* should be applied to speech in the university or college context": *Hudson v. Craven*, 403 F.3d 691, 700-01 (9th Cir. 2005); *Pugel v. Bd. of Trustees of the Univ. of Illinois*, 378 F.3d 659, 667 n.7 (7th Cir. 2004); *Pitt News v. Pappert*, 379 F.3d 96, 105 n.5 (3d Cir. 2004); *Kincaid v. Gibson*, 236 F.3d 342, 347-54 (6th Cir. 2001) (en banc); *Fox v. Bd. of Trustees of State Univ. of New York*, 841 F.2d 1207, 1214 (2d Cir. 1988), *rev'd on other grounds*, 492 U.S. 469 (1989). *Id.* at 170, n.79. The final case identified in the survey, *Student Gov't Ass'n v. Bd. of Trustees of the Univ. of Massachusetts*, 868 F.2d 473, 480 n.6 (1st Cir. 1989), is discussed below. *See id.* at 169 n.75. One other case, not mentioned in the survey — and the only one that directly applied *Hazelwood* to extracurricular student speech outside the class setting — is *Alabama Student Party v. Student Government Ass'n*, 867 F.2d 1344, 1346-47 (11th Cir. 1989) (using *Hazelwood* to support public university's authority to place restrictions on student electioneering that would not have been permissible off campus).

79   See *Ward v. Polite*, 667 F.3d 727, 730-31 (6th Cir. 2012).

80   *Id.* at 733.

81   See Frank D. LoMonte, ""The Key Word is 'Student'": *Hazelwood* Censorship Crashes the Ivy-Covered Gates," 11 First Amend. L. Rev. 305 (2013) (discussing *Ward* case and growing tendency of courts to cite *Hazelwood* in determining free-speech rights of college students); Dan Kozlowski, "Unchecked Deference: *Hazelwood*'s Too Broad and Too Loose Application in the Circuit Courts," UB Journal of Media Law & Ethics, Vol. 3, No. 1/2 (Winter/Spring 2012) (critiquing courts' tendency to apply *Hazelwood* to

student speech in settings beyond strictly "curricular" speech).

82 *Student Gov't Ass'n v. Bd. of Trustees of the Univ. of Massachusetts*, 868 F.2d 473 (1st Cir. 1989).

83 *Id.* at 480 n.6.

84 *See also DiBona v. Matthews*, 269 Cal. Rptr. 882, 893 (Cal. Ct. App. 1990), *cert. denied*, 498 U.S. 998 (1990) ("We question whether the rationale underlying the 'school sponsorship' rule [of *Hazelwood*] would allow its wholesale extension to educational settings involving adults."); *Walko v. Kean College of New Jersey*, 561 A.2d 680, 687 n.5 (N.J. Super. Ct. Law Div. 1988) (declining to apply *Hazelwood* to a college student newspaper).

85 *Joyner v. Whiting*, 477 F.2d 456, 460 (4th Cir. 1973).

86 *Lueth v. St. Clair County Community College*, 732 F. Supp. 1410 (E.D. Mich. 1990).

87 *Id.* at 1414.

88 See *id.* and *Hazelwood Sch. Dist. v. Kuhlmeier*, 484 U.S. 260, 270 (1988). The *Lueth* court listed the following six criteria that it believed the Supreme Court used to determine that the paper at Hazelwood East High School was not a public forum: 1. A formal school board policy provided that the newspaper was developed within the school's adopted curriculum and the curriculum's educational implications. 2. The school's curriculum guide described the journalism course through which the newspaper was produced as a 'laboratory situation' allowing application of skills learned in a prerequisite journalism course. 3. The journalism course was taught by a faculty member during regular class hours, and students received graded credits for participation. 4. The teacher of the journalism class selected the newspaper's editors, set publication dates, assigned stories, advised in the development of stories, edited and negotiated with printers. 5. The school principal conducted final review of each issue of the newspaper prior to publication. 6. School officials did not deviate in practice from the policies surrounding the newspaper's publication. *Id.* at 1414 (citing *Hazelwood*, 484 U.S. at 267).

89 *Id.*

90 *Id.* at 1414-15.

91 *Id.* at 1415.

92 *Antonelli v. Hammond*, 308 F. Supp. 1329, 1336 (D.Mass. 1970).

93 *Kincaid v. Gibson*, Civ. No. 95-98 (E.D. Ky. Nov. 14, 1997), *aff'd*, 191 F.3d 719 (6th Cir. 1999), *reh'g granted and opinion vacated*, 197 F.3d 828 (6th Cir. 1999), *reh'g en banc and rev'd*, 236 F.3d 342 (6th Cir. 2001).

94 *Kincaid v. Gibson*, 236 F.3d 342, 354 (6th Cir. 2001).

95 *Id.* at 352.

96 *Id.* at 346 n.5.

97 *Id.* at 354 ("[O]ur review of KSU's policy and practice with regard to *The Thorobred*, the nature of the yearbook and its compatibility with expressive activity, and the university context in which the yearbook is created and distributed, all provide strong evidence of the university's intent to designate the yearbook as a limited public forum.").

98 *Id.* at 348 n.6. ("Our decision to apply the forum doctrine to the student yearbook at issue in this case has no bearing on the question of whether and the extent to which a public university may alter the content of a student newspaper. Likewise, we note that a college yearbook with features akin to a university student newspaper might be analyzed under a framework other than the forum framework.") (citations omitted). *See also Husain v. Springer*, 494 F.3d 108, 124 (2nd Cir. 2007) (declining to decide issue of whether forum analysis is appropriate for college student media, but finding that "at the very least, when a public university creates or subsidizes a student newspaper and imposes no ex ante restrictions on the content that the newspaper may contain, neither the school nor its officials may interfere with the viewpoints expressed in the publication without running afoul of the First Amendment."). But see *Coppola v. Larson*, No. Civ. 06- 2138(SRC), 2006 WL 2129471, *2 (D. N.J. Jul. 26, 2006) (unpublished opinion) (finding that "[s]tudent journalists at public colleges generally operate in a 'limited public forum'" (citing Kincaid, 236 F.3d at 346)).

99 *Hosty v. Carter*, 325 F.3d 945, 946 (7th Cir. 2003)

100 *Id.*

101 *Id.* at 948-49.

102 *Id.* at 948. The opinion cited U.S. Census Bureau Statistics finding that only 1 percent of those enrolled in American colleges or universities were under the age of 18, and 55 percent were 22 years of age or older. *Id.* at 948-49.

103 *Id.* at 949.

104 *Hosty v. Carter*, 412 F.3d 731, 734 (7th Cir. 2005).

105 *Id.* at 735.

106 College Campus Press Act, 110 Ill. Comp. Stat. 13/1-97 (2007). "All campus media produced primarily by students at a State-sponsored institution of higher learning is a public forum for expression by the student journalists and editors at the particular institution. Campus media, whether campus-sponsored or noncampus-sponsored, is not subject to prior review by public officials of a State-sponsored institution of higher learning." 110 Ill. Comp. Stat. 13/10.

107 National Association of College and University Attorneys & Laura Merritt, *How the Hosty Court Muddled First Amendment Protections by Misapplying Hazelwood to University Student Speech*, 33 J.C. & U.L. 473 (2007); Chris Sanders, *Censorship 101: Anti-*Hazelwood *Laws and the Preservation of Free Speech at Colleges and Universities*, 58 Ala. L. Rev. 159 (2006); Virginia J. Nimick, *Schoolhouse Rocked:* Hosty v. Carter *and the Case Against* Hazelwood, 14 J.L. & Pol'y 941 (2006); Daniel A. Applegate, *Stop the Presses: The Impact of* Hosty v. Carter *and* Pitt News v. Pappert *on the Editorial Freedom of College Newspapers*, 56 Case W. Res. L. Rev. 247 (2005); Richard M. Goehler, Hosty *is a "Recipe for Confusion and Conflict*, 23 Comm. Law. 21 (Summer 2005).

108 *See, e.g.*, "Memo Linking California with Hosty Decision Worries Students," SPLC *News Flash*, Sept. 15, 2005, *available at* http://www.splc.org/newsflash_archives.asp?id=1064&year=2005; "Grambling State Student Paper Elects to Shut Down for Fear of Adviser Termination," SPLC *News Flash*, January 24,

2007, *available at* http://www.splc.org/newsflash.asp?id=1415.

109 *Hosty v. Carter*, 412 F.3d 731, 744 (7th Cir. 2005) (en banc) (Evans, J., dissenting).

110 In addition to the nearly four decades of pre-*Hosty* court decisions protecting college student press freedom, neither of the only two federal court cases involving censorship of college student media decided after *Hosty* at the time this book went to press have adopted the Seventh Circuit's opinion. *Husain v. Springer*, 494 F.3d 108, 124 (2d Cir. 2007) (noting the disparity between *Hosty* and pre-*Hosty* cases and finding that it "need not decide in this case which of the two approaches embraced by other circuits governs evaluations of the First Amendment protections afforded student media outlets at public colleges"); *Coppola v. Larson*, No. Civ. 06-2138(SRC), 2006 WL 2129471 (D.N.J. July 26, 2006) (unpublished opinion) (citing *Kincaid* and many of the pre-*Hosty* cases upholding student press freedom, but making no mention of *Hosty*).

111 Much more information about the *Hosty* case, including suggestions for countering its impact on college student media, is available at http://www.splc.org/gsu.

112 College Campus Press Act, 110 Ill. Comp. Stat. 13/1-97 (2007).

113 *Moore v. Watson*, 838 F.Supp.2d 735 (N.D. Ill. 2012). The defeat resulted in Chicago State paying more than $210,00 in attorney fees and court costs. *Moore v. Watson*, No. 09 C 0701, 2013 WL 1337153 (N.D. Ill. March 29, 2013).

114 CAL. EDUC. CODE Sec. 66301 (2008).

115 Oregon HB 3279, 74th Oregon Legislative Assembly – 2007 Regular Session, *available at* http://landru.leg.state.or.us/07reg/measures/hb3200.dir/hb3279.intro.html (codified at OR. REV. STAT. Secs. 336.477, 351.649).

116 It is important to distinguish between "prior review," which is discussed here, and "prior restraint," which has been addressed earlier in this chapter. Mandatory prior review refers only to the act of demanding to read or otherwise preview content before it is published and/or distributed. Where those reading the content then demand that changes be made or where they prohibit publication or distribution altogether, they are engaging in prior restraint. While both acts are considered forms of censorship, different legal standards may apply to each.

117 *Antonelli v. Hammond*, 308 F. Supp. 1329 (D. Mass. 1970).

118 *Id.* at 1335.

119 *Id.* at 1335-36 n.6

120 *Mazart v. State*, 441 N.Y.S.2d 600, 605 (N.Y. Ct. Cl. 1981). *See also Milliner v. Turner*, 436 So. 2d 1300 (La. Ct. App. 1983), *cert. denied*, 442 So.2d 453 (La. 1983).

121 *Trujillo v. Love*, 322 F. Supp. 1266 (D. Colo. 1971).

122 *Hosty*, 412 F.3d at 739. The court rejected the students' claim that the Supreme Court's decision in *Hazelwood* v. Kuhlmeier, which allowed for prior review of high school student newspapers, was limited to high schools. "[*Hazelwood*] does not even hint at the possibility of an on/off switch: high school papers reviewable, college papers not reviewable." *Id.* at 734.

123 During the 1992-93 school year 22 student newspaper thefts were reported to the Student Press Law Center. That number rose to 38 thefts during the 1993-94 school year. Those numbers were in sharp contrast to the approximately 2-3 thefts per year that previously had been reported to the Center. In 2012, 27 newspaper thefts were recorded. Newspaper thefts nationwide are tracked in the Student Press Law Center's Newspaper Theft Forum, www.splc.org/theft.

124 "Students 'Pay' for Paper Theft," *The Gainesville Sun*, March 26, 1988.

125 See Kissel, K., "Journalism Students Won't Stand Trial for Newspaper Thefts," Associated Press, Aug. 12, 1993; "No Trial in Newspaper Thefts/Probation for PSU Suspects in Campus 'Speech' Case," *Pittsburg Post-Gazette*, Aug. 12, 1993, at B6; Leo, J., "Censorship by Theft," *U.S. News and World Report*, Nov. 15, 1993, at 24.

126 News accounts and court documents are *available at* the Student Press Law Center: Successful Newspaper Theft Prosecutions, http://www.splc.org/nptheftdocuments.asp.

127 *Id. But see State v. Morice*, No. 67693-D (21st Jud. Dist. Ct. Tangipahoa Parish, La., Jan. 13, 1994) (unpublished) (court dismissed charges of criminal mischief against a student government leader at Southeastern Louisiana University accused of "instigating" the theft of a campus newspaper).

128 *See, e.g.*, "Students at Three Colleges Disciplined for Stealing Newspapers," SPLC *News Flash*, July 1, 2003, *available at* http://www.splc.org/newsflash_archives.asp?id=635&year=2003; "Colleges Discipline Thieves," Student Press Law Center *Report*, Fall 2002, at 10.

129 CAL. PENAL CODE Sec. 490.7 (West 2008).

130 COLO. REV. STAT. Ann. Sec. 18-4-419 (West 2008).

131 MD. CODE Ann., Crim. Law Sec. 7-106 (West 2008).

132 *Id.* at Sec. 7-106(c).

133 *See, e.g., Coming Up, Inc. v. City and County of San Francisco County*, 857 F. Supp 711 (N.D. Calif. 1994). Following a September 1994 jury trial finding they violated the First Amendment, a federal district court judge ordered San Francisco Police Chief Richard Hongisto and two police officers to pay damages and legal fees of more than $338,000 to *The Bay Times*, a gay weekly newspaper distributed free throughout the San Francisco area. Hongisto ordered his officers to seize the paper from newsracks after it criticized and mocked the police chief. "Police Chief's Confiscation of 'Free' Newspaper Violates Publisher's Civil Rights," Student Press Law Center Newspaper Theft Forum, http://www.splc.org/pdf/sftheft.pdf.

134 *Joyner v. Whiting*, 477 F.2d 456, 463 (4th Cir. 1973).

CHAPTER 7

Private Schools and Press Freedom

Do students at a private high school or college have to check their free speech rights at the campus gate when they arrive at school each morning?

The answer to that question is a resounding maybe. Because the First Amendment begins, "*Congress* shall make no law … ," courts hold that only the government and those acting on the government's behalf are constitutionally barred from denying a person the right to free speech. Private institutions, including private high schools and colleges, are not usually subject to the limitations imposed by the First Amendment.[1] Unfortunately, this has allowed some private campus officials to routinely censor student media stories they dislike and punish those students who refuse to comply with their censorship demands.

> Private institutions, whose officials do not act on behalf of the state, are generally not subject to limitations imposed by the First Amendment.

But contrary to popular belief, all is not lost on the private school campus. The First Amendment is not the only weapon available to defenders of free expression. There are valid legal theories, along with strong policy arguments, that may help the private school journalist who faces the threat of censorship.

POLICY ARGUMENTS

The most powerful arguments against administrative censorship at private schools often have little to do with the law. There are a number of policy arguments that private school student journalists can present to school officials to help persuade them that censorship is — above all else — simply a bad practice.

First, the simple fact that the law may not always prevent censorship at a private school does not make it right. Just because private school officials can censor does not mean they should. This is the nation where Thomas Jefferson said, "[w]ere it up to me to decide whether we should have a government without newspapers or newspapers without a government, I should not hesitate a moment to prefer the latter." One can argue that any official censorship of a newspaper, whether by a private school administrator or a state or local government official, is simply un-American. If a private school's ultimate function is to turn students into informed and active citizens, then the students' basic experiences with the workings of a free society are key, regardless of where the students attend school. A student journalist who has experienced censorship and prior restraint throughout his academic career will approach journalism —and its role in American society — with a warped perspective. Free expression and a flourishing marketplace of ideas are a vital part of what separates America from the totalitarian nations we condemn.

> The First Amendment is not the only weapon available to defenders of a free campus press. There are valid legal theories and strong policy arguments that may help the private school journalist confronted with threats and acts of censorship.

Second, a private school that stifles the expression of its students is retarding one of the basic necessities of the learning process — the free flow of ideas. Minds need exposure to new ideas and new means of expression to grow. When censored, students at private schools receive a lesser education than their counterparts in public schools.

Encouragingly, some private schools wholeheartedly embrace this belief. Yale University, for example, has endorsed a policy that stirringly recognizes the "paramount obligation of the university" to protect students' and faculty's right to free expression if it is to fulfill its function "to discover and disseminate knowledge."[2] "We take a chance," the policy states, "as the First Amendment takes a chance, when we commit ourselves to the idea that the results of free expression are to the general benefit in the long run, however unpleasant they may appear at the time."[3]

Third, because many private schools are affiliated with a religious organization, a special affinity for the First Amendment should create a common bond with journalists and their free expression rights. If it were not for the First Amendment and its protection of the free exercise of religion, many of the schools themselves might not exist. It would seem incumbent upon religious schools to advocate the guarantees that protect both journalists and themselves from excessive intrusion by those in power.

Even if this kind of reasoning does not work in closed-door meetings with school officials, public and political pressure may lessen an administrator's desire to censor. Publicly aired grievances communicated to the local press by students, professional organizations, alumni groups and others frequently get results when internal discussions fail. Appeals by well-placed outsiders (especially those who happen to be alumni of the school) can have a powerful effect on administrators who might otherwise turn a deaf ear to students' arguments that censorship is wrong.

School administrators who are quick to censor may hesitate if they realize that their actions will lead to bad publicity for the school. Administrators have been known to have a change of heart when it appears that their decision to censor student expression might have a negative impact on next year's enrollment figures or fundraising. In addition, demonstrating to school officials that you are willing to fight for free expression rights may cause administrators to reconsider their position.

Ultimately, it may be possible to go to court and seek legal redress for wrongs done, even when those wrongs are committed by a private institution. The prospects for obtaining relief are, admittedly, uncertain. Nevertheless, there are at least four different legal theories under which students might win a favorable verdict in court cases involving the censorship of media at a private school, given the right circumstances.

CONTRACT RIGHTS/LAW OF ASSOCIATIONS

In the right situation, the legal remedy most likely to protect student journalists at a private school is a claim based on a breach of the guidelines or rules established by the private school itself.

As courts have frequently noted, "a student-college relationship is essentially a contractual one."[4] Catalogs, student handbooks and recruiting brochures distributed by schools (both on paper and online) usually contain pages of policies and rules. Many courts have ruled that the distribution of these documents and the offer of admission to the school — both of which can include explicit and implicit promises that can be mutually agreed upon — and an acceptance of this offer and payment of tuition by a student create a contractual relationship.[5] Other courts have found that the law of associations, rather than strict contract law, is more appropriate to the student/private school relationship.[6] The law of associations has been applied to private schools, churches, civic groups and other private organizations to address situations where contract rights, property rights and other personal rights merge. While the legal theories vary slightly, the general notion is the same: where a private school voluntarily establishes a set of guidelines or rules, it must follow them. Otherwise, there exists a breach of a legally enforceable promise, for which the recipient of the broken promise may obtain legal relief.

> Where private schools have promised to protect students' free expression rights, they may be contractually bound to honor that promise.

For example, a private university is not legally required to establish a procedure that provides students with the opportunity to respond when the school wants to take disciplinary action, such as a hearing to answer a charge that could result in a student's expulsion. With no government rules to limit it, a private school generally enjoys a significant degree of freedom in disciplining — or even expelling — its students. However, if that school has a written policy outlining the procedures to be followed in a student disciplinary action, those procedures must be followed.[7] If not, there is a breach of contract or an associational promise, and the student may seek damages or reinstatement. This "due process" does not need to meet the standards of the federal Constitution, but it does need to meet the standards specified in the student handbook, catalog or other policy statement.

While this legal theory has come up mainly in the context of students being expelled or denied diplomas, there is no reason this rationale should not be extended to cover other promises made by a college or university. Indeed, in a case that involved the *Dartmouth Review* (an independent student publication at Dartmouth College) and promises made by the school in its student handbook, a New Hampshire state court judge ruled that a "private college is equally obliged not to violate any of the contractual rights of its students."[8]

While the judge limited his ruling to a section of the handbook that dealt with student disciplinary proceedings, the court indicated that other campus promises made in the handbook had to be kept as well. Importantly, prior to the ruling, lawyers for the students had submitted arguments to the judge that pointed out sections in the handbook that guaranteed Dartmouth students the right to express themselves freely.[9]

In some cases, student journalists may even find themselves the beneficiaries of contractual rights extended to their advisers. A faculty member's contract with her school — or sometimes a faculty manual or handbook — frequently contains an academic freedom provision. While the specific protections vary, academic freedom commonly protects the right of a professor to teach her students as she deems appropriate. For a faculty member whose contractual duties include advising student media, this arguably might include the right to teach her students to publish free from administrative control and editorial interference.

Whether one is attempting to enforce a provision in a student handbook or a clause in a faculty contract, problems arise when a private school's promise to respect free speech lacks sufficient clarity or specificity to constitute a binding promise. As one commentator noted, "passages [in a school's student handbook or other official publication] that simply express aspirations are not normally considered part of the contract."[10] For example, a highminded but vague statement in a school's student handbook that "Doe University believes that freedom of speech is essential to receiving a well-rounded education" probably will not help much in court. On the other hand, a statement that "Doe University, recognizing the essential role of a free and independent press, respects the right of *The Student Times* to publish free of administrative interference and agrees to abide by the law as established by the First Amendment to the United States Constitution," will likely create specific and legally enforceable rights.

Another possibility arises where a school employee or agent acts in violation of these rights out of self-interest; for example, a private high school administrator might discipline a student because the student wrote a negative review of the administrator's favorite restaurant (which happens to be owned by her brother). While this action could be viewed as a breach of contract, it could also be viewed as a tortious interference with the contract between the student and the school.[11] The difference in the claims is the motivation behind them. A *breach of contract* happens when the school (or employees acting on its behalf) chooses to violate the rights that it granted. A *tortious interference with contract* occurs when an individual, for his own reasons, tries to prevent a party to the contract from performing the duties he owes under the contract. Of course, if the school defends the administrator's action after the fact, the school would seem to be endorsing the conduct, making the action a traditional breach of contract.

If a private school clearly promises or states that its students have the right to express their viewpoints openly or that student publications will be free of administrative interference with final editorial control left to the students, any action contrary to that policy may be a breach of a promise for which a court could give relief. Students should check to see if such a policy exists at their school, and if not, encourage the adoption of one.[12]

STATE ACTION

Regardless of whether a contract exists, a court may exercise its jurisdiction and invoke the First Amendment's protections if it is shown that a private school is really taking what amounts to governmental action when it censors the student press. This so-called "state action" doctrine comes in three forms, each rare and fairly difficult to demonstrate. The first is proof that the private school and the state have developed an interdependent, symbiotic relationship.[13] This is possible when the school is heavily dependent on state support for its existence, in return for providing services that the state otherwise would perform itself.

Initially, it might seem that practically all private schools fall into this category because of the massive amounts of money provided by the state and federal governments, including research grants and student aid. However, this is not the case. In several instances, courts have ruled that financial support is not enough.[14]

State action might also be found without this dependent relationship if the action of the private school is taken at the direction of the government. This is called the "close nexus" test: a citizen is deprived of his rights because a private institution is adhering to a government regulation, or a government entity has encouraged or compelled the institution to infringe on legally guaranteed liberties.[15] Under this rule, student journalists would receive First Amendment protection if a government regulation or a government official forced a private school to censor speech or otherwise violate the students' constitutional rights. An example might be a federal FBI agent ordering a private school official to conduct an unauthorized search of a student newspaper's newsroom. Such a scenario, while possible, is rare.

Finally, state action may be found if a private institution is performing duties and functions that traditionally have been discharged by the government.[16] However, courts generally say that a private entity is performing a public function only if that function has been done exclusively by the government in the past.[17] It might be difficult for education, which has both a private and a public history,[18] to meet this standard.[19] For instance, in a 2002 ruling, a federal appeals court rejected the claims of a Maine student who alleged he was suspended in violation of his due process rights, finding that no constitutional claim could be brought against a private school. The court held that education was not a "traditional public function," so a private school was not performing "state action" in providing educational services.[20]

CHARTER SCHOOLS: PUBLIC OR PRIVATE?

One of the latest developments in education has been the emergence of so-called charter schools. In 1991, Minnesota enacted the first charter school law in the country. Since that time, all but two states (Maine and Mississippi) have followed suit. As of December 2011, it was estimated that there were nearly 5,200 charter schools serving more than 1.94 million students in the United States.[21]

While it is not specifically known how many student journalists attend charter schools, some form of journalism exists at almost every type of school. A 1998 study found that nearly 97 percent of all high schools have at least some form of media-related activity at their school (newspaper, yearbook, literary magazine, etc.).[22] A more recent survey by the Kent State University Center for Scholastic Journalism found near-identical results in 2011.[23] These statistics suggest that the number of charter schools offering participation in student media likely exceeds 5,000 nationally.

Charter schools are created by contract (a charter) between the operators of the school and the chartering authority. While charter schools come in many shapes and sizes and are, by design, intended to stray at least somewhat from the traditional public school model, they share two common characteristics: "(1) a charter contract that establishes their authority to exist and binds them to accountability standards; (2) some form of relief from the statutory and regulatory requirements imposed on traditional public schools."[24]

Given their unique structure, charter schools have sometimes been described as "quasi-public"[25] or "hybrid public schools."[26] Unfortunately, such gray terms would be of little help to charter school student media confronting a battle over administrative censorship or access to school information. As this chapter makes clear, the categorization of a charter school as either public or private has serious legal implications. Among other things, the First Amendment protects students attending a public school; private school students must look elsewhere for help in defending against administrative censorship. In spite of their differences and the obvious institutional independence evident at many charter schools, there is a general consensus that charter schools — for purposes of law — are public schools, albeit with a twist.[27]

In every state but one, the authority to grant a charter to a school is limited to a governmental body, such as a state educational agency or a local school district (or, in a few states, a college or university).[28] All state charter laws — and federal law — hold charter schools to the same health and safety standards mandated for traditional public schools.[29] Charter schools — including those that may have been converted from being a private school — are funded primarily by public education dollars. Federal law and the laws of almost all states prohibit charter schools, like ordinary public schools, from charging tuition.[30] In fact, the charter school laws of several states[31] and the federal school charter law[32] specifically define charter schools as "public."

A growing number of court decisions have found that charter schools are public bodies and that their employees are "government" or "state" actors, subject to the same constitutional limitations imposed on other public school and government employees, as well as compliance with state freedom of information laws and anti-discrimination laws.[33] For instance, in one of the first cases to address the issue directly, an Ohio federal court found that a charter school, administered by a private company and organized under Ohio's charter law, and the school's principal were both "state actors" subject to a federal civil-rights lawsuit. In that case, a kindergarten teacher at the school claimed that the principal fired her after she complained that the school was providing inadequate assistance to a troubled student. In rejecting the school's request that it be dismissed from the First Amendment lawsuit because it was a private company, the court found that since the charter school "was created only with the help of the state, the [c]ourt must consider its actions to be those of the State."[34]

So, while charter schools may have freedom from some of the traditional and regulatory red tape that confronts mainstream public schools, the law clearly sets limits. Charter schools should be treated as public entities and their administrators and faculty as government officials. Consequently, student journalists at charter schools should enjoy the same First Amendment and other legal rights enjoyed by their public school counterparts.

STATE CONSTITUTIONS

Some state constitutions may provide an additional shield for defending free expression. In 1980, the U.S. Supreme Court said that the states are free to provide protection in their own constitutions beyond that of the federal Constitution – including protection for speech on private property, such as a private campus, where the U.S. Constitution normally would give no recourse.[35] The Court said that states may provide greater, even affirmative, protection for free speech on private property, provided that the value of the property is not diminished and the purposes for which the property is used are not disrupted.

State constitutions — all of which contain a free speech provision — may provide broader free speech protection than the federal First Amendment.

A 2002 survey by the Student Press Law Center found that the constitutions of forty-four states contained language that affirmatively protects free expression,[36] unlike the federal Constitution, which prohibits only *governmental* interference with free speech. For example, the Alaska State Constitution's free speech clause states: "Every person may freely speak, write, and publish on all subjects, being responsible for the abuse of that right."[37] The Alaska Supreme Court has said that the provision protects free speech "in a more explicit and direct manner" than does the First Amendment.[38]

A few states have construed their state constitutions to forbid the abridging of free press protections by private parties. Of these states, the constitutions of New Jersey, Massachusetts and Pennsylvania have been successfully used in the courts to protect the free expression rights of students on private campuses.[39] However, to date there has been no ruling specifically addressing whether student media at a private school enjoys freedom from censorship under a state constitution with an affirmative right of free speech and freedom of the press.

STATUTORY PROTECTION

As just discussed, lawmakers are always free to provide greater free speech protections to their citizens than those required by the federal First Amendment. Taking that cue, lawmakers in at least seven states — California, Connecticut, Florida, Massachusetts, Maine, New Jersey and North Dakota — have enacted state laws that would appear, on their face, to protect the free press and speech rights of individuals while on private property. Federal lawmakers have also introduced legislation — so far unsuccessfully — and enacted a "Sense of Congress" provision squarely aimed at protecting the free speech rights of private college students.

State (Private) Civil Rights Laws

Because of unfavorable court decisions and other limitations, the civil rights laws of the three New England states are probably — at least for now — of limited help to private school student media.

Connecticut's law is directed primarily at protecting employee whistleblowers at private companies from retaliation for their speech activities, a situation that rarely arises in the context of student media.[40]

On the other hand, the plain language of Massachusetts' Civil Rights Act would seem to provide significant legal protection from censorship by private school administrators.[41] The law eliminates the "state action" requirement and prohibits private individuals or entities from engaging in acts that would be unconstitutional if committed by a government body or official. The Maine law, which was patterned after the Massachusetts law, is largely identical except that it requires that any violation be "intentional."[42] However, despite the promising language of these statutes, courts in both states have caught cases of "judicial cold feet" when asked to interpret and apply the laws, going out of their way to rein in the groundbreaking legislation.[43] This prompted dissenting judges in at least one case to chide their colleagues for their "manipulative" and narrow reading of the law, which they said was "so wedded to 'traditional' thinking that they [the judges writing the majority opinion] simply refuse to accept the basis for Massachusetts' innovative...law."[44] More recently, at least one court has used the Massachusetts law to protect student speech, albeit on a public college campus, and it is possible that other courts could interpret the law more broadly in the future.[45]

So far, courts have not meaningfully weighed in on similar laws in New Jersey[46] and North Dakota,[47] and both — at least on their face — could offer private school student journalists significant free speech protection. Both contain language that specifically prohibits public officials and private individuals — presumably including private school administrators — from interfering with another person's First Amendment and other constitutionally protected rights. As one court has noted, however, the North Dakota law is a criminal statute and does not provide a private cause of action.[48]

Florida's law, also untested in court, is narrower in scope.[49] Like the laws discussed above, it also protects persons from unlawful acts by both public officials and private individuals. However, its protections are limited to acts that violate Florida's state constitution, which does include a free speech and press provision[50], or another state law. While it may prove to be an effective deterrent to private school censorship, the law does not extend federal First Amendment protection to Florida's private schools.

California's "Leonard Law": Unique Relief for California Students

"Judicial cold feet" has not been a problem so far for students attending California private schools. They have a unique weapon in the fight against censorship: a short, but remarkable, state law. Adopted in 1992 with near-unanimous bipartisan support, the "Leonard Law," named after its primary sponsor, former state Sen. Bill Leonard, R-San Bernardino, reads in part: "It is the intent of the Legislature that a student shall have the same right to exercise his or her right to free speech on campus as he or she enjoys when off campus."[51] The "Leonard Law" expressly forbids administrators from taking disciplinary action against a student for engaging in speech that would be protected by the First Amendment outside of campus. What makes the law so unique — in addition to its exceptionally broad and protective language guaranteeing student free speech rights — is that it applies to students at both public and private high schools and colleges. Widely regarded as a bold stroke for student free speech rights, the law goes where no other federal or state law has gone before, essentially converting the private school into a public forum.

> "It is the intent of the Legislature that a student shall have the same right to exercise his or her right to free speech on campus as he or she enjoys when off campus."
> — California Education Code Secs. 48950 and 94367

The law explicitly states that it does not "authorize any prior restraint of student speech" at private universities,[52] and allows all students the right to file a civil lawsuit against school officials who violate its provisions.[53] Although the law does not allow a student to sue for monetary damages, the court can order the school to pay a student's attorney fees if the student wins. There are, however, exceptions in the law that allow private religious schools to suppress student speech where it is shown that such speech "would not be consistent with the religious tenets of the organization." "Hate speech" is also punishable, though the term is very narrowly defined. In addition, school officials are permitted to regulate free expression using content-neutral "reasonable time, place and manner regulations." (See discussion of time, place and manner regulations in Chapter 8.)

In the nearly two decades since its passage, the "Leonard Law" has had a significant effect on student speech at private schools. In the first case to actually go to court under the law, a group of Stanford University students successfully challenged the school's speech code, which, among other things, prohibited speech "intended to insult or stigmatize an individual or group of individuals on the basis of their sex, race, color, handicap, religion, sexual orientation or national or ethnic origin." The students, led by Stanford Law School graduate Robert Corry, claimed that such vague language had a substantial "chilling effect" on meaningful, honest communication. In addition, the Santa Clara County Superior Court held that Stanford's speech code was both facially overbroad and underinclusive under the First Amendment, and therefore invalid under the "Leonard Law."[54]

The importance of the "Leonard Law" appears to be in its deterrent effect on school censorship. Administrators in California must consider whether their desire to suppress student speech is important enough to face a possible legal challenge under the "Leonard Law." Indeed, several students have avoided threatened punishment for otherwise-protected speech once they made it known that they were prepared to pursue lawsuits under the "Leonard Law."[55]

Noted constitutional law professor Julian N. Eule once remarked, "Suffice it to say that, were I representing a California school district, I would be less than confident about advising my client that it could exercise editorial control over the contents of a high school's newspaper."[56] All in all, the "Leonard Law's" transport of the First Amendment onto private school property is a noteworthy step forward for protecting student free expression rights on campus.

Sense of Congress

Although legislation similar to the "Leonard Law" has not caught on in the rest of the country, the United States Congress has indicated its support for free expression rights for students at both public and private colleges. While an attempt to create a federal "Leonard Law" fell short,[57] Congress adopted revisions to the Higher Education Act in 1998 that included a "sense of Congress" espousing non-binding guidelines addressing student free expression rights. The provision states, "It is the sense of Congress that no student attending an institution of higher education on a full- or part-time basis should, on the basis of participation in protected speech or protected association," be punished for engaging in conduct that would otherwise be protected by the First and Fourteenth Amendments if it occurred at a public college.[58]

While this legislation, sponsored by former Rep. Robert Livingston, R-La., and Sen. Larry Craig, R-Idaho, has been described as "a welcome step forward for press rights on the private campus,"[59] a "sense of Congress" is merely a reflection of Congress' views and recommendations, and should not be regarded as a binding law that imposes penalties for noncompliance. However, students can and should use the words of Congress in their attempts to persuade administrators to be more sensitive to campus free speech concerns.

CAN STUDENTS BE PUNISHED BY PRIVATE SCHOOL OFFICIALS FOR OFF-CAMPUS SPEECH?

The ability of the private school to affect free expression does not always end at the schoolhouse gate. Absent a school policy or state statute to the contrary, a private school may have substantial leeway in punishing or even expelling a student for off-campus speech. For example, in 1999, Peter Ubriaco was expelled from Albertus Magnus High School in Rockland County, New York, for hosting a personal website, which — among other items — jokingly encouraged visitors to his site to "walk into the local mall and shout the word 'penis' at the top of their lungs." The school found the site to be "violent and pornographic," even though the website contained no threats or pornographic images. Although the First Amendment likely would have provided significant legal protection had Ubriaco been punished by public school officials,[60] his attempts to seek legal redress were thrown out of federal court for one simple reason: he attended a private school.[61] The court ruled that because there was no state action involved, it lacked jurisdiction to prevent private school officials from punishing Ubriaco for his off-campus conduct.

Still, at least a handful of courts have refused to allow private school officials to exercise unfettered authority over off-campus student misconduct. In November 2002, a Minnesota state judge ordered a private school to reinstate a high school student who was expelled after a school official found him in possession of marijuana just off of school grounds.[62] That same month, a judge in Philadelphia ordered a private all-boys school to re-enroll a student expelled after he used a digital movie camera to secretly record a classmate in an "intimate moment" with a former girlfriend.[63] In both cases, judges expressed concern over the fairness of the schools' actions.

While the cases above are unusual, they do make clear that private school officials do not act in a vacuum. Punishing students for their purely private, off-campus conduct — and particularly for speech that is not unusually egregious or shocking — strikes many as unfair and heavy-handed. Students who publish a generally responsible, if controversial, off-campus student newspaper or website will usually find support — if not in a court of law, then at least in the court of public opinion.

Requiring a Free Private School Press

Winning free speech protections for student journalists by legally compelling private schools to protect student speech — by a state or federal law or by a constitutional provision — poses some risks for journalism as a whole, and has its critics.[64] Forcing a private institution to allow use of its newspaper for public expression, for example, comes close to the state forcing privately owned newspapers to publish mandated material, an effect that the Supreme Court has said is generally not permissible under the First Amendment.[65] The Court has also ruled that the government cannot force a private citizen to affirm a belief he does not share.[66]

With these precedents, the question arises whether the state, through its constitution and courts, should be permitted to intervene with private schools so that student media can freely advocate ideas with which school officials disagree. Providing such a right to student journalists requires a careful delineation between a private school's student newspaper, where the school has traditionally and willingly given editorial control to its students or has indicated that it would do so, and a private publishing company, which clearly retains ultimate control of its publications. While sorting these competing interests may be a challenge, it can be done. As other sources have noted, such balancing falls precisely within the role of courts.[67] In recent years, several commentators have put forward thoughtful, well-reasoned proposals for how such a balance might be struck — and persuasive arguments for why it should be.[68] However, if the past is any indication, the law — and specifically judges — will likely have to be pushed and prodded before such ideas are seriously considered. Still, given the potential rewards of a healthy and vigorous campus "marketplace of ideas" and a free, uncensored private school press, such proposals deserve serious consideration.

INDEPENDENCE

Even in law, the best defense may be a good offense. Rather than trying to formulate after-the-fact arguments as to why an administrator's act of censorship is illegal, many private school student journalists have found it more effective to take away the means by which school officials can censor in the first place. To limit administrative control, a publication can separate itself from the school by becoming a separate entity or corporation.

For a number of reasons, complete independence, either through formal incorporation or by other means, is practical for only a few publications. An independent newspaper or magazine at a private school should not expect any financial or material support from its school if it wants to guarantee freedom from censorship. Because of the costs involved in supporting a full-fledged student media program, only a relatively small number of student publications have found independence to be a realistic alternative. However, the proliferation of personal computers and the Internet has made going independent easier and less costly than in the past.

While independence may be an attractive alternative, it does not, by itself, overcome the ability of a private school to restrict distribution of a publication on its campus or to punish students for their off-campus expression. Nevertheless, in the right situations, declaring independence from the school has worked well for a number of student publications.

SUMMARY

Although official control of student journalism remains a legal and practical reality at many private schools, students who find themselves becoming victims of censorship and prior restraint should not give in quietly. Ideally, control of the press should be as repugnant to the school as it is to student journalists. But where school administrators cannot be convinced of the reasons for a strong, viable and editorially independent campus press, some private school students may have reasonable legal arguments available to them. Whether there is state action, a contract or other enforceable promise, a state constitution, a statute such as California's "Leonard Law" — or the power of persuasion — press freedom on private campuses can realistically be fought for and won.

> To limit administrative interference, a student media organization capable of financially supporting itself can achieve independence from the school by becoming a separate entity or corporation.

D.J. Fritz, ace investigative reporter for the St. Holy *Student Times*, was exhausted. After almost a year of extensive reporting he had just finished writing a story that was bound to cause a major shake-up among the powers-that-be at his private school. It had taken more time and more effort than he ever imagined, but after conducting dozens of interviews, reviewing hundreds of documents and triplechecking everything, he was proud of the job he had done. St. Holy school officials might not like the news story they were going to read the next morning, but they would not be able to dispute its truth.

As Fritz was leaving the newsroom, his editor, Patty Peachtree, frantically called him to her office. "Deej," she said, visibly shaking, "we've got a problem!"

She tells Fritz that the printer had tipped off St. Holy officials about the story. Word had quickly made its way to the top. The president's first call was to the printer, whom he ordered to stop the presses. His second call was to Peachtree. She tells Fritz that the president has removed her as editor, effective immediately. His third call, Peachtree says, was to Fritz's home. Waiting on his voicemail, she tells him, will be a message from the president informing him that he has been permanently expelled from St. Holy.

"They can't do that!" D.J. yells. "This is America. What about freedom of the press? What about all that free speech stuff I read in the student media policy they made us sign at the beginning of the year? And kicking me out of school — by voicemail? You've gotta be kidding!"

D.J. worriedly calls you for advice. What can you tell him? What questions might you want to ask?

ANSWER:
To begin, you can give Fritz some good news and some bad news. First the bad: since St. Holy is a private school, you tell him, it is probably not subject to the First Amendment's press freedom protections. The First Amendment limits censorship only by government officials or those acting directly on their behalf. Unless there are very unusual circumstances in play, St. Holy administrators probably do not fall into that category. The fact that St. Holy receives state or federal financial support (for example, federal financial aid, research grants, etc.) is not enough to change the result. Unfortunately, you tell D.J., he is going to have to wage his defense without relying on the First Amendment, which leads to the good news: there are other options.

From what Fritz tells you, the most obvious option might be to look to promises that the school has made. While private schools are not required to guarantee a censorship-free student media, if they do promise to allow free speech, they may be legally bound to keep their word. In this case, Fritz provides you with a copy of St. Holy's student media policy. In addition to some fairly grandiose — but not very specific — wording in the preamble about the importance of a free and independent press, the policy also contains the following provision: "The editor in chief is ultimately responsible for determining the editorial content of *The Student Times*." That, you tell Fritz, is reasonably specific and may, in fact, constitute a legally enforceable contractual promise that St. Holy school officials would not censor the student media. The same theory, you tell him, would hold true when it comes to challenging St. Holy's decision to fire Peachtree and expel him. Again, while private schools typically have more leeway than public schools when it comes to taking disciplinary action against their students, most also have policies and procedures in place that determine how such punishment is to be meted out. Most disciplinary policies, for example, require that, at a minimum, students be told what they've done wrong and provided with an opportunity to present their side of the story prior to being punished. Clearly, that did not happen here. Even where a specific, written promise might not exist, courts will often find an implied contractual promise by parties to deal fairly with one another. Using voicemail to expel a student who has paid his tuition and otherwise reasonably relied on the assumption that he will be permitted to continue, absent some clear wrongdoing (which most courts would likely find does not include writing an accurate story that embarrasses the school), probably falls into the category of "unfair dealing."

In addition to examining the school's own promises and policies, you tell Fritz that he will want to check into state law to find out if the school officials might have crossed any lines. Like the federal Constitution's First Amendment, the constitutions of each state contain a provision protecting free expression rights. In some states, the state free expression provision actually provides greater legal protection than the First Amendment and has been used to limit private school censorship. In other states, lawmakers have passed statutes that may prove helpful.

Even if turns out that their options in a court of law are limited, Fritz and Peachtree can still look to the "court" of public opinion for help. Fritz's story, as it has been relayed to you, is airtight. His research is sound, his facts accurate and the reporting fair. Even if St. Holy officials have the legal right to censor the story and penalize the student staff, that does not make it the right thing to do. If, after discussion, school officials refuse to back down from their position, you suggest that Peachtree and Fritz might want to meet with the rest of the *he Student Times* staff to discuss their public response, which in most cases should include contact with local media, press organizations (including the Student Press Law Center), community groups and St. Holy student and alumni groups. Censoring is one thing. Being loudly and very publicly identified as a censor is something else. If the president cannot be legally compelled to do the right thing, he might be embarrassed into doing it.

ENDNOTES

1   *See Hudgens v. NLRB*, 424 U.S. 507 (1976).
2   Yale.edu, Undergraduate Regulations 2007-2008: Free Expression, Peaceful Dissent, and Demonstrations (quoting the *Report of the Committee on Freedom of Expression* at http://yalecollege. yale.edu/content/general-conduct-and-discipline (last visited July 30, 2013).
3   *Id.*
4   *See Russell v. Salve Regina College*, 890 F.2d 484, 488 (1st Cir. 1989), *rev'd on other grounds*, 499 U.S. 225 (1991), *reinstated on remand*, 938 F.2d 315, 316 (1st Cir. 1991). *See generally* Ralph D. Mawdsley, *Litigation Involving Higher Education Employee and Student Handbooks*, 109 Ed. Law Rep. 1031 (1996).
5   *See, e.g., Ross v. Creighton Univ.*, 957 F.2d 410, 416 (7th Cir. 1992) (recognizing the contractual nature of the student-school relationship and finding that "[t]he catalogues, bulletins, circulars, and regulations of the institution made available to the matriculant become a part of the contract"); *Swartley v. Hoffner*, 734 A.2d 915, 919 (Pa. Super. Ct. 1999), *appeal denied*, 747 A.2d 902 (Pa. 1999) (finding that students may bring suits "where the institution ignores or violates portions of the written contract" such as a student handbook); *Kuritzky v. Emory Univ.*, 669 S.E.2d 179 (Ga. App. 2008); *Morehouse College, Inc. v. McGaha*, 627 S.E.2d 39 (Ga. App. 2005); *Larson v. Snow College*, 189 F. Supp. 2d 1286, 1301 n.14 (D. Utah 2000); *Doe v. Gonzaga Univ.*, 24 P.3d 390, 402-03 (Wash. 2001), *rev'd on other grounds*, 536 U.S. 273 (2002) (provisions in student handbook created implied contract); *Alsides v. Brown Institute, Ltd.*, 592 N.W.2d 468 (Minn. Ct. App. 1999); *Ward v. N.Y. Univ.*, No. 99-CIV-8733(RCC), 2000 WL 1448641, at *4 (S.D.N.Y. Sept. 25, 2000) (failure to provide "state of the art facilities" as implicitly promised in university promotional materials might be actionable); *Guckenberger v. Boston Univ.*, 957 F. Supp. 306, 317 (D. Mass. 1997) (noting "[u]niversities are capable of forming legally cognizable contractual relationships with their students"). *See also Thornton v. Harvard Univ.*, 2 F. Supp. 2d 89, 93-94 (D. Mass. 1998); *Brody v. Finch Univ. of Health Sciences*, 698 N.E.2d 257, 265 (Ill. App. Ct. 1998), *appeal denied*, 705 N.E.2d 434 (Ill. 1998); *Gomes v. Univ. of Maine Sys.*, 304 F. Supp. 2d 117, 130-31 (D. Me. 2004). *Steinberg v. Chicago Med. Sch.*, 371 N.E.2d 634, 640-41 (Ill. 1977); *Zumbrun v. Univ. of Southern California*, 101 Cal. Rptr. 499, 504 (Cal. App. 1972); *Univ. of Texas Health Sci. Ctr. at Houston v. Babb*, 646 S.W.2d 502, 506 (Tex. App. 1982); *Stanoch v. Breck Sch.*, No. CT 02- 019852 (Dist. Ct. Hennepin County Nov. 21, 2002) (temporary restraining order). See also the discussion of the *Dartmouth Review* case, below at n.8. However, some courts have given substantial deference to private universities where the interpretation of the rules and regulations found in a student handbook is in dispute (*See, e.g., Schaer v. Brandeis Univ.*, 735 N.E.2d 373 (Mass. 2000) and to religious institutions where they can show that the complained-of action was done for "ecclesiastical reasons" or for "the good of the church" (*See Sabatino v. Saint Aloysius Parish*, 672 A.2d 217, 219 (N.J. Super. Ct. App. Div. 1996)).
6   *Tedeschi v. Wagner College*, 404 N.E.2d 1302, 1305-06 (N.Y. 1980); *Christ the King Reg'l High Sch. v. Catholic High Sch. Athletic Ass'n*, 624 N.Y.S.2d 755, 756 (N.Y. App. Div. 1995); *Clayton v. Princeton Univ.*, 519 F. Supp. 802, 804-06 (D.N.J. 1981); *A. v. C. College*, 863 F. Supp. 156, 158 (S.D.N.Y. 1994); *Abbariao v. Hamline Univ. Sch. of Law*, 258 N.W.2d 108 (Minn. 1977); *Baltimore Univ. v. Colton*, 57 A. 14 (Md. 1904).
7   *Jansen v. Emory Univ.*, 440 F. Supp. 1060 (N.D. Ga. 1977). *See also Tedeschi v. Wagner College*, 404 N.E.2d. 1302, 1306; *Centre College v. Trzop*, 127 S.W.3d 562, 568 (Ky. 2003).
8   *Dartmouth Review v. Dartmouth College*, CIV No. 88-E-111 (N.H. Super. Ct. Grafton Div., Jan. 3, 1989).
9   Plaintiff's Petition for Damages and Equitable Relief, *Dartmouth Review v. Dartmouth College*, CIV No. 88-E- 111.
10 Michael Zolandz, *Storming the Ivory Tower: Renewing the Breach of Contract Claim by Students Against Universities*, 69 Geo. Wash. L. Rev. 91, 102 (2000).
11 *Jacobs v. Ethel Walker Sch. Inc.*, No. CV020515279S, 2003 WL 22390051, slip op. at 8, 9 (Conn. Super. Ct. Sept. 30, 2003) (finding that a claim could proceed to trial where a student alleged that a

dean, "for improper reasons known only to her," intentionally held an unfair hearing).

12 For a discussion of student media policies, *See* J. WILLIAM CLICK, GOVERNING COLLEGE STUDENT PUBLICATIONS (NCCPA Publications 2d ed. 1993). The book is out of print, but is on file with the authors and is available in libraries or through online retailers such as Amazon.com.

13 *See, e.g., Burton v. Wilmington Parking Auth.*, 365 U.S. 715 (1961) (finding state action in race discrimination by privately owned coffee shop that operated as an "interdependent" part of the publicly owned garage in which it was located).

14 *Rendell-Baker v. Kohn*, 457 U.S. 830 (1982) (finding no state action in teacher's dismissal for speech activities even though private high school that helped educate troubled youths received up to 99 percent of its annual budget from state tax receipts); *Yeo v. Town of Lexington*, 131 F.3d 241, 253-54 (1st Cir. 1997) (en banc), *cert. denied*, 524 U.S. 904 (1998); *Powe v. Miles*, 407 F.2d 73, 81-82 (2d Cir. 1968); *Blackburn v. Fisk Univ.*, 443 F.2d 121, 123 (6th Cir. 1971); *Tynecki v. Tufts Univ. Sch. of Dental Med.*, 875 F. Supp. 26, 33 (D. Mass. 1994). Indeed, this interdependent relationship has been recognized only in Pennsylvania. There, the state not only provided money to the private schools in question, but it also designated representatives to serve on the schools' boards of trustees. In addition, state statutes specified how the private schools would interact with the state university system. The name of a private school was even changed because of a statutory provision. Based on these laws, the courts ruled that the private schools were, in effect, part of the public university system, making them subject to restrictions on government action. *Krynicky v. Univ. of Pittsburgh*, 742 F.2d 94 (3rd Cir. 1984), *cert denied*, 471 U.S. 1015 (1985); *Braden v. Univ. of Pittsburgh*, 552 F.2d 948 (3d Cir. 1977) (en banc); *Isaacs v. Bd. of Trustees of Temple Univ.*, 385 F. Supp. 473 (E.D. Pa. 1974). *Compare Williams v. Discovery Day Sch.*, 924 F. Supp 41 (E.D. Pa. 1996) (distinguishing *Krynicky* and rejecting the claim that a day school authorized by Congress and housed in a federal government office building was state actor).

15 *Jackson v. Metropolitan Edison Co.*, 419 U.S. 345 (1974); *Denchy v. Educ. & Training Consultants*, 803 F. Supp. 1055, 1060-61 (E.D. Pa. 1992).

16 *Marsh v. Alabama*, 326 U.S. 501 (1946) (ruling that where a company-owned town performed all of the functions traditionally performed by a local government, the town was subject to the same federal guidelines as a government).

17 *Flagg Bros., Inc. v. Brooks*, 436 U.S. 149 (1978); *Rendell-Baker v. Kohn*, 457 U.S. 830, 840-841 (1982). But *See* Brian Steffen, *Freedom of the Private-University Student Press: Constitutional Proposal*, 36 J. MARSHALL L. REV. 139, 157 n.112 (2002), where the author points to *Edmonson v. Leesville Concrete Co., Inc.*, 500 U.S. 614 (1991), in which the Supreme Court appeared to veer away from the rigid "exclusivity" test, suggesting that private school student media in future cases might benefit from a more relaxed "public function" test of state action analysis, which asks only "whether the action in question involves the performance of a traditional function of the government." *Id.* at 624. The *Edmonson* Court also allowed for the examination of a combination of factors (public function, close nexus, state regulation) to determine the existence of state action.

18 *Trustees of Dartmouth College v. Woodward*, 17 U.S. 518 (1819) (rejecting attempt to subject private college to greater governmental oversight and noting the distinct roles played by public and private educational institutions in the early 19th century). But *See Riester v. Riverside Community Sch.*, 257 F. Supp. 2d 968, 972 (S.D. Ohio 2002) (finding that "free, public education, whether provided by public or private actors, is an historical, exclusive, and traditional state function"); Robert O'Neil, *Private Universities and Public Law*, 19 BUFF. L. Rev. 155, 157 (1970) (questioning the Supreme Court's decision in *Trustees of Dartmouth College* case).

19 *See, e.g., State v. Schmid*, 423 A.2d 615, 621-22 (N.J. 1980) (holding that despite the relationship between the State of New Jersey and Princeton University, i.e., state accreditation, participation in state programs, tax-exempt status, and some state funds, the university was wholly private and its actions did not rise to the level of state action for First Amendment purposes); *Powe v. Miles*, 407 F.2d 73, 80 (2d Cir. 1968) (noting that "[e]ducation has never been a state monopoly in this country, even at the primary or secondary levels, and New York's entry into higher education on a significant scale came more than a century after Alfred [University's] establishment").

20 *Logodice v. Trustees of Maine Cent. Inst.*, 296 F.3d 22, 26 (1st Cir. 2002).

21 Center for Education Reform, *2011-12 National Charter School & Enrollment Statistics*, available at http://www.edreform.com/wp-content/uploads/2012/03/National-Charter-School-Enrollment-Statistics-2011-12.pdf (last viewed June 21, 2013).

22 JACK DVORAK, INDIANA UNIV. HIGH SCHOOL JOURNALISM INSTITUTE, STATUS OF JOURNALISM AND NEWS MEDIA IN THE NATION'S SECONDARY SCHOOLS (1998).

23 For a summary of the Kent State survey results *See* Katina Paron, "This Just In: Students Love Print," WNYC SchoolBook blog, Dec. 22, 2011, available at http://www.wnyc.org/blogs/schoolbook/2011/dec/22/this-just-in-students-love-print/ (last viewed June 21, 2013).

24 Julie Mead, *Devilish Details: Exploring Features of Charter School Statutes That Blur the Public/Private Distinction*, 40 HARV. J. ON LEGIS. 349, 350 (2003).

25 SANDRA VERGARI, THE CHARTER SCHOOL LANDSCAPE (2002) (Introduction).

26 THOMAS L. GOOD & JENNIFER S. BRADEN, THE GREAT SCHOOL DEBATE: CHOICE, VOUCHERS, AND CHARTERS 120 (2000).

27 The Center for Education Reform, one of the leading proponents of the charter school movement, describes charter schools as "independent public schools." *See, e.g.,* Neal McClusky, *Beyond Brick and Mortar: Cyber Charters Revolutionizing Education* (Jan. 11, 2002), https://virtualschooling.wordpress.com/2005/11/23/beyond-brick-and-mortar-cyber-charters-revolutionizing-education-cer-action-paper//

28 Minnesota is alone in having granted authority to certain charitable organizations, and even that grant is subject to approval by the state commissioner of education. MINN. STAT. Sec.124D.10-3(a) (2007).

29 Mead, *supra* note 24, at 369. *See, e.g.,* ALASKA STAT. Sec. 14.03.255(d) (2004); MINN. STAT. Sec. 124D.10-8(a) (2007); N.Y. EDUC. LAW SEC. 2854(1)(b) (McKinney 2007); 20 U.S.C. 7221i(1)(J) (West 2008).

30 Mead, *supra* note 24, at 367. *See* 20 U.S.C. 7221i(1)(F) (West 2008).

31 *See, e.g.,* MINN. STAT. SEC. 124D.10-7 (2007) ("A charter school is a public school and is part of the

state's system of public education"); CAL. EDUC. CODE Sec. 47615(a)(1) (West 2008) ("Charter schools are part of the Public School System..."); N.C. GEN. STAT. Sec. 115C-238.29E(A) ("A charter school that is approved by the State shall be a public school within the local school administrative unit in which it is located."); N.Y. EDUC. LAW Sec. 2850(2)(e) (McKinney 2007) (stating that a charter school is "an independent and autonomous public school" performing "essential public purposes and governmental purposes of this state")"; OHIO REV. CODE ANN. Sec. 3314.01(B) (West 2008) ("A community school created under this chapter is a public school, independent of any school district, and is part of the state's program of education.").

32 20 U.S.C. 7221i(1)(A)-(L) (West 2008).

33 *Nampa Classical Academy v. Goesling*, 447 Fed. Appx. 776, 778 (9th Cir. Aug. 5, 2011) (unpublished) ("Because Idaho charter schools are governmental entities, the curriculum presented in such a school is not the speech of teachers, parents, or students, but that of the Idaho government."); *Riester v. Riverside Community Sch.*, 257 F. Supp. 2d 968 (S.D. Ohio 2002) (holding that a private company operating a charter school and its employee, who was acting as the school's principal, were both "state actors" that could be sued under federal law for violating a teacher's First Amendment rights); *Jones v. Sabis Educ. Sys., Inc.*, 52 F. Supp. 2d 868 (N.D. Ill. 1999) (finding that a charter school was a governmental body subject to suits under the federal Civil Rights Act of 1866, 42 U.S.C. Sec. 1981); *Daugherty v. Vanguard Charter Sch. Academy*, 116 F. Supp. 2d 897 (W.D. Mich. 2000) (finding that a Michigan charter school could be sued for its alleged Establishment Clause violations because it was defined as a public school under a Michigan statute); *Wilson v. State Bd. of Educ.*, 89 Cal. Rptr. 2d 745, 752-53 (Cal. Ct. App. 1999), *reh'g denied* (Nov. 24, 1999) ("[I]t is apparent that charter schools are part of California's single, statewide public school system....They cannot discriminate against students on the basis of ethnicity, national origin, gender or disability"); *Council of Organizations and Others for Educ. About Parochiaid, Inc. v. Governor*, 566 N.W.2d 208, 228 (Mich. 1997) (Boyle, J., dissenting) ("[W]hile [charter] schools are bound to comply with some restrictions that are generally applicable to all public schools, such as the Freedom of Information Act, . . . [these] schools have significant independence . . . from state or local regulation"); *Scaggs v. New York Dept. of Educ.*, No. 06-CV-0799, 2007 WL 1456221, at *13 (E.D.N.Y. May 16, 2007) (slip op.) (finding that a corporation operating a charter school in New York "may properly be viewed as having engaged in state action . . . where it allegedly failed to provide . . . students with adequate special education programs and safe physical conditions"). The Ninth Circuit's position is in flux, because in a 2009 ruling, *Caviness v. Horizon Com'ty Learning Ctr.*, 590 F.3d 806, the court decided that a fired Arizona teacher had no constitutional claim against the corporate owner of a charter school, because Arizona law did not make charter schools "state actors" for employment purposes. The same court then reached an opposite result two years later, applying the law of Idaho, in the aforementioned *Goesling* case. The *Caviness* case represents a minority view and it has not been followed to date by any other circuit.

34 *Riester v. Riverside Community Sch.*, 257 F. Supp. 2d 968, 973 (S.D. Ohio 2002). Note, however, that the federal Ninth Circuit reached a different result in a 2010 ruling in which a fired teacher tried to bring a constitutional claim challenging his dismissal. In *Caviness v. Horizon Community Learning Center, Inc.*, 590 F.3d 806, 816 (9th Cir. 2010), the court found that the private contractor operating an Arizona charter school was not a state entity that could be held liable for violating the Constitution, because providing educational services was "not a function that is traditionally and exclusively the prerogative of the state".

35 *PruneYard Shopping Ctr. v. Robins*, 447 U.S. 74, 88 (1980).

36 For example, state courts in Alaska, California, Colorado, Indiana, Massachusetts, New Jersey, Oregon, Pennsylvania, Washington and Wyoming have indicated that the affirmative language in their constitutional free speech provisions provides broader protection than the federal Constitution's First Amendment. Other state courts, however, have said that, despite such affirmative language, their state constitutional provisions offer no free speech protection greater than the federal Constitution. Some of these states include Arizona, Connecticut, Georgia, Florida, Hawaii, Iowa, Maryland, Michigan, Minnesota, New Hampshire, New York, North Carolina, Ohio, South Carolina, South Dakota, Texas and Wisconsin. *See also* Burt Neuborne, *State Constitutional Protection of Free Speech and Establishment Clause Values*, PRACTISING LAW INSTITUTE, 277 PLI/ Lit 205, 209-12 (1985).

37 ALASKA CONST. art. I, Sec. 5 (2007).

38 *Messerli v. State*, 626 P.2d 81, 83 (Alaska 1980).

39 *Abramowitz v. Boston Univ.*, CIV No. 82680 (Mass. Sup. Ct. Suffolk Div., Dec. 2, 1986); *Commonwealth v. Tate*, 432 A.2d 1382 (Pa. 1981); *State v. Schmid*, 423 A.2d 615 (N.J. 1980), *appeal dismissed*, 455 U.S. 100 (1980) (holding that Princeton University violated the state constitutional rights of a nonstudent when it had him arrested for distributing political literature on campus). But *See State v. Guice*, 621 A.2d 553 (N.J. Super. Ct. Law Div. 1993) (upholding trespassing convictions against students who had distributed political literature on a private university campus where the institution, unlike Princeton University in the *Schmid* case, had not traditionally opened its grounds to such activity).

40 CONN. GEN. STAT. Sec. 31-51q (2008).

41 MASS . GEN. LAWS, ch. 12, Sec. 11H (2008) ("Whenever any person or persons, whether or not acting under color of law, interfere by threats, intimidation or coercion, or attempt to interfere by threats, intimidation or coercion, with the exercise or enjoyment by any other person or persons of rights secured by the constitution or laws of the United States, or of rights secured by the constitution or laws of the commonwealth, the attorney general may bring a civil action for injunctive or other appropriate equitable relief in order to protect the peaceable exercise or enjoyment of the right or rights secured.").

42 ME. REV. STAT., tit. 5, Sec. 4681(1), 4682-1-A (2007).

43 *Redgrave v. Boston Symphony Orchestra, Inc.*, 855 F.2d 888 (1st Cir. 1988), *cert. denied*, 488 U.S. 1043 (1989). Relying heavily on certified answers elicited from the Massachusetts Supreme Judicial Court in *Redgrave v. Boston Symphony Orchestra*, 502 N.E.2d 1375 (Mass. 1987), the majority noted: "The MCRA is an unusual statute, a civil rights law that abolishes the state action requirement for constitutional claims of deprivation of rights. This is not difficult to understand in the context of racial

discrimination, the prohibition of which was the statute's primary object . . . . But where the issue is the plaintiff's 'right' to free speech, the analogy is strained . . . . The courts, noting that free speech guarantees protect citizens against governmental restraints upon expression, have hesitated to permit governments to referee disputes between speakers lest such mediation, even when it flies the banner of 'protecting speech,' interfere with the very type of interest it seeks to protect." 855 F.2d at 904. *See also Phelps v. President of Colby College*, 595 A.2d 403 (Me. 1991) (rejecting a claim by students at a private college that the school's punishment of their unauthorized fraternity activities violated their free speech-rights under Maine's Civil Rights Act).

44 *Redgrave*, 855 F.2d at 919, 921 (Brownes, J., and Selva, J., dissenting).

45 *Reproductive Rights Network v. President of Univ. of Massachusetts*, 699 N.E.2d 829 (Mass. App. Ct. 1998) (finding that the University of Massachusetts at Boston violated the free-speech rights of students under Massachusetts civil-rights law when it ordered campus police to bar their access to university meeting facilities).

46 N.J. Stat. Ann. Sec. 10:6-2 (West 2008). So far, the statute has been interpreted only against state entities. *See, e.g., Kandil v. Yurkovic*, No. 06-4701, 2007 WL 4547365 (D.N.J. Dec. 18, 2007) (slip op.) (finding that police officers and a police department retained Eleventh Amendment immunity from suit under the New Jersey statute); *Citizens For a Better Lawnside, Inc. v. Bryant*, No. 05-4286, 2006 WL 3825145 (D.N.J. Dec. 22, 2006) (slip op.) (finding a Section 10:6-2 claim to be indistinguishable from a federal Section 1983 civil-rights claim, and further finding no violation of the law where a borough council restricted the public comment time allocated to speakers opposed to redevelopment plan); *Marjac, LLC v. Trenk*, No. 06-1440, 2006 WL 3751395, at *7-8 (D.N.J. Dec. 19, 2006) (slip op.) (refusing to dismiss a section 10:6-2 claim against a city planning board where substantive due process rights were denied); *K.J. v. Div. of Youth & Family Services*, 363 F. Supp. 2d 728 (D.N.J. 2004) (refusing to dismiss a section 10:6-2 claim against a state agency where minor children were allegedly malnourished).

47 N.D. Cent. Code Sec. 12.1-14-05 (West 2007).

48 *Riemers v. G. K. Development, Inc.*, No. 2:06-CV-97, 2007 WL 2746895 at *4 (D.N.D. Sept. 20, 2007) (slip. op) (holding that the defendant shopping mall did not violate the plaintiff's civil rights when it refused to rent him a space to solicit signatures for a political cause).

49 Fla. Stat. Ann. Sec. 760.51 (2008).

50 Fla. Const. art. 1, Sec. 4 (1998).

51 Cal. Educ. Code Sec. 48950 (West 2008) (pertaining to high schools); Cal. Educ. Code Sec. 94367 (West 2008) (pertaining to colleges). In addition to the "Leonard Law," discussed here, California attorneys are also urged to look at Cal. Civil Code Sec. 52.1, which has its roots in Massachusetts' pioneering civil-rights law, discussed above. Section 52.1, like the laws of Massachusetts and Maine, appears on its face to be essentially a state version of 42 U.S.C. Sec. 1983, the federal civil-rights statute, but one which eliminates the requirement for state action. Like its New England cousins, the law has —at least thus far— largely been neutered by the California courts. *See, e.g., Jones v. Kmart Corp.*, 949 P.2d 941 (Cal. 1998) (statute does not apply to private actors' violations of laws that limit only state's power).

52 Cal. Educ. Code Sec. 94367(d).

53 *Id.* at Sec. 48950(b), 94367(b).

54 *Corry v. Leland Stanford Junior Univ.*, No. 740309 (Cal. Super. Ct. Feb. 27, 1995), available at http://www.ithaca.edu/faculty/cduncan/265/corryvstanford.htm (last visited July 30, 2013).

55 For example, fraternity members at Occidental College avoided disciplinary action for publishing a lewd poem in a private newsletter that was then inadvertently made public. Linda Seebach, *PC in LA*, National Review, July 19, 1993, available at http://lindaseebach.net/columns/1993/07/01/july-1993/ (last visited July 30, 2013).

56 Julian N. Eule, as completed by Jonathan D. Varat, *Transporting First Amendment Norms to the Private Sector: With Every Wish There Comes a Curse*, 45 UCLA . L. Rev. 1537 (1998).

57 Congress has made at least two attempts to protect the free-speech rights of private college students. The Collegiate Speech Protection Act of 1991 was introduced by the late Rep. Henry Hyde (R-Ill.), H.R. 1380, 102d Cong. (1st Sess. 1991). The legislation would have allowed private college students and faculty to sue for injunctive and declaratory relief where they believed that their school's speech code interfered with their First Amendment rights. The bill died in committee. The next attempt was the Freedom of Speech and Association on Campus Act of 1997. H.R. 980, 105th Cong. (1st Sess. 1997). Sponsored by then-Rep. Robert Livingston, R-La., and inspired by the banishment and punishment of fraternity and sorority members from several private universities, the bill (H.R. 980), which also died in committee, would have denied federal funding to any institution found guilty of violating the free-speech and association rights of its students.

58 H.R. Conf. Rep. 105-750 Sec.112(a), at 12 (1998).

59 Brian Steffen, *Freedom of the Private-University Student Press: A Constitutional Proposal*, 36 J. Marshall L. Rev. 139, 170 (2002).

60 *See* discussion of off-campus speech in Chapter 8.

61 *Ubriaco v. Albertus Magnus High Sch.*, No. 99 Civ. 11135 (JSM) (S.D.N.Y. July 21, 2000).

62 *Stanoch v. Breck Sch.*, No. CT 02-019852 (Dist. Ct. Hennepin County Nov. 21, 2002) (temporary restraining order); Norman Draper, *Breck Must Readmit Expelled Teen*, Minneapolis Star Tribune, Nov. 27, 2002, at 1A.

63 Martha Woodall, *Judge Says Student Can Stay in School*, The Philadelphia Inquirer, Nov. 20, 2002, at B1.

64 *See, e.g.,* Frank Michelman, *Universities, Racist Speech and Democracy in America: An Essay for the ACLU*, 27 Harv. Civil Rights-Civil Liberties L. Rev. 339, 341-42 (1992) (introducing his opposition to the federal Collegiate Speech Protection Act of 1991, discussed above, which he said gave him an "allergic reaction"); Julian N. Eule, as completed by Jonathan D. Varat, *Transporting First Amendment Norms to the Private Sector: With Every Wish There Comes a Curse*, 45 UCLA L. Rev. 1537 n.a1 (1998) (similarly noting that certain free speech laws imposed on private entities had given him a "rash"). *See also Redgrave v. Boston Symphony Orchestra, Inc.*, 855 F.2d 888, 904 (1st Cir. 1988), *cert. denied*, 488 U.S. 1043 (1989) (rejecting the argument that a Massachusetts civil-rights law prohibited censorship by

private arts groups and finding that "[t]he freedom of mediating institutions, newspapers, universities, political associations, and artistic organizations and individuals themselves to pick and choose among ideas, to winnow, to criticize, to investigate, to elaborate, to protest, to support, to boycott, and even to reject is essential if 'free speech' is to prove meaningful.").

65   *Miami Herald Publ'g Co. v. Tornillo*, 418 U.S. 241 (1974).

66   *See Wooley v. Maynard*, 430 U.S. 705 (1977). *See also Gay Rights Coalition of Georgetown Univ. Law Ctr. v. Georgetown Univ.*, 536 A.2d 1, 5 (D.C. 1987) (holding that a private university could not be compelled by the District of Columbia's Human Rights Act to grant official "university recognition" to gay student groups; however, the university could not deny such groups "tangible benefits" such as use of facilities, as the law required that student organizations be treated equally).

67   *Redgrave*, 855 F.2d at 924 n.9 (Brownes, J., dissenting) ("First amendment claims are not made of absolutes, they involve the balancing of competing interests. Each case must be judged on its own specific facts…").

68   *See, e.g.*, Brian Steffen, *Freedom of the Private-University Student Press: A Constitutional Proposal*, 36 J. MARSHALL L. REV. 139 (2002); Erwin Chemerinsky, *More Speech is Better*, 45 UCLA L. Rev. 1635 (1998); Elizabeth Mertz, *The Burden of Proof and Academic Freedom: Protection for Institution or Individual?* 82 Nw. U. L. Rev. 492 (1988).

CHAPTER 8

Independent Student Media

FROM THE SPLC CASE FILES

After administrators shut down the official high school student newspaper, former student staffers decided to start their own. Meeting at home, conducting interviews on their private telephones and using personal computers and printers, the staff was ready to distribute their first issue when the editor-in-chief was called to the principal's office. The principal warned the editor that he would immediately suspend any student who distributed the paper at school. When the editor attempted to explain his understanding of the law, the principal gave him Saturday detention. After contacting the Student Press Law Center and local news media, the editor met with the school district's lawyer. After their meeting, the lawyer acknowledged that the principal was "mistaken" in his understanding of the law and that as long as the paper contained no seriously disruptive or unlawful content, the students had the right to distribute their paper on school grounds during the school day without interference. Two days later, as TV news cameras and the principal looked on, the staffers handed out their independent newspaper to students (and some teachers) who waited in long lines for a copy.

Student journalists traditionally have developed their skills working for school-sponsored newspapers, yearbooks and other media. In recent years, however, an increasing number have turned to independent, non-school-sponsored — so-called "underground" — student media. Personal computers, desktop printers, inexpensive copying services, software publishing programs and the Internet have made it possible for students to produce high-quality, independent publications or websites with limited resources, staff and money.

Students choose to go it alone for many reasons. Unfortunately, the decision often comes as a result of a school's attempt to censor or shut down school-sponsored student media. This has become more common since the U.S. Supreme Court permitted greater censorship of school-sponsored public high school newspapers in its 1988 decision, *Hazelwood School District v. Kuhlmeier*.[1] While the decision was bad news for many "official" high school student publications that were published as part of a class or that relied on school resources or funding, the *Hazelwood* Court reaffirmed that non-school sponsored student speech — which the Court explicitly said included independent student media distributed on campus — continued to enjoy substantial First Amendment protection.[2] Examples abound of high school students across the country turning to independent student media after being frustrated by administrative censorship and other free-speech hurdles.[3]

> "Underground" student media means a medium that it is produced apart from any class and without any school materials, resources or official assistance.

For other students, independent student media may simply provide an alternative to more traditional student publications, whose editorial policies may not lend themselves to focusing on minority viewpoints or on less popular and less commercially viable content. For example, politically conservative students, student poets and artists, gay and lesbian students, and Latino students have all been among those who have looked to an alternative student media to find their voice.

While independent student media often allow students more editorial and artistic freedom, these forums can also create headaches for those unfamiliar with where the lines of freedom and responsibility are drawn. Students who exercise their rights as an independent publisher are — just like all publishers — accountable for everything they produce. Additionally, students forced "underground" miss out on learning opportunities that come from participation in well-supported journalism programs headed by trained and experienced journalism faculties. While students who strike out solo face a significant learning curve and the accompanying risks, these hurdles are not insurmountable.

This chapter will attempt to identify for a would-be underground publisher some of the legal rights and risks that accompany independence. Many of these risks – copyright violation, unlawful invasion of people's privacy, and so forth – are the same as those faced by publishers of official, on-campus media and are discussed in greater depth elsewhere in this book. This chapter will briefly flag such possible perils, and will emphasize the ways in which the law may view independent media differently from its official school-affiliated cousins. Note that this chapter will often use the phrase "underground newspaper" as a shorthand to refer to non-school-affiliated media, but except where noted, the same rules apply to all forms of media, whether in print, over the airwaves, or online.

WHAT IS "UNDERGROUND" STUDENT MEDIA?

Independent student media can be any type of publication or media not officially affiliated with a school. Independent student media are often referred to as the "underground press," after their predecessors from the 1960s. Unfortunately, the term often connotes a dark, subversive activity carried out by radical anarchists and their ilk. While it is true that independent student media can be critical of school officials and policies and do sometimes use strong language or include articles on sensitive or controversial topics, the "underground" press also includes a "tips sheet" published by a community youth chess club, a hand-stapled "zine" published by student fans of a local band, or a religious newsletter published and handed out to students by an off-campus youth church group. Additionally, an increasing number of students are utilizing the Internet to disseminate non-school-sponsored media.

Independent media are often small operations, sporadically published and produced by staffs that are loosely organized. In some places, however, there is nothing "underground" about an alternative student publication that has become a well-funded, well-respected rival or substitute for its school-sponsored counterpart. By and large, the law discussed here applies to independent student media in all its forms.

The distinguishing feature of underground student media is not its format but rather that it is produced apart from any course and without any school materials, resources or other official assistance. The publication's connection to a school is that students are usually its sole producers and primary audience. (Note that nonstudents may not have the same legal rights as students in distributing material on campus.[4]) Although student newspapers distributed off campus may be referred to as "underground" publications, the term is more accurately limited to those publications that come onto school grounds. Students who produce and distribute their publications or websites apart from school, and whose impact on school is limited, generally cannot be censored or punished by school officials, although clearly many administrators do not understand this.[5]

The law has recognized three categories of student speech, each of which is entitled to different degrees of protection: (1) School-sponsored student speech; (2) Non-school-sponsored student speech that occurs on school grounds; (3) Non-school-sponsored speech that occurs entirely off campus.

KNOW YOUR STUDENT MEDIA

Not all student speech is created equally, nor treated equally by the law. Take a moment to determine into which category your speech falls.

Category 1: School-sponsored student speech. This category includes most "official" student media (print, online, cable and broadcast) that receive funding and/or support from the school. They are usually assisted by a teacher or faculty adviser and are physically produced using school equipment and resources and distributed primarily on school grounds. Sometimes, but not always, they are produced as part of a class. At the high school level, student publishers of school-sponsored speech receive the least First Amendment protection — with some important exceptions. High school students are often subject to the Supreme Court's ruling in *Hazelwood School District v. Kuhlmeier*, which gives school officials considerable — though not unlimited — leeway in regulating student media content under certain circumstances. School-sponsored student media at public colleges, on the other hand, generally retain strong First Amendment protection. Student media rights at private schools, which are not governed by the First Amendment, can vary considerably. (For more information, see Chapters 5 (public high schools), 6 (public colleges) and 7 (private institutions)).

Category 2: Non-school-sponsored student speech that occurs on school grounds. This category, which is the primary focus of this chapter, includes independent or "underground" student media that is created and published outside of school using private funding and resources, but which is physically distributed or intentionally made available or directed to students on campus. Such publications range from one-page, handwritten flyers to incorporated student dailies with multimillion-dollar annual budgets. At public high schools and universities, student publishers of independent student media are protected, at a minimum, by the Supreme Court's ruling in *Tinker v. Des Moines Independent Community School District.* This case provides substantial legal protections from censorship.

Category 3: Non-school-sponsored student speech that occurs entirely off-campus. This category — off-campus student speech — includes publications or other media that, like independent (or "underground") student media (Category 2 speech), are produced by students entirely outside of school, using private funds and resources. Unlike independent student media, off-campus student speech is not intentionally distributed or substantially promoted on school grounds. While its content may include school-related news or opinion, that is its only connection to a school. This category includes off-campus websites that are not created, viewed or promoted by the publishers at school. It also generally includes private youth club publications (for example, a Girl Scouts or church group newsletter) distributed in the outside community, a private diary or blog written and kept entirely outside of school, and any privately published newspaper or publication physically distributed outside of school property (and not intentionally designed to be carried onto campus), even if the publishers or authors are students. Off-campus student speech, which is generally entitled to the strongest free speech protection, is discussed at the end of this chapter and in Chapter 9.

THE FIRST AMENDMENT AND INDEPENDENT STUDENT MEDIA

In America, students do not "shed their constitutional rights to freedom of speech or expression at the schoolhouse gate."[6] The U.S. Supreme Court made that statement in its landmark 1969 case *Tinker v. Des Moines Independent Community School District*, in which it upheld the right of public junior high and high school students to wear black armbands to school to protest the Vietnam War. The First Amendment's protection of free speech, the Court ruled, does not stop simply because students are in a classroom instead of at a political rally or on a public street. A school policy completely preventing students from engaging other students in open discourse on issues they deem important violates their fundamental rights as human beings and hampers their opportunity to become well-informed, contributing citizens.

However, as a concurring justice in *Tinker* noted, it cannot be assumed that "the First Amendment rights of children are co-extensive with those of adults."[7] Schools cannot be expected to complete their mission of educating young people if the First Amendment permits a limitless campus speech free-for-all. Accordingly, student speech rights can be limited when their exercise "materially disrupts classwork or involves substantial disorder or invasion of the rights of others."[8] In other words, under the *Tinker* standard, school officials can censor independent student speech where it causes a serious physical disruption to school activities or where it includes content that is otherwise unprotected by the law (libelous statements, obscenity, or speech that unlawfully invades another's right to privacy would be common examples). Determining the scope of *Tinker*'s free speech protections often sparks debate. It is clear that administrators do not need to wait for a riot or fight to occur before limiting student speech. However, school officials must provide a "reasonable forecast" of disruption supported by facts, and not merely speculation or a dislike of the speech.[9]

Although the Court in *Tinker* dealt with armbands, the *Tinker* standard also protects other forms of non-school-sponsored student expression, including independently produced student media that is distributed on school grounds. Protecting such expression is an important part of the educational process, encouraging students to become active, thinking participants in their world and well-informed citizens of their communities and country. As one court noted when it struck down a Colorado high school policy that restricted independent student media:

> "High school students, who… include persons of voting age, must develop the ability to understand and comment on the society in which they live and to develop their own sets of values and beliefs. A school policy completely preventing students from engaging other students in open discourse on issues they deem important cripples them as contributing citizens. Such restrictions do not advance any legitimate governmental interest. On the contrary, such inhibitions on individual development defeat the very purpose of public education in secondary schools."[10]

Sadly, as the constant battles between independent student journalists and school officials attest, far too many "professional educators" have lost sight of such vital educational goals, instinctively treating independent student media as a nuisance to be swept aside or even an enemy to be quashed.

Though the United States Supreme Court has had many opportunities to overrule *Tinker* during the last three decades, it has never done so.[11] Instead, it has frequently cited the decision in other cases involving campus speech, including *Hazelwood*.[12] Accordingly, for independent student media, *Tinker* remains the law of the land. (The *Tinker* case and its "disruption" standard are discussed at length in Chapter 4.)

Public vs. Private Schools

The type of school that students attend can greatly affect their rights to produce and distribute independent student media. As a general rule, students at public high schools and colleges have the right to distribute their own publications on school grounds during the school day.[13] Assuming their speech is otherwise lawful (not libelous or obscene, for example), public school students are typically governed by the *Tinker* standard concerning disruption.

Unfortunately, private school students are on less secure legal footing in protecting themselves from administrative censorship. Because the First Amendment protects against censorship only by local, state, or federal government officials — a group that does not include private school officials — *Tinker* does not prevent administrators at private schools from censoring their students' underground publications. Other protections may be available to private school student journalists, including more expansive state laws or constitutions,[14] public pressure, policy arguments, or previous guidelines or rules the school may have established. Courts, for example, have held that contract law or the law of associations can establish relationships that may prevent private schools from violating policies advertised or included in their own handbooks, catalogs and recruiting brochures once they have accepted tuition payments.[15]

Absent a school policy or some other specific legal protection (other than the First Amendment), private school officials probably have the right to prohibit or limit the on-campus distribution of outside publications and other media if they choose to do so. And, while private school officials cannot legally prevent their students from distributing media off-campus, they may be able to punish or expel students who do so in violation of school rules, though courts have occasionally limited the authority of private schools to punish their students' off-campus conduct.[16] Fear of bad publicity has been effective in reeling in overzealous private school officials in other cases. For more information on the rights of private school students, see Chapter 7.

K-12 School v. College

The grade level of school can also make a difference to courts dealing with independent

The law clearly protects the right of public high school and college students to distribute publications — or other material they have created independently — on school grounds during the school day.

student media cases. Several courts have recognized, at least implicitly, something of a sliding scale for First Amendment protections based on the age of the speaker. College-aged publishers of independent student media probably have more leeway making content decisions than their high school counterparts because they have an older, and theoretically more mature, audience that is demographically closer to the community at large.[17] This seems to be particularly true with respect to sexually graphic speech or content deemed "lewd" or "indecent," where courts have increasingly allowed for greater administrative controls at the elementary and secondary school levels.[18] In addition, the physical grounds of college campuses are typically larger than those of high schools, posing fewer possibilities for disruptions and interference, such as the blocking of hallways. At the same time, high school students arguably have more editorial freedom than junior high school students. They certainly enjoy more editorial freedom than elementary-aged students, since lower courts have increasingly been less-than-friendly to the country's very youngest citizens.[19]

PROTECTED SPEECH

Depending on the type and level of school, students working on independent student media enjoy legal and editorial freedoms that are not always available to those working on school-sponsored media. Indeed, such freedoms are often what attract students to work for alternative media in the first place.

Discussion of School Issues

Many students want to publish an underground newspaper to air grievances about their school and issues of concern to them. Others are simply looking for a creative and fun outlet to show off literary or artistic talents or to talk about favorite hobbies or interests. Whether they are commenting about a school board's controversial decision or reviewing rap music, independent student journalists often have more freedom to cover topics that might be deemed "too sensitive" by a newspaper affiliated with the school.

Thus, some of the school-related topics discussed in underground newspapers in recent years have included pregnancy counseling services, dress codes, student elections, political correctness, flag salutes, sex education, athletic programs, military recruiting on campus, and searches of students. Political and social issues, including commentaries on war, the economy, sexual promiscuity, drug and alcohol abuse, gay rights and curfews are also frequent topics in independent student media. Courts have come to respect frank, opinionated discussions of these serious topics, which can help teach students how to speak out on important issues. As one court noted, an out-of-class discussion among students does not "interfere with what the school teaches; it enriches the school environment for the students."[20]

PAYING THE PIPER: THE RIGHT TO ADVERTISE AND SELL STUDENT PUBLICATIONS

Although many underground (and school-sponsored) newspapers get by on meager donations of money and supplies, those able to sell advertising or sell copies of the paper as a way to recover costs may have to defend themselves against new opposition. Many schools will quickly argue that a newspaper that is sold or that contains advertisements is a commercial solicitor, like a T-shirt vendor or cell phone salesperson hawking a commercial product, which can more easily be restricted or banned from school grounds.[21]

But advertising — or "commercial speech" as courts often refer to it — is entitled to substantial First Amendment protection and can be banned or regulated only government officials have sufficient legal justification for doing so.[22] While students should steer clear of accepting misleading advertisements or publishing ads for illegal services or products because the law does not protect such ads,[23] courts have generally refused to penalize independent student media based on their decision to include otherwise lawful advertisements. However, if administrators can prove that the particular advertisement caused a substantial and material disruption, a court might then accept a ban on papers with advertising.[24] In fact, most school-sponsored newspapers include

Courts have generally struck down administrative attempts to ban a student publication simply because it is sold (or contains ads) rather than distributed freely.

---

advertisements, and schools generally cannot discriminate against an unofficial paper in favor of the official one.[25]

Similarly, courts generally have struck down school policies or attempts to ban a student publication simply because it is sold rather than distributed freely.[26] As the Supreme Court has said, "freedom of speech and freedom of the press are available to all, not merely to those who can pay their own way."[27] For more information on advertising and the law, see Chapter 20.

Religious Speech

Students who try to distribute religious materials such as Bibles or invitations to a church party sometimes run into additional roadblocks from school officials who worry that on-campus distribution might be a violation of the Establishment Clause's requirement of the separation of church and state.[28] But courts have consistently found that there is no church/state conflict when schools merely permit students to publish and distribute religious publications in the same way they publish and distribute other non-school-sponsored publications, such as fliers for a Girl Scout meeting or a youth sports league.[29] Contrary to what even many school attorneys believe, a public school that prevents an individual student from engaging in non-disruptive religious expression is far more likely to be successfully sued for a constitutional violation than a school that allows such expression.

> Courts have consistently held there is no church/state conflict when public school officials allow students to create and distribute religious-themed material on campus in the same manner that other student-created material is permitted.

School officials do not unlawfully endorse students' religious speech just by passively allowing it to occur. As one federal appeals court noted: "private speech endorsing religion is constitutionally protected — even in school. Such speech is not the school's speech even though it may occur in school."[30] Courts have held that public high school and junior high school students generally have an affirmative First Amendment right to disseminate religious materials on campus subject only to the *Tinker* standard and reasonable time, place and manner restrictions (see discussion, below).[31]

Some courts in the years after *Hazelwood* have chosen to use "forum analysis" to evaluate students' distribution rights in the context of religious materials cases.[32] This approach likens public schools to other public spaces such as parks, airports and street corners, and generally allows less freedom to distribute materials because schools are not usually freely open to the public. In any event, whether courts use forum analysis, the *Tinker* standard or some combination of the two, they have all recognized that public school officials cannot completely bar students from handing out religious materials while on campus.[33]

Student religious speech in elementary schools presents a special case, and many (though not all) courts afford less regard for the speaker's rights and more regard to the potential impact of the message on impressionable young listeners. [34] Two recent court rulings illustrate this tension. In 2008, a federal appeals court ruled that a Michigan fifth-grader had no constitutionally protected right to distribute religious messages on Christmas cards that he was "selling" as part of a school-organized "market" designed to teach about principles of retailing. Applying *Hazelwood*, the court ruled that the market was a curricular school activity and that limiting the subject matter to school-approved messages was reasonable.[35] But in 2011, a different federal appeals court found a First Amendment violation in a Texas school's decision to ban students from handing out candy canes, pencils and party invitations bearing religious messages, either during class time or during out-of-class in-school parties.[36] (However, the court declined to award the families any damages, finding that the law was so unclear that school officials would not have known they were acting unconstitutionally at the time.)[37] As these seemingly comparable cases exemplify, the level of protection afforded to speech at the lower K-12 grades is an intensely fact-specific question, and rulings will vary based on rather small distinctions in the wording of a student's message and its setting.

UNPROTECTED SPEECH

While students working on independent student media enjoy significant legal protections, the freedom to publish has never been unlimited. Legal boundaries exist, and as with any publisher, student publishers of independent media can be held legally responsible and unprotected from censorship if they cross the line. Some of the more common legal traps for independent student media are discussed below.

Libel

Just like any journalist, writers of underground newspapers must be careful not to damage people's reputations wrongfully. The size of a newspaper's audience or the informality of the publication's appearance or tone does not insulate students from potential legal liability for libel.

Potential libel problems may arise when student publishers lapse into personal attacks and name-calling. Because off-campus publishers enjoy the freedom of distributing without prior review, there may be a temptation to try to shock and to "push the envelope" by using inflammatory accusations. While not everything negative or offensive is actionable as libel, a provably false allegation of fact – "the coach is a convicted felon" when in fact he was only ticketed for speeding – can be defamatory and expose the publisher to liability whether the publication is *The New York Times* or a student blog read by three people.

Steering clear of potential libel law problems will enable an underground newspaper to live a longer life. While school officials will often cite libel as a reason for penalizing an underground newspaper's leaders, at least one court has held that high school officials must be able to prove that they would be liable for the statement they are attempting to censor — a difficult test.[38] Regardless of the analysis, a careful and reasonable assessment of potential libel issues will help underground journalists intelligently rebut possible accusations. For much more information on libel law, see Chapter 13.

Invasion of Privacy

Underground newspapers can also get into trouble when they unlawfully invade a person's privacy. One way to do this is to disclose private or embarrassing facts that would tend to humiliate the target. This might happen if a student's confidential school transcript or medical history were discussed in an underground newspaper or if a gossip column revealed intimate details about a teacher's romantic life. Although newsworthiness can protect some uses of personal information, truth is not a defense in a privacy case, as it is with libel. And although consent is a defense to a privacy claim, the consent must come from someone who is legally capable of giving it (which probably rules out young children) and must be verifiable in court.

Another common privacy problem can arise when journalists physically intrude on someone's privacy. This can happen when students trespass where they are not supposed to be (including "hacking" into a private computer system), use surveillance equipment to observe or record people secretly without proper permission, or misrepresent themselves to gain access to somewhere they would not otherwise be entitled to go. For more information on invasion of privacy, see Chapter 14.

Obscenity

Some underground publications attempt to attract attention or emphasize a point by using profane or crass language. While the law has traditionally protected simple poor taste or offensiveness, independent journalists should know that obscenity creates a potential, if unlikely, danger zone.

Unfortunately, "obscenity" is misunderstood by many school officials. The term is frequently thrown about with little thought to describe any material considered objectionable or immoral. In fact, obscenity is a specific category of unprotected speech, defined by law, and includes only what is sometimes referred to as "hard core," sexually explicit speech that has no value — artistic, literary, political, scientific or otherwise — other than to provide sexual stimulation. (A similar but slightly broader definition of obscenity has been applied to cases involving minors.[39] Thus, a high school underground publication could run into obscenity problems even if the same material would not be considered obscene on a college campus.)

While mere offensive content —including so-called "four-letter words" or profane or "earthy" language or ideas— is not legally obscene,[40] it can create unwelcome controversy and headaches. The same is true for nudity or sexually oriented images. Such materials may be offensive to some, but as long as the images do not show explicit sex acts, they are not legally obscene. Still, even if the material is legally protected, student publishers are urged to weigh its value carefully against its potential costs before going to press.

Indecent/Vulgar Speech

As discussed above, only the most sexually explicit or inappropriately targeted material can be correctly categorized as legally obscene. Despite the claims of misguided school officials, student publications almost never approach, let alone cross, the line of legal obscenity. To date, there are no reported cases of student media being successfully prosecuted for obscenity. In fact, there are a number of older court cases — most dating back to the early 1970s — upholding the right of students to use "earthy" language and crass references in unofficial publications.[41] These courts acknowledged that while such content may offend some people, it is — for better or worse — part of our society and how people communicate. In recent years, however, courts have begun expanding the zone of unprotected speech to include student speech (at least at the high school level) that is "lewd," "vulgar," "plainly offensive" or "indecent,"[42] however vague the definitions of such terms might be.[43]

The Supreme Court has allowed restrictions on school-sponsored speech by high school students where the speech is lewd and vulgar but not legally obscene. In 1986, the Court ruled in *Bethel School District v. Fraser*[44] that school officials could punish a student who delivered a student government campaign speech to a school assembly using repeated innuendos that were sexual but not obscene. The court reasoned that schools have a responsibility to teach the "'habits and manners of civility' essential to a democratic society."[45]

Courts have disagreed on the reach of *Bethel* when applying it to independent student media. One appeals court relied on *Bethel* in upholding the suspension of students who used profanity and vulgarity in their underground publication.[46] Other courts have disagreed on whether "vulgar, lewd and plainly offensive" non-school-sponsored student speech that does not rise to the level of a disruption can be banned.[47]

Thus, although underground journalists are not likely to run into problems with full-fledged obscenity in most cases, students — particularly high school students — should keep in mind the audience of the publication, the pervasiveness of any offensive material (i.e., is every other word or phrase crude or are such usages more sporadic?) and the possibility of communicating ideas in other ways so as to avoid potential problems.

A more complete discussion of obscenity law and its "indecency" progeny is available in Chapter 15.

Advocating Illegal Drug Use

As it did in 1986 when it carved out an exception to the First Amendment's protections for sexually "lewd and indecent" speech, in 2007 the Court created another topic that can be declared off-limits to high school students: speech during a "school-sanctioned" and "school-supervised" event that is perceived as advocating illegal drug use.[48] In a 5-4 decision the Court ruled in *Morse v. Frederick* that Deborah Morse, principal at Juneau-Douglas High School in Juneau, Alaska, acted lawfully when, as the Olympic torch passed through town in 2002, she crossed the street in front of the school and ripped down a banner with the cryptic message, "Bong Hits 4 Jesus," being held by then 18-year-old senior Joseph Frederick. The Court majority concluded that given the special nature of the school environment and the "serious and palpable" dangers posed by student drug abuse, public schools may "take steps to safeguard those entrusted to their care from speech that can reasonably be regarded as encouraging illegal drug use."[49]

While siding with the majority, however, Justice Samuel Alito's concurring opinion in *Morse* included an important limitation on school officials' censorship authority not only in the context of student speech about drugs but student speech generally. The Court's opinion, he wrote, "provides no support for any restriction of speech that can plausibly be interpreted as commenting on any political or social issue...."[50] In other words, "school-sanctioned" and "school-supervised" student speech that includes a political or social component — speech that is at the core of what the First Amendment was meant to protect — cannot be censored by school officials absent some other legally justified reason (for example, the speech is libelous or obscene). Indeed, had Frederick held up a banner (or presumably passed out flyers or an independent newspaper, created a private website or worn a T-shirt) that said "Legalize Marijuana" rather than the nonsensical gibberish he chose, the First Amendment should have protected it and, under Justice Alito's reasoning, he likely would have won his case.[51]

Material That Disrupts School

School officials frequently cite *Tinker*'s exception for "substantial disruption" as another reason for limiting student free speech rights. But while "substantially disruptive" allows some leeway for administrators' judgment calls, the leeway is not boundless. Indeed, the U.S. Supreme Court has recognized that protecting spirited campus debate about controversial subjects is, in part, why the First Amendment exists.[52] School officials may not prohibit speech simply because they wish to avoid the "unpleasantness" or "discomfort" that often accompanies controversial speech.[53] As one court has said: "disliking or being upset by the content of a student's speech is not an acceptable justification for limiting student speech under *Tinker*."[54] Still, *Tinker*'s protection is by no means unlimited and there are some things that independent journalists would do well to avoid.

First, underground publications should not cause or incite illegal conduct. It is one thing to report on (or even describe arguments in favor of) advocate violent political protest, sex between unmarried minors or illicit drug use. But actually leading readers through a how-to lesson on such topics probably crosses the line into incitement and makes it easier for school officials to argue students are disrupting school.

Such was the case in Wisconsin when a high school student was expelled from school his senior year after writing an article in an underground paper that gave instructions on hacking the school's computers.[55] An Oregon case involved a student expelled for writing "how-to" articles on exploding a toilet, setting off stink bombs in school, phoning in bomb threats and taking over the school intercom system.[56] Similarly, high school students in Virginia ran into trouble with school officials when they published a recipe — which they said was intended as a joke — for a marijuana dessert called "Apple Pot."[57] In an extraordinary case, a New York high school student was actually arrested in 1995 for inciting a riot after asking students to throw trash on the ground, urinate on the floor and wear certain types of T-shirts to school.[58] Incitement to engage in illegal activity is not protected in either the student press or the non-student press.

Second, specific calls to stage walkouts or protests can be banned or punished when school officials can point to recent events making it likely that students will respond to the plea.

For example, a federal court upheld an Indiana high school's decision to suspend students for handing out leaflets calling for a school walkout. The court said that a walkout by fifty-four students the day before, the noisy and rowdy atmosphere in the halls, an increase in tardiness and predictions by administrators of an even bigger walkout the next day all combined to make the leaflet distribution disruptive.[59] On the other hand, a general plea to students urging them to protest administrative action — without additional inducements — should not be sufficient to support a claim of disruption. For example, a California court found that a flier handed out by a high school student that "merely urged students to meet in the quad, the next day, to speak out on what was happening at school" and which "did not explicitly encourage students to miss class or advocate 'imminent unlawful conduct,'" could not be "construed as advocating a clear and present danger of the commission of unlawful acts on school premises, or the violation of lawful school regulations, or the substantial disruption of the orderly operation of the school."[60] (Emphasis in original).

Third, pointed ridicule or statements aimed at humiliating particular groups of students or administrators can play into the hands of school officials, who may argue — sometimes successfully, sometimes not — that such insults may lead to disruptions at school. For example, a Pennsylvania court upheld the expulsion of a junior high student based on disruption that occurred after he created a website containing offensive remarks and images about school personnel, including a depiction of a teacher's severed head dripping with blood and a "joke" solicitation for funds to cover the cost of a hit man for her execution.[61] Subsequently, however, another Pennsylvania judge ruled that a student's joking "Top Ten" list ridiculing the high school athletic director, which the student e-mailed to his friends from his home computer, did not create enough disruption to justify the author's tenday suspension.[62] In Ohio, students were disciplined for making fun of learning-disabled students and women with facial hair in their newspaper.[63] Racist messages can also fall into this category, although a school's prediction that unrest would result from racially motivated statements still might be speculative without supporting facts.[64]

Whether administrators can legally support their claims or not, students should always be conscious of giving school officials ammunition to punish or prevent speech on the grounds of potential for substantial disruption. For example, a North Carolina student who published unconfirmed reports about a principal canceling school social events and keeping bomb threats secret was accused of inciting a riot because students allegedly could not stop talking about the news during classes and even started to leave the building.[65] False announcements of class cancellations could also fall into the category of disruptions for which underground publications are held responsible. On the other hand, school officials would have a difficult time arguing that their censorship was justified if the only disruption that resulted was because of the censorship itself (for example, a student protest demanding that confiscated newspapers be released), and not because of the publication.

Keep in mind that school officials do not have to wait for a disruption; they merely must be able to reasonably forecast it. Still, underground journalists accused of causing a disruption through the content of their paper — regardless of how justified the accusation may be — can always point to the fact that no real disruption occurred after the paper was distributed. This has helped students in a number of cases.[66]

True Threats

Another related area that is becoming increasingly problematic for independent and off-campus student media is speech that represents a genuine or so-called "true threat" to the safety of others. Following the 1999 tragedy at Colorado's Columbine High and other highly publicized incidents of school violence, school officials have become increasingly sensitive to what one court described as "latent signs that a student may undertake to bring guns to school and embark on a shooting rampage. Such signs may include violence-laden student writings."[67] For example, in the summer of 2000, an Arkansas middle school student was expelled for writing an angry page of song lyrics about his former girlfriend.[68] Even though the student wrote the lyrics outside of school and never intended to send the lyrics to anyone or otherwise make them public – a "friend" surreptitiously stole them from his bedroom – the fact that they ended up on school grounds gave the court what it considered to be a sufficient justification to uphold the expulsion.[69]

A court should categorize a statement as a "true threat" unprotected by the First Amendment only where a reasonable person could believe (courts have split on whether it is the speaker's or the recipient's belief that counts)[70] that it was a serious expression of an intent to cause harm.[71] As the California Supreme Court noted in overturning a fifteen-year-old student's criminal conviction for writing and distributing so-called "dark poetry" at his high school, "ensuring a safe school environment and protecting freedom of expression... are not necessarily antagonistic goals."[72] However, as the Arkansas decision — and others — illustrate, courts have given school officials considerable leeway, and student publishers are urged to exercise caution when discussing violence.[73] Indeed, even where a court declines to find that a student's threatening or hostile speech constituted a "true threat," it may still find that the speech constituted a material and substantial disruption of regular school activities and is thus unprotected by the First Amendment.[74]

Copyright Infringement

Copyright protects authors of stories, photographs, artwork or graphics — whether they appear in print, online or in some other tangible form — from unauthorized use of their work.

Federal copyright laws do not, however, completely prevent an underground publication from using copyrighted material. Underground journalists, like anyone else, can seek permission to reproduce a photograph published in the local newspaper. The doctrine of "fair use" also allows journalists to use copyrighted materials, such as excerpts in a book review, news reporting or commentary, so long as they use no more than necessary to make their point. In addition, parodies and originally produced caricatures of cartoons necessarily use copyrighted materials as their source, and are permitted as long as they are not used merely for their recognition value or to usurp opportunities for the original author to make money off the same idea.[75] For more information on copyright law, see Chapter 16.

PRIOR REVIEW

One of the primary reasons students decide to produce independent media is to avoid the possibility of administrative interference before publication and distribution. Such systems of mandatory prior review are a type of governmental prior restraint,[76] which courts are required to examine very carefully to make sure they do not violate the Constitution's free speech guarantees.[77] At the public college level, courts have held neither independent nor school-sponsored student media can be required to submit their publications for approval by school or government officials before distribution.[78] However, lower courts continue to disagree whether high school students working on independent media are protected from mandatory administrative prior review.[79] Until the Supreme Court issues clear rulings, there will be some risk – depending on the court decisions in each local jurisdiction (some of which are described below) – that administrators might be able to insist on reviewing editorial content even if the medium is not an official school publication.[80]

In the meantime, it is important to remember that even where the law may not clearly prohibit the practice, school officials are never required to conduct prior review.[81] In fact, public pressure has sometimes been as effective — or more effective — than the law in persuading school administrators to adopt policies prohibiting administrative prior review.[82]

Courts That Forbid Prior Review

In the first post-*Hazelwood* case to address the question of administrative prior review of non-school-sponsored student media, a federal appellate court held that high school

At a public college, school officials do not have the right to require prior review of an independent student publication. At the high school level, courts are divided.

No school official is ever *required* to exercise prior review. Those that do only increase the possibility that they or their school will be held legally responsible for what non-school-sponsored student media publish.

administrators have no general right to review and change an underground newspaper before it is distributed.

In *Burch v. Barker*,[83] Washington state high school students were punished not for the content of their publication or for any disruption it caused, but solely for not submitting it for prior approval as school policy required. The U.S. Court of Appeals for the Ninth Circuit rejected the school's arguments that review was necessary to identify damaging or distracting information. The court said that *Tinker* did not call for censorship based on "undifferentiated fears of possible disturbances or embarrassment to school officials" and added that a heavy presumption exists against any prior review.[84]

The *Burch* decision, however, applies only to the Western states and territories within the Ninth Circuit. Those states and territories are Alaska, Arizona, California, Guam, Hawaii, Idaho, Montana, Nevada, Northern Mariana Islands, Oregon and Washington. Students could be forced to submit to prior review in those jurisdictions only if school officials present real evidence of a likelihood of disruption under the *Tinker* test. As always, however, students can still be held responsible for the consequences of their actions after publication, regardless of any prior review.[85]

Other courts have also been tough on schools trying to inspect and censor underground publications. In *Fujishima v. Board of Education*,[86] the Seventh Circuit ruled that high school students who produced an underground newspaper did not have to comply with a school policy requiring prior review. The court said *Tinker* allowed for after-the-fact punishment of disruptive speech, but did not create "a basis for establishing a system of censorship and licensing designed to prevent the exercise of First-Amendment rights."[87] *Fujishima*, however, also has its limits. The Seventh Circuit's jurisdiction includes only Wisconsin, Illinois and Indiana. And the Seventh Circuit has allowed prior review in other contexts. For example, in 1996, the court called prior review an "important tool in preserving a proper educational environment" in a case analyzing the distribution of religious handbills to fourth-graders.[88]

Where prior review is permitted, a prior review policy must clearly establish in writing what is forbidden and establish procedures by which students can challenge decisions to censor.

In an exceptionally pro-student decision, the California Supreme Court, relying primarily on state law, struck down a school district's prior review policy. While the court allowed that school officials were permitted to halt on-campus distribution or punish students for publishing unlawful speech, such as obscenity, they could do so only after distribution had begun.[89]

The First Circuit — which covers Maine, Massachusetts, New Hampshire, Puerto Rico and Rhode Island — also has hinted that prior review is impermissible. In *Riseman v. School Committee of City of Quincy*, the court struck down a vague rule against distributing advertising on school grounds, implying that advance content review may not be acceptable.[90]

Finally, the Fifth Circuit — which covers Louisiana, Mississippi and Texas — struck down a prior review policy that school officials used to censor parents who wished to pass out materials opposing the school's new math curriculum at an after-school public meeting.[91] Unfortunately, the decision, which was specifically limited to parental distribution rights, may be of limited help to the independent student media.

Courts That Examine School Policies

Some of the other federal appeals courts (there are 13 in all) take a different approach to prior review. They believe that prior review is acceptable — at least in theory — with sufficient safeguards.[92] In these jurisdictions, there is no hard-and-fast rule, and the legality of any prior review regime will depend on the details of how it is applied. Thus, even where a court does not categorically disapprove of prior review, a particular school's practice may provide inadequate safeguards to survive a First Amendment challenge.

TYPICAL NON-SCHOOL-SPONSORED STUDENT MEDIA POLICY

Most school policies that apply to non-school sponsored student media will have certain elements in common. Typically, they will:

1. Apply not only to underground newspapers but also any book, tract or other publication to be distributed on school grounds.
2. Require submission of a copy of the material to a designated school official at a specified time before the material is to be distributed, typically 24 or 48 hours.
3. Provide a set of reasons that the school official can cite as grounds for rejecting the proposed distribution. These often include bans on materials that are substantially disruptive, obscene or libelous.
4. Specify that a student can appeal the official's ruling within a certain period of time.

Common Flaws in a Policy

Just because school administrators adopt a policy does not mean a court will uphold it. Many courts have pointed out pitfalls that schools must avoid when creating prior review policies. A survey of some of these observations may help in spotting an unenforceable provision that will prevent school officials from unlawfully censoring independent student media.

While a school's conduct code or speech policy "need not define the forbidden conduct with mathematical precision,"[93] such guidelines must inform a reasonably intelligent student of what is prohibited[94] and prohibit arbitrary enforcement by school officials.[95] This means that key terms such as "substantial disruption," "libel" or "obscenity" should be correctly defined in the policy.[96] Other terms, such as a policy that prohibits "inappropriate,"[97] "abusive,"[98] "irresponsible,"[99] or "demeaning" language or that bans material that is of "poor taste," are simply so vague that they would almost always be struck by a court. The policy should include examples of or criteria related to any prohibited expression.[100] Unwritten or poorly distributed policies will likely be void.[101]

The policy also cannot be "overbroad," or include unlimited administrative discretion or legally unnecessary reasons to censor a publication. Policies with these provisions could leave censorship decisions to administrators' whims or the "mere desire to avoid the discomfort and unpleasantness of speech."[102] Schools that conduct prior review cannot suppress underground papers solely because they are vigorous critics of a school system or take a controversial political or social stance that differs from that of the majority of the community.[103]

Vague and overbroad language has also frequently doomed so-called "speech codes,"[104] which have sometimes been used by schools to ban independent student media.

Among the actual school policies struck down by courts are those allowing school officials to censor a publication because it: did not conform to "the journalistic standards of accuracy, taste and decency maintained by the newspapers of general circulation in the city;"[105] was "alien to school purposes;"[106] "advocates illegal actions, or is grossly insulting to any group or individual;"[107] or was "productive of, or likely to produce a significant disruption of the normal educational processes, functions or purposes in any of the city schools or injuries to others."[108]

Finally, a policy must also clearly tell students to whom the material must be submitted for approval.[109] A decision must be reached on the status of the publication within a reasonable time after submission, and the policy should specify what happens if school officials fail to make a timely decision.[110]

Due Process Rights for Independent Student Journalists

In addition to the more substantive protections discussed above, students may have a defense where school rules — or the way school officials apply those rules when handing down discipline — violate their right to a full and fair procedural review. A meeting in the principal's office may be less formal than a trial in a courtroom, but an administrator's failure to treat a student fairly and provide sufficient "due process" rights can create significant legal problems for the school.[111]

For example, students must have adequate written "notice" of the relevant school distribution policy. This does not mean that each student must actually receive the policy or be told of it personally. Instead, it means that a school district must publish the policy in school publications or circulate it in the same manner as other official school materials.[112] This prevents schools from relying on oral policies, keeping policies secret or enforcing policies haphazardly. To satisfy the publication requirement, many schools may simply include the policy in a student rights handbook given out annually, publish it in a beginning-of-the-year newsletter or post it on the school's website.

In addition, school officials must provide a student accused of wrongdoing with any evidence they have in support of the student's guilt, and must give students a chance to argue why distribution of their publication should be allowed.[113] Again, this hearing does not have to be particularly formal, but it does have to be granted promptly and allow the affected students a chance to present their side.[114] There is no guarantee the school official will listen or agree, but students should at least have a chance to explain their legal rights and their reason for wanting to distribute the publication.

Finally, students should be given the chance to appeal a school official's decision to censor or ban a publication. Again, the appellate review must be prompt and allow students a chance to state their case.[115] While the person overseeing the appeal is likely to be a school district administrator who may not be any more sympathetic to a student's case than a principal or other lower-level administrator, the process nevertheless provides an opportunity for a second hearing before resorting to the public court system.

These same "due process" principles also apply to a student's right to contest his or her punishment when suspended or expelled.[116] In such cases, the due process that must be afforded a student depends on the length of the sanctions and the particular circumstances involved, with more serious punishments requiring greater procedural protections.[117]

The law protects the publication and distribution of anonymous material.

TO BE (IDENTIFIED) OR NOT TO BE? ANONYMOUS PUBLICATIONS

Many independent journalists want to expose their ideas, but not their identities. They may justifiably fear retribution from teachers and administrators or scorn from their classmates. In fact, the U.S. Supreme Court has recognized that an "honorable tradition" of anonymous speech has existed throughout American history.[118] However, while the law clearly protects anonymous (or pseudonymous) speech, complete anonymity may not always be possible to achieve.

For example, in states that permit prior review of underground publications, at least one person often will need to be identified as a contact to communicate with administrators reviewing the publication. School officials may also want a contact in case problems arise during distribution. This need not be an individual or student responsible for having produced the content of the publication, but rather an "agent" willing to act as a go-between.

Beyond these minimal conditions, however, there is no requirement that everyone involved with a student newspaper be identified in its pages or to school officials (though school officials may attempt to track down such information on their own). As one court has said, a prohibition against anonymous literature can unlawfully deter campus free speech because "without anonymity, fear of reprisal may deter peaceful discussion of controversial but important school rules and policies."[119]

Disclaimers of School Sponsorship

One of the best and easiest things independent student journalists can do to stay out of trouble is to alert readers clearly — typically by way of a prominently published, written disclaimer — that their publication is, in fact, independent and that school officials have nothing to do with it. Such a disclaimer can strip school officials of one of their more common arguments against an independently produced student publication: namely, that people will be confused by it and believe it was created and supported by or affiliated with the school.

This happened at a North Carolina university, where school officials complained that the paper's name incorporated the school's name and used the school's seal in its masthead. The paper denied using protected material or trying to confuse people, but did change its secondary title from an "independent journal of" the school to an "independent journal at" the school.[120] In Missouri, a student was expelled from his private college because school officials alleged his alternative newspaper had misled advertisers into thinking it was affiliated with the school.[121]

A disclaimer need not be fancy. For example, a simple statement in the flag or masthead of a publication that reads "this publication is not affiliated with Anytown High School and its contents are not endorsed by the school" is probably sufficient. Such a phrase may not shield you from all legal problems, but it does show you are taking reasonable steps to prevent confusion. It also provides school officials with some cover when trying to explain to upset readers and community members why they are powerless to censor or punish students working on media published apart from the school.

The Right of Students to Distribute at School

Public schools cannot enforce an outright ban on the distribution of independently produced student newspapers any more than they can ban their creation.[122] However, schools can legally adopt reasonable rules regarding on-campus distribution of which students should be aware.

First, independent journalists should remember that *Tinker* allows schools to prevent reasonably anticipated substantial and material disruptions. No matter how eloquent the articles in an underground newspaper may be, students who want to form a human chain across a hallway to hand out their paper will have a tough case. So will students who insist on handing out the latest issue in the middle of a science class. Administrators are entitled to make sure the normal operations of a school proceed without interruption.

School officials may impose what are called reasonable "time, place and manner" regulations on an independent student publication's distribution.[123] These policies may not unreasonably stifle a paper's freedom, or deter or discriminate against its message, but should be aimed at "promoting the orderly administration of school activities by preventing disruption."[124]

School officials can enforce reasonable regulations as to the time, place and manner of campus distribution of student media.

WHEN IS DISTRIBUTION DISRUPTIVE?

Reported cases provide some insight into what kind of disturbances are necessary for school officials to be able to restrict distribution of an underground newspaper.

For example, there is little doubt that school officials can legally prohibit students from distributing papers in the middle of a class.[125] School officials can also likely prohibit the reading of newspapers or discussion of their content during class and punish people who disobey the rule, but neither is an adequate reason to ban distribution of the paper in the first place.[126]

Other possibly legitimate reasons for stopping distribution are direct threats to student safety and damage to property resulting from the actual act of distribution. In its *Tinker* decision, for example, the Supreme Court cited as an example of disruption a case in which buttons advocating equal rights for African-Americans were forced on students and thrown through windows.[127]

Still, in the vast majority of cases little disruption is likely to result from the orderly distribution of a publication (and of course, none at all if distribution is via the Web). Mere objection by other students to the distribution or disagreement with a publication's content (the so-called "heckler's veto") is not enough, for that would create "a license to prohibit virtually every type of expression."[128]

"Time, Place And Manner" Regulations

In real life, reasonable "time, place and manner" regulations often mean that schools establish a general area and a time for students to hand out their media. Making a blanket policy heads off a case-by-case debate every time some individual or organization seeks to hand out materials.

To be "reasonable," time, place and manner regulations must advance a "significant" government interest rather than the mere whim of those in power.[129] Ensuring the safety of persons on school property and preventing disruption of the educational process are commonly accepted by courts as being significant government interests.[130] On the other hand, restricting distribution simply to keep a campus pretty and litter-free is probably not a sufficient government interest, unless it can be accomplished with little adverse effect on the underlying speech.[131] Any restrictions must also be narrowly tailored: school officials should strive to develop and choose the least restrictive distribution rules that will accomplish their goal. In addition, regulations must be "content-neutral" and must not be based on any attempt to restrict what is being said.[132] Finally, regulations must leave open ample and effective alternative channels of communication. For example, it would not be reasonable to restrict distribution of an independent student newspaper to a time when students are no longer in the building or to a place where students never venture. Some schools may find it easiest to restrict distribution of an underground paper to the same time and place used by the school-sponsored paper.[133] Schools will generally have a tough time justifying a policy that gives alternative papers less favorable distribution settings than those provided to an official campus publication.[134]

Typically, distribution policies will instruct students to distribute their work in an area away from active school classrooms (for example, in the cafeteria, near the library and at or near school entrances and exits) and outside of teaching hours. Such was the result of negotiations at a Washington State high school, where students agreed to give school officials two hours notice and then peacefully distribute their independent newspaper near key school entrances and exits and in the cafeteria for fifteen minutes before school, during lunch and after school.[135]

OFF-CAMPUS STUDENT MEDIA: THE THIRD CATEGORY

So far, this chapter has focused on the rights of publishers of independent, or "underground," student media. Earlier chapters discussed the rights of high school, college and private school students when working on "official," school-sponsored student media. But there is a third category: off-campus student media.

In recent years, courts have recognized these three separate categories when determining the degree of censorship or control that school officials — more specifically, public high school officials — are permitted to exercise over the speech activities of their students.[136] (Public college officials have more limited ability to regulate or punish student speech, regardless of the setting.[137] Private school officials, who are not bound by the First Amendment, are also governed by different rules that can vary significantly by school.[138])

Time, place and manner regulations are limited to concerns related to distribution. They must be "content-neutral" and must not be based on any attempt to restrict what is being said.

While the law remains fluid, student publishers of off-campus speech traditionally have been entitled to the strongest First Amendment protections from administrative censorship or punishment. Where school officials are unable to show that students conducted speech-related activities at school or as part of an official school event, courts have traditionally concluded that school officials lack authority to limit such speech or to punish the students involved.[139]

When outside of school, these courts have concluded that students should have the same free speech rights as any other citizen. As the Supreme Court has said, "students in school as well as out of school are 'persons' under our Constitution. They are possessed of fundamental rights which the State must respect...."[140]

In *Thomas v. Board of Education, Granville Central School District*,[141] for example, four high school students published an underground newspaper with their own money and distributed it off-campus before and after school. The students were suspended for five days, had to write essays on the harm their speech caused and had suspension letters included in their permanent files. The school alleged that the students' speech had caused a disturbance on campus and that their paper was obscene; the court found no evidence to support either claim.[142]

The students had asked an English teacher occasional questions and typed a few of the articles on school typewriters. Even so, such a minimal use of school resources did not change the court's assessment that the students were essentially operating off campus.[143] The court noted that no school funds were used to produce the paper and that a notice disclaiming any connection to the school was included in the paper.

In ruling for the students, the *Thomas* court was clear: "the First Amendment forbids public school administrators and teachers from regulating the material to which a child is exposed after he leaves school each afternoon."[144]

After-school hours are traditionally the realm of parents, the court said, and therefore the court was loath to allow the school to regulate that time.[145] As members of the public, students are subject to the same laws as any other citizen, and therefore school regulations are unnecessary, the court said.

In addition, the court was wary of the potential consequences of allowing such regulation. If the court upheld the regulation, it wondered whether school officials might not then be able to punish a student who lawfully purchased a "bad" magazine off-campus and then lent it, or "distributed" it, to a friend while visiting the friend's house. The court rejected such far-reaching administrative control and commented that after-school activities are "the proper subjects of parental discipline"[146] The court held that in such situations, school officials were not empowered to assume the role of parens patriae (surrogate parent).[147]

A Texas court responded in a similar vein, chastising school officials who sought to punish students for the off-campus distribution of an independent newspaper the students had created:

> "It should have come as a shock to the parents of five high school seniors... that their elected school board had assumed suzerainty [control] over their children before and after school, off school grounds, and with regard to their children's rights of expressing their thoughts. We trust that it will come as no shock whatsoever to the school board that their assumption of authority is an unconstitutional usurpation of the First Amendment."[148]

Courts have, however, sometimes expressed a willingness to "fudge" the geographic boundaries of on-campus speech to include some off-campus speech that had a direct and significant impact on school grounds.

For example, a Texas court upheld the ability of school officials to regulate the distribution of publications handed out "near" campus in a "manner calculated to result in their presence on the campus."[149] Another court stated that "the width of a street might very well determine the breadth of the school board's authority,"[150] suggesting its willingness to adopt a "sliding scale" to determine how far off campus school authorities' power extends. Under this court's rationale, peaceful and orderly student speech that took place just outside school grounds could not be subject to school regulation while speech that significantly disrupted school activities might be regulated, even when it occurred some distance away.

This sliding scale approach appears to have gained momentum in recent years — particularly with the growth of online speech and the pervasiveness of smartphones — as a growing number of courts have been more open to the idea that where student speech takes place is less important than how the speech affects a school.[151] For these courts, the test is not one of geography, but rather the impact — or, in many cases, the anticipated impact — of the student's off-campus speech. Under this approach, where school officials can demonstrate that it is: (1) reasonably foreseeable that the speech (or the effects of the speech) will appear on school property and (2) reasonably foreseeable that the speech will materially and substantially disrupt normal school activities (the *Tinker* standard), punishment of students' off-campus speech is permissible.

The U.S. Supreme Court has yet to say directly how much authority school officials are permitted to exercise over students when they are off school grounds and not involved in a school-sponsored activity. In its 2007 *Morse v. Frederick* decision (better known by many as the "Bong Hits 4 Jesus" case), the Court dodged the question when it upheld the authority of school officials to punish an 18-year-old Alaskan high school student for holding up a banner on a public sidewalk across the street from his high school while the Olympic torch passed through downtown Juneau. The Court conceded the event was not "school-sponsored," but because of heavy school involvement — students were permitted to leave class to watch, and were under teacher supervision — the event was "school sanctioned," and so the speech was regarded as being on-campus. *Morse* does not answer how the Court might (or might not) allow school authorities to regulate truly off-campus speech that reaches the school only through its effects.

Finally, a few courts have allowed schools to punish students for engaging in otherwise lawful speech off school grounds not because of the content of the speech, but rather because of the students' inappropriate conduct. In 1973, for example, a high school student in Texas distributed a newspaper off campus and after school. The principal suspended him for violating a prior review policy.[152] As the student left the principal's office, he slammed the door and swore at the secretary. The student continued to come on campus during his suspension and swore again, this time at the principal.

In upholding the student's suspension the court did not deal with the question of his published speech or the validity of the school's policy. Rather, it concentrated on the student's actions. The court was clearly disturbed by what it viewed as a flagrant disregard of authority. The court found that the student's actions after distribution of his newspaper disrupted the school day; therefore, his speech rights were trumped by the school's interest in maintaining a peaceful school environment.

As the court wrote: "we ask only that the student seeking equitable relief from allegedly unconstitutional actions by school officials come into court with clean hands."[153] For more information on free speech protections for student publishers of off-campus websites and other online speech — including practical tips for staying out of trouble — see Chapter 9.

SUMMARY

Sadly, many students today have found that "official," school-sponsored media no longer provide an opportunity to meaningfully express their ideas or inform their peers about news and issues they deem important. Censorship has become the rule at many schools, leading to bland publications that are often more administrative "P.R. puff pieces" than a genuine forum for expression by and for students. Even where censorship is not a problem, students may simply want a change or the freedom to create a fresh "voice" that is all their own.

Whatever their motivation, students in the 21st century have more alternatives than ever to make their voices heard. Personal computers, desktop printers, e-mail, blogs and text-messaging allow students to appoint themselves "publishers" and "distributors" (and such technology also forces students to assume responsibility for everything that they create).

Unfortunately, school officials too often fail to understand or respect the significant legal limitations placed upon their authority to control or punish non-school-sponsored, "private" student speech; administrative battles with student "underground" publishers are common.

For off-campus student speakers, the legal protections remain strong, but courts appear increasingly willing to blur the boundaries between on and off-school speech. Unfortunately, lacking clear guidance from the Supreme Court, it is likely that the confusion for school officials and the conflict among lower courts faced with the question of deciding where, when and how much authority school officials have over the off-campus lives of their students will continue. Some courts continue to recognize what they believe is a reasonably hard line between in-school and out-of-school student speech and conduct. Other courts seem to be okay with the idea that the authority of school officials can extend far beyond the schoolhouse gate, allowing them virtually 24/7 authority to punish students for speech that clearly would be protected were the speaker a non-student.

Still, while the path to true freedom of the press may sometimes take nontraditional routes and often seem like an uphill battle, the rewards — for many students — are worth it.

CASE STUDY

Riley Rambo had had it. For the third issue in a row, the principal had cut his article from the student newspaper, *Hi Tales*. The latest, which he'd worked on for more than two weeks, detailed health code violations that had been issued to his public high school's cafeteria. The principal simply said it was "too negative." After talking it over with a half-dozen similarly frustrated staff members, they reluctantly decided that the time had come to cut their ties to *Hi Tales* and strike out on their own. *Lo Tales* was born.

The staff met at Rambo's house. Rambo's aunt was the publisher of the local newspaper and agreed to print 1,000 copies of *Lo Tales* once a month for free. In putting together their first issue, the staff used their home computers, with one exception: because of a tight deadline, Rambo used a computer in the school library to make final edits to one article during his lunch period. The staff interviewed students and teachers both at home and during non-class periods at school. At the same time, they also took some photos around school using personal cameras.

A week before the first issue was ready, the principal, having gotten wind of *Lo Tales*, called Rambo into the office and handed him a copy of the school's newly adopted "Student Media Policy," which read: "School-sponsored student media are subject to review and approval by the principal prior to distribution. The principal reserves the right to prevent distribution where he has a reasonable educational justification for doing so. Once approved, school-sponsored media can be distributed to students in the lunchroom, outside the library and at the school's main entrance 15 minutes before and after school and during the lunch period.

Non-school-sponsored student media must be submitted to the principal for review and approval one week prior to distribution. Material will not be approved that is libelous, indecent, ungrammatical, unfair, poorly written, demeaning, disrespectful to school authorities or otherwise objectionable. Advertising is not permitted. Violations of this policy will result in suspension or expulsion. All decisions by the principal are final. If approved, material may only be distributed from behind a table in front of the main office between 7:30 - 7:45 a.m. The table and all material must be cleared away before school starts at 8:00 a.m."

The *Lo Tales* staff is upset and Rambo calls you for help. He doesn't see how they can work under such a policy. "Heck," Rambo says, "even if anything got past the principal under this policy, nobody even gets to school much before 7:45 in the morning anyway." Rambo calls you for help. What can you tell him?

ANSWER : First, *Lo Tales* is properly categorized as non-school-sponsored student media. Simply using a school computer once, during a student's personal time, to edit a story should not jeopardize *Lo Tales*' status as non-school-sponsored student media. You tell Rambo, however, that to be absolutely safe from here on you don't want him using school computers (or any other school resource or equipment) for anything — deadline or not. The fact that students conduct interviews or take photos while at school — again, during non-class periods — should have no bearing on *Lo Tales*' "independent" status. Students have the right to observe and record what goes on around them in public areas at school.

As for the policy itself, it is clearly unconstitutional — at least as it applies to non-school-sponsored student media.

The first problem with the policy is that it contains terms that are so vague that no student (or administrator, for that matter) could reasonably determine what is allowed and what is forbidden. For example, how does one determine whether an article is "poorly written" or whether it is "unfair?" Such terms are undefined by law and are incapable of providing *Lo Tales* staffers with a reasonable understanding of what they can and cannot publish. Courts routinely strike down government speech policies or laws that contain such vaguely defined terms because they give government officials too much personal discretion.

Second, the policy appears to ban speech that is clearly protected by the Constitution. Non-schoolsponsored student speech in public high schools is protected by the Supreme Court's decision in Tinker. Under the Tinker standard, school officials can restrict independent student speech only where they can show that it will cause a serious, physical disruption to normal school activities or is otherwise unlawful. The excessively broad "Student Media Policy" plainly restricts speech far beyond that. While the principal has the right to restrict "libelous" material and may, according to some courts, have the right to restrict "indecent" speech (although the term indecency arguably suffers from the same vagueness problems as described above[154]), the First Amendment does not permit him to restrict speech that is, for example, "ungrammatical," "disrespectful," or — the catchall — "otherwise objectionable." The law protects speech that contains misplaced commas or that criticizes government officials. Indeed, if the policy protected only speech to which no one "objected," there would be nothing left of the First Amendment. Finally, a blanket prohibition on advertising is unlawful. The First Amendment protects speech whether it is paid for or not.

Whether the principal has the right to look over and approve *Lo Tales* before it is distributed will probably depend on where the high school is located. So far, courts in different jurisdictions have been split on the issue of whether school officials can require that independent student media be submitted for prior review. Even if *Lo Tales* will be distributed in a state where courts have allowed for such prior review (or if they have not yet addressed the issue and *Lo Tales* does not want to legally contest it), it is still clear that the policy needs to be fixed. Requiring that the paper be submitted one week in advance is almost certainly unreasonable. News goes stale and the *Lo Tales* staff probably has the right to expect an answer from administrators within about 48 hours of submitting the paper for review. Moreover, the policy lacks an adequate appeal process. Simply because the principal says "the principal's decision is final" does not make it so. Courts have frequently struck down policies that fail to provide for a meaningful appeal.

Finally, while the principal has the right to establish time, place and manner regulations regarding how, when and where *Lo Tales* is distributed, they must be reasonable. These are not. Time, place and manner regulations must not only make sense and be content-neutral, they must also provide speakers with a reasonable opportunity to get their message out. Limiting *Lo Tales* distribution to one sequestered location and a 15-minute time period when few students will be in school to pick up a copy is not reasonable. An independent student publication should have pretty much the same distribution rights that are provided to "official," school-sponsored student media (assuming their distribution rights are also reasonable). If the official student newspaper has distributed its copies just before, during and after school with no problems, the principal will be hard-pressed to explain why providing *Lo Tales* with the same privileges would be unworkable.

You suggest to Rambo that he take this information back to his principal and politely ask that he revise his policy. If he refuses, Rambo should appeal the principal's decision to the superintendent and, if necessary, to the school board. Depending on the response he receives from the principal and superintendent, you tell him, it would probably help to alert parents, community groups and the local media. The good news is the law is clearly on their side. The bad news is —as any teacher will tell you— it can take a great deal of time and energy to teach those who don't really want to learn.

ENDNOTES

1   *Hazelwood Sch. Dist. v. Kuhlmeier*, 484 U.S. 260 (1988).
2   The *Hazelwood* Court noted that its decision applied only to "school-sponsored publications, theatrical productions, and other expressive activities that students, parents and members of the public might reasonably perceive to bear the imprimatur of the school." 484 U.S. at 271. The Court explicitly excluded "underground" newspapers from *Hazelwood*'s reach. Id. n.3.
3   *See, e.g.*, Taylor Moak, "Out from Under," Student Press Law Center *Report*, Fall 2012, http://www.splc.org/news/report_detail.asp?id=1644&edition=59 (Kentucky students created paper and online alternative newspaper after principal refused to allow mentions of homosexuality in student media); Britt Hulit, "Wisc. student journalists create independent publication to counter official's censorship," SPLC *News Flash*, May 18, 2005, http://www.splc.org/news/newsflash.asp?id=1011; "Underground papers also fall prey to censorship," Student Press Law Center Report, Spring 2002, p. 23 (Massachusetts high school students started an independent paper after attempts to work with the principal to create a school-sponsored newspaper failed); "The tiger uncaged," Student Press Law Center *Report*, Fall 1994, p. 4 (Arkansas high school students published and distributed a four-page newspaper off school grounds after their principal ordered the paper's staff to apologize and submit the paper to prior review); "Alternative press is battlefront in today's post-*Hazelwood* world," Student Press Law Center *Report*, Fall 1992, p. 3; "Hammer makes waves, keeps on publishing," Student Press Law Center *Report*, Fall 1990, p. 14 (California high school students created an underground paper after school officials censored a letter to the editor that was critical of the school's principal).
4   *See, e.g.*, *Widmar v. Vincent*, 454 U.S. 263, 268 n.5 (1981) ("We have not held, for example, that a campus must make all of its facilities equally available to students and nonstudents alike"); *Hays County Guardian v. Supple*, 969 F.2d 111, 121 (5th Cir. 1992) (arguing that the "[u]niversity need not give students and nonstudents equal access to the [u]niversity campus" (referencing *Perry Educ. Ass'n v. Perry Local Educators' Ass'n*, 460 U.S. 37, 44)); *ACLU Student Chapter-Univ. of Maryland, College Park v. Mote*, 321 F. Supp. 2d 670 (D. Md. 2004) (holding that a state university's decision to restrict outsider access to its campus did not violate the First Amendment). *See also Hedges v. Wauconda Community Unit Sch. Dist.*, 9 F.3d 1295 (7th Cir. 1993) (upholding the constitutionality of a school policy that limited the distribution of materials created primarily by nonstudents to ten copies or less); *Gilles v. Torgersen*, 71 F.3d 497 (4th Cir. 1995) (dismissing a challenge to a university policy that required potential campus speakers to obtain an official university sponsor). *But cf. Chiu v. Plano Indep. Sch. Dist.*, 339 F.3d 273 (5th Cir. 2003), *cert. dismissed*, 540 U.S. 1071 (2003) (upholding parents' claim against a school district after administrators prevented them from circulating a petition and distributing materials opposing a new math curriculum while attending a parents-only informational meeting held on school grounds); *Hills v. Scottsdale Unified Sch. Dist. No. 48*, 329 F.3d 1044 (9th Cir. 2003), *cert. denied*, 540 U.S. 1149 (2004) (holding that a school district could not prohibit the distribution of flyers by a nonstudent group advertising a religious summer camp); *Peterson v. Bd. of Educ.*, 370 F. Supp. 1208 (D. Neb. 1973) (finding that a high school's on-campus ban against independent newspapers distributed by nonstudents was an invalid prior restraint on free speech).
5   *See* "Utah student sings censorship," Student Press Law Center *Report*, Spring 1999, p. 7 (a Utah high school principal threatened to arrest a student editor of an underground paper if the student tried to distribute the paper on the sidewalks adjacent to school property; the principal subsequently confiscated copies of the paper that were distributed off campus). *See also Thomas v. Bd. of Educ.*, 607 F.2d 1043, 1051 (2d Cir. 1979) (holding that a high school violated its students' constitutional rights when it suspended them for publishing an off-campus newspaper).
6   *Tinker v. Des Moines Indep. Community Sch. Dist.*, 393 U.S. 503, 506 (1969).
7   *Id.* at 515.
8   *Id.* at 513.
9   *Id.* at 509, 514.
10 *Rivera v. East Otero Sch. Dist.* R-1, 721 F. Supp. 1189, 1194 (D. Colo. 1989).
11 To date, only one Supreme Court justice — Clarence Thomas — has indicated a desire to overrule *Tinker*. *Morse v. Frederick*, 127 S. Ct. 2618, 2636 (2007) (Thomas, J., concurring).

12 *Hazelwood* Sch. Dist. v. Kuhlmeier, 484 U.S. 260, 266 (1988).

13 For high school cases, *See, e.g., Burch v. Barker*, 861 F.2d 1149 (9th Cir. 1988); *Bystrom v. Fridley High Sch.* (Bystrom I), 822 F.2d 747 (8th Cir. 1987); *Baughman v. Freienmuth*, 478 F.2d 1345 (4th Cir. 1973); *Fujishima v. Bd. of Educ.*, 460 F.2d 1355 (7th Cir. 1972); *Shanley v. Northeast Indep. Sch. Dist.*, 462 F.2d 960 (5th Cir. 1972); *Eisner v. Stamford Bd. of Educ.*, 440 F.2d 803 (2d Cir. 1971); *Riseman v. Sch. Committee of Quincy*, 439 F.2d 148 (1st Cir. 1971); *Slotterback v. Interboro Sch. Dist.*, 766 F. Supp. 280 (E.D. Pa. 1991); *Rivera v. East Ottero Sch. Dist.*, 721 F. Supp. 1189 (D. Colo. 1989); *Cintron v. State Bd. of Educ.*, 384 F. Supp. 674 (D.P.R. 1974); *Hatter v. Los Angeles City High Sch. Dist.*, 452 F.2d 673 (9th Cir. 1971); *Barcik v. Kubiaczyk*, 912 P.2d 408 (Or. Ct. App. 1996); *Hedges v. Wauconda Community Unit Sch. Dist. No. 118*, 9 F.3d 1295 (7th Cir. 1993); *Clark v. Dallas Indep. Sch. Dist.*, 806 F. Supp. 116, 120 (N.D. Tex. 1992); *Thompson v. Waynesboro Area Sch. Dist.*, 673 F. Supp. 1379 (M.D. Pa. 1987); *Johnston-Loehner v. O'Brien*, 859 F. Supp 575 (M.D. Fla. 1994); *Nelson v. Moline Sch. Dist. No. 40*, 725 F. Supp. 965 (C.D. Ill. 1989). For college cases, *See, e.g., Papish v. Bd. of Curators of Univ. of Missouri*, 410 U.S. 667, 670 (1973); *Hays County Guardian v. Supple*, 969 F.2d 111 (5th Cir. 1992); *Spartacus Youth League v. Bd. of Trustees*, 502 F. Supp. 789 (N.D. Ill. 1980); *Channing Club v. Bd. of Regents*, 317 F. Supp. 688 (N.D. Tex. 1970).

14 *See, e.g.*, CAL. EDUC. CODE SEC 48950 (high schools), *available at* http://www.splc.org/knowyourrights/law_library.asp?id=13 § 94367 (colleges and universities) *available at* http://www.splc.org/knowyourrights/law_library.asp?id=14.

15 *See Steinberg v. Chicago Medical Sch.*, 69 Ill.2d 320 (1977). *See also Clayton v. Trustees of Princeton Univ.*, 519 F. Supp. 802 (D.N.J. 1981).

16 *See, e.g., Stanoch v. Breck Sch.*, No. CT 02-019852 (Minn. Dist. Ct., 4th Judicial Dist. Nov. 21, 2002) (granting temporary restraining order against private school that expelled a student for off-campus possession of drug paraphernalia, as the punishment violated the school's contract with the student).

17 *See Healy v. James*, 408 U.S. 169, 180-81 (1972); *Bd. of Regents of the Univ. of Wisconsin Sys. v. Southworth*, 529 U.S. 217, 239 n.4 (2000) (Souter, J., concurring in the judgment) ("Our . . . cases dealing with the right of teaching institutions to limit expressive freedom of students have been confined to high schools, whose students and their school's relation to them are different and at least arguably distinguishable from their counterparts in college education") (citations omitted); *Thonen v. Jenkins*, 491 F.2d 722 (4th Cir. 1973); *Nuxoll v. Indian Prairie Sch. Dist. #204*, 523 F.3d 668, 671, 674 (7th Cir. 2008) (finding a distinction between the First Amendment protection accorded "adult debates on social issues," which are "more valuable than debates among children" because "the contribution that kids can make to the marketplace in ideas and opinions is modest") (citing *Rosenberger v. Rector & Visitors of University of Virginia*, 515 U.S. 819, 829); *Bystrom v. Fridley High Sch.* (Bystrom I), 822 F.2d 747, 750 (8th Cir. 1987); *Schwartz v. Schuker*, 298 F.Supp. 238, 242 (D.C.N.Y. 1969) (noting that "the activities of high school students do not always fall within the same category as the conduct of college students, the former being in a much more adolescent and immature stage of life and less able to screen fact from propaganda").

18 *Bethel Sch. Dist. No. 403 v. Fraser*, 478 U.S. 675, 683 (1986) (holding that "[t]he schools, as instruments of the state, may determine that the essential lessons of civil, mature conduct cannot be conveyed in a school that tolerates lewd, indecent, or offensive speech...."); *Bystrom*, 822 F.2d at 751-53; *Saxe v. State College Area Sch. Dist.*, 240 F.3d 200, 213 (3d Cir. 2001).

19 *See, e.g., Walker-Serrano v. Leonard*, 325 F.3d 412, 416-17 (3d Cir. 2003) (finding that school administrators did not violate an elementary school student's First Amendment rights when they prevented her from circulating a petition against a class field trip to the circus, for "if third graders enjoy rights under *Tinker*, those rights will necessarily be very limited"); *S.G. v. Sayerville Bd. of Educ.*, 333 F.3d 417, 423 (3d Cir. 2003), *cert. denied*, 40 U.S. 1104 (2004) (upholding a school's three-day suspension of a kindergarten student who said "I'm going to shoot you" during a game of cops-and-robbers at recess and finding that "a school's authority to control speech in an elementary school setting is undoubtedly greater than in a high school setting"); *Walz v. Egg Harbor Township Bd. of Educ.*, 342 F.3d 271 (3d Cir. 2003), *cert. denied*, 541 U.S. 936 (2004) (holding that an elementary school did not violate the First Amendment when it prohibited students from distributing gifts with religious messages during classroom holiday parties); *Sonkowksy v. Bd. of Educ. for Indep. Sch. Dist. No. 721*, 327 F.3d 675, 677 (8th Cir. 2003) (rejecting a Minnesota elementary school student's claim that the school violated his rights by not permitting him to wear a Green Bay Packers jacket on a field trip to the Minnesota Vikings' practice facilities and by not allowing him to color an associated project with rival team colors, for even if it could be assumed that "a fourth-grader. . . has a constitutionally protected right to free expression at school, that right was not violated when school officials required adherence to directions on school projects"); *C.H. v. Oliva*, 990 F.Supp. 341 (D.N.J. 1997), *aff'd*, 166 F.3d 1204 (3d Cir. 1998), *aff'd* in part on reh'g en banc, 226 F.3d 198 (3d Cir. 2000), *cert. denied* sub. nom., *Hood v. Medford Township Bd. of Educ.*, 533 U.S. 915 (2001) (finding no First Amendment violation where elementary school officials prohibited a student from reading a religious story to classmates and moved the student's drawing of Jesus to a less prominent location). *But see Morgan v. Swanson*, 659 F.3d 359, 409 (5th Cir. 2011) (en banc) (stating, in case involving religious speech by Texas elementary-school students, "viewpoint discrimination against private, student-to-student, non-disruptive speech is forbidden by the First Amendment"); *Slotterback v. Interboro Sch. Dist.*, 766 F. Supp. 280, 296, 301 (E.D. Pa. 1991) ("Even at the elementary school level...the school district's current content-based ban [on 'material(s) that proselytizes a particular religious or political belief'] is substantially overbroad.").

20 *Burch v. Barker*, 861 F.2d 1149, 1159 (9th Cir. 1988).

21 *Texas Review Society v. Cunningham*, 659 F. Supp. 1239 (W.D. Tex. 1987) (upholding a university regulation requiring that student publications with advertising be distributed from newsstands rather than by hand, as the school had an interest in protecting its unique campus-based "marketplace of ideas" from commercial intrusion). More recent decisions by the U.S. Supreme Court and the federal Fifth Circuit have greatly expanded the First Amendment protection for commercial speech and have likely undermined the continued validity of the *Texas Review* decision. *See, e.g., Greater New Orleans*

Broad. Ass'n v. United States, 527 U.S. 173 (1999); *Hays County Guardian v. Supple*, 969 F.2d 111 (5th Cir. 1992), *cert. denied*, 506 U.S. 1087 (1993) (striking down a Texas university policy that restricted the on-campus distribution of independent newspapers with commercial advertisements). *See* Chapter 20 for a full discussion of the evolution of commercial speech rights.

22 *Central Hudson Gas & Electric Corp. v. Public Service Commission of New York*, 447 U.S. 557 (1980); *Pitt News v. Pappert*, 379 F.3d 96 (3d Cir. 2004) (striking down state law that prohibited advertisers from placing alcohol ads in college student media); *Burbridge v. Sampson*, 74 F. Supp. 2d 940 (C.D. Cal. 1999) (striking down policy at a community college that imposed greater restrictions on commercial speech than on noncommercial speech); *Peterson v. Bd. of Educ.*, 370 F. Supp. 1208, 1213-1214 (D. Neb. 1973) (striking down high school's attempt to ban independent student publications with advertising); *Pliscou v. Holtville Unified Sch. Dist.*, 411 F. Supp. 842, 849 (S.D. Cal. 1976) (finding that a school cannot arbitrarily deny an independent student newspaper's request to solicit ads).

23 *Williams v. Spencer*, 622 F.2d 1200 (4th Cir. 1980).

24 *See Hernandez v. Hanson*, 430 F. Supp. 1154 (D. Neb. 1977). *See also Hays County Guardian*, 969 F. 2d at 118.

25 *See Hays County Guardian*, 969 F.2d at 120-21.

26 *Bright v. Los Angles Unified Sch. Dist.*, 556 P.2d 1090, 1100 (Cal. 1976) (holding that a school district cannot ban the sale of underground newspapers and finding that "[t]he right to publish a newspaper would be meaningless indeed if it did not include the right to sell it"); *Jacobs v. Board of Sch. Commissioners*, 490 F.2d 601, 607-609, vacated as moot, 420 U.S. 128 (1975) (ruling against a high school that had a policy of prohibiting the sale of publications on school grounds); *Peterson v. Bd. of Educ.*, 370 F. Supp. 1208 (D. Neb. 1973) (holding that a high school could not restrict the distribution of independent publications that contain advertising and solicit voluntary donations where the distribution takes place on campus but outside of school buildings); *Hernandez v. Hanson*, 430 F. Supp. 1154, 1161 (D. Neb. 1977) ("as a matter of law... the outright prohibition of commercial literature [on a high school campus] is inconsistent with the First Amendment"). *See also Nitzberg v. Parks*, 525 F.2d 378, 383 n.4 (4th Cir. 1975) (finding that a provision in a high school policy that distinguished between "free" literature and commercial literature distributed by students was constitutionally suspect); *New Left Educ. Project v. Bd. of Regents*, 326 F. Supp. 158, 165 (W.D. Tex. 1970), vacated, 414 U.S. 807 (1973) (finding that a university's prohibitions on commercial and non-commercial solicitation on campus were unconstitutionally overbroad); *New Times, Inc. v. Arizona Bd. of Regents*, 519 P.2d 169, 176 (Ariz. 1974) (striking down university regulations that affected an off-campus publisher's ability to distribute its materials on campus, as "[t]he commercial nature of the activity is no justification for narrowing the protection of expression secured by the First Amendment"); *Spartacus Youth League v. Bd. of Trustees of Illinois Industrial Univ.*, 502 F. Supp. 789 (N.D. Ill. 1980) (enjoining a university from requiring that publications get administrative approval before being sold on campus).

27 *Murdock v. Pennsylvania*, 319 U.S. 105, 111 (1943) (noting also, among other things, that Thomas Paine's Common Sense pamphlets were sold).

28 *See, e.g., Rivera v. East Otero Sch. Dist. R-1*, 721 F. Supp. 1189 (D. Colo. 1989); *Clark v. Dallas Indep. Sch. Dist.*, 806 F. Supp. 116, 120 (N.D. Tex. 1992); "Student sues to distribute religious texts at school, Student Press Law Center *Report*, Winter 1999-2000, p. 27.

29 *See, e.g., Hedges v. Wauconda Community Unit Sch. Dist.*, 9 F.3d 1295 (7th Cir. 1993); *Slotterback v. Interboro Sch. Dist.*, 766 F. Supp. 280 (E.D. Pa. 1991); *Clark*, 806 F. Supp. at 120; *Rivera*, 721 F. Supp. at 1189; *Thompson v. Waynesboro Area Sch. Dist.*, 673 F. Supp. 1379 (M.D. Pa. 1987). *See also Rosenberger v. Rector and Visitors of Univ. of Virginia*, 515 U.S. 819 (1995) (finding that a university could pay the publication expenses of a student Christian newspaper, in accordance with its general policy of funding student newspapers); *Bd. of Educ. of Westside Community Sch. v. Mergens*, 496 U.S. 226 (1990) (noting that a high school must officially recognize a student religious club and afford it the same benefits as other student clubs); *Westfield High Sch. L.I.F.E. Club v. City of Westfield*, 249 F. Supp. 2d 98 (D. Mass. 2003) (rejecting a high school's claim that allowing a student Bible club to distribute religious materials would be school sponsorship of religion, and prohibiting the school from suspending club members for distributing candy canes with a religious message); *Good News Club v. Milford Central Sch.*, 533 U.S. 98 (2001) (holding that a public school violated the First Amendment when it refused to permit a private children's religious club to use school facilities after hours); *Lamb's Chapel v. Center Moriches Union Free Sch. Dist.*, 508 U.S. 384 (1993) (holding that a public school must allow a religious group use of its after-hours facilities where the group was showing a film and where the school had made its facilities generally available to a wide variety of public organizations); *Child Evangelism Fellowship of Maryland, Inc. v. Montgomery County Public Sch.*, 457 F.3d 376 (4th Cir. 2006) (finding a school district's policy to be overbroad where it reserved unfettered discretion over take-home flyer distribution and where — as a result — a private religious organization was not allowed to send informational flyers home with students); *Donovan v. Punxsutawney Area Sch. Bd.*, 336 F. 3d. 211 (3d Cir. 2003) (holding that a school violated a high school student's First Amendment rights when it precluded her from forming a Bible Club that would meet on school grounds during non-instructional time); *Hills v. Scottsdale Unified Sch. Dist. No. 48*, 329 F.3d 1044 (9th Cir. 2003), *cert. denied*, 124 S. Ct. 1146 (2004) (holding that a school district could not prohibit the distribution of flyers by a non-student group that was advertising a religious summer camp). *But see Phillips v. Oxford Separate Mun. Sch. Dist.*, 314 F. Supp. 2d 643 (N.D. Miss. 2003) (upholding a school's decision to remove a humorous, religious-themed poster created by a seventh grade student government candidate and finding that the school had legitimate Establishment Clause concerns about the poster); *Fleming v. Jefferson County Sch. Dist. R-1*, 298 F.3d 918 (10th Cir. 2002) (holding that Columbine High School could reject religious-themed tiles from a memorial project because the project was school-sponsored speech).

30 *Chandler v. Siegelman*, 230 F.3d 1313, 1316-17 (11th Cir. 2000), *cert. denied*, 533 U.S. 916 (2001) (explaining how its decision differed from Supreme Court's decision in *Santa Fe Indep. Sch. Dist. v. Doe*, 530 U.S. 290 (2000), where the Court struck down a high school's practice of holding a student

election to determine whether students would lead a prayer before a school-sponsored football game).

31 *See, e.g., Thompson*, 673 F. Supp. at 1379 (holding that students' distribution of a religious newspaper in the hallways of a junior high school was speech protected by First Amendment); *Rivera*, 721 F. Supp. 1191 (finding that a school acted unlawfully where it prohibited students from distributing "[m]aterial that proselytizes a particular religious or political belief"). *See also Johnston-Loehner v. O'Brien*, 859 F. Supp 575 (M.D. Fla. 1994) (holding that an elementary school distribution policy violated the First Amendment because it gave the superintendent the discretion to approve or reject religious materials).

32 *See Hedges v. Wauconda Community Unit Sch. Dist.* No. 118, 9 F.3d 1295 (7th Cir. 1993); *Hemry v. Sch. Bd. of Colorado Springs*, 760 F. Supp. 856 (D. Colo. 1991) (upholding a school policy that prohibited students from handing out a religious newspaper in high school hallways — which the court found to be non-public forum — where other means of distribution were made available by the school); *Nelson v. Moline Sch. Dist. No. 40*, 725 F. Supp. 965 (C.D. Ill. 1989) (noting that forum analysis is an appropriate means for determining the constitutionality of unwritten high school regulations that prohibit the distribution of political or religious literature on school grounds); *Muller v. Jefferson Lighthouse Sch.*, 98 F.3d 1530 (7th Cir. 1996) (finding that an elementary school is a nonpublic forum and upholding the legality of the school's prior review policy for non-school-sponsored publications).

33 The right to non-disruptively hand out religious literature on campus is in contrast with the ability to use a school-provided platform to deliver religious speech to a "captive" audience. Applying *Hazelwood*, courts generally are allowing schools to forbid overt religious references in students' graduation speeches, on the grounds that listeners might regard a valedictory speech as a school-approved message. *See Corder v. Lewis Palmer Sch. Dist No. 38*, 566 F.3d 1219 (10th Cir. 2009) (finding no First Amendment violation when graduation speaker was disciplined for going off her school-approved text to urge students to "find out more" about Jesus); *Lassonde v. Pleasanton Unified Sch. Dist.*, 320 F.3d 979 (9th Cir. 2003) (finding no First Amendment violation when school ordered graduation speaker to deliver school-revised speech, removing Bible quote and passages urging listeners to "seek out the Lord, and let Him guide you"); but *See Griffith v. Butte Sch. Dist. No. 1*, 244 P.3d 321 (Mont. 2010) (declining to apply *Hazelwood* to legitimize censorship of student's religious-themed graduation speech, finding that no reasonable listener would mistake individual student's speech for an official school message, given prominent disclaimers in graduation program).

34 *See, e.g., Walz ex rel. Walz v. Egg Harbor Township Bd. of Educ.*, 342 F.3d 271 (3d Cir. 2003), *aff'g* 187 F. Supp. 2d 232 (D.N.J. 2002), *cert. denied*, 541 U.S. 936 (2004) (holding that a school could legally prevent the in-class distribution of "evangelical candy canes" by an elementary school student because they proselytized a particular view and might be interpreted by young, impressionable students as bearing the school's seal of approval); *C.H. v. Oliva*, 990 F. Supp. 341 (D.N.J. 1997), *aff'd*, 166 F.3d 1204 (3d Cir. 1998), *aff'd* in part on reh'g en banc, 226 F.3d 198 (3d Cir. 2000), *cert. denied* sub. nom., *Hood v. Medford Township Bd. of Educ.*, 533 U.S. 915 (2001) (finding no First Amendment violation where elementary school officials prohibited a student from reading a religious story to classmates and moved the student's drawing of Jesus to a less prominent location); *Peck v. Upshur County Bd. of Educ.*, 155 F.3d 274 (4th Cir. 1998) (upholding a school board policy that allowed private groups to distribute Bibles at public high schools, but prohibited such distribution at elementary schools). *See also Muller v. Jefferson Lighthouse Sch.*, 98 F.3d 1530 (7th Cir. 1996). But *See Johnston-Loehner v. O'Brien*, 859 F. Supp 575 (M.D. Fla. 1994) (finding that elementary school students have a constitutional right to distribute lawful, non-disruptive written materials on school grounds).

35 *Curry ex rel. Curry v. Hensiner*, 513 F.3d 570 (6th Cir. 2008).

36 *Morgan v. Swanson*, 659 F.3d 359 (5th Cir. 2011) (en banc).

37 *Id.* at 382-84.

38 *Kuhlmeier v. Hazelwood Sch. Dist.*, 795 F.2d 1368, 1375-76 (8th Cir. 1986), rev'd on other grounds, 484 U.S. 260 (1988).

39 *Ginsberg v. State of New York*, 390 U.S. 629 (1968).

40 *See Papish v. Bd. of Curators of Univ. of Missouri*, 410 U.S. 667, 670 (1973) (finding that a cartoon and a headline with profanity and offensive content was not "constitutionally obscene").

41 *See, e.g., Scoville v. Bd. of Educ.*, 425 F.2d 10 (7th Cir. 1970); *Jacobs v. Bd. of Sch. Commissioners*, 490 F.2d 601 (7th Cir. 1973); *Baughman v. Freienmuth*, 478 F.2d 1345 (4th Cir. 1973); *Koppell v. Levine*, 347 F. Supp. 456 (E.D.N.Y. 1972); *Sullivan v. Houston Indep. Sch. Dist.*, 333 F. Supp. 1149 (S.D. Tex. 1971).

42 *See, e.g., Canady v. Bossier Parish Sch. Bd.*, 240 F.3d 437, 442 (5th Cir. 2001) (noting that high schools can regulate student expression that involves "lewd, vulgar, obscene or plainly offensive speech").

43 *See, e.g., Reno v. ACLU*, 521 U.S. 844, 874 (1997) (holding that the term "indecent," as used in a federal law restricting online speech, "lacks the precision that the First Amendment requires").

44 *Bethel Sch. Dist. v. Fraser*, 478 U.S. 675 (1986).

45 *Id.* at 681.

46 *Bystrom v. Fridley High Sch.* (Bystrom I), 822 F.2d 747, 752 (8th Cir. 1987).

47 *Chandler v. McMinnville Sch. Dist.*, 978 F.2d 524, 529 (9th Cir. 1992); (stating that "vulgar" but nondisruptive speech can be limited by school officials). *But see Pyle v. Sch. Committee of South Hadley*, 667 N.E.2d 869 (Mass. 1996) (finding that a state law protects high school students who engage in vulgar but non-disruptive expression); *Meyer v. Los Angeles Unified Sch. Dist.*, Case No. CV-00-4360 LGB (C.D. Cal. June 8, 2000) (finding that the CAL. EDUCATION CODE SEC. 48950 protects the use of vulgar language in underground high school newspapers).

48 *Morse v. Frederick*, 127 S. Ct. 2618 (2007).

49 *Id.* at 2622.

50 *Id.* at 2636. Despite Justice Alito's admonition that the Court's ruling in *Morse* was specifically limited to student speech that encouraged illegal drug use, at least two lower courts have nevertheless cited the decision to carve out other categories of unprotected speech. *See, e.g., Ponce v. Socorro*, 508 F.3d 765 (5th Cir. 2007) (citing Justice Alito's opinion in ruling that school officials can punish student

speech if they believe it advocates behavior that endangers students' physical safety); *Nuxoll v. Indian Prairie Sch. Dist. #204*, 523 F.3d 668, 673, 675 (7th Cir. 2008) (finding that Alito's concurrence was not a "controlling" opinion and refusing to enjoin enforcement of Illinois high school rule that banned "derogatory comments ... that refer to race, ethnicity, religion, gender, sexual orientation, or disability").

51 *Morse*, 127 S. Ct. at 2636.

52 *Tinker v. Des Moines Indep. Sch. Dist.*, 393 U.S. 503, 512-513 ("A student's rights, therefore, do not embrace merely the classroom hours. When he is in the cafeteria, or on the playing field, or on the campus during authorized hours, he may express his opinions, even on controversial subjects like the conflict in Vietnam, if he does so without 'materially and substantially interfer(ing) with the requirements of appropriate discipline in the operation of the school' and without colliding with the rights of others."); *Healy v. James*, 408 U.S. 169 (1972); *Rosenberger v. Rectors and Visitors of the Univ. of Virginia*, 515 U.S. 819 (1995).

53 *See Saxe v. State College Area Sch. Dist.*, 240 F.3d 200, 212 (3d Cir. 2001).

54 *Beussink v. Woodland R-IV Sch. Dist.*, 30 F. Supp. 2d 1175, 1180 (E.D. Mo. 1998).

55 *Boucher v. Sch. Bd. of the Sch. Dist. of Greenfield*, 134 F.3d 821 (7th Cir. 1998).

56 *Pangle v. Bend-Lapine Sch. Dist.*, 10 P.3d 275 (Or. Ct. App. 2000), review denied, 34 P.3d 1176 (Or. 2001).

57 "Students push for new policy," Student Press Law Center *Report*, Spring 1986, p. 20.

58 "Student arrested for distributing paper," Student Press Law Center *Report*, Spring 1995, p. 6.

59 *Dodd v. Rambis*, 535 F. Supp. 23 (S.D. Ind. 1981).

60 *Meyer v. Los Angeles Unified Sch. Dist.*, Case No. CV-00-4360 LGB (C.D. Cal. June 8, 2000). *But see Doninger v. Niehoff*, 527 F.3d 41 (2d Cir. 2008) (denying public high school student's motion for preliminary injunction after school disqualified her from student office after she referred to administrators as "douchebags" on her personal blog and urged others to contact school district officials to voice their disagreement with a school policy, which the court said created a "foreseeable risk of substantial disruption to the work and discipline of the school").

61 *J.S. ex rel. H.S. v. Bethlehem Area Sch. Dist.*, 807 A.2d 847 (Pa. 2002).

62 *Killion v. Franklin Reg'l Sch. Dist.*, 136 F. Supp. 2d 446, 455-56 (W.D. Pa. 2001).

63 "Magazine spurs six suspensions," Student Press Law Center *Report*, Winter 1993-94, p. 17. But *See* "Indie press assured of rights," Student Press Law Center *Report*, Spring 2003, p. 24 (reporting on a Minnesota school that charged five girls with "sexual harassment" for the content of their underground newspaper).

64 *See, e.g., Leibner v. Sharbaugh*, 429 F. Supp. 744 (E.D. Va. 1977); "Underground's fight ends," Student Press Law Center *Report*, Fall 1996, p. 9.

65 "Principal claims student underground caused near-riot," Student Press Law Center *Report*, Spring 1995, p. 7.

66 *See, e.g., Killion*, 136 F. Supp. 2d at 455-56; *Scoville v. Bd. of Educ.*, 425 F.2d 10 (7th Cir. 1970); *Channing Club v. Bd. of Regents of Texas Tech Univ.*, 317 F. Supp. 688, 691 (N.D. Tex. 1970); *Shanley v. Northeast Indep. Sch. Dist.*, 462 F.2d 960 (5th Cir. 1972); *Westfield High Sch. L.I.F.E. Club v. City of Westfield*, 249 F. Supp. 2d 98, 112-13 (D. Mass. 2003). *See also Chalifoux v. New Caney Indep. Sch. Dist.*, 976 F. Supp. 659 (S.D. Tex. 1997) (finding that a school violated the First Amendment when it prohibited Catholic students from wearing rosaries to school on the grounds that some gangs had adopted the rosary as their identifying symbol, as the school did not have sufficient evidence of actual disruption).

67 *In re George T.*, 93 P.3d 1007, 1019 (Cal. 2004).

68 *Doe v. Pulaski County Special Sch. Dist.*, 306 F.3d 616 (8th Cir. 2002).

69 *Id.* at 625.

70 Compare *Doe*, 306 F.3d at 622 (determining whether a threat existed by analyzing whether a reasonable person in the statement recipient's circumstances would believe that he was being threatened) with *Lovell v. Poway Unified Sch. Dist.*, 90 F.3d 367, 373 (9th Cir. 1996) (determining whether a threat existed by analyzing whether a reasonable person in the speaker's circumstances should have foreseen that his or her words would be perceived as a threat).

71 *Watts v. United States*, 394 U.S. 705 (1969); *Mahaffey v. Aldrich*, 236 F. Supp. 2d 779, 785-86 (E.D. Mich. 2002) (finding that a high school student's off-campus website, which was created "for laughs" and included a list of people he wished "would die," did not constitute a "true threat"); *J.S. ex rel. H.S. v. Bethlehem Area Sch. Dist.*, 807 A.2d 847 (Pa. 2002) (finding that a middle school student's website did not constitute a "true threat" even though the site listed reasons a teacher should die, showed a picture of the teacher's head severed from her body and solicited funds for a hit man. The court found that the website, taken as a whole, was a "sophomoric, crude, highly offensive, and perhaps misguided attempt at humor or parody," but that it did not reflect a serious expression of intent to inflict harm, though the teacher took offense and experienced fear after viewing the website); *Emmett v. Kent Sch. Dist.*, 92 F. Supp. 2d 1088, 1090 (W.D. Wash. 2000) (rejecting a school's claim that "mock obituaries" published on a student's off-campus website "were intended to threaten anyone, did actually threaten anyone, or manifested any violent tendencies whatsoever"); *Bauer v. Sampson*, 261 F.3d 775 (9th Cir. 2001) (finding that a community college professor's statements, which were critical of the administration and published in an underground campus newspaper, did not constitute a true threat). Compare to *Pitchford v. Union R-XI Sch. Dist.*, Case No. 2001- CV-1868 (E.D. Mo. 2003) (finding, by a jury verdict, that an 8th grade student's parody story about the murder of students and teachers was a "true threat" that justified her suspension). *See also Murphy v. Fort Worth Indep. Sch. Dist.*, 258 F. Supp. 2d 569 (N.D. Tex. 2003), vacated as moot, 334 F.3d 470 (5th Cir. 2003) (concerning a high school student who was "effectively expelled" from school because he read a rap poem in class that was initially labeled as a "terroristic threat"); *Ponce v. Socorro*, 508 F.3d 765, 767 (5th Cir. 2007) (declining to decide whether speech constituted "true threat," but upholding a Texas high school principal's punishment of a student after he discovered a violent fictional story in the student's notebook at school that the principal concluded constituted a "terroristic threat"); *LaVine v. Blaine Sch. Dist.*, 257 F.3d 981 (9th Cir. 2001), reh'g en banc denied, 279 F.3d 719 (9th Cir. 2002), *cert. denied*, 536 U.S. 959 (2002) (finding that a high school student's First Amendment rights were not violated when the student was expelled on an "emergency basis" because of a poem that he had

written about a school shooting); *S.G. v. Sayreville Bd. of Educ.*, 333 F.3d 417 (3d Cir. 2003), *cert. denied*, 540 U.S. 1104 (2004) (upholding the three-day suspension of a five-year-old kindergarten student who said "I'm going to shoot you" during a recess game of cops and robbers, as the school's policy prohibited speech that made threats or referred to the use of firearms).

72 *In re George T.*, 93 P.3d 1007, 1019 (Cal. 2004).

73 For more information on the application — or misapplication — of the true threat doctrine to an ever-growing number of student speech cases, *See* Jonnie Macke, *The True Threat Doctrine as Misapplied in Doe v. Pulaski County Special Sch. Dist.*, 57 ARK. L. REV. 303 (2004) and Fiona Ruthven, *Is the True Threat the Student or the School Board? Punishing Threatening Student Expression*, 88 IOWA L. REV. 931 (2003).

74 *See, e.g., Wisniewski v. Bd. of Educ. of Weedsport Cent. School Dist.*, 494 F.3d 34, 38 (2d Cir. 2007), *cert. denied*, 128 S. Ct. 1741 (2008) (holding that student's Internet-based instant message depicting shooting of teacher would materially and substantially disrupt work and discipline of school, and ruling that "school officials have significantly broader authority to sanction student speech" under the Supreme Court's *Tinker* standard than would be allowed in an adult setting under the *Watts* ("true threat") standard).

75 *Campbell v. Acuff-Rose Music, Inc.*, 510 U.S. 569 (1994); *Walt Disney Productions v. Air Pirates*, 581 F.2d 751 (9th Cir. 1978).

76 *See Slotterback v. Interboro Sch. Dist.*, 766 F. Supp. 280, 298 (E.D. Pa. 1991) ("To be sure, these paragraphs [establishing mandatory prior review of 'non-school written materials'] form a system of prior restraint on students' protected, personal first amendment speech.").

77 *Near v. Minnesota*, 283 U.S. 697, 714 (1931) (noting that the First Amendment's primary purpose is to prevent "previous restraints upon publications" by the government (citing *Patterson v. Colorado*, 205 U.S. 454 (1907)); *Lovell v. City of Griffin*, 303 U.S. 444 (1938) (holding that a city ordinance was unconstitutional because of its requirement that written materials be pre-approved by the city manager before distribution).

78 *See, e.g., Antonelli v. Hammond*, 308 F. Supp. 1329 (D. Mass. 1970). *See also Burbridge v. Sampson*, 74 F. Supp. 2d 940 (C.D.Cal. 1999) (striking down a "reservation" system for a free speech zone on a community college campus, as the system required students to submit materials to administrators for advance approval before distribution) and related proceeding, *Khademi v. South Orange Community College Dist.*, 194 F. Supp. 2d 1011 (C.D. Cal. 2002); *Crue v. Aikin*, 370 F.3d 668, 678 (7th Cir. 2004) (holding that a college's directive was unconstitutional where it prohibited university students and faculty members from contacting prospective student athletes without prior permission from the school about "a matter of significant importance and public concern").

79 *See, e.g.*, "Distribution rights under examination," Student Press Law Center *Report*, Spring 2004, p. 7; "Student who was not allowed to distribute anti-abortion fliers sues Fla. school," Student Press Law Center *News Flash*, Apr. 6, 2004, http://www.splc.org/newsflash_archives.asp?id=784&year=2004.

80 For the time, the Supreme Court's official position on the issue of prior review of independent, on-campus student speech seems to be to look the other way. It explicitly declined to address the question in its *Hazelwood* decision, ruling: "We need not now decide whether [specific written regulations] are required before school officials may censor publications not sponsored by the school that students seek to distribute on school grounds." *Hazelwood*, 484 U.S. 260, 273 n.6.

81 *Bystrom v. Fridley High Sch.* (Bystrom I), 822 F.2d 747, 755 (8th Cir. 1987) ("[W]e are certainly not holding that [prior review] guidelines of the type we have upheld in this opinion are wise or advisable policy. That is not a judicial question. It is for school boards and administrators to decide whether to attempt to write and apply similar guidelines.").

82 "School policy knocks out prior review," Student Press Law Center *Report*, Fall 1992, p. 18; "New Dade County policy adopted: prior review prohibited; next step is educating administrators," Student Press Law Center *Report*, Fall 1994, p. 5.

83 *Burch v. Barker*, 861 F.2d 1149 (9th Cir. 1988).

84 *Id.* at 1153-55, 1159.

85 *Id.* at 1159 (noting that the case holding does not "affect the ability of the school to punish students for unacceptable or disruptive conduct after it occurs").

86 *Fujishima v. Bd. of Educ.*, 460 F.2d 1355 (7th Cir. 1972).

87 *Id.* at 1358 (emphasis in original).

88 *Muller v. Jefferson Lighthouse Sch.*, 98 F.3d 1530, 1540 (7th Cir. 1996), *cert. denied*, 520 U.S. 1156 (1997).

89 *Bright v. Los Angeles Unified Sch. Dist.*, 556 P.2d 1090 (Cal. 1977).

90 *Riseman v. Sch. Committee of Quincy*, 439 F.2d 148, 149 (1st Cir. 1971) (noting that the school's prior distribution rule was "vague, overbroad, and d[id] not reflect any effort to minimize the adverse effect of prior restraint") (citations omitted).

91 *Chiu v. Plano Indep. Sch. Dist.*, 339 F.3d 273, 283 (5th Cir. 2003), *cert. dismissed*, 540 U.S. 1071 (2003).

92 *Eisner v. Stamford Bd. of Educ.*, 440 F.2d 803 (2d Cir. 1971); *Baughman v. Freienmuth*, 478 F.2d 1345 (4th Cir. 1973); *Shanley v. Northeast Indep. Sch. Dist.*, 462 F.2d 960 (5th Cir. 1972); *Muller v. Jefferson Lighthouse Sch.*, 98 F.3d 1530 (7th Cir. 1996), *cert. denied*, 520 U.S. 1156 (1997); *Bystrom v. Fridley High Sch.*, 822 F.2d 747 (8th Cir. 1987). *See also Harless v. Darr*, 937 F. Supp. 1351, 1353 (S.D. Ind. 1996) (approving an elementary school's prior approval policy where the policy did not, on its face, give the superintendent the power to reject materials for publication on the basis of content).

93 *Coy v. Bd. of Educ. of North Canton City Sch.*, 205 F. Supp. 2d 791, 802 (N.D. Ohio 2002).

94 *See Baughman v. Freienmuth*, 478 F.2d 1345, 1350 (4th Cir. 1973) ("[A] regulation requiring prior submission of material for approval before distribution must contain narrow, objective, and reasonable standards by which the material will be judged.").

95 *See Flaherty v. Keystone Oaks Sch. Dist.*, 247 F. Supp. 2d 698, 704 (W.D. Pa. 2003) (finding that a school policy on speech was unconstitutionally overbroad where it was not limited to "those circumstances that cause a substantial disruption to school operations as required under *Tinker*"). *See generally Wiemerslage*

v. Maine Township High Sch. Dist. 207, 29 F.3d 1149, 1151 (7th Cir. 1994) (noting that "a school's disciplinary rules need not be drafted as narrowly or with the same precision as criminal statutes").

96 *See Nitzberg v. Parks*, 525 F.2d 378, 383 (4th Cir. 1975) (holding that school board's student media "regulations are void for vagueness and overbreadth"); *Leibner v. Sharbaugh*, 429 F. Supp. 744, 748 (E.D. Va. 1977) (finding that a school district regulation which proscribed distributing "obscene" or "libelous" material without defining those terms was unconstitutionally vague). *But see Muller*, 98 F.3d at 1541, 1543 (refusing to strike down a prior review policy that failed to specifically define its terms and finding that school officials "must be allowed the space and discretion to deal with the nuances" of performing their functions).

97 Coy, 205 F. Supp. 2d 802 (holding that a school district's conduct code was unconstitutionally vague where it was used by administrators to punish a student website publisher for "inappropriate" conduct).

98 Flaherty, 247 F. Supp. 2d at 704.

99 *Westfield High Sch. L.I.F.E. Club v. City of Westfield*, 249 F. Supp. 2d 98, 126-127 (D. Mass. 2003) (striking down a prior review policy on vagueness grounds, as the policy allowed only "responsible speech" and established no time limits for administrative review).

100 *See Nitzberg*, 525 F.2d at 383. *See also Baughman*, 478 F.2d at 1349.

101 *See, e.g., Nelson v. Moline Sch. Dist. No. 40*, 725 F. Supp. 965 (C.D. Ill. 1989); "Mich. school district revokes students' suspensions for underground paper, revises policy," Student Press Law Center *News Flash*, March 27, 2003, *available at* http://www.splc.org/newsflash.asp?id=586 (reporting a settlement after Michigan high school students were suspended for violating a publications policy that had never been included in the student handbook).

102 *See Vail v. Bd. of Educ. of Portsmouth Sch. Dist.*, 354 F. Supp. 592, 599 (D.N.H. 1973), vacated, 502 F.2d 1159 (1st Cir. 1973); *Rivera v. East Otero Sch. Dist. R-1*, 721 F. Supp. 1189, 1194 (D. Colo. 1989) (striking down a school district's prior review policy, as a school district "cannot completely muzzle the students to save itself the difficulty of determining which speech it may constitutionally proscribe"); *Johnston-Loehner v. O'Brien*, 859 F. Supp. 575 (M.D. Fla. 1994) (striking down a prior review policy where the district superintendent had the discretion to unilaterally approve or reject the distribution of elementary school students' non-school-sponsored written material); *Nelson v. Moline Sch. Dist. No. 40*, 725 F. Supp. 965, 977 (C.D. Ill. 1989) (holding that a high school's content-based, unwritten prohibition against distributing political or religious literature on school grounds violated the First Amendment, as did its subsequent, unconstitutionally vague prior-review requirement).

103 *See Bystrom v. Fridley High Sch.*, 822 F.2d 747, 755 (8th Cir. 1987).

104 *See Saxe v. State College Area Sch. Dist.*, 240 F.3d 200 (3d Cir. 2001) (striking down a school district's anti-harassment policy that prohibited speech or conduct that "offends, denigrates or belittles" after the policy was challenged by Christian students who feared that they would be punished for speaking out against homosexuality and distributing religious literature); *Sypniewski v. Warren Hills Reg'l Bd. of Educ.*, 307 F.3d 243 (3d Cir. 2002), *cert. denied*, 538 U.S. 1033 (2003) (striking down a high school harassment policy that prohibited any written expression creating "ill will"); *Flaherty v. Keystone Oaks Sch. Dist.*, 247 F. Supp. 2d 698 (W.D. Pa. 2003) (finding that a high school's policies against "abusive," "offensive," "harassing" or "inappropriate" behavior were unconstitutionally overbroad and vague after a student was punished for posting Internet messages about a school volleyball game to an off-campus website).

105 *Leibner v. Sharbaugh*, 429 F. Supp. 744, 748 (E.D. Va. 1977).

106 *Cintron v. State Bd. of Educ.*, 384 F. Supp. 674, 679 (D.P.R. 1974).

107 Baughman, 478 F.2d at 1349.

108 *Jacobs v. Bd. of Sch. Commissioners*, 490 F.2d 601, 604 (7th Cir. 1973), vacated as moot, 420 U.S. 128 (1975).

109 *See Eisner v. Stamford Bd. of Educ.*, 440 F.2d 803, 811 (2d Cir. 1971).

110 *Baughman v. Freienmuth*, 478 F.2d 1345, 1348-49 (4th Cir. 1973); *Eisner*, 440 F.2d at 810; *Quarterman v. Byrd*, 453 F.2d 54, 59-60 (4th Cir. 1971); *Westfield High Sch. L.I.F.E. Club v. City of Westfield*, 249 F. Supp. 2d 98, 125-126 (D. Mass. 2003).

111 *See, e.g., Goss v. Lopez*, 419 U.S. 565 (1975); Eisner, 440 F.2d at 803; Quarterman, 453 F.2d 54; Baughman, 478 F.2d at 1351; Nitzberg, 525 F.2d at 383-84.

112 *See Nitzberg*, 525 F.2d at 383 n.4.

113 *Cf. Murphy v. Fort Worth Indep. Sch. Dist.*, 258 F. Supp. 2d 569, 573 (N.D. Tex. 2003), vacated as moot, 334 F.3d 470 (5th Cir. 2003) (finding that a school violated the due process rights of a high school student when it "effectively expelled" him for reading a threatening rap poem in class, as the student "was not told what he was accused of doing and what the basis of the accusation was" and he did not "have an opportunity to tell his side of the story in order to make sure than an injustice was not done.") (Citations omitted).

114 Leibner, 429 F. Supp. at 749.

115 *See Hall v. Bd. of Sch. Commissioners*, 681 F.2d 965, 969 (5th Cir. 1982); *Shanley v. Northeast Indep. Sch. Dist.*, 462 F.2d 960, 977-78 (5th Cir. 1972); *Leibner*, 429 F. Supp. at 749.

116 *Killion v. Franklin Regional Sch. Dist.*, 136 F. Supp. 2d 446, 450-51 (W.D. Pa. 2001) (finding that a school's failure to provide prior written notification of a suspension violated the student's due process rights); *Vail v. Bd. of Educ.*, 354 F. Supp. 592, 603-04 (D.N.H. 1973) ("It is settled law that a school must afford some opportunity for a hearing when dealing with expulsions."); *Donovan v. Ritchie*, 68 F.3d 14 (1st Cir. 1995).

117 *See generally Vail*, 354 F. Supp. at 602-04 (outlining due process requirements for suspensions and expulsions).

118 *McIntyre v. Ohio Elections Commission*, 514 U.S. 334, 357 (1995) ("Under our Constitution, anonymous pamphleteering is not a pernicious, fraudulent practice, but an honorable tradition of advocacy and of dissent. Anonymity is a shield from the tyranny of the majority.").

119 *Jacobs v. Bd. of Sch. Commissioners*, 490 F.2d 601, 607 (7th Cir. 1973) (citing *Talley v. California*, 362 U.S. 60 (1960)). *See also McIntyre*, 514 U.S. 334 (holding that an Ohio ban on the distribution of anonymous campaign literature violated the First Amendment); *ACLU v. Miller*, 977 F. Supp. 1228 (N.D. Ga. 1997) (permanently enjoining enforcement of a state law that criminalized anonymous and pseudonymous Internet communications).

120 "Wake Forest asks political paper to drop university's name and seal," Student Press Law Center *Report*, Spring 1993, p. 18.

121 "Unofficial student paper not welcome," Student Press Law Center *Report*, Spring 1997, p. 27.

122 *See, e.g., Vail v. Bd. of Educ.*, 354 F. Supp. 592 (D.N.H. 1973), *vacated*, 502 F.2d 1159 (1st Cir. 1973) (finding that a public high school's blanket prohibition against the distribution of all non-school-sponsored written materials on school grounds was unconstitutional).

123 *See, e.g., Pliscou v. Holtville Unified Sch. Dist.*, 411 F. Supp. 842, 849 (D.C. Cal. 1976); *Slotterback v. Interboro Sch. Dist.*, 766 F. Supp. 280, 299 (E.D. Pa. 1991).

124 Vail, 354 F. Supp. at 598.

125 *Cf. Peck v. Upshur County Bd. of Educ.*, 155 F.3d 274, 281, 284 (4th Cir. 1998) (finding that a school policy limiting nonstudents' ability to distribute religious materials was reasonable and constitutional where it was based on time and place restrictions "pursuant to a neutral, open access policy").

126 *Sullivan v. Houston Indep. Sch. Dist.*, 307 F. Supp. 1328, 1340 (S.D. Tex. 1969) (Sullivan I).

127 *Blackwell v. Issaquena County Bd. of Educ.*, 363 F.2d 749, 751, 753 (5th Cir. 1966).

128 *Clark v. Dallas Indep. Sch. Dist.*, 806 F. Supp. 116, 120 (N.D. Tex. 1992).

129 *Grayned v. City of Rockford*, 408 U.S. 104, 117-18 (1972) (holding that expressive activity outside a school may be prohibited only where it "materially disrupts classwork or involves substantial disorder or invasion of the rights of others" (quoting *Tinker v. Des Moines Indep. Community Sch. Dist.*, 393 U.S. 503, 513 (1969)).

130 *Slotterback v. Interboro Sch. Dist.*, 766 F. Supp. 280, 299 (E.D. Pa. 1991).

131 *See City of Cincinnati v. Discovery Network, Inc.*, 507 U.S. 410 (1993); *Hays County Guardian v. Supple*, 969 F.2d 111, 119 (5th Cir. 1992) ("Even a content-neutral restriction on such a basic and traditional medium of distribution cannot be justified by trivial gains in convenience or insignificant reductions of litter."); *Miller v. City of Laramie*, 880 P.2d 594 (Wyo. 1994).

132 *See* Grayned, 408 U.S. at 115-16.

133 "Underground paper still subject to review, restraint," Student Press Law Center *Report*, Winter 1991-92, p. 14.

134 Hays County Guardian, 969 F.2d at 111; "Iowa school must pay fees for restricting distribution," Student Press Law Center *Report*, Winter 1998-99, p. 27.

135 "Underground paper wins minutes for distribution," Student Press Law Center *Report*, Spring 1994, p. 8. *See also Slotterback v. Interboro Sch. Dist.*, 766 F. Supp. 280, 299 (E.D. Pa. 1991) (declaring a school distribution policy to be unconstitutionally overbroad where it limited student distribution of religious materials to only one exit and only at the end of the school day).

136 *See, e.g., Emmett v. Kent Sch. Dist. No. 415*, 92 F. Supp. 2d 1088 (W.D. Wash. 2000); *Killion v. Franklin Regional Sch. Dist.*, 136 F. Supp. 2d 446, 454 (W.D. Pa. 2001).

137 For more information on college press freedom, *See* Chapter 6.

138 For more information on the rights of private school student journalists, *See* Chapter 7.

139 *See, e.g., Bystrom v. Fridley High Sch., Indep. Sch. Dist. No. 14*, 822 F.2d 747, 750 (8th Cir. 1987) (noting that the legal burdens involved with censoring off-campus student speech at the high-school level would be greater than those involved with censoring on-campus speech at the high-school level, and that such burdens might prove insurmountable); *Thomas v. Board of Educ., Granville Central Sch. Dist., 607* F.2d 1043 (2d Cir. 1979), *cert. denied*, 444 U.S. 1081 (1980); *Shanley v. Northeast Indep. Sch. Dist.*, 462 F.2d 960 (5th Cir. 1972) (holding that a high school's attempt to discipline students for distributing a student publication off-campus and during out-of-school hours violated their constitutional rights); *Sullivan v. Houston Indep. Sch. Dist.*, 307 F. Supp. 1328, 1340-41 (S.D. Tex. 1969) (Sullivan I) ("School officials may not judge a student's behavior while he is in his home with his family nor does it seem to this court that they should have jurisdiction over his acts on a public street corner.").

140 *Tinker v. Des Moines Indep. Sch. Dist.*, 393 U.S. 503, 511 (1969). *See also Bethel Sch. Dist. No. 403 v. Fraser*, 478 U.S. 675, 688 (1986) (Brennan, J., concurring) ("If respondent had given the same speech outside of the school environment, he could not have been penalized simply because government officials considered his language to be inappropriate….").

141 *Thomas v. Bd. of Educ., Granville Central Sch. Dist., 607* F.2d 1043 (2d Cir. 1979), *cert. denied*, 444 U.S. 1081 (1980).

142 *Id.* at 1052.

143 *Id.* at 1045.

144 *Id.* at 1051.

145 *Id.*

146 *Id.*

147 *Id.*

148 Shanley, 462 F. 2d at 964.

149 *Sullivan v. Houston Indep. Sch. Dist.* (Sullivan II), 475 F.2d 1071, 1073 (5th Cir. 1973). *See also Baker v. Downey City Bd. of Educ.*, 307 F. Supp. 517 (C.D. Cal. 1969) (finding that school officials can regulate student conduct that occurs "while going to and from school").

150 Shanley, 462 F.2d at 974.

151 *Morse v. Frederick*, 127 S. Ct. 2618 (2007) (holding that a high school student who was standing across the street from his school for a school-sponsored event did not have a constitutional right to display a banner that could be seen as promoting illegal drug use); *Layshock v. Hermitage Sch. Dist.*, 496 F. Supp. 2d 587, 598 600 (W.D. Pa. 2007) (acknowledging that the "test for school authority is not geographical," but finding that "no nexus" existed between creation of Internet parody of principal on student's MySpace.com social networking site and a substantial disruption of school environment where no classes were canceled and no widespread disorder occurred); *J.S. ex rel. H.S. v. Bethlehem Area Sch. Dist., 807* A.2d 847 (Pa. 2002) (upholding the punishment of a middle school student who created an off-campus website that caused a teacher to take medical leave and otherwise disrupted school); *Doninger v. Niehoff*, 527 F.3d 41, 50-52 (2d Cir. 2008) (rejecting a student's claim that her off-campus blog that referred to school officials as

"douchebags" and called upon students to contact school officials to protest school policy was protected by First Amendment, because it was "reasonably foreseeable" that posting would reach school property and create a risk of substantial disruption to the school environment); *Wisniewski v. Bd. of Educ.*, 494 F.3d 34, 40 (2d Cir. 2007), *cert. denied*, 128 S. Ct. 1741 (2008) (finding that school discipline of middle school student who sent an instant message from a home computer with a crude drawing suggesting a teacher be shot and killed was permissible because it was reasonably foreseeable that the icon would come to the attention of school authorities and that it would create a risk of substantial disruption); *Baker v. Downey City Bd. of Educ.*, 307 F. Supp. 517 (C.D. Cal. 1969). The outcome in cases involving off-campus student conduct (sometimes mixed with elements of speech) frequently is decided based upon the nexus between the conduct and its effect on the school. *See, e.g., Klein v. Smith*, 635 F. Supp. 1440 (D. Me. 1986) (holding that a school violated the First Amendment when it disciplined a student for making a vulgar gesture to a teacher off school grounds and after school hours); *Fenton v. Stear*, 423 F. Supp. 767 (W.D. Pa. 1976) (upholding the in-school suspension of a high school student who made a vulgar remark about a teacher to other students off school grounds when the teacher drove by in a shopping center parking lot); *O'Rourke v. Walker*, 128 A. 25 (Conn. 1925) (upholding the punishment of a male student who annoyed young girls on their way home from school, as his conduct was "detrimental to the good order and best interests of the school"); *Clements v. Bd. of Trustees of Sheridan County Sch. Dist. No. 2*, 585 P.2d 197 (Wyo. 1978) (upholding the punishment of a high school student for "harassing a school bus" on its way to school where the student cut off the bus with his car and repeatedly dropped to very low speeds in front of it); *Tucson Public Sch., Dist. No. 1 v. Green*, 495 P.2d 861 (Ariz. Ct. App. 1972) (holding that school officials may punish students who precipitate a fight on the campus of a rival school); *Lander v. Seaver*, 32 Vt. 114 (Vt. 1859) (upholding the punishment of a student who called his teacher "old Jack Seaver" in front of other pupils after school hours, as the student's act had "a direct and immediate tendency to injure the school and bring the master's authority into contempt." The Supreme Court of Vermont noted that punishment would not have been appropriate "in matters in no ways connected with or affecting the school."). *See* Chapter 9 for a more detailed discussion of administrative authority over off-campus websites.

152 *See* Sullivan II, 333 F. Supp. 1149, vacated, 475 F.2d 1071 (5th Cir. 1973), *cert. denied*, 414 U.S. 1032 (1973).

153 Sullivan II, 475 F.2d at 1077. *See also Schwartz v. Schuker*, 298 F. Supp. 238 (E.D.N.Y. 1969) (upholding the punishment of a high school publisher of an independent newspaper who violated a direct order not to distribute the newspaper at school, encouraged other students to do likewise and entered school grounds while suspended); *Smith ex rel. Lanham v. Greene County Sch. Dist.*, 100 F. Supp. 2d 1354, 1364 (M.D. Ga. 2000) (upholding the suspension of an elementary school student who wore a controversial T-shirt to school, as the shirt was not the sole reason for his punishment).

154 *See Reno v. ACLU*, 521 U.S. 844, 874 (1997) (holding that the term "indecent," as used in a federal law restricting online speech, "lacks the precision that the First Amendment requires").

CHAPTER 9

Online Student Media

Recent years have marked the explosive growth of Internet-aided electronic communications. Websites, apps, e-mail, chatrooms, bulletin boards, listservs, streaming video and audio, newsgroups, texting — all are part of the so-called "new media" that, like the printing press, telegraph, telephone, radio and television that preceded it, have changed the way the world communicates. We now live in a world of nearly ubiquitous, instant communication, with individuals regularly checking email wirelessly, messaging friends while walking down the street, and surfing the Internet on mobile phones from anyplace they choose. Our lives are saturated with media.

Such change has come with breakneck speed. While the Internet was "born" in the late 1960s, it existed primarily on the computers of a handful of computer experts and educators.[1] It was really not until the mid 1990s — with the advent of Web browsers that allowed for user-friendly navigation of the World Wide Web — that the growing international network of linked computers really took off. When the second edition of this book was published in 1994, the words "Internet," "website," and "email" did not even appear in its pages. Today, by contrast, questions concerning Internet-based communication and student media represent much of the SPLC's workload. It is estimated that, as of 2012, more than 78 percent of Americans regularly used cyberspace to communicate — a number certain to continue growing.[2] And students — perhaps more than any other demographic group — have led the charge in embracing the new media, incorporating it into nearly every facet of their lives. The U.S. Department of Education found that, in fall 2003, 93 percent of all U.S. public schools' instructional rooms had Internet access, up from just 3 percent in 1994.[3] The unparalleled communications opportunities make this a particularly exciting time for student journalists. Never before have students had such ready access to exhaustive sources of information or been able to so easily share ideas and collaborate with their peers — or a global audience.

CYBERSPACE AND THE LAW

Notwithstanding such excitement and opportunity, the emergence of the Internet as a publishing and research tool for student journalists has created "new" legal problems — some real, others imagined.

Despite ongoing rumors and the claims of some school officials and others, student media published on the Internet is not inherently more dangerous than its print-based counterparts. There are, to date, no known cases of an image or information published by student media on the Internet being used to bring physical harm to a student.[4] Nor does publishing online create liability or trigger new regulations simply because of the choice of media. For example, despite persistent misperceptions and widely adopted — yet wildly inconsistent — administrative policies to the contrary, no federal privacy laws prohibit the publication of student names or photos on student-edited websites, with or without parental consent.[5] Except for a small handful of states that restrict what can be published on K-12 school districts' own servers, any material that can legally be published in traditional print format can legally be published online as well. An editor who knows how to avoid publishing libelous statements in a newspaper can use that knowledge to avoid the same mistakes when publishing on a website.

Still, "old" legal questions have found new life in cyberspace. While the fundamentals of copyright, libel and invasion of privacy law remain unchanged, the inherent uniqueness of the Internet means that questions cannot always be easily compared to those that have arisen in print or other "traditional" media. For instance, is a defamatory statement written and edited by journalists in New York, posted to a website hosted on a computer

Did You Know? 94 percent of public school instructional rooms had Internet access in the fall of 2005, compared with just 3 percent in 1994.

Student media published on the Internet is not inherently more dangerous than print publication. There are, to date, no known cases of an image or information published by student media on the Internet being used to bring physical harm to a student.

in New Jersey and intended primarily for the American audience of a Delaware-based company deemed "published" in Australia — and therefore subject to that country's laws and court system — simply because it can be pulled up via the Internet on a computer in Sydney?[6] Or are the community standards of Memphis applicable in judging whether sexually graphic material created and posted by a husband and wife in California — and determined by California officials to be lawful — violates Tennessee obscenity law simply because the material can be accessed on a computer in that location?[7]

Such emerging questions aside, student journalists must also confront the added hurdle that — just as in disputes that arise with more traditional media — schools and student media often find themselves immersed in more complex legal predicaments than the rest of the world because of the added challenge of balancing administrative concerns with education and the free flow of ideas.

Unfortunately, school administrators who view the Internet as somehow a completely different animal from earlier forms of media have often felt justified in inventing new grounds for restricting it. In the process, errant administrators have sometimes wholly abandoned established protocol used in resolving past First Amendment or other legal disputes. Online media proponents argue that it is not the complex nature of the technology that is causing problems; it is — just as accompanied the introduction of telephones, TV's and other "new media" of their day — the confusion, paranoia and uninformed fear that surrounds it.

In recent years, state legislators fearful of the reach of the Internet have been swept up in a frenzy to regulate students' online communications in ways that are doubtfully constitutional and that never would have seriously been entertained in other media. For instance, North Carolina in 2012 enacted a statute exposing students to as much as a year in jail for ridiculing school employees online in ways intended to "torment" them.[8] The law is believed to be the nation's first criminal statute that singles out "students" as a special class of citizens subject to differential criminal liability.

This chapter will attempt to address some of the more common questions that have arisen for student media when using the Internet as a publishing tool or as a newsgathering resource. Keep in mind that the law for online speech is, in most cases, no different from the law that governs speech that occurs in more traditional media. Therefore, be sure to consult other relevant chapters in this book (for example, "Defamation Law" in Chapter 13 or "Copyright Law" in Chapter 16) and the SPLC website for help in answering questions on specific legal topics.

Finally, a word of caution. One thing you will hear from virtually every authority on cyberspace law is that the subject is "fluid." Both the law and the technology are continuously evolving. But while technology moves forward by leaps and bounds, the law tends to work at a steady crawl. As many of the questions raised below have yet to be directly addressed by a court, some of which follows represents the Student Press Law Center's best attempt to predict the law's direction.

CENSORSHIP OF ONLINE SPEECH

The explosion of universal Internet access, and the development of ready-made publishing platforms from Facebook to Twitter to Wordpress to Tumblr, has fueled the perception that censorship is a relic as relevant to the 21st century as quill pens and inkwells. That perception is both right and wrong. It's true that today's students can more easily reach a public audience without the need for a school-subsidized printing press. But the potentially unlimited reach of online speech is in fact heightening schools' interest in censoring what students write. Remarks about school officials that used to go unpunished when spoken across the lunch table at the shopping mall food court are now targets for suspension, expulsion or even criminal charges when published online.[9]

As a matter of law, students do not lose their First Amendment protection just because their speech is on the Web rather than the printed page. In fact, the Supreme Court has said that online media is legally equivalent to print media.[10] The Court specifically rejected the government's argument that online media should be treated like broadcast media, which have traditionally been subject to far more government control, and concluded that the same strong protections that apply to print newspapers should apply equally to online speech.[11] Personal home pages, the Court said, are "the equivalent of individualized newsletters about that person or organization" and should be treated as such.[12] Because the Court chose to equate the Internet with print publications, a student website should be protected by the same laws and in the same way as more traditional forms of student media.

Because the degree of legal protection available to students will often depend on the category of school they attend (for example, public/private, high school/college, etc.), the discussion is divided accordingly below. The chapter will look first at the status of publishing on a school-affiliated website that is the online equivalent of a "school newspaper," and then turn to the rapidly growing body of law that addresses students' rights when they publish off campus on their personal time.

Public High Schools

Since the Supreme Court's 1988 ruling in *Hazelwood School District v. Kuhlmeier*,[13] many public high school administrators have had substantial — though not unlimited — leeway in controlling school-sponsored student media. Where applicable, *Hazelwood* allows school officials to restrict student speech provided they have a "valid educational purpose."[14]

However, where a public high school has established a "policy or practice" of allowing a publication to operate as a "public forum" where students express themselves freely, the administration's ability to censor student speech is more limited.[15] In other words, while a school is not required to designate a student news medium as a public forum, once it does, it cannot restrict speech without a compelling reason.[16] Courts have indicated that a compelling reason arises only where the expression causes a "material and substantial" disruption of school activities, invades the rights of others, or is otherwise unprotected by the First Amendment.[17] (A libelous statement, an imminent threat to the safety of another, or an obscene photo would be examples.) So the amount of leeway that courts will give student speech depends on the type of "forum" — public or nonpublic — in which the speech takes place.

A school's Acceptable Internet Use Policy — just like any school policy — must be in compliance with state and federal laws.

There is no reason that the same rules would not apply in the online context. Computers and other facilities used to post student publications or websites are generally the property of the school. The amount of legal protection available to online high school journalists will therefore largely turn on whether the online publication is designated, through school policy and other factors, as a forum for free expression.

A school's Acceptable Use Policy (AUP), often found in a student handbook or in district guidelines, typically sets out the rules governing student (and sometimes faculty) use of school computer networks. Looking at such a policy might help to determine whether a network has been designated a public forum. If the policy language is cautionary, referring to access as a "privilege," and includes stringent restrictions regarding the type of communication permitted, the facilities will more likely be viewed as a non-public forum where the school has reserved the right to control the content.[18] If the policy refers to student access as a "right," on the other hand, or if students have been permitted reasonably free access to the system, schools will have a more difficult time justifying acts of censorship.[19]

Of course, a school's AUP — just like any school policy — must be in compliance with state and federal laws.[20] Public school officials never have unlimited authority to control their students' online speech. Among other checks on administrative power, the

First Amendment probably requires that schools have, at the very least, a reasonable justification for banning online student speech. Moreover, the law probably also requires that an AUP be "viewpoint neutral," meaning that school officials may not, for example, use an AUP to prohibit the discussion of a particular opinion with which they disagree. Likewise, some states have enacted laws or state constitutions that offer broad protection of student expression across a variety of media, presumably including online media, that school officials are required to take into account in adopting an AUP or otherwise restricting online student speech.[21]

Unfortunately, determining the forum status of a student publication or website — which, in turn, establishes the amount of legal protection available to it — can get tricky. For a more thorough discussion of public forum analysis and high school censorship generally, please see Chapter 5.

Even where the entire online publication itself has not been declared a public forum, a certain area of a website, such as a chat room or a bulletin board system, might nevertheless qualify as a public forum if the school has explicitly designated it as such.[22] Also, chat room and bulletin board systems are often owned by third-party companies that offer the service for free in exchange for the right to place advertisements on the pages, suggesting that those pages might not be the property of the school at all. In fact, though courts have yet to rule in a case involving school-sponsored high school media, establishing a privately hosted website could help students avoid some of the censorship problems that can occur when a website is hosted on the school's computers. Fortunately, there are ample platforms for high school students seeking to find an off-campus host for their website, which helps minimize (but does not entirely avoid) the school's ability to interfere with publication.

Public Colleges

While the Supreme Court has muddied the law when it comes to determining the degree of free speech protection available to students in public high schools, it is a different story at the college level. As discussed at length in Chapter 6, the law protecting editorial content in public college student media has, for the most part, remained simple and consistent: school officials — and those acting on their behalf — must keep their hands off.

While there are few reported court decisions addressing free speech protections for online student media at public colleges or universities, there is no reason that the same simple rule should not apply with equal force. However, while public college students have the right to publish a website or post an online version of their student newspaper free from administrative censorship, the right to do so on a school-sponsored computer server may be more limited.

Because computer facilities used on college campuses are generally the property of the school, some of the public forum doctrine principles discussed above and in Chapter 5 may be applicable.[23]

A public university would not be legally required to provide its students with university e-mail accounts or its student newspaper with space on a university server to host the paper's website. However, once a college decided to do so — and after, for example, it has allowed the student newspaper to regularly create and post its website on the school server without interference — a public forum is created and the school would be prohibited from placing further restrictions on the website without a compelling interest.[24] As with high schools, a college's written Acceptable Use Policy may also be a factor in determining the status of an online forum.

Fortunately for college student media, where a school refuses to allow unrestricted access to the college server, or places unacceptable restrictions on the types of material

While most public college students have the right to publish a website or post an online version of their student newspaper free from administrative censorship, the right to do so on a school computer server may be more limited.

that can be posted, the solution is easy: go somewhere else. Private Web hosting services are reasonably inexpensive, easy to use and virtually indistinguishable to readers. Once the logistics of where the website is to be physically hosted are solved, student editors at virtually all public colleges or universities should remain free to determine the editorial and advertising content of the site free from administrative restraints (although not, perhaps, from disciplinary action following publication).[25]

As is the case with print-based media, the right of private school students to publish online free from administrative censorship may be more limited.

Private Schools

Students attending private schools do not enjoy First Amendment protection from censorship by school officials. Only government officials — or those acting on their behalf — are subject to the First Amendment's prohibitions on limiting free speech.[26] Many private schools, however, voluntarily grant free expression rights to students through written school policies.

Courts have suggested that where a private school adopts a particular policy, whether it is a disciplinary code, a student handbook or an Acceptable Use Policy, the school may be contractually bound by the policy.[27] Private school students might also be able to look to their state constitution or statutes for protection. For more information on private school press rights, see Chapter 7.

FROM THE SPLC CASE FILES

(1) Working from home, after school, on his family's computer, a public high school student created his own website and posted it on a private Internet server. Among other things, the site criticized the student's band teacher for being overly demanding and playing favorites. Among the comments posted about the teacher: "[he is] an overweight middle-aged man who doesn't like to get haircuts." Upon discovering the website, which contained no defamatory or other unlawful material, school officials suspended the student for ten days, claiming that the site violated a school policy that prohibited students from demonstrating "physical, written or verbal disrespect/threat" to a school employee.

As a result of his suspension, the student received an "F" in his band class and lower grades in other classes. The student sued. A federal district judge — in a preliminary ruling — ordered school officials to allow the student to return to classes. The judge also prohibited school officials from further restricting what the student put on his private website. A month later, the student agreed to drop his lawsuit and settle the claim after the school district agreed to pay him $30,000, remove the suspension from his records and issue a letter of apology.[28]

(2) In the spring of 2007, a student at a Connecticut high school wrote a blog post, using the website LiveJournal, criticizing school officials' decision to cancel a yearly music festival at the school. The post called the school officials "douchebags" and asked fellow students and their parents to complain to the school superintendent "to piss [the superintendent] off" even more than a previously sent mass e-mail on the subject. The school responded to the blog post by banning the student from seeking re-election as class secretary for her senior year.

The day of the election, school officials also prevented a group of students from wearing T-shirts in support of the blogger's election. The student sued, arguing that her state and federal free-speech rights had been violated. She sought an injunction that would prevent an election without her name on the ballot, and to prevent other disciplinary action against her or her supporters who wore the T-shirts. A Connecticut federal district court denied the injunction, finding that the student failed to demonstrate a likelihood of success on the merits of her constitutional claims. The court found that the blog post constituted on-campus speech for First Amendment purposes because "the blog was related to school issues, and it was reasonably foreseeable that other . . . students would view the blog and that school officials would become aware of it."

The court determined that the student did not have a First Amendment right to run for voluntary

---

office and that the school officials may have had the authority to prevent the student from running as a punishment for her statements, to promote civility in school functions. The court expressed reservations, however, about the school's power to ban the students from wearing the protest T-shirts, which the court found comparable to the protest armbands in the *Tinker* case. The student appealed the ruling to the U.S. Court of Appeals for the Second Circuit, which in 2008 affirmed the district court's ruling, though — like the district court — emphasizing that the finding of no First Amendment violation was premised on the relative leniency of the punishment imposed.[29]

INDEPENDENT/OFF-CAMPUS WEBSITES AND ONLINE MEDIA

One of today's most fiercely debated First Amendment issues among judges, attorneys and legal scholars is when (if ever) a school can regulate what students say using electronic media when they are off school premises and not attending school functions. Wave after wave of such cases began hitting the federal courts beginning in about 2007, all following a variation of the same factual situation: A student is suspended or expelled for online speech that offends or alarms school officials, and the student challenges the punishment as unconstitutional.[30]

The Supreme Court has long recognized that students, like all citizens, are protected by the First Amendment when it comes to expressing themselves off-campus.[31] In shielding student journalists from overreaching school administrators, lower courts have been even more specific.[32] As a federal court in Texas ruled: "School officials may not judge a student's behavior while he is in his home with his family nor does it seem to this court that they should have jurisdiction over his acts on a public street corner."[33] Another court noted that administrators cross well-established lines when they attempt to transform themselves into de facto parents by asserting 24-hour control over students' speech activities.[34]

The first round of online-speech cases to reach the courts largely followed these earlier cases, resulting in rulings that public school officials cannot legally censor or punish a student for material on a personal homepage or blog, or for using a personal account to send messages outside of school from a home computer, even if the subject matter of the speech is school-related or offends people at school.[35]

But a key ruling from the federal Second Circuit U.S. Court of Appeals in 2007 seemed to turn the tide against students' online freedom. Eighth-grader Aaron Wisniewski was suspended from his New York middle school for using an Instant Messaging icon that was meant to resemble a cartoon of his English teacher being shot in the head.[36] Although Wisniewski created the icon at home and sent messages while off campus to only a handful of friends, one of the recipients printed a message and brought it to school, where the teacher saw the cartoon and was traumatized. Finding that it was foreseeable that the cartoon would reach school and cause a disruptive impact there, the Second Circuit turned aside the student's First Amendment challenge and upheld the punishment.[37] The *Wisniewski* ruling appeared to unleash school authority to treat off-campus speech — which, after all, is portable and can almost always foreseeably reach a school audience — as legally no more protected than on-campus speech. In subsequent cases, courts have been willing -- especially where speech refers to violence or attacks named students personally — to erase the on-campus/off-campus line and allow schools to punish speech even where there is no proof that the author used school time or school computers, or even intended the speech to be read at school.[38] However, if a student's off-campus speech is merely critical of school employees — even if it is harsh and offensive — courts so far have been less willing to allow administrators to punish it.[39]

The zeal to expand school authority over students' online speech escalated with the nationwide furor over "cyberbullying," the use of social networking sites for cruel personal harassment.[40] In 2011, the Indiana legislature nearly enacted a law giving principals the

A 2008 national survey found that exactly 50 percent of those polled believed school officials should be allowed to discipline students who, while at home, posted entries to a social networking site like Myspace.com that might be disruptive to school classes.
Source: Fist Amendment Center, *State of the First Amendment 2008*

power to suspend or expel students who said or did anything, anywhere, that "interfered with school purposes."[41] But even in an age of "cyberbullying" hysteria, there are limits. Courts have hesitated to allow schools to intervene in purely off-campus personal disputes that are better settled by families. For instance, when a school punished a high school athlete for posting a bawdy online video in which she and a friend engaged in sexual humor at a slumber party, a federal district judge threw out the discipline on the grounds that the behavior, which merely caused some gossip at school, was not disruptive.[42]

While these cases, taken together, make clear that the First Amendment imposes limitations on the ability of school officials to punish students who create and publish off-campus websites or engage in other forms of private, online communication, some key questions remain. Chiefly, what is the appropriate legal standard for protecting such speech? Do young people have the same free speech rights as others outside of school or are they always subject to a lesser "student standard" — even when the speech exists entirely apart from school? Courts could still reasonably conclude — as some legal commentators have urged[43] — that no separate standard (including *Tinker*) is necessary or appropriate. Students who speak off-campus apart from an official school activity, it is argued, do so as private citizens and should be protected from administrative control or punishment by the same strong constitutional protections that are enjoyed by all citizens. Unfortunately, few courts have yet to go that far. In fact, most courts have so far either ducked the question or appear to have given it little serious thought.

As a result, two ideas have arguably — and with scant legal basis — begun to take root in the lower courts. First, *Tinker*'s "material disruption" standard seems to be, for now, the standard of choice for the majority of courts in applying the First Amendment to independent student speech on the Internet where at least some parts of it trickle on campus. For example, if a student regularly views his website at school or urges others to do so, that activity could cause the website to be treated the same as other independent publications that are distributed on school grounds, which are subject to *Tinker*.[44] Second, even in situations where Internet speech takes place entirely outside of school, administrators may — particularly in cases where the speech references violence — persuade a court to extend their *Tinker*-based authority to reach beyond the schoolhouse gate.[45]

FROM THE SPLC CASE FILES

Almost all court cases involving discipline for postings on Facebook, Twitter and other social media sites have originated in K-12 schools. But in a rare exception, the University of Minnesota fought one of its students all the way to the state Supreme Court over punishment imposed for the student's crude Facebook jokes about the mortuary science class she was taking. The college argued that, even though the student wrote her posts entirely on personal time using a home computer, she was still subject to discipline because the jokes indicated unfitness for her chosen profession, funeral director. The Minnesota Supreme Court allowed the discipline to stand, ruling that "a university does not violate the free speech rights of a student enrolled in a professional program when the university imposes sanctions for Facebook posts that violate academic program rules that are narrowly tailored and directly related to established professional conduct standards."[46] We will never know how the U.S. Supreme Court might have ruled, because the student, Amanda Tatro, died just days after the state-court ruling came down. The chances of a further appeal died with her.[47]

> A student's legal right to access the Internet and receive information online will often depend, in part, on the level (high school/college) and status (public/private) of the school the student attends.

AVOIDING CYBERTRAPS: TIPS FOR OFF-CAMPUS WEBSITE PUBLISHERS

While the law offers substantial protection to students who publish private, off-campus websites, students can help themselves by keeping a few tips in mind:[48]

(1) STEER CLEAR OF SCHOOL. The more contact you have with the school, the more likely a court will find that school officials have some authority to control or punish you for your actions. To be independent, you should act independently. If you are creating a website, do it at home, on your own

computer, on your own time, using your own Internet service. Do not use the school's equipment or resources. Likewise, do not encourage students to look up your website or read your social-media posts while at school.

(2) PROCLAIM YOUR INDEPENDENCE. It is strongly suggested that independent student websites include a prominent statement, or disclaimer, that the school is not involved with the site. (For example, "*The CyberVoice* is an independent student website written and published privately by students attending Central High School. *The CyberVoice* uses no school funds or other resources and all work occurs outside of school. The information and views expressed on the website are those of the author and not necessarily those of Central High School or its employees.") Similarly, the name and look of your website should abstain from anything that could reasonably confuse readers that it is officially affiliated with the school. For example, it is best to avoid publishing an official school logo or mascot as a mainstay on your homepage or calling your site by a name that is similar to an official school website or publication.

(3) VIOLENCE IS NO JOKE. Following a number of highly publicized school shootings and other violent incidents, school officials are extremely jumpy when it comes to threats to teachers, students or administrators posted on students' personal websites, even if the "threats" are remote or never intended to be taken seriously. Students across the country — with no evil intentions — have found themselves in hot water for writing poetry, creating artwork or even posting jokes with a violent or threatening theme. While such overreaction is unfortunate — and in many cases illegal — student publishers are cautioned to exercise discretion and sensitivity when covering violent topics.

(4) KNOW YOUR BOUNDARIES. Even if your school cannot legally regulate or punish you, you are still bound by the same laws of privacy, libel, obscenity and copyright that govern every publisher. If you are going to exercise your free-speech rights, take the time to understand the responsibilities that go along with such rights. This book is an excellent place to start. Don't give school officials or others an easy excuse for pulling the plug on your site.

(5) THE BEST DEFENSE IS A GOOD OFFENSE. As with traditional print publications, being able to stand — publicly and proudly — to defend a well-reported, well-written, fair and balanced Web story or a carefully crafted editorial is always the single best defense to censorship. Practice sound journalism. In most cases, that means avoiding gratuitous profanity or sexually graphic content, name-calling, rumor mongering and other cheap shots. Always strive for the high road.

More information and help for independent online publishers is available in the *SPLC Guide to Off-Campus Student Web Sites*.[49]

ACCESS TO INTERNET RESOURCES

In addition to creating new ways to publish and reach the audience, the Internet also presents student journalists with unprecedented access to information and sources when researching and reporting stories. Unfortunately, the Internet's usefulness as a research tool — for both students and faculty — has been significantly limited in some cases by administrative and technological restrictions.

As with the right to publish, a student's legal right to access the Internet and receive information online will often depend, in part, on the level (high school/college) and status (public/private) of the school the student attends.

Public High Schools

While courts have yet to specifically address the question, it is likely that high school administrators can constitutionally limit access to at least some websites and other Internet content.

The Supreme Court has upheld a law requiring the use of filtering software on public library computers to block images that constitute obscenity or child pornography, and to prevent minors from obtaining access to material that is harmful to them.[50] Another provision of the law actually requires some schools to install Internet filters on their computers.[51] Though the school provision has yet to be challenged, it seems likely, given its decision regarding public library filters and some of its past decisions involving student speech, that the Court would view at least some use of filtering software in schools as permissible.

That school administrators could block access to some websites, however, does not mean they can block access to any website. While no court has yet ruled on a constitutional standard a school must meet before blocking a website, it seems clear that a school could not block a particular site for no stated reason whatsoever, or simply because school administrators disagree with the viewpoints expressed on the site. The Constitution does not permit blatant censorship or otherwise unlawful suppression of newsgathering activities merely because the medium involved is digital rather than print-based.

Nor does a school's ability to ban or filter a website during school hours mean it automatically has the right to ban a site at all times. While courts have often upheld content-neutral "time, place, and manner" restrictions on otherwise constitutional speech, an outright ban is more likely to offend the First Amendment. Consequently, a site that might be a distraction in a computer-filled classroom might be perfectly acceptable after school hours in the library or in a student newspaper's newsroom.

The question of how best to balance government restrictions on school Internet access remains unsettled. One possibility is that judges will approach the Internet as an information resource similar to a library and look to past library censorship cases for guidance. In one such case, *Board of Education v. Pico*,[52] a board of education ordered high school officials to remove books from the school library that the board deemed inappropriate, including books the board claimed were "anti-American, anti-Christian, anti-Semitic, and just plain filthy."[53] In *Pico*, a plurality — but not a majority — of the Supreme Court held that the board had selected books for removal in a "narrowly partisan or political manner" and the board's action was therefore unconstitutional.[54]

Significantly, the *Pico* Court recognized that the right to receive information is inherent in the right to speak. Writing for the Court, Justice William Brennan noted "the State may not, consistently with the spirit of the First Amendment, contract the spectrum of available knowledge."[55] Justice Brennan explained that this principle was particularly important in school library censorship cases given the library's special role as a focal point for free and independent inquiry.

In almost the same breath, however, Brennan said that public school officials should be given broad discretion to make decisions about educational materials that "transmit community values."

Unfortunately, proclaiming such dual goals has proven much easier than achieving them, and fights between those who view a public school's library as place of intellectual freedom and those determined to impose their version of "community values" are frequent. The Internet, which can provide students with access to resource material on an unprecedented scale, is sparking similar battles.

In 1998, a federal court in Virginia was the first to address a public library's restrictions on Internet access. Citing *Pico*, the court suggested that a public library's (not a school library) decision to block access to certain websites based on content alone could be viewed as the equivalent of removing particular books from the library shelves. Such content-oriented "removal," the court stated, would probably be unconstitutional.[56]

However, in reaching its decision, the court explicitly pointed to distinctions the Supreme Court had made in *Pico* between public libraries and school libraries. The court made special note of Justice William Rehnquist's dissenting remarks that "unlike university or public libraries, elementary and secondary school libraries are not designed for freewheeling inquiry."[57] The court suggested that school officials at the elementary or high school level may enjoy more discretion in what they block, as long as the rationale for doing so is educationally sound and not based on disagreement with a particular message.[58]

It remains to be seen whether other courts will adopt such reasoning when faced with a case specifically addressing the authority of public high school officials to restrict Internet access.

INTERNET FILTERS 101

The goal of filtering software is to prevent the user of a computer from accessing websites that are inappropriate as determined by the software's installer. The mechanics of this process, however, make it far from perfect.

Broadly speaking, filtering software monitors Internet communications software (such as Web browsers, newsgroup readers, chat programs, e-mail tools and instant message applications) for material that matches its list of banned words or sites. When a user attempts to access a banned site, or another computer sends a banned word or combination of words to the filtered computer, the filter stops the information from displaying on the screen. Instead, it will show a page identifying the content as blocked, or a blank page, or sometimes even the same type of generic error a user sees when entering a page that does not exist. (Some variations of commercially available filtering software also send e-mail alerts to the installer when a user attempts to access forbidden content, or even copy the installer on the text of messages sent over the computer; these products typically are marketed to parents as a means of monitoring their children's online communications.)

Typically, two types of filtering techniques are used. First is something filter manufacturers call "content-based" filtering, which looks for banned words in the text portions of a website, e-mail or chat conversation. When a forbidden word or phrase appears, the page is blocked. Because this filter does not actually judge a site's content — it cannot tell whether the subject matter of the site is inappropriate, only whether a word that appears on the site is on its watch list — the term "content-based" is something of a misnomer. In reality, the filtering is merely word-based.

The second type of filtering is known as site-based filtering. In this method, Internet addresses known to have material considered unwelcome are added to a list by the filter's authors. When a request for that machine is entered by the user (by typing in the site's Web address, for example), the filter blocks it. Site-based filtering is much more effective than word-based filtering, both because it does not attempt to make judgments about a site's content from the words it uses and because, to get on the filtered list, a human being must generally determine that the site should be blocked. However, site-based blocking can block only sites that have been reviewed in advance; new sites will be able to pass through undetected. Additionally, most manufacturers of filtering software keep the list of blocked URLs a secret, meaning the only way to know whether the software will block a site is to install a copy and try it out.[59]

While this is how filtering software works in theory, in practice, it accomplishes its goals only about two-thirds of the time. The rest of the time, sites that should be blocked manage to get through and sites that should be available are improperly blocked.[60] Critics of filtering software regularly point to harmless and even educationally valuable sites blocked by overzealous filters; one experiment found that a website with model guidelines for Colorado high school theatre programs got filtered as "pornography" while a page displaying actual pornography from *Hustler* magazine went unfiltered.[61] In fact, the Student Press Law Center has occasionally received reports from students that the SPLC's own website has been blocked from school computers.

The FCC revisited its Internet filtering rules in 2011 and issued guidance to school districts clarifying their duty to block "harmful" websites. The Commission specifically advised that there is no legal obligation to prevent students from accessing social-networking sites on school computers: "Although it is possible that certain individual Facebook or MySpace pages could potentially contain material harmful to minors, we do not find that these Web sites are per se 'harmful to minors' or fall into one of the categories that schools and libraries must block."[62]

Public Colleges

Though courts have yet to specifically address the issue, restrictions on Internet access by public college journalists engaged in legitimate newsgathering activities would seem to be permissible only in rare, very specific cases. On more than one occasion the Supreme Court has made clear that college campuses are the quintessential "marketplace of ideas," fully protected by the First Amendment's free speech guarantees.[63] And in the 21st century, the Court has recognized that such a marketplace cannot legitimately exist without the Internet. The Supreme Court has repeatedly rejected government attempts to impose restrictions on the right of adults to engage in otherwise lawful Internet-based speech, including attempts to ban or unduly restrict speech that might not be suitable when viewed by minors.[64]

Consequently, where they exist, regulations or filters limiting access to Internet-based research material by college students — the vast majority of whom are legal adults[65] — presumably would need to be carefully tailored to limit very specific types of speech. For example, an Acceptable Use Policy (AUP) prohibiting access to sites that a court has determined to be legally "obscene," probably would pass constitutional muster; the Supreme Court has ruled that obscenity is not a category of speech protected by the First Amendment.[66]

However, broad-reaching policies that are lax in their wording or Internet filters lax in their programming, prohibiting access to material, for example, that is "indecent," "offensive," "vulgar," "derogatory," "harmful," or "sexual in nature" almost certainly would be unconstitutional. Such vaguely worded policies or imprecise technological filters reach beyond obscenity or other forms of unlawful speech to prohibit material protected by the First Amendment.[67]

Private Schools

Because private school administrators are not limited by the First Amendment, they will generally — absent a clear school policy or promise to the contrary — have greater authority to restrict how their students use school computers to surf the Web or engage in other online activities. Such restrictions may be imposed through the adoption of an Acceptable Use Policy or the installation of Internet filters. Hopefully, most private school officials — understanding the value of the Internet as an education resource and reporting tool and recognizing its place in a free society — will exercise their authority judiciously.

LIABILITY FOR ONLINE SPEECH

As mentioned above, libel is libel whether it occurs in an online news article posted to a student website or in an advertisement reproduced in a print newspaper. The same holds true for content that invades an individual's legal right to privacy or that violates a person's copyright. The medium through which an unlawful statement is published does not affect its suitability — or unsuitability — for publication.

The choice of medium may, however, affect who can be held responsible for such unlawful content.

Section 230 of the federal Communications Decency Act limits the liability of users or providers of "interactive computer services " (which specifically includes systems operated by "educational institutions"[68]) for material created or provided by someone else.[69] In other words, where school employees have played no editorial role in creating an online student newspaper, the law will protect the school from responsibility even where the offending material is housed on the school's computers.

In addition to shielding its school host, Section 230 would also likely protect student media from liability for libelous or other unlawful material posted on their website by a third party. For example, Section 230 probably limits a student newspaper's liability for reader comments or statements posted to a bulletin board or survey forum on the newspaper's website.

Note that the law provides a shield from liability only for content created or provided by an outside party. A student newspaper remains responsible for anything the newspaper staff itself produces and posts online.

A "Good Samaritan" provision in the CDA allows for the voluntary screening of "material that the provider or user considers to be obscene, lewd, lascivious, filthy, excessively violent, harassing, or otherwise objectionable...."[70] While removing such material is okay, it probably is not safe for student media staff to add to content provided by others, or to rewrite it, if immunity is to apply in full force. If a court concluded that a school official or student media staff was a content provider because it contributed "in part" to unlawful content, immunity might be lost.[71]

More information regarding the liability provisions in the federal Communications Decency Act can be found in Chapter 17.

Additionally, Congress has also provided some protection to online media for copyright law violations. The "Online Copyright Infringement Liability Limitation Act"[72] (OCILLA) exempts "online service providers" (OSP's) — a broadly defined term that specifically includes schools[73] that provide or operate their own computer network (and presumably website or chat room "operators" that allow outsiders to directly post material online) from liability for copyright violations committed by others where certain conditions are met.

Under the law, liability for storing copyrighted material on a computer network or website can be avoided if the OSP registers its address and an administrator's name with the Register of Copyrights.[74] This person would be the designated contact person when a copyright owner wants to complain about his work being infringed on the school's site. Registering requires paying a modest, one-time fee and mailing a form to the Copyright Office.[75] Once an OSP has a registered agent, it will not be liable for infringement by a third party as long as it acts promptly to resolve complaints as specified in the statute.[76]

SUMMARY

Thirty years ago, the Internet was little more than a crude concept, a nebulous idea in the minds of industry pioneers. Most developers thought it would be used primarily by the military; a few thought it might prove helpful to some businesses. Almost no one predicted that it would become the household fixture that it has.

But as with the advent of television, the telephone and other formerly "new" media, there are skeptics; those self-professed, often well-intentioned folks who fear change and attempt to stymie the growth of communications technology through restrictions. As history tells us, though, the real hazard does not come from the invention. Rather, it comes from public officials "who try to protect outdated, incumbent technologies" and who fear or misunderstand those that replace it.[77]

Fortunately, the unknown eventually becomes commonplace and the fear gradually subsides. Unfortunately, the path to such acceptance can leave behind a formidable wake. The Supreme Court has indicated that the Internet should be viewed, at least legally, as simply another means to get one's message out. While the apparatus may be revolutionary, its function is not; the age-old practice of storytelling is just as valuable whether it is accomplished with drums, paper or digitized electrons.

CASE STUDY

After Central High School's cheerleading team placed first at the Minnesota state cheerleading trials, the public high school's student newspaper published a special photo spread featuring shots taken during the competition. Mindy Moore, the mother of one of the cheerleaders called the paper's editor, Riley Reed, to compliment the staff and to request extra copies of the paper to mail to distant friends and family.

Unfortunately, all of their copies were gone, so Reed suggested that Moore check out the online version of the paper since the same photos and articles were posted there.

An hour later, the principal walked into the newsroom. He tells Reed that he just got off the telephone with Mrs. Moore, who was very upset that her daughter's photos are on the Internet. She told the principal that she had not given permission to post the photos and wants them immediately removed. She told the principal that she's heard stories of all the wackos on the Internet and doesn't "want someone down in Florida driving up to stalk my daughter." The principal — who also loved the print version of the photo spread — claims he's pretty sure the law prohibits student photos from being published online and orders you to remove them. Reed has called you for help. What can you tell him?

ANSWER:
As you see it, there are two separate issues. First, does publishing a student's photos on the Internet — with or without parental consent — violate the law even though the same photos appeared lawfully in the print version of the student newspaper? Reed tells you he wants to comply with the law and that he is willing to voluntarily remove the photos if the principal is right.

Fortunately, you tell Reed, this one is a pretty easy call. Assuming that the newspaper and the Web site are student-edited — in other words, that a student (not a school official) made the decision to include the shots in the photo spread — and assuming that the photos have none of the other legal problems that you must always be concerned about (for example, they are not obscene, there are no copyright problems, they weren't taken with a hidden camera snuck into the cheerleaders' locker room, etc.), there is no legal barrier to publishing the photos online. In this case, the photos were taken by a student staff photographer and show Moore's daughter — along with her teammates — on the stadium field where the competition was held and watched by an audience of about 8,000. (It's worth noting that both Mrs. Moore and the principal were pleased with the spread as it appeared in the print newspaper, suggesting that the photos are otherwise "clean" and appropriate.) It's clear to you that the photos present no legal problems. You tell Reed that there are no special laws prohibiting student photos — or names for that matter — from being published online. If you can publish the photos legally in the print version of the newspaper, you can publish them online as well, with the caution that New Jersey and Maine state law require consent if the website is on a school server.

Having determined that the photos can be legally published, the second question is whether Reed has the right to publish them even though the principal has ordered that they be taken down. Or, to put it another way, does the principal have the legal authority to censor otherwise lawful photos from the student website? Unfortunately, the answer to this question, you tell Reed, can get fairly complicated. Hopefully, once he informs the principal that posting the photos online is lawful, the matter will be resolved. If the principal sticks to his position, however, it becomes a case of censorship.

Like all public high school censorship cases — print or online — the amount of free speech protection available will vary depending on the "forum status" of the censored media. Whether a student website qualifies as a public or a closed forum depends on a number of different factors. Among them:

(1) The school's location (for example, is the school in a state with a student free expression law?);

(2) Existing school policies (for example, does the school district have a student media policy or an Acceptable Use Policy for Internet usage that specifies who is responsible for content decisions?);

(3) Website logistics and structure (for example, is the site hosted on a school or a private server? Is the website produced as part of a class? Where do the newspaper and website get their funding? Who physically posts new material to the site?); and

(4) Past and existing editorial practices (for example, have student editors historically been allowed to determine the content of the website? Do school officials have to review and approve Web site material before it is posted?).

The ability to contest the principal's censorship legally, you tell Reed, will depend on the answers to these questions. As with print publications, if the website qualifies as a forum for student expression, the school's ability to censor non-disruptive, lawful material (such as the photos at issue here) would be limited. On the other hand, if the website is a closed forum, school officials have greater — though not unlimited — authority to control the material that is posted. In this case, the principal still would likely have to show that he has a reasonable educational justification for banning student photos (or names) from the website. Absent something more substantive than an unsubstantiated fear of "wackos in Florida," it's by no means certain that he could do so.

ENDNOTES

1   It is generally accepted that the present-day Internet evolved from a small network of computers known as ARPANET. The Internet Society: History of the Internet (http://www.isoc.org/internet/history/brief.shtml) (last visited August 21, 2013).
2   As of June 30, 2012, 78.6 percent of North Americans and more than 245 million people in the United States are estimated to be regular Internet users. *See Internet World Stats, Internet Users in the Americas,* http://www.internetworldstats.com/stats2.htm (last visited June 21, 2013).
3   *Internet Access in U.S. Public Schools and Classrooms: 1994-2003,* National Center for Education Statistics (Publication No. NCES 2005-015) at 4 (February 2005), http://www3.northern.edu/rc/pages/Reading_Clinic/distance_education.pdf (last visited May 3, 2013).
4   *See, e.g.,* Associated Press, "School districts carefully weigh using online images," April 29, 2001 (in response to fears that pedophiles were using school websites to track down children, FBI admitted that there had been no known cases where online child pornography could be traced to a school website).
5   For a fuller discussion of this issue, *See* Chapter 14.
6   *See Dow Jones & Co. v. Gutnick* (HCA 56 Dec. 10, 2002) (Australian High Court ruled that its country's courts do have jurisdiction to hear libel case brought against U.S. publisher). For more information, *See* Chapter 13. At least domestically, an approach to this jurisdictional question is beginning to emerge for defamation cases. *See, e.g., Best Van Lines, Inc. v. Walker,* 490 F.3d 239 (2d Cir. 2007) (finding that merely posting information on a website that is accessible in a state is not sufficient to provide jurisdiction without demonstrating additional contacts with the state); *Cybersell, Inc. v. Cybersell, Inc.,* 130 F.3d 414, 418 (9th Cir. 1997) (same).
7   *See United States v. Thomas,* 74 F.3d 701 (6th Cir. 1996), *cert. denied,* 519 U.S. 820 (1996) (upholding obscenity convictions by Tennes*See* jury of California couple who published "Nastiest Place on Earth" computer bulletin board system). *Cf. United States v. Rowe,* 414 F.3d 271 (2d Cir. 2005) (finding venue was proper in New York to prosecute individual who resided in Kentucky for publishing an advertisement on the Internet to trade obscene materials (child pornography)).
8   N.C.G.S.A. Sec. 14-458.2 (2012).
9   *See, e.g.,* N.C. Sess. Law 2012-149 (North Carolina statute enacted in 2012 making it a misdemeanor for a student to post a photo of a school employee online with an intent to "torment" or "intimidate").
10 *Reno v. American Civil Liberties Union,* 521 U.S. 844, 870 (1997), *aff'g* 929 F. Supp. 824 (E.D. Pa. 1996).
11 *Id.* (rejecting the government's assertion that the Internet should, like broadcast speech, be subject to more stringent regulation and finding that there is "no basis for qualifying the level of First Amendment scrutiny that should be applied to [the Internet]").
12 *Id.* at 853 n.9.
13 484 U.S. 260 (1988).
14 *Id.* at 273. *See also Ward v. Hickey,* 996 F.2d 448, 452 (1st Cir.1993) ("[I]t is well-settled that public schools may limit classroom speech to promote educational goals."). *Planned Parenthood of S. Nevada v. Clark County Sch. Dist.,* 941 F.2d 817, 829-30 (9th Cir. 1991) (en banc) (ruling that schools'

restrictions on access must be viewpoint neutral).

15 *Hazelwood Sch. Dist. v. Kuhlmeier*, 484 U.S. 260, 267 (1988) (citing *Perry Educ. Assn. v. Perry Local Educators' Assn.*, 460 U.S. 37, 47 (1983)). "[U]nless the schools affirmatively intend to open a forum for indiscriminate use, restrictions reasonably related to the school's mission that are imposed on the content of school-sponsored publications do not violate the first amendment." *Planned Parenthood*, 941 F.2d at 819.

16 *Perry Ed. Ass'n*, 460 U.S. at 45 ("In these quintessential public forums, the government may not prohibit all communicative activity. For the state to enforce a content-based exclusion it must show that its regulation is necessary to serve a compelling state interest and that it is narrowly drawn to achieve that end.").

17 *Tinker v. Des Moines Indep. Community Sch. Dist.*, 393 U.S. 503, 511 (1969). *See also, e.g., Morse v. Frederick*, 127 S. Ct. 2618 (2007) (holding that the school did not violate student's First Amendment rights in confiscating banner he displayed at school-affiliated event and suspending student for his actions that promoted illegal drug use); *Pinard v. Clatskanie Sch. Dist. 6J*, 446 F.3d 964 (9th Cir. 2006) (holding that the court must consider all circumstances presented to the school when determining whether speech could materially and substantially disrupt the school environment); *Wisniewski v. Bd. of Ed. of Weedsport Central Sch. Dist.*, 494 F.3d 34 (2d Cir. 2007) (concluding that school reasonably believed student's cartoon depiction of teacher being shot had the potential to materially and substantially disrupt the school environment).

18 The Virginia Department of Education, Division of Technology, has a website including various examples — some quite restrictive, others more free-speech friendly — of high school AUPs. Virginia Dept. of Ed., *Acceptable Use Policies: A Handbook*, http://www.doe.virginia.gov/support/safety_crisis_management/internet_safety/acceptable_use_policy.shtml (last visited Oct. 8, 2012). *See also Making Progress: Rethinking State and School District Policies Concerning Mobile Technologies and Social Media*, Consortium on School Networking, April 2012, http://www.splc.org/pdf/making_progress_2012.pdf (last visited October 8, 2012). The SPLC Model Guidelines also refer to student online media and can provide a useful reference point. Student Press Law Center, *Student Press Law Center Model Guidelines for High School Student Media*, http://www.splc.org/hsguidelines.

19 *Hazelwood*, 484 U.S. at 271-72.

20 *See, e.g., Sypniewski v. Warren Hills Reg'l Bd. of Educ.*, 307 F.3d 243, 258 (3d Cir. 2002) (enjoining enforcement of a school's anti-harassment policy as violative of First Amendment rights because it was overly vague); *Saxe v. State Coll. Area Sch. Dist.*, 240 F.3d 200, 214 (3d Cir. 2001) (same); *Flaherty v. Keystone Oaks Sch. Dist.*, 247 F. Supp. 2d 698 (W.D.Pa. 2003) (striking down as unconstitutional high school policy prohibiting "abusive," "offensive," "harassing," or "inappropriate" behavior that was used to punish student who posted messages to an off-campus, online message board).

21 *See, e.g.,* CAL. ED. CODE SEC. 48907 (2003).

22 *See generally United States v. American Library Ass'n*, 539 U.S. 194 (2003) (holding that Internet terminals in public libraries were not public fora because libraries never declared them to be public fora), *rev'g* 201 F. Supp. 2d 401 (E.D. Pa. 2002). *See also Cornelius v. NAACP Legal Defense & Educ. Fund, Inc.*, 473 U.S. 788, 802 (1985) (stating that the government expressly creates a public forum by "intentionally opening a non-traditional forum for public discourse."). *But cf. Hazelwood*, 484 U.S. at 267 (holding that a school creates a public forum by establishing a "policy and practice" of allowing free expression).

23 *See Loving v. Boren*, 956 F. Supp. 953 (W.D. Okla. 1997), *aff'd*, 133 F.3d 771 (10th Cir. 1998) (applying forum doctrine to university server and Internet service); *See also Landers v. State Univ. Sys. of Calif.*, No. BC 160005 (Calif. Sup. Ct., L.A. County Jan. 14, 1997) (unpublished) (trial court order granting preliminary injunction against university's enforcement of regulations on content of online speech transmitted using university server, based on court's finding that server is a designated public forum for use by students and employees, and that restrictions on content of speech must be narrowly tailored to survive strict scrutiny).

24 *See Kincaid v. Gibson*, 236 F.3d 342 (6th Cir. 2001) ("we find that forum analysis is the appropriate framework under which to proceed in this case" (involving censorship of a public college student yearbook).

25 *See, e.g., Yoder v. Univ. of Louisville*, No. 12-5354. 2013 WL 1976515 (6th Cir. May 15, 2013) (unpublished). In the *Yoder* case, a federal appeals court upheld a public university's decision to punish a graduate student in the nursing program who made a string of jokes on her off-campus personal blog about observing childbirth, describing the family she was observing with such detail that the college believed patient confidentiality might have been compromised.

26 *See Hudgens v. N.L.R.B.*, 424 U.S. 507 (1976). *See also Shanley v. Northeast Indep. Sch. Dist.*, 462 F.2d 960 (5th Cir. 1972); *Blackburn v. Fisk Univ.*, 443 F.2d 121 (6th Cir. 1971); *Post v. Payton*, 323 F. Supp. 799 (E.D.N.Y. 1971).

27 *Steinberg v. Chicago Med. Sch.*, 371 N.E.2d 634 (Ill. 1977).

28 *See O'Brien v. Westlake City Schools Bd. of Educ.*, No. 1:98CV 647 (E.D. Ohio 1998); Ohio school district settles with student over Web page that criticized teacher, Student Press Law Center *Report*, Spring 1998, at 35.

29 *See Doninger v. Niehoff*, 514 F. Supp. 2d 199 (D. Conn. 2007), *aff'd*, 527 F.3d 51 (2d Cir. 2008). Notably, the first round of court rulings in the *Doninger* case involved the student's request for an injunction restoring her class office as the case was ongoing. The courts' observations about the strength of Doninger's First Amendment claims were made in the context of deciding whether she was so likely to prevail that she was entitled to the immediate relief she sought. These preliminary rulings are of less significance than the ultimate ruling in Doninger's case, which came in 2011 when the matter was back before the Second Circuit. The judges somewhat backed away from their preliminary ruling that no First Amendment violation took place. Instead, the court merely decided that school officials could, in light of the confusing state of student First Amendment rights online, have reasonably believed they were acting constitutionally; because of that reasonable belief, the officials were immune from paying Doninger any damages, which ended her case. *See Doninger v. Niehoff*, 642 F.3d 334, 339 (2d Cir. 2011) (affirming dismissal of First Amendment claim

on qualified immunity grounds). In light of this more moderated subsequent ruling, it would be risky for a school to rely on the initial round of *Doninger* decisions to punish a student for speech on an off-campus blog seeking to stir up opposition to school policy decisions.

30 *See* Frank D. LoMonte, *Reaching Through the SchoolHouse Gate: Students' Eroding First Amendment Rights in a Cyber-Speech World*, American Constitution Society Issue Brief, March 2, 2009 http://www.acslaw.org/publications/issue-briefs/reaching-through-the-schoolhouse-gate-students-eroding-first-amendment-r-0 (last viewed October 8, 2012).

31 *Tinker v. Des Moines Indep. Community Sch. Dist.*, 393 U.S. 503, 511 (1969) (holding that "students in school as well as out of school are 'persons' under our Constitution.").

32 *See, e.g., Thomas v. Granville Sch. Dist.*, 607 F.2d 1043 (2d Cir. 1979); *Shanley v. Northeast Indep. Sch. Dist.*, 462 F.2d 960 (5th Cir. 1972); *Hatter v. Los Angeles City High Sch. Dist.*, 452 F.2d 673 (9th Cir. 1971); *Sullivan v. Houston Indep. Sch. Dist.*, 307 F. Supp. 1328 (S.D. Tex. 1969).

33 *Sullivan*, 307 F. Supp. at 1340-41.

34 *Shanley*, 462 F.2d at 966.

35 *Layshock v. Hermitage Sch. Dist.*, 496 F. Supp. 2d 587 (W.D. Pa. 2007) (school violated student's First Amendment rights by punishing him for creating a false and derogatory profile of school principal on Myspace. com while off campus); *Flaherty v. Keystone Oaks Sch. Dist.*, 247 F. Supp. 2d 698 (W.D. Pa. 2003) (high school policy used to punish student who posted messages to an off-campus, online message board from his home struck down as unconstitutional, in part, because it failed to distinguish between on-campus and offcampus speech); *Mahaffey ex rel. Mahaffey v. Aldrich*, 236 F. Supp. 2d 779 (E.D. Mich. 2002) (suspension of student contributor to off-campus Web site called "Satan's Web Page" violated First Amendment, where court found that material did not constitute a "true threat"); *Killion v. Franklin Regional Sch. Dist.*, 136 F. Supp. 2d 446 (W.D. Pa. 2001) (First Amendment prohibited school from imposing a 10-day suspension on a student who sent an e-mail from his home to other private e-mail accounts that made disparaging remarks about a school official's sex life even where an unidentified student distributed copies of the e-mail at school); *Emmett v. Kent Sch. Dist.*, 92 F. Supp. 2d 1088 (W.D. Wash. 2000) (emergency expulsion of high school honor student who published "mock obituaries" of his friends on his private website held to have violated First Amendment); *Beussink v. Woodland Sch. Dist.*, 30 F. Supp. 2d 1175 (E.D. Mo. 1998) (high school officials violated student's First Amendment rights when they suspended him for ten days for publishing off-campus Web site criticizing school and school officials); *O'Brien v. Westlake City Schools Bd. of Ed.*, No. 1:98CV 647 (E.D. Ohio 1998) (unpublished) (ordering public high school officials to refrain from further interference with student's private Web site and to reinstate student suspended for publishing Web site that violated school policy prohibiting "disrespect" of school employees); *Beidler v. North Thurston County (Wash.) Sch. Dist.*, No. 99-2-00236-6 (Thurston Cty. Super. Ct. July 18, 2000) (unpublished) (school district held to have violated First Amendment in suspending a student for the remainder of the school year after discovering that he had created private Web site that ridiculed a school administrator). *See also Coy ex rel. Coy v. Bd. of Educ. of North Canton City Schools*, 205 F. Supp. 2d 791 (N.D. Ohio 2002) (in motion for summary judgment, court held that the suspension of a student who merely visited his skateboarding website, which was created at home, likely violated First Amendment).

36 *Wisniewski v. Bd. of Ed. of the Weedsport Central Sch. Dist.*, 494 F.3d 34 (2d Cir. 2007).

37 *Id.* at 40.

38 *See Kowalski v. Berkeley County Sch.*, 652 F.3d 565 (4th Cir. 2011) (applying Supreme Court's *Tinker* standard and rejecting First Amendment challenge to suspension of student who created MySpace social networking page devoted to accusing a classmate of spreading herpes); *D.J.M. v. Hannibal Pub. Sch. Dist. No. 60*, 647 F.3d 754 (8th Cir. 2011) (applying *Tinker* and upholding suspension of student who used Facebook to chat online with friends about obtaining guns and shooting particular disliked classmates). *See also J.S. v. Bethlehem Area Sch. Dist.*, 807 A.2d 847 (Pa. 2001) (upholding expulsion of junior high school student who published website that included an image of his teacher's bloody and severed head and "mock" solicitations for hit man fund to execute her).

39 *See, e.g., J.S. v. Blue Mountain Sch. Dist.*, 650 F.3d 915 (3d Cir. 2011) (en banc) (overturning school district's punishment of middle school student who created a mock MySpace profile parodying her principal, including coarse references to the principal's family and sexual habits); *See also Layshock v. Hermitage Sch. Dist.*, 650 F.3d 205 (3d Cir. 2011) (en banc) (affirming district court's ruling in favor of high school student who mocked principal on MySpace page in which "principal" claimed to be a "big steroid freak" who smoked "big blunts" and was a "big whore").

40 The National Conference of State Legislatures defines cyberbullying as "the willful and repeated use of cell phones, computers, and other electronic communication devices to harass and threaten others." National Conference of State Legislatures, "Issues & Research: Cyberbullying," *available at* http://www.ncsl.org/issues-research/educ/cyberbullying.aspx (last visited June 21, 2013). Harvard University's Berkman Center published an overview of bullying statutes, including those specifically singling out electronic bullying for distinct punishment, in February 2012. As of that survey, 48 states had enacted laws requiring schools to address bullying, including eight states that imposed criminal penalties for bullying. *See* Dena T. Sacco et al., "Overview of State Anti-Bullying Legislation and Other Related Laws," Berkman Center for Internet & Society, Feb. 23, 2012, *available at* http://cyber.law.harvard.edu/sites/cyber.law.harvard.edu/files/State_Anti_bullying_Legislation_Overview_0.pdf (last viewed June 21, 2013).

41 Frank LoMonte, "Bill letting Indiana schools punish off-campus conduct gets shipped to study committee, buying students a reprieve," SPLC Blog, March 8, 2012, *available at* http://www.splc.org/wordpress/?p=3329.

42 *T.V. v. Smith-Green Com'ty Sch. Corp.*, 807 F.Supp.2d 767 (N.D. Ind. 2011)

43 *See, e.g.,* Aaron Caplan, *Public Sch. Discipline for Creating Uncensored Anonymous Internet Forums*, 39 Willamette L. Rev. 93 (2003); David Hudson, *Censorship of Student Internet Speech: The Effect of Diminishing Student Rights, Fear of the Internet, and Columbine*, 2000 L. Rev. M.S.U.-D.C.L. 199 (2000).

44 Courts have sent mixed signals about how much of a role student publishers must play in on-campus

distribution to be held responsible when their site is visited at school. For more information, *See* the *SPLC Guide to Off Campus Student Web Sites* (available online at http://www.splc.org/legalresearch. asp?id=13).

45 *See, e.g.,* J.S., 807 A. 2d at 847.
46 *Tatro v. Univ. of Minn.*, 816 N.W.2d 509, 521 (Minn. 2012)
47 Seth Zweifler, "Amanda Tatro, who fought free speech battle against the University of Minnesota, dead at 31," SPLC Blog, June 26, 2012, *available at* http://www.splc.org/wordpress/?p=3844.
48 Adapted from Hiestand, M., "It's the Law: Tips for Student Publishers of Off-Campus Web Sites," *Trends in High School Media* (July 2004) (National Scholastic Press Association).
49 Available on the SPLC website at: http://www.splc.org/legalresearch.asp?id=13.
50 *United States v. American Library Ass'n*, 539 U.S. 194 (2003) (challenging library filter provisions in Child Internet Protection Act, (CIPA), 47 U.S.C. Sec. 254(h)(6)).
51 Schools receiving E-rate discounts for Internet services or that are receiving Title III funds for technology are required to install Internet filters on their computers. Child Internet Protection Act (CIPA), 47 U.S.C. Sec. 254(h)(5); 20 U.S.C. Sec. 6777. One of the confusing aspects of the federal laws that require filtering is that their provisions, while parallel, are not the same. For example, schools that receive discounts on their Internet connections fall under a portion of the law that requires the school to "monitor" the behavior of students using the system and only allows monitors to disable the filters for adults engaged in "lawful" activity. 47 U.S.C. Sec. 254(h)(5)(B)(i) and (D). Schools that receive federal funding but do not receive discounts on their Internet service are only required to install filters — that is, the law says nothing about monitoring users. *See generally* 20 U.S.C. Sec. 6777(a)(1)(A). Additionally, these schools are permitted to disable the filters for anyone, adult or minor, engaged in "lawful" use. 20 U.S.C. Sec. 6777(c).
52 457 U.S. 853 (1982).
53 *Id.* at 856.
54 *Id.* at 870.
55 *Id.* at 866 (quoting *Griswold v. Connecticut*, 381 U.S. 479, 482 (1965)); *See also Stanley v. Georgia*, 394 U.S. 557, 564 ("the Constitution protects the right to receive information and ideas").
56 *Mainstream Loudoun v. Bd. of Trustees of the Loudoun County Library*, 2 F. Supp. 2d 783 (E.D. Va. 1998) (quoting *Reno*, 929 F. Supp. at 838). *See also Minarcini v. Strongsville*, 384 F. Supp. 698 (N.D. Ohio 1974), *aff'd*, 541 F.2d 577 (6th Cir. 1976) (holding that once a library is established, the school board cannot place conditions on use of the contents based on the personal views of the school board members).
57 *Mainstream Loudoun*, 2 F. Supp. 2d at 794 (quoting *Pico*, 457 U.S. at 915 (Rehnquist, J., dissenting)).
58 *Id.* at 795.
59 For example, the owners of CyberPatrol sought and obtained permanent injunctions against two hackers who distributed a utility that allows users to *See* CyberPatrol's list of filtered sites. *Microsystems Software, Inc. v. Scandinavia Online AB*, 226 F.3d 35 (1st Cir. 2000), dismissing appeal from 98 F. Supp. 2d 74 (D. Mass. 2000). Later, the Copyright Office of the Library of Congress issued regulations stating that accessing the list solely for the purpose of criticism could constitute fair use. Exemption to Prohibition on the Circumvention of Copyright Protection Systems for Access Control Technologies, 65 Fed. Reg. 64,555 (October 27, 2000) (to be codified at 37 C.F.R. pt. 201).
60 COPA Commission, *Final Report of the COPA Commission*, Oct. 20, 2000, at II(B), *available at* http://www.copacommission.org/report/recommendations.shtml (last visited Sept. 12, 2013); *See also COPA Commission, Filtering/Blocking*, Oct. 20, 2000, *available at* http://www.copacommission.org/report/filteringblocking.shtml (last visited Sept. 14, 2008). *See also* Adam Goldstein, *Like a Sieve: The Child Internet Protection Act and Ineffective Filters in Libraries*, 12 FORDHAM INTELL. PROP. MEDIA & ENT. L.J. 1187, n.36 and accompanying text (2002) (averaging out the success rates in the COPA report and explaining why the filters are not cumulative in effect).
61 *See* Electronic Fontier Foundation & Online Policy Group, "Internet Blocking in Public Schools: A Study on Internet Access in Educational Institutions," June 2003, *available at* http://w2.eff.org/Censorship/Censorware/net_block_report/net_block_report.pdf (last visited July 11, 2013).
62 FCC Final Rule, "Schools and Libraries Universal Service Support Mechanism and a National Broadband Plan for Our Future," 47 C.F.R. Part 52, 76 FR 56295-01 at 56297 (Sept. 15, 2011).
63 *Rosenberger v. Rectors and Visitors of the Univ. of Virginia*, 515 U.S. 819 (1995); *Healy v. James*, 408 U.S. 169 (1972); *Widmar v. Vincent*, 454 U.S. 263 (1981) (there can be "no doubt that the First Amendment rights of speech and association extend to the campuses of state universities.")
64 *Ashcroft v. American Civil Liberties Union*, 124 S.Ct. 2783 (2004) (striking down federal Child Online Protection Act [COPA], 47 U.S.C. Sec. 231, that made it a crime to post material on the Internet for commercial purposes that was "harmful to minors" because of burden law placed on constitutionally protected speech enjoyed by adults); *Reno v. American Civil Liberties Union*, 521 U.S. 844 (1997) (striking down as unconstitutional provisions in the federal Communications Decency Act [CDA], 47 U.S.C. Sec. 223(a) and (d), that made it a crime to transmit "indecent" material or display "patently offensive" material on the Internet). *See also Ashcroft v. Free Speech Coalition*, 535 U.S. 234 (2002) (striking down as unconstitutional provisions of federal Child Pornography Prevention Act [CPPA] that banned "virtual child pornography"). In addition to striking down federal legislation aimed at prohibiting otherwise lawful Internet speech, courts have also struck down similar attempts by state lawmakers. *See, e.g., American Civil Liberties Union v. Johnson*, 194 F.3d 1149 (10th Cir. 1999) (New Mexico law criminalizing online dissemination of material deemed "harmful to minors" violated First Amendment by burdening otherwise protected adult speech); *PSINet, Inc. v. Chapman*, 362 F.3d 227 (4th Cir. 2004) (Virginia law criminalizing dissemination over Internet, for commercial purposes, of materials harmful to minors violated First Amendment because of burden it imposed on protected adult speech); *American Library Ass'n v. Pataki*, 969 F. Supp. 160 (S.D.N.Y. 1997) (striking down New York statute making it a crime to use a computer to disseminate obscene material to minors); *State v. Weidner*, 611 N.W. 2d 684 (Wis. 2000) (state law criminalizing the transmission of harmful material to minors over the Internet is unconstitutional). There appears to be more judicial willingness to allow for regulation

of access to online material by minors rather than for regulations or prohibitions on the material itself. *See United States v. American Library Ass'n*, 539 U.S. 194 (2003) (upholding library filter provisions in federal Child Internet Protection Act [CIPA], 47 U.S.C. Sec. 254(h)(6)); *FTC v. Toysmart.com*, 2000 WL 34016434, No. 00- 11341-RGS (D.Mass. July 21, 2000) (stipulated consent agreement and final order enjoining toy company from violating federal Child Online Privacy Protection Act [COPPA], 15 U.S.C. Sec. 6501-6506, which requires that commercial websites or online services directed at children obtain parental consent before collecting personal information from children under the age of 13).

65 According to the U.S. Census Bureau survey, 99 percent of those enrolled in American colleges or universities during the fall of 2000 were 18 years of age or older. The full survey is *available at*: http://chronicle.com/weekly/almanac/2001/nation/0102001.htm (subscription required) (last visited July 8, 2007).

66 *Miller v. California*, 413 U.S. 15 (1973), *reh'g denied*, 414 U.S. 881 (1973).

67 *See* cases cited above. *See also* Marjorie Heins, *Academic Freedom and the Internet*, Academe, May-June 1998, at 21. Note, though, that in one of the few cases to address the issue of Internet access on a public college computer network, the U.S. Court of Appeals for the Fourth Circuit upheld a state law prohibiting state employees from accessing sites that were "sexually explicit" in nature. *Urofsky v. Gilmore*, 216 F.3d 401 (4th Cir. 2000) (en banc), *cert. denied*, 531 U.S. 1070 (2001). The court ruled against professors who claimed the law was overbroad in that it prohibited access to vast studies in the health sciences, not to mention thousands of masterpieces of art and poetry. The effect of this ruling on student journalists arguably is limited, as there is a significant difference between the right of an employer to prohibit his employee from accessing sexually explicit materials while at work and the authority of public college officials to limit student journalists engaged in lawful newsgathering activities. *Compare Loving v. Boren*, 956 F. Supp. 953 (W.D. Okla. 1997), *aff'd*, 133 F.3d 771 (10th Cir. 1998) (university professor lacked standing to challenge university policy that conditioned access to full Internet newsgroup service on bases of age and academic purposes); *Pichelmann v. Madsen*, No. 01-3736, 2002 WL 442248 (7th Cir. Mar. 19, 2002) (university did not violate First Amendment in ordering student employee to stop using feminist quote on work-related e-mail because speech was matter of private, not public, concern).

68 47 U.S.C. Sec. 230 (f)(2). *But see* Ray August, *Issues in Higher Education: Gratis Dictum! The Limits of Academic Free Speech on the Internet*, 10 J. Law & Pub. Pol'y 27, 47 (1998) (law professor argues the statute provides immunity only for private organizations and believes that public schools could be held liable as publishers for unlawful content posted to their Web sites if they screen content).

69 47 U.S.C. Sec. 230.

70 47 U.S.C.A. Sec. 230(c)(2)(A).

71 *See generally Fair Housing Council of San Fernando Valley v. Roommates.Com*, LLC, 521 F.3d 1157 (9th Cir. 2008) (en banc) (concluding that website operator could be "information content provider" and therefore not entitled to Section 230 immunity from housing discrimination claim, where website was designed to require users to enter demographic information prohibited by Fair Housing Act and to match up responses with landlords seeking to rent based on tenants' characteristics).

72 17 U.S.C. Sec. 512(a) - (k).

73 17 U.S.C. Sec. 512(e).

74 17 U.S.C. Sec. 512(c). Note subsection (c)(2) requiring the designation of agent.

75 *Id*. Forms are available online at: http://www.copyright.gov/onlinesp/) (last visited Sept. 12, 2013)

76 17 U.S.C. Sec. 512(3).

77 David Bartlett, *Soul of a News Machine*, 47 Fed. Communications L.J. 1, 22 (1996).

CHAPTER 10

Broadcast Student Media

This chapter is brief, but necessary. It is brief because, in many respects, there is no need to distinguish between the legal challenges faced by student journalists working in television and radio and those faced by their print-based counterparts. In the areas of libel, invasion of privacy, copyright, reporter's privilege and freedom of information law, the legal issues confronting broadcast and print reporters are virtually identical. Those topics are discussed elsewhere in this book.[1] This chapter is necessary because broadcasters, unlike journalists in print and other "off-the-air" mediums, are subject to federal regulation, most in the form of rules established by the Federal Communications Commission (FCC). This regulation, however, must be limited because like print journalists, student broadcasters — at least those at public schools — are also entitled to important First Amendment protections.

BROADCAST VS. NON-BROADCAST SPEECH

Courts have allowed government regulation of broadcasting in ways that, as a constitutional matter, would never be tolerated in the print or non-broadcast electronic media, such as the Internet, cable, satellite or closed-circuit systems. But as some critics have pointed out, it is not always clear why. "Although the courts have justified these apparent contradictions on the grounds that different media present different First Amendment considerations, they do not often explain in any rigorous analytical detail how the differences in media result in constitutional distinctions. It is even rarer for a court to test the breadth or scope of its holding against the constitutional justification for differences in regulation."[2]

> Courts have allowed government regulation of broadcasting in ways that would never be tolerated in the print or non-broadcast electronic media.

One of the historical justifications given for the regulation of broadcasting is the limited number of broadcast frequencies that are available to be assigned by the FCC.[3] As numerous critics have pointed out, however, technological advances in broadcasting raise serious questions about the continued validity of this "scarcity" argument.[4] Cable, satellite, cellular, broadband Internet and other emerging, widely available new media technologies — with their seemingly boundless supply of programming "channels" — strain the credibility of the scarcity argument.

> Technological advances in broadcasting and the Internet have raised serious questions about the continued validity of the "scarcity" justification for the FCC's regulation of broadcasting.

Another justification for FCC regulation is related to broadcast frequency "pollution." For example, if all radio stations in a city wanted to call themselves "Mighty 100" and broadcast at 100 megahertz, the result would be unintelligible. To the extent that the FCC oversees "technical compliance" to ensure that all those who wish to broadcast can do so without stepping on (or being stepped on by) other broadcasters, the regulatory distinction between print and broadcast media might be justified. Still, a rationale based on controlling frequency pollution would not justify restrictions on a particular broadcast's content.

More recently the FCC has increasingly pointed to another reason to justify its content-based restrictions: harm to minors or children. Emphasizing that broadcast speech is "uniquely accessible"[5] to children and that there is a "compelling interest in protecting the physical and psychological well-being of minors,"[6] the Supreme Court has upheld some FCC restrictions aimed at limiting such harm.[7] Not surprisingly, defining what is "harmful to minors" and then determining what can and should be done to prevent it, while balancing such restrictions against the free speech rights of adults, has proven easier said than done.[8]

> The Supreme Court has permitted restrictions on broadcast content deemed "harmful to minors."

While a loosely defined and unchecked FCC goal of restricting material that is "harmful to minors" certainly poses risks to broadcast and non-broadcast media alike, the more stringent restrictions imposed on over-the-air communications have not been applied to "off-the-air" systems such as cable or closed-circuit systems.[9] Nor have such restrictions been imposed on satellite or Internet-based communication systems.[10] For the most part, individuals working on student-run non-broadcast television or radio stations are entitled to First Amendment protections similar to those that protect the print media.

FCC REGULATIONS

Because the FCC's primary statutory function is issuing broadcast licenses, most of its regulations concern either the license application process or the technical operation of a broadcast radio or television station once a license is obtained. These can be fairly complex and generally are not directly related to broadcast content.

Notably, a handful of other regulations are aimed specifically at controlling broadcast programming content, control that in most cases would be unconstitutional if directed at non-broadcasters. For example, current FCC regulations address: (1) political broadcasting and equal time rules; (2) lottery and contest programming; (3) station promotions; (4) broadcast of telephone conversations; (5) broadcast hoaxes; (6) underwriting announcements on noncommercial-educational stations and (7) "indecent" programming (see Chapter 15 for more information on the broadcast "indecency" standard). Further, at various times, FCC regulations — or as is more often the case, the threat of FCC regulations — have also resulted in programming controls over such areas as "family viewing time," "children's television," television violence and drug lyrics. Though the FCC, in 1987, repealed the Fairness Doctrine, which required broadcasters to provide individuals with opposing viewpoints to an issue a reasonable opportunity to respond, both lawmakers and the FCC have at times suggested reviving the doctrine.[11]

A thorough discussion of FCC regulations is beyond the scope of this book. Student broadcasters are urged to consult the sources listed at the end of this chapter for more information about compliance with specific regulations.

KEEPING A PUBLIC FILE

When an educational broadcast licensee, which is generally the university's board of directors or university itself, seeks to renew its broadcast license, the station must submit FCC Form 303-S.[12] Section III, Item 3 of that form asks the applicant to certify that the station has kept a "public file" at the station during the previous license term.

A public file is a list of documents that every broadcast television and radio station must keep on-hand and available for public inspection during regular business hours. Failure to follow the FCC's public file rules may result in a fine – which the Commission calls a "forfeiture order."[13]

In 2009, WEAX(FM), which was licensed to Tri-State University in Angola, Indiana, was ordered to pay $9,000 after admitting that the station did not maintain all of the information that the FCC requires to be in a public file.[14] The FCC did not find it relevant whether anyone had ever attempted to inspect the file, stating that failure to maintain the required documents "diminishes the public's ability to determine and comment on whether the station is serving the community."[15]

Moreover, the penalty levied was not reduced because WEAX was a noncommercial, educational station that would have a hard time paying an FCC fine. When determining how much to fine a broadcast station for FCC violations, the Commission will only consider the finances of the licensee, which is normally the university, and not the finances of the station.[16] It would be difficult for a university to claim that a four-figure fine would cause undue financial hardship, even if it is clear that any fine will be taken directly out of the broadcast station's operations budget.

Additionally, when assessing forfeiture orders, the FCC will not take mercy on a station

A 2008 national survey found that 66 percent of those polled believed the government should be allowed to require television bradcasers to offer equal time to conservative and liberal commentators. The same survey also found that 38 percent of the respondents felt the government should be allowed to require broadcasters to air a specified amount of "positive news" as a condition of granting their FCC license.
Source: First Amendment Center, *State of the First Amendment 2008*

because it is noncommercial. It is the FCC's policy that "there is no proposed forfeiture exemption or reduction based on the noncommercial status of a station."[17]

With unforgiving penalties awaiting the station that is not to keep a public file, it is important to know exactly what documents an educational radio or TV station must have on hand. The FCC's public file rules are embodied in FCC rules 73.352618 for commercial stations and 73.352719 for noncommercial educational stations. These rules do not apply to Low Power FM and Low Power television stations. The FCC offers a brief description of a station's responsibilities on its website,[20] but a general explanation of what a noncommercial educational station must keep in its public file follows:

What must be in the public file?

- A copy of the current FCC authorization to operate and construct the broadcast station.
- A copy of any filed FCC application, related documents, opposition to the application served upon the broadcast station, and the Commission's response to those applications.
- Service contour maps submitted with an FCC application showing the location of a station's main studio, transmitter location street address.
- The station's ownership reports (FCC Form 323-E), which are due on the first anniversary of licensure and then ever two years thereafter.
- Documents concerning broadcasts by candidates for public office.
- Documents relating to the station's Equal Employment Opportunity policy.
- The most recent version of an FCC manual, titled "The Public and Broadcasting."[21]
- For television stations, a copy of a completed "Standardized Public Interest Reporting Form." This form must detail the station's efforts to determine the issues facing its community and the programming aired during the preceding three-month period in response to those issues.
- A list of donors supporting specific programs.
- Local public notice announcements.
- Documents relating to FCC investigations or complaints.
- For television stations, copies of requests for mandatory carriage on any cable system.
- Some television stations must also retain a DTV Consumer Educational Quarterly Activity Report (FCC Form 388), describing methods used to educate the public about the industry-wide conversion from analog to digital television signal technology.[22]

FCC rulings indicate that where a licensee retains sufficient oversight and takes meaningful steps to ensure that there are no violations of FCC regulations, universities should be able to turn over day-to-day operation of the station to students.

Where must the public file be located?

- A copy must be kept at the main studio of the radio station.
- If a main studio is located outside of the station's broadcasting area, the station must mail the file to requesting individuals within the service area.
- A copy of the public file may either be in paper form or accessible on a computer database, as long as a computer is made available to the public to access the database and the database can be printed upon request.
- Television stations must also make the public file available on the station's website or on the state broadcasters association's website. If a television station chooses to put its public file on a broadcaster association's website, the station's own website must link to it.

When must a copy of the public file be accessible to the public?

- A copy of the file must be available during regular business hours, either in hard copy or through a computer terminal.

UNAUTHORIZED OPERATION OF A RADIO STATION

Before a radio or television station can begin broadcasting, it must first obtain an operating frequency from the FCC. A station cannot "purchase" an operating frequency from the FCC, but rather must lease, or license, it for a set period of time. Generally, stations are licensed a broadcast frequency for renewable two-year periods.[23]

A broadcast station can renew its license by filing the appropriate paperwork with the FCC.[24] However, an application to renew a broadcast license must be submitted four months prior to a license's expiration.[25] Failure to apply for a license renewal will result in possible fines by the FCC, even if the mistake was unintentional or came as a result of a clerical error.[26] The FCC requires this four-month period in order to give the community an opportunity to comment on the station's service and, if warranted, oppose the station's renewal application.[27]

Colby Community College, which operates the FM radio station KTCC, failed to submit a license renewal application four months before the station's license was set to expire.[28] In letters to the FCC, the station's radio broadcasting instructor noted that the oversight was the result of his "predecessor's failure to document the license renewal process, as well as his own unfamiliarity with the license renewal process." Given the personnel turnover that is sometime's common with educational broadcast operations, and the lack of training that personnel sometimes receive prior to taking over a broadcast facility, KTCC's explanation was not unique.[29]

Although KTCC's operators did not know they had to file a renewal application four months prior to their license's expiration, the Commission still found the station's actions to be a "willful" violation of FCC rules. The FCC stated that rules violations "resulting from inadvertent error or failure to become familiar with the FCC's requirements are willful violations," even if they were not purposeful. The FCC has stated that "the term 'willful' means that the violator knew that it was taking (or in this case, not taking) the action in question, irrespective of any intent to violate the Rules."[30]

Failing to renew a broadcast license will result in that station's license lapsing. When a broadcast facility continues to operate on a frequency without a license from the FCC, it is operating an unauthorized station, which is a violation of FCC rules and will result in further fines.[31]

If a station has not submitted its renewal application form four months prior to license expiration, the station can apply for Special Temporary Authority to broadcast on its frequency even after the license expires. During this time period, the Commission will consider the station's renewal application and the community's comments about the station. Special Temporary Authority will not, however, excuse a station from a fine for violating the FCC's four-month renewal time period.

The FCC will grant a station special temporary authority "for a period of 180 days, but the applicant must show that extraordinary circumstances warrant such an extension."[32] Requests should be filed electronically using FCC Form 601 Main Form, specifying the purpose as "Renewal/Modification." Once Special Temporary Authority has been granted, a station may operate until the FCC has made a final decision regarding the license renewal application or the authority expires.

PENALTIES FOR NONCOMPLIANCE

In a potential breakthrough for educational broadcasters, the FCC announced in May 2013 that it would refrain from imposing heavy financial penalties on student-run noncommercial stations for first-time violations of Commission rules, such as failure to submit ownership reports or maintain an adequate public file. In recognition of "the fragile environment in which student-run stations operate," the Commission said it will give violators a chance to enter into a "consent decree" accompanied by a "voluntary payment" rather than a fine (though the distinction may be more of terminology than substance). Crucially, the Commission said the "voluntary payment" would be calculated in light of the financial resources of the station rather than (as had long been the practice) the financial resources of the deeper-pocketed license-holder, typically the college itself.[33] In the case that prompted the policy shift, the Commission allowed a student-run station in Iowa to pay $2,500 for a public file infraction that normally would have drawn a fine of $20,000 or more, in recognition that the station's entire annual budget was just $6,650. The order emphasized the uniquely valuable role that student-run radio occupies: "Student-run radio stations ... are a unique subset of media outlets that provide opportunities for student volunteers to obtain training and real-world experience in radio programming, production, operations and management while they take part in the academic life of the school."[34] The Commission emphasized that forgiveness would apply only to stations that are entirely student-programmed and student-managed.

NONCOMMERCIAL RADIO UNDERWRITING

Educational radio stations may be licensed to operate as "noncommercial" broadcasters — but what it means to be "noncommercial" can be confusing. FCC reserves the 87.9(MHz) through 91.9(MHz) frequency ban for "nonprofit educational organization[s] ... upon showing that the station will be used for the advancement of an educational program."[35] In exchange for a broadcasting license, a noncommercial educational station agrees not to broadcast certain commercial speech. For instance, an educational noncommercial station may not broadcast commercial "advertisements," although "sponsorship" messages are allowed. Violations of the FCC's rules, even by collegiate[36] or high school stations,[37] can result in a FCC fine.

FCC rule 399b prohibits noncommercial educational stations from broadcasting "advertisements," which the FCC defines as material, broadcasted in exchange for payment, that (1) promotes any for-profit company's service, facility or product; or (2) expresses the views of any person with respect to any matter of public importance; or (3) supports or opposes any candidate for political office. Although "advertisements" are banned, noncommercial educational stations may broadcast programming that bears a resemblance to an advertisement.

Section 399a of the United States Code governs the use of business or institutional "logograms," which are audio or visual signs "used for the exclusive purpose of identifying ... and which is not used for the purpose of promoting the products services, or facilities of such corporation, company, or other organization."[38] A noncommercial educational station may include logograms in broadcasts in exchange for payment so long as they do not interrupt regular programming[39] and are used for identification purposes, not promotional purposes. Determining what constitutes a slogan that is used for the purpose of identifying, as opposed to promoting, can be difficult.[40]

Notwithstanding the FCC's rule that "promotional" announcements are prohibited, a noncommercial broadcaster may air a for-profit entity's "promotional" announcement if it qualifies as a "program-related" material. In order to qualify for this exception to the FCC's informational/promotional divide, the broadcaster must: (1) receive no consideration for the program-related announcement; and (2) the materials must be offered on the basis of public interest considerations and not the private economic interests of the offeror; or (3) the price of the materials offered is only nominal.[41]

The FCC has stated that there is no restriction on broadcasting promotional announcements on behalf of non-profit organizations, although the broadcaster must identify the sponsor.[42]

In addition to permitting the use of some logograms, the FCC permits "enhanced" donor or underwriter acknowledgements.[43] Under FCC rules, a noneducational station may broadcast: (1) logograms or slogans that identify an underwriter but do not promote it;

(2) locational information of an underwriter; (3) contain value neutral descriptions of an underwriter's product line or service; and (4) brand and trade names and product or service listings of the underwriter.[44] Similar to the term "promotional," what constitutes a "value neutral" description of a product is difficult to define. For example, broadcasters may not air underwriting announcements or acknowledgements that include "qualitative and comparative descriptions of the donor's products or services."[45] Thus, announcements of price information, calls to action, and announcements containing an inducement to buy, sell, rent or lease a product are prohibited.[46]

The Commission has approved the following phrases as permissible underwriting announcements: "professional equipment and supplies,"[47] "home style food,"[48] "an intelligent four-wheel drive system,"[49] "surgery never has to be unpleasant,"[50] and the use of the term "only" if used to indicate that a store has the only goods of an identified kind within a geographic area (so long as the phrase is not otherwise promotional or comparative).[51] The FCC proscribes comparative underwriting terms such as: "more,"[52] "best,"[53] "most,"[54] "greatest,"[55] "special,"[56] and "hottest."[57] Moreover, the FCC bans impermissibly qualitative terms, regardless of their truth, like: "efficient, economical, dependable, dedicated, prompt, fair price, reliable and excellent,"[58] in addition to terms such as "quality financial services,"[59] "friendly efficient crew,"[60] "convenient,"[61] "established,"[62] and "beautiful."[63]

The base forfeiture amount (otherwise known as a fine) for a violation of Section 399b is $2,000,[64] although that amount can be adjusted up or down based upon the "nature, circumstances, extent and gravity of the violation."[65] The Commission will also consider a broadcaster's degree of culpability, history of prior offense, ability to pay a FCC forfeiture, and any other factor "as justice may require" when fining a broadcaster.[66]

Generally, the two most significant factors in determining the severity of a FCC fine are the number of broadcasts that violate the Commission's rules and the durational period thereof. The FCC has levied a $20,000 forfeiture for 10 improper announcements over a 15-month period,[67] a $10,000 forfeiture for 288 announcements over a 1-month period,[68] a $5,000 forfeiture for eight announcements on two days over a week-long period,[69] and a $2,500 forfeiture for four announcements on two days over a week long-period.[70]

MUSIC LICENSING FOR BROADCASTING AND WEBCASTING

There are a host of laws and licensing schemes that apply to student broadcasters wishing to play music over the radio, television, or Internet. Failing to comply with these requirements, even inadvertently, can result in legal action.

Federal copyright law gives the holder of a musical copyright, which is usually the recording artist or recording company, an exclusive right to publicly perform their song.[71] According to the law, a "public performance" is a performance that occurs in any place open to the public or a performance of a song that is transmitted or otherwise made available to a group of people. Thus, in order to play a song over radio, television, or the Internet, a broadcaster must obtain permission from a copyright owner in the form of licenses.

In the context of a broadcaster playing a song over the radio, television, or Internet, there are actually two copyrights at stake within the broad right of "public performance."[72] The first is the right to the musical work itself (the notes and lyrics that make up the underlying composition of the musical piece). The second is the right to the musical recording (the song recorded on a CD, in MP3, or other formats). Thus, broadcasters have two copyright issues to worry about when playing a song: (1) the copyright in the musical work; and (2) the copyright in the musical recording that is being broadcast. If a station is playing music over the radio or television, it only needs to obtain a license to publicly perform the musical work itself, not the sound recording. However, when webcasting a song, a broadcaster must obtain a license from the copyright holder to publicly perform the actual song and a separate license to publicly perform the musical recording.

In order to obtain the required licenses, a broadcaster must go to a "Performance Rights Organization," or PRO.[73] There are four major PROs that broadcasters should know about: ASCAP, BMI, SESAC, and SoundExchange. Each of these companies charges broadcast stations a fee for the necessary copyright licenses, which is then passed on to the copyright holder. With the exception of SESAC, fees are negotiated and set by the Copyright Royalty Board. Although nearly every musical artist is a member of either ASCAP, BMI, or SESAC, no artist is a member of all three. Thus, if a station wishes to broadcast a song, it must get a license from the respective copyright holder's PRO.

ASCAP[74] offers blanket radio licenses for noncommercial, educational radio stations. These licenses allow student broadcasters to pay a fee based on the number of full-time students at a host educational institution and play any song in the ASCAP repertoire. ASCAP's Per Program license requires stations to report the amount of music content a broadcaster airs and pay accordingly. The blanket and Per Program licenses cover a copyright holder's right to the musical performance, not the sound recording, which must also be licensed to play a song on the Internet. As a result, ASCAP also offers three different license types for "news media" performances. A license for non-interactive services, which is the one most likely to apply to a school station, covers webcasts, streaming background music and previews or "samples" (excerpts lasting 60 seconds or less) of music.[75]

BMI,[76] like ASCAP, offers blanket licenses for educational stations in the form of Music Performance Agreements (MPA). MPAs for college or university stations include the licenses to musical compositions for live or recorded performances via Internet or Intranet websites, webcasts of campus radio station broadcasts, regular campus radio broadcasts, school-promoted musical attractions, music-on-hold and a variety of other types of musical public performances. A BMI "one-tier" license allows a school station to make a single annual payment to BMI and, in return, to play all music in the BMI library — similar to ASCAP's blanket license. BMI's "two-tier" option allows stations to pay a smaller annual payment and a separate fee for any musical event on a college premises promoted only by the college. Both of these options require a campus broadcast station to provide BMI with a performance list as well as information about whether performances were transmitted over the Internet. BMI licenses the right to publicly perform a musical composition, not the right to publicly perform a musical recording. Thus, when playing a song via the Internet, which requires a license to publicly perform a sound recording in addition to a license to publicly perform a musical composition, just a BMI license will not suffice.

In order to obtain a license to publicly perform a sound recording, which is required when playing a song on the Internet, broadcasters may go to SoundExchange.[77] Although Congress has allowed traditional radio broadcasts that perform copyrighted sound recordings to be aired without having to obtain a separate sound recording license, two relatively recent pieces of legislation — the Digital Performance Right in Sound Recordings Act[78] and the Digital Millennium Copyright Act[79] — created separate performance rights in sound recordings for digital and satellite transmissions, including Internet transmissions.

This digital public performance right in sound recordings means that if your station is simulcasting a signal over the Internet or via satellite, it must pay performance royalties. SoundExchange is the only U.S. organization that collects and distributes these royalties and the U.S. Copyright Office has specifically designated it to collect and distribute royalties relating to webcasting. The royalties that SoundExchange collects are split, with 50 percent going to the copyright holder in the recording (usually the record company) and 50 percent going to the performers.

Since webcasting is relatively new, stations that want to webcast often forget to obtain a sound recording license from SoundExchange. Recently, however, SoundExchange has made an effort to reverse this trend by sending letters to broadcasters who were streaming without a license.[80] Additionally, the Federal Communications Commission ("FCC") has the power to fine stations that do not have the proper licenses. Thus, it is important to obtain a license from SoundExchange if your station plans to play music over the Internet.

SoundExchange has entered into a Webcasters Settlement Act, a series of settlement agreements that cover noncommercial educational webcasters such as schools. These agreements are negotiated annually so it is important that, in addition to getting the coverage in the first place, your school obtains a timely renewal of its license by filing a Notice of Election with SoundExchange. Although SoundExchange usually imposes a reporting requirement as a condition of the license, this requirement may be waived for educational stations that have fewer than 55,000 monthly Aggregate Tuning Hours.

PENALTIES FOR BROADCASTING OR WEBCASTING WITHOUT A LICENSE

Acquiring all of the necessary licenses to broadcast or webcast can be difficult, but the consequences for being caught publicly performing music without a license are harsh. For instance, a station that publicly performs any copyrighted song without the proper licenses can be held liable for damages up to $30,000 — or in extreme cases up to $150,000 — for each song played without authorization.[81]

The FCC has made it clear in past decisions that it does not have a reduced fine scale when it comes to noncommercial broadcasters.[82] This means that even though your station may not be making a profit, it can be fined as much as commercial stations. For example, in 2009 the FCC fined a noncommercial radio station $7,200 for failure to have its program lists available for public inspection. Around the same time, the FCC fined a college radio station $7,000 for failure to file its annual license renewal application on time.[83] The FCC turned a deaf ear to stations that complained that they did not have the resources to pay the fines. In fact, the only way to get a fine reduced based on a showing of financial hardship is to provide the FCC with a financial statement showing that the institution as a whole (your school or college) cannot pay the fine. A statement of the radio or television station's budget is not sufficient. Furthermore, ignorance of the law is no excuse: it is always the music user's responsibility to make sure that he/she has obtained all proper copyright clearances for all works to be used before broadcasting.

PORTIONS AND FAIR USE

For those stations that do not use music often, copyright law allows broadcasters to play music without paying a fee if it is a "fair use."

Fair use is an exception to the general rule that copyrighted material cannot be used without consent and is an important principle for student broadcasters to understand. It allows limited portions of copyrighted material to be used for certain purposes—mainly teaching, research, criticism, news reporting or parody—without the user having to obtain prior authorization from the copyright owner. Traditionally, courts have used the following four factors to determine whether a use constitutes fair use: (1) The purpose and character of the use; (2) The nature of the copyrighted work; (3) How much of the original work is used; and (4) The effect of the use on the commercial value of the copyrighted work.[84]

Unfortunately, these factors are far from clear-cut and there is no magic formula for determining whether fair use applies in a given situation. Fair use most commonly applies in situations where only a portion of a work is being used, where someone is commenting on the work in some manner and where the use is not of a type for which someone would generally obtain a license. In the music field, there is a well-established licensing scheme, meaning that courts may be less likely to find fair use when it is relatively easy—and practical—for the user to obtain a license.

Students and advisers frequently ask, for example, about a "30 second rule" or a "10 second rule" for fair use. These mythical rules supposedly allow use of music or video clips no longer than the specified time (30 seconds, 10 seconds or some other fixed limit) without the need to obtain a license. Unfortunately, there exist no such rules in copyright law. Although courts do consider the amount of the work used, this is only one of four factors courts consider in evaluating fair use. This means that even if the clip used amounts to only a few seconds, a court could still find that the other factors weigh against a finding of fair use. Additionally, the Supreme Court has stated that even if a use is minimal, it could still constitute infringement if it takes the "heart" of the work.[85] This means that a clip of even a few seconds could be infringing if a court finds that the clip has captured the "heart" of the song.

If you want to use music in your broadcast without obtaining a license, don't rely on a "30 second" or "10 second" rule. While there are no hard-and-fast rules for fair use, there are some guidelines you can follow. For example, use of a small portion of music for the purpose of reviewing or commenting on that music or the artist is most likely going to be a fair use, especially if you haven't used the "heart" of the work— for example, the most well-known parts of a song. And while there really is no magic number for the length of your clip, using the shortest clip possible can reduce the chance that a court will find the use to be infringing.

CENSORSHIP AND STUDENT BROADCASTERS

Although a school, particularly a public college or university, may be required to afford its student newspaper virtually unfettered editorial freedom, the same is not always true of its student broadcast media. As the Supreme Court has said, "Balancing the various First Amendment interests involved in the broadcast media...is a task of great delicacy and difficulty. The process must necessarily be undertaken within the framework of the regulatory scheme that has evolved over the course of the past half-century."[86] This "delicate balance" is perhaps nowhere more evident than on America's public college and university campuses, where student journalists working on school radio or television broadcast stations face very different hurdles regarding the exercise of their free press rights than their print counterparts.

It is important to note that the court rulings described in this chapter only apply to broadcast radio and television stations. Closed circuit media are not subject to FCC regulations or licensing and thus should receive the same First Amendment protections provided to print media. Cable stations are subject to some FCC regulation, though generally less than broadcast stations.[87]There is a significant question as to whether the FCC has the authority to regulate content on the Internet. In December, 2010, the FCC issued a Network Neutrality Report & Order that gave the Commission the authority to limit Internet Service Providers' (ISPs) ability to completely block or slow the operation of a website.[88] ISPs have twice, as of the publication of this book, challenged the FCC's order, claiming that it does not have the authority to enact this policy.[89] Among their arguments, ISPs have claimed that the First Amendment prohibits the government from interfering in an ISP's decision about what content it will allow users to receive.[90]

In most cases, the school's board of regents or the university itself will hold the broadcast license for the station, making them ultimately responsible to the FCC for any regulatory violations.[91] Yet even with the university's concern over its responsibilities as licensee, the First Amendment rights of the students working at the station must be considered. Courts consistently have held that at public educational institutions, the First Amendment limits the ability of college and university officials to control the content of student media.[92] It is this dichotomy between student editorial control and university control as licensee that can raise significant and complex First Amendment issues, some of which have not been fully settled.

NOTE TO HIGH SCHOOL AND PRIVATE SCHOOL STUDENT BROADCASTERS

For practical reasons, this chapter focuses on the legal rights of student broadcasters at public colleges and universities. Student-run, high school broadcast stations in the United States are fairly rare. Likewise, student broadcast media at private schools — like all private school student media — are not protected from administrative censorship by the First Amendment (see full discussion of private school student media in Chapter 7). However, while the free-speech protections for high school and private school student broadcasters may be comparatively more limited, some of the discussion that follows (for example, the role of the FCC) remains relevant.

ROLE OF FCC LICENSEE

Even where university officials want to allow their students greater control over the school radio or television station, the FCC still requires that the license-holder exercise a minimum degree of oversight. The FCC has ruled that while a licensee can delegate much of the day-to-day responsibilities to others, it cannot wholly insulate itself from such responsibility.[93] For instance, when a University attempts to license a Low Power FM station (LPFM), but already licenses a full power station, the FCC will consider the University's license application only if the station is "managed and operated by students of the university, although as the licensee, the University must retain ultimate control of the station's operations."[94] According to the FCC, the "touchstone of control 'is not divining who executes the station's programming, personnel and finance responsibilities,' but rather who establishes policies governing time brokerage agreements, local marketing or management agreements and exercises ultimate control."[95] Thus, licensees, such as a University, may delegate the day-to-day operations of a radio station to non-university employees, such as student broadcasters, so long as it is the University keeps ultimate control of the broadcast operation and establishes policies governing student control. Without such policies, the University-licensee may be liable to the FCC for unlawfully transferring its license.[96]

In one of the earliest cases involving a campus radio station, a federal appeals court reaffirmed that broadcast licensees have a duty to know the content of their programming.[97] The court rejected a challenge brought by the Yale University Broadcasting Company arguing that an FCC Notice regarding "drug oriented" music constituted an illegal censorship threat. The Notice included a reminder to licensees that they had a duty to know the content of records being played on their station and to make a judgment regarding the wisdom of playing such music if they were to fulfill their obligation to broadcast in the "public interest."[98] In a dissenting opinion to the court's refusal to hear an en banc appeal, Chief Judge Bazelon sharply criticized the FCC's "chameleon-like directives...couched in code words for license renewal such as 'public interest' or 'licensee responsibility,'" which the judge noted were commonly understood as "euphemisms for self-censorship," and which enabled the FCC to accomplish indirectly what it could not do directly.[99]

A few years later, the FCC actually revoked the license of a radio station at the University of Pennsylvania after finding that the school had abdicated to students all of its responsibility to supervise and control the station. The loss of control, the FCC alleged, resulted in allegations regarding the broadcast of obscenity, the use of drugs and alcohol at the station, and various technical violations that caused interference with other radio and television stations.[100] Still, the Commission recognized student-operated stations as valuable "educational resources." Noting that most such university stations had operated for years without problem, the Commission stated it did not "wish to discourage university licensees from operating student-run stations."[101] While a system of "shared responsibility" could work, the Commission found, it said University

---

of Pennsylvania officials had gone too far. "Its abdication was total," the Commission ruled, "and cannot be tolerated...."[102]

About ten years later, in an unreported case involving the University of California at Santa Barbara (UCSB), the Commission apparently found a balance it liked, ruling that a "hands-off" policy in the context of UCSB's student-run station was "workable."[103] The Commission accepted the school's policy that university officials had the right to control or punish students for playing content that violated FCC regulations, such as the ban on indecency. However, the policy prohibited officials from controlling content that did not violate FCC regulations even where school officials disagreed with or found the content otherwise offensive.[104] The Commission's ruling indicates that where a licensee retains sufficient oversight and takes meaningful steps to ensure that there are no violations of FCC regulations, universities should be able to turn over the day-to-day operation of the station to students.

FORUM ANALYSIS

While the UCSB case prescribes what may be the lower limits of editorial control an FCC licensee can safely exercise over student-operated stations, no court has addressed the question of where the upper boundaries might lie. In other words, how much editorial control — or censorship — can a public university, as licensee, exercise over the programming of a student-run broadcast station when its actions are at odds with the student operators of the station?

In cases not involving "student-run" stations, courts have allowed government officials to exercise some control over editorial content, although they have required that the degree of such control be considered in the context of the type of forum involved.

As a general principle of First Amendment law, property owned or controlled by the government will fall into one of three legal categories: (1) the traditional public forum, (2) the public forum created by government designation (also known as a limited public forum) or (3) the nonpublic forum. The distinction between a public forum and a limited or nonpublic forum will depend on the degree of access to the property speakers have been allowed.[105]

In traditional public forums, such as streets and parks where there is an established tradition of the property being devoted to assembly and debate by the general public, the government can prohibit speech only in extraordinary circumstances and only in a content-neutral manner; the government may reasonably control when, where and how speech is disseminated but not the message.[106]

On the other hand, the government creates a limited public forum when it "has opened for use by the public a place for expressive activity." Alternatively, the government may open the forum "for use by certain groups, or for the discussion of certain subjects."[107] Those who do not fall within the prescribed class of speakers may be reasonably excluded. Where an individual does fall within the class of speakers for which the limited public forum was created, the government's ability to control the speech within that forum is significantly restricted.

Finally, where the "property is not a traditional public forum and the government has not chosen to create a designated public forum, the property is either a nonpublic forum or not a forum at all."[108] While access to a nonpublic forum can be restricted simply upon a showing that the restrictions are reasonable, the government violates the First Amendment if it denies access merely because it opposes the speaker's view.[109]

Most public university stations — including those that are "student-operated" — would be categorized as either limited or nonpublic forums. In such cases, the First Amendment protections available to students working at those stations would depend on the station's actual polices and practices.[110] As in the UCSB case, some stations specifically charge students with the responsibility for deciding what news or programs are to be aired. A strong argument could be made in such cases that the station operates as a limited public forum for speech by the student broadcast staff. As such, the ability of school officials to regulate otherwise lawful student programming would be limited to maintaining the obligations of the FCC license. Other stations are managed by non-student employees who may serve as station managers or program directors. The degree of control exercised by these individuals differs, and the forum status of such stations would likely vary accordingly. At other stations, students may be cast more in the role of interns who have little say in deciding what is aired. In such cases, students would likely have limited recourse in mounting a successful legal challenge if the administration overrules their programming decisions.

The bottom line is that administrative oversight, if it goes too far, will almost certainly weaken the forum status of the station. By extension, it will also weaken the First Amendment protections available to students wishing to exercise editorial control at the station.

JUDICIAL BALANCING

The First Amendment exists to prevent government censorship of private speech. However, where it is determined that the government itself is the speaker, the government may determine the content of its speech free from First Amendment scrutiny.[111] Unfortunately, it is not always clear who is the speaker. In the case of public broadcast stations, including university-licensed stations, the government is put in the dual and complicated role of being both speaker and censor, and courts are left to try and sort things out.[112]

In one of the first cases to tackle the issue, *Muir v. Alabama Educational Television Commission*,[113] the U.S. Court of Appeals for the Fifth Circuit rejected a First Amendment claim by viewers and upheld the authority of two state-owned public television stations, neither of which were student-run or operated, to refuse to air a controversial program. The court found that the public television stations at issue were not supposed to function as "a pure marketplace of ideas." Therefore, as a nonpublic forum, the state could regulate content "in order to prevent hampering the primary function of the activity."[114]

The *Muir* court's decision heavily influenced a later ruling in *Schneider v. Indian River Community College Foundation*.[115] The case involved a noncommercial, educational station licensed to the Board of Trustees of Indian River Community College. The station employed a full-time station manager and program director as well as other paid staff, some of whom taught at the college. The paid staff was "assisted" by student interns. Nothing in the record suggests that the students exercised any control over the station's programming. The station manager and programming director sued the school, claiming that the community college's president violated their First Amendment rights by engaging in censorship and prior review of the station's programming.[116]

In finding for the college, the court wrote "the degree of control which can be exercised consistently with the First Amendment depends on the mission of the communicative activity being controlled."[117] The president of the college regularly monitored the commentary that went on the air. He also exercised his opinion about what upcoming events could be covered by the radio station. As in *Muir*, the court found that the station was "not designed to function as a pure marketplace of ideas."[118] Moreover, the court said it was the First Amendment rights of the FCC licensee — in this case the college trustees — that were protected by the First Amendment and not the rights of the employees. Because the station was not operated as a "public access" broadcaster, the court found that the trustees' control of the programming did not violate the First Amendment rights of the employees.[119] The court said that although it is "ill-advised" for government institutions to make content-based decisions, it "does not warrant judicial scrutiny."[120]

In 1994, a federal district court in Washington State heard a case whose facts probably come the closest to framing the legal issues that would likely arise in a student broadcast media case. The case involved KCMU, a noncommercial radio station owned and operated by the University of Washington. The university employed three full-time employees (a station manager, programming director and fundraiser) and two part-time disc jockeys. All others who worked at the station, including several disc jockeys and members of its news department staff, were community volunteers, a diverse group that included a handful of students.

Trouble began when university employees proposed to change the station's alternative music format, a move that was strongly opposed by most of the volunteer staff. At the same time, the station manager and programming director began to vigorously enforce a policy that, among other things, prohibited on-air criticism of the radio station, university policies and university staff. As tensions increased, station management removed several volunteers from their positions for speaking out, both on and off the air, against the changes at KCMU. The volunteers sued alleging that the terminations violated their First Amendment rights.

In its defense, the university argued that, as the holder of the FCC license, it had sole, unlimited discretion to decide what would be broadcast and to exclude all broadcasting of material that was critical of the radio station or the university. Rejecting the university's argument, the court said that the case did "not concern KCMU's right, as licensee, to control its own programming."[121] The radio station was not, as the school contended, simply a vehicle for government speech where the school had an unfettered right to control its own message and the First Amendment was irrelevant. Instead, the court employed traditional forum analysis to resolve the case.

In a somewhat confusing, roller-coaster decision in which the court upheld the station's firing of some staff members but found the station's termination of others unlawful, the court ruled that KCMU was a nonpublic forum. It noted that while staff members had been allowed to develop and broadcast stories of their choosing, the evidence nevertheless indicated that the university had not intentionally opened the radio station as a public forum. In a nonpublic forum, the court ruled that the university enjoyed "relatively broad discretion under the First Amendment to regulate speech at the station, but may not do so based solely on the content of that speech."[122] "Suppression of particular news stories because of their content," the court found, "constitutes the type of pure viewpoint discrimination prohibited by the First Amendment."[123]

Finally, in a later decision, the Supreme Court held that a state public television broadcaster's decision to exclude a "fringe" congressional candidate from a televised debate was a reasonable, viewpoint-neutral exercise of journalistic discretion and therefore did not violate the First Amendment.[124] The case largely followed the reasoning used by both the *Muir* and *Schneider* courts, finding that the political debates were nonpublic forums.

Though their outcomes sometimes differed, all of these cases make clear that a court is obligated to first examine the forum status of the speech in a state-owned broadcast station. Unlike the situation at professionally run public broadcast stations, the stated mission of many student-run stations is to provide a forum for student news and opinion. Moreover, at some stations, student program or news directors have been charged with the day-to-day task of deciding what is aired. Both factors could weigh heavily in the judicial balance.

Indeed, the *Muir* court actually cites a landmark student press case to suggest that not all public broadcast stations are necessarily created equal.[125] While a college or university is not required to open its broadcast station to student news and opinion, once it does, the First Amendment may prevent school officials from casually taking away their microphones. The view of student-run stations as protected forums has been supported by various commentators, who have argued that when a state, operating as a licensee, opens a platform for others to use, the ability of the state (in this case the public university) to regulate content should be limited. As one writer noted, "The state has a great deal of discretion in its initial decision to delegate editorial responsibility, but once it has been delegated, the state 'cannot selectively intervene to delete material or discipline editors.'"[126] The state licensees should not be able to require a departure from the normal editorial process and make decisions that are politicized or ad hoc.[127] If the government's "sole purpose was to suppress speech, the government's decision would become presumptively unconstitutional."[128]

Finally, it is worth bearing in mind that the U.S. Supreme Court has generally been very protective of campus speech. As the Court has said, "the college classroom and its surrounding environs is peculiarly the marketplace of ideas ... and the vigilant protection of constitutional freedoms is nowhere more vital than in the community of American schools."[129] Consequently, where an initial showing can be made that a university-licensed broadcast station has opened itself as a forum for expression by student staff members and where it can be demonstrated that allowing such expression can be accomplished in a way that does not violate FCC rules, it is certainly reasonable to conclude that this delicate balance would tip in favor of the students.

SUMMARY

In many areas of the law, such as libel, copyright and freedom of information, the differences between broadcast and print journalism are minimal. In other areas, particularly content regulations imposed by the FCC, broadcasters are subject to more control and less First Amendment protection. It is important to note, however, that for purposes of the First Amendment, there is a distinction between true "broadcast" media, using the public airwaves, versus "off-the-air" mediums such as cable, satellite, closed-circuit and Internet-based communications. "Off-the-air" media receive the same higher standard of constitutional protection traditionally afforded print-based media.

Sorting out the mixture of FCC-imposed restrictions and First Amendment freedoms at a public school can prove tricky. When a broadcast license is granted to a school, school officials can probably justify certain acts of censorship by showing that the censorship was necessary under the terms of their license with the FCC. For example, a student broadcaster who uses a string of four-letter words during her daytime broadcast probably would not be able to claim a First Amendment violation if the school punished her for her speech. But the weight of student media law makes clear that a school official would have a heavy burden demonstrating that the school's duties as broadcast licensee required him to censor or punish a student for expression on a student-run broadcast station that did not clearly violate FCC regulations. Vague references to FCC requirements without substantial evidence to back them up likely would not suffice.

ADDITIONAL SOURCES FOR INFORMATION ON BROADCAST LAW AND REGULATIONS

1. *The Public Radio Legal Handbook*, 4th Edition (2002), John Crigler. An online edition is distributed by the National Federation of Community Broadcasters (www.nfcb.org). Members of College Broadcasters, Inc. are eligible to obtain a discounted price on access to the online edition. Visit www.collegebroacasters.org for more information.
2. National Association of Broadcasters, *Legal Guide to Broadcast Law and Regulation: 1998 Legal Guide Update* (1998).
3. The Federal Communications Commission (FCC) Web site (www.fcc.gov) includes information on broadcast regulations, including links to relevant laws, regulations and FCC rules.
4. *Media Law for Talk Radio,* by Richard Goehler, published by the National Association of Broadcasters (www.nab.org).
5. *Media Law Handbook for Radio Broadcasters*, 2d Edition, by Jerianne Timmerman, distributed by the National Association of Broadcasters (www.nab.org).

"Did she just say what I think she did?"

Lisa Jade, adviser to State College's student media program, felt her jaw drop as she and her student staff watched videotape of the press conference held by SC's softball coach an hour earlier. "Sure did," one of her reporters tells her. "And if you think that's bad, wait until you hear what she calls the first baseman in just a minute."

In all her years as an adviser, Jade had never heard a school official use such coarse and vulgar language to describe students — at least not publicly. Sure the softball team's season had been a disaster so far, and sure the coach had a reputation as one of the most successful — and volatile — in the country (she'd once been featured on the cover of *SportsWeek* magazine after throwing a bat in the direction of an umpire) and she was frustrated, but Jade was pretty sure some of the words used by the coach would have expanded the vocabulary of an Army drill sergeant.

"So what do we do?" The question seemed to spring simultaneously from KSCR's (the school's broadcast radio station) news director, SCTV's (the school's closed circuit TV station) news producer, the editor of *The Student Times* student newspaper and the Webmaster of i-Student, State College's student website. "How do we report this?"

Before giving any advice, she tells her students she needs to call her trusted legal expert for some help. That's you. What can you tell her?

ANSWER:
First things first. After hearing the coach's comments for yourself you determine that (1) the comments are not legally obscene (no reasonable person could conclude that were meant to sexually arouse the listener, a requirement of obscenity[130]), but (2) they certainly might be considered indecent by the FCC — defined to include language that contains "patently offensive sexual or excretory references" — because there was definitely some of that.[131]

That said, you tell Jade that as far as SCTV, *The Student Times* and i-Student are concerned, it's up to their student news director, editor-in-chief or website news editor to decide how to cover the coach's news conference and what quotes or sound bites, if any, they want to include. Publishing the coach's comments on a closed-circuit TV station, in a print newspaper or on the Internet would break no laws and — at least with respect to such student media on a public college campus — would be protected by the First Amendment. Obviously, the coach's language — though certainly newsworthy — will be shocking to readers and viewers. For that reason, the student staffs should carefully weigh their editorial options before publishing or airing anything.

Things are more complicated for the student radio station. As an over-the-air broadcast station, KSCR is subject to FCC regulation. Among other things, FCC regulations prohibit the broadcast of indecent programming during times when children are likely to be listening. That means — as the regulations are currently interpreted — KSCR is prohibited from broadcasting the coach's more "colorful" comments between 6 a.m. and 10 p.m. The station is permitted to air news reports during the day that more generically describe the coach's statements ("With language that might have made Howard Stern blush, the coach today blasted her own players...") or air sound bites that "bleep" out the offensive language, but any broadcast that includes her unedited remarks will have to wait until the "safe harbor" hours of late-night and very early morning radio.

Even then, while broadcasting the coach's unedited comments won't break any laws, it is less clear whether the First Amendment would protect the student news director's rights if State College officials ordered him not to air the comments at any time. The FCC requires that a broadcast station's licensee, in this case the State College Board of Trustees, exercise some oversight over programming to ensure compliance with FCC regulations. In this case, the college not only has the right, but likely the responsibility, to prohibit broadcast of the coach's indecent remarks outside of the safe harbor hours. Whether school officials have the authority to exercise programming controls in excess of FCC regulations, however, may depend on the forum status of KSCR.

If school officials, after ensuring compliance with FCC regulations, have traditionally turned over all other programming decisions to the KSCR student staff, a reasonable argument could be made that the radio station operates as a limited public forum, much like the student newspaper and other off-the-air student media. In such case, school officials would be hard-pressed to censor the broadcast of otherwise lawful, non-disruptive programming — meaning, in this case, that the college could not lawfully overrule the students if they decided to air the un-bleeped remarks after 10 p.m.

If, on the other hand, school officials (or other non-student employees acting on their behalf) have traditionally played a significant role in determining the radio station's programming, the students may be out of luck mounting a successful legal challenge if censored.

ENDNOTES

1   Broadcasters face some unique issues when it comes to acquiring the rights to "bumper" music and other copyrighted third-party content used on the air. The intellectual property issues raised by the use of copyrighted music in broadcasting are discussed in Chapter 16.

2   T. BARTON CARTER ET AL., MASS COMMUNICATIONS LAW (6th ed. 2007) at 469.

3   See, e.g., National Broad. Co. v. United States, 319 U.S. 190, 210-15 (1943); Red Lion Broad. Co. v. FCC, 395 U.S. 367, 377 (1969).

4   See Telecomm. Res. & Action Ctr. v. FCC, 801 F.2d 501, 508 (D.C. Cir. 1986) (Bork, J.); FCC v. Fox Television Stations, Inc., 556 U.S. 502, (2009) (Thomas, J., concurring).

5   FCC v. Pacifica Found., 438 U.S. 726, 748-49 (1978).

6   Sable Communications of California, Inc. v. FCC, 492 U.S. 115, 126 (1989).

7   Pacifica Found., 438 U.S. at 729 (upholding the power of the FCC "to regulate a radio broadcast that is indecent but not obscene"). See also Action for Children's Television v. FCC, 58 F.3d 654, 669-70 (D.C. Cir. 1995) (en banc), cert. denied, 516 U.S. 1043 (1996) (federal appeals court upheld ban on indecent broadcasts from 6 a.m. to 10 p.m., when children are more likely to be watching).

8   See Brown v. Entertainment Merchants Ass'n, 131 S. Ct. 2729, n.3 (2011).

9   See, e.g., ACLU v. Reno, 521 U.S. 844, 868 (1997) (striking down attempt to apply a broadcast-like indecency standard to Internet speech). But see Denver Area Educ. Telecomm. Consortium, Inc. v. FCC, 518 U.S. 727, 745 (1996) (plurality opinion upholding federal law permitting cable operators to prohibit indecent material on leased access channels, citing, among other reasons, cable TV's accessibility to children, and thus apparently retreating somewhat from its position in its 1994 Turner Broad. Sys., Inc. v. FCC, 512 U.S. 622 (1994), that cable TV was entitled to full First Amendment protection).

10 See United States v. Playboy Entm't Group, 529 U.S. 803, 827 (declaring unconstitutional a federal statute restricting access to cable programming). See also Letter from W. Kenneth Ferree, Chief, Media Bureau to Saul Levine, Mt. Wilson FM Broadcasters, Inc., DA 04-3907 (Dec. 15, 2004) (denying Petition of Mt. Wilson FM Broadcasters, Inc. in the Matter of Establishment of Rules and Policies for the Digital Audio Radio Satellite Service in the 2310-2360 MHz Frequency Band (filed Oct. 29, 2004) to add indecency provisions applicable to satellite radio).

11 Kathleen Kirby, RTNDA and NAB vs. FCC: A Brief History (Oct. 11, 2000) available at: http://transition.fcc.gov/ogc/documents/opinions/1999/rtnda.html (last visited Aug. 16, 2013).

12 www.fcc.gov/Forms/Form303-S/303s.pdf.

13 47 C.F.R. Sec. 1.80 (2010).

14 In re Tri-State Univ., DA 09-930, Forfeiture Order (Rel. April 28, 2009).

15 Id. See Forfeiture Policy Statement, 12 FCC Rcd 17087, 17104-05 (1997).

16 See In re Tri-State, DA 09-930 at *3; In re Colby Community College, DA 10-603, Forfeiture Order (Rel. April 6, 2010); Wayne State College, 24 FCC Rcd 2484, Forfeiture Order (MB 2009); Washington and Lee Univ., 23 FCC Rcd 15821 (MB 2008). See also Discussion Radio, Inc, 19 FCC Rcd 7433, 7441, Memorandum Opinion and Order and Notice of Apparent Liability (2004).

17 See In re Little Miami Local Schools, DA 10-598, Forfeiture Order (Rel. April 6, 2010); Des Moines Independent Community School District, 24 FCC Rcd 2869, 2871, Memorandum Opinion and Order (MB 2009); Bible Broadcasting Network, Inc., 23 FCC Rcd 8743, Forfeiture Order, (MB 2008) (rejecting licensee's argument that its forfeiture order should be reduced because of its noncommercial educational status; Lebanon Educational Broadcasting Found., 21 FCC Rcd 1442, 1446, Memorandum, Opinion and Order (EB 2006); Little Miami Schools fn 19 (On occasion, it is possible to obtain some forgiveness if the station's record is clear of violations, as with WEAX, which was able to get its penalty reduced to $7,200.); In the Matter of Metropolitan School District of Wayne Township, Forfeiture Order, 26 F.C.C. Rcd. 11093 (MB Aug. 3, 2011), available at http://hraunfoss.fcc.gov/edocs_public/attachmatch/DA-11-1344A1.pdf; In the Matter of University of South Carolina, Forfeiture Order, 26 F.C.C.R. 11134 (MB Aug. 4, 2011), available at http://hraunfoss.fcc.gov/edocs_public/attachmatch/DA-11-1351A1.pdf.

18 47 C.F.R. § 73.3526 (2010), available at edocket.access.gpo.gov/cfr_2010/octqtr/pdf/47cfr73.3526.pdf.

19 47 C.F.R. § 73.3527 (2010), available at edocket.access.gpo.gov/cfr_2010/octqtr/pdf/47cfr73.3527.pdf.

20 See http://transition.fcc.gov/eb/broadcast/pif.html.

21 See www.fcc.gov/mb/audio/decdoc/public_and_broadcasting.html.

22 *See* http://www.fcc.gov/Forms/Form388/388.pdf.
23 To determine when a broadcast license expires, use the FCC's Universal Licensing System search website, http://wireless2.fcc.gov/UlsApp/UlsSearch/searchLicense.jsp.
24 To renew a license, a licensee must submit FCC Form 303-S.
25 47 C.F.R. 73.1020, 73.3539(a) (2010).
26 *See Five Star Parking d/b/a/ Five Star Taxi Dispatch*, 23 FCC Rcd 2649, Forfeiture Order (EB 2008); *PJB Communications of Virginia, Inc.*, 7 FCC Rcd 2088, Memorandum Opinion and Order (1992); *Southern California Broadcasting Co.*, 6 FCC Rcd 4387, Memorandum Opinion and Order (1992); *"Standard Communications Corp."*, 1 FCC Rcd 358, Memorandum Opinion and Order (1986).
27 The FCC's license renewal process is briefly described on the FCC's website: http://www.fcc.gov/guides/license-renewal-applications-radio-broadcast-stations.
28 *In re Colby Community College*, DA 10-603, Forfeiture Order (Rel. April 6, 2010).
29 *See Little Miami Local Schools*, DA 10-598, Forfeiture Order (Rel. April 6, 2010); *Educational Media Foundation*, 23 FCC Rcd 15366, Letter (MB 2006).
30 *See*, e.g., *In re Board of Trustees, Davis & Elkins College*, DA 09-988, Forfeiture Order (Rel. April 28, 2009).
31 *See In re Colby Community College*, DA 10-603, Forfeiture Order (Rel. April 6, 2010); *In re Board of Trustees, Davis & Elkins College*, DA 09-988, Forfeiture Order (Rel. April 28, 2009).
32 The FCC's rules regarding Special Temporary Authority can be found on the FCC's website: http://transition.fcc.gov/pshs/services/sta.html.
33 *In re Application of William Penn University*, DA 13-1074, FCC Policy Statement and Order, May 13, 2013, available at http://transition.fcc.gov/Daily_Releases/Daily_Business/2013/db0513/DA-13-1074A1.pdf (last visited May 20, 2013).
34 *Id.* at 8.
35 47 C.F.R. Sec. 73.503(a).
36 *In re Xavier Univ.*, Memorandum Opinion and Order, 5 F.C.C.R. 4920, 4921 (1990).
37 *Letter to the chief, Complaints & Political Programming Branch, Enforcement Division, to Evansville-Vanderburgh School Corporation WPSR(FM)* (March 23, 1999) (unpublished letter ruling).
38 47 U.S.C. Sec. 399a(a); see 47 C.F.R. Sec73.503(a), (b).
39 47 U.S.C. Sec. 399a(b).
40 *See In re Comm'n Policy Concerning the Noncommercial Nature of Educ. Broad. Stations*, 90 f.c.C.2d 895, 911 (1982) (Second Report).
41 *See In re Comm'n Policy Concerning the Noncommercial Nature of Educ. Broad. Stations*, 86 F.C.C.2d 141, 152 (1981) (First Report).
42 Second Report, 90 F.C.C.2d at 907.
43 *See In re Comm'n Policy Concerning the Noncommercial Nature of Educ. Broad. Stations*, 97 F.C.C.2d 255, 263 (1984) (Third Report).
44 *Id.*
45 *See In re Comm'n Policy Concerning the Noncommercial Nature of Educ. Broad. Stations*, 7 F.C.C.R. 827, 827-28 (1992) (Fourth Report).
46 *Id.* at 828.
47 *In re Family Vision Ministries, Inc.*, Memorandum Opinion and Order, 18 F.C.C.R. 1418, 1419 n.5 (2003).
48 *Id.*
49 *Id.*
50 *Id.*
51 *Agape Brdcst. Found., Notice of Apparent Liability for a Forfeiture*, 13 F.C.C.R. 13154, 13155 (1998).
52 *Letter to Window to the World Comm. (WTTW-TV)*, Notice of Apparent Liability, 12 F.C.C.R. 20239, 20240 (1997); *Letter to KRM-FM*, 8 F.C.C.R. 1 (1992).
53 *Minority TV Project, Inc.*, Notice of Apparent Liability for Forfeiture, 17 F.C.C.R. 15646, Sec. 20 (2002).
54 *Caguas Educ. TV, Inc.*, Notice of Apparent Liability for Forfeiture, Para. 7 (2005), *available at* http://www.fcc.gov/eb/Orders/2005/DA-05-725A1.html; *Letter to Frank Sobrino (WNYE-TV)*, Sept. 6, 1995; *In re Nat'l Farmworkers Serv. Center, Inc.*, Notice of Apparent Liability for Forfeiture, 2010 WL 2407953, *4 (June 15, 2010); *In re Independence public Media of Phil., Inc.*, 24 F.C.C.R. 857, 860 (2009).
55 *Caguas Educ. TV, Inc.*, Notice of Apparent Liability for Forfeiture, Para. 7 (2005).
56 *In re Jones College*, 24 F.C.C.R. 231, 234 (2009).
57 *In re Nat'l Farmworkers Serv. Center, Inc.*, Notice of Apparent Liability for Forfeiture, 2010 WL 2407953, *4 (June 15, 2010).
58 *Letter to WBHL*, Notice of Apparent Liability, 7 F.C.C.R. 19144, Para. 9 (2002).
59 *Letter to KRTM-FM*, 8 F.C.C.R. 1 (1992).
60 *Russellville Educ. Brdcst. Found.*, Notice of Apparent Liability for Forfeiture (1999), *available at* http://www.fcc.gov/bureaus/Mass_Media/Orders/1999/da991280.txt.
61 *Tri-State Inspirational Brdcst. Corp.*, Memorandum Opinion and Order, 16 F.C.C.R. 16800, Para. 6 (2001).
62 *In re Nat'l Farmworkers Serv. Center, Inc.*, Notice of Apparent Liability for Forfeiture, 2010 WL 2407953, *4 (June 15, 2010).
63 *In re Cayuga Co. Community Coll.*, 24 F.C.C.R. 8573, *3 (2009).
64 *See the Commission's Forfeiture Policy Statement and Amendment of Section 1.80 of the rules to Incorporate the Forfeiture Guidelines*, 12 F.C.C.R. 17087, 17115 (1997), *recons. denied*, 15 F.C.C.R. 303 (1999); 47 C.F.R. Sec. 1.80(b).
65 47 U.S.C. Sec. 503(b)(2)(E).
66 *Id.*

67 *Christian Voice of Cent. Ohio, Inc. (WCVZ-FM)*, 19 F.C.C.R. 23663 (2004) (reduced later to $9,000 for good compliance history and after reevaluating the acceptability of one of the announcements).
68 *Hispanic Broad. Sys., Inc.*, Notice of Apparent Liability for Forfeiture, 20 F.C.C.R. 2411 (2005)
69 *In re Jones College*, 24 F.C.C.R. 231 (2009).
70 *In re Independence Pub. Media of Phil., Inc.*, 24 F.C.C.R. 857 (2009).
71 David D. Oxenford and Robert J. Driscoll, *The Basics of Music Licensing in Digital Media*, Davis Wright Tremaine LLP (March 10, 2010). The text of the Copyright Act can be found in 17 U.S.C. Sec. 101 *et seq.*
72 *Copyrights Basics for Radio Stations & Webcasters*, College Broadcasters, Inc., *available at* http://www.askcbi.org/?page_id=129 (last visited Sept. 26, 2013).
73 David Oxenford, *Copyright Office Issues Letter in Support of Broadcast Performance Royalty - Suggests that Economic Comeback for Radio Makes Royalty More Affordable*, Broadcast Law Blog (June 8, 2010).
74 Information in this section was taken from the Web site of The American Society of Composers, Authors and Publishers, *available at* http://www.ascap.com (last visited Sept. 26, 2013).
75 *The ASCAP RateCalc* is available by following this link: https://www.ascap.com/weblicense/license.html
76 Information in this section was taken from the Web site of Broadcast Music, Inc., *available at* http://www.bmi.com (last visited Sept. 26, 2013).
77 For more information, please visit SoundExchange's website at www.soundexchange.com.
78 Pub. L. No. 104-39, 109 Stat. 336 (1995).
79 Pub. L. No. 105-304, 112 Stat. 2860 (1998).
80 *See* David Oxenford, *SoundExchange Sending Reminders to Broadcasters who are not Paying Royalties for Streaming Music Sound Recordings*, Broadcast Law Blog (Mar. 23, 2010).
81 *Frequently Asked Questions: General Licensing*, SESAC Licensing, *available at* http://www.sesac.com/Licensing/FAQsGeneral.aspx (last visited Sept. 26, 2013). Specifically, the Copyright Act provides that before final judgment, the copyright owner can elect to recover statutory damages ranging from $750 to $30,000, as the court considers just. If, however, the copyright owner can prove that there was willful infringement, the penalty can be increased up to $150,000 per song played. On the other hand, if a court finds that the infringement was not done in bad faith, it has discretion to reduce the damages to a minimum of $200 per song played. *See* 17 U.S.C. Sec. 504(c)(1)-(2).
82 For more information on FCC fines, see David Oxenford, *FCC Gives No Special Consideration to Noncommercial Broadcasters who Violate the Rules - Colleges Pay Attention to your Radio Station!* Broadcast Law Blog (Apr. 30, 2009).
83 *Id.*
84 For an example of how a court would analyze these factors, look at the Supreme Court's decision in *Campbell v. Acuff-Rose Music*, 510 U.S. 569 (1994).
85 *Harper & Row Publishers, Inc. v. Nation Enterprises,* 471 U.S. 539, 565 (1985).
86 *Columbia Broad. Sys., Inc. v. Democratic Nat'l Committee*, 412 U.S. 94, 101-102 (1973).
87 *See Turner Broad Sys. v. FCC*, 512 U.S. 622 (1994).
88 *In re Preserving the Open Internet, Report and Order*, FCC 10-201 (2010), *available at* http://hraunfoss.fcc.gov/edocs_public/attachmatch/FCC-10-201A1_Rcd.pdf.
89 *Comcast Corp. v. FCC*, 600 F.3d 642 (D.C. Cir. 2010) (first challenge); Marguerite Reardon, *D.C. Court to Hear Challenges to Net Neutrality Rules*, Cnet, http://news.cnet.com/8301-30686_3-20117222-266/d.c-court-to-hear-challenges-to-net-neutrality-rules/ (second challenge).
90 Remarks by Kyle McSlarrow, President & CEO, National Cable & Telecommunications Association before the Media Institute in Washington, D.C., Dec. 9, 2009, *available at,* http://betanews.com/2009/12/15/do-isps-have-first-amendment-rights-net-neutrality-vs-voip-connectivity/.
91 *See, e.g., In re Tri-State Univ.*, 24 F.C.C. Rcd. 2946, 4963-64 (MB 2009); *Alabama Educ. Television Commission*, 50 FCC 2d 461, para. 7 (1975).
92 *See generally Gambino v. Fairfax County Sch. Bd.*, 429 F. Supp. 731 (E.D.Va. 1977) (finding "the extent of state involvement in providing funding and facilities …does not determine whether First Amendment rights are applicable") (citing *Antonelli v. Hammond*, 308 F. Supp. 1329 (D. Mass. 1970)); *Stanley v. Magrath*, 719 F.2d 279, 282 (8th Cir. 1983); *Bazaar v. Fortune*, 476 F.2d 570, *aff'd en banc with modification*, 489 F.2d 225 (5th Cir. 1973) (per curiam)). *See also Joyner v. Whiting*, 477 F.2d 456 (4th Cir. 1973). Private schools are not limited by these same constraints, as they are not government organizations.
93 47 C.F.R. 73.3540.
94 *In re Creation of Low Power Radio Service*, 15 F.C.C. Rcd. 19208, 19241 (2000).
95 *In re Long Island University Public Radio Network*, Order, 25 F.C.C. Rcd. 13571, 13574 (EB 2010) (quoting WGPR, Inc., Memorandum Opinion & Order, 10 F.C.C. Rcd. 8140, 8142 (1995)).
96 A "transfer of control" can come in many forms, including the acquisition of a majority share of a licensee's company.
97 *Yale Broad. Co. v. FCC*, 478 F.2d 594, 602 (1973), *cert. denied*, 414 U.S. 914 (1973).
98 *Id.* at 596.
99 *Id.* at 605. Such criticisms of the FCC's overreaching persist to this day. *See, e.g.,* Julie Hilden, "The FCC tries to silence Howard Stern: Can the radio shock jock sue?" FindLaw's Writ (April 13, 2004). (http://writ.news.findlaw.com/hilden/20040413.html) (last visited Aug. 20, 2012).
100 *Trustees of the Univ. of Pennsylvania*, 69 F.C.C.2d 1394, paras. 23-38 (1978), recon. denied, 71 F.C.C.2d 416 (1979) (WXPN).
101 71 F.C.C.2d at 421.
102 71 F.C.C.2d at 428.
103 "KCSB-FM responds to FCC investigation," Student Press Law Center *Report*, Fall 1987, pp. 28-31.
104 *See Id.* To ensure students did not violate FCC regulations, school officials provided station employees with written guidelines and on-site training.

105 *See Jersawitz v. People TV,* 71 F. Supp. 2d 1330, 1339 (N.D. Ga. 1999) (citing *Perry Educ. Ass'n v. Perry Local Educators' Ass'n,* 460 U.S. 37 (1983)).

106 *See Perry Education Ass'n,* 460 U.S. at 45.

107 *Id.*

108 *Arkansas Educ. Television Commission v. Forbes,* 523 U.S. 666, 678 (1998).

109 *Id.* at 677-78.

110 A brief discussion of the various organizational structures of student electronic media is *available at* Howard M. Kleiman, "Student Electronic Media and the First Amendment," *Journalism & Mass Communication Educator* (Summer 1996), pp. 7-12.

111 *See Rosenberger v. Rector & Visitors of the Univ. of Va.,* 515 U.S. 819, 833 (1995) ("We have permitted the government to regulate the content of what is or is not expressed when it is the speaker or when it enlists private entities to convey its own message.").

112 *See, e.g., Arkansas Educ. Television Commission,* 523 U.S. at 673 (public television station permitted to exclude "fringe" political candidate from televised debate); *Knights of the Ku Klux Klan v. Univ. of Missouri,* 203 F.3d. 1085, 1091 (8th Cir. 2000) (no First Amendment right to sponsor public radio station programming and have underwriter's message read over the air). *But see Aldrich v. Knab,* 858 F. Supp. 1480, 1486-87 (W.D. Wash. 1994) (university-licensed station's policy prohibiting criticism of station violates First Amendment).

113 *Muir v. Alabama Educ. Television Comm'n,* 688 F.2d 1033, 1047 (5th Cir. 1982), *cert. denied,* 460 U.S. 1023 (1983) (en banc), *cert. denied,* 460 U.S. 1023 (1983).

114 *Id.* at 1050.

115 *Schneider v. Indian River Community College Foundation, Inc.,* 875 F.2d 1537, 1541 (11th Cir. 1989).

116 *See Schneider,* 875 F.2d. at 1540-42.

117 *Id.* at 1541 (citing *Muir,* 688 F.2d at 1050).

118 *See id.* at 1541.

119 *See id.*

120 *Id.* (citing *Muir,* 688 F.2d at 1052-53).

121 *Aldrich v. Knab,* 858 F. Supp. 1480, 1492 (W.D. Wash. 1994).

122 *Id.* at 1493.

123 *Id.* at 1494. However, the Court of Appeals later reversed, holding that the case should have been dismissed below, though not for its legal analysis. *Aldrich v. Knab,* No. 93-35423 1994 U.S. App. LEXIS 23843 (9th Cir. Aug. 29, 1994).

124 *Arkansas Educ. Television Commission,* 523 U.S. at 683.

125 *Muir,* 688 F.2d at 1043 (citing *Bazaar v. Fortune,* 476 F.2d 570, 574 (5th Cir. 1973) (public university officials did not have authority to censor student literary magazine recognized as forum for student expression simply because the school provided financial support and administrators disapproved of the content)).

126 *See* Linda L. Berger, Note: Government-Owned Media: the Government as Speaker and Censor, 35 Case W. Res. L. Rev. 707, 737 (1985) (citing William C. Canby, Jr., *The First Amendment and the State as Editor: Implications for Public Broadcasting,* 52 Tex. L. Rev. 1123, 1148 (1974)).

127 *See* Berger at 740-41.

128 *Id.* This principle was adopted by the dissenting opinions in *Muir,* 688 F.2d at 1060 (Reavely, J., dissenting).

129 *Healy v. James,* 408 U.S. 169, 180 (1972). *See also Widmar v. Vincent,* 454 U.S. 263, 267 (1981); *Rosenberger,* 515 U.S. at 836 (describing college and university campuses as one of the vital centers for the nation's intellectual life).

130 *See* Chapter 15 for more information on the law of obscenity.

131 The FCC's indecency standard is discussed in Chapter 15.

CHAPTER 11

The Rights of Advisers

A veteran adviser for an award-winning student newspaper at a public college found himself under fire. Minority student groups and administrators were upset after student editors at the newspaper failed to cover a minority student conference on their campus. The student editors admitted their mistake and apologized, promising to address their critics' concerns. Despite the fact that the adviser was legally prohibited from exercising control over the content of the publication — which he did not do — some students and administrators called for his removal. Three months later, school officials fired the adviser, citing what they claimed was the newspaper's "sub-par scope and quality of news coverage...."[1]

Student media advisers exist in a kind of limbo. They are both collaborators in a common cause with their student staff and, at the same time, teachers often responsible for assigning those same students a grade. They are advocates for an independent student voice, and professional colleagues of faculty members upon whom student criticism sometimes falls. They are watchdogs of school officials and employed by the same. Unfortunately, they frequently find themselves in a legal limbo as well, with ill-defined and amorphous legal concepts circumscribing their rights and responsibilities. Confronted by the dilemma of how to be a "good" and supportive adviser to their students — and at the same time keep their job — many student media advisers find themselves between the proverbial rock and hard place.

> Courts have ruled that when public school officials censor a student publication, it is the *students'* First Amendment rights that are affected — not the adviser's.

But, while advisers often share the pain of administrative censorship with their students, they generally do not share the same legal right to challenge such actions. Courts have generally ruled that when public school officials censor a student publication, it is the *students'* First Amendment rights that are affected — not the adviser's.[2] While censorship may implicate other legal rights an adviser might have — some which are discussed below — and while courts have permitted students to sue when their adviser is removed (see discussion, below) and have also sometimes allowed advisers to sue *on behalf of their students* (see discussion, "Legal Standing to Sue," below) it has been generally accepted that advisers cannot sue for violation of their own First Amendment rights based solely on censorship of their students' journalism.

This chapter examines several legal issues that impact advisers, including a possible right to disobey unconstitutional orders, a right to speak out on matters of public importance, academic freedom and curriculum control issues, contract-based employment remedies, and third-party standing to sue when students' rights are violated. Finally, it provides some practical tips on surviving what may be the toughest — but most rewarding — job in school.

RIGHT TO DISOBEY

All school officials — including advisers — are prohibited from censoring student publications where it violates federal or state law. But while student media advisers may be mindful of the legal protections against censorship, their bosses — be it through ignorance or deliberate indifference — often are not. Moreover, instead of censoring a student publication themselves, school officials too frequently delegate their dirty and sometimes illegal work to the student media adviser, a situation that can leave the adviser in a legal and ethical quandary.

Some court decisions have found that there exists a right to disobey clearly illegal or unconstitutional orders from one's superiors. If a teacher were to embezzle funds on an administrator's order, she would likely find herself arrested in short order. If a custodian plants a hidden camera in the shower area of a school locker room, it is unlikely that he would escape punishment simply by claiming he did so on orders from the principal. At some point even employees have an obligation and a right to say "no" to their bosses. Similarly, a teacher or adviser at a public school should be able to refuse to violate a student's First Amendment or other constitutionally guaranteed civil rights. (Different rules would likely apply to private school advisers.[3])

A teacher or adviser at a public school should be able to refuse to violate a student's First Amendment or other constitutionally guaranteed civil right.

Courts have recognized a right to be protected against retaliation for defying clearly unlawful orders in cases involving other public employees.[4] A Pennsylvania court, for example, upheld the right of a county prison guard to sue his employer after being fired for refusing to follow his boss's order to use what the guard believed to be excessive and unlawful force on an inmate. The court found:

> "The Duty to refrain from acting in a manner which would deprive another of constitutional rights is a duty created and imposed by the Constitution itself.... Therefore, we hold that the right to refuse to perform an unconstitutional act is a right 'secured by the Constitution' within the meaning of federal law."[5]

Similarly, the Washington Supreme Court acknowledged the law's obligation to protect the "conscientious dissenter" when it held that a state administrative judge could not be dismissed for refusing to follow a directive from his superiors that he reasonably believed violated state law and his profession's code of professional ethics:

> "We would do individual courage and integrity a great injustice were we to require employees to follow unquestioningly their master's bidding. A person with courage enough to risk employer sanctions, hostile reactions from colleagues, or possible discharge and the disgrace that accompanies it by disobeying a superior's order on the belief that it would be illegal or unethical for him to act otherwise, is entitled to a determination of the reasonableness of his belief."[6]

In 2011, an Iowa appeals court decided that a high school journalism adviser who was reprimanded for failing to censor edgy material in an April Fool's parody edition that offended some readers was entitled to have his record cleared, because censoring the material would have been unlawful under Iowa's Student Free Expression Law.[7] Although the case did not involve the direct defiance of an order to censor — the reprimand followed distribution of the offending newspaper — the court's reasoning supports the idea that an adviser cannot be punished for refraining from violating students' legal rights.

Alternatively, an adviser might be able to claim a right to disobey an order to unlawfully censor or engage in other illegal activity where she can reasonably show that doing so might make her the defendant in a lawsuit brought by her students. For example, a Minnesota federal appeals court heard a case involving college administrators who refused to perform certain actions they felt would violate students' civil rights. The court decided in favor of the school officials, holding that they had grounds to contest NCAA ineligibility rulings because they would be personally burdened if the ruling did violate the students' constitutional rights.[8]

Under both of these "right to disobey" theories it will be up to the adviser to show either that the ordered censorship was, in fact, illegal or the adviser reasonably believed it to be illegal. This, of course, is easier in some cases than in others. Unfortunately, advisers risk a charge of insubordination and being disciplined or fired "for cause" if a court later determines the censorship was permissible.[9] In close cases — or where no irreparable harm would occur — advisers may be better served by following orders, but challenging or questioning questionable directives through a formal grievance process.[10] (For help in identifying unlawful censorship, see Chapters 6 (public college), 5 (public high school) or 7 (private schools)).

While advisers face an uphill battle claiming violation of their free-press rights when student media are censored, the right of students to publish free from administrative interference — at least at a public college or university — is expansive and can include any act, direct or indirect, taken by an administrator where the intent is to control, manipulate or punish otherwise protected content.[11] Not surprisingly, courts have found that removing a student media adviser — if done to improperly influence or punish protected content — can violate, or "chill," the First Amendment rights of student editors.[12]

For example, when Ocean County College officials, unhappy with the New Jersey student newspaper's criticism of school officials and school policy, announced that they would not rehire the newspaper's thirty-five-year veteran adviser, Karen Bosley, the student editors of the *Viking News* cried foul. The court agreed, ruling that the college should not be permitted to do an end-around the First Amendment rights of students by punishing or removing their adviser for material they published. Allowing such action to stand, the court found, would unlawfully deter students from producing otherwise protected "articles critical of the college administration in the future."[13]

The court granted the students' petition that the school be required to keep Bosley in her position while the students' lawsuit continued.[14] The court found sufficient evidence that the school's removal of the adviser was, indeed, content-related. Specifically, the court noted: (1) college administrators had sent letters to the newspaper and had many conversations with the student editors where they "specifically expressed their displeasure with the Paper and its criticism of college administrators";[15] (2) college administrators had expressed a long-standing concern about the adviser's possible influence over the newspaper's publication of material critical of the school and school officials, and (3) despite the school's claim that the adviser's position was being eliminated due to "budgetary constraints," other advisers' positions were not similarly targeted. "Such disparate treatment of similarly situated groups," the court found, "further supports the students' claims that the adviser's removal was motivated by the Paper's content."[16]

"It is clear," the court concluded, "that such a retaliatory removal of a student media adviser would…have an impermissibly chilling effect on the Paper's student editors' freedom of expression in future issues of the Paper, and inflict irreparable harm on the student editors."[17]

RIGHT TO SPEAK OUT:
EXTRACURRICULAR SPEECH BY PUBLIC EMPLOYEES

Some school officials will threaten to fire teachers or staff members who criticize the administration, school board or school. As a result, student media advisers frequently have questions about how much support they can give their publication staffs as students wage a battle against administrative censorship. Do they, for example, have the right to talk openly to outside media when contacted for comment on such matters?[18] Can they safely testify before the school board in opposition to a proposed prior review policy? Can they help edit a student press release detailing acts of administrative censorship?

Before 2006, an established body of case law maintained that public employees enjoy a limited, but constitutionally protected, right to free speech.[19] The Supreme Court's 1968 ruling in *Pickering v. Board of Education* specifically addressed the issue for public school teachers, concluding that a teacher can speak out on a "matter of legitimate public concern" without reprisal.[20] However, the right to publicly discuss matters of private concern is more limited, if not altogether unprotected.

Unfortunately, distinguishing between speech on a matter of public concern, which is protected, and more individual, private speech, which is not protected, is not always easy. Law books are full of cases where judges have struggled — with mixed success, it can be argued — to arrive at a decision, which can make for a risky guessing game for student media advisers. At times, courts have found that employee speech about school

Courts have found that removing a student media adviser — if done to improperly influence or punish protected content — can chill the First Amendment rights of student editors.

The right of public school advisers to publicly discuss matters of private concern is limited, if not altogether unprotected.

A 2006 Supreme Court decision found that internal criticism of an employer made during the course of one's official duties does not involve a matter of public concern and is unprotected by the First Amendment.

conditions is First Amendment-protected speech even where there is some element of self-interest in the speech.[21] In other instances, courts have found that the speaker was not addressing a protected matter of public concern, even where the subject matter clearly related to school policies going beyond the speaker's personal self-interest.[22] As these diverging court decisions illustrate, advisers stand on unsteady footing when they speak out publicly about school matters.

In an often-cited employee speech case, *Connick v. Myers*, the Supreme Court held that complaints made in public by an individual employee about internal office policies or matters that primarily affect only the employee generally are not protected.[23] In one case from 1992, for example, a South Carolina schoolteacher was discharged after he circulated a letter to other teachers complaining about a payroll change, criticizing the district for "budgetary mismanagement" and calling for a "sick-out" during finals.[24] The federal appeals court held that the "essential thrust" of his letter was a private grievance, and stated that "personal grievances, complaints about conditions of employment, or expressions about other matters of personal interest do not constitute speech about matters of public concern that are protected by the First Amendment, but are matters more immediately concerned with the self-interest of the speaker as employee."[25]

By contrast, in 1989 a federal appeals court ruled that the First Amendment protected an Oklahoma public school cafeteria worker who complained about unsanitary cafeteria practices — including serving spoiled food to children — and the school's refusal to address the issue. The worker complained to the principal, school board and state and county health departments. The school board then adopted a policy forbidding cafeteria workers from complaining to individuals outside the school. The worker filed suit (which she later withdrew after the school board rescinded the policy) alleging her First Amendment rights were violated. In a later suit awarding attorney's fees, the court said, "plaintiff's complaints about unsanitary practices in the school's cafeteria and the administration's refusal to address them clearly dealt with matters of public concern."[26] In a more recent case, from 1994, a federal appeals court found that a public elementary school teacher's published letters to the editor of her local newspaper criticizing school board members for planning a taxpayer-funded convention trip to San Francisco, which she described as a "luxurious vacation," and her filing of a Freedom of Information Act request asking for the names of those seeking to attend the conference, constituted speech about a matter of public concern.[27] Unfortunately for advisers, even where a public employee's speech does involve a matter of public concern, a court may still find the speech unprotected if the speaker went too far and unreasonably interfered with or undermined the school's mission.[28]

The U.S. Supreme Court's 2006 decision in *Garcetti v. Ceballos* has further muddied these waters, adding a new layer to how courts define and evaluate the free-speech rights of public employees. In *Garcetti*, the Supreme Court focused its free-speech analysis on whether a deputy district attorney's statements were made "pursuant to his duties."[29] The attorney, following his own fact-finding and investigation, had drafted a memo to his supervisors that expressed concerns that a prosecution his office had undertaken was based on "serious misrepresentations." He was subsequently reassigned, transferred and denied promotion.[30] In a 5-4 ruling, the Supreme Court rejected the attorney's employee speech claim and concluded that the repercussions were lawful. The majority concluded that because the deputy district attorney's statements were made in the course of his official duties, they did not and could not involve a matter of public concern, which left him with no recourse under the First Amendment.[31]

A vigorous dissent opposed the Court's new approach, noting that "public employees are still citizens while they are in the office. The notion that there is a categorical difference between speaking as a citizen and speaking in the course of one's employment is quite wrong."[32] Predictably, the *Garcetti* case has had chilling repercussions for public employee First Amendment claims. The American Bar Association, for instance, reported in 2008 that "lower courts applying the decision have increasingly ruled against public employee plaintiffs who previously might have won."[33] At least two federal appeals courts have applied the *Garcetti* reasoning to the claims of public school teachers disciplined for speech, although in those cases, the speech involved an in-class lecture, in which teachers' free-expression rights have always been recognized as being at their lowest.[34]

The combination of the *Connick* and *Pickering* rulings, which can leave public employees guessing about whether a court will find their public speech to be about a "matter of public concern," and *Garcetti*, which now also makes it risky to express such criticism internally, leaves student media advisers — like all whistleblowers who dare speak out against perceived wrongs committed at their workplace — in an extremely difficult position. *Garcetti* raises a caution flag that advisers who question their supervisors about censorship of student media in an attempt to resolve the problem internally are at risk of demotion, retaliation or other professional discipline with no constitutional recourse (though of course they may have other remedies, such as contract-based appeals).

Finally, it is must be noted that even where a public employee's speech is legally protected, it can still be difficult to prove that speech was the motivating factor for the employee's punishment or dismissal. As discussed below (see "Filing a First Amendment Lawsuit"), such a showing may be necessary for an adviser to prevail.

RIGHT TO CONTROL CURRICULUM

To what extent, if any, does the First Amendment give student media advisers the right to determine the content or method of their teaching? Whether it is defined as a right of "academic freedom" or something else, courts continue to struggle in their attempt to decide how much control teachers and professors have over what goes on in their own classrooms. For example, does a high school adviser — believing it to be the best way to teach journalism — have the right to insist on a student-only edited newspaper? Or does the First Amendment prohibit college administrators from punishing a journalism professor who, as part of a classroom exercise, encourages her students to file freedom of information requests to obtain public records from university officials? Unfortunately, as the following discussion suggests, clear answers to such questions can be difficult to come by.

> The Supreme Court has never clearly defined the scope of the right of academic freedom.

Academic Freedom

While most people have heard of "academic freedom," there is little agreement — either among courts or commentators — about precisely what it is, who it protects, or where it comes from.[35] The Supreme Court has never clearly defined the scope of the right of academic freedom, though it has on more than one occasion indicated that expressive activity in the academic setting deserves special constitutional protection.[36]

Lower courts have been more specific, but frequently at odds with one another in their attempts to clarify what is meant by academic freedom.

> First Amendment-based claims of "academic freedom" to teach fare better at the college level than in high schools.

At the college level, most courts have recognized at least some loosely defined right of academic freedom, but increasingly, individual professors are having a tough time convincing courts that such a right protects their decisions to determine their own curriculum or teaching methods.[37]

For high school teachers the situation is considerably bleaker, with most courts rejecting teachers' claims that they have a First Amendment-based right of academic freedom to determine what they teach in their classrooms.[38] But there are exceptions. For example, a Colorado appellate court held that school officials could not refuse to renew the contract of Judith Watson, a middle-school student newspaper adviser, if their only reason for doing so was that Watson: (1) allowed her students to publish articles that the principal felt "portrayed the school in a negative light," (2) refused to retract the articles and (3) advised her students in the newspaper class of their right to refuse to retract them.[39] The First Amendment, the court ruled, protected Watson's actions:

> "Academic freedom is within the protections of the First Amendment... This includes a teacher's interest in choosing a particular pedagogical method for a course, so long as the course is part of the school's official curriculum and the teaching method serves a demonstrable educational purpose ... Watson's class, 'School Newspaper,' was part of the school's official curriculum, and it was the plaintiff's responsibility to teach her students about the legal concepts applicable to journalism. Accordingly, her conduct was constitutionally protected."[40]

While a more thorough discussion of the right of academic freedom is beyond the scope of this chapter, several sources of additional information are available.[41]

Other First Amendment Protection
In addition to — or as part of an academic freedom analysis — courts have frequently used two other approaches to analyze teacher classroom speech cases.

Public/Private speech approach
Some courts have looked to the *Pickering* and *Connick* public/private speech standard, discussed above in the context of extracurricular teacher speech, to determine whether a teacher's in-class speech is protected. Under this approach, a teacher's classroom speech about a matter of public concern is protected; speech about a matter of private concern is not. Unfortunately, as in the case of extracurricular employee speech, courts have had little success settling on a uniform test for determining which type of speech is which.

One group of courts apparently thinks the test is easy. Under their analysis, teachers in the classroom setting are first and foremost employees and all questions about curriculum are simple employment disputes that are never matters of public concern. These courts reject all notions of academic freedom for public high school teachers and have made clear their belief the First Amendment never protects individual teachers' decisions about curriculum.[42] The U.S. Court of Appeals for the Fourth Circuit (which covers professors in Maryland, North Carolina, South Carolina, West Virginia and Virginia) has applied a similar test to the speech of college professors.[43]

Other courts applying the public/private speech test have relied on a much broader definition of what constitutes a matter of public concern. For example, in *Cockrel v. Shelby County School District*, a federal court of appeals explicitly ruled that matters of public concern are those that can "be fairly considered as relating to any matter of political, social or other concern to the community."[44] Applying such a standard, the court found that school officials had violated the First Amendment rights of a Kentucky elementary school teacher when they fired her for allowing actor Woody Harrelson to give a controversial talk to her class about industrial hemp as an alternative to cutting down trees, despite her principal having pre-approved the actor's visit. The court noted that the "discussion of industrial hemp plainly meets the broad concept of 'public concern' as defined by the Supreme Court in a 1983 case," and that "the key question is not whether a person is speaking in his role as an employee or citizen, but whether the employee's speech in fact touches on matters of public concern."[45]

It appears likely, however, that the usefulness of the *Cockrel* ruling has been weakened by more recent decisions. While the U.S. Supreme Court's *Garcetti* holding purported to avoid touching on issues of academic freedom,[46] a Seventh Circuit appeals court — writing that "*Garcetti* applies directly" — denied any First Amendment protection to an elementary school teacher who personally espoused anti-war views during a current-events lesson.[47]

Hazelwood approach

Other courts have ignored the public/private speech test and have instead turned to the Supreme Court's standard in *Hazelwood School District v. Kuhlmeier*, a case discussed in detail in Chapter 5.[48] While *Hazelwood* specifically addressed the First Amendment rights of students working on a school-sponsored newspaper, a number of courts have seen fit to apply the standard to the school-sponsored speech of teachers as well.

Under this approach, a teacher's classroom speech is protected by the First Amendment unless school officials can show that they have a legitimate pedagogical (educational) interest in restricting the speech.

Unfortunately — just as has been the case for student speech — such a vague standard has provided limited protection in practice and teachers have had a difficult time convincing courts that administrative regulation or punishment of their in-class speech was unlawful. For example, a federal appellate court had little trouble concluding that school officials acted lawfully in disciplining a Colorado high school teacher for his classroom criticism of two unnamed students for "making out" on a tennis court.[49] The court concluded that the school's asserted interest in preventing the teacher from spreading unsubstantiated rumors and in ensuring that "teacher employees exhibit professionalism and sound judgment" were legitimate educational interests that justified the school's punishment.[50]

While most *Hazelwood*-based teacher speech cases have involved secondary school teachers, at least one court has applied *Hazelwood* to the classroom speech of a college professor. The court readily acknowledged that it had serious reservations about whether a high school-based censorship standard was appropriate in the context of a college classroom and it refused to "decide definitively...whether *Hazelwood* does in fact govern a public college or university's control over the classroom speech of a professor or other instructor."[51]

Contract-based academic freedom

While most high school teachers, and even some college professors, may have a tough time arguing that they have a First Amendment-based right of "academic freedom," such protection can be found in other sources. Most college — and many high school — faculty members have a contract or letter of appointment that spells out, with varying degrees of specificity, the faculty member's terms and conditions of employment.

Often such documents make reference to more detailed policies, rules or procedures that are found in a faculty handbook, union agreement or other outside document. These documents frequently contain provisions relating to faculty academic freedom and have been held to be legally binding contracts.[52] In certain states, provisions in a state law or state constitution may be relevant as well.[53]

Due Process

Even if a faculty handbook, union agreement, or state tenure law, for example, does not contain explicit language forbidding administrators from punishing or removing an adviser based on her work with student media, such agreements frequently set up specific rules, or a process, for how such disciplinary measures can be meted out. Where administrators fail to comply with the rules, an adviser may find some relief by filing a "due process" complaint.[54]

For example, an agreement may require that an administrator provide written notice to a newspaper adviser three months before failing to renew her contract or it may require that the school provide the teacher with a hearing, perhaps with the opportunity to have a lawyer or union representative present, before imposing any disciplinary measures. Student media advisers in the Anchorage School District, for instance, bargained to include in their union agreement a provision that school officials consider putting a veteran publication adviser (or coach) on probation for one year before resorting to

At least one court has applied *Hazelwood* to the classroom speech of a college professor.

Faculty handbooks and union agreements often contain provisions relating to faculty academic freedom that have been held to be legally binding contracts.

Due Process: The requirement that the specific rules or process for how disciplinary measures can be imposed be both fair and followed.

termination.[55] Such a provision could be used to dissuade administrators from hot-headedly firing qualified advisers because of complaints from disgruntled school officials or parents about published stories — an unfortunately common occurrence at many high schools. An administrator's failure to follow established rules often voids the punishment and can at least temporarily provide advisers a reprieve. Absent a formal agreement or written procedures, a court may still require a school to adhere to a reasonable and fair process for handing down punishment or removing an adviser from his position where the school's action deprives the adviser of an established property interest in continued employment. Such cases are likely to be productive only in the case of tenured faculty whose adviser role is clearly part of the faculty position. Due process claims for untenured, temporary, extra-duty, or contract employees, whose property interest in continued employment terminates with the ending date of their current contract, are generally of limited help.[56]

> An administrator's failure to follow established rules often voids the punishment and can — at least temporarily — provide advisers a reprieve.

Miscellaneous Rights

In addition to some of the rights discussed above, courts have also ruled, for example, that a Wyoming adviser could not be fired for assisting students with the publication of a non-school-sponsored or "underground" newspaper,[57] and a New Jersey college adviser could not be fired because of an editorial she wrote for the paper she advised.[58] Another pre-*Hazelwood* decision suggested that a high school adviser could not be fired when the student paper "upset" certain school board members, but upheld the dismissal when the adviser failed to prove that the offending content was the reason for the board's decision.[59]

FILING A FIRST AMENDMENT LAWSUIT: OTHER OBSTACLES

As mentioned above, to assert a First Amendment claim, an adviser must first show that the speech at issue was, in fact, protected. Unfortunately for advisers (and other public employees) that is not the end of it. Even if an adviser shows that she was punished after engaging in protected speech or allowing her students to do so, an adviser must still prove that the protected speech was a substantial and motivating factor in any punitive action.[60] Assuming the adviser can meet this burden, the school then has a chance to rebut the adviser's claim and show that there were, nevertheless, other legitimate grounds for the punishment.[61]

All of this can make for an uphill legal battle for advisers. For example, in *Nicholson v. Board of Education Torrance Unified School District*, the adviser of a California high school paper claimed that he was put on probationary status for refusing to follow an administrative order to submit the paper to the principal for prior review. The court ruled that the prior review request was not unconstitutional.[62]

Furthermore, the court said that even if the prior review had been unconstitutional, the adviser needed to show that the protected expression was a motivating factor in the punitive action against him. If he could do so, then the burden would shift back to the school to show that there were other legitimate grounds for the punishment. In the *Nicholson* case, the court found that the school board did have other legitimate reasons for the punitive action, including the adviser's failure to follow rules governing bookkeeping duties.[63]

In short, even if the adviser had been able to show that his speech was protected, the court said he would still have lost the case because there were other lawful grounds for his firing. The lesson of *Nicholson* is that it is imperative that advisers not give administrators other legitimate reasons for punishment. Advisers who are consistently late for class, turn in grade reports late, or otherwise flout school regulations unrelated to First Amendment issues do not tend to win otherwise legitimate First Amendment firing cases.

Despite the legal obstacles sometimes faced by advisers who feel they have been wrongly punished or terminated for standing up for a free and independent student press, advisers have often attained success at the settlement stage of a lawsuit, sometimes being offered substantial sums of money by the schools involved.[64] Schools will often agree to settle a case to avoid the bad publicity that can accompany particularly egregious (even if lawful) censorship attempts, or to avoid protracted litigation where an adviser has a strong claim.

For example:

- Attorneys for fired East Carolina University media adviser Paul Isom negotiated a $31,200 buyout, compensating him for the unexpired portion of his one-year contract, after Isom was fired because his students published a front-page photo of a naked man "streaking" an ECU football game.[65]
- Fired Indiana high school adviser Kelly Short got a $40,000 settlement plus legal fees after suing her school alleging that her First Amendment rights were violated when she stuck up for her students, whose principal imposed mandatory prior review of newspaper content and tried to micro-manage the schedule and appearance of the yearbook.[66]
- California's Fallbrook High School reinstated adviser Dave Evans and gave him $7,500 in back pay and $20,000 in legal fees to resolve a suit over the principal's cancellation of the journalism program, which followed the students' decision to publish an editorial critiquing the effectiveness of the sex education curriculum and a news story that highlighted a controversy over the school's participation in an emergency-preparedness exercise.[67]
- Fort Valley State University in Georgia agreed to pay adviser John Schmitt $117,000 in legal fees and $75,000 in personal damages for the non-renewal of his contract after the student newspaper reported, among other things, that a university vice president was involved in questionable financial dealings at her previous school and that campus security failed to properly treat a student with asthma, who later died. The school also agreed, as part of the 2002 settlement, to adopt a stronger publications policy that included provisions to protect future advisers.[68]
- New Mexico high school poetry club adviser Bill Nevins was awarded $205,000 as part of his 2004 settlement with his employer, Rio Rancho Public Schools, after he claimed he was suspended because of anti-war poetry written by his students.[69]
- Barton County Community College in Kansas agreed to pay newspaper adviser Jennifer Schartz $130,000 as part of a 2006 settlement. Schartz claimed in her lawsuit that her contract was not renewed because students published a letter to the editor criticizing the college's basketball coach, which the school called a "personal attack."[70]

LEGAL STANDING TO SUE

In some cases, advisers may have the right to sue on behalf of their students when the students' rights are violated. Students whose publications are censored are sometimes reluctant or unable to sue, due to lack of parental support, community pressure, graduation, or a host of other issues. In these situations, an adviser may have "legal standing" to go to court on behalf of their students.

The law is split on this issue. In *Olson v. State Board for Community Colleges and Occupational Education*, the Colorado Supreme Court found that while the adviser herself had no constitutionally protected rights relating to censorship of the student newspaper, she was a proper third-party plaintiff and could continue the case on behalf of her students.[71] Similarly, a New York court allowed a high school newspaper adviser to file suit on behalf of his students for violation of their First Amendment rights, although the court rejected the adviser's claim that his own rights were violated when he was fired.[72] The court noted that the law more readily allows third-party standing in First Amendment cases.[73] In a 2001 case, a Georgia court found that a college newspaper adviser also had third-party standing to sue.[74] And in 1985, in allowing a high school

Standing to Sue: A jurisdictional requirement that the party bringing a lawsuit has been injured or threatened with injury. If a court finds that person lacks standing, it cannot hear a case.

Third-Party Standing to Sue: An exception to the traditional standing requirement that allows a third party (such as an adviser) to sue on behalf of a person with a claim (such as a student journalist) who cannot reasonably bring his own lawsuit.

adviser to sue on behalf of her students, a Wyoming judge wrote that "in cases like this where the rights of high school students to freedom of expression are at issue, teachers are often the only logical adult litigants."[75] The Ninth U.S. Circuit Court of Appeals reached a similar conclusion in the *Nicholson* case, discussed above.[76]

However, in a 1992 case, a Louisiana court found differently. Geraldine Moody, a social studies teacher, allowed her students to publish a newspaper for class credit. The newspaper, called *Your Side*, was unrelated to the official school paper and the students undertook the project to learn more about the First Amendment's guarantee of press freedom. The school administration felt *Your Side* contained inappropriate material. They were also disturbed that the paper had been sold instead of distributed for free. Moody was transferred and reprimanded. She subsequently resigned. The court found that she did not have standing to sue on behalf of her students because she neither wrote nor edited the students' publication; the court also noted its belief that the students could have sued on their own behalf.[77]

A fired adviser at Illinois' Chicago State University won reinstatement and back pay in a 2011 ruling from a federal district court, which found that the adviser had legal standing to sue in his own right for violation of the First Amendment.[78] However, that ruling, *Moore v. Watson*, may be of limited usefulness beyond Illinois, because the court was influenced by the mention of adviser rights in Illinois' College Campus Press,[79] and concluded that, under Illinois law, the adviser was a "participant" in the protected forum of the campus newspaper.

Another case to note is *Cullen v. Gibson*, in which the Sixth U.S. Circuit Court of Appeals dismissed a case brought by a college student media adviser at Kentucky State University. The adviser had sued on both her own and her students' behalf after the student yearbook was censored and she was removed as adviser. The court ruled she had no standing to continue her lawsuit because she had voluntarily resigned from KSU before the legal proceeding concluded, which, the court said, rendered her case moot.[80]

ADVISER'S TOP TEN TIPS FOR SURVIVING A CENSORSHIP STORM

1. Let Your Students Lead

At the beginning of each year, explain to your students the difficult position in which you, as adviser, operate. You are on their side, of course. But you — unlike the students themselves — are also a school employee. Let them know you support them, but that they must be willing and able to take the leadership role should it be necessary to challenge administrative action. It's their publication. Courts have made clear that it is also their legal rights — not the adviser's — that are at stake. If a fight must be waged, it must be their fight (and ideally, one that parents and other community members are willing to join). It is also important that school officials understand early on that any battle will be with students and parents, not you.

2. Avoid Insubordination

Remember that the boss is still the boss. Allowing administrators to confuse the censorship issue with complicated contract and labor claims never helps. Of course, you must follow your conscience. Censorship flies in the face of everything that journalists and journalism educators stand for. It's tough to stomach and you must determine your personal and professional comfort zone. But generally — unless the acts of your superiors are clearly illegal — you must do as you are told.

If your superiors won't back down or agree to an acceptable compromise, your only other options are to quit or be fired. If you believe that your boss' actions have crossed some line you should contact your union, file a formal grievance or seek independent legal counsel.

3. Let Others be the "Bad Guy"

If your students need guidance or simply a "pep talk" in fighting their censorship battle, they should contact an outside group — such as the Student Press Law Center or your state's scholastic press group — for help. Such groups can provide direction and inspiration to your students without fear of administrative retaliation. Ideally, you should provide a list of outside resources to your students at the beginning of each school year so they will know where to turn without having to seek your assistance in a time of crisis.

4. Establish a Paper Trail

Stories change, especially once the heat is on. Protect yourself. You should not rely on the handshake or verbal promise of an administrator. If you are asked to do something you find questionable, ask (respectfully) for a directive in writing, and whether you receive it or not, you should always send a written memo confirming your understanding of the directive and the action you plan to take.

If ordered to do something with which you disagree, note your disagreement and, if applicable, your intention to reluctantly comply. Also be sure to keep hard copies of those glowing evaluations from years gone by. Finally, because your students may be able to successfully sue the school if they are able to show your removal is content-based, it is important to document and retain records (for example, e-mail, minutes, notes from informal meetings or contacts) that show administrative unhappiness with what is published. Such records — maintained as part of a "First Amendment File" — comprise an important history of the student media organization and should never be destroyed, but carefully passed to succeeding staffs for use should the need arise.

5. Watch What You Say and Write

Courts have not been protective of the right of employees to criticize their employers — even when it's deserved. This is especially true when the matter is one of private rather than public concern. For example, while you probably have the right to address a school board meeting about why you generally think censorship is educationally unsound (without tying your comments to any specific situation), you might find yourself in hot water if you write a letter to the editor detailing how your principal "unfairly reprimanded" you for allowing the publication of a story she disliked.

Likewise, unless you are following a formalized internal grievance process, recent court decisions warn that you must also be wary of criticizing your employer in internal, professional communications, such as a memo to your superintendent or board of regents, as statements made pursuant to your official duties no longer enjoy First Amendment protection. Because of the vague and generally flimsy legal protections that currently exist for employee speech, the safest course is usually to keep quiet and let your students and others do the talking and writing.

6. Put Your Union Dues to Work

If you feel your job being threatened, notify your union representative immediately (if you have one). When a censorship battle becomes an employment battle, complications can quickly set in and you need help from those with labor law experience. Unions are paid to stick up for teachers when they are mistreated. Use yours.

7. Secure the Line

Be careful when using school resources to discuss your case. This is particularly true of e-mail, which can be easily (and usually legally) monitored by school officials. Consider using your private telephone or home e-mail account.

8. Toot Your Own Horn

Enter your publications in competition. Being able to show that a third party has honored your student publications and/or your work as an adviser can be helpful in deflecting administrative criticism and building public support.

9. Bring in the Pros

Establish regular contact with members of the professional local media. Bring in local journalists as guest speakers. Ask a reporter or editor to act as an "informal consultant" to your publication. Consider starting an internship or a "Teen Page" program with local media. If properly cultivated and educated, the commercial press can be the student media's ally. Take advantage. Once local journalists know and perhaps even take some "ownership" in your student journalism program, the more likely they will be to support you and your students' times of need.

While it will seem at times as though it is you against the world, you have many supporters. Any student media adviser that has been in the business for more than a few years probably has endured a crisis or two. Seek them out. Ask for their advice — or at least their ear. Contact the SPLC or one of the national or regional journalism education organizations. There is strength (and comfort) in numbers. If you advise college media, the group College Media Association provides an Adviser Advocate Committee as a member benefit. Since its inception in 1998, the committee has investigated numerous claims of improper retaliation against advisers.[81] The AAC will work with advisers and schools to resolve disputes and has publicly censured institutions that violate CMA principles.

CASE STUDY

You are adviser to the *Student Times* newspaper, which is published by students in your Journalism II class. The student editor has decided to publish a story on drug use at your public high school. The reporter interviewed several students who, on the condition of anonymity, admitted to using drugs and at least one who said that he sold drugs on campus. (So far, only the reporter and editor know the names of the students.) The draft article, which you've told your students is well-reported and written, paints an eye-opening picture and exposes a side of your school that many have never seen.

An hour ago, your principal, after being contacted by *Student Times* reporters seeking comment for the story, called you in to her office. Though she hasn't read the article, she said the topic is "sensationalist." She is concerned that parents and others in the community will be upset and has ordered you to stop it from going to the printer. She has also demanded that you provide her with the names of the students interviewed for the story who admitted to being involved with drugs.

You leave the office in a state of shock. Though you were concerned that your school district did not have a student media policy when you were hired three years ago, the principal has generally left the paper alone. In fact, the only other time the principal got involved was two years ago when she asked the editors to delay a story about a security glitch in the school's computer system for a couple of days until the problem could be fixed, which your students agreed to do.

As you return to your classroom, and before you can tell your students what has happened, you're handed a telephone message from a local reporter who has somehow heard about the drug story and would like to talk to you. What do you do?

ANSWER:
Unfortunately, many experienced student media advisers have found themselves in a situation not too different from the above. Even more unfortunate is that there is, in most cases, no perfect solution. Some responses, however, are definitely better than others.

RESPONDING TO THE PRINCIPAL'S CENSORSHIP DEMAND

First, it is important to take a deep breath. Administrative censorship can feel like a professional slap in the face. After all, it's unlikely the principal tells the chemistry teacher how to run her classroom or the basketball coach how to manage his team. She trusts them to use their professional judgment. Why should you be treated any differently? Moreover, for many journalism teachers, censorship (especially for the reasons given by the principal in this case) strikes a moral chord that is hard simply to shrug off. But while such a reaction is understandable, automatically going on the defensive is unlikely to resolve the conflict and could make things worse.

It is essential to keep in mind that the principal's censorship of the drug story, if found to be unlawful, would violate the students editors' free press rights, not yours. Courts have consistently ruled that advisers do not have a First Amendment right to publish material in a student publication. Moreover, as an employee, you are generally required to follow the orders of your superiors or risk facing charges of insubordination. Therefore, if the principal's actions are to be effectively challenged, your students must be willing to assume the bulk of that responsibility themselves.

Hopefully, prior to the censorship, you will have discussed — at least generally — your students' rights and responsibilities under the law (as well as reminded them of the limits placed on you as an employee of the school) and alerted them of resources, such as the Student Press Law Center or your state scholastic press association, to which they can independently turn for information and guidance.

While it may be frustrating, both you and your students are usually best served by your staying on the sidelines and letting your students (and hopefully their parents, other community members and the various support groups) use the knowledge and tools they have to fend for themselves. While any First Amendment-based free press rights belong to your students, the law may offer you other legal protections. For example, if you are certain that the principal's order to censor is unlawful, some courts have recognized an employee's right to disobey. The key is that you must be able to show that the order to censor is clearly unlawful. Had this censorship taken place at a public college — where the First Amendment protections against censorship are generally well established — or at a high school in one of the handful of states that has a law protecting student press freedom, such censorship likely would be held unlawful.

To be sure, there are reasonable arguments to be made that the principal may be overstepping her authority. For example, because the principal generally has not interfered with the newspaper and has allowed student editors to determine its content, an argument can be made that the paper has, by practice, been operated as a public forum, a legal status that would almost certainly shield the *Student Times* from the censorship demanded by the principal in this case. However, three years is a relatively short period of time and, when combined with the principal's earlier "request" for a delay in publication of the computer glitch story, a court may conclude that the school's intent to create a public forum is, at best, unclear.

Even if the paper is not found to be a public forum, however, a reasonable argument can still be made that the principal has failed to meet her legal burden to censor the *Student Times*. As you have said, you found the story well-written and well-reported. Neither you nor the principal have suggested that there is any reason to doubt its accuracy or its fairness. In fact, it appears that your students have done just what any good journalists should: they have found and truthfully reported the news.

Unfortunately, allowing the principal to censor material if she has a "reasonable educational justification" (mirroring language from the Supreme Court's *Hazelwood* standard, which the Court said applies to non-forum high school student newspapers) gives the principal considerable, though not unlimited, leeway. And while it seems your principal's reasons for censoring the story (that is, that the topic is "sensationalist" and likely to upset the community) are based largely on public relations concerns rather than educational ones, it is probably best, in questionable cases such as this, not to risk an insubordination charge by refusing the principal's order outright. If you wish to challenge her order to censor the newspaper, it is probably best to appeal the principal's orders through a formal, internal grievance procedure. (Of course, your students can continue to act independently to challenge the censorship.)

Advisers may also have contract-based academic freedom rights. Now is the time to dust off your employee handbook and dig up any collective bargaining agreements or district policies to search for relevant language. Schools are generally bound to honor promises they have made and follow procedures they have established. Unfortunately, absent a formal, written agreement, your options may be limited, as most courts have said that public high school teachers do not have a First Amendment-based right of academic freedom to teach their classes as they choose. (College advisers probably have a stronger claim, though some courts have whittled away at their academic freedom protection in recent years.)

Assuming that your school has not made such promises, you have two main choices: you can follow your principal's directive to censor or resign your position. You, of course, have to follow your conscience and in the worst of cases that may mean resignation. Keep in mind, however, that administrators may be delighted to see a competent, professional journalism adviser walk out the door, allowing them to replace you with a "puppet adviser" of their choosing. Generally, your students and your program will be best served if you stick around.

In such a case, you should send a memo to the principal asking for confirmation of her order to censor the newspaper and her reasons for doing so. If you believe the censorship to be misguided, use the memo to inform her of your belief, but make it clear that you understand that she is the boss and that if she orders you to censor the paper, you will do so.

While censoring the paper may ultimately result in your being named as a defendant in a lawsuit brought by your students, the record will show that you were simply doing what an employee must sometimes do in following questionable, if not clearly unlawful, orders from the boss.

REVEALING CONFIDENTIAL SOURCES
This is one of those cases where ignorance is bliss. Advisers should never know the identity of secret sources or be the custodian of confidential records. As long as only your student reporter and student editor know the names of the sources, they are generally under no obligation to reveal that information to you — or any other school or law enforcement official absent a properly served subpoena. If students receive a subpoena, they should immediately contact a media law attorney or the Student Press Law Center for assistance in challenging it in court. (For more information on the Reporters' Privilege, see Chapter 18). Once again, if your principal tells you that you must ask your students for the names, go ahead and do so. But also once again, your students hopefully understand that they have the right to tell you (and all other school officials) "no."

TALKING WITH THE NEWS MEDIA
Under the circumstances, it would be safest for you to refrain from making any on-the-record comment to the news media. While you have a right as a government employee to speak out on matters of public concern when such statements are not made pursuant to your duties, there is a lack of consistency among courts about where to draw the line between public and private matters. Your students, however, are not bound by such rules and are free to speak without prompting — or interference — from you. Moreover, this is one of those times where it frankly makes more sense for the student editor — rather than the adviser — to respond to questions concerning the student newspaper.

SUMMARY

Advisers have a tough task. They must teach their students responsible, incisive journalism. But doing so can endanger the adviser's job when school officials are unfriendly to a free press that covers the inadequacies of the school, the failings of administrators or controversial topics that upset the community.

Advising is not easy, but it shapes the journalists of the future. As veteran high school media adviser Wayne Brasler of the University of Chicago Laboratory School has said, "I find advisers are overworked, underpaid, underappreciated and overpressured. I am convinced, however, God put us here to teach journalism and that's why we do it, warts and all."[82]

ENDNOTES

1   *Lane v. Simon*, No. 04-4079-JAR, 2005 WL 1366521 (D. Kan. June 2, 2005), *vacated as moot*, *Lane v. Simon*, 495 F.3d 1182 (10th Cir. 2007) (holding that because public college newspaper adviser exercised no control over the content of the paper, his right to freedom of the press was not affected by his removal as adviser); *Romano v. Harrington*, 664 F. Supp. 675, 679 (E.D.N.Y. 1987) (holding that a public high school adviser of student-edited newspaper could not allege a violation of his First Amendment rights even if his dismissal was due to the content of the newspaper); *Moody v. Jefferson Parish School Bd.*, 803 F. Supp. 1158, 1163 (E.D. La. 1992) (holding that a public high school

adviser's role in supervising publication of student newspaper was "not independently protected by the Constitution" because she neither wrote nor edited the newspaper, but merely critiqued the students' work (quoting *Romano*, 664 F. Supp. at 681)).

2   *See Lane* at *4 ("Because Johnson exercises no control over the content of the Collegian, his right to freedom of the press was not at all affected by his removal as adviser").

3   Because the First Amendment prohibits censorship only by government officials, private school advisers who have had the courage to stand up to administrative censorship have faced some tough battles over the years. For example, College Media Advisers censured Mount St. Mary's College in Maryland after the CMA found that school officials had reprimanded the student newspaper's adviser, William Lawbaugh, and denied him a $3,800 raise for refusing to review the newspaper before it went to press. Lawbaugh eventually resigned. "Mount Saint Mary adviser steps down," Student Press Law Center *Report*, Winter 2002-2003, p. 15. In 1989, the dean of journalism at Marquette University, a private, Catholic university, fired adviser Judy Riedl and suspended two student newspaper staff members after the newspaper published an advertisement for an abortion rights rally. "Marquette U. newspaper staff resigns," Student Press Law Center *Report*, Spring 1993, p. 20. A more recent example of a Marquette adviser being fired can be found at "Marquette adviser's firing stands after SPJ inquiry," Student Press Law Center *Report*, Fall 2005, p. 16. *See also* "Pennsylvania college adviser resigns for fear of losing promotion after trustees complain about coverage," SPLC *News Flash*, Feb. 21, 2003, *available at* http://www.splc.org/newsflash_archives.asp?id=560&year=2003) (regarding Thiel College). In most cases, a private school adviser's options for challenging retaliatory acts have been limited to contract-based protections and public support. For more information on private school press freedom, see Chapter 7.

4   *See, e.g., Parrish v. Civil Service Comm'n of Alameda*, 425 P.2d 223 (Cal. 1967) (holding that a social worker who refused order to participate in illegal raids on homes of welfare recipients could not be fired for insubordination); *Stephens v. Dep't of State Police*, 532 P.2d 788 (Or. 1975) (finding that a state police officer could not be charged with insubordination for refusing to follow order his superior had no legal authority to give); *Chaney v. Civil Service Comm'n*, 412 N.E.2d 497 (Ill. 1980) (holding that state law enforcement agents could not be discharged for insubordination for refusing to participate in illegal "sting" operation).

5   *Harley v. Schuylkill County*, 476 F. Supp. 191, 194 (E.D. Pa. 1979) (quoting Civil Rights Act of 1871, 42 U.S.C. Sec. 1983).

6   *Lowry v. State Bd. of Industrial Insurance Appeals*, 684 P.2d 678, 682 (Wash. 1984).

7   *Lange v. Diercks*, No. 11-0191 (Iowa Ct. App. Nov. 9, 2011)(unpublished).

8   *Regents of the Univ. of Minnesota v. Nat'l Collegiate Athletic Ass'n*, 560 F.2d 352 (8th Cir. 1977), *cert. denied*, 434 U.S. 978 (1977). *But see Romano v. Harrington*, 664 F. Supp. 675, 680 (E.D.N.Y. 1987) (noting that the "amorphous approach of the NCAA case has not been widely followed").

9   "Yearbook claim fails: court throws out Indianapolis adviser's claim that removal was retribution for supporting students," Student Press Law Center *Report,* Spring 1993, p 22.

10 *See Pickett v. Potter*, No. 04-CV-73722-DT, 2005 WL 3465723, at *13 (E.D. Mich. Dec. 15, 2005) ("The principle 'obey now, grieve later' is a fundamental tenet of arbitral law.").

11 *Joyner v. Whiting*, 477 F.2d 456, 460 (4th Cir. 1973) (finding school administrators' acts such as "suspending the editors, suppressing circulation, requiring imprimatur of controversial articles, excising repugnant material, withdrawing financial support, or asserting any other form of censorial oversight based on the institution's power of the purse" to constitute unlawful censorship of a college newspaper when motivated by content); *Stanley v. Magrath*, 719 F.2d 279, 282 (8th Cir. 1983) (holding that any adverse administrative action taken against college student publication "substantially motivated by...content" violates the First Amendment); *Coppola v. Larson*, No. Civ. 06-2138(SRC), 2006 WL 2129471, *7 (D.N.J. July 26, 2006) (unpublished opinion) *available at* http://www.splc.org/pdf/occopinion.pdf ("Impermissible editorial control over student-run publications may also include actions by school administrators that have an indirect but adverse impact on a publication's ability to publish.").

12 *Moore v. Watson*, 838 F. Supp. 2d 735 (N.D. Ill. 2012) (retaliatory removal of college media adviser was, under Illinois' College Campus Press Act, a violation both of the advisers' rights and of the student editors' rights); *Lane v. Simon*, No. 04-4079-JAR, 2005 WL 1366521, *4 (D. Kan. June 2, 2005), *vacated as moot, Lane v. Simon*, 495 F.3d 1182 (10th Cir. 2007) (noting that removal of a college student newspaper adviser can be a "particularized, actual injury" to the editors of the paper); *Coppola v. Larson*, No. Civ. 06-2138(SRC), 2006 WL 2129471, *8 (D.N.J. Jul. 26, 2006).

13 *Coppola*, 2006 WL 2129471, at *8.

14 *Id.* at *10. *But compare David et al. v. Board of Educ. of Blue Springs*, No. 4:98-CV-01152-DW (W.D. Mo. Feb. 3, 1999) (denying high school student journalists' request to reinstate their newspaper adviser who had allowed publication of controversial article and ruling that only adviser, who was not a party to the case, could request such relief) and, "Judge throws out students' plea," Student Press Law Center *Report,* Spring 1999, p. 14.

15 *Coppola*, 2006 WL 2129471, at *16.

16 *Id.* at *9.

17 *Id.* at *10.

18 In 1998, an Idaho state court judge ruled that a school district's policy flatly prohibiting teachers from contacting or being interviewed by news media during the school day (including during lunch breaks and at other times when they were not teaching) and a requirement that school administrators pre-approve all press contact was unconstitutional. *Jefferson County Educ. Ass'n v. Bd. of Trustees*, No. CV-97-377 (Idaho, 7th Dist. Sept. 15, 1998); "Idaho judge ungags teachers," Student Press Law Center *Report,* Winter 1998-99, p. 26. Note, however, that teachers must still be mindful of what they actually say to the press. *See Fogarty v. Boles*, 938 F. Supp. 292, 299 (E.D. Pa. 1996), aff'd, 121 F.3d 886 (3rd Cir. 1997) ("The First Amendment does not protect a public employee's right to talk to the press; rather, it protects the public employee's right to speak on matters of public concern." (quoting *Fogarty*, 938 F. Supp. at 299)).

19 It is likely that some of the precedents in this area have since been circumscribed by the Supreme Court's holding in *Garcetti v. Ceballos*, 547 U.S. 410 (2006), discussed later in this chapter.

20 *Pickering v. Bd. of Educ.*, 391 U.S. 563, 572 (1968) (holding that "absent proof of false statements knowingly or recklessly made by him, a teacher's exercise of his right to speak on issues of public importance may not furnish the basis for his dismissal from public employment").

21 Pre-*Garcetti* cases finding public employee speech to involve a matter of public concern include: *Reidenbach v. U.S.D. No. 437*, 912 F. Supp. 1445, 1450 (D. Kan. 1996) ("the safety of school children is a matter of significant public concern.... Plaintiff's statements that overcrowding on her bus may cause safety problems are of obvious interest to members of the community, and particularly to parents of the defendant school district"); *Cirelli v. Town of Johnston Sch. Dist.*, 897 F. Supp. 663, 666 (D.R.I. 1995) (dust and heath risks were a matter of public concern even though such risks came to the plaintiff's attention because of her personal problems with them, because "plaintiff's personal interest in an issue that potentially affects all of the members of the staff and student body does not strip such issue of its public nature"); *Hall v. Marion Sch. Dist. No. 2*, 31 F.3d 183, 193 (4th Cir. 1994) (holding that a teacher's "letters to the editor, FOIA requests, and a questionnaire distributed to fellow teachers involved a public employee speaking as a citizen" and were thus "issues of public concern"); *Rich v. Montpelier Supervisory Dist.*, 709 A.2d 501 (Vt. 1998) (noting that a teacher's speech at a community forum criticizing a basketball cut policy touched upon matters of public concern); *Cioffi v. Averill Park Central Sch. Dist. Bd. of Educ.*, 444 F.3d 158 (2d Cir. 2006) (holding that a high school athletic director's criticism of the school district's handling of hazing incident involved a matter of public concern); *Seemuller v. Fairfax County Sch. Bd.*, 878 F.2d 1578 (4th Cir. 1989) (concluding that a high school P.E. teacher's satirical letter to a student newspaper commenting on allegations of sexual discrimination against female students by teachers in the P.E. department addressed a matter of public concern); *Mills v. Steger*, 64 F. App'x. 864, 873 (4th Cir. 2003) (unpublished opinion) (holding that a public radio station manager's comments to the media about a change in station programming involved matter of public concern).

22 Pre-*Garcetti* cases finding public employee speech not to involve a matter of public concern include: *Lancaster v. Indep. Sch. Dist. No. 5*, 149 F.3d 1228 (10th Cir. 1998) (holding that an internal personnel matter involving a football coach suspended from a coaching position was not a matter of public concern); *Love-Lane v. Martin*, 201 F. Supp. 2d 566 (M.D.N.C. 2002) (finding that an assistant principal's criticism of school disciplinary practices did not constitute a matter of public concern); *Ryan v. Shawnee Mission Unified Sch. Dist. No. 512*, 437 F. Supp. 2d 1233 (D. Kan. 2006) (holding that a physical therapist working for a school district was not speaking as a matter of public concern when she complained about treatment being provided to some special-needs students by the district). *See also Fogarty v. Boles*, 938 F. Supp. 292, 299 (E.D. Pa. 1996), *aff'd*, 121 F.3d 886 (3d Cir. 1997) (dismissing First Amendment claim of high school teacher non-renewed as yearbook adviser after principal accused him of contacting newspaper reporter about environmental hazards at school. Teacher denied contacting reporter and therefore, the court concluded, there was no speech to protect).

23 *Connick v. Myers*, 461 U.S. 138, 154 (1983) (holding that a district attorney's employee questionnaire touched on matters of public concern only in the most limited sense and finding no First Amendment violation in the questionnaire, while recognizing the importance of protecting a public employee's right to free expression).

24 *Stroman v. Colleton County Sch. Dist.*, 981 F.2d 152, 154 (4th Cir. 1992).

25 *Id.* at 156.

26 *Luethje v. Peavine Sch. Dist. of Adair County*, 872 F.2d 352, 355 (10th Cir. 1989).

27 *Hall v. Marion Sch. Dist. No. 2*, 31 F.3d 183, 195 (4th Cir. 1994) (noting that "when an employee's speech substantially involves matters of public concern, as is the case here, the state must make a stronger showing of disruption in order to prevail").

28 In one particularly troubling case, an Oklahoma school nurse spoke out against the district's medication policy, arguing that allowing a nurse to dispense prescription and non-prescription drugs with only parental permission violated state law. Afraid of losing both her job and her nursing license, she gathered a great deal of information in support of her position from outside agencies. She also filed a formal complaint with the district and spoke at a school board hearing discussing the proposed changes to the medication policy. After the hearing, the policy was revised to address most of the nurse's concerns. At the next meeting, however, the board voted not to renew the nurse's contract, which she alleged was in retaliation for speaking out. She filed suit. A federal court of appeals held that while the medication policy and its impact on children was a matter of public concern, the nurse's speech was not constitutionally protected because it had "disrupted the operation of the school system, undermined the administration's authority and impaired the working relationships of the health services." *Johnsen v. Indep. Sch. Dist. No. 3*, 891 F.2d 1485, 1489 (10th Cir. 1989).

29 *Garcetti v. Ceballos*, 547 U.S. 410, 421 (2006) (holding "that when public employees make statements pursuant to their official duties, the employees are not speaking as citizens for First Amendment purposes, and the Constitution does not insulate their communications from employer discipline").

30 *Id.* at 414-15.

31 The Court did note, however, that academic freedom principles might require a different outcome for employee speech cases in the educational setting. Noting the half-century of First Amendment rulings by the Court as well as the academic freedom concerns expressed by the dissenting justices, Justice Kennedy, writing for the majority, found "some argument that expression related to academic scholarship or classroom instruction implicates additional constitutional interests that are not fully accounted for by this Court's customary employee-speech jurisprudence." *Garcetti*, supra, at 425. That is not, however, the way *Garcetti* appears to be playing out, at least in the K-12 setting. When a K-12 teacher is disciplined for in-class expression, courts are less likely to find a First Amendment violation than if the teacher is disciplined for conduct unrelated to curricular decisions. *See, e.g., Johnson v. Poway Unified Sch. Dist.*, 658 F.3d 954, 966 n.12 (9th Cir 2011) (rejecting First Amendment claims brought by math teacher who was forced to remove banners from his classroom about the role of God in America's history, and specifically finding that greater First Amendment solicitude for matters implicating academic freedom applied only at the college level); *see also infra* at n. 17.

32 *Id.* at 427 (Stevens, J., dissenting).

33 David L. Hudson, Jr., "The *Garcetti* Effect," ABA Journal, January 2008, *available at* http://www. abajournal.com/magazine/the_Garcetti_effect/.

34 See *Mayer v. Monroe County Comm. Sch.*, 474 F.3d 477, 480 (7th Cir. 2007), *cert. denied*, 128 S.Ct. 160 (2007) (finding that "*Garcetti* applies directly" to the speech of an elementary school teacher who personally espoused anti-war views during a current-events lesson and rejecting her First Amendment claim); *Evans-Marshall v. Board of Educ. of Tipp City Exempted Village Sch. Dist.*, 624 F.3d 332 (6th Cir. 2010) (ruling against teacher whose contract was not renewed on the grounds of her choice of controversial materials in assigned readings and in exemplar writing samples). *Garcetti*'s withdrawal of First Amendment rights should not apply, however, when a teacher tries to inform the general public about school wrongdoing, including unlawful censorship. *See, e.g.*, *McAvey v. Orange–Ulster Boces*, No. 07 Civ. 11181, 2009 WL 2744745 (S.D.N.Y. Aug. 29, 2009) (citing but rejecting *Garcetti* and *Mayer* in ruling in favor of a school social worker who alleged she was reprimanded and transferred in retaliation for speaking to the police and news media about school's failure to respond adequately to sexual misconduct allegations against a teacher).

35 *See, e.g.*, David M. Rabban, "A Functional Analysis of 'Individual' and 'Institutional' Academic Freedom Under the First Amendment," 53 Law & Contemp. Probs. 227 (Summer 1990); Donna R. Euben, "Academic Freedom of Individual Professors and Higher Education Institutions: The Current Legal Landscape," AAUP: Resources on Academic Freedom, May 2002, *available at* http://www.aaup.org/ issues/academic-freedom/resources-academic-freedom (last visited Sept. 23, 2013).

36 *See, e.g.*, *Keyishian v. Bd. of Regents*, 385 U.S. 589, 603 (1967) (holding that "our Nation is deeply committed to safeguarding academic freedom, which is of transcendent value to us all and not merely the teachers concerned. That freedom is therefore a special concern of the First Amendment, which does not tolerate laws that cast a pall of orthodoxy over the classroom."); *Sweezy v. New Hampshire*, 354 U.S. 234, 250 (1957) (finding that government's inquiry into the subject matter of university lecturer's presentations "unquestionably was an invasion of the lecturer's liberties in the areas of academic freedom and political expression...."); *Bd. of Regents of the Univ. of Wisconsin System v. Southworth*, 529 U.S. 217, 237 (2000) (Souter, J., concurring in the judgment) ("Our understanding of academic freedom has included not merely liberty from restraints on thought, expression, and association in the academy, but also the idea that universities and schools should have the freedom to make decisions about how and what to teach.").

37 Classroom speech by university professors has been protected if the speech is "germane to the subject matter." However, a growing number of courts appear willing to second-guess professors. *Bonnell v. Lorenzo*, 241 F.3d 800, 821 (6th Cir. 2001), *cert. denied*, 534 U.S. 951(2001) (finding a professor's use of vulgar language in the classroom "not germane to the subject matter" and thus unprotected speech); *Kracunas v. Iona College*, 119 F.3d 80, 88 (2d Cir. 1997) (rejecting an academic freedom claim because the professor's "conduct could not reasonably be seen as appropriate to further a pedagogical purpose"). See also *Edwards v. California Univ. of Pennsylvania*, 156 F.3d 488, 491 (3d Cir. 1998) (concluding that "a public university professor does not have a First Amendment right to decide what will be taught in the classroom"); *Urofsky v. Gilmore*, 216 F.3d 401, 410 (4th Cir. 2000), *cert. denied*, 531 U.S. 1070 (2001) ("any right of 'academic freedom'...inheres in the University, not in individual professors...."). *But see Parate v. Isibor*, 868 F.2d 821 (6th Cir. 1989) (noting that "it has long been recognized that the purpose of academic freedom is to preserve the 'free marketplace of ideas' and protect the individual professor's classroom method from the arbitrary interference of university officials"). In a noteworthy 2011 decision, a federal appeals court cited academic freedom in refusing to dismiss the First Amendment claims of a University of North Carolina-Wilmington professor who claimed that he was denied tenure because of the conservative political views he expressed in columns that were included in his tenure application. *Adams v. Trustees of the University of N.C.-Wilmington*, 640 F.3d 550 (4th Cir. 2011).

38 *See, e.g.*, *Miles v. Denver Pub. Schools*, 944 F.2d 773 (10th Cir. 1991) ("case law does not support teacher's position that a secondary school teacher has a constitutional right to academic freedom"); *Boring v. Buncombe County Bd. of Educ.*, 136 F.3d 364, 369 (4th Cir. 1998) (en banc), *cert. denied*, 525 U.S. 813 (1998) (teacher's dispute over curriculum is "nothing more than an ordinary employment dispute, it does not constitute protected speech and has no First Amendment protection"); *Kirkland v. Northside Indep. Sch. Dist.*, 890 F.2d 794, 800 (5th Cir. 1989), *cert. denied*, 496 U.S. 926 (1990) (noting that "although... the concept of academic freedom has been recognized in our jurisprudence, the doctrine has never conferred upon teachers the control over public school curricula"); *Bradley v. Pittsburgh Bd. of Educ.*, 910 F.2d 1172, 1176 (3d Cir. 1990) (stating that "no court has found that teachers' First Amendment rights extend to choosing their own curriculum or classroom management techniques in contravention of school policy or dictates"). *See also Downs v. Los Angeles Unified Sch. Dist.*, 228 F.3d 1003, 1016-17 (9th Cir. 2000), *cert. denied*, 532 U.S. 994 (2001) (holding that a public high school teacher has no First Amendment right to post material on a school bulletin board that conflicts with the school district's message, as the bulletin boards are "vehicles for conveying a message from the school district... the school district may formulate that message without the constraint of viewpoint neutrality.").

39 *Watson v. Eagle County Sch. Dist.*, 797 P.2d 768 (Colo. Ct. App. 1990).

40 *Id.* at 770. Unfortunately, the *Watson* court's expansive reading of secondary school teacher academic freedom rights has not been widely followed, even by other Colorado courts. *See Bd. of Educ. of Jefferson County Sch. Dist. R-1 v. Wilder*, 960 P.2d 695, 701 (Colo. 1998) (noting that "the First Amendment allows extensive regulation of school-sponsored expression. Such expression includes that which 'may fairly be characterized as part of the school curriculum.'"(citing *Hazelwood Sch. Dist. v. Kuhlmeier*, 484 U.S. 260, 271 (1988)).

41 Some additional Web resources include the American Association of University Professors (AAUP), http:// www.aaup.org; the American Civil Liberties Union (ACLU), http://www.aclu.org; and The Thomas Jefferson Center for the Protection of Free Expression, http://www.tjcenter.org.

42 *See, e.g.*, *Boring v. Buncombe County Bd. of Educ.*, 136 F.3d 364 (4th Cir. 1998) (en banc), *cert. denied*, 525 U.S. 813 (1998) (upholding a school's transfer of an award-winning high school drama

coach to a junior high school because the selection of a play for the students' drama performance was an ordinary employment dispute that did not present a matter of public concern); *Lee v. York County Sch. Div.*, 418 F. Supp. 2d 816, 824-25 (E.D. Va. 2006) (finding that removal of high school teacher's religious posters from classroom wall did not violate the First Amendment because the materials were "curricular speech" and therefore not a matter of public concern); *Kirkland v. Northside Indep. Sch. Dist.*, 890 F.2d 794, 795 (5th Cir. 1989), *cert. denied*, 496 U.S. 926 (1990) (concluding that the selection of a supplemental reading list by a high school history teacher was not a matter of public concern). Many have criticized the *Boring* court's analysis. *See*, e.g., Harvard Law Review Association, *Fourth Circuit Rules that a Teacher's Selection of School Curriculum is Not Protected Speech*, 112 HARV. L. REV. 982 (Feb. 1999).

43 *Urofsky v. Gilmore*, 216 F.3d 401 (4th Cir. 2000), *cert. denied*, 531 U.S. 1070 (2001).
44 *Cockrel v. Shelby County Sch. Dist.*, 270 F.3d 1036, 1050 (6th Cir. 2002), *cert. denied*, 537 U.S. 813 (2002).
45 *Id.* at 1051-52.
46 *Id.*
47 *Mayer v. Monroe County Community School*, 474 F.3d 477, 480 (7th Cir. 2007). Notably, the district court in *Mayer* also found for the school, but did not resort to relying on *Garcetti*. The lower court reasoned that "because military intervention in Iraq is an issue of public importance, Mayer had a right to express her views on the subject, but that the right is qualified in the workplace by the requirement that expression not disrupt an employer's business unduly." *Mayer*, 474 F.3d at 478.
48 *See*, e.g., *Silano v. Sag Harbor Union Free Sch. Dist. Bd. of Educ.*, 42 F.3d 719 (2d Cir. 1994), *cert. denied*, 515 U.S. 1160 (1995); *Bd. of Educ. of Jefferson County Sch. Dist. R-1 v. Wilder*, 960 P.2d 695 (Colo. 1998); *Webster v. New Lenox Sch. Dist.*, 917 F.2d 1004 (7th Cir. 1990) (holding that school officials committed no First Amendment violation when they ordered a junior high school social studies teacher not to teach a subject matter from a "Christian viewpoint," because – under *Hazelwood* – school officials had a "legitimate pedagogical concern" where the possibility of an Establishment Clause violation existed). *See also Lacks v. Ferguson Reorganized Sch. Dist. R-2*, 147 F.3d 718 (8th Cir. 1998), reh'g denied, 154 F.3d 904 (8th Cir.1998), *cert. denied*, 526 U.S. 1012 (1999) (holding that a school board's termination of a teacher who permitted students to use profanity in plays and poetry did not violate the teacher's right to free speech under the First Amendment, as the teacher had notice that the use of profanity in creative writing was prohibited and the school district had a legitimate academic interest in prohibiting profanity).
49 *Miles v. Denver Pub. Schools*, 944 F.2d 773 (10th Cir. 1991).
50 *Id.* at 778-79.
51 *Vanderhurst v. Colorado Mountain College Dist.*, 208 F.3d 908, 915 (10th Cir. 2000). See also *Bishop v. Aronov*, 926 F.2d 1066, 1074 (11th Cir. 1991) (using what the court described as an "amorphous" balancing test that adopts "as its polestar *Hazelwood*'s concern for the 'basic educational mission' of the school" in upholding university's directive to professor that he refrain from interjecting religious belief or preferences in classroom). The Ninth Circuit has also indicated that it might be open to a *Hazelwood*-based standard for curricular speech. *Brown v. Li*, 308 F.3d 939, 951-52 (9th Cir. 2002) ("In view of a university's strong interest in setting the content of its curriculum and teaching that content, *Hazelwood* provides a workable standard for evaluating a university student's First Amendment claim stemming from curricular speech." (emphasis added)). The *Brown* dissent noted that only one judge on the panel applied the *Hazelwood* standard to college students and that, therefore, no binding precedent should be created by the case. *Brown*, 308 F.3d at 960 (Reinhardt, J., dissenting).
52 *See*, e.g., *Cary v. Bd. of Educ.*, 598 F.2d 535 (10th Cir. 1979) (regarding the constitutional rights of high school teachers under a collective bargaining agreement); *Morris v. Clifford*, 903 F.2d 574 (8th Cir. 1990) (regarding a terminated professor's rights to proceed with a claim based on regulations found in the faculty handbook); *Zuelsdorf v. Univ. of Alaska, Fairbanks*, 794 P.2d 932 (Alaska 1990) (regarding a policy manual found to be incorporated into an employment contract between the university and its professors). *See generally* American Association of University Professors (AAUP), Faculty Handbooks as Enforceable Contracts: A State Guide (5th ed. 2005). The 1940 Statement of Principles on Academic Freedom and Tenure (*available at* http://www.aaup.org/AAUP/pubsres/policydocs/contents/default.htm) was developed by the American Association of University Professors (AAUP) and the Association of American Colleges and Universities and is the fundamental statement on academic freedom for college and university faculty. According to the AAUP, the principles have been incorporated into hundreds of college and university handbooks. For a discussion of contractually guaranteed academic freedom in the high school context see Department of Education and Hawaii State Teachers Association, 66 LA 1221 (Hi. 1976) (Tsukiyama, Arb.). In the case, an arbitrator found that a high school policy prohibiting the showing of "R"-rated movies conflicted with the basic education values promoted by an academic freedom clause in the teachers' contract and ordered that the movie policy be rescinded. The relevant clause of the collective bargaining agreement provided: "The parties seek to educate young people in the democratic tradition, to inspire meaningful awareness and respect for the Constitution and the Bill of Rights, to instill appreciation of the value of individual personality and to foster a recognition of individual freedom and social responsibility. It is recognized that these democratic values can best be transmitted in an atmosphere which is conducive to inquiry and learning and in which academic freedom for teacher and student is encouraged. Academic freedom shall be guaranteed to teachers and they shall be encouraged to study, investigate, present and interpret objectively facts and ideas concerning man, society, the physical and biological world, and other branches of learning subject to established courses of study." Another example of a high school-based academic freedom provision is found in the Anchorage School District's union agreement, the latest version of which states: "Members enjoy academic freedom in the District. Members are free to present instructional materials that are pertinent to the subject and level taught, within the outlines of the appropriate course content, the planned instructional program, and in accordance with School Board policy. Members shall also be entitled to freedom of discussion within the classroom on all matters relevant to the subject matter under study within their areas of professional competence. Facts concerning controversial issues shall

be presented in a scholarly and objective manner and shall be pedagogically justifiable and discussion shall be maintained within the outlines of the teacher's course content. Members shall not be censored or restrained in the performance of their duties exclusively on the grounds that the material discussed and/ or opinions expressed are controversial." "Agreement between the Anchorage Education Association and the Anchorage School District" (7/1/2010 - 6/30/2013), Sec. 402 Academic Freedom, at 24, *available at* http://www.nctq.org/docs/Anchorage.pdf (last visited Sept. 21, 2013). Ideally, an academic freedom provision would protect not only teaching materials, but teaching methods as well.

53 *Karetnikova v. Trustees of Emerson College*, 725 F. Supp. 73 (D. Mass. 1989) (holding that the cancellation of a private university professor's contract because of her political expression violated state law).

54 *See, e.g., Morris v. Clifford*, 903 F.2d 574 (8th Cir. 1990) (finding that provisions in a faculty handbook created a right to substantive due process); *Mills v. Steger*, 64 Fed. App'x 864 (4th Cir. 2003) (noting that a radio station manager who was an employee of a public university was entitled to the protections of the Faculty Handbook). *See also* "Adviser reinstated following contract violation," Student Press Law Center *Report,* Winter 1988-89, p. 9.

55 "Agreement between the Anchorage Education Association and the Anchorage School District" (7/1/2010-6/30/2013), Sec. 150(J) Added Duty Activities, p. 11, *available at* http://www.nctq.org/docs/Anchorage.pdf (last visited Sept. 21, 2013).

56 *See, e.g., Mills v. Steger*, 64 Fed. App'x 864 (4th Cir. 2003) (holding that a public radio station manager who was dismissed from a job could not claim a due process violation where his twenty-four years of employment were based on a series of annually renewable contracts, and further holding that the station manager did not have a property interest in continued employment past the end date of his current contract).

57 *Bertot v. Sch. Dist. No. 1, Albany County*, Wyoming, 522 F.2d 1171 (10th Cir. 1975). *See also* "Wash. adviser fired for helping underground paper regains job," SPLC *News Flash*, April 14, 2008, *available at* http://www/ splc.org/newsflash.asp?id=1741 (reporting on settlement in appeal of Washington teacher's dismissal).

58 *See Endress v. Brookdale Community College*, 364 A.2d 1080 (N.J. Sup. Ct. App. Div. 1976).

59 *Calvin v. Rupp*, 471 F.2d 1346 (8th Cir. 1973).

60 *See Nethersole v. Bulger*, 287 F.3d 15 (1st Cir. 2002) (finding that a college vice president's complaints about the potential effects of a new admissions policy on minority recruitment were a motivating factor for her forced transfer to another job).

61 *Mount Healthy City Sch. Dist. v. Doyle*, 429 U.S. 274 (1977).

62 *Nicholson v. Bd. of Educ. Torrance Unified Sch. Dist.*, 682 F.2d 858 (9th Cir. 1982).

63 *Id.* at 864.

64 "Adviser Bosley settles case with Ocean County College," SPLC *News Flash*, July 23, 2007, *available at* http://www.splc.org/newsflash.asp?id=1583&year=2007; "Adviser gets $74,000, attorney's fees in settlement with school district," SPLC *News Flash*, Oct. 14, 2005, *available at* http://www.splc.org/newsflash_archives. asp?id=1100&year=2005; "Fla. district pays $20,000 to settle adviser's lawsuit," Student Press Law Center *Report,* Fall 2004, p. 26; "Mo. college newspaper adviser settles suit over firing," SPLC *News Flash*, Aug. 7, 2002, *available at* http://www.splc.org/newsflash.asp?id=464&year=2002; "Former paper adviser receives cash, award," Student Press Law Center *Report,* Spring 1999, p. 14; "Adviser receives $20,000 settlement," Student Press Law Center *Report,* Spring 1999, p. 15; "Florida school district settles with ousted adviser," SPLC *News Flash*, July 2, 1998, *available at* http://www.splc.org/newsflash.asp?id=77&year=1998.

65 "ECU, former student media adviser reach financial settlement," SPLC *News Flash*, April 23, 2012, *available at* http://www.splc.org/news/newsflash.asp?id=2370.

66 "Former adviser's lawsuit will cost Indiana district $40,000, unspecified legal costs," SPLC Blog, May 22, 2012, *available at* http://www.splc.org/wordpress/?p=3671.

67 "Calif. high school settles censorship lawsuit," SPLC *News Flash*, Dec. 23, 2009, *available at* http:// www.splc.org/news/newsflash.asp?id=2007.

68 "Adviser settles with Ga. university," Student Press Law Center *Report,* Spring 2002, p. 12.

69 "N.M. school district pays $205,000 in settlement with ex-poetry club adviser," SPLC *News Flash*, August 3, 2004, *available at* http://www.splc.org/newsflash_archives.asp?id=860&year=2004.

70 "Adviser gets $130,000 in settlement with college," SPLC *News Flash*, Aug. 10, 2006, *available at* http:// www.splc.org/newsflash_archives.asp?id=1309&year=2006.

71 *Olson v. State Bd. for Community Colleges and Occupational Educ.*, 687 P.2d 429 (Colo. 1984).

72 *Romano v. Harrington*, 664 F. Supp. 675 (E.D.N.Y. 1987).

73 *Id.* at 681

74 *Schmitt v. Prater*, No. 1:99-CV-1659-WBH (N.D. Ga. Aug. 24, 2001) (unpublished).

75 *Worth v. Campbell County Sch. Dist. No. 1*, No. C84-0362-B (D. Wyo. Apr. 26, 1985) (unpublished) (order denying motions for summary judgment).

76 *Nicholson v. Bd. of Educ. Torrance Unified Sch. Dist.*, 682 F.2d 858 (9th Cir. 1982).

77 *Moody v. Jefferson Parish School Bd.*, 803 F. Supp. 1158 (E.D. La. 1992), *aff'd,* 2 F.3d 604 (5th Cir. 1993). The court ruled against Moody on all other claims as well. *See also* "Yearbook claim fails: court throws out Indianapolis adviser's claim that removal was retribution for supporting students," Student Press Law Center *Report,* Spring 1993, p. 22.

78 *Moore v. Watson*, 838 F. Supp. 2d 735 (N.D. Ill. 2012).

79 110 ILCS 13 (2007).

80 *Cullen v. Gibson*, 124 F.3d 197 (6th Cir. 1997) (unpublished opinion), *cert. denied*, 522 U.S. 1117(1998).

81 For more information, see College Media Association, www.collegemedia.org.

82 Dow Jones, Adviser Update, Jan. 2001, at 6A-7A.

CHAPTER 12

Defamation

FROM THE SPLC CASE FILES

The Student Times publishes a routine feature story about how students balance the competing demands of work and college. The reporter interviews a number of students, all identified by name, about their fairly normal experiences in fairly typical student jobs. One is a busboy at a local restaurant, another a retail clerk at a pharmacy, another works at a fast-food joint. However, a fourth student, "Jennifer," the story notes, has a job that is a bit different.

"Some students think there are no interesting jobs that will keep them working at the same place for an extended amount of time. Junior Jennifer Jones found an appealing job that most only dream about. She sings at Ed's Kountry Kastle, a local bar. 'It's not hard work and I like it. I also get free beer,' Jennifer says."

A few days later, the *Student Times* editor gets a phone call from the angry owner of Ed's Kountry Kastle. He says that Jennifer does sing at his club. But, he says, she was certainly never served alcohol. He also tells you that Jennifer is just 19 years old. He reminds you that serving a minor is against the law and would endanger his liquor and business license. He tells the editor he's calling his lawyer.

The nursery rhyme tells us that while sticks and stones can break your bones, words will never hurt you. Obviously, Mother Goose was not a libel lawyer. The law sees things differently. When a person has been hurt by the inaccurate words of a speaker or writer, the law allows the injured party to seek redress.

Defamation law, which encompasses injury both by written words (libel) and spoken words (slander), has been around for centuries. In ninth century England a person convicted of defamation had his tongue cut out.[1] By the 17th century, judges had substituted ears, genitals and entrails for the tongue.[2] Fortunately, in 21st century America, a defamer retains all body parts. But, as many a person who has been through the ordeal of a libel lawsuit might tell you, simply lopping off an ear might actually be less painful.

Haphazardly picking up a pen or banging away on a keyboard can be costly. Multi-million dollar jury awards against commercial news media have become a common occurrence.[3] Threats of imprisonment for defamation — though exceedingly rare and generally unsuccessful — have also occurred.[4] In fact, one of the longest-running cases involving criminal libel involved a Colorado college student, whose home was searched and personal computer seized after he distributed a satirical newsletter making fun of one of his professors at the University of Northern Colorado.[5] (Fortunately, the case ended not only with no criminal prosecution, but with the overzealous prosecutor who authorized the raid paying a substantial financial settlement.[6])

Even when the media win the case, the news is still bad. For almost as "chilling" as the multi-million dollar court awards is the skyrocketing cost of defending against a lawsuit. This is especially true for a student publication whose entire legal defense fund (if one even exists) could be wiped out with a single telephone call to a $300-an-hour media-law attorney.[7] Although exact figures are not available, the cost of hiring an attorney to defend a publication against even a "small" libel lawsuit that goes to trial easily can reach into the tens of thousands of dollars. And the cost of an appeal, which can drag on for years, routinely pushes defense costs into the six-figure range. Complex or high-profile libel cases have cost media defendants millions.[8] With the cost of "winning" an average libel case enough to bankrupt even the largest student publication, the message is clear: libel is to be avoided. But to do so, it must first be understood.

Did You Know? The average jury award in a libel lawsuit between 1980-2007 was approximately $2.8 million. Source: Media Law Resource Center (2008)

To date, the Student Press Law Center is aware of no published court decisions reporting a successful libel claim against a high school student publication, and only a handful on the college level.

Fortunately for student journalists, the risk of being sued for libel is, relatively speaking, small. To date, the Student Press Law Center is aware of *no* published court decisions reporting a successful libel claim against a high school student publication, and only a handful on the college level. Despite what school administrators (and school attorneys) may claim in trying to censor controversial content, student publications are not magnets for libel claims (and in fact, schools are more likely to be successfully sued for censoring content than for letting it run).

Still, claims occasionally arise, at times from unexpected places. In 2011, NBA basketball legend Scottie Pippen sued a variety of print, broadcast and online publications —including student media at Arizona State University and the University of Tampa — for suggesting that he was "bankrupt," when in fact he had experienced large investing losses but had never declared bankruptcy.[9] It is the responsible student journalist's duty to be aware of the dangers of defamatory content, and to take common-sense precautions to head off libel claims. And by understanding the law of defamation, the well-informed student journalist can be ready with an educated response when an administrator bent on censoring a controversial story starts, inaccurately, labeling the material "libelous."

As discussed later, even on the rare occasion when student media are faced with a threat of a defamation lawsuit, threats can often by resolved using a combination of common sense and courtesy. At other times, an experienced media-law attorney may be needed.

The purpose of this chapter is to describe in as clear and "un-legalese" terms as possible what libel is, how the law addresses it, and, most importantly, how to avoid getting into potentially libelous situations in the first place. While the particulars of libel law can vary from state to state, this chapter provides student journalists with enough information to avoid the most common libel problems. In the end, however, even journalists who have a thorough understanding of libel law and take every reasonable precaution to avoid trouble cannot prevent a disgruntled subject from filing a lawsuit. The chapter ends, therefore, with some common-sense suggestions to avoid libel and some defense tactics to use if a lawsuit is threatened.

WHAT IS LIBEL?

Simply stated, libel is any published communication — words, photos, pictures, symbols — that falsely harms a person's reputation. If a statement is true, it legally cannot be the basis of a successful libel claim.

Any communication that is memorialized (on paper, on a website, in a text message) can be libelous. There are no restrictions in form or context. Cartoons, editorials, headlines, e-mails, messages in Internet chat rooms, photos, captions, website postings, interview transcripts, graphics, display advertisements, classifieds and letters to the editor can all contain libelous statements. As musician Courtney Love found out when she was sued for calling a rival a "thief" with "a history of dealing cocaine" in a series of rants on Twitter, even casual observations on social media can give rise to a claim for libel.[10] Also, defamatory statements made in a television or radio broadcast usually qualify as libel because, like writings, they have broader and longer exposure than the fleeting spoken word that typifies slander.[11]

One pervasive misconception among journalists is that if they put quotation marks around a statement made by someone else or simply reprint a letter to the editor and identify the source, they will not be responsible for those comments. But according to the law, the republication of a libel is still a libel. In repeating the libel in their publication or on their broadcast, the media are said to have "adopted" the libel as their own. A student newspaper that reprints a libelous classified ad or letter to the editor simply gives the person libeled two targets to sue — the original author and the

---

Libel is any published communication — words, photos, pictures, symbols — that falsely harms a person's reputation.

Libel is written defamation. Slander refers to spoken defamation. Defamatory statements made in a television or radio broadcast usually qualify as libel, because, like writings, they have broader and longer exposure than mere spoken words.

If a particular statement is not defamatory when published in traditional print media, it does not become defamatory simply because it is published online.

publication. A letter to the editor or a quoted remark in a story containing a potentially libelous "fact" statement must — just like everything else in a publication — be verified and should not be published unless it is found to be true.

LIBEL IN THE INTERNET AGE

The exact birthday of the Internet is hard to pinpoint.[12] The completion date of the first known libel trial in America based on Internet content, however, is much easier to trace: June 9, 1999.[13] Online media — websites, e-mail, chat rooms, listservs, instant messaging, blogs — continue to change the way the world communicates. Unfortunately, but inescapably, they have also changed the way the world gets in legal trouble for communication gone awry. Online content can be defamatory. It can result in lawsuits. And, just like carelessly published print-based content, it can result in significant liability. But, contrary to the claims raised by some school officials seeking to control or even prohibit online student media because of their concerns over liability, online speech — simply because it is online — poses no more of a legal threat, and sometimes much less, than its print-based counterpart.

There are a couple of important points to keep in mind. First, if a particular statement is not defamatory when published in traditional print-based media, it does not become defamatory simply because it is published online. A statement is or is not defamatory regardless of how widely it can be viewed. Second, federal law provides significant protection to Internet Service Providers — and probably website operators — who do not create content, but only provide the means to post it online.[14]

Still, while courts have attempted — mostly successfully — to apply traditional libel law to the new, non-traditional online medium, the transition has not been without some wrinkles. Jurisdictional issues, for example, continue to cause some headaches for judges. When something is posted to a website, it is posted to a potential worldwide audience. Can a newspaper in Connecticut, for example, be sued in a Virginia court — and required to bear the expense of defending itself hundreds of miles from home — simply because the newspaper's online news stories can be viewed by individuals sitting at their computers in Roanoke?[15] If so, what about those who view the site in Australia?[16]

Another interesting question concerns the application of statutes of limitation to online speech. Typically, a statute of limitations requires that a person bring a libel lawsuit within one or two years after publication of an allegedly defamatory statement or lose the opportunity to complain. However, some have claimed that online material, largely because of the Internet's ability to store and a user's ability to search vast quantities of data, tends to have a longer shelf life than printbased publications, which frequently are discarded soon after they are read. Can a newspaper, therefore, be sued for a story that it first posted on the Internet almost three years ago just because the story can be retrieved today by readers searching the newspaper's online archives?[17]

Courts are also struggling with the question of how to deal with comments posted on websites by readers, often under a false name or no name at all. Do persons or organizations that feel they have been libeled by an anonymous author of online material have the right to demand that an Internet service provider or website operator reveal the author's true identity or contact information?[18] The right to speak anonymously, or to use a pseudonym (in 21st century terms, a screen name), is a firmly established principle as old as the First Amendment itself. Benjamin Franklin, Alexander Hamilton and James Madison all published political commentary in reliance on the safety of a false identity. At the same time, because the operator of the website has immunity from liability for defamatory material authored by outsiders, it sometimes may feel unjust to leave a defamed person with no remedy -- a publisher who is immune, and an author who cannot be found.

When asked to force the operator of a website to disclose information about the author of an anonymous online comment, many judges resolve the question by applying the "*Dendrite* factors" that originated with an influential ruling from a New Jersey appeals court.[19] The *Dendrite* test puts the burden on the person seeking to unmask an anonymous commenter to show that he has

You do not avoid libel problems simply "because someone else said it." Reprinting or re-broadcasting a libelous statement made by someone else (such as a quote or letter to the editor) can subject the media to a libel lawsuit.

P-I-H-F-F
• Publication
• Identification
• Harm
• Falsity
• Fault

A statement is "published" if it is communicated to someone other than the person it is about.

A statement "identifies" a person if it is shown that it is "of and concerning" that person.

used the Internet to notify the commenter of the legal proceeding, that the underlying defamation claim is well-supported, and that the need for the commenter's identity outweighs the speaker's First Amendment right to remain unnamed. As with many aspects of online publishing, the law governing the rights of anonymous website commenters is still evolving as courts come to grips with the way online publishing works.

FROM THE SPLC CASE FILES

A columnist at a high school student newspaper, writing an opinion piece about a well-known local landlord, alleges that the businessman has faced accusations of "racist renting policies." The businessman sues for defamation. The defense attorney presents the court with 11 local newspaper articles describing allegations of abusive practices by the landlord's hired property manager, who has been convicted of racial hate crimes. A state appeals court affirms the dismissal of the case, finding that even if small details in the column were imprecise, the "sting" of the story — that accusations of racial bias had been made — was substantially true.[20]

THE PIHFF CHECKLIST

Packed within the simple definition of libel are five elements that a plaintiff (the person who is suing) must establish to prove he has been defamed by the defendant (the person or publication being sued): Publication, Identification, Harm to reputation, Falsity (i.e., the statement is untrue) and Fault. Remember "PIHFF." If a plaintiff cannot prove each of these five elements, his claim will fail:

I. P - PUBLICATION. The plaintiff must show that the statement was "published," that is, communicated to someone other than the person it was about. This does not mean that the statement has to be in a newspaper and circulated; the defamatory statement's presence on a computer screen in the newsroom where it is read by other students or in a draft provided to an editor could constitute publication.

II. I - IDENTIFICATION. The person claiming that he was libeled must show that he was identified by the statement. If the publication does not specifically refer to the individual by name, it must be shown that a sufficient number of people who read the story reasonably believed the plaintiff was the one identified.[21] For example, a story that reports only that the school's "starting quarterback" was seen using illegal drugs identifies the subject just as surely as if he was named.

Disguising a Subject's Identity

While hiding or disguising the identity of the subject of a highly sensitive and unverifiable story is a valid method of avoiding a libel lawsuit, it must be done carefully. Two problems regularly arise. First, a common practice is to disguise a subject by giving him a fake name and changing any identifying characteristics. Where this is done, care must be exercised to ensure that: (1) the subject's identity has been disguised enough so that no one can reasonably make an accurate identification and (2) the "disguised" subject does not resemble some third party to whom you might never have intended to refer.[22]

When disguising a person's identity you must not only obscure the person's name but also avoid facts that might point an identifying finger. Revealing enough distinctive facts about the unnamed figure ("a 6-foot-5 sophomore from Honduras whose father is a judge") or even one uniquely identifying fact ("the nine star-shaped piercings in her lower lip") is as good as printing the person's name, making the disguise ineffective to preclude a libel claim.

But be careful. While you must fictionalize enough of the subject to protect his identity, you can go too far. For example, in a story on the cause of suicide among students, it would be factually incorrect to say that a student attempted suicide because he was diagnosed with schizophrenia when he was really suffering from depression. It may help you disguise your subject, but you will be giving your readers false information. Attention should be paid to the style and content of the story so that its basic message is not distorted in an effort to avoid identification.

When altering an identity, keep in mind that few names are unique. Changing the name of your subject to "Juanita Jones from Peoria" is great — until the three Juanita Joneses in Peoria call you to complain that your story has libeled them.[23]

Still, there are a few things you can and should do to avoid libeling unknown third persons. Most importantly, a story should clearly state when names and other characteristics have been altered. A disclaimer that "The names in this story have been changed," puts the reader on notice and should significantly reduce the chances that you will be hauled into court by someone you have never heard of.[24] Another good practice is to quickly scan the campus and local telephone directory of the story's location. You can also conduct an Internet search to see if anyone else bears the fictionalized name. Although this is certainly not foolproof, it will help your case to show that you at least made the effort.

Finally, disguising a person's identity in a news story should be the exception, not the rule. Altering facts or withholding information from readers raises important ethical issues. In fact, some journalists flatly refuse to disguise or withhold a subject's identity, feeling that any intentional deception compromises their credibility with readers.

Group Libel
Yet another way to libel someone without mentioning his name is to make defamatory statements about an entire group to which he belongs. Saying that a private college's seven-member admissions committee is "knee deep in bribes" could entitle any of the committee members who had not accepted bribes to successfully sue for libel. On the other hand, reporting that "one Central High School teacher" was seen using illegal drugs would not libel any one of the 100 teachers at the school. The key question is whether a statement can reasonably be interpreted to refer to a specific individual in the group because only individuals, not groups of people, can sue for damage to personal reputation. The most important factor when answering that question is usually group size. Most state courts have yet to draw a clear line distinguishing small groups, whose members can sue for libel, and large groups, whose members cannot, though it is often said that a statement about a group with more than 25 members cannot defame individual members of that group.[25]

Corporations and other "business entities," including private schools and foundations, can be defamed.

For example, in one case, 27 Kentucky school teachers sued a local newspaper after it reported that during a meeting with school officials a group of parents had sought an investigation of "teachers having affairs with students." When the story was published, the school employed between 29 and 35 teachers. The court dismissed the teachers' claim, referring in part to the 25-person "rule," and found that the news account could not "reasonably be said to have impugned the integrity of every teacher at [the school]."[26]

The "25-person rule," however, should be used only as a general guide. Where stories have associated each member of a group with a defamatory statement or where a particular member plays an especially prominent role in the group, courts have permitted individual members to sue even when the group referred to was larger than 25.[27]

As a federal magistrate in the Kentucky case above noted: "Although a minority analysis, the 'intensity of suspicion' test is gaining favor in some jurisdictions. These jurisdictions have abandoned the numerical approach in favor of a three-part factual inquiry into the definiteness and composition of the group, the prominence of the group, and the prominence of each individual plaintiff within the group."[28]

When writing your story, be precise in your descriptions. If only two persons of the 45-member student government are being accused of mismanaging student activity fees, do not characterize the two people as "members of the student government..." or even "a number of student government members." Instead, accurately say that the investigation involves "two members of the student government."

Some courts may recognize an exception to the group libel rule where a statement is made about a group consisting solely of government employees, which would presumably include public school officials. The Virginia Supreme Court rejected a police officer's defamation claim for comments by the city's mayor that the "Elkton police" were engaged in various unlawful acts. The comments appeared in several local newspapers. In dismissing the lawsuit, the court said that the First Amendment does not permit government employees to use the group libel theory as their only basis for bringing a defamation claim.[29]

Corporate or Entity Libel

Corporations and other "business entities" — including, for example, private schools,[30] religious organizations, partnerships, associations, foundations and charities — can be defamed. Like individuals, their reputations affect their ability to conduct their affairs in a community. And like individuals, falsely identifying a particular entity as being unethical, financially unstable, dishonest or the like can defame its reputation, subjecting the author to potential liability.

III. H - HARM. The plaintiff must prove that the statement harmed his reputation in the eyes of members of the community. Any statement that says something negative about a person, group or business is potentially libelous. Take a close look. Statements that shame, disgrace or ridicule an individual's reputation or that injure a person's livelihood are sufficiently harmful to meet this test. The term "community" can mean a small segment of society. For example, falsely reporting that the school's valedictorian used a calculator on an exam could be libelous even though his reputation was damaged only among a relatively small group of students and teachers who knew that use of a calculator on that particular exam was considered cheating.

> A statement is "harmful" if it shames, disgraces or injures a person's reputation.

Finally, depending on the type of libel, a person may be required to prove he actually lost money because of the libel (as opposed to claiming that he should be compensated solely for his embarrassment or pain and suffering).

Once you have spotted a "red flag," consider whether the information is necessary. It makes no sense to include potentially harmful material if the story can be told as well without it. Irrelevant background or "parenthetical" details can often be edited without significantly changing a story's core message.

Of course, there are many stories that simply cannot be told without including information that will harm an individual's reputation. For example, if a school administrator takes a personal vacation to Hawaii using school funds, a news story on the subject would certainly harm her professional reputation. But that story is news, and reporting information about the misuse of public funds is the duty of a journalist. If the red flag statement goes to the heart of your story or if you believe the story's impact would be significantly diminished without it, leave it in — but give it the extra attention it demands, as discussed below.

IV. F - FALSITY. If a person cannot prove that a harmful statement made about him by the news media is false, then the person generally cannot win a libel lawsuit.[31] Truth is an absolute defense to a charge of libel. If a statement is true — even if it ruins a person's reputation for the rest of his life — the person making the statement cannot be held liable. It goes without saying, however, that saying or believing something is true and proving it in court are two different things. In many situations, only the person who claims she has been libeled will have access to the information necessary to establish a statement's truth.

Fortunately for media defendants, the Supreme Court has ruled that the burden of proving a statement false will usually rest with the person who claims she has been libeled.[32] In other words, before a media defendant has to present evidence to a jury that a statement is true, a plaintiff must first present enough proof to persuade a jury that the statement is false. This procedural distinction can be significant at trial and makes winning a libel suit substantially more difficult for some libel plaintiffs.

Moreover, a statement need only be "substantially true." It is not necessary to show that every reported fact in publication or broadcast is 100 percent accurate.[33] For example, if a newspaper were to report that Fred Smith was a habitual criminal, it might be libelous if Smith could prove that he had been convicted only once. However, the charge that Fred Smith was convicted of embezzling $1.3 million would not be libelous if the evidence showed that the amount involved in the embezzlement was really only $1.1 million. The statement published would not result in significantly greater injury to reputation than would the correct information if it had been published. As courts have frequently noted: a statement is substantially true if the substance, the "gist" or the "sting" of the statement is true.[34]

In the end, however, knowing the truth and having absolute confidence in its accuracy is not always possible. In such cases, you should always ask yourself the following question: Do you believe the statement is true? If not, leave the information out. You are not ready to publish it. If you do believe the information is accurate, your next step is to determine whether you can adequately support or defend the statement if you are sued.

V. F - FAULT. The plaintiff must show that the defendant was at fault in publishing the statement. There can be no liability without fault.[35] In other words, before you can be required to pay damages for a defamatory statement, the person suing you must prove that you did something you should not have done (for example, you published the statement even though you personally believed the information untrue) or that you failed to do something you should have done (for example, you did not check police records to confirm that a person had actually been arrested, you did not provide the person with an opportunity to respond or you used unreliable sources). If, on the other hand, you did everything a reasonable reporter should do to verify the information in your story before publishing it, you are not "at fault" and cannot be forced to compensate the plaintiff for his injuries. Note, however, that claiming you either "didn't see" or "didn't mean" a libelous statement you published is no easy out. Lack of knowledge or intent may provide you with a defense to a libel claim, but it does not magically "cleanse" an otherwise defamatory statement.

> To prove "fault," the person suing must prove that the publication did something it should not have or failed to do something it should have done.

People suing for libel who are public officials (such as government office holders and top-ranking public school administrators) or public figures (such as rock stars and professional athletes) must prove a higher level of fault than an ordinary person. But this really has nothing to do with the definition of defamation. Famous persons can be defamed as easily as private persons.

> People suing for libel who are either public officials or public figures must prove a higher level of fault than an ordinary person.

Often, callers to the Student Press Law Center get bogged down in trying to determine whether, for example, their campus police chief is a "public figure" because they vaguely remember something from their journalism class about public figures being treated differently. The fact is, whether a campus police chief is a public or private figure pertains only to the standard by which a news organization might avoid financial liability if the statements they publish about the police chief turn out to be false. If a court determines that the police chief is a public figure, the statement can still be defamatory, but the publication may be legally excused from liability because society has recognized the importance of protecting the media's ability to engage in aggressive reporting about public figures without being in constant fear of a lawsuit. Note, however, that the rules for avoiding liability come into play only after a lawsuit begins. The journalist's objective — and the reason for the PIHFF checklist — is to avoid inadvertent or unnecessary defamation in the first place and thereby avoid a lawsuit completely.

The Public Official/Public Figure Rule

New York Times Company v. Sullivan[36] is often referred to by the press and media-law attorneys as "The Great Case." Decided by the United States Supreme Court in 1964, the case created a new constitutional defense to libel suits. Before 1964, public officials and public figures in most states could win a libel suit whenever the publisher failed to prove that a statement was true. Because of the relative ease of winning and the high cost of defending such cases, intimidation by libel suit was a common strategy employed, for example, by southern officials intent on repressing the civil-rights movement. Indeed, by the time the Supreme Court decided *New York Times v. Sullivan*, southern officials had brought nearly $300 million in libel actions against the press.[37] Of that figure, $3 million was against *The New York Times* alone, a sum that threatened the newspaper's existence.[38]

New York Times Company v. Sullivan (1964) is often referred to as "The Great Case."

In the *New York Times* case, the Supreme Court ruled that states had to require libel plaintiffs who were public officials to prove "actual malice." The term "malice" does not necessarily mean ill will or mean-spiritedness; rather, it means that the person who claims he was libeled must prove that the challenged statement was published by people who either knew it was false or who were reckless in verifying its accuracy.

Three years later, the Supreme Court extended the actual malice standard to cover many cases involving public figures (even if they are not public officials).[39]

Application of the actual malice standard creates a difficult hurdle for public official and public figure libel plaintiffs to overcome. It means that even if a story eventually is proven false, the publication cannot be held responsible for the libel if, in the court's view, the author did not know that what she wrote was false when it was first published and she made at least a modest attempt to verify the facts prior to publication.

The "actual malice" standard means that the person who claims he was libeled must prove that the challenged statement was published by people who knew it was false or were reckless in verifying it.

As a practical matter, many libel lawsuits are won or lost on the question of whether the plaintiff qualifies as a public official or public figure or is a purely "private" individual. Unfortunately, the determination of a person's status is not always easy. In most states private persons who file a libel suit need only show that the person who communicated the defamatory statement was "negligent" (that is, she did not use a reasonable amount of care in reporting or verifying the information), and not that she either knew a story was false or entertained serious doubts about its accuracy.[40] As a result, there is a huge incentive on the part of libel plaintiffs to avoid having the actual malice standard applied to their cases. Plaintiffs' lawyers will go out of their way to argue that their client is simply a private citizen, not worthy of the title "public official" or "public figure." And sometimes — much to the surprise of media defendants who thought they were on safe ground — these arguments are successful.

Consequently, journalists should never try to predict whether an individual is a public official or public figure for libel purposes. Ultimately, only the courts can make this determination and their decisions can vary significantly depending on the facts and the jurisdiction involved. Therefore, while the public person defense is of enormous value to the media, it should never be relied on as an excuse for sloppy reporting. Because a person's status is significant only after a lawsuit is filed, predicting the status of a particular individual is best left to media lawyers and judges. For your part as a journalist, it is best to assume that every one of your subjects is a private person and that you will be held to lowest fault standard if you publish inaccurate information.

Who is a Public Official?

There is no easy method for determining who qualifies as a public official. The courts have provided some guidance, but no black and white line to distinguish a low-level government bureaucrat who is not a public official from a mid-level government bureaucrat who might be. The Supreme Court has said that a public official is one who, at the very least, has or appears to the public to have a substantial responsibility for or control over the conduct of governmental affairs.[41] Note that the Court has said that a person is not a public official just because he is paid with government funds.[42] A public official also holds a position that has "such apparent importance that the public has an independent interest in the qualifications and performance of the person who holds it, beyond the general public interest in the qualifications and performances of all government employees."[43] Finally, public officials hold positions that would "invite public scrutiny and discussion of the person holding it, entirely apart from the scrutiny and discussion occasioned by the particular charges in the controversy" that the journalist is writing about.[44]

School board members,[45] school superintendents,[46] principals,[47] coaches,[48] trustees[49] and other upper-level school administrators[50] usually — but not always — will be considered public officials (or in some cases, public figures). Law enforcement personnel (including campus police officials) almost always will be categorized as public officials because of the significant interest the public has in monitoring their activities.[51]

Prominent students, particularly student government officers, have occasionally been held to be public officials (or public figures). For example, an Arizona court held that a university student senator was a public official and could not recover against a student newspaper that compared him to Mussolini, Hitler and Stalin and called him a "campus demagogue" that was "hissing in another pit."[52] And a federal appellate court in Ohio found that a public high school student, a senior who: (1) served as president of his school's student senate, (2) was an announced candidate for the local school board, (3) served as a peer counselor at a drug center and (4) had intentionally, the court found, thrust himself into a controversy between the school board and students, was a public figure.[53] More recently, however, West Virginia's highest court ruled that a star high school athlete, recognized as the state's top football player and known for having led his basketball team to the state championship, was not a public figure.[54]

Dangerously for student journalists, perhaps the most difficult public employees for courts to classify as either a public or private person have been teachers and professors. Although the Supreme Court has not yet spoken directly on the issue, most lower courts — particularly in recent years — have found that public high school and college teachers are public officials (or public figures) because they have substantial responsibility for the education of young people.[55] Many of these courts have found that because the public has a keen interest in the operation of its school systems, application of the public official/figure rule was necessary to ensure that threats of libel suits would not protect incompetent teachers. Courts in other states have disagreed.[56]

To be shielded by the actual malice standard (again, the most favorable to a media defendant), the statement about a public official must relate to the person's conduct in or fitness for office. Even if the person has left public office, the statement should continue to be protected as long as he has not been out of office an unreasonably long period of time.[57]

Who is a Public Figure

Defining a public figure is like "trying to nail a jellyfish to the wall," said one frustrated judge.[58] It is often more difficult to predict who will be considered a public figure than it is a public official because the standards are even less clear-cut. Nevertheless, there are two characteristics that tend to distinguish a public figure from ordinary (or private) persons:

Because of the uncertainties involved, journalists should never try to determine whether an individual is or is not a public official or public figure for libel purposes prior to publishing a story. It is best to assume that every one of your subjects is a private person and that you will be held to the lowest fault standard if you publish inaccurate information.

The Supreme Court has said that a public official is one who, at the very least, has, or appears to the public to have, a substantial responsibility for or control over governmental affairs.

Courts are divided on whether public school teachers are public or private persons.

(1) They have voluntarily increased their exposure to the public spotlight by assuming roles of special prominence in the affairs of society. This is generally accomplished either by virtue of their achievements or by their attempt to influence resolution of a public controversy. For example, a New York state court ruled that a high school coach, whom the court said would normally have been considered a private individual, nevertheless became a public figure by storming onto a football field and verbally abusing the officials.[59] A federal court in Michigan ruled that a high school student became a public figure because of his active and public role as a member of the school's student government.[60] In Georgia, a federal judge decided that a former "star" player on a top-ranked University of Alabama football team was a limited-purpose public figure, even decades after his playing days were over, for purposes of a sports story looking back at whether a memorable tackle in a rivalry game was a "cheap shot."[61]

(2) Public figures usually enjoy preexisting access to the media that allows them a greater opportunity to respond to false statements than that enjoyed by private individuals.

To complicate the matter further, there are two subcategories of public figures: a general-purpose public figure and a limited purpose public figure.

A general purpose public figure is the easiest to spot because he or she is a "celebrity," whose pervasive fame or notoriety has made their name a "household word" in their community. Widely known entertainers (Taylor Swift), athletes (Tiger Woods), political figures or social critics (Hillary Clinton) and leading professionals in their fields (Bill Gates) usually fall into this category. While some public figures are pervasively known, it is possible to be a public figure in a local market and a private person elsewhere for libel purposes (for example, a musician who performs in local nightclubs in Minneapolis might be a public figure there, but a private figure if defamed in Phoenix).

Once a person has been declared a general public figure, the actual malice standard may be applied to any defamatory statement about their lives, even those having nothing to do with their line of work or their area of expertise or influence. Because categorizing a person as a general public figure significantly reduces the chance that they will ever win a libel suit, courts have interpreted the category fairly rigidly.

Limited public figures, on the other hand, are those individuals who have voluntarily assumed a leading role in a particular public controversy in order to influence its outcome. Unlike general public figures, whose "celebrity status" extends beyond their particular area of expertise, limited public figures tend to be closely identified and associated with a specific public issue.

Probably the most important step in classifying a person as a limited public figure is the court finding the event with which that person is associated to be: (1) sufficiently public and (2) sufficiently controversial. Courts will usually take a hard look to ensure that a "public controversy" is just that. There usually must be real public debate and any outcome must be "felt by persons who are not direct participants."[62] Public curiosity and concern (even if legitimate) or the mere "newsworthiness" of an event is not supposed to figure into the test (although it sometimes seems to). For example, the arrest and conviction of a private person will not usually convert that person into a public figure, although there may be exceptions where the crime involved is particularly heinous or noteworthy (for example, a triple-murder).[63] Finally, the person must have voluntarily assumed a special role in the controversy, one that attempts to affect the controversy's outcome and one that invites public attention and comment.

Once a person has been classified a limited public figure, the actual malice standard may be applied only to defamatory statements that are directly connected to the public controversy with which the person is associated. All other topics are subject to the private person standard, usually negligence. You will remember that this differs from

A general-purpose public figure is a "celebrity" whose pervasive fame or notoriety has made his or her name a "household word."

A limited purpose public figure is someone who has voluntarily assumed a leading role in a particular public controversy.

the treatment given general public figures, where any subject is fair game.

Private Persons (Everyone Else)

A "private person" is anyone who is neither a public official nor a public figure. Because the public's interest in receiving information about private individuals is thought to be less important than information about public persons, most courts have been less forgiving of the press when they make a mistake.

The Supreme Court has allowed each state to define its own "private person" fault standard as long as it does not impose liability on a reporter without some showing of fault for publishing a libelous statement.[64] With a few exceptions,[65] most states require that a private person prove that a reporter was negligent, that is, that the reporter made a mistake — perhaps an innocent one — that a "reasonable" reporter should not have made. It may help to think of negligence as simply a test for common sense, which is why many private person cases come down to the reporter attempting to show the jury that he did everything he should have done as a responsible journalist while the plaintiff tries show how the reporter acted unreasonably, doing something (or forgetting to do something) that shows a lack of reasonable care.

Arguments frequently occur about such things as whether a reporter contacted all the sources she should have prior to publication, whether the reporter took accurate notes, whether the reporter was sloppy in interpreting documents, whether the information obtained by the reporter was truly "believable," whether a source was trustworthy, whether a story was so "hot" that further investigation was excused, whether a story was so important or newsworthy that a minor lapse in common sense might be forgiven, whether a reporter came to an unreasonable conclusion based on the facts she found and whether a newsroom's policy for catching mistakes was adequate.

Where a journalist exercises good judgment and common sense and is careful to observe sound research and reporting practices, she is not likely to be found negligent — and thus will not be held liable — even if the information she reports later turns out

> In most states, a private person need only prove that a reporter was negligent, that is, that the reporter made a mistake that a "reasonable" reporter should not have made.

RED FLAGS: JOURNALIST BEWARE

The following is a list of particularly sensitive categories and topics that, if inaccurate, will almost always satisfy the "harm to reputation" requirement to support a claim of libel. These topics should be given special attention prior to publication:

1. Statements that accuse or suggest that a person has been involved in serious sexual misconduct or is sexually promiscuous. A special problem: incorrectly identifying an unmarried woman as pregnant.

2. Statements that associate a person with a "loathsome" (to use the colorful term favored by the courts) or socially stigmatizing disease. For example: leprosy, some mental illnesses and any sexually transmitted disease such as herpes or HIV-infection.

3. Statements that accuse another of committing a crime, of being arrested, jailed or otherwise involved in criminal activity. For example, depending on the context or inferences made, it might be defamatory to report that a person was "questioned by police." And be careful: for example, even if you do not flatly accuse a person of committing the crime of perjury (lying while under oath), you might still invoke a red flag by reporting that a person had answered "yes" to a question on the witness stand yesterday but had responded "no" to the same question over a year ago.

4. Negative statements that affect a person's ability to engage in his livelihood, business, trade, profession or office. For example, a story that accused a teacher of being erratic, disorganized, absent from the classroom for extended periods and otherwise unfit to teach was held to be libelous.[66] Statements by co-workers about a school psychologist, including that she was abrasive,

unprofessional and rude, that she sometimes lied and that she failed to meet professional standards were held to be potentially defamatory.[67] Likewise, the North Dakota Supreme Court upheld a $3 million verdict against a former college student who had posted an Internet article accusing a college professor of, among other things, making inappropriate sexual advances toward her.[68] As libel attorney and author Neil Rosini has pointed out, this is an especially broad category and lawsuits can come from unexpected sources.[69] For example, a story that reported that a section of a new hospital was "plagued with air conditioning problems relating to the design of the system" was found to have injured the professional reputation of the building's architect even though the architect was never named.[70] And a high school football coach successfully argued that his professional reputation was damaged when a newspaper falsely reported that he cursed and belittled his players from the sidelines, yelling such statements as, "Come on, get your head out of your &!(!!(&. Play the game." The coach claimed he said "Get your head up."[71]

5. Statements that attack a person's honesty or integrity. For example: calling a person a "liar" or a "thief" or stating that a person has a "selective memory."

6. Negative statements about grades or academic ability. A special problem: stories about "special education" or remedial learning programs.

7. Statements that allege racial, ethnic or religious bigotry.

8. Statements that accuse a person of associating with criminals, "shady characters," or publicly disfavored groups.

9. Statements that attack a person's patriotism or that raise questions about a person's affiliation with groups thought to be associated with anti-American or terrorist organizations.

10. Statements that question a person's creditworthiness, financial stability, or economic status.

11. Any negative statement about a lawyer. As one writer has noted, "lawyers, in a class by themselves, are the most prolific libel plaintiffs in America...."[72] Because lawyers do sue and do know their way to the courthouse, all references to them should be flagged and verified. Therefore, while knowing the intricacies of libel law is certainly valuable, journalists can avoid all of it by remembering one simple idea: there is no substitute for thorough investigation, accurate reporting and responsible editing.

APPLYING THE PIHFF CHECKLIST

You should use the PIHFF list as a quick mental checklist anytime you have a question about whether something is defamatory.

For example, in a story about sexual harassment you interview a student who gives you the name of a teacher who, she says, made sexually explicit remarks and tried to kiss her when they were alone in the classroom. Because the alleged harassment occurred when no one else was present, there are no other sources available to confirm the accusation. Can you use the information in your story? To answer the question, go down the list.

First, if the story is printed in the student newspaper, it is obviously "published." Answer yes to "publication."

Second, if the teacher is named or otherwise identified in the story (for example, if the story says the student stayed after school to get help with her math homework and there is only one male math teacher at the school), the answer to "identification" is also yes. Third, could the statement harm the teacher's reputation in the eyes of the community? Another easy one. (The "red flags" are flapping wildly.) Common sense tells you that a story claiming that a teacher tried to kiss one of his students after making sexually explicit comments not only exposes that teacher to public shame and disgrace, it will likely get him fired. Another yes, then, to "harm."

Fourth, is the statement false? This is really the $64,000 question, isn't it? If the statement is true, it cannot support a libel claim. Only false statements can be defamatory. (This is why some libel lawyers also sometimes refer to truth as a defense — an absolute defense — to a libel claim.) Unfortunately, in this case — absent a hidden camera in the classroom — the truth is known by only two people. And assuming they are telling different stories, one of them is lying.

If a lawsuit is filed, it will ultimately be up to a jury (or in a few cases, a judge) to decide who is telling the truth. But that happens later. You need to know what to do now. For your part as a journalist deciding whether the story can be safely published, you should ask yourself whether you believe the charges to be true. And just as important — why or why not? If, after gathering and weighing all reasonably available evidence and the factoring in the credibility of the sources, you doubt the student's claim, you should go no further. You should never publish a story where you entertain serious doubts about its truthfulness. If, however, you believe the student and have found evidence that supports — even if it does not prove — her claim (perhaps you have interviewed another student who has independently told you of similar encounters with the same teacher, but she is not willing to go on the record), you should continue with your PIHFF analysis. In this case, the best you can do is answer that, while you believe otherwise, the statement may be false.

The final element is "fault." The basic question is one of common sense: Did you do everything a good reporter should do to confirm the accuracy of the information? Did you ask whether the student had reported the teacher's actions to anyone else? If, for example, she said she told the principal, did you contact the principal? Did you obtain and carefully read any formal, written complaints that might have been filed by the student? Did you try to find witnesses who might have observed inappropriate contact between the two? Did you try and find out whether other claims had ever been filed against the teacher? Did you contact the teacher for a response to the allegation? Did you check to see if the student making the claim had a reputation for telling the truth or if there was any indication she was out to "get" the teacher because of a bad grade or some other reason?

These are by no means the only questions that might come up in court. But answering "yes" to the above questions tends to show that you carefully and thoughtfully did your job as a reporter.

If you use solid reporting habits in putting your stories together, you should pass the "fault" test. But "fault" is, unfortunately, an infamous gray area of libel law, and judges differ on what constitutes the appropriate level of care. For example, one judge might think one reliable source is enough to run a particular story, another might be satisfied with no fewer than three.

So our checklist score so far: (1) the statement is to be published, (2) the teacher is identified, (3) it will harm the teacher's reputation, (4) the student's claim may be false (even though you personally believe otherwise) and (5) you probably will not be found "at fault." You do not need a libel lawyer to tell you that with three yes's and two maybes it does not look good for your story at this point.

A person who consents to the media's use of a libelous statement cannot later sue if the statement does, in fact, injure his reputation.

In this case, with no other proof available and no more students coming forward with similar accusations, it comes down to the teacher's word against the student's. Though you sincerely believe the student, you reasonably decide that you cannot be confident enough of the accuracy of the accusation or provide sufficient proof to justify publishing it. Still, you believe that sexual harassment is a problem among a significant number of students at your school and having an actual example of harassment greatly enhances the impact that your story might have in helping students — and teachers — understand and resolve the problem. What to do?

One solution might be that you not identify the teacher. But be careful. Changing the teacher's name to "Mr. Smith" will not protect you if you then say that the incident took place in the teacher's real classroom, Room 310, or if you describe "Mr. Smith" or his room in a way that people will recognize him. Also, if you identify the student victim, you probably narrow your list of possible teachers to those who have had the student in their class, which also poses problems. Be certain that you do not identify "Mr. Smith" in any way. Finally, be sure not to mislead others into thinking that someone else is responsible. This may be difficult (or impossible) if your school is small, where, for example, an accusation against one unnamed male teacher may cast a shadow on all 10 male teachers at the school. (See page 193 for a discussion of the problem of group libel.)

Assuming that such barriers do not exist in your case — and with all of these warnings in mind — you successfully disguise the teacher's identity.

So, the final "PIHFF Checklist" tally: yes to publication, no to identification, yes to harm, maybe to truth, maybe to fault. Fortunately, because the teacher must prove each of the five elements, one "no' is all it takes. There is no libel and you are protected from a successful lawsuit.

But what if the teacher had shown each of the five PIHFF elements? Does he win? Not necessarily. Read on.

DEFENSES

If a person claiming she was libeled shows the five elements contained in the PIHFF checklist are present (that is, the statement was published, the person was identified, his reputation was harmed, the statement was false and the news organization was at fault), the burden then shifts to the publication, which must show that even though the statement was defamatory, there still should be no award of money damages because the statement was either justified or excused. These defenses, as they are called, are discussed below. Generally, a media defendant has the burden of proving the defense in court. If they are successful, the libel plaintiff recovers nothing.

Consent

Simply stated, a person who consents to the media's use of a libelous statement cannot later sue if the statement does, in fact, injure his reputation.[73] To be valid, the consent must be voluntary. It must also be given by someone capable of understanding what he is consenting to. For this reason, obtaining valid consent from a minor can sometimes be tricky. (See discussion regarding minor consent in Chapter 14.)

Privilege

One of the most effective and easiest to use of the libel defenses is also one of most overlooked by journalists. Most states allow the media to publish fair and accurate accounts of official public proceedings and reports without fear of later being successfully sued for libel. For example, a reporter who fairly and accurately reports that a witness at a murder trial testified that she "saw Ming Li shoot the victim," would be protected from a libel suit even if it later was proven that the witness lied and Ms. Li was innocent. The public records and proceedings privilege, also sometimes called the "fair report" privilege, is based on the rationale that keeping citizens informed about matters of public concern is more important than avoiding occasional damage to individual reputations.[74]

In some situations this privilege offers even more protection to the media than the truth defense, discussed above, because it applies even where a published defamatory statement is later proven false. Although ethical considerations and professionalism

Most states allow the media to publish fair and accurate reports of official public proceedings and reports without fear of later being successfully sued for libel. The scope of the privilege varies considerably from state to state.

might demand more, the privilege permits media defendants to avoid liability without regard to whether the information reported is true or false and with no obligation to verify the information's accuracy. If the information is part of an official proceeding or report and if it is reported fairly and accurately — the privilege attaches.

Because the privilege is such a useful one, the three requirements for using it are worth mentioning:

(1) The information must be obtained from a record or proceeding recognized by the state as "official." This is the most difficult requirement to understand because the scope of the privilege varies considerably from state to state. Records and meetings privileged in one state are not automatically privileged in another. For example, reporters in Alabama can publish information obtained from a police incident report without independent verification and still be protected by the privilege if the report proves untrue.[75] Reporters in Vermont, however, must independently confirm all factual statements in a police report to be protected by the privilege.[76]

Despite the variations, the following types of proceedings and records are usually privileged: open court hearings; public criminal and civil trials; judicial documents kept in a court's open file (including motions, exhibits and deposition transcripts that have been signed and filed with the court); school board or board of regents meetings and records;[77] meetings and records of certain other school officials;[78] meetings and records of legislative and executive proceedings and reports; individual and business filings with a government agency for regulatory, real estate and tax purposes; coroner reports; arrest reports (particularly after a person formally pleads to the charges); and publicly filed birth, adoption, marriage, divorce and death certificates.

One category that courts have disagreed on, however, are reports or statements made by law enforcement officials in the early, investigatory stages of a case (before an arrest warrant is issued). For this reason, reporters should be cautious when relying on such records or when reporting "off-the-cuff" remarks made by police.

Because the definition of an "official record" will ultimately depend on where you live, it is always a good idea to consult a local media-law attorney, your state press association or the Student Press Law Center for help.

(2) The media report must be fair and accurate. A "fair" report is one that is balanced and presented in context. For example, it would not be fair to present only the plaintiff's side when covering a civil trial if the defendant denied or answered the plaintiff's charges. Another common example: if a person was arrested but subsequently found not guilty, it would be unfair to report only that he had been arrested. "Accurate" means "substantially accurate." Of course, what constitutes substantial accuracy to one judge may not satisfy another so it is always best to dot every "i" and cross every "t."

Statements of pure opinion, even if highly critical, are generally immune from defamation claims.

Police and court records are a particular source of trouble for journalists. To report that a person was arrested when the police blotter states that he was only picked up for questioning would not be privileged because it is not accurate. A story reporting that a person was convicted of a crime when he was only charged would also lose its privilege. You must also be careful interpreting legal documents into "laymen's terms." Oversimplifying some legal terms can lead to inaccuracy and loss of privileged status.

(3) The source of the statement should be clearly noted in the media report. While not all states require that the source of the information be included in the story to invoke the privilege, it is certainly a good practice to follow. An explicit attribution to a privileged source is not only sound journalism, it also prevents a person from claiming that the information was obtained from a non-privileged source. Preventing such confusion could avoid an expensive courtroom battle to settle the issue.

Doing the legwork to obtain information directly from a privileged record is sometimes more work than relying on a second-hand, non-privileged source, but the additional protection of the fair report privilege rewards the thorough journalist. Always ask yourself whether the information you intend to publish — particularly where it relates to sensitive "red flag' issues — might not also be found in an official report that you could cite as your source.

FROM THE SPLC CASE FILES

Case 1: As part of its preseason review of women's college basketball teams, a magazine writes that the team is "loaded with talent.... But coach Marian Washington usually finds a way to screw things up. This season will be no different."

The coach sues for libel. The court dismisses the complaint, finding the statement is protected opinion.[79]

Case 2: A college student was charged with sexual battery after he had sex with a classmate, who witnesses claimed was too drunk to consent. The student was acquitted after his criminal trial ended in a hung jury, but he was nevertheless expelled from the university. Following the trial, a school official told the local newspaper that she knew what was in the evidence and despite the outcome in court she believed that the student "definitely committed a sexual battery." The student sued for defamation. The court upheld his claim, dismissing the school official's argument that the statement was protected opinion.[80]

Simply leading off a statement with "In my opinion..." provides no automatic protection from a libel lawsuit.

Opinion Versus Fact - The Fair Comment Defense

"There is no such thing as a false idea," the Supreme Court wrote in 1974.[81] Because a statement must be false to be defamatory, statements that are solely a speaker's opinion are generally protected, even when they are not very nice.[82]

The biggest problem in using the constitution-based "opinion defense" and its relative, the common law-based "fair comment defense," is that it is not always easy to label a statement either "pure fact" or "pure opinion." As the examples above show, many statements tend to fall in that grey area in between, which can leave journalists and lawyers (and courts) guessing.[83]

Consider, for instance, the statement "Tom Peterson is an awful cook." Is that a statement of fact or opinion? If the statement stood alone, most would probably see it as simply one person's opinion, a subjective comment that might easily change along with the particular taste of the person who said it. (Perhaps Tom Peterson likes garlic and the reviewer does not.) But what if the person making the statement is the dean of Peterson's cooking school? And what if he goes on to list specific examples of Peterson's culinary ineptitude: he undercooks fish, burns bread, leaves eggshells in his cake batter and never washes his hands. Now the statement seems more one of fact than opinion. And if the claims are inaccurate anyone who publishes the dean's comments may find themselves up Libel Creek without a paddle.

To distinguish potentially defamatory fact from constitutionally protected opinion, courts have devised various tests. Most are focused on whether the statement can be objectively verified, or in other words, proven true or false. Only facts are true or false. If a statement cannot reasonably be verified, it will be considered protected opinion. For instance, in the case brought by the college basketball coach in the example cited above, a federal appeals court applied what it called a "supportable interpretation standard."[84] The court said the coach had to show that the statement (the coach tends to "screw things up") was based on facts that were demonstrably untrue or that no reasonable person could characterize as a supportable interpretation of the underlying facts. The court noted the practical difficulty in a jury weighing all the facts (watching

---

videos of games, listening to the testimony of basketball "experts," etc.) to determine whether the coach actually "screwed things up" or not. In the end, the court found that the underlying facts were open to different interpretations by reasonable persons.

In *Milkovich v. Lorain Journal Co.*,[85] decided in 1990, the Supreme Court also partly addressed the fact/opinion question. The Court said that an opinion based on a description of facts, which themselves would be considered libelous, is no less libelous merely because it is labeled opinion.[86] Simply leading off a statement with "in my opinion..." (or using the word "alleged") provides no automatic protection from a libel charge. As the Court pointed out, "the statement, 'in my opinion Jones is a liar,' can cause as much damage to reputation as the statement, 'Jones is a liar.'"[87]

In *Milkovich,* the Court found that statements in a reporter's column that said that a high school wrestling coach lied during a state athletic association hearing were sufficiently based in fact to be measured as true or false. Even though the offending column contained many of the characteristics of an opinion piece — it was located on the sports page ("a traditional haven for cajoling, invective and hyperbole") under the large caption "TD Says..." (the columnist's initials) accompanied by a small box photograph of the columnist, the Court nevertheless determined that statements contained in the piece alleging that the coach lied during an official hearing (for example, "[a]nyone who attended the meet...knows in his heart that [the coach] lied at the hearing after...having given his solemn oath to tell the truth") could be proved false and libelous.

The Court also noted that it believed that there were enough constitutional safeguards in place to ensure that its decision would work no hardship on the press. In particular, a person claiming an injury in a lawsuit against the media must still prove that the statement is false. Additionally, statements that no reasonable person would believe, such as satire and rhetorical hyperbole, remain protected.[88] (See discussion, below.)

Most libel experts seem to agree that the *Milkovich* decision has had little impact on how stories are screened for libel. While statements of opinion remain protected, false factual statements can be a problem wherever or however they are published. Columnists, editors, lawyers and others should continue to exercise common sense and use reasonable care in verifying all potentially damaging statements that readers might perceive as stating or implying facts and in making clear that any opinions offered are just that.

FROM THE SPLC CASE FILES

A controversial big-city lawyer was successful in having sexual assault charges dropped against two university fraternity members by arguing that the victim had consented to the sexual encounter. The student newspaper ran an editorial condemning the court's decision, saying that the acts should not have been so easily excused. The editorial detailed some of the lawyer's courtroom argument casting responsibility on the woman, a position that the editors found deplorable. The editorial called the lawyer "a scumbag," which prompted him to file a libel lawsuit. A court later dismissed the case.[89]

Epithets and Insults

Courts have generally held that epithets and insults are protected statements of opinion, which are not intended to be taken literally and cannot be proven true or false.[90] For example, describing a high school teacher as a "babbler" was held not libelous.[91] Similarly, use of the expressions "fat bitch,"[92] "chicken butt,"[93] "big skank,"[94] and "raving maniac"[95] were also, in specific cases, held not to be actionable. A Connecticut court ruled that calling a man a "bastard" did not give rise to a cause of action by his mother.[96] A federal appeals court found that describing a retail outlet as "trashy" could not support a libel claim because it could not be objectively verified.[97]

Likewise, another court found that talk show host Geraldo Rivera's use of the phrase "accomplice to murder," during an emotional television debate to describe an abortion opponent who maintained a website that identified doctors who performed abortions, was "absolutely protected as rhetorical hyperbole by both the First Amendment and applicable state defamation law."[98] And a federal appeals court judge, apparently tired of litigants whining to his court about name calling, ruled that a toy company spokesperson's use of the term "bank robber" to describe acts committed by a record company accused of trademark infringement was protected rhetorical hyperbole.[99] "The parties," the judge wrote, "are advised to chill."[100]

But there is no blanket license to engage in outlandish name-calling. Where a statement has the "feel" of actual or implied fact, courts have not been so forgiving. For example, a federal court in Texas ruled that calling a person a "despicable human being" could be defamatory.[101] A federal appeals court said that describing an attorney as an "ambulance chaser" was not rhetorical hyperbole and could reasonably imply that the attorney engaged in unethical behavior and solicitation.[102] And, in what is certainly a bit of a stretch, a Wyoming court said that describing a well-known lawyer as a "vermin-infested turd dispenser" could also support a libel claim.[103]

THE BIG OOPS!

> Humor columns, spoofs, cartoons and satire are protected as long as readers understand the material is not intended to be taken seriously.

The scenario is usually pretty much the same. A staffer, hoping to lighten the mood, includes a funny line or "joke" in an otherwise serious story that he submits, knowing that the editor will pull it. Unfortunately, in the madhouse that can be deadline night, the make-believe copy is missed or the uncorrected version of the story is imported into the layout program. In the rush to make it to the printer, it is also missed during the final proofread and the "joke" is not caught until it is seen by thousands of readers, including the joke's target, who does not think it is very funny.

Sadly, there is no shortage of real-life examples.

At Ohio State University, an editor of the university-produced media guide, in what school officials later called a "foolish and thoughtless moment of humor," added the word "drunk" to a photo caption describing a well-known comedian and former OSU graduate who had appeared in public service spots that addressed the problem of binge drinking on campus. Fortunately for the editor, who lost his job because of the slip-up, the comedian displayed his sense of humor in deciding not to sue.[104]

The student newspaper staff at Virginia Tech University was not so lucky. A school official sued the newspaper for $850,000 after it published a story that identified her as the university's "Director of Butt-Licking." The fictitious title accidentally appeared when editors of *The Collegiate Times* forgot to remove it from the "dummy copy" stored on computer templates. A pullout quote — part of a story that detailed the success of one of the school official's programs — included the crude phrase. The editors promptly sent her a letter apologizing for the mistake, but she sued anyway, claiming that the phony title implied the "commission of a crime involving moral turpitude" and had damaged her career. Hours of work, a stack of attorney bills and a lot of red faces later, a Virginia circuit court dismissed the case when it determined that "the use of the title is too absurd to be taken seriously."[105] The state's high court subsequently agreed.[106]

Finally, two members on a high school yearbook staff in Colorado learned the lesson the hard way after they were sued for accidentally inserting the letters "B-i-t-c-h" beneath a classmate's yearbook photo. Described as a computer prank that went awry, one of the students named in the lawsuit said, "It was just weird goofing around. It wasn't supposed to be printed." About 500 of the 2,700 yearbooks were distributed before the blunder was caught. The case was eventually settled out of court. [107]

Everyone likes a good joke. But in the media business, the stakes are simply too high — and a mistake too easily made — for any staff to tolerate such foolishness. Staff members should be instructed that no copy or image should ever be inserted into a story on the production line unless the writer intends for that copy to actually be published. Most editors have enough real-life editing to do without being given intentional blunders.

SATIRE AND CARTOONS: WALKING THE FINE LINE OF FUNNY

The student media love a good joke. Satire, spoofs, cartoons, April Fools' Day parodies — all are part of a student press tradition. Unfortunately, attempts at humor sometimes can be carried too far or not far enough. While relatively uncommon, the publication of satire and humor occasionally prompts threats of libel or other lawsuits by individuals who find themselves the subject of a student publication's ridicule.[108]

Generally, it is not a defense to a libel suit to claim that you were "just trying to be funny" or "meant it only as a joke." "Humor" is not necessarily the same as "opinion," and does not enjoy blanket protection from lawsuits. For example, while cartoons are typically viewed as a forum for farce and jokes, strips such as Gary Trudeau's *Doonesbury* or Aaron McGruder's *Boondocks* often walk a fine line, mixing facts and fun. This can be dangerous. As courts have noted: "The principle is clear that a person shall not be allowed to murder another's reputation in jest."[109] Even so, if a statement cannot reasonably be interpreted to be one of express or implied fact, it cannot be libelous.[110] This means that humor columns, spoofs, cartoons and satire are completely protected as long as it is clear that the material is not intended to be taken seriously.

The importance of readers "getting the joke" was illustrated by a 1988 New Jersey court decision.[111] In that case, a college administrator who was the subject of a "phony ad" sued Kean College's student newspaper, the *Independent*. The student newspaper's 1985 spoof insert issue, called the *Incredible*, included a parody advertisement for a telephone sex fantasy service called the "Whoreline" and listed the assistant dean of the school of education and other school officials among those who staffed the line. The spoof insert contained no serious articles and the "Whoreline" ad was surrounded by what the court described as "obviously 'fake' ads, in the middle of what was unquestionably a parody of the usual student newspaper." This was all the court required to rule in favor of the student newspaper.

A parody or spoof that no reasonable person would read as a factual statement, or as anything other than a joke — albeit a bad joke — cannot be actionable as a defamation, the court said.[112] The court also refused to allow the dean to recover damages based on her claim for intentional infliction of emotional distress.[113]

Courts do not always have such a clear sense of humor, however.[114] So-called "Senior Wills" or "Senior Prophecy" sections — or any section where students, especially those who are not part of the publication staff, are allowed to submit their own material — have been a particular problem for student publications. For instance, in an unreported decision, an Oklahoma court awarded a teenage mother $5,001 in a libel suit against the Tulsa school district for various statements published in her alma mater's student newspaper.[115] For example, a "Rumors of the Year" section of the newspaper said, "T.M. is pregnant again." And during her senior year, a "Predictions" section stated, in part, "In the year 2010 maybe T.M. will finally figure out who the father of her child really is." Although most of the comments used only the student's initials, the jury found that the student was sufficiently identified.

It is widely believed that the media's initial response to a complaint can be the single most important factor in discouraging — or encouraging — further legal action.

Because of the risks, journalists must exercise judgment and common sense in publishing satire or humor. A biting personal attack that seemed hilarious at 3 a.m. in the newsroom might not appear as funny to a jury in a brightly lit courtroom. If you intend something as a joke, be sure that everyone will recognize it as a joke. For instance, resist inserting spoof columns between genuine news stories or editorials. Tip readers off as to your humorous intentions by saving your funny stuff for a "Funny Page," an "On the Lighter Side" section or a clearly labeled "April Fools'" edition. Some newspapers have gone so far as to print their spoof section upside down.[116] A prominent disclaimer (for example, "Parody — Not to be Taken Seriously") might not provide absolute protection from liability, but it can be a helpful safeguard. Subtlety may be tempting and fun; it is also dangerous.

In close cases, it may even be helpful to obtain the consent of the person satirized. Generally, a person who consents to the publication of an article about himself cannot later sue for libel. If the target of the joke does not see the fun and refuses to consent, perhaps it is time to rethink your humor. Mean is rarely funny. Finally, remember that the law is more forgiving when your satire or spoof column addresses an issue of public — as opposed to merely a private — interest.[117]

RESPONDING TO LIBEL LAWSUIT THREATS

One can hope that you have taken every precaution: Conscientious reporting; careful layout; meticulous editing. Nevertheless, the dreaded telephone call arrives: "How could you publish that garbage? I'm going to sue you!"

We live in a lawsuit-happy world, and if you spend much time in journalism, you will, in all likelihood, eventually receive "the call." Every journalist needs to be prepared for that possibility because it is widely believed that the media's initial response to a complaint can be the single most important factor in discouraging — or encouraging — further legal action.[118] Here are a few thoughts:[119]

Be prepared. You need to think about your response before the telephone rings. Complaints are part of the business. They will come, so have a game plan in place and make sure everyone on the newsroom staff knows what is expected should they be the lucky one to answer the phone (or receive the angry e-mail or open the newsroom door). One person — ideally a senior editor, but most importantly, a "people person" and someone not directly involved with the story — should be appointed to field reader or audience complaints. Unless there is absolutely no one else available, advisers should stay clear. It is essential that the caller understand that his beef (and later, his lawsuit if there is one) is with the student editorial staff that made the decision to publish the story, not the school itself. Remind staff members that all complaints must be treated seriously — no matter how "kooky" the caller might be or outrageous the claim might appear. "Kooks" can — and do — sue. Every complaint should be treated as the first step to the filing of a libel lawsuit. Consequently, you must assume that every communication you have with the complainant is being carefully documented or recorded and might later be used as evidence against you.

Be polite. Understand that being exposed for one's follies and foibles — even when deserved — is unpleasant. Particularly if the subject of the story is not accustomed to the glare of the media, being held up for public scrutiny can provoke strong, even irrational, feelings. Often subjects of negative news stories are angry or embarrassed. They may need and want to vent those feelings. Let them. Don't take their ranting personally (certainly easier said than done sometimes) and, above all, don't get into a shouting match. At this stage, the chance of your bringing them around to your point of view is nil. An argument will only fan the flames. Moreover, as cautioned above, anything you say during the heat of an argument could later be used against you at trial. Instead, treat callers with respect. Encourage them to provide whatever facts or copies of documents you might need to evaluate the complaint. Assure them that your news organization strives to report the news accurately and fairly and if mistakes have been made, it is your general policy to correct them. Inform them that their complaint will be taken seriously and investigated to determine the proper response. End the call by telling the complainant that you will respond within a set period of time and then be sure to do so, even if only to tell them that you are still investigating the matter. Don't let them stew. Again, do your best to help them see you as a person trying to do the right thing, not the enemy.

Listen — and keep quiet. If you remember nothing else, remember this: listen to the caller. Listen carefully and purposefully. Take accurate notes, or if your state law allows, record the conversation. Listening can help you. Talking at this point usually hurts. Just as you must assume that the caller may be recording your conversation to later use against you in a lawsuit, you should be sure to listen and document any statements that might be helpful to use as evidence against the caller. Be empathetic. ("I understand why you might be upset. We'll look into this.") Do not admit to error. ("I never meant it that way. We will definitely need to run a clarification.") As tactfully as you can, decline any request to provide details about who your reporters talked to or how they obtained the information for the story. ("I'm sorry, but right now, I'm just collecting information so that we can get to the bottom of things.") Don't explain your editing process or fact-checking policy. Don't explain how photos are selected, how headlines are written or how pages are designed. Empathize — but don't apologize or make excuses. At least not now.

Bring in help — maybe. After hearing the initial complaint, you may have a pretty good idea of its validity and the seriousness of the threat. If you are convinced the complaint is legitimate or if you are certain the complainant is determined to follow through on his threat of a lawsuit, now is probably the time to seek legal counsel. In special cases, your lawyer may want to talk to the responsible reporter or the editor on his own, where information can be revealed in a confidential and legally privileged setting. If you have libel insurance, now is also the time to contact your insurer. Most policies require that you notify the insurer about a serious libel complaint to ensure coverage.

Many states now have "retraction statutes," which typically limit the news media's financial liability if the law's requirements are adhered to.

Gather the facts. If the validity of the complaint remains unclear, you need to do some digging. Obtain copies of all published versions of the article (including online editions) and any previous stories on the topic. Talk briefly with the reporter about how the story was put together, what sources she talked to, what other information was relied on and who else on the newspaper staff was involved (editors, copy editors, design staff). Inform all staff members involved that they should gather and preserve all materials (for example, reporter notes, supporting documents, hand-edited versions, etc.) that have anything to do with how the story was prepared, edited or laid out.

Be a good winner. If, after evaluating the information you have compiled, you determine that your coverage was accurate and the complaint without merit, you should notify the complainant of your conclusion. (Even if you are able to quickly dismiss the complaint, you may want to wait a day or so before responding to allow emotions to cool.) Now is not the time to gloat. Even people with losing claims can still *file* lawsuits. Explain to the complainant that your news organization will consider reporting new information and developments about his story as matters warrant. Also, point out that if he still feels the coverage was unfair, he should consider explaining his position in a letter to the editor or station manager. Assure him that thoughtful letters critical of the news organization and its coverage are routinely considered for publication.

Bring in help — definitely. If you find there is a reasonable basis for the complaint, you will now want to notify legal counsel for help on how to proceed. Sometimes complaints can be handled simply by a clarification, correction or retraction, which are discussed below.

Take a deep breath and relax. Sure, easier said than done. But the reality is that while many threats are made, few lawsuits are actually filed, particularly against student media. Threatening a lawsuit is easy. Filing a lawsuit can be a fairly involved — and expensive — step. For most complainants, being able to vent to someone who is listening and who takes their complaint seriously is enough to move them out of the "red zone" — which should be your goal.

SLAPPING DOWN FRIVOLOUS LAWSUITS

During the fall of 2011, students in an undergraduate course at Vermont's St. Michael's College, "Media and American Politics," got more of an education in the workings of the justice system than they'd signed up for. Assigned to profile little-known presidential candidates competing in the New Hampshire primary, students Chris Hardy and Logan Spillane wrote about John D. Haywood, a lawyer and former Navy officer from Durham, N.C. Haywood saw the story on a school-created website and sued both the college and the student authors for libel, claiming the profile contained false statements that harmed his chances of winning the election.[120] Among his many claims was that the students had damaged his reputation by interviewing his Republican associates in North Carolina and making them aware — truthfully — that Haywood had entered the race on the Democratic side. The students and the school argued that Haywood's lawsuit arose from their exercise of the right to freedom of speech in connection with a public issue.

The lawsuit was dismissed under a Vermont "anti-SLAPP" law that protects the right to speak and publish on matters of public concern. The Vermont law, which was passed in 2005, provides that "a defendant in an action arising from the defendant's exercise, in connection with a public issue, of the right to freedom of speech or to petition the government for redress of grievances under the United States or Vermont Constitution may file a special motion to strike(.)" A U.S. magistrate judge found the suit to be groundless and threw it out, ordering Haywood to pay the defendants' legal fees.[121]

A "SLAPP" is a Strategic Lawsuit Against Public Participation, a misuse of the legal system to intimidate citizens from getting involved in issues of public importance. Anti-SLAPP statutes provide a hurry-up method for a person targeted by a frivolous libel suit to have the case dismissed at the earliest possible stage, and to recover money wasted defending against the claim. As of May 2013, 28 states and the District of Columbia had anti-SLAPP statutes,[122] while two others (Colorado and West Virginia) had court-created SLAPP mechanisms that protect the right to petition the government on issues of public importance without fear of being dragged into court.

SLAPP laws protect all speakers, even unpaid high school journalists. A high school editor used Nevada's anti-SLAPP statute when faced with a lawsuit by a music teacher who claimed she was libeled by a news story. The student newspaper at Churchill County High School reported that the teacher failed to forward some entries to a statewide choir competition as she had promised to do. The teacher sued for libel, but in August 2010, a state district-court judge found that the article was "truthful" and ordered the entire case dismissed.[123] A SLAPP motion generally must be made at the very beginning of a lawsuit, so as soon as a libel claim is brought or even seriously threatened, those on the receiving end should check their state laws and consider whether the claim is so groundless that it can be SLAPPed aside.

RETRACTIONS

The media makes mistakes. When mistakes happen, they should be acknowledged and corrected. This is accomplished by means of a clarification, correction or retraction. A retraction (or a clarification or correction) should be brief and businesslike. It should "sincerely seek to repair the harm done by the defamatory statement."[124] It should refer to and explicitly retract the harmful statement and it should generally include an appropriate apology. Begrudging, snide or deceptive retractions are better left unpublished.

The following retraction is typical: "The Crime Beat report in the May 18, 2013, issue of *The Student Times* incorrectly identified the person arrested for shoplifting at the University Bookstore on May 15. The Crime Beat should have reported that John Q. Doe, of 555 Main Street, was arrested and charged with shoplifting in the incident, according to campus police records. *The Student Times* sincerely apologizes for the error."

Retractions should generally be published as prominently as the original statement.[125] Unlike a correction, which might pertain to a harmless typographical error (such as a photo cutline misidentifying the arena where a concert was held), a retraction typically refers to a broader acknowledgment that the thrust of the story was false, incomplete or misleading. The term "retraction" should therefore be used sparingly.

If the correction is published in response to a complaint from a person identified in the story, it is advisable to obtain the consent of the complainant prior to publishing a correction, to make sure that the correction puts the complaint to rest rather than aggravating it. Note, too, that corrections/retractions can sometimes be a valuable negotiating tool in securing a binding release or agreement not to sue. These are usually matters to discuss with a media-law attorney.

While retractions or clarifications can serve an important function, they are not a cure-all and, if not handled properly, can cause additional problems. For example, admitting in a retraction that a statement is false if the truth of the statement is still at issue, apologizing for "shoddy" reporting, or providing a detailed narrative of the publication's failed editorial process are things that can later come back to haunt you should the defamed person decide to sue. Care should also be exercised to avoid republishing or compounding a libelous statement (for example, "*The Student Times* apologizes for reporting that Jane Doe was arrested for shoplifting.").

As of June 2013, 32 states had enacted "retraction statutes," which typically limit the media's financial liability if a timely retraction is published and the law's requirements are otherwise followed.[126] While the laws vary by state and should be consulted to ensure compliance, they typically address such things as the timing, size and wording of a retraction. Many also require that a person submit a written demand for a retraction prior to initiating a lawsuit. In addition to the various state laws, there continues to be a glimmer of hope, for the adoption of a national, uniform retraction statute.[127] Note, however, that a retraction statute is not a "free pass" to commit libel; it merely enables a publisher to minimize damages.

The decision to publish a retraction can be difficult; writing it can be tricky. Unless you are especially competent in this area it may be worth consulting an attorney before proceeding. The Student Press Law Center's legal staff is also available to assist you.

AVOIDING LIBEL: A DOZEN TIPS FROM THE SPLC

1. Activate your common sense. While the nitty-gritty details of libel law can be confusing, the main ideas are straightforward, generally conforming to common sense. Libel law in a nutshell: (1) don't publish things that aren't true or that you don't have the evidence to reasonably support and (2) don't be a sloppy reporter. Common sense dictates that if you don't understand something or if a story simply doesn't make sense, ask enough questions of enough people until it does. If you are confused, rest assured that your readers would be as well.

2. Remember you role as a journalist. Your job is to accurately relate the facts of a story to your readers. Go into a story with an open mind and not just looking for information that supports any preconceived version of the story that you might have. Your job is to find and report the facts as they exist. Do not be content with anything less. Good reporting is hard work. Be prepared to invest the time and energy necessary to get the story right. No excuses. If you're not willing or can't do so, leave the story for someone else.

3. Take (and keep?) good notes. The "Golden Oldie" of libel lawyer advice. Record facts and interviews scrupulously, including who said what and when. If you know you are a weak note-taker, invest in a digital recorder. While there continues to be some debate over the subject, a growing number of libel lawyers are suggesting that news organizations retain reporters' notes and story documentation for up to two years after the story is first published, which is, in most cases the time limit for filing a lawsuit.[128] All lawyers agree on two things. First, every newsroom should have a note retention policy that is uniformly enforced. If notes are generally destroyed following publication, all notes

should always be destroyed. If notes and old photo memory cards are kept until the start of the next school year, this should always be done. Second, you should never destroy notes for a particular story simply because you feel they may be the subject of litigation. Not only does this make it look like you are hiding something, it can also be illegal.

4. Documents, documents, documents. Get it in writing. If your source tells you during an interview that she acquired her information from an internal memo, ask for a copy of the memo. Read it to make sure that what your source told you jibes with what's in the memo. Whenever possible, cite a public record as your source for information. In most cases, doing so will protect you from liability even if it later turns out the information contained in the public record was wrong.

5. Don't overstate the facts. You are a reporter, not a salesman. Get rid of the "bigger is better" mentality. A football coach who can't account for $1,000 of the team's budget does not need to be labeled "corrupt" or the "ring-leader of the largest financial scandal in school history." Two sources is not "many sources" or "a number or sources" — it is "two sources." And it is perfectly okay for a problem to just be a "problem" and not a "crisis." In most cases, you should avoid the temptation to interpret the facts or reach a conclusion or an opinion for your readers. It is safest to let the facts speak for themselves.

6. Don't overstate the credibility of a source
Either to yourself or to your readers. When interviewing a source, ask yourself if you think he's telling the truth. Does he have a reputation as a liar? Does he have any reason to harm the subject? If you are relying on statistical data or some other published report, establish that source's reliability. If, for example, the manner in which the statistics were compiled has been reasonably questioned, say so in your story. Remember that one exceptionally credible source is worth more than a dozen shaky sources. Finally, anonymous sources should be used sparingly. And at least you should know the identity of your confidential source.

7. Always give the subject of your story an opportunity to present his or her side. Not only does this give a story an essential element of fairness, it also provides you with an opportunity to catch — or at least confirm — parts of a story that may be subject to question.

8. Eliminate the non-essential. Sensitive or complex news stories are not the place to show off your literary talents. Leave the flowery prose and melodrama for your journal. Write carefully and purposefully. Edit out sources or subjects that add nothing to the story. They are potential plaintiffs. When possible, avoid personal attacks. Address criticism to specific issues. Delete unnecessary (even though interesting) allegations. Tell what you know and how you know it. No more. No less.

9. Seek the input of others. Before publication, ask others to look at your story and offer their criticisms or suggestions. After working endless hours on a story, you need "fresh eyes" to catch gaps, inconsistencies, confusing phraseology, mistaken attributions and all of the other small traps that are invisible to one who has already read the copy 20 times. If you have discomfort about specific legal issues that the material might raise, consider getting pre-publication review by a lawyer. An ounce of prevention sure beats sitting in court.

10. Look at the "Big Picture." Forget the little details upon which you have focused so long and hard. Before publication, step back and read the story through one last time. Taken as a whole, are there any obvious questions you failed to ask or glaring sources you didn't contact (for example, a person in a room who witnessed a key — and disputed — meeting)? Look at your story from different points of view. Do you believe your subjects and sources would feel they were treated fairly (even if they didn't like the story itself)? What about headlines and subheads — are they fair and accurate? Are the graphics, photos and accompanying captions correct and not misleading? The bottom line: Make sure the story makes sense to you and fairly presents the facts as you know them.

11. Respond to post-publication complaints courteously and fairly. Studies have shown that a person who perceives that he has been treated rudely or arrogantly by a media organization is far more likely to sue than one who believes that he has been shown the proper respect.

12. Finally, if you need help - legal or otherwise -don't be afraid to ask for it. As a student, you're not supposed to know it all. If you need legal help, select an attorney with media law experience and an understanding of the role of the press in a free society. The Student Press Law Center can help you with this. And ask for that help sooner rather than later. It's much easier to put out a campfire than a forest fire.

CASE STUDY

You are the editor of *The Student Times*. *Times* staff reporter Keisha Keyes, who has been with the paper for two years, just submitted the following story:

> The swim team hit a patch of rough water on Tuesday when President Leroy Williams punished three swimmers for their conduct violations during a recent road trip.
>
> According to sources close to the team, Williams kicked two students off the squad and stripped them of their scholarships after swim team coach Splash Johnson found them drinking alcohol on the team bus. A third, who was not drinking but who admitted to trying to hide his teammates' empty bottles from the coach, was put on probation but will still be allowed to compete.
>
> Campus reaction has been mixed.
>
> "It's about time," said junior Mary Walsh. "I've heard about those wild swim team bus trips for weeks. The coach simply ignored things until now. They say empty beer cans actually rolled down the aisle every time the bus stopped."
>
> "I think the punishment is way too harsh," said senior Todd Jones. "President Williams is being totally unfair. It's ridiculous! Why take away their scholarships and ruin their lives because of one mistake?"
>
> One of the swim team members, who was not punished but who asked not to be identified, said that he saw his teammates drinking on the bus. While he agrees that some punishment was necessary, he is upset that the whole team must now pay the price.
>
> "This pretty much ruins our season. How are we supposed to win without our team captain? She was the best swimmer on the team."
>
> President Williams refused to comment for the story.

Can the story be safely published? What problems, if any, do you see?

ANSWER:
This is clearly an important and newsworthy story. If it is true that students were drinking on the team bus and were kicked off the team — and certainly if it is true that the drinking had been "ignored" by the coach for a while — it is news. However, those are big "ifs" and the story needs more work before publication.

Bring out the PIHFF Checklist.

First, the story is or will be published. Check off "P."

The second element is identification. Four people are identified by name: Mary Walsh, Todd Jones,

Coach Johnson and President Williams. That's easy.

Others are referred to by title: the swim team "captain," an unnamed swim team member who was quoted for the story and the "three unnamed swimmers" who were punished as a result of the drinking incident. Go through these one at a time.

Assuming that there was only one team captain, you must conclude that he or she is easily identifiable. The name of the team captain is not a secret.

The swim team member quoted in the story who asked for anonymity, however, does not appear to be identified. In addition to not using his name, your reporter has avoided other details that would identify the swimmer (although you may want to watch the use of gender pronouns if that could narrow down the pool of possible sources too much).

What about the "three swimmers" that were punished? We've already determined that one of them — the team captain — has probably already been identified by title. It does not appear that the story discloses any other information that would single out the other swimmers for identification. Still, information travels fast, especially in small schools, and their names may already be widely known. Or perhaps the local commercial paper has published their names. If that is the case, you may not be safe hiding behind a cloak of anonymity and should assume that they are effectively identified. The last and hardest "identification" question, however, is whether referring to "three swim team members" unfairly points a finger at those on the team who were not drinking. The key question is the group's size. If there are just 10 swimmers on the team, the charge that three of them were illegally drinking may unfairly cast a shadow over the seven who were not. In such cases, your only safe option may be to name names or drop the story. We'll assume here, though, that the team has 40 members. In such a case, it will be difficult — probably impossible — for any of the 37 "innocent" students to argue that their individual reputations were harmed by the accusation. The pool of suspects is too large.

So, now that you've determined who is identified and who is not, the next element to address is "harm." Of those identified in the story, are there any statements about them that might harm their reputations?

First, the swimmers. Drinking alcohol on a team bus violates both school rules and, if they were underage, the law. Accusing a person of unlawful activity is an automatic "red flag" statement that meets the "harm to reputation" test. But what about the swimmer who did not drink, but hid his friends' empty bottles from the coach? The charge is much less serious and any harm to his reputation much less severe. Indeed, in the eyes of some of his peers, his actions in trying to keep his teammates out of trouble may even help his reputation. But the deception did violate school rules and does cast some doubt on his reputation for honesty. The harm test is probably satisfied.

Second, the individuals named in the story. No statements are made by others about Mary Walsh or Todd Jones. Assuming that you have accurately recorded their comments, they have suffered no harm.

Third, Coach Johnson. There are two statements made by others about Coach Johnson. The first is the claim that he found some of his swimmers drinking on the school bus. No harm there. That is just doing his job. The second statement, by Mary Walsh, is much more problematic. Walsh alleges that the coach knew about the drinking for weeks — she says that empty beer cans were rolling down the aisles — but did nothing until now. That is a very serious charge and casts significant doubt on his ability to perform his job. Walsh's allegation clearly hurts the coach's reputation and could cost him his job.

Fourth, President Williams. There are two statements made about President Williams. The first is that he handed down the punishments to the swimmers. No apparent harm to Williams' reputation there. The second is the comment made by Todd Jones criticizing the harshness of the punishment and claiming that "President Williams is being totally unfair." While Jones' statements may raise questions about how the president handled the situation, the Supreme Court has made clear that only statements alleging facts can support a libel claim. Statements of opinion are protected. While courts have adopted different tests for distinguishing fact from opinion, it is clear that

Jones' statement is not one that can be proven either true or false. Some people may agree with Jones that the president's punishment was too harsh. Others may disagree. That is the essence of an opinion. As opinion, Jones' statement does not meet the "harm" test. Also, in an effort to be fair, your reporter did give the president an opportunity — which he declined — to comment and explain his actions. Bottom line: Williams would have no defamation claim.

So you have narrowed your concerns. The following statements remain at issue: (1) Two of the swimmers (one of which is the team captain) were drinking on the team bus and kicked off the team. (2) One of the swimmers tried hiding his teammates' empty alcohol bottles and was put on probation with the team. (3) Coach Johnson knew that drinking was taking place on the bus during earlier trips and did nothing.

The next element is falsity. Only false statements can be libelous. If the above statements are true and if you can prove them, you cannot be successfully sued for libel. The accuracy of some statements will be obvious. If, for example, the coach had held a press conference during which he publicly acknowledged that he knew drinking had taken place during previous team outings but he had failed to stop it, the truth of the statement would no longer be at issue. Unfortunately, all you have are Walsh's secondhand allegations. While you might not be able to conclude the allegation against Coach Johnson is false, you are a long way from being able to say for sure that the statement is true. You can proceed to the last part of the checklist — but with caution. Ask yourself the same question about the charges against the swimmers. Do you have reason to believe that the accusations against them are false? If not, move on.

Unfortunately, the truth can be elusive. Journalists typically cover a news story from the outside; but the full truth is often only known by those on the inside: the newsmakers themselves. In such cases, the press must simply do the best that it can to get the story right. That brings you to the final element in our PIHFF checklist: fault. You cannot be held responsible for a defamatory statement — even if you later discover the statement was false — unless you have done something wrong. The big question, then, when addressing fault: Have you done everything that a reasonable journalist should have done to confirm the accuracy and fairness of the story? Look at the statements and carefully examine the support you have for each. In other words, what do you know and how do you know it?

The first potentially defamatory statement involves the swimmers kicked off the team for drinking. Your reporter lists her source for the information as "sources close to the team." Who are they, and why can't she name them? A confidential source who is unwilling to come forward will be of little help in court if you are sued for libel. You need something more. Your reporter quotes one unnamed team member who says he witnessed the drinking. Is this witness credible? Did your reporter try to talk with other team members? How many? What did they say? Are their stories consistent? How about the coach? The bus driver? How about school officials who might have been involved in the investigation? Underage drinking is a crime. Were police involved? Were reports filed? A glaring omission is that the story reflects no attempt to talk to the punished students themselves. While the students might decline to comment, a good reporter doesn't assume a no-comment. Always give the subject of an accusatory statement the opportunity to respond to or clarify the charges prior to publication.

The second statement involves the student put on probation. The story says that the student "admitted" that he had tried to hide the empty bottles. Admitted to whom? Did he admit this to your reporter or is this also from "sources close to the team?" There is a big difference and that point should be clarified. If the admission was to your reporter, had she identified herself as a journalist to the student and did she clearly record what the student said? Look at the reporter's notes. During the two years that she has worked for the paper have you known the reporter to be reliable? If the admission did not come directly from the accused team member, you will need to address the same questions as with the other two swimmers, above. Namely, what are the sources for the information? How many? Are their stories consistent? Are the sources credible? Was this swimmer given the opportunity to comment? Reporting the story thoroughly will take a lot of work, but assuming you are diligent and obtain satisfactory answers for all the questions above, you should be in a position to publish your story.

Finally, what about the charge that Coach Johnson knew about the drinking but did nothing? What do you know about the accuser, Mary Walsh? How does she know this? Read her quotes carefully. She does not claim to have witnessed the scene on the team bus firsthand, and may be simply relating gossip. For a charge as serious as this, a reasonable journalist would not publish what could be nothing more than a third-hand rumor. And good journalism would demand that the coach be given an opportunity to respond. While additional reporting may yield additional information about what the coach did or didn't know about team drinking problems, the statement by Walsh is clearly not safe to publish as-is and should be deleted.

As the above illustrates, you don't have to be a libel lawyer to avoid defamation. You do, however, have to activate your common sense and be willing to do what it takes to get the story right. Good reporting is hard work. There are few shortcuts.

SUMMARY

While the details of libel law can get complicated for lawyers, avoiding much of the libel trap as a journalist is not especially difficult. Understanding the basic elements of libel: (1) Publication, (2) Identification, (3) Harm, (4) Falsity and (5) Fault (PIHFF) and developing an awareness of some of the key libel defenses, such as consent, fair comment and the fair report privilege, is not too hard and can help reporters — young and old — steer clear of trouble.

But while having a basic understanding of the law is important, the best all-around defense to libel problems is simply good reporting. American defamation law gives the press a fair share of wiggle room and protects journalists who act reasonably in carrying out their obligation to truthfully, accurately and vigorously report the news. While nothing can stop the disgruntled subject of an unflattering news story from suing, journalists who adhere to sound reporting practices will generally prevail in the end.

ENDNOTES

1   BARBARA DILL, THE JOURNALIST'S HANDBOOK ON LIBEL AND PRIVACY (The Free Press 1986), p. 9.
2   RODNEY A. SMOLLA, JERRY FALWELL v. LARRY FLYNT: THE FIRST AMENDMENT ON TRIAL (St. Martin's Press 1988), p. 215. The author cites the 1663 court sentence given to John Twyn, an Englishman convicted of treason for his book, *A Treatise on the Execution of Justice*, in which he argued that the King owed a duty to the people and that "the people may take up arms against a king and his family and put the king to death if he refuses accountability." Mr. Twyn's words obviously peeved the powers that be; the court handed down the following sentence: "The judgment is that you be led back to the place from whence you came and from thence be drawn upon a hurdle to the place of execution; and there you shall be hanged by the neck, and being alive, shall be cut down, and your privy-members shall be cut off, your entrails shall be taken out of your body, and you living, the same to be burnt before your eyes; your head to be cut off, your body to be divided into four quarters and your head and quarters to be disposed of at the pleasure of the King's Majesty. And the Lord have mercy upon your soul." (quoting from Richard Labunski's book, *Libel and the First Amendment* (Transaction Books, 1987), p. 34).
3   The Media Law Resource Center reported that the average jury award in libel lawsuits from 1980 through 2007 was $2.8 million. *MLRC 2008 Report on Trials and Damages*, 2008 MLRC Bulletin No. 1 (Feb. 2008).
4   Criminal libel, once thought to be a relic of American history, emerged in a much-watched case involving a Utah high school student who, among other things, used his website to accuse his principal of being "the town drunk" and of sleeping with the school secretary. A local prosecutor charged him with criminal libel in violation of the state's criminal code. The Utah Supreme Court eventually held that the law was overbroad and unconstitutional. *I.M.L. v. State*, 61 P.3d 1038 (Utah 2002). In 2002, however, a publisher and owner of a monthly political newspaper was fined $3,500 and sentenced to one year's unsupervised probation after being convicted by a Kansas jury of seven misdemeanor counts of criminal libel. *Kansas v. Carson*, No. 01-CR-301 (Kan. Dist. Ct., Wyandotte County jury verdict July 17, 2002), aff'd, 95 P.3d 1042, 2004 Kan. App. LEXIS 877 (Kan. Ct. App. Aug. 20, 2004), *review denied*, No. 90,690, 2004 Kan. LEXIS 821 (Kan. Dec. 15, 2004); see also *Developments in Criminal Defamation Law Since 2002*, 2004 MLRC Bulletin No. 4 (Dec. 2004) at 6-7. For more information, see *Criminalizing Speech About Reputation: The Legacy of Criminal Libel in the U.S. after Sullivan & Garrison*, 2003 MLRC Bulletin No. 1 (March 2003).
5   The facts of Thomas Mink's case are described in *Mink v. Knox*, 613 F.3d 995, 998-99 (10th Cir. 2010).
6   Brian Schraum, "Former Colo. student publisher reaches $425k settlement with prosecutor, ending Howling Pig legal marathon," SPLC Blog, Dec. 12, 2011, *available at* http://www.splc.org/wordpress/?p=2959.

7   The chilling effect of the mere threat of libel litigation, particularly on smaller publications, is addressed in Anthony Lewis's book, MAKE NO LAW: THE SULLIVAN CASE AND THE FIRST AMENDMENT (Random House 1991), at 200-218.

8   It has been reported that CBS spent in excess of $2 million defending itself against a libel suit brought by General William Westmoreland in the early 1980s. The discovery phase of the case alone produced 400,000 pages of documents. CBS filed a motion and supporting brief for summary judgment that ran an epic 1,342 pages. Westmoreland's attorney, not to be outdone, responded with a 1,380-page brief of his own. Westmoreland eventually dropped his case. Lewis, *supra* note 7, at 216.

9   *Pippen v. Comcast Corp.*, No. 1:11-cv-08834 (E.D. Ill. complaint filed Dec. 13, 2011).

10 Shea Bennett, "The Price of Defame—Courtney Love's Twitter Rant Costs Her $430,000," Mediabistro. com, March 4, 2011, *available at* www.mediabistro.com/alltwitter/courtney-love-defame-lawsuit_b6126 (last viewed Aug. 22, 2013).

11 RESTATEMENT (SECOND) OF TORTS Sec. 568A (1977).

12 Historians trace the origin of the present-day Internet to ARPANET, a small network intended to allow researchers to share super-computers in the United States. Some contend that the "birthday" of the Internet was the day ARPANET was launched in 1969, connecting "host" computers at Stanford Research Institute, U.C.L.A., University of California at Santa Barbara and the University of Utah. Barry M. Leiner et al., *Brief History of the Internet*, Internet Society.org, *available at* http://www.isoc.org/internet/history/brief.shtml (last visited Aug. 22, 2013).

13 According to the Media Law Resource Center, the first completed Internet libel case was *SNA v. Array*, 51 F. Supp. 2d 554 (E.D. Pa. June 9, 1999) (bench verdict). MLRC 2008 *Report on Trials and Damages, supra* note 3; *see also* LDRC (nka MLRC) 2002 *Report on Trials and Damages*, 2002 LDRC Bulletin No. 1 (Feb. 2002).

14 Communications Decency Act (CDA), 47 U.S.C.A. Sec. 230 (West Supp. 2008). A more thorough discussion of the CDA's liability provisions is available on the SPLC website at http://www.splc.org/legalresearch.asp?id=24. *See also Fair Housing Council of San Fernando Valley v. Roommates.com, LLC*, 521 F.3d 1157 (9th Cir. 2008) (finding that CDA did not immunize website operator whose rental site required the user to submit personal information that federal housing discrimination laws forbid landlords from gathering).

15 *See, e.g., Young v. New Haven Advocate*, 315 F.3d 256 (4th Cir. 2002) (Virginia court does not have jurisdiction over Connecticut newspapers that posted stories online absent showing that Virginia readers were directly targeted); *see also Carefirst of Md., Inc. v. Carefirst Pregnancy Ctrs.*, 334 F.3d 390 (4th Cir. 2003) (Maryland company cannot sue Illinois company in Maryland courts based solely on fact that Illinois company's website was accessible in Maryland); *Revell v. Lidov*, 317 F.3d 467 (5th Cir. 2002) (Harvard professor who posted material on Columbia University website could not be sued in Texas court); *Pavlovich v. Superior Court*, 58 P.3d 2 (Cal. 2002) (California courts do not have jurisdiction over website operator in Indiana), *aff'd*, 93 Fed. Appx. 297 (2d Cir. 2004); *Realuyo v. Villa Abrille*, 2003 WL 21537754 (S.D.N.Y. July 8, 2003) (New Jersey resident who practiced law in New York could not sue Philippines-based company and residents for website article).

16 *See Dow Jones & Co. v. Gutnick* (2002) HCA 56 (Australian High Court ruled that its country's courts do have jurisdiction to hear libel case brought against U.S. publisher. The court ruled that personal jurisdiction existed solely because the article in question, posted on the *Barron's Online* website based in New Jersey, could be viewed on the Internet in Australia.).

17 So far, most courts have said no, ruling that the statute of limitations begins to run the day the story is first posted. *See Van Buskirk v. N.Y. Times Co.*, 325 F.3d 87 (2d Cir. 2003) (Internet posting subject to single publication rule for purposes of statute of limitations); *Firth v. New York*, 775 N.E.2d 463 (N.Y. 2002) (New York's highest court adopts "single publication rule," under which statute of limitations for action based on defamatory statement on website begins to run on date that statement is first posted).

18 *In re Baxter*, CIV No. 01-MC-00026-M (W.D.La. Feb. 4, 2002) (ruling staying court order requiring an Internet service provider to reveal identity of University of Louisiana at Monroe professor who operated website critical of university). *See also America Online, Inc. v. Anonymous Publicly Traded Co. v. John Does 1-5*, 542 S.E.2d 377 (Va. 2001); *Polito v. AOL Time Warner, Inc.*, 78 Pa. D. & C.4th 328, 2004 Pa. Dist. & Cnty. Dec. LEXIS 340 (Lackawanna County C.P. Jan. 28, 2004).

19 *Dendrite Int'l, Inc. v. Doe No. 3*, 775 A.2d 756 (N.J. Super. A.D. 2001).

20 *Sisley v. Seattle Sch. Dist. No. 1*, 171 Wash.App. 227, 286 P.3d 974 (Wash. App. 2012).

21 *Geisler v. Petrocelli*, 616 F.2d 636, 639 (2d Cir. 1980) (holding that "[I]t is not necessary that all the world should understand the libel; it is sufficient if those who knew the plaintiff can make out that (she) is the person meant.") (citation omitted).

22 Not intending to identify a particular person is no excuse. As one court has said, the test is "not who is meant but who is hit" in the mind of the reasonable reader. *Sims v. KIRO, Inc.*, 580 P.2d 642, 645 (Wash. Ct. App. 1978), *review denied*, 91 Wash.2d 1007 (Wash. 1978), *cert. denied*, 441 U.S. 945 (1979).

23 A New York judge recognized the problem journalists face in coming up with an appropriate disguise. Noting that an "infinite variety" of names exists in our multi-ethnic society, he observed that disguising a name like "Jones" by spelling it backwards "would be little protection, for somewhere in this wondrous land there must be someone name Senoj." *Landau v. Columbia Broad. Sys. Inc.*, 205 Misc. 357, 360-61, 128 N.Y.S.2d 254 (N.Y. Sup. Ct. 1954) *aff'd mem.*, 1 A.D.2d 660, 147 N.Y.S.2d 687 (N.Y. App. Div. 1955).

24 *See, e.g., Allen v. Gordon*, 86 A.D.2d 514, 446 N.Y.S.2d 48 (N.Y. App. Div. 1982) (prominent disclaimer indicating that names used in book were fictitious was a factor preventing the real "Dr. Allen" of Manhattan from claiming author's use of name referred to him), *aff'd*, 437 N.E.2d 284, 56 N.Y.2d 780 (N.Y. 1982).

25 *See* RESTATEMENT (SECOND) OF TORTS Sec. 564(A) cmt. b (1977); *see also* Bruce W. Sanford, *Libel and Privacy* Sec. 4.4, at 110.1-111 (2d ed. & Supp. 2004).

26 *O'Brien v. Williamson Daily News*, 735 F. Supp 218 (E.D. Ky. 1990), *aff'd mem.*, 931 F.2d 893 (6th Cir. 1991).

27 A rather absurd example of a case in which a court allowed a defamation claim against a group larger than 25 is *Fawcett Publications Inc. v. Morris*, 377 P.2d 42 (Okla. 1962), *cert. denied*, 376 U.S. 513 (1964), *reh'g denied*, 377 U.S. 925 (1964). In that case, which is now more than 40 years old and probably of little significance, the court allowed a single player on the 60-plus man Oklahoma football team, a fullback on the team's alternate squad, to sue when a writer accused the entire team of taking drugs to improve performance; *see also Barger v. Playboy Enters.*, 564 F. Supp. 1151 (N.D. Cal. 1983), *aff'd*, 732 F.2d 163 (9th Cir. 1984), *cert. denied*, 469 U.S. 853 (1984); *McCullough v. Cities Serv. Co.*, 676 P.2d 833 (Okla. 1984).

28 *O'Brien*, 735 F. Supp. at 223.

29 *Dean v. Dearing*, 561 S.E.2d 686 (Va. 2002). "An allegedly defamatory statement which imputes misconduct generally to a governmental group constitutes libel of government, for which there is no cause of action in American jurisprudence." Id. at 689.

30 *See, e.g., Ithaca Coll. v. Yale Daily News Publ'g Co.*, 433 N.Y.S.2d 530 (N.Y. Sup. Ct. 1980) (private liberal arts college that is pervasively involved in affairs of society held to be a "public figure"), *aff'd on other grounds*, 85 A.D.2d 817, 445 N.Y.S.2d 621 (N.Y. App. Div. 1981).

31 *See, e.g., Stanley v. Gen. Media Communications, Inc.*, 149 F. Supp. 2d 701 (W.D.Ark. 2001) (dismissing libel and false light claim brought against Penthouse Magazine by two high school students involved in spring break "condom-fitting" contest where they failed to show that photographs and accompanying captions in magazine were false).

32 *Phila. Newspapers v. Hepps*, 475 U.S. 767 (1986). A possible exception to this rule involves the situation where a private individual sues the media for a statement that does not involve a matter of public concern (the so-called "Private/Private" situation).

33 As the Restatement (Second) of Torts (1977) points out: "Slight inaccuracies of expression are immaterial provided that the defamatory charge is true in substance." Sec. 581A cmt. f.

34 *See, e.g., Tilton v. Capital Cities/ABC, Inc.*, 905 F. Supp. 1514 (N.D. Okla. 1995), *aff'd*, 95 F.3d 32 (10th Cir. 1997), *cert. denied*, 519 U.S. 1110 (1997).

35 *Gertz v. Robert Welch, Inc.*, 418 U.S. 323 (1974), appeal after remand, 680 F.2d 527 (7th Cir. 1982), *cert. denied*, 459 U.S. 1226 (1983).

36 *New York Times Co. v. Sullivan*, 376 U.S. 254 (1964).

37 Anthony Lewis, Make No Law: The Sullivan Case and the First Amendment (Random House 1991), pp. 34-36.

38 Lewis, *supra* note 37, at 35.

39 *Curtis Publ'g Co. v. Butts*, 388 U.S. 130 (1967).

40 *See* note 65, below, for a list of states with standards other than negligence for private persons.

41 *Rosenblatt v. Baer*, 383 U.S. 75 (1966), *on remand*, 237 A.2d 130 (N.H. 1967).

42 *Hutchinson v. Proxmire*, 443 U.S. 111 (1979), *on remand*, 605 F.2d 560 (7th Cir. 1979).

43 *Rosenblatt*, 383 U.S. at 86.

44 *Id.* at 87, n.13.

45 *Matta v. Burton*, 721 A.2d 1164 (Pa. Commw. Ct. 1998) (school board director is a public official), *appeal dismissed*, 736 A.2d 606 (Pa. 1999); *Strong v. Okla. Publ'g Co.*, 899 P.2d 1185 (Okla. Ct. App. 1995) (school board member is a public official); *Sanders v. Prince*, 403 S.E.2d 640 (S.C. 1991) (implied recognition that county school board member is a public figure); *Angle v. Easton Publ'g Co.*, 33 Pa. D. & C.3d 315 (Northampton County C.P. 1984) (school board candidate held to be a public figure).

46 *Kefgen v. Davidson*, 617 N.W.2d 351 (Mich. Ct. App. 2000) (superintendent is a public official); *Beck v. Lone Star Broad. Co.*, 970 S.W.2d 610 (Tex. Ct. App. 1998) (assistant superintendent for business services of a public school district is a public official); *Purvis v. Ballantine*, 487 S.E.2d 14 (Ga. Ct. App. 1997) (former superintendent is a public official); *Dow v. New Haven Indep., Inc.*, 549 A.2d 683 (Conn. Super. 1987); *Scott v. News-Herald*, 496 N.E.2d 699 (Ohio 1986); *State v. Defley*, 395 So.2d 759 (La. 1981); *Cone v. John H. Phipps Broad. Stations*, 5 Media L. Rep. 1972 (M.D. Ga. 1979); *Palm Beach Newspapers, Inc. v. Early*, 334 So.2d 50 (Fla. App. 1976), *appeal dismissed*, 354 So.2d 351 (Fla. 1977), *cert. denied*, 439 U.S. 910 (1978); *Nusbaum v. Newark Morning Ledger Co.*, 206 A.2d 185, 86 N.J. Super 132 (N.J. App. Div. 1965) (former member of municipal board of education held to be a public figure), *cert. denied*, 209 A.2d 138 (N.J. 1965).

47 *Williams v. Detroit Bd. of Educ.*, 523 F. Supp. 2d 602 (E.D.Mich. 2007) (terminated public school principal was a public official); *Sovchik v. Roberts*, 2001 WL 490015, 2001 Ohio App. Lexis 2047 (Ohio Ct. App. May 9, 2001) (former assistant principal of public high school held to be a limited purpose public figure); *Jee v. N.Y. Post Co.*, 671 N.Y.S.2d 920 (N.Y. Sup. Ct. 1998) (former public high school principal is a public official), *aff'd*, 260 A.D.2d 215, 688 N.Y.S.2d 49 (N.Y. App. Div. 1999); *Jordan v. World Publ'g Co.*, 872 P.2d 946 (Okla. Ct. App. 1994) (public middle school principal held to be a public figure); *Johnson v. Robbinsdale Indep. Sch. Dist. No. 281*, 827 F. Supp. 1439 (D. Minn. 1993) (public elementary school principal held to be a public official); *Palmer v. Bennington Sch. Dist.*, 615 A.2d 498 (Vt. 1992) (public elementary school principal held to be a public official); *Junior-Spence v. Keenan*, 1990 WL 17241, 1990 Tenn. App. LEXIS 130 (Tenn. Ct. App. Feb. 28, 1990) (public high school principal held to be a public official); *Stevens v. Tillman*, 855 F.2d 394, 403 (7th Cir. 1988) (finding that principal was a public official); *Kapiloff v. Dunn*, 343 A.2d 251, 258 (Md. Ct. App. 1975) (public high school principal held to be a public official), *cert. denied*, 426 U.S. 907 (1976); *Reaves v. Foster*, 200 So.2d 453, 456 (Miss. 1967) (public high school principal held to be a public official). *But see Beeching v. Levee*, 764 N.E.2d 669, 679 (Ind. Ct. App. 2002) (concluding that school principal was not a "public official" or "public figure" for purposes of defamation action, where statements related to "work-place dispute" rather than issues of broader public concern); *Goodwin v. Kennedy*, 552 S.E.2d 319 (S.C. Ct. App. 2001) (public high school assistant principal held not to be a public official), *reh'g denied*, Sept. 19, 2001; *East Canton Educ. Ass'n v. McIntosh*, 709 N.E.2d 468 (Ohio 1999) (public high school principal held not to be a public official), *cert. denied sub nom., Slick v. McIntosh*, 528 U.S. 1061 (1999); *Ellerbee v. Mills*, 422 S.E.2d 539 (Ga. 1992) (public high school principal not a public official), *cert. denied*, 507 U.S. 1025 (1993); *McCutcheon v. Moran*, 425 N.E.2d 1130 (Ill. Ct. App.

1981) (public school principal not a public official).

48 *See McGarry v. Univ. of San Diego*, 154 Cal.App.4th 97, 64 Cal.Rptr.3d 467 (Cal. Ct. App. 2007) (former college football coach was "limited-purpose" public figure in relation to defamation claim for statements concerning his job performance and termination as coach); *Blackwel v. Eskin*, No. 02098, 2006 WL 678577 (Pa. Com. Pl. March 16, 2006) (unpublished) (former assistant basketball coach at Temple University, who was a star player at Temple and played pro basketball for two years, was a public figure); *Daubenmire v. Sommers*, 805 N.E.2d 571 (Ohio Ct. App. 2004) (former high school football coach was limited-purpose public figure for defamation claims based on statements concerning non-renewal of his contract; coach had been publicly involved in controversy over use of religion in coaching and made multiple media appearances in connection with the controversy); *Time, Inc. v. Johnston*, 448 F.2d 378 (4th Cir. 1971) (private college assistant basketball coach, a former professional basketball player, held to be a public figure); *Johnson v. Southwestern Newspapers Corp.*, 855 S.W.2d 182 (Tex. Ct. App. 1993), *writ denied*, Sept. 29, 1993, *reh'g of writ of error overruled*, Nov. 17, 1993 (athletic director and football coach at a Texas public high school held to be a public official); *Mahoney v. Adirondack Publ'g Co.*, 517 N.E.2d 1365 (N.Y. 1987) (public high school teacher and football coach "conceded that he was a public figure"); *Kirk v. Houston's Rest., Inc.*, 1988 Tenn. App. LEXIS 292 (Tenn. Ct. App. May 26, 1988) (state university basketball coach held to be a public official); *Johnston v. Corinthian Television Corp.*, 583 P.2d 1101, 1103 (Okla. 1978) (elementary school teacher and wrestling coach held to be a public official); *Grayson v. Curtis Publ'g Co.*, 436 P.2d 756 (Wash. 1967) (former public university basketball coach held to be a public figure); *Standridge v. Ramey*, 733 A.2d 1197 (N.J. Super. Ct. App. Div. 1999) (former athletic director for school district conceded he was a public official); *Campanelli v. Regents of the Univ. of Cal.*, 51 Cal.Rptr.2d 891 (Cal. Ct. App. 1996) (university basketball coach is a public figure). *See also Brewer v. Times-Journal, Inc.*, 19 Media L. Rep. 2125 (Ga. Super. Ct. 1991) (high school football coach held to be a public figure in an invasion of privacy case). *But see O'Connor v. Burningham*, 165 P.3d 1214, 1219 (Utah 2007) (women's basketball coach at public high school not a public official because her work "does not affect in any material way the civic affairs of a community — the affairs most citizens would understand to be the real work of government"); *Folse v. Delgado Cmty. Coll.*, 776 F. Supp. 1133 (E.D. La. 1991) (community college basketball coach not a public figure); *Moss v. Stockard*, 580 A.2d 1011 (D.C. App. 1990) (women's public university basketball coach who did not "shape or try to shape the outcome of a particular public controversy" ruled not a public official or public figure); *Warford v. Lexington Herald-Leader*, 789 S.W.2d 758 (Ky. 1990) (assistant basketball coach at NCAA Division I state-related school not a public figure), *cert. denied*, 498 U.S. 1047 (1991). *See also Milkovich v. News-Herald*, 473 N.E.2d 1191 (Ohio 1984) (well-known high school wrestling coach not a public figure despite his involvement in a local controversy). Note, however, that the Ohio Supreme Court decision in *Scott v. News-Herald* 496 N.E.2d 699 (Ohio 1986) generally disapproves of *Milkovich's* determination of the public figure issue, *rev'd on other grounds*, 497 U.S. 1 (1990).

49 *Bowes v. Wis. Vocational, Tech. & Adult Educ. Bd.*, 9 Media L. Rep. 2372, 2379 (Wis. Cir. Ct. 1983) (appointed members of state technical college's board of directors held to be public officials); *Scott v. McCain*, 250 S.E.2d 118, 120 (S.C. 1978) (member of county school district's board of trustees held to be a public official), *appeal after remand*, 274 S.E.2d 299 (S.C. 1981).

50 *See, e.g., Lewis v. Univ. Chronicle*, No. A06-2281 (Minn. Ct. App. Jan. 25, 2008) (unpublished) (former dean of public college was public figure); *Paul v. News World Communications*, No. 01CA917, 2003 WL 23899002 (D.C. Super. Ct. 2003) (school district's chief information officer, who made six-figure salary and supervised eight departments with 149 employees, was a public official); *Davis v. Borskey*, 660 So.2d 17 (La. 1995) (purchasing agent for a state university held to be a public official); *Wollen v. Brown, et. al.*, 1992 WL 219317, 1992 Conn. Super. LEXIS 2598 (Conn. Super. Ct. 1992) (former member of school building committee who "thrust himself into the forefront of the controversy" surrounding referendum on bond for school renovation "with the intention of influencing the outcome" was a public figure on issues related to referendum); *Walko v. Kean Coll. of N.J.*, 561 A.2d 680 (N.J. Super. Ct. Law Div. 1989) (assistant dean at public college held to be a limited purpose public figure); *Renwick v. News & Observer Publ'g Co.*, 304 S.E.2d 593 (N.C. Ct. App. 1983) (associate dean of public university ruled a public figure), *rev'd on other grounds*, 310 S.E.2d 405 (N.C. 1984), *reh'g denied*, 315 S.E.2d 704 (N.C. 1984), *cert. denied*, 469 U.S. 858 (1984); *Byers v. Southeastern Newspapers Corp. Inc.*, 288 S.E.2d 698 (Ga. Ct. App. 1982) (public college dean held to be a public figure); *A.H. Belo Corp. v. Rayzor*, 644 S.W.2d 71 (Tex. Ct. App. 1982) (trustee of public university's foundation is a public figure); *Torgerson v. Minneapolis Star & Tribune Co.*, 7 Media L. Rep. 1805 (Minn. Dist. Ct. 1981) (Minnesota law school dean held to be a public figure); *Avins v. White*, 627 F.2d 637 (3d Cir. 1980) (Delaware public law school dean held to be a public official), *cert. denied*, 449 U.S. 982 (1980); *Gallman v. Carnes*, 497 S.W.2d 47 (Ark. 1973) (assistant dean and professor of public law school held to be a public official). *But see Churchill v. Univ. of Me. Sys.*, 2002 WL 32068344, 2002 Me. Super. LEXIS 226 (Me. Super. Ct. Dec. 13, 2002) (project director of Maine Community Policing Institute at the University of Maine held not to be a public official).

51 *See Nungaray v. Cuesta Coll.*, No. CV71542 (Cal. Super. Ct. San Luis Obispo County, Sept. 24, 1993) (campus safety officer held to be a public official); *Roche v. Egan*, 433 A.2d 757, 762 (Me. 1981) ("Our research has disclosed that every court that has faced the issue has decided that an officer of law enforcement, from ordinary patrolman to Chief of Police, is a 'public official' within the meaning of federal constitutional law."). *See also Waterson v. Cleveland State Univ.*, 639 N.E.2d 1236 (Ohio Ct. App. 1994) (holding a public university campus police officer to be a public official).

52 *Klahr v. Winterble*, 418 P.2d 404 (Ariz. Ct. App. 1966).

53 *Henderson v. Kaulitz*, 6 Media L. Rep. 2409 (6th Cir. 1981). *But see Frasca v. Andrews*, 463 F. Supp. 1043, 1052 (E.D.N.Y. 1978) (suggesting that vice president of student government at a public high school would not be a public official).

54 *Wilson v. Daily Gazette Co.*, 588 S.E.2d 197 (W.Va. 2003).

55 *See Martin v. Roy*, 767 N.E.2d 603 (Mass. App. Ct. 2002) (private college professor held to be a public

figure); *Featherstone v. CM Media, Inc.*, 2002 Ohio 6747, 2002 WL 31750286, 31 Media L. Rep. 2336 (Ohio Ct. App. Dec. 10, 2002) (retired school teacher found to be limited-purpose public figure based on evidence that he regularly participated at school board meetings and hosted talk show that discussed school board), *appeal denied*, 785 N.E.2d 473 (Ohio 2003), *recons. denied*, 787 N.E.2d 1232 (2003); *Corbally v. Kennewick Sch. Dist.*, 973 P.2d 1074 (Wash. Ct. App. 1999) (middle school teacher's "conduct" held to be that of a public official); *Pendleton v. City of Haverhill*, 156 F.3d 57 (1st Cir. 1998) (public school substitute teacher and vocation counselor who granted an interview to a local newspaper regarding minority hiring in the school system one year earlier held to be a limited purpose public figure); *Campbell v. Robinson*, 955 S.W.2d 609 (Tenn. Ct. App. 1997) (public school teacher held to be a public official); *Faltas v. State Newspaper*, 928 F. Supp. 637 (D.S.C. 1996) (physician and professor at public university held to be a limited public figure), *aff'd*, 155 F.3d 557 (4th Cir. 1998), *cert. denied*, 525 U.S. 1157 (1999); *Abdelsayed v. Narumanchi*, 668 A.2d 378 (Conn. Ct. App. 1995) (state college professor held to be a public figure), *appeal denied*, 676 A.2d 397 (Conn. 1996), *cert. denied*, 519 U.S. 868 (1996); *Elstrom v. Indep. Sch. Dist. 270*, 533 N.W.2d 51 (Minn. Ct. App. 1995) (public high school teacher held to be public official); *Stein v. Redlion Citizens for Decency, Inc.*, No. 85 SU 00134-d (York County May 14, 1993) (Pennsylvania public high school teacher held to be a public official); *Kelley v. Bonney*, 606 A.2d 693 (Conn. 1992) (public junior high school teacher held to be a public official); *Hayes v. Smith*, 832 P.2d 1022 (Colo. Ct. App. 1991) (Colorado Court of Appeals noted that a public school teacher was probably a public official even though the plaintiff did not contest the application of the actual malice standard), *cert. denied*, 1992 Colo. LEXIS 625 (Colo. 1992); *Mahoney v. Adirondack Publ'g Co.*, 517 N.E.2d 1365 (N.Y. 1987) (teacher and football coach at public high school conceded he was a public official); *Luper v. Black Dispatch Publ'g Co.*, 675 P.2d 1028, 1031 (Okla. Ct. App. 1983) (public school teacher held to be a public official); *Sewell v. Brookbank*, 581 P.2d 267, 270 (Ariz. Ct. App. 1978) (public high school teacher held to be a public official); *Johnston v. Corinthian Television Corp.*, 583 P.2d 1101, 1103 (Okla. 1978) (elementary school teacher and wrestling coach held to be a public official); *Johnson v. Bd. of Junior Coll. Dist. #508*, 334 N.E.2d 442, 447 (Ill. App. Ct. 1st Dist. 1975) (junior college professors who had been active in college controversy were limited public figures); *Gallman v. Carnes*, 497 S.W.2d 47, 50 (Ark. 1973) (assistant dean and professor of public law school held to be a public official); *Rose v. Koch*, 154 N.W.2d 409, 426 (Minn. 1967) (university professor who was also a former state legislator held to be a public figure).

56 *See Snitowsky v. NBC Subsidiary*, 696 N.E.2d 761 (Ill. App. Ct. 1998) (public school teacher held not to be a public figure), *appeal denied*, 705 N.E.2d 450 (Ill. 1998); *Kumaran v. Brotman*, 617 N.E.2d 191 (Ill. App. Ct. 1993) (former substitute teacher held not to be a public figure); *Grossman v. Smart*, 807 F. Supp. 1404 (C.D. Ill. 1992) (assistant professor at state university); *Staheli v. Smith*, 548 So.2d 1299 (Miss. 1989) (public university professor engaged in geology research); *Richmond Newspapers v. Lipscomb*, 362 S.E.2d 32 (Va. 1987) (public high school teacher), *cert. denied*, 486 U.S. 1023 (1988); *True v. Ladner*, 513 A.2d 257 (Me. 1986) (former public high school teacher); *Nodar v. Galbreath*, 462 So.2d 803, 808 (Fla. 1984), superseded by statute as stated in *Linafelt v. Beverly Enters. Florida, Inc.*, 745 So.2d 386 (Fla. Ct. App. 1999); *Stevens v. Tillman*, 568 F. Supp. 289 (N.D. Ill. 1983), later proceeding, 661 F. Supp. 702 (N.D. Ill. 1986) (public elementary school teacher), supplemental op., 1986 U.S. Dist. LEXIS 16392 (N.D. Ill. 1986), *aff'd*, 855 F.2d 394 (7th Cir. Ill. 1988); *Poe v. San Antonio Express News Corp.*, 590 S.W.2d 537, 540 (Tex. Ct. App. 1979), writ of error refused (Feb. 27, 1980), *reh'g of writ of error overruled* (April 2, 1980) (public high school teacher); *Franklin v. Lodge 1108, Benevolent and Protective Order of Elks*, 159 Cal. Rptr. 131, 136-37 (Cal. Ct. App. 1979).

57 *See, e.g., Zerangue v. TSP Newspapers, Inc.*, 814 F.2d 1066, 1069 (5th Cir. 1987) (period of six years did not erode public official status); *Gray v. Udevitz*, 656 F.2d 588, 590 n.3 (10th Cir. 1981); *Pierce v. Capital Cities Communication, Inc.*, 576 F.2d 495, 510 n.67 (3d Cir. 1978) (former mayor and port authority head still public official as to his activities in office more than three years after leaving office), *cert. denied*, 439 U.S. 861 (1978). *See also Milgroom v. News Group Boston, Inc.*, 586 N.E.2d 985, 986 (Mass. 1992).

58 *Rosanova v. Playboy Enter., Inc.*, 411 F. Supp. 440, 443 (S.D. Ga. 1976), *aff'd*, 580 F.2d 859 (5th Cir. 1978).

59 *Winter v. Northern Tier Publ'g Co.*, 4 Media L. Rep. 1348 (N.Y. Sup. Ct. 1978) (order granting summary judgment).

60 *Henderson v. Van Buren Pub. Sch.*, 4 Media L. Rep. 1741 (E.D. Mich. 1978), *aff'd*, 6 Media L. Rep. 2409 (6th Cir. 1981).

61 *See Holt v. Cox Enter.*, 590 F.Supp. 408 (N.D. Ga. 1984).

62 *Warford v. Lexington Herald-Leader*, 789 S.W.2d 758, 768 (Ky. 1990) (citing *Hutchinson v. Proxmire*, 99 S.Ct. 2675 (1979)), *cert. denied*, 498 U.S. 1047 (1991).

63 *See Ruebke v. Globe Communications Corp.*, 241 Kan. 595, 601, 738 P.2d 1246 (Kan. 1987).

64 *Gertz v. Robert Welch, Inc.*, 418 U.S. 323, 347 (1974).

65 States with standards other than negligence for private individuals currently include the following: (1) New York — defendant must be "grossly irresponsible." *See, e.g., Chapadeau v. Utica Observer-Dispatch, Inc.*, 341 N.E.2d 569 (N.Y. 1975); (2) Colorado — "actual malice." *See, e.g., Diversified Mgt. v. Denver Post*, 653 P.2d 1103 (Colo. 1982); (3) Indiana — which appears to require "actual malice," though court rulings are in some flux. *See, e.g., Journal-Gazette Co. v. Bandido's, Inc.*, 712 N.E.2d 446 (Ind. 1999), *cert. denied*, 528 U.S. 1005 (1999); *See also Beauchamp v. City of Noblesville, Ind.*, 320 F.3d 733, 746 (7th Cir. 2003); *But see Med. Informatics Eng'g, Inc. v. Orthopaedics Northeast, P.C.*, 458 F. Supp. 2d 716, 721, n.3 (N.D. Ind. 2006) ("In the case of a private individual bringing a defamation action over a matter of private concern, only negligence with regard to the truth or falsity of the statement is required."). The following states have apparently not yet settled on a libel standard for private person plaintiffs: (1) Idaho, *See, e.g., Wiemer v. Rankin*, 790 P.2d 347 (Idaho 1990) (courts *seem* to be leaning toward negligence standard); (2) Nebraska, *See, e.g., Hoch v. Prokop*, 507 N.W.2d

626 (Neb. 1993) (something less than "actual malice"); (3) North Dakota (no reported cases).

66 *See Richmond Newspapers v. Lipscomb*, 362 S.E.2d 32 (Va. 1987), *cert. denied*, 486 U.S. 1023 (1988). *But see Harris v. School Annual Publ'g Co.*, 466 So.2d 963 (Ala. 1985) (cartoon published above teacher's name in elementary school yearbook of monkey sitting on swing, holding a banana, with caption "out munching" was not defamatory inference that teacher was somewhere eating when she should have been in classroom or defamatory as a racial insult).

67 *Echtenkamp v. Loudon County Pub. Schs.*, 263 F. Supp. 2d 1043 (E.D.Va. 2003).

68 *Wagner v. Miskin*, 660 N.W.2d 593 (N.D. 2003), *cert. denied*, 540 U.S. 1154 (2004).

69 Neil J. Rosini, The Practical Guide to Libel Law (Praeger Publishers 1991), pp. 9-12.

70 *McDowell v. Paiewonsky*, 769 F.2d 942, 947 (3d Cir. 1985).

71 *Mahoney v. Adirondack Publ'g Co.*, 123 A.D.2d 10, 12, 509 N.Y.S.2d 193 (N.Y. App. Div. 1986) (court opinion used substitute characters for profanity). The newspaper later won the case on appeal when the court ruled the coach failed to show actual malice. 517 N.E.2d 1365, 71 N.Y.2d 31, 14 Media L. Rep. 2200 (N.Y. 1987).

72 *Dill*, supra, note 1 at 114.

73 *See, e.g., Walters v. Linhof*, 559 F. Supp. 1231 (D. Colo. 1983); *Lee v. Paulsen*, 539 P.2d 1079 (Ore. 1975) (en banc); Restatement (Second) of Torts Sec. 583 (1977).

74 *See* Neil J. Rosini, The Practical Guide to Libel Law (Praeger Publishers 1991), p. 129, n.389. Rosini notes three policies that underlie the privilege: (1) the media is thought to act as an agent of the public who have a right to attend and report on the proceedings of information themselves; (2) the theory of "public supervision," which holds that the public should be able to oversee the manner in which public duties are discharged; and (3) the notion of the public's "right-to-know," a concept often noted in freedom of information law. Rosini notes that different judicial decisions have justified the privilege emphasizing different rationales.

75 *Wilson v. Birmingham Post Co.*, 482 So.2d 1209 (Ala. 1986) (privilege applies to article based on police incident report).

76 *Stone v. Banner Publ'g Co.*, 677 F. Supp. 242 (D. Vt. 1988) (privilege does not extend to articles relying on preliminary police investigation, including police incident report).

77 *See, e.g., Heuer v. Kee*, 59 P.2d 1063 (Cal. Ct. App. 2d Dist. 1936) (resolution presented by a parent to a public meeting of the chamber of commerce and board of education privileged); *Stablein v. Schuster*, 455 N.W.2d 315 (Mich. Ct. App. 1989) (contents of a letter read at a board of education meeting were privileged as part of a public and official proceeding; newspaper publishers immune from defamation liability because report of letter was fair and accurate); *Vaadeland v. Indep. Sch. Dist.*, No. C3-99-152, 1999 Minn. App. LEXIS 903 (Minn. Ct. App. April 3, 1999) (statement made at school board meeting was privileged as a matter of public record; defendants not liable for defamation even though the statement was false because the report accurately reflected its source); *Freier v. Indep. Sch. Dist.*, 356 N.W.2d 724 (Minn. Ct. App. 1984) (publication of a school board's written decision resulting from a school board hearing to consider the discharge of a teacher absolutely privileged as a report issuing from a quasi-judicial proceeding); *Weissman v. Mogol*, 462 N.Y.S.2d 383 (N.Y. Sup. Ct. 1983) (parents' petition to board of education is absolutely privileged despite no formal hearing being commenced to consider the petition); *Lent v. Underhill*, 66 N.Y.S. 1086 (N.Y. App. Div. 1900) (report read at a public school meeting, as is a newspaper's fair and accurate publication of it).

78 *Steven H. v. Duval County Sch. Bd.*, No. 99-500-CIV-J-20C, 1999 WL 1427666, 1999 U.S. Dist. LEXIS 23349 (M.D. Fla. Sept. 3, 1999) (statements made by a public high school teacher and football coach privileged), *summary judgment granted in part, denied in part*, 2001 U.S. Dist. LEXIS 25814 (M.D. Fla. May 7, 2001); *Jimenez v. United Fed'n of Teachers*, 657 N.Y.S.2d 672 (App. Div. 1997) (newspaper's publication of statements made by teachers union members was privileged as a substantially true report of an official proceeding), *appeal dismissed*, 684 N.E.2d 283 (N.Y. 1997).

79 *Washington v. Smith*, 80 F.3d 555 (D.C. Cir. 1996).

80 *Mallory v. Ohio Univ.*, 2001 Ohio 8762, 2001 WL 1631329, 2001 Ohio App. LEXIS 5720, (Ohio Ct. App. Dec. 20, 2001), *appeal denied*, 767 N.E.2d 272 (Ohio 2002), *on remand*, 782 N.E.2d 173 (Ohio Ct. Cl. 2002).

81 *Gertz v. Robert Welch, Inc.*, 418 U.S. 323, 339 (1974).

82 *See Epstein v. Bd. of Trustees of Dowling Coll.*, 543 N.Y.S.2d 691 (N.Y. App. Div. 1989), where the court found that a letter to the editor, published in Dowling College's student newspaper, that purported to be a compilation of complaints about a university professor was protected opinion. The letter included the following random comments about the professor: "[L]ying, deceiving, making false promises, not advising, ill advising, misleading, unfair/contradictory grading policies and statements, ludicrous amount of failures, lost time and credits...poor treatment of students, insulting, harassing, limited office hours, long lines of students waiting for extra help...poor teaching abilities, lack of organization, losing assignments."

83 *See, e.g., Ansorian v. Zimmerman*, 627 N.Y.S.2d 706 (N.Y. App. Div. 1995) (oral and written statements by high school student and her parents that alleged that student's teacher was incompetent were protected as "pure opinion"), *cert. denied*, 486 U.S. 1023 (1988). Compare *Richmond Newspapers v. Lipscomb*, 362 S.E.2d 32 (Va. 1987) (story that accused a teacher of being erratic, disorganized, absent from the classroom for extended periods and otherwise unfit to teach was held to be libelous).

84 *Washington*, 80 F.3d at 557.

85 *Milkovich v. Lorain Journal Co.*, 497 U.S. 1 (1990).

86 *Id.* at 18. ("If a speaker says, 'In my opinion John Jones is a liar,' he implies a knowledge of facts which lead to a conclusion that Jones told an untruth.... Simply couching such statements in terms of opinion does not dispel these implications. . . . ").

87 *Id.* at 19.

88 *Id.* at 21.

89 *See Judge finds editorial not defamatory, dismisses libel suit against newspaper*, Student Press Law Center *Report* (Spring 1997), at 35. Though the judge found that the statements in the editorial were protected opinion and not capable of defamatory meaning, he criticized the student newspaper for using

"tasteless language . . . which rings of language sometimes used by fifth-graders at recess."

90 *See, e.g., Milkovich v. Lorain Journal Co.*, 497 U.S. 1 (1990).

91 *Moyer v. Amador Valley Joint Union High Sch. Dist.*, 275 Cal. Rep. 494, 498 (Cal. Ct. App. 1990).

92 *Evarts v. Downey*, 16 Media L. Rep. 2449 (N.Y. Sup. Ct. 1989).

93 *Seelig v. Infinity Broad. Corp.*, 97 Cal.App.4th 798 (Cal. Ct. App. 2002).

94 *Id.*

95 *DeMoya v. Walsh*, 441 So.2d 1120, 1121 (Fla. Dist. Ct. App. 1983).

96 *Weinberg v. Pollock*, 19 Media L. Rep. 1442 (Conn. Super. Ct. 1991).

97 *Levinsky's Inc. v. Wal-Mart Stores, Inc.*, 127 F.3d 122 (1st Cir. 1997) (this case contains an in-depth analysis of the issue of rhetorical hyperbole and the distinction between fact and opinion).

98 *Horsley v. Rivera*, 292 F.3d 695, 697 (11th Cir. 2002).

99 *Mattell, Inc. v. MCA Records, Inc.*, 296 F.3d 894 (9th Cir. 2002), *cert. denied*, 537 U.S. 1171 (2003).

100 *Id.* at 908.

101 *Smith v. McMullen*, 589 F. Supp. 642 (S.D. Tex. 1984).

102 *Flamm v. Am. Ass'n of Univ. Women*, 201 F.3d 144 (2d Cir. 2000).

103 *Spence v. Flynt*, 816 P.2d 771 (Wyo. 1991), *cert. denied*, 503 U.S. 984 (1992).

104 *See Comedian isn't laughing after Ohio State Univ. publication accidentally calls him a drunk*, Chronicle of Higher Educ., January 13, 2000.

105 *Yeagle v. Collegiate Times*, 41 Va. Cir. 448; 1997 Va. Cir. LEXIS 52 (Va. Cir. Ct. 1997).

106 *Yeagle v. Collegiate Times*, 497 S.E.2d 136 (Va. 1998).

107 Marlys Duran, *Cherry Creek grad sues over yearbook slur*, *Rocky Mountain News*, Nov. 1, 1995, at 4A, *available at* 1995 WL 10614873.

108 *See, e.g., Nungaray v. Cuesta College*, No. CV71542 (Cal. Super. Ct. San Luis Obispo County, Sept. 24, 1993) (comic strip depicting college public safety officer as ignoring a burning car to chase down a cyclist riding outside the bike lane not libelous because "average reader would easily recognize the subject as a caricature in comic strip form"); *Stone v. Brooks*, 322 S.E.2d 728 (Ga. 1984) (court upheld libel lawsuit against student editors of the Medical College of Georgia's lampoon newspaper, the Cadaver, for publishing a sarcastic response to the author of a letter to editor — whom the court noted was a married student nurse, two months pregnant at the time — criticizing the publication for its "sick" humor. In part, the response stated: "Our mothers were German shepherds; our fathers were Camels, so naturally we love to hump bitches in heat. Say, Ms. Brooks, when do you come in season?" The court said its result would have been different if the final line in the editor's response had been omitted), *aff'g*, 317 S.E.2d 277 (Ga. Ct. App. 1984); *Salek v. Passaic Collegiate Sch.*, 605 A.2d 276 (N.J. Super. Ct. App. Div. 1992) (publication in section of high school yearbook captioned "The Funny Pages" of a photo of a female teacher next to a male teacher with the caption "Not tonight Ms. Salek, I have a headache" cannot be libelous or invasive of privacy because photo was clearly understood as parody and no reasonable person could believe them to be factual); *Havalunch, Inc. v. Mazza*, 294 S.E.2d 70 (W.Va. 1981) (court dismissed libel lawsuit against student newspaper reporter who wrote tongue-in-cheek restaurant reviews for paper that read: "HAVALUNCH — Bring a can of Raid if you plan to eat here. And paint your neck red: looks like a truck stop. You'll regret everything you eat here, especially the BLT's" because "the total tone of the story was one of humor and overstatement which would be obvious to any reasonable reader." *Id.* at 72); *See also Murray v. Bd. of Trustees of the Univ. of Louisville*, 659 F.2d 77 (6th Cir. 1981) (allowing First Amendment claim by editor of student newspaper fired for publishing April Fools' issue that court said contained cartoons and articles that "arguably" might have been libelous).

109 *Frank v. Nat'l Broad. Co.*, 119 A.D.2d 252, 257 (N.Y. App. Div. 1986) (quoting *Donoghue v. Hayes*, 1831 Hayes Exch 265, 266 (1831) (Ireland)), *appeal granted*, 69 N.Y.2d 607, 507 N.E.2d 320 (N.Y. 1987), *appeal withdrawn*, 70 N.Y.2d 641, 512 N.E.2d 558 (N.Y. 1987).

110 *Milkovich v. Lorain Journal Co.*, 497 U.S. 1, 20 (1990) (statements that "cannot 'reasonably be interpreted as stating actual facts' about an individual," such as rhetorical hyperbole, are protected from libel actions); *Pring v. Penthouse Int'l, Ltd.*, 695 F.2d 438 (10th Cir. 1982) (story describing the outlandish sexual talents of a fictional "Miss Wyoming" could not be the basis for a libel suit brought by a real Miss Wyoming), *cert. denied* 462 U.S. 1132 (1983); *See also Hustler Magazine v. Falwell*, 485 U.S. 46 (1988) (U.S. Supreme Court rejected claim of intentional infliction of emotional distress brought by Rev. Jerry Falwell for ad parody that facetiously asserted that Falwell's first sexual experience was with his mother in an outhouse and that he regularly drank Campari liquor before preaching. A jury earlier rejected a libel claim on the ground that no reasonable person would believe the cartoon described actual facts.).

111 *Walko v. Kean Coll. of N.J.*, 561 A.2d 680 (N.J. Super. Ct. Law Div. 1988).

112 *Id.* at 683.

113 *Id.* at 684, citing *Falwell*, 485 U.S. at 46.

114 For an eye-opening example of a court's utter lack of humor, *see New Times, Inc. v. Isaacks*, 91 S.W.3d 844 (Tex. App. 2002), rev'd, 146 S.W.3d 144 (Tex. 2004), *cert. denied*, 545 U.S. 1105 (2005). In that case a Texas appellate court refused to dismiss a libel case filed against the publisher of a satirical article about a 6-year-old being arrested, shackled and jailed for 10 days for writing a book report on Maurice Sendak's classic children's tale, *Where the Wild Things Are*. Among other things, the story "quoted" the child's purported reaction to the charge that the book could corrupt children's minds: "Like I'm sure. It's bad enough people think like Salinger and Twain are dangerous, but Sendak? Give me a break, for Christ's sake. Excuse my French." Said the funny-boneless judge: "A reasonable reader could find this story to be believable." 91 S.W.3d at 859.

115 *Ex-student gets $5,001 in McLain libel suit*, Tulsa Tribune, Nov. 8, 1990; *see also Tulsa School District Loses Libel Suit*, Student Press Law Center *Report* (Winter 1990-91), at 33.

116 *See San Francisco Bay Guardian, Inc. v. Superior Court*, 21 Cal. Rptr.2d 464 (Cal. Ct. App. 1993) (fake letter to editor published in April Fools' issue of newspaper that was printed upside down and labeled "special parody section" could not support a libel claim because average reader would recognize that letter was published in jest), *review denied*, 1993 Cal. LEXIS 5847 (Cal. 1993).

117 *See, e.g., Garvelink v. Detroit News*, 522 N.W.2d 883 (Mich. App. 1994), *appeal denied*, 534 N.W.2d 530 (Mich. 1995). In that case, a Michigan court dismissed a libel suit filed by real-life school superintendent Roger Garvelink against the *Detroit News*, which had published a spoof interview with a fictitious superintendent named Roger Gravelhead. The satirical interview, published on the newspaper's editorial page, contained a series of questions and answers about a recent school levy defeat and its effect. Among the fictional superintendent's responses to the levy defeat was a plan to enact "punishment cuts" to "make the kids hurt and the parents howl." The court noted that in this area of parodies, political cartoons, and satirical columns, especially involving public officials, while the tenor of the column may be caustic or even vicious, the Supreme Court has clearly recognized that "[t]he sort of robust political debate encouraged by the First Amendment is bound to produce speech that is critical of those who hold public office or those who are 'intimately involved in the resolution of important public questions....'" *Id.* at 887 (citing *Hustler Magazine v. Falwell*, 108 S.Ct. 876, 879 (1988)).

118 Gilbert Cranberg, *Fanning the Fire: The Media's Role in Libel Litigation*, 71 Iowa L. Rev. 221 (1985).

119 Adapted from Mike Hiestand, "It's the Law: Responding to Libel Complaints," *Trends in College Media* (July 2002), Associated Collegiate Press.

120 Daniel Moore, "Rarely used statute in Vermont helps student journalists escape a frivolous libel lawsuit," SPLC *News Flash, available at* http://www.splc.org/news/newsflash.asp?id=2510.

121 *Haywood v. St. Michael's College*, Civ. Action No. 2:12-CV-164, 33 (D. Vt. Dec. 14, 2012).

122 States with anti-SLAPP statutes are: Arizona, Arkansas, California, Delaware, District of Columbia, Florida, Guam, Georgia, Hawaii, Illinois, Indiana, Louisiana, Maine, Maryland, Massachusetts, Missouri, Nebraska, Nevada, New Mexico, New York, Oklahoma, Oregon, Pennsylvania, Rhode Island, Tennessee, Texas, Utah, Vermont, and Washington state. *See* Harvard University Berkman Center Digital Media Law Project, "Responding to Strategic Lawsuits Against Public Participation (SLAPPs)," Feb. 4, 2013, *available at* http://www.dmlp.org/legal-guide/responding-strategic-lawsuits-against-public-participation-slapps (last viewed Aug. 22, 2013).

123 Brian Schraum, "Judge dismisses teacher's libel suit against student newspaper," SPLC *News Flash*, Aug. 12, 2010, *available at* http://www.splc.org/news/newsflash.asp?id=2124.

124 12 Am. Jur. Legal Forms 2d *Libel and Slander* Sec. 163:4 (2002).

125 50 Am. Jur. 2d *Libel and Slander* Sec. 346 (2002).

126 Laura Lee Prather, "Texas Adopts the Defamation Mitigation Act," Freedom of Information Foundation of Texas, June 21, 2013, *available at* http://www.foift.org/transparency/texas-adopts-the-defamation-mitigation-act/ (last visited Aug. 22, 2013). For more information, see Sack on Defamation: Libel, Slander and Related Probs., Sec. 11.2 (Practising Law Institute 2001).

127 In August 1993 the National Conference of Commissioners on Uniform State Laws gave its final approval to the "Uniform Correction or Clarification of Defamation Act." The Act attempts to both reduce legal costs and protect reputation by encouraging retractions, thereby resolving libel claims without extended litigation. In February 1994, the American Bar Association endorsed the Act, paving the way for its consideration by Congress and state legislatures. (H. Kaufman, *LDRC Special Report: The Potential Reform of State Retraction Law Under the Uniform Correction of Clarification of Defamation Act,* 1993.)

128 Byron, D. and McGinley, J., *Libel Defense Resource Center Pre-Publication/Pre-Broadcast Committee Reports on: Note Retention Policies of Reporters and Use of "Advice of Counsel" as a Defense by Reporters* (Sept. 24, 2002).

CHAPTER 13

Invasion of Privacy

The legal right of privacy has been defined as the right to be let alone, the right of a person "to withhold himself and his property from public scrutiny if he so chooses."[1] Privacy, however, is not a right explicitly guaranteed by the United States Constitution. In fact, as legal claims go, invasion of privacy is relatively new, being traced back to a 1890 *Harvard Law Review* article written by Samuel D. Warren and his then law partner Louis D. Brandeis, who would later serve on the U.S. Supreme Court.[2] Responding to the yellow press that peddled sensationalism, the two maintained that privacy claims were necessary to protect private people from "mental pain and distress far greater than could be inflicted by mere bodily injury."[3]

If Warren and Brandeis were disturbed by the sensationalistic newspapers of the late 1800s, one can only imagine their reaction to the media-saturated 21st century. In our Information and Internet Age — where comprehensive and sometimes intimate details about a person's life are often just a mouse click away — personal privacy has become an increasingly controversial topic.

Over the last 100-plus years, invasion of privacy law has developed into four different legal claims: (1) Public Disclosure of Private and Embarrassing Facts, (2) Intrusion Upon Seclusion, (3) False Light and (4) Misappropriation. The last two have little to do with "privacy," as most people would think of the term. False light claims resemble defamation claims in that a person is complaining that he has been portrayed inaccurately. Misappropriation typically involves the use of a person's name or likeness in advertising without consent. On the other hand, intrusion upon seclusion claims and public disclosure of private fact claims are brought by those who believe that their personal privacy has been violated.

> Their are four types of invasion of privacy claims:
> • Public disclosure of private and embarrassing facts
> • Intrusion
> • False light
> • Misappropriation

PUBLIC DISCLOSURE OF PRIVATE AND EMBARRASSING FACTS

This is probably the most troublesome and important type of invasion of privacy for student journalists to understand. Americans hold dear their constitutionally protected right to freely speak (or write) what is on their minds. But Americans are also increasingly protective of their right to control access to their private lives, to do their own thing without anyone else peeking over their shoulders. When these two rights conflict, a privacy lawsuit may be filed to resolve the dispute. Indeed, at their core, all public disclosure cases address one very important — and complicated — question: at what point does the right to publish truthful information about a person give way to his right to be left alone, free from embarrassment or unwanted publicity? Consider the following example.

FROM THE SPLC CASE FILES

In 1977, Toni Ann Diaz became the first woman ever elected student body president of the College of Alameda, a two-year public community college just outside Oakland, California. Some time after taking office Diaz accused college officials of improperly withdrawing money from a student activity fund by affixing her signature to checks with a rubber stamp. *The Oakland Tribune* and the *Reporter*, the college's student newspaper, covered the dispute.

Not long after the story appeared, a columnist for the *Oakland Tribune* received a tip that Toni Ann Diaz was actually born Antonio Diaz. Confidential sources confirmed — and Diaz later acknowledged — that she was a transsexual who had undergone a sex change operation several years earlier. Since the operation, Diaz had gone to great lengths to keep her secret, which was known only by her family. Before enrolling at Alameda she had changed her name on her high school records and her driver's license and had attempted to have her birth certificate changed.

Having satisfied himself that the information about Diaz was true, the *Tribune* reporter published the information in his column.

Diaz sued the reporter and the *Tribune* for invading her privacy.[4]

As you consider the above example, ask yourself where you would draw the line. Would Diaz's past sexual identity ever be of legitimate public concern? Would it make any difference to your answer if Diaz had been the mayor of Oakland instead of a college student government president? What if she were the state's first woman governor? What if Diaz had made an issue of a political opponent's gender? What if she were an Olympic athlete? Most people can probably imagine circumstances that would make a private fact, such as Diaz's sex change operation, something that the public had a bona fide reason in knowing. But where to draw the line?

Courts are in the business of having to draw such lines. And in their attempt to sort out the competing rights in an invasion of privacy case, most courts in jurisdictions that recognize a private facts claim (not all do[5]) have settled on one key question: is the information newsworthy? If the information is a matter of public interest or concern, then there cannot be a claim for public disclosure of private facts, regardless of how embarrassing the information.

Before a news organization would have to defend itself against a privacy lawsuit by arguing that a story was newsworthy, however, the person claiming his privacy was invaded must convince the court that the information involved met three requirements: It must be:

(1) Sufficiently private. Information about a person that is already known by those outside a person's small circle of family and friends or information that could easily and lawfully be discovered will generally not support a private facts privacy claim. For example, a person making a privacy claim will have a difficult time winning her case if she has voluntarily revealed — by words or actions — the alleged "private" information to a number of other people. In addition, material that can lawfully be obtained from public records will rarely be considered private.[6] Generally, any public court record or open court testimony is in the public domain, including details of divorce proceedings or criminal prosecutions for everything from drunk driving to murder.[7] Even information contained in sealed or confidential government records usually can be published safely as long as the reporter did nothing unlawful to obtain the information.[8]

In one of the few privacy suits involving a college publication, the Vanderbilt University student newspaper was sued after reporting on a privacy and libel suit filed against the campus humor magazine. The magazine had been sued for invasion of privacy and libel by the father of a four-year-old girl for publishing his daughter's photograph and a caption, which the father claimed implied that his daughter was "amenable to acts of illicit sexual intercourse." Even though the paper's news account reprinted the disputed magazine page, the Tennessee Supreme Court ruled that it was not an invasion of privacy because the photograph was already a matter of public record, having been included in papers filed with the court in the first lawsuit.[9]

Other types of public records that courts have permitted to be publicized include: motor vehicle registration records,[10] military service records,[11] birth certificates,[12] salaries of public employees,[13] applications for public employment,[14] licenses authorizing the possession of concealed weapons,[15] autopsy reports of murder victims[16] and lists of delinquent real estate taxpayers.[17]

In the context of schools, courts have permitted to be publicized a teacher's sick leave record,[18] allegations by students and parents concerning a teacher's conduct that are submitted to the state board of education,[19] portions of letters between a high school and the state's interscholastic athletic conference concerning violations of conference regulations by the school's football team,[20] the nature of a school board's disciplinary action against school officials,[21] the names of applicants for a school superintendent position,[22] and the names and salaries of individual teachers in a school district.[23] (Note that these cases involve the right to publish information lawfully obtained, not the right under state open-records laws to obtain the documents in the first place. The two bodies of law are not necessarily equivalent. In other words, the fact that a document contains matters of public record that can be published without unlawfully invading privacy does not guarantee that the government can be forced to turn over the document.)

On the other hand, grade transcripts, student evaluations, medical histories and information obtained from personal correspondence or similar private sources, such as a diary or private e-mails, are generally not matters of public record. Consequently, disclosing this information might give rise to a claim for invasion of privacy. Also, a handful of courts have suggested that a matter of public record might lose its protected status over time where the information is no longer "newsworthy,"[24] although this now appears to be the minority view.[25]

(2) Sufficiently intimate: Personal habits, details or history that a person ordinarily does not reveal are at the center of a private facts complaint. Sensational stories that address a person's sexual behavior, medical/psychological history or financial affairs should be carefully reviewed. Student "gossip columns" can be a dangerous source of invasion of privacy lawsuits. While "inquiring minds" may want to know who is romancing whom, how late a couple stayed out Saturday night or what student cannot afford a new prom dress because her mother was just laid off from work, such information could seriously embarrass the subject of the gossip.

(3) Highly offensive: The revealed information must be more than just annoying, bothersome or mildly embarrassing to the person who is claiming an invasion of privacy — it must be information that would humiliate or seriously offend an average person if it were revealed. Reporting that an adult likes to watch cartoons secretly every Saturday morning may mildly embarrass a person; reporting that he likes to watch hard-core pornography every Saturday night may humiliate him. Note that the character and tone of the story and the motivation of the publisher can also play a role in determining whether a piece of information is highly offensive.

OBTAINING MEDICAL INFORMATION: HIPAA

When people are hurt in an accident or get sick, especially when they are well known, it is often news. But a federal privacy law, the "Health Insurance Portability and Accountability Act of 1996,"[26] better known by its acronym, HIPAA, is often misused to obstruct journalists' attempts to obtain newsworthy information.

Part of the law limits the ability of health care providers, insurance companies, medical billing companies and the business associates of such groups (for example, a hospital's accounting firm) from providing protected "health information" about an identifiable patient without that patient's consent.[27] The Department of Health and Human Services adopted regulations implementing HIPAA that took effect in 2003.[28] Among the records required to be kept confidential by HIPAA: physical or mental health information created or received by a health care provider or public health authority, health care claims and attachments, insurance applications and health care payment information. The law also limits the disclosure of physical or mental health information created or received by a school or university.[29] Violations of HIPAA can result in fines and/or jail time.

While HIPAA does prohibit some previously available sources from providing medical information

Journalists that lawfully obtain and publish medical information about an individual do not violate the Health Insurance Portability and Accountability Act (HIPAA).

to reporters, it does not close down the information pipeline entirely as some apparently believe. (Indeed, there is at least some reason to believe HIPAA does not apply whatsoever to medical information that appears in a public record, because HIPAA allows for the release of otherwise-protected medical information when release is "required by law," and a public records law should certainly qualify as a "requirement."[30])

HIPAA restricts the release of health information only by "covered entities," a finite group defined by regulation.[31] Journalists are not "covered entities," and student reporters who lawfully obtain and publish medical information about an individual do not violate HIPAA. The journalist is protected even when the information is obtained from a "covered entity," unless the journalist improperly induced the source to break the law. (Of course, the traditional law regarding invasion of privacy still applies.) HIPAA does not prohibit student journalists from asking questions of health care providers or patients or engaging in other lawful newsgathering efforts, such as taking photographs or video of a hospital or accident scene from a public street or sidewalk.

HIPAA also does not apply to most other government service providers not engaged in healthcare. For example, law enforcement agencies and fire departments are not "covered entities" and HIPAA does not prohibit disclosure of police or fire incident reports. Similarly, court records that contain medical information, autopsy records and courthouse birth and death records are not affected and continue to be available as required by a state open records law. Family members, witnesses to an accident, clubs and associations and religious organizations can also provide medical information to reporters without violating HIPAA.

Even where health care information is protected it can always be released with a patient's consent, or a parent's consent if the patient is a minor. In addition, the law allows health care providers to release limited "directory information" about a patient after that patient has been given the opportunity to restrict the disclosure of this information, which usually occurs during the admissions process.[32] Where a patient has not objected, the hospital can then confirm for a reporter the patient's name and provide his location in the hospital and general condition (for example: "good," "fair," "serious," "critical," or "treated and released").

Finally, HIPAA applies only to "individually identifiable health information." So while a school nurse or a university medical clinic is a "covered entity," HIPAA would not prevent them, for example, from providing anonymous statistical information about the number of students treated for the flu or the number of students seeking birth control information.

While HIPAA does provide some new hurdles to medical reporting, it is not the towering obstacle that some claim. Knowing where the lines are drawn should help reporters navigate the HIPAA maze.

WATCH OUT FOR BODY PARTS!

On occasion, student media have found themselves in the hot seat for inadvertently publishing photographs that reveal a bit more of a subject than either the subject or the photographer intended. Sports photos, in particular, should be carefully reviewed for "wandering" body parts. While these photos usually do not result in liability (provided they are unintentional, otherwise "newsworthy" and taken in a public area), they are embarrassing and can generate litigation threats.[33]

THE "NEWSWORTHINESS" DEFENSE

Where revealed information meets each of the above requirements, it will then be up to the news organization to argue that its publication of the information should nevertheless be protected because it is newsworthy.[34] As any media lawyer will tell you, however, "newsworthiness" can be a slippery concept to grasp.

Courts have often given the news media wide latitude to decide what is newsworthy. For example, in a fairly widely followed decision, one federal appeals court recognized "a broad constitutional privilege" to publish matters of "public interest," which the court found "extends to information concerning interesting phases of human activity and embraces all issues about which information is needed or appropriate so that individuals may cope with the exigencies of their period."[35]

Such broad pronouncements aside, however, there are limits. California courts, for example, have been particularly reluctant to defer to the media on the issue of newsworthiness and have balanced the social value in information against the interest of the individual in maintaining privacy. For example, in the *Diaz* case, discussed above, the court weighed three factors in its attempt to determine whether a college student government president's history as a transsexual was "newsworthy":

> (1) the social value of the facts published;
> (2) the depth of the article's intrusion in ostensibly private affairs; and
> (3) the extent to which the party voluntarily acceded to a position of public notoriety.

Additionally, a more recent California decision added a fourth prong to the *Diaz* test. It requires that:

> (4) a logical connection exists between the events or activities that brought the person into the public eye and the particular facts disclosed by the news report.[36]

Truth is not a defense in a private facts privacy case.

A number of other courts appear to follow the similar definition of "newsworthiness" set forth in the *Restatement (Second) of Torts* Sec. 652D:

"[A]ccount must be taken of the customs and conventions of the community; and in the last analysis what is proper becomes a matter of the community mores. The line is to be drawn when the publicity ceases to be the giving of information to which the public is entitled, and becomes a morbid and sensational prying into private lives for its own sake, with which a reasonable member of the public, with decent standards, would say that we had no concern."[37]

And, also like California, some of these courts have refined the Restatement's definition by asking whether there is a logical relationship between the events or activities that brought the person into the public eye and the particular facts[38] For example, the revelation that a person had been in rehab for alcoholism might be relevant to that person's appointment to judicial office, but not to the person's victory in the local flower show.

One factor that has weighed against finding that a story is newsworthy is the passage of time. In 1971, a California court found that it was an invasion of privacy to expose a rehabilitated man's crime of truck hijacking eleven years after its commission, but this holding was overruled by the California Supreme Court in 2004. In California today, published information about criminal proceedings that was obtained from public records is protected by the First Amendment.[39] Indeed, other recent court decisions suggest that the passage of time will not defeat a claim of newsworthiness, particularly where the information can be obtained from public records.[40]

While a finding of newsworthiness will always depend on the specific facts of a given situation, the following types of stories have been held to be newsworthy: reports on criminal activity,[41] suicide,[42] marriage,[43] divorce,[44] accidents,[45] the abandonment of a newborn baby at a hospital,[46] death from narcotics,[47] records of campus parking violations,[48] runaway youth,[49] arrests,[50] police raids,[51] a graphic description of an attack on a high school student by other students while on school grounds[52] and a television report identifying a college student who worked as a nude dancer in a nightclub where illegal activities took place.[53]

A famous example of a story that was found not to be newsworthy occurred when an Alabama woman successfully sued a newspaper that published a photo of her emerging from a carnival funhouse with her dress blown above her waist.[54] The woman probably would have lost the suit if she had been jumping from a burning building rather than walking out of a funhouse.

A more troubling case for the student media upheld a verdict against a newspaper that had published a story concerning teenage pregnancies. The newspaper had accurately identified the individual who claimed his privacy was invaded as the teenage father of an illegitimate child.[55]

Information about a well-known public figure or a public official will usually be considered newsworthy. For example, if an individual is running for public office, it is permissible to publicize information that may be damaging or embarrassing, which relates to her potential performance in office. Note, however, that even celebrities and other well-known figures retain some privacy rights about the most private and intimate details of their lives.[56]

A private person's life is less open to scrutiny, but his secrets may be newsworthy and reportable when they are closely connected to a significant public issue.

As a general rule, the deceased have no right to privacy; the right dies with the person.[57] Heirs cannot file suit on behalf of a deceased person, although some states make exceptions for misappropriation or right of publicity claims.[58]

The First Amendment protects the right of journalists to use the names of minors in newsworthy stories as long as the information is "lawfully obtained" and "truthfully" reported.

PUBLISHING THE NAMES AND PHOTOS OF MINORS

Good high school journalists take seriously the obligation to cover their peers in meaningful ways. As student publications struggle to provide both a voice for other students and serve as a watchdog of student misbehavior, many reporters and editors are facing challenges when it comes to telling student stories that some would prefer not be told. A growing number of young journalists are being asked by school administrators to leave out of their stories information that identifies individual students. And many, questioning the wisdom and legality of these restrictions, have begun to ask why.

What the Courts Say

In a unanimous 1979 decision, the U.S. Supreme Court ruled in *Smith v. Daily Mail* that the First Amendment protects the right of journalists to use the names of minors in newsworthy stories as long as the information is "lawfully obtained" and "truthfully" reported.[59] In that case, the Court struck down a West Virginia law that had been used to prosecute two West Virginia newspapers that printed the name of a 14-year-old junior high school student alleged to have shot and killed a 15-year-old classmate.

Following the *Daily Mail* ruling, other courts have, for example, ruled that newspapers can publish the name of a minor charged with unauthorized use of a motor vehicle and hit-and-run driving,[60] the name of a juvenile who was kidnapped and sexually assaulted,[61] the name of a high school student viciously attacked by his classmates at school,[62] the name and photograph of a 12-year-old who was charged with the attempted murder of a police officer,[63] the names of juveniles who testified in a trial in which the adult defendants were charged with supplying alcohol to minors,[64] the photograph of a minor child taken while in the arms of her mother on the courthouse steps following a much-publicized paternity hearing[65] and the name and course of mental health treatment of an individual convicted of sexual assault when he was 14, but who was no longer a minor at the time of publication.[66]

Even where a court proceeding or government record can be lawfully closed by government officials, courts generally have said that the government may not restrict the press from publishing newsworthy information contained in such records or proceedings — including minors' names — when such information has been lawfully obtained through other means.[67] However, where a reporter agrees to confidentiality ahead of time in exchange for access to information that would otherwise be off-limits, that agreement must generally be honored.

For example, in most states juvenile court proceedings and records can be closed to the public. Some states also allow judges to close the portions of adult trials that require juvenile testimony or evidence. In such cases, the decision whether to allow access is often left to the discretion of the judge. As a result, judges have occasionally placed conditions on reporters' access to otherwise closed juvenile proceedings by allowing reporters in — but only after they have promised not to disclose certain information about minor participants that might be revealed during the proceeding. Such conditions are probably valid.[68]

But even in such cases, the power of judges to restrict press coverage is limited. For example, a California appellate court struck down an order that prohibited reporters admitted to a juvenile custody proceeding from revealing virtually any information about the minors involved, including a ban on interviewing the minors without an attorney present, interviewing their caretakers with the minors present, interviewing any mental health professional to whom the minors had been referred or "doing any act in the future that might interfere with reunification or have a negative impact upon the providing of reunification services." While the media could have been denied access to the proceeding altogether, the appeals court said, it was beyond the juvenile court's power to restrict the press's right to investigate and publish information it had lawfully obtained outside of the courtroom.[69]

Despite the Supreme Court's clear ruling in *Daily Mail* and the lower court cases that have followed, the misconception that juvenile names are strictly "off-limits" persists. Student journalists continue to battle — and educate — school officials over their right to publish student names or other identifying information as part of their regular news coverage. This seems to be particularly true when students seek to publish "student information" (information about student grades, discipline, etc.) or when they publish online.

Of course, the same invasion of privacy rules that limit the publication of identifying information about adults in certain situations apply to information about minors as well.[70] But these limitations are based on restrictions that apply to all, not just minors.

Student Information and FERPA

Many school officials — predominately at the high school level — have become needlessly squeamish about allowing student journalists to publish information about their classmates. In some cases, they have even required parents to sign consent forms before a child's name or photo can be published in student-edited media. In rare instances, they have simply banned the use of student names or photos entirely. Often, they justify their censorship or restrictions by pointing to a federal law known as the Family Educational Rights and Privacy Act (FERPA), also sometimes called the Buckley Amendment.[71] While their intentions in such cases is usually not sinister, their interpretation of the law is misguided.

FERPA was enacted in 1974 after Congress found that some school officials were mishandling student records. The law has two parts. First, the law requires that students and parents be given access to the students' own school records. Second — and this is the provision that causes most of the confusion — FERPA penalizes schools that indiscriminately release certain student "education records" to third parties.

Where the policies directed at student media miss the mark is that FERPA restricts the release of information only by school officials or those acting for them. Outside parties — including student reporters, who are neither state actors, employees nor agents of the school[72] — are not restricted by the law. Unfortunately, school and government officials sometimes do not understand — or simply choose to ignore — this distinction.

While it is entirely appropriate, for example, that school districts create a policy regarding a principal's disclosure of protected student information to a student reporter (or anyone else) during

The Family Educational Rights and Privacy Act (FERPA) restricts the release of information only by school officials or those acting for them. Outside parties — including student reporters — are not restricted by the law.

an interview, it is wrong for the school to impose the same limitations on student-edited media, prohibiting them from disclosing to their readers accurate information lawfully obtained during the newsgathering process. Despite the claims of some school officials, any policy that imposes a flat ban on the publication of accurate, newsworthy and lawfully obtained information by student-edited media would almost certainly be unconstitutional.[73]

For example, in the only published court decision to address the issue, a New York federal court refused to extend FERPA to cover the release of student information published in a high school student newspaper, ruling "the prohibitions of the [FERPA] amendment cannot be deemed to extend to information which is derived from a source independent of school records."[74]

Limiting permissible news coverage to "approved" students destroys the student media's ability to pursue the news. It also creates a logistical nightmare, forcing staff to consult an ever-changing master list of "approved" students who had consented to coverage before writing or publishing a story about them or including their photo in the yearbook. Under such a complicated scheme it is inevitable that students or school officials will make mistakes. "Unapproved" names or photos invariably will be published and "approved" students mistakenly omitted from student publications such as the yearbook. Such mistakes could expose a school district to liability — or certainly accusations of incompetence — that had previously not existed.

Student news organizations have published millions of individual publications — full of student names and photos — without incident. In FERPA's 35-plus years in force, no school has ever been fined under the law because of anything published in a student publication. It is unclear why school district lawyers and administrators now believe it necessary to enforce such policy changes. FERPA does not require it, the Constitution almost certainly prohibits it — and common sense suggests straining the law to cover student journalism is fraught with problems and just plain foolish.

Online Publications

From the moment the first high school student media websites went online in the mid-1990's, school officials began imposing special restrictions on their use by student journalists. Among the more common restrictions were limitations, or outright bans, on the posting of student photos or names in the online version of student-edited publications. Such policies were often justified by pointing to some unspecified privacy or safety concern, often accompanied by a blanket claim that the law required such restrictions.[75]

In fact, there are no federal laws that require school officials to prohibit or restrict student journalists from publishing the names or photos of students in their online publications when that information is lawfully obtained, accurate and newsworthy.[76] Only two states, New Jersey and Maine, are known as of August 2013 to have state statutes that restrict the use of students' photos with the full names on school-hosted websites without advance parental permission.[77] With the exception of those states, any information that can be published lawfully in the print version of a publication can be published lawfully online as well. And contrary to all the dire warnings, there remains no hard evidence to suggest that online student publications pose any more of a danger to students than their print counterparts.[78] But a fear of the unknown has always accompanied the introduction of new technology and media and, until the dust settles, battles over online publishing are regrettable, but probably inevitable.

Besides merely being silly, restrictive online publishing policies could have serious legal implications for the student media and school districts. Every libel law primer begins with essentially the same advice: publish only complete and accurate information. By requiring the publication of misleading or incomplete information, a strong argument can be made that the policies prohibiting the use of full names or other identifiers like photos increase, not decrease, the odds that student media — and possibly the school district that created such a faulty system — will be subjected to libel or invasion of privacy lawsuits because of misidentifications created from the confusion. Such polices — which have been criticized by various journalism groups[79] — also hurt an online publication's reputation as a serious and credible news source.

The Decision to Publish or Not Publish

Even though there generally should be no across-the-board legal barriers to student media publishing minor names — in print or online — there sometimes are valid reasons for not doing so voluntarily. For example, many news organizations do not, as a rule, publish the names of young people accused of less serious crimes. Children, the thinking goes, should not be stigmatized for the rest of their lives for an error in judgment they made while growing up.

The Poynter Institute's Al Tompkins, who has written widely on media ethics, has created a useful list of questions and factors that student journalists may want to consider when deciding whether to identify juveniles, particularly those involved in criminal activities. Among them: (1) Who is served by identifying the juvenile? (2) How newsworthy is the story? (3) What is the juvenile's history? (4) Would others be harmed if the minor was not named or if rumors were allowed to circulate unchecked?[80]

The decision about when and how to identify young people involved in news stories can sometimes be tough. In the end, the decision should be an editorial and ethical choice — not one dictated by law.

FALSE LIGHT

Simply stated, a false light claim can arise anytime you unflatteringly portray — in words or pictures — a person as something that he or she is not. While lumped together with other invasion of privacy suits, it is really more like a libel claim. Both involve complaints based on a false report. The major difference between the two is that a libel complaint requires that the statement in question "defames," or seriously injures a person's reputation. A statement in a false light claim, on the other hand, need only be "highly offensive" to a reasonable person.

For a time it was thought that a statement need only be false for the subject of the statement to bring a false light claim. Under that view, even a compliment could be actionable if it was untrue. Today, the prevailing standard seems to be reflected in the *Restatement (Second) of Torts*, Section 652E, which defines the elements of a false light claim as follows:

> "One who gives publicity to a matter concerning another that places the other before the public in a false light is subject to liability to the other for invasion of his privacy, if: (a) the false light in which the other was placed would be highly offensive to a reasonable person, and (b) the actor had knowledge of or acted in reckless disregard as to the falsity of the publicized matter and the false light in which the other would be placed."[81]

Some of the more common situations that have prompted false light claims include:

(1) Publishing a photo with an incorrect or misleading caption (for example, labeling a bystander an actual participant in a photo of a Ku Klux Klan demonstration) or using the wrong photo to illustrate a story (for example, incorrectly publishing an old yearbook photo of "John Doe" (Class of 1996) to illustrate a story on the arrest of "Jonathan Doe" (Class of 1998);[82]

(2) Attributing to individuals political or other views that they do not hold (for example, incorrectly stating that an abortion opponent is a member of a pro-choice organization);

(3) Careless cropping or digital alteration of a photograph (for example, cutting off or exaggerating part of a subject's body so that he appears deformed);

(4) Use of an individual's photograph or remarks out of context (for example, use of

> A false light claim can arise anytime you unflatteringly portray a person as something that he is not.

an old file photo or video of a randomly photographed student as "filler" to illustrate a feature story on "Alcoholism on Campus");

(5) The intentional fictionalization or embellishment of the life or activities of an identifiable person (for example, a docudrama or biography in which the creator makes up events, thoughts, quotations and attitudes involving the subject);

(6) Falsely attributing to an individual authorship of certain writings or remarks (for example, printing a letter to the editor with the wrong or forged name attached or careless editing of a letter so that the author's views are misconstrued);

(7) Falsely attributing to a person certain actions or motivations (for example, manipulating a photo to show individual engaged in an activity in which he did not actually participate).[83]

More than the other three types of invasion of privacy claims, the law regarding false light is in a period of flux. While the majority of states recognize false light claims, a minority of states do not.[84] And some states have rules that require a plaintiff to sue for either false light or libel, not both.

In 2004, the Colorado Supreme Court held that a claim for false light does not exist under Colorado law.[85] Likewise, the Florida Supreme Court decided in 2008 that a right to sue for false light was unnecessarily duplicative of other legal claims, and also raised First Amendment problems.[86] On the other hand, in 2007, the Ohio Supreme Court held that false light claims are allowed under Ohio law.[87] If you are involved in a false light situation, contact a local media-law attorney or the Student Press Law Center to find out what the law is in your state.

Where a false light claim is allowed, the Supreme Court has established some important constitutional limitations that help protect the public's interest in a free press. Since 1967, plaintiffs in false light suits have been required to show that the defendant was at fault in printing the false statement. Just like in a libel case, a public person must show that a media defendant either knew the statement was false when he published it or had serious reservations about the accuracy of the statement but published it anyway, i.e., "actual malice."[88] The Supreme Court has not clearly answered the question of whether a different standard should apply to a false light claim brought by a private figure, and lower courts have been divided on the issue.[89]

FROM THE SPLC CASE FILES

Deadline was less than an hour away. The photograph of empty beer cans that was supposed to illustrate the front-page story in the Campus Life section about student alcohol abuse was nowhere to be found. Needing something — anything — to fill the void, the layout editor desperately hunted through the photo morgue file. She came up with a three-year-old photo of students in a campus bar, drinks in some of their hands. Skipping a photo caption, she made deadline. A couple of days later, a woman called the newsroom, upset and angry. The caller demanded to know why some of her old college friends, who had seen or heard about the photo in the newspaper, had called to ask about her "drinking problem."

INTRUSION

In the pages of fiction, the intrepid reporter stops at nothing to get her story.

Disguised as an "insider," armed with a telephoto lens, a hidden audio "bug" taped under her sweater and a stolen key to open the safe where the incriminating evidence is hidden

— she will not be denied. So goes the myth. In fact, if our mythical reporter had to work in the real world she would probably be sued for invasion of privacy based on intrusion. Intrusion, unlike the other three forms of invasion of privacy, concerns itself not with the news or information that is reported but with how a reporter gathers that news in the first place. This type of invasion of privacy can occur when a zealous reporter uses some type of eavesdropping device, voice recorder or camera to record a person's private life without permission. It also occurs by misrepresenting oneself to gain access to a private person or place or by trespassing upon private property. Significantly, a reporter can be sued even when he does not publish the information he obtained. The improper "newsgathering act" is itself the basis for the suit. On the other hand, even where a reporter is guilty of intrusion, the information he has obtained can sometimes still be legally published (if, for example, it is "newsworthy").[90] The law treats the "news" and the "newsgathering act" separately.

The idea in an intrusion case is fairly simple: when a person is in a place where she has a reasonable right to expect privacy, a reporter must respect that right. Reporters are given no special privilege to gather the news.[91] Determining when a person has such a "reasonable expectation of privacy" is sometimes an easy call for a reporter to make. For example, a couple cannot reasonably expect privacy while walking through (or even "making out" in) a crowded campus plaza. They are, in a legal sense, fair game for photographers and journalists who wish to report what they do and say during their walk.[92] At the other extreme, the couple is obviously entitled to privacy once they close the door to their apartment. Any attempt to invade their privacy without their permission, whether it is physically barging in the front door, donning a disguise as a refrigerator repairman or planting a hidden microphone in one of their lamps, would constitute an invasion of privacy for which a reporter could be sued.

In between the public plaza and the private apartment, however, are situations that are not so clear-cut. And for student journalists who do much of their work on school property the question can get especially complicated. For example, bathrooms or locker rooms[93] are obviously private places for which the permission of those individuals present should always be obtained prior to engaging in any newsgathering. A school hallway or cafeteria, on the other hand, would probably be considered a public space, allowing a student journalist to report freely. A more difficult question is whether students in a classroom would be able to claim that they have a reasonable expectation of privacy that would, for example, prevent a yearbook photographer from safely taking photographs without first obtaining the permission of the teacher, making his presence known to the students and giving them an opportunity to object.

> Intrusion is a claim often based on the act of newsgathering. A reporter can be sued even when the information obtained is never published.

> The Supreme Court ruled in 2001 that journalists can lawfully use confidential records, audio tapes, e-mail transcripts or other material about a matter of public interest that is blindly provided them.

WHAT TO DO WHEN THE UNMARKED ENVELOPE ARRIVES IN THE MIDDLE OF THE NIGHT

You've seen it in movies. A darkened figure slides an envelope under the intrepid reporter's hotel room door. Inside is a document from the bad guy's locked filing cabinet proving that the alleged conspiracy the reporter is investigating goes all the way to the top. In Hollywood, the reporter always publishes the information and brings the bad guy to his knees — but how does it play out in real life?

While journalists cannot break the law to obtain newsworthy information — or actively aid others in doing so — the Supreme Court ruled in its 2001 decision, *Bartnicki v. Vopper*,[94] that where journalists are blindly provided confidential records, audio tapes, e-mail print-outs or other material about a matter of public interest, the materials generally are fair game.

However, before using any information that might have been unlawfully obtained, journalists must ensure that: (1) they played no part in the illegal acquisition; (2) they lawfully received the information even though it might originally have been obtained unlawfully; and (3) the subject matter is truthful and of public interest.

Information unlawfully obtained that is not of public concern — or newsworthy — falls outside of First Amendment protection, and could subject both the person who gathered the information and the publisher of the information to an invasion of privacy claim.

Most Common Types of Intrusion

Intrusion claims are among the easiest to avoid, provided that reporters and editors remain alert to those types of situations that tend to spark trouble. Generally, intrusion claims fall into three categories:

(1) Trespass. Examples include entering a crime scene without the permission of someone entitled to give it, climbing a high fence, picking a door lock or otherwise breaking into private property without consent of the owner,[95] hacking into private computer files, intercepting personal e-mail or remaining on private property when asked to leave. As a general rule, reporters have a right to enter privately owned public places (private school campuses, restaurants, shopping malls) or property (a private company's computer server) without permission but must leave or stop gathering information if asked to do so. Note, however, that any photos or other information a reporter obtains prior to being asked to leave belong to the reporter and neither the police nor the property owner has the right to confiscate a camera, film, laptop or notebook on the spot.

When a person is in a place where she has a reasonable right to expect privacy, a reporter must respect that right.

While public places are generally open to newsgathering, a different rule applies to a special class of "limited" public places, including schools,[96] courthouses, prisons, airports, military facilities, hospitals, civic centers or stadiums when used for a commercial rather than a governmental purpose, and "private" spaces within a public building (such as a judge's personal office in a courthouse). Insofar as access is controlled to these places, journalists should obtain permission to move beyond the public receiving areas.[97] Note, however, that student journalists, who have a right to be on school grounds, generally need not obtain special permission to venture into those areas where students are routinely allowed. Note also that at least one court has found that school officials have no legal obligation to shield students from members of the press.[98]

(2) Secret Surveillance. Examples include the use of a telephoto lens or a hidden camera to photograph a person in a private setting without consent, secretly "bugging" a private room or telephone, or strapping on a tiny microphone or video camera to record a conversation with someone without their knowledge. As technology has improved and audio and video recording devices such as "Hat-Cams" and microphones embedded in pencils have moved from James Bond movies to real life, the temptation to employ such newsgathering gadgetry can be strong. But these new gadgets also bring new legal risks.

The law on this subject can vary from state to state. For example, while some states — and the federal Wiretapping Act — allow reporters to tape a conversation without telling the other participants, such a practice is currently illegal in at least twelve states.[99] Fifteen states prohibit the use of hidden cameras in private places.[100] The use of audio devices ("bugs") to record or eavesdrop on oral communications without the consent of all parties is illegal in ten states.[101] Recording a telephone or oral communication without the consent of at least one party is illegal in most states.[102] If your story plans include secret surveillance, check out the specifics of your state law first. When in doubt, err on the side of caution.

As a general rule, reporters can legally photograph or record anything they want from a public area, such as a public sidewalk. You generally cannot, however, use technology to improve upon what an unaided person would be able to see or hear. It is not, for example, an unwarranted invasion of privacy to photograph a person who appears at the window or inside the door of their private home. It is potentially an invasion of privacy, however, to use a telephoto lens to peer deep inside the house.

(3) Misrepresentation (invalid or exceeded consent). Examples include: misrepresenting

oneself to gain access to a private place or person (such as posing as a lawyer to get an interview with an inmate on death row) and obtaining consent to enter a private place from someone not authorized to give that consent (for example, asking a resident adviser to let you into a student's dorm room to take photos). Note that "undercover" reporting is generally protected as long as the disguise is not used as a means to trespass or engage in an activity you would not otherwise be allowed to do. For example, a television network was not liable for invasion of privacy or trespass when its employees, equipped with concealed cameras, posed as patients and requested eye exams from several eye clinics.[103] The court said that even though the employees gained entry into the eye clinics by misrepresenting their purposes, they did not trespass or invade the privacy of the doctors working there because the offices were open to anyone who expressed a desire for their services, and the doctors were videotaped engaging in professional communications with strangers. More recently, an Oklahoma court dismissed fraud and trespass claims brought against TV reporters who posed as parents in need of child care to obtain a tour of and secretly tape the day care facility for a story on the state of local child care.[104] Thus, it probably would not be an intrusion for a black student reporter to pose as a potential pledge to investigate a story about racial discrimination inside a fraternity. The reporter has a right to apply as a pledge, whether he is serious about it or not. On the other hand, posing as a doctor to talk with the family of an accident victim would much more likely be considered an invasion of privacy. For most reporting, however, good legal sense suggests — and professional ethics demand — that journalists identify themselves as reporters and explain to their sources that the information they obtain may be used in a news story.

Reporters must also be careful not to violate any criminal laws when they are investigating a story. Journalists do not have special license to break the law — even where their intentions are good.[105] For example, student journalists who try to buy alcohol as part of an undercover investigation of liquor stores that sell alcohol to people under 21 may find themselves arrested and charged with the unlawful attempt to purchase an alcoholic beverage. In most states this is a misdemeanor that could result in a fine, community service and/or the suspension of one's driver's license.[106]

Practical Tips for Covering a Hot News Scene

When confronted by police or other officials, immediately identify yourself as a member of the press. Find out now if law enforcement agencies in your area issue press passes or credentials. If so, obtain one. If not, it can still be helpful to create an "unofficial" press pass/I.D. card that clearly identifies you as a journalist. Avoid the appearance of being a participant in the news event. For example, wearing insignia, carrying signs or joining in chants with participants in a protest lessens your credibility as a reporter and sends a mixed message to police about your purpose for being at a news scene. Also find out ahead of time if your local police have issued any sort of media guidelines. Such nonbinding guidelines typically address the release of information to the media, access to crime scenes and issuance of press credentials. They often represent a bargained compromise between the police and press, and can provide a helpful reminder to overzealous officers.

Remain calm and professional. At a "hot" scene, the adrenaline can run high. Resist being swept away by it. When confronted by police, explain your intentions and ask for their cooperation. Persuade, don't argue. Your job is to report the news — not win a shouting match. Challenging officers' authority or spouting off about the "First Amendment" rarely improves your bargaining position. Keep the high ground. Never push or grab a police officer.

Obey all lawful police commands. The U.S. Supreme Court has said that in most cases members of the press have no more — or less — right to gain access to newsworthy events than the general public. Police have the authority to limit media access when they believe such restrictions are needed for public safety or to prevent interference with an investigation. Do not cross clearly marked police lines. Do not take anything from a crime

A state-by-state guide to taping telephone conversations is available on the Reporters' Committee for Freedom of the Press' Web site at: **www.rcfp.org/taping**

scene. Reporters who ignore police orders regarding access risk arrest and prosecution.

Contest police misconduct. While courts tend to give law enforcement officials considerable leeway when it comes to controlling a "hot" news scene, there are limits. For example, police do not have the right to engage in excessive verbal or physical abuse. Also, any restrictions must be reasonable. Finally, police cannot, under any circumstances, zero in on members of the news media, subjecting them to greater restrictions than others. Still, refusing to obey even an apparent illegal or unreasonable order can be risky. In most cases, the better course is to comply with the order, but to challenge the conduct through formal administrative or judicial channels as soon as possible.

Do not voluntarily surrender your notes or equipment to police. Police do not have a right to confiscate a reporter's camera, film or notes without a subpoena. (And even then, a state shield law or qualified privilege may offer protection.) They *never* have a right to destroy such material. Nevertheless, if a reporter or photographer is ordered by the police at the scene to turn over his equipment, it is usually best to comply. However, make it clear to the officer that you believe he is violating the law and that you would not be relinquishing the material absent his order to do so. Contact a media-law attorney as soon as possible.

Preserve a record. If it is clear that a confrontation is inevitable, do what you can to document the scene. Jot down the names of any police or witnesses. If you're using a tape or video recorder, keep it running. It is likely that your version of the events will differ significantly from that of the police. As long as you have acted reasonably, such hard evidence can prove invaluable.

Stay in touch. If detained or threatened with arrest, the ability to contact outside help quickly can be important. Carry a cellphone and, where possible, plan for all reporters and photographers on the scene to check in periodically with an editor outside of the protest area who will be available during the protest. If you're able, give your notes or memory card to another journalist who can get them back to your newsroom promptly.

Be prepared. If you're covering a demonstration or other event likely to result in arrests, carry at least $50 cash in your pocket to purchase a bail bond. Also have available a government-issued photo ID (in addition to a press pass) and the telephone numbers of your editors, an attorney and the police department spokesperson (saved in a place other than the memory of your cellphone, which police will take away as soon as they arrest you). All of these may help speed your release from custody.

If you are arrested, keep quiet. You have the right to remain silent — exercise it. After you have once again identified yourself as a reporter, ask only that you be allowed to contact your news organization or attorney. Do not agree to plead guilty (or "no contest" or pay a "post and forfeit fee") to any charge without first talking to legal counsel or fully understanding what you are doing. If you believe you are not guilty, you only preserve all of your legal rights by pleading "not guilty."

Recording Police and Security Personnel

The explosion of pocket-sized video recording devices has made some police agencies ultra-sensitive to the filming and recording of officers on duty. State and federal laws make "wiretapping" — the secret recording of a private conversation — a criminal offense. Some police agencies have tried to use wiretapping laws to punish journalists and witnesses who record officers' voices as they are conducting police business, such as at the scene of an arrest. But at least two federal circuit courts have said there is a First Amendment right to record police doing official business in areas visible to the public,[107] so it is doubtful that a wiretapping charge against a journalist covering police activity would hold up if challenged in court. Of course, if the journalist actually obstructs police or firefighters trying to do their jobs, or otherwise violates the law, the

---

First Amendment will offer no recourse.[108]

Since the terrorist attacks of Sept. 11, 2001, there have been increasing clashes between security personnel and photojournalists over the right to take pictures of "sensitive" areas such as military bases, federal courthouses, and even subway stations. In response to a lawsuit by the New York Civil Liberties Union, the U.S. Department of Homeland Security issued a memo in October 2010 clarifying that anyone may photograph or videotape the exterior, lobby, hallways and other public visible parts of federal buildings.[109]

GOING UNDERCOVER? A FEW MORE THINGS TO THINK ABOUT

In recent years, companies and individuals upset by damaging —but truthful —undercover investigations have found inventive ways to strike back at news organizations.[110] Because the stories that result from the investigations are accurate — complete with hidden camera footage to back up the reporters' claims — the subjects of the stories cannot sue for libel. Instead, creative lawyers for the companies have sued the press for things like fraud, trespass, conversion of property, intentional infliction of emotional distress, breach of loyalty or tortious interference with contract.[111]

That is what the supermarket chain Food Lion did after two producers from the ABC newsmagazine program "PrimeTime Live" conducted an undercover investigation of food-handling practices at two of the chain's stores in the early 1990s.[112] Food Lion hired the producers — one as a meat wrapper and the other as a deli clerk — after they used false identities and submitted falsified employment applications.[113] The producers used hidden cameras and microphones to obtain the information for their story, ultimately airing footage that appeared to show Food Lion employees repackaging and redating fish that had passed the expiration date, grinding expired beef with fresh beef, and applying barbecue sauce to chicken past its expiration date to mask the smell and sell it as fresh in the gourmet food section.[114]

Food Lion, which claimed it suffered a significant loss due to reduced sales and a decline in its stock price, filed suit against ABC, alleging myriad claims.[115] Notably, however, the chain did not claim the story was libelous. A federal jury returned a verdict for Food Lion on its claims of fraud, trespass, and breach of loyalty and awarded the chain $1,402 in actual damages and $5.5 million in punitive damages.[116]

Although an appeals court ultimately threw out the punitive damage award and reduced Food Lion's actual damages to just $2,117 this case demonstrates the perils of engaging in misrepresentation to uncover a story. While truth is still the best defense, it may not always be enough. Student journalists should be prepared to defend their newsgathering tactics as well.

MISAPPROPRIATION OF A PERSON'S NAME OR LIKENESS

Also called "commercialization," this type of invasion of privacy is fairly straightforward and should rarely present a problem for alert student journalists. Misappropriation is the unauthorized use of a person's name, photograph, likeness, voice or endorsement to promote the sale of a commercial product or service.[118] It recognizes that every person has the right to benefit from his own publicity or celebrity.

For example, before accepting an advertisement that features a school's all-star quarterback enjoying a meal at a local restaurant, a student newspaper should require written proof that the quarterback consented to the endorsement.[119] Note, however, that the right of publicity is not limited to the famous or near-famous. Similar caution should be exercised any time an advertisement is submitted that includes photos or statements of endorsement by anyone other than the person who actually submitted the ad. Having subjects sign a model release form should be a standard practice. Where the subject of an advertisement is a minor, some states require that the consent form be signed by a

> Misappropriation is the unauthorized use of a person's name, photo, likeness, voice or endorsement to promote the sale of a commercial product or service.

parent or legal guardian to be enforceable.[120]

As a general rule, a person cannot bring a misappropriation claim for the use of his photo or likeness that is reasonably related to a bona fide article, book or broadcast story on a matter of public interest. (Of course, there may still be copyright or other legal issues to consider.)

New York actually goes a step further. State courts there have rejected a common law right to privacy and have limited "right to publicity" claims to those able to show that the use of their name or likeness was "for advertising purposes or for the uses of trade." For example, in one of the only student press cases involving a claim of misappropriation, a student magazine at the University of Rochester in New York was sued for publishing a woman's photograph on its cover without permission.[121] The photograph was not used in connection with any advertising nor was it used to illustrate an article of public interest. Noting that the magazine was a nonprofit venture and that all copies were distributed free of charge, the court found that the magazine's use was not for "advertising purposes or for the uses of trade," so there was no violation of New York's misappropriation statute.

Courts have generally allowed media outlets to reuse their own editorial photos or clips as part of a self-promotion campaign.[122] For example, a student magazine could reproduce one of its old covers that included a photo of a celebrity to use in an advertisement seeking new subscriptions provided there was no suggestion that the celebrity actually endorsed the publication.

CONSENT AS A DEFENSE TO INVASION OF PRIVACY CLAIMS

With every form of invasion of privacy, consent is a valid defense. If you want to do a story that involves the private and intimate details of a person's life, such as a story on sexual abuse, teenage pregnancy, substance abuse/treatment, family problems, grades or sexual orientation, it is always a good idea to obtain the consent of your subject first. When reporting on or photographing a story in an obviously private setting, obtaining the consent of the subject should be a routine practice. If you can convince your subjects that you will treat their story with respect, sensitivity and professionalism, you will find many people willing to share their personal experiences. Where your subject remains reluctant, or where editorial discretion dictates, you might consider disguising the person's identity. A story that does not identify a specific person cannot be the basis for an invasion of privacy lawsuit based on private facts, false light or misappropriation (but not intrusion). But again, remember, the disguise must be complete to be successful. Simply changing a name may not be enough.

If you intend to rely on consent as your defense you must make sure you obtain the consent from someone with a legal right to give it. This is not always as easy as it might sound. For example, the Supreme Court ruled in two separate cases in May 1999 that law enforcement officers who permit the news media to accompany them into a home or onto private property while serving a search warrant violate the Fourth Amendment's prohibition against unreasonable searches and seizures.[123] As a result, both law enforcement officers and the news media may face civil liability for violating the Fourth Amendment rights of property owners when members of the media accompany officers during a search if the search turns out to lack proper legal basis.[124] Other trouble spots: landlords cannot automatically give consent for their tenants, school officials for students, parents for their children[125] or employers for their employees (or vice versa).

It is also important that a journalist not exceed the scope of the consent given. For example, one court ruled that the fact that a restaurant was open to the public did not automatically include consent for a television camera crew to obtrusively film inside without permission.[126] In asking for consent, be candid with your subject about what information you want to use and how you plan to use it.

In most cases, it is not necessary to obtain student or parental consent — written or verbal — to publish student photos, names or other information in student-edited media. As long as material is lawfully obtained, accurate and newsworthy, nothing in the law requires student journalists to obtain consent from the subject of the news story or photo prior to publication.[127] Schools that require student-edited media to obtain written parental consent prior to the publication of *any* student names or photos in student media not only create a logistical nightmare for student media staff, they also invite potential legal trouble and confusion where it need not exist.

When is consent necessary?

The general rule aside, there are some occasions where consent is necessary or at least a good idea to protect your news organization from potential liability. The most common reasons:

(1) Publication of a story that involves the private and intimate details of a person's life (for example, a story on mental illness, sexuality, substance abuse or treatment, poor grades, serious and previously confidential family problems);

(2) Reporting or photographing a story from a clearly private setting (for example, a hospital room, a private bedroom or dorm room, an invitation-only party, a counseling session);

(3) Reporting a story involving a potentially defamatory topic where the subject of the story is your primary source (for example, a student admits to cheating on a test or using drugs);

(4) Any use of an individual's name, photo, voice or likeness in an advertisement, promotion or for other commercial reason.

Verbal or written?

Though verbal consent is legally sufficient, it can be harder to prove. Written consent provides physical evidence that consent was provided by the subject of an article, advertisement or photograph. A well-written consent agreement also provides all parties with a clear understanding of the nature and scope of the consent both before and after the agreement.

What should be in the consent form?

The complexity of the consent form, often called a "release," usually depends on the nature of the intended use. A release for a multi-million dollar endorsement deal involving a well-known celebrity can run for pages. A written acknowledgment from a teen mother confirming her consent to be interviewed and have her story published in the student newspaper can be a single paragraph.

All consent forms should, of course, include the name of the subject of the story or photograph. They should also describe what will be used (for example, "any or all information obtained from the interview conducted on April 10, 2013, related to my experiences as a teenage mother"), and how it will be used (for example, "for publication in the *Student Times* and on its Web site"). A consent form should be extensive enough to cover all intended uses of the material. A limited release that allows a particular photograph to be published in a specified publication would not authorize its use in other publications or for other purposes now or in the future. Likewise, it may not permit the use of other photos taken during a photo session or the extensive alteration of an image. If you anticipate using the material in such ways, say so in your release. Remember, though, a release is an agreement and, if you go too far, the model or subject may balk.

For release forms involving minors, it is a good idea to specify that extra lengths that have been taken to ensure that the subject understands what she is consenting to and the ramifications of that consent (for example, "I understand that information from my interview may be used in a story to be published in the *Student Times*, the student newspaper at Central High School. I understand the *Student Times* is distributed both on school, throughout the community and nationally, for example, to paid mail subscribers and at student press conventions. I also understand that the story may be reproduced on the *Student Times* Web site, which can be read by anyone in the world with access to the Internet and may be available for years to come. I have been advised by the *Student Times* staff that I may wish to discuss my decision with my parents and others whose opinion I respect. I am providing this information of my own free will because I believe others may

A sample release form for the noncommercial use of material by student media is available in the appendix.

Courts have generally concluded that a minor's consent is valid when the minor seems to be sufficiently mature and capable of realizing the possible repercussions of the consent.

benefit from knowing of my experiences.").

Unless the form states that a person has been paid or provided with some other specified benefit for providing consent, some jurisdictions allow the consent to be revoked at any time. This is not typically a problem for student media when the source has cooperated in telling her story, but it can be a big problem where, for example, a model for a bikini shop ad in your yearbook gets cold feet and decides at the last minute that she does not want her photo included — just as all 5,000 copies of the yearbook are delivered to your doorstep.

A basic, sample release form for the noncommercial use of material by student media has been included in the Appendix.

Who should sign?

For student media — in the business of working with minors — this can be a complicated question. Generally, a model release form used for commercial purposes (i.e., advertisements, promotions, endorsements) should be signed by both the minor subject and her parent or legal guardian. The same would be applicable for any release involving young children or other individuals incapable of fully understanding the nature and ramifications of their consent. For noncommercial uses involving older minors (for example, high school students) capable of understanding what they are doing, the law — as is discussed below — is less clear. Based on existing legal authority, the Student Press Law Center believes that parental consent — while it is a good idea to obtain it if you can — is not required for a release to be valid.

> When obtaining consent from a minor, journalists should take extra precautions to ensure that the minor is fully informed of what is taking place.

Can a Minor Give Valid Consent?

A question of particular interest to the student press is whether or not minors (typically a person under the age of 18) can validly consent — without a parent — to the publication of stories about themselves that either could invade their privacy or libel their reputation. A story on alcoholism, in which a recovering addict agrees to share her experience with the student newspaper, would be a common example.

The American Law Institute has noted in its *Restatement*, a widely accepted legal authority, that consent should be effective as long as the person giving the consent has the legal capacity to do so.[128] In a comment explaining that section, the *Restatement* notes that a child's consent is and should be effective if he is "capable of appreciating the nature, extent and probable consequences of the conduct [to which he consents]," even if parental consent is not obtained or even expressly refused.[129]

Courts have followed the reasoning of the Restatement in cases of invasion of privacy and defamation, finding that a minor's consent is valid when the minor seems to be sufficiently mature and capable of realizing the possible repercussions of the consent.[130] Courts also have found that if a story falls within the broad definition of "newsworthy," then a minor's privacy rights are no greater than those of adults, and it is not necessary for a publication to gain the consent of minors or their parents merely to report the story.[131] However, at least one court has recognized the limits of newsworthiness and found that when news media deal with children, particularly those under the age of 12, reporters must think about the probable consequences of their conduct and operate within the bounds of basic decency.[132]

There are exceptionally strong policy and legal arguments in favor of recognizing a minor's consent as valid in the right circumstances. Such reasoning is in line with that adopted by courts in determining whether a minor may consent to other kinds of actions that may harm them,[133] and whether a child is responsible for injuries he causes,[134] his crimes,[135] and confessions to crimes.[136]

Such a position also takes into account the importance of recognizing the First Amendment right of minors to have their voices heard. For example, without legal recognition of a minor's right to consent, a 17-year-old recovering drug addict seeking to persuade other teens to "stay clean" by relating his experiences would likely find few media outlets willing to touch his story for fear of being sued by his parents, or by the subject himself when he is older. The *Restatement* view strikes a sensible middle ground. It recognizes a person's age as simply one factor, among others, to be considered in determining if consent is valid. As long as a person understands what she is consenting to and realizes the consequences of allowing such information to be published, the consent should stand up. Where a person — irrespective of age — is too immature or is otherwise unable to appreciate the significance of giving consent, the consent is invalid. Under this view, most high school students could provide valid consent. Most elementary-aged children, because of their immaturity, probably could not.

When obtaining consent from a minor, it is essential that a student journalist take extra precautions to insure that the minor is fully informed of what is taking place. Make sure that the minor understands that you are a reporter working on a story that will be published. Tell him what your story will be about and how you intend to use the information he provides. Let him know that your publication is read not only by other students, but by parents, faculty, neighbors, potential employers and even other larger media, which could pick up on the story. When the information is especially "sensitive," you should convey to him some of the possible consequences — both immediate and future — of publishing his information. Most importantly, tell him he is under no obligation to give you the information you are requesting. You may also want to suggest that he talk with a parent or some other adult before proceeding. While not necessary to be legally enforceable, the Student Press Law Center strongly encourages that — in cases involving disclosure of private and potentially embarrassing personal information — you obtain the consent in writing.

FROM THE SPLC CASE FILES

Editors and reporters for *JagWire*, an award-winning high school student newspaper in Washington state, wanted to open the public's eyes to what they regarded as an epidemic level of casual sexual promiscuity among their classmates. They chose a method they knew would pack a punch: Getting students (even "good kids" from "good families") to go on the record candidly discussing their sexual attitudes and behavior. The result was an alarming wake-up call to the entire community. But some of the sources, having agreed verbally to be quoted by name, started having remorse. They claimed that the journalists led them to believe their identities would be protected, and their families filed a lawsuit against the school district claiming invasion of privacy.

A superior court jury returned a verdict in favor of the school district on all counts, finding (a) that the student sources had consented to the disclosure, and (b) that the school district could not be held liable for what its student journalists wrote in any event. On appeal, the Court of Appeals of Washington agreed. The appeals court rejected the families' claim that the school district unfairly prejudiced the jury by arguing that censoring the article would have infringed on the students' First Amendment rights.[137]

Although the student journalists' side ultimately prevailed, the case probably would never even have reached the courthouse if the journalists had recorded their sources' agreement to go on the record (either with a signed agreement or with a verbal recording of the understanding).

SUMMARY

Invasion of privacy is a relatively new and evolving area; caution should be the watchword. Nevertheless, knowing the "basics" of the four privacy claim — (1) public disclosure of private facts, (2) intrusion upon seclusion, (3) false light and (4) misappropriation — and being able to identify potential or common trouble spots will serve any journalist well.

You're editor of *The Student Times*. One of your reporters, Scoop Johansen, has heard about a police sting operation to crack down on illegal drug sales in your city. He successfully persuades police to let him follow the operation from the inside and write a story when it's over. He learns that the investigation is focusing on Christopher Edwards, the man police believe is the ringleader in the drug community. Police provide Johansen with background information on Edwards and he learns from them that the suspect is a graduate of your high school. Digging through old yearbooks you find a photo of Christopher Edwards. You learn that Edwards had been a star football player and a member of the homecoming king's court.

In anticipation of what looks to be an important and very interesting story, you decide that, in addition to news about the police operation, you also want to do a feature story on how drugs have affected students at your school. A staff member tells you that one of her friends, Misty Nomore, is a former drug user who is now back in school after missing much of her sophomore year while she participated in a drug treatment program. After thinking it over, Misty, now 16, tells you that she would be willing to tell her story to you for the first time. She's proud of her recovery and eager to help others avoid her mistakes. She tells you that drugs are much more prevalent in your high school than people would guess. She even gives you a photo taken at the treatment facility and points out two other students at your school whom she met there. You're surprised. One, Peter Perfect, is an old acquaintance that you never would have guessed had a substance abuse problem.

The day of the sting operation arrives. Scoop rides along with police, who allow him to take photos as they bust down Edwards' door without knocking (and, you later learn, without a search warrant). Unfortunately, he's not there, but Polly Pure, and her six-year-old daughter are — in their nightgowns, which you can see from the photos Scoop took. Between terrified sobs, Polly tells police they've made a mistake. Edwards, she tells them, lives next door. Police later arrest him without incident.

It's time to go to press. Scoop has filed his story. The feature on Misty Nomore is also complete. In addition, you've got photos from Scoop, the yearbook and Misty. One of your section editors, Laura Law, has looked over everything first and approaches you shaking her head. "Boss," she says, "I think we might have a few problems." What do you think she might be talking about?

ANSWER:
Laura Law brings out her yellow legal pad.

First, she says, "I'm really worried about Scoop being with police and shooting photos when they accidentally busted down Polly Pure's door. Not only is it bad form, but if she sues I'm worried we might be in trouble."

Laura is right. While Scoop had permission from police to accompany them on the raid, a pair of Supreme Court decisions makes clear that police "ridealongs" are a risky affair for reporters regardless of such permission.[138] Even worse, in this case the police themselves didn't have the right to unlawfully break down Polly's door in the middle of the night or to consent to the invasion of Polly and her daughter's privacy by allowing Scoop to shoot photos of them in their nightgowns. Only Polly could consent to that. And she obviously didn't.

Next, Laura says, "I'm also concerned about the feature story on Misty Nomore. She is only 16 and she's telling us some pretty revealing stuff about her life. What if she changes her mind in a few months when she goes to find a summer job and a potential employer tells her he doesn't want to hire a former drug addict? Could she sue us?"

Probably not. As long as Misty is a "normal" high school student able to understand that her story is going to be published in the student newspaper and read by students, faculty, community members (including potential employers) and others, most legal authority suggests that Misty can validly consent to the publication of a story that might otherwise invade her privacy. Here, Misty feels strongly about using her experience to help others — a noble act and something that she should be allowed to do if she so decides. Still, the law is not fully developed on this issue and it would be wise to go the extra mile to ensure that Misty understands the ramifications of going public. You should have her sign a written consent form and, while her consent is probably valid on its own, it would be nice if her parents signed it as well.

Laura is also worried about including Peter Perfect's name or the photo of him and Misty. "After all," Laura says, "just because Misty wants to go forward with her story doesn't mean that Peter wants everyone to know about his struggles."

Laura has a good point. As a legal matter, it's a close call. Misty does not have the right to consent to a "private facts" invasion of Peter's privacy. However, Peter might not have an invasion of privacy claim in the first place. The use of illegal drugs is against the law. News coverage of criminal activity is almost always newsworthy, which is a defense to any invasion of privacy claim. This would be particularly true if Peter was someone in the public eye. Moreover, Misty probably has the right to tell her own story — including providing accurate, newsworthy information about other people that have played prominent roles in her life — even if those people would rather that information be kept quiet. As one court said, any other rule would have the unwelcome result "that one's autobiography must be written anonymously."[139] (Of course, Misty might have promised the treatment facility that she wouldn't talk about other patients without permission, a promise she may be legally bound to keep.) Still, legal issues aside, the decision about whether to "out" Peter against his wishes raises some serious ethical issues that you and your staff should carefully consider.

"Finally," Laura says, "There is something about Edwards' yearbook photo that is bugging me. Are you sure we have the right guy?"

Listen to Laura. While she may sound paranoid, as an editor you sometimes have to be. As one Illinois commercial newspaper found out the hard way, "Christopher Edwards" is a pretty common name. In that case, the paper accidentally used the high school yearbook photo of "Christopher Edwards" to illustrate their news story on the drug-related arrest of "Christopher A. Edwards" — a different person. The innocent Mr. Edwards sued the newspaper for, among other things, false light invasion of privacy.[140]

CASE STUDY #2

Scoop Johansen, your star reporter, is back knocking on your door: "Boss, have I got a story for you!" He tells you that the school board president's son, Tom Trouble, was part of a group of students caught vandalizing the school Friday night, resulting in thousands of dollars of damage. Police were involved and all of the students were suspended — except for Tom.

"Wow!" you tell Scoop. "How did you hear about this?"

Scoop tells you that when he got to school this morning he found an envelope shoved through the slots of his locker. He has no idea where it came from, but it was clearly from someone pretty high up. It contained the whole story, plus lots of school district documents — some stamped "Confidential" — about the investigation and suspensions.

Just after Scoop leaves, Ally Baba, another one of your top reporters, comes knocking: "You won't believe this, boss." She then tells you that she, too, had heard rumors about the vandalism story. She immediately headed down to the police station and spoke to her contact who confirmed the story and gave her all of the police reports related to the investigation, which she shows you. "But there's a problem, boss. They want all this stuff back." She tells you that her contact at the police station called her about an hour ago and told her that he'd made a terrible mistake. He didn't realize that all of the students involved were minors. State law, he said, prohibits him from releasing the records. He told Ally that not only does she have to return the documents — she also can't publish any of the information contained in the records.

As you sit in your office pondering your options, there is another knock on your door. It's your technology reporter, Luis Laptop. He, too, has heard about the vandalism story and he's very excited. "You'll never guess what I found," he says. He tells you that after hearing all the rumors he hacked into the personal e-mail account of a school board member. Along with finding some juicy information about the school board member's marital problems, Luis says he also found a flood of e-mail between board members. A couple of the board members, he says, are outraged by the preferential treatment they feel has been given the school board president's son.

Just as Luis finishes, Jessica James, your news photographer, pops in to tell you that — you guessed it — she's also heard about the vandalism story. In fact, she tells you, she was walking to school this morning just behind Tom Trouble and overheard him bragging to his companion about how even though he'd done most of the spray painting, he's getting off scot-free. She says that since she figured it was news, she jogged ahead, snuck behind a parked car and snapped a photo of him (with the camera she always carries — just in case news happens) as he walked past her on the sidewalk just outside of school. She says she also just got off the phone with Chris Crime, one of the students she heard Tom say was suspended, who confirmed Tom's story and gave her all the details. Just before he hung up, Chris told Jessica that he's worried about being quoted because everyone signed a confidentiality agreement and the school board president threatened to expel anyone who talked. "Fortunately," Jessica tells you, "I have the whole telephone conversation on tape, which I secretly turned on."

You close your office door. The phone rings. It's Tom's mom. She's heard that your reporters are snooping around and she's livid. "Don't you dare publish Tom's name! He's only 15. You can't put a kid's name in the paper like this. You better have some good lawyers!"

Your head is spinning, but deadline is approaching. What information can you use? What information is off-limits? Have any of your reporters crossed the line in gathering information on what will likely be your biggest news story of the semester?

ANSWER:
First of all, it's clearly news. Despite Tom's mother's claim, you have the right to publish Tom's name when he's involved in a newsworthy story — whether he's 50, 15, or 5 years old — as long as the information you report is accurate and you have obtained it lawfully. We'll assume here that the report of Tom's involvement and lack of punishment is accurate. It looks like you have plenty of solid sources to back up the claim. Of course, you will need to go through the normal process of verifying all information about the incident prior to publication, including carefully reviewing all documents and attempting to contact Tom, the other charged students, school officials and police for comment. So while it appears you have plenty of accurate information, the tougher question is determining what information has been obtained lawfully. Let's take a look at what each of your reporters dug up.

Scoop: Assuming that he's telling the truth, Scoop has done nothing illegal. Even though it sounds like he has obtained records that he probably shouldn't have, Scoop neither stole the records nor aided or actively encouraged anyone else to do so. They just showed up in his locker. As long as the documents are authentic (which you must do your best to confirm), some of the records are probably "education records" about individual students that — under the federal Family Educational Rights and Privacy Act —school officials are not supposed to release without student or parental consent. But that's neither your nor Scoop's problem. FERPA applies only to school officials and their agents. As editor of the student newspaper, you're not covered by FERPA. Of course, there may be other private information in the documents, unrelated to the vandalism, that is not newsworthy (for example, student transcripts, medical information, etc.). Publishing such information (or even carelessly letting the records fall into someone else's hands) could constitute an invasion of privacy, so be careful. But the bottom line is that you can use the information provided to Scoop so long as it is accurate and newsworthy.[141]

Ally: Like Scoop, Ally also did nothing wrong. It wasn't her fault that her source at the police department screwed up and gave her copies of records that he wasn't supposed to. As long as Ally didn't aid him or knowingly encourage him to break the law, the problem is solely the police department's. Ally obtained the records lawfully and, to the extent that the information is newsworthy and accurately reported, it's fair game to use.[142] There is, of course, something else to think about, though — something that has nothing to do with the law. Apparently, Ally has used this source before. If you burn him here, you can rest assured he's not going to be helping Ally on any stories in the future. There is no right or wrong, but it is something to consider.

Luis Laptop: By breaking into the school board member's personal mailbox without authorization, Luis has almost certainly broken the law.[143] Among other claims, the board member probably has an intrusion invasion of privacy claim against Luis. It is no excuse that you haven't yet published the information Luis obtained; the intrusion was complete when Luis viewed personal e-mails without permission (although, obviously, publishing the information will clearly reveal the computer break-in and make legal action more likely). The board member probably will not, however, have a claim against the newspaper for the public disclosure of private facts, even if the newspaper chooses to print the results of Luis' fishing expedition. The newsworthiness of the information – that some school board members think Tom is being given preferential treatment – should counteract any privacy claim. There are, however, strong arguments both ethically and legally against publishing; the newspaper's publication will appear to ratify the intrusion and increase the risk that the newspaper, rather than just Luis, will be sued by the board member whose account was hacked. Bottom line: tell Luis to keep his mouth shut and his computer turned off for a while. Except in extraordinary circumstances, you will probably not want to use Luis' information.

Jessica: With one potential glitch, it sounds like Jessica has lawfully obtained her information. First, Jessica is free to accurately report any newsworthy information she hears while walking down a public street. Tom had no "expectation of privacy" in such circumstances. Of course, if Tom denies things, it may prove difficult to verify what Tom said during his morning stroll. But that's a problem of proof, not an invasion of privacy concern. Second, Jessica is free to take a photo of pretty much anything or anyone as long as, as in this case, the subject of the photo is in a public spot. Again, Tom had no reasonable "expectation of privacy" while walking to school on public streets and sidewalks. It makes no difference that Jessica was hiding when she took the photo. Finally, as long as Jessica accurately identified herself to Chris Crime (including, for ethics sake, telling him she was a reporter), there is no legal problem in reporting what he told her during the telephone call. Again, verifying what Chris said on the telephone — especially if he gets cold feet about talking and denies his conversation with Jessica — could be a problem. But this time Jessica secretly taped her telephone conversation with Chris so you've got proof. The one potential glitch: secretly taping a telephone call without the consent of everyone involved is illegal in a small number of states. (In most states, you can tape any telephone call to which you are a party.) While you can still use the information Chris gave Jessica, you will need to check your state's law before you can safely rely on the tape.

ENDNOTES

1   *Federal Trade Comm'n v. American Tobacco Co.*, 262 U.S. 276, 298 (1923).
2   Samuel D. Warren & Louis D. Brandeis, *The Right to Privacy*, 4 HARVARD L. REV. 193 (1890).
3   *Id.* at 195.
4   *See Diaz v. Oakland Tribune, Inc.*, 188 Cal. Rptr. 762 (Cal. App. Ct. 1983). A jury awarded Diaz $775,000, but an appeals court overturned the judgment because it said the trial court judge's instructions to the jury were flawed. Diaz eventually settled her case out of court for between $100,000 and $200,000.
5   *See, e.g., Miller v. Brooks*, 472 S.E.2d 350 (N.C. App. Ct. 1996), *review denied*, 483 S.E.2d 172 (N.C. 1997) (private facts claims not recognized in North Carolina); *Anderson v. Fisher Broad.*, 712 P.2d 803 (Ore. 1986) (Oregon recognizes private facts claims in limited circumstances only).
6   *See Cox Broad. Co. v. Cohn*, 420 U.S. 469 (1975) (Atlanta television station was sued by victim's father after it broadcast the name of a 17-year-old deceased gang rape victim. The U.S. Supreme Court found that the information was not private because it was obtained at a public trial.).
7   *See, e.g., Doe 2 v. Associated Press*, 331 F.3d 417 (4th Cir. 2003) (dismissing privacy claim against reporter for publishing name of former student who testified at the sentencing hearing of teacher who pled guilty to sexually molesting him and several of his classmates, despite trial court judge's order not to identify victims).
8   *Florida Star v. B.J.F.*, 491 U.S. 524 (1989) (newspaper could not be punished for publishing confidential information accidentally provided to reporter). *See also Bartnicki v. Vopper*, 532 U.S. 514 (2001) (First Amendment protected defendant radio host that aired material provided to him by third party who had unlawfully obtained it.). The *Bartnicki* case is discussed more fully on page 235. Note that while many states have enacted shield laws that prohibit government officials from disclosing the names of sexual

assault victims, the names of individuals testing positive for HIV, or material obtained from certain juvenile proceedings, such laws — either expressly or by judicial interpretation — have been held inapplicable to news media where the information is lawfully obtained and accurately reported. Those statutes that remain on the books are constitutionally suspect in light of the Supreme Court's ruling in the *Florida Star* case. (For a list of so-called "rape shield" statutes, *See* 2003 COMMUNICATIONS LAW, PLI, p. 182-183.)

9   *Langford v. Vanderbilt Univ.*, 287 S.W.2d 32 (Tenn. 1956). The libel case against the magazine was also later dismissed. *Langford v. Vanderbilt Univ.*, 318 S.W.2d 568 (Tenn. 1958).

10 *Bombardieri v. Registrar of Motor Vehicles*, 688 N.E.2d 954 (Mass. 1998).

11 *In re Application of Martin*, 447 A.2d 1290 (N.J. 1982).

12 *Atwell v. Sacred Heart Hosp.*, 520 So. 2d 30 (Fla. 1988).

13 *Int'l Ass'n of Fire Fighters v. Mun. of Anchorage*, 973 P.2d 1132 (Alaska 1999).

14 *City of Kenai v. Kenai Peninsula Newspapers*, 642 P.2d 1316 (Alaska 1982).

15 *CBS, Inc. v. Block*, 725 P.2d 470 (Cal. 1986).

16 *Galvin v. Freedom of Information Comm.*, 518 A.2d 64 (Conn. 1986).

17 *Attorney Gen. v. Collector of Lynn,* 385 N.E.2d 505 (Mass. 1979).

18 *Perkins v. Freedom of Information Comm.*, 635 A.2d 783 (Conn. 1993).

19 *Kelley v. Bonney*, 606 A.2d 693 (Conn. 1992).

20 *Ottochian v. Freedom of Information Comm.*, 604 A.2d 351 (Conn. 1992).

21 *Rose v. Freedom of Information Comm.*, 602 A.2d 1019 (Conn. 1992).

22 *Attorney Gen. v. School Committee of Northampton*, 375 N.E.2d 1188 (Mass. 1978).

23 *Mans v. Lebanon Sch. Bd.*, 290 A.2d 866 (N.H. 1972).

24 *See Briscoe v. Reader's Digest Ass'n*, 483 P.2d 34, 93 Cal. Rptr. 866 (Calif. 1971) (it was an invasion of privacy to expose a rehabilitated man's crime of truck hijacking eleven years after its commission even though the information could easily be found in publicly available records). A federal district court, however, found the same facts newsworthy and public, notwithstanding the passage of time. *Briscoe v. Reader's Digest*, 1 Med. L. Rptr. 1852 (C.D. Cal. 1972). More importantly, the California Supreme Court partially overruled *Briscoe. Gates v. Discovery Communications, Inc.*, 34 Cal. 4th 679 (Cal. 2004). In *Gates*, the court held that the First Amendment bars invasion of privacy claims when the facts are obtained from public records of a criminal proceeding. *See also Wolston v. Reader's Digest*, 443 U.S. 157 (1979) (reclusive plaintiff, who had been convicted of contempt of court sixteen years earlier, had acquired "public figure" status in 1958, but had lost it by 1974); *Norris v. King*, 357 So.2d 1165, 1978 La. LEXIS 7459 (La. Ct. App. 1982) (plaintiff's conviction and fine of $100 for stealing money from a Coke machine lost its public interest after 15 months).

25 Most courts have concluded that the passage of time does not dilute the newsworthiness or lessen the legitimacy of the public's concern and, often pointing to the Supreme Court's decision in *Cox Broad. v. Cohn*, 420 U.S. 469 (1975), have said that once information is disclosed in public documents, the press cannot be sanctioned for fairly and accurately reporting it. *See Gates v. Discovery Communications, Inc.*, 34 Cal. 4th 679 (Cal. 2004); *Uranga v. Federated Publ'ns, Inc.*, 67 P.3d 29 (Idaho 2003) (newspaper not liable for publishing 40-year-old document contained in court record open to public); *Romaine v. Kallinger*, 537 A.2d 284 (N.J. 1988) (no liability for publishing book based on 8-year-old murder and hostage incident); *Dresbach v. Doubleday*, 518 F. Supp. 1285, 1290 (D.D.C. 1981) (no liability for book that gave account of plaintiff's brother's murder of his parent 19 years earlier); *Montesano v. Donrey Media Group*, 668 P.2d 1081, 1085- 86 (Nev. 1983), *cert. denied*, 466 U.S. 959 (1984) (no liability for reporting plaintiff's 23-year-old hit-and-run conviction). *See also McCall v. Oroville Mercury*, 191 Cal. Rptr. 280 (Cal. Ct. App. 3d Dist. 1983) (criminal record of public official is publishable "no matter how remote in time or place").

26 42 U.S.C. Sec. 1320d et seq.

27 42 U.S.C. Sec. 1320d-6(a)-(b).

28 45 CFR Parts 160-164.

29 42 U.S.C. Sec. 1320d(4).

30 This was the interpretation of the Connecticut Freedom of Information Commission in a case involving an author's request for decades-old records about a state mental hospital's treatment of a notorious local criminal. *See Robillard v. Freedom of Information Officer*, State of Conn., Conn. FOI Comm'n, Docket #FIC 2011-297 (April 25, 2013) (citing 45 C.F.R. Sec. 164.512(a)).

31 45 CFR Part 160.103.

32 45 CFR 164.510.

33 *See, e.g., Carroll v. Parks*, 755 F.2d 1455 (11th Cir. 1985) (high school yearbook not liable for publishing photograph of student competing in foot race in which his genitals were accidentally exposed). *See also McNamara v. Freedom Newspapers, Inc.*, 802 S.W.2d 901 (Tex. Ct. App. 1991) (newspaper's publication of a photograph, taken at a high school soccer game, which shows a soccer player with his genitals exposed, does not support claim of invasion of privacy or intentional infliction of emotional distress).

34 Some courts put the burden on the person claiming invasion of privacy to show that the disputed information was not newsworthy. *See, e.g., Shulman v. Group W Prods., Inc.*, 955 P.2d 469 (Cal. 1998); *Diaz v. Oakland Tribune*, 188 Cal. Rptr. 762 (Cal. Ct. App. 1983).

35 *Campbell v. Seabury Press*, 614 F.2d 395, 397 (5th Cir. 1980). *See also J.C. v. WALA-TV, Inc.*, 675 So.2d 360 (Ala. 1996) (Alabama Supreme Court, citing Campbell, dismissed privacy claim brought by the parents of a 15-year-old girl accurately identified as a "runaway" by TV station since girl's safety was of "great interest to the Alabama public.").

36 *Shulman*, 955 P.2d at 484 (Cal. 1998).

37 *See, e.g., Howard v. Des Moines Register & Tribune Co.*, 3 Media L. Rep. 2304 (Iowa Dist. Ct. 1978), *aff'd* by, 283 N.W.2d 289 (Iowa 1979), *cert. denied*, 445 U.S. 904 (1980).

38 *See, e.g., Romaine v. Kallinger*, 537 A.2d 284 (N.J. 1988).

39 *Gates v. Discovery Communications, Inc.*, 34 Cal. 4th 679 (Cal. 2004). *See* note 24, above, for discussion of *Gates*.

40 *Jenkins v. Bolla*, 600 A.2d 1293 (Pa. Super. Ct. 1992) (publication of boarding home operator's convictions for criminal sex acts 50 and 30 years earlier and commitment to a state hospital 28 years

earlier was "newsworthy," given the legitimate public interest regarding the state care provided the mentally ill housed in plaintiff's boarding home); *Sidis v. F-R Pub. Corp.*, 113 F.2d 806 (2d Cir. 1940), *cert. denied*, 311 U.S. 711 (1940). *Sidis* is a well-known case involving an adult who, while renowned years earlier as a child prodigy, had gone out of his way to avoid the public eye for twenty years. Though recognizing Sidis' "passion for privacy," the court nevertheless ruled that the adult life of a famous child prodigy was "newsworthy" and protected. *See also* discussion at note 24, above.

41   *Sanchez v. Affiliated Publ'ns, Inc.*, 1993 WL 818736, 22 Med. L. Rptr. 1188 (Mass. Super. Ct. Oct. 15, 1993) (news story describing rape and subsequent pregnancy of 14-year-old girl — unidentified in article but known to some readers — by gang member); *Gallo v. Princeton Univ.*, 656 A.2d 1267 (N.J. Super. Ct. App. Div. 1995), *cert. denied*, 663 A.2d 1359 (N.J. 1995) (statements made to media by university officials about investigation into improprieties by school official); *Romaine v. Kallinger*, 537 A.2d 284 (N.J. 1987).

42   *State ex rel. Findlay Publ'g Co. v. Schroeder*, 669 N.E.2d 835 (Ohio 1996).

43   *Aquino v. Bulletin W.*, 154 A.2d 422 (Pa. Super. Ct. 1959).

44   *Boston Herald, Inc. v. Sharpe*, 737 N.E.2d 859 (Mass. 2000).

45   *Scott, Sardano & Pomeranz v. Records Access Officer*, 480 N.E.2d 1071 (N.Y. 1985).

46   *Pasadena Star-News v. Superior Court*, 249 Cal. Rptr. 729 (Cal. App. Ct. 1988).

47   *Royhan v. Triangle Publ'ns*, 230 F.2d 359 (7th Cir. 1956).

48   *Kirwan v. The Diamondback*, 721 A.2d 196 (Md. 1998), criticized in, *United States v. Miami Univ.*, 91 F. Supp.2d 1132 (S.D. Ohio 2001), *a'ffd*, 294 F. 3d. 797 (6th Cir. 2002) (ruling that student disciplinary records can be protected by FERPA even if the records do not relate to academic matters).

49   *J.C. v. WALA-TV, Inc.*, 675 So.2d 360 (Ala. 1996); *Goldman v. Time, Inc.*, 336 F. Supp. 133 (N.D. Cal. 1971) (runaway American youth in Europe).

50   *Smith v. Daily Mail Publ'g Co.*, 443 U.S. 97 (1979); *Hogan v. Hearst Corp.*, 945 S.W.2d 246 (Tex. 1997).

51   *Hagler v. Democrat-News, Inc.*, 699 S.W.2d 96 (Mo. App. Ct. 1985).

52   *Tucker v. News Publ'g Co.*, 397 S.E.2d 499 (Ga. App. 1990).

53   *Puckett v. ABC*, 1990 WL 170425, 18 Med. L. Rptr. 1429 (6th Cir. 1990) (unpublished).

54   *Daily Times Democrat v. Graham*, 162 So.2d 474 (Ala. 1964).

55   *Hawkins v. Multimedia*, 344 S.E.2d 145 (S.C. 1986), *cert. denied*, 479 U.S. 1012 (1986). *But see Meetze v. Associated Press*, 95 S.E.2d 606 (S.C. 1956) (report that a twelve-year-old married girl gave birth did not invade mother's privacy).

56   *See, e.g., Michaels v. Internet Entm't Group, Inc.*, 5 F. Supp. 2d 823 (C.D. Cal. 1998) (finding that videotape of actress Pamela Anderson Lee and former husband, Brett Michaels of rock band Poison, having sex was not sufficiently newsworthy to overcome couple's right of privacy and allow its broadcast over Internet by thirdparty); but compare *Jones v. Turner*, 1995 WL 106111 (S.D.N.Y. 1994) (finding that right of publicity claim against Penthouse magazine by Paula Corbin Jones, who had accused President Clinton of sexual harassment, for publication of semi-nude photos of her that the magazine purchased from her former boyfriend was unlikely to succeed because it was a matter of public interest).

57   *See, e.g., Flynn v. Higham*, 149 Cal. App. 3d 677 (Cal. App. 1983).

58   *See, e.g.,* Calif. Civil Code Sec. 3344.1(g) (70 years after death); Fla. Stat. Ann. Sec. 540.08 (40 years after death).

59   *Smith v. Daily Mail Publ'g Co.*, 443 U.S. 97 (1979). *See also Oklahoma Publ'g Co. v. District Court*, 430 U.S. 308 (1977) (Supreme Court lifted an injunction that prohibited publication of the name or photograph of an 11-year-old boy charged with second-degree murder). A narrow variation to this general rule may exist in cases involving the publication of the names of minors obtained during otherwise closed hearings. Where reporters have agreed not to disclose information as precondition to attending such proceedings, they may be legally bound to honor their agreements (See discussion, below).

60   *Mikan v. Valley Publ'g*, 589 P.2d 1201 (Ore. App. Ct. 1979).

61   *Poteet v. Roswell Daily Record*, 584 P.2d 1310 (N.M. 1978).

62   *Tucker v. News Publ'g Co.*, 397 S.E.2d 499 (Ga. App. 1990).

63   *Arkansas Democrat-Gazette v. Zimmerman*, 20 S.W.3d 301 (Ark. 2000).

64   *George W. Prescott Publ'g Co. v. Stoughton Div. of the Dist. Court*, 701 N.E.2d 307 (Mass. 1998).

65   *Heath v. Playboy Enter. Inc.*, 732 F. Supp. 1145 (S.D. Fla. 1990) (adult magazine's publication of photograph of minor child — the grandson of former talk show host Johnny Carson — did not give rise to private facts case brought by child's court-appointed guardian despite lack of consent to photo by child).

66   *Register-Herald v. Canterbury*, 449 S.E.2d 272 (W.Va. 1994).

67   *See, e.g., In re H.N.*, 632 A.2d 537 (N.J. Super. Ct. App. Div. 1993) (New Jersey appellate court upheld the right of a newspaper to publish the name and other identifying information about a 16-year-old charged with scalding her two-month-old nephew to death while bathing him. The court noted that the information was lawfully obtained from press conferences and other disclosures made by law enforcement officials.).

68   *Austin Daily Herald v. Mork*, 507 N.W.2d 854 (Minn. 1993) (Minnesota Supreme Court upheld lower court order permitting media to attend closed trial only if they agreed not to reveal the names of the juvenile victims and witnesses); *In re A Minor*, 595 N.E.2d 1052 (Ill. 1992) (Illinois Supreme Court ruled that a reporter admitted to a juvenile proceeding after agreeing not to disclose names could not publish the identities of two minor children, which he had learned during the course of the proceedings); *In re Minor*, 563 N.E.2d 1069, 1077 (Ill. App. 1990). *See also Edward A. Sherman Publ'g Co. v. Goldberg*, 443 A.2d 1252 (R.I. 1982).

69   *San Bernardino County Dep't of Public Social Serv. v. Superior Court*, 283 Cal.Rptr. 332 (Cal. App. Ct. 1991). *See also In re A Minor*, 595 N.E.2d 1052 (Ill. 1992) (information obtained by reporter outside of closed juvenile hearings not subject to non-publication agreement).

70   *See* SPLC *Legal Brief: Invasion of Privacy Law, available online at* http://www.splc.org/legalresearch. asp?id=29.

71   20 U.S.C. Sec. 1232g.

72   *See, e.g., Owasso Indep. Sch. Dist. No. I-011 v. Falvo*, 534 U.S. 426 (2002) (a student is not a person

"acting for" educational institution for purposes of FERPA); *Yeo v. Lexington*, 131 F.3d 241 (1st Cir. 1997) (en banc), *cert. denied*, 524 U.S. 904 (1998) (student editors of high school yearbook were not "state actors" and their editorial acts must be judged apart from school administrators); *McEvaddy v. City Univ. of New York*, 633 N.Y.S.2d. 4 (1995). *See also Sevier County Bd. of Educ. v. Worrell*, 1994 WL 666926 (Tenn. App. Ct. 1994) (distinguishing between information about students obtained by reporter and student records maintained by the school and protected from disclosure by state's version of FERPA). The U.S. Department of Education, the agency charged with enforcing FERPA, has said: "FERPA was not intended to apply to campus newspapers or records maintained by campus newspapers. Rather, FERPA applies to 'education records' maintained by an educational agency or institution, or by a person acting for such agency or institution." *Letter from LeRoy S. Rooker*, Director, Family Policy Compliance Office, U.S. Department of Education (Sept. 1993).

73   For a thorough discussion of the Family Educational Rights and Privacy Act and its application — or misapplication – to student media, see the SPLC's *FERPA Fundamentalism: How a federal law designed to protect student privacy is being misinterpreted to injure press freedom, available at* http://www.splc. org/ferpa. For a discussion of public high school students' First Amendment rights, see the SPLC's *Hazelwood Guide, available at* http://www.splc.org/legalresearch.asp?id=4. For information about the rights of students attending private schools, see the SPLC's *Legal Guide for the Private School Press, available at* http://www.splc.org/legalresearch.asp?id=52.

74   *Frasca v. Andrews*, 463 F. Supp. 1043, 1050 (E.D.N.Y. 1979).

75   *See, e.g.*, Josh Moore, "Missing faces, missing names," Student Press Law Center *Report*, Fall 2010, at 28; "New school district Internet policies give rise to nameless, faceless Web," Student Press Law Center *Report*, Fall 2001, at 36; "Policy restricts newspaper's online edition," Student Press Law Center *Report*, Fall 1998, at 20.

76   There has been some question about whether a provision in the Children's Internet Protection Act (CIPA), 47 U.S.C. Sec. 254, could be construed to prohibit school-sponsored online student publications from publishing identifiable information about students. CIPA, a federal law that requires schools and libraries receiving subsidized rates for Internet access to install filtering software on their computers, contains a provision that requires schools to adopt and implement an Internet safety policy that addresses unauthorized disclosure, use and dissemination of personal identification information regarding minors. 47 U.S.C. Sec. 254(I)(1)(A)(iv). Some school districts have interpreted this provision as prohibiting the publication of minors' names or photos in student-edited publications that are hosted by school websites. In fact, the Federal Communications Commission has offered no guidance as to what constitutes personal identification information. Instead, the FCC has concluded that local authorities are best situated to choose which Internet safety policies will be most appropriate for their relevant communities. *In the Matter of: Federal-State Joint Board on Universal Service Children's Internet Protection Act*, FCC Report and Order CC Docket No. 96-45, at p. 3 (April 5, 2001), available at www. fcc.gov/Bureaus/Common_Carrier/Orders/2001/fcc01120.doc (last visited Aug. 28, 2013); *See also* 47 CFR Sec. 54.520 (2007). This vague directive and the lack of a mandated definition regarding what constitutes personal identification information — not to mention the significant constitutional questions raised by a flat ban on the publicity of otherwise accuarate, lawful and newsworthy information — hardly supports the leap that CIPA compels schools to prohibit the publication of students' names or photos online. Where school officials remain unconvinced, however, students may want to explore alternatives to school-sponsored websites, such as using a blogging platform like WordPress, because CIPA does not apply to private Web hosting services.

77   See ME. REV. STAT. Ann., tit. 20-A, Sec. 6001 (2009); N.J. STAT. Ann. Sec. 18A:36-35 (2009).

78   *See, e.g.*, "School districts carefully weigh using online images," Associated Press, April 29, 2001 (reporting that there have been "no known cases where child online pornography could be traced to a school Web site").

79   *See, e.g.*, "Journalism Education Association, NPPA endorse use of student names and photos on the Internet," SPLC *News Flash* (January 12, 2000), *available at* http://www.splc.org/newsflash. asp?id=126&year=2000.

80   Al Tompkins, "Identifying Juveniles," The Poynter Institute (Feb. 29, 2000), *available at* http://www. poynter.org/content/content_view.asp?id=5555 (last visited Sept. 1, 2013).

81   The specific language of the *Restatement* aside, it has been pointed out that many false light cases involve material that falls well short of being "highly offensive." This is particularly true when combined with misappropriation allegations. *See* Practicing Law Institute, COMMUNICATIONS LAW (2003), vol. 3, pp. 333-334.

82   *See Edwards v. Paddock Publ'g*, 763 N.E.2d 328 (Ill. App. Ct. 2001).

83   *See Stanley v. General Media Communications, Inc.*, 149 F. Supp. 2d 701 (W.D. Ark. 2001) (dismissing false light claim brought by high school students involved in spring break "condom-fitting" contest using plastic phallus where they failed to show that photographs and accompanying captions were false).

84   Courts in at least nine states – Colorado, Massachusetts, Minnesota, New York, North Carolina, South Carolina, Texas, Virginia and Wisconsin – have decided that false light claims will not be recognized as part of the state's common law. *Denver Publ'g Co. v. Bueno*, 54 P.3d 893 (Colo. 2002); *Ayash v. Dana-Farber Cancer Inst.*, 443 Mass. 367 (Mass. 2005); *Lake v. Wal-Mart Stores, Inc.*, 582 N.W.2d 231 (Minn. 1998); *Messenger v. Gruner + Jahr Printing & Publ'g*, 94 N.Y.2d 436 (N.Y. 2000); *Renwick v. News & Observer Publ'g Co.*, 310 N.C. 312 (N.C. 1984); *Brown v. Pearson*, 326 S.C. 409 (S.C. 1997); *Cain v. Hearst Corp.*, 878 S.W.2d 577 (Tex. 1994); *WJLA-TV v. Levin*, 264 Va. 140 (Va. 2002); *Zinda v. Louisiana Pacific Corp.*, 149 Wis. 2d 913 (Wis. 1989). In addition, Missouri has rejected false light claims, but left open the possibility that the claim might be recognized in the future given the right factual scenario. *Sullivan v. Pulitzer Broad. Co.*, 709 S.W.2d 475 (Mo. 1986).

85   *Denver Publ'g Co. v. Bueno*, 54 P.3d 893 (Colo. 2002).

86   *Jews for Jesus, Inc. v. Rapp*, 997 So. 2d 1098 (Fla. 2008).

87   *Welling v. Weinfeld*, 2007 Ohio 2451 (Ohio 2007); *see also West v. Media Gen. Convergence, Inc.*, 53 S.W.3d 640 (Tenn 2001) (Tennessee law recognizes false light claims).

88 *Time, Inc. v. Hill*, 385 U.S. 374 (1967).

89 A recent tally of how different jurisdictions have answered the question regarding the application of the actual malice standard to private person false light claims can be found in the 2006 edition of Communications Law, published annually by the Practising Law Institute (New York City, NY). *See* Communications Law 2006, Vol. 1 (2006), pp. 850-855.

90 *See, e.g., Sevier County Bd. of Educ. v. Worrell*, 1994 WL 666926 (Tenn. App. 1994) (finding that even if newspaper photographer violated state statute restricting public access to schools, law did not allow for court order prohibiting publication of photographs of school); *In re King World Prods., Inc.*, 898 F.2d 56, 59 (6th Cir. 1990) (holding that prior restraint of the press is not allowed even if the press's conduct clearly violates the law).

91 *See generally Branzburg v. Hayes*, 408 U.S. 665 (1972).

92 Extreme examples of this general rule can be seen in the wave of cases involving the video series "Girls Gone Wild," where young women in otherwise public places (for example, during Mardi Gras, on Daytona Beach during spring break, etc.) expose themselves to cameras. As a judge said, in dismissing three women's invasion of privacy claims in one such case, "when you expose your body on Bourbon Street or in a club and you know there is an individual with a video camera, certainly you must expect that this is going to be shown all over the place." *Doe v. Mantra Films*, No. 01-12450 (La. Dist. Ct. Orleans Parish March 8, 2002) (oral ruling). *See also Lane v. MRA Holdings*, 242 F. Supp. 2d 1205 (M.D.Fla. 2002).

93 *See John Does v. Franco Prods.*, 2002 U.S. Dist. LEXIS 24032 (N.D. Ill. Nov. 25, 2002), *aff'd, Doe v. GTE Corp.*, 347 F.3d 655 (7th Cir. 2003) (companies involved in secretly taping college athletes in their locker room and distributing videotape on Internet as pornography ordered to pay more than $500 million). *See also Doe v. Mobile Video Tapes, Inc.*, 43 S.W.3d 40 (Tex. App. Ct. 2001) (female band members not depicted in clandestine security videotapes made in changing area at high school did not have invasion of privacy claim).

94 532 U.S. 514 (2001).

95 Law enforcement officials may not have the authority to grant a journalist permission to enter private property. *See, e.g., Green Valley School v. Cowles Florida Broad.*, 327 So.2d 810 (Fla. App. Ct. 1976).

96 For example, the California Attorney General's office issued an advisory opinion in June 1996 giving school administrators the authority to deny commercial news media access to school grounds if their presence "would interfere with peaceful conduct of the activities of the school," 79 Ops. Cal. Atty. Gen. 58 (1996), even though California law specifically exempts the news media from the definition of "outsiders" who must check with administrators before visiting schools. Calif. Penal Code Secs. 627.1(a) (7) & 627.2; Calif. Evid. Code Sec. 1070. *See also Sevier County Bd. of Educ. v. Worrell*, 1994 WL 666926 (Tenn. App. Ct. 1994) (court declined to decide whether newspaper photographer violated Tenn. Code Ann. Sec. . 49-6-2008, which restricted access to school grounds to students, staff, parents and "other persons with lawful and valid business.).

97 A good source for reporters seeking additional information on this topic is, "A Reporter's Field Guide," Reporters Committee for Freedom of the Press (Fall 1997), *available at* http://www.rcfp.org/reporters-field-guide (last visited Sept. 1, 2013).

98 *Prescott v. Newsday*, 541 N.Y.S.2d 501 (N.Y. App. Div. 1989) (finding that neither newspaper nor high school officials had a legal duty to obtain parental permission before 17-year-old student was interviewed by newspaper reporter at school about his participation in alternative education program).

99 Secret recording of telephone conversations by one party is currently prohibited in the following states: California (Cal. Penal Code Secs. 631, 632); Connecticut (Conn. Gen. Stat. Sec. 52-570d); Florida (Fla. Stat. Sec. 934.03); Illinois (720 Ill. Comp. Stat. 5/14-1 to 2); Maryland (Md. Code Ann., Cts. & Jud. Proc. Sec. 10-402; Massachusetts (Mass. Gen. Laws ch. 272, Sec. 99); Michigan (Mich. Comp. Laws 750.539c); Montana (Mont. Code Ann. Sec. 45-8-213(1)(c)); Nevada (Nev. Rev. Stat. Sec. 200.620); New Hampshire (N.H. Rev. Stat. Ann. Sec. 570-A:2); Pennsylvania (18 Pa. Cons. Stat. Ann. Sec. 5703); Washington (Wash. Rev. Code Sec. 9.73.030). Delaware law is unclear; *See* Del. Code. Ann. tit. 11, Sec. 1335(a)(4), *but see* Del. Code. Ann. tit. 11, Sec. 2402(c)(4). Section 2402(c)(4) appears to allow secret telephone recordings, but Del. Code. Ann. tit. 11 Sec. 1335(a)(4) does not.

100 The secret photographing or videotaping of a person in a place where there is a reasonable expectation of privacy is currently prohibited in the following states: Alabama (Ala. Code Sec. 13A-11-32); Arkansas (Ark. Code Ann. Sec. 5-16-101); California (Cal. Penal Code Sec. 632); Delaware (Del. Code Ann. tit. 11 Sec. 1335(a)(4), *but see* Del. Code. Ann. tit. 11, Sec. 2402(c)(4)); Georgia (Ga. Code Ann. Sec. 16-11- 62); Hawaii (Haw. Rev. Stat. Sec. 711-1111); Maine (Me. Rev. Stat. Ann. tit. 17-A, Sec. 511); Maryland (Md. Code Ann., Crim. Law Secs. 3-901 to -903); Michigan (Mich. Comp. Laws Sec. 750.539d); Minnesota (Minn. Stat. Sec. 609.746); New Hampshire (N.H. Rev. Stat. Ann. Sec. 644:9); South Carolina (S.C. Code Ann. Sec. 16-17-470) (Statute's prohibition of hidden cameras does not apply to bona fide newsgathering activities. S.C. Code Ann. Sec. 16-17-470(E)(5)); South Dakota (S.D. Codified Laws Sec. 22-21-1); Tennesee (Tenn. Code Ann. Sec. 39-13-605); Utah (Utah Code Ann. Sec. 76-9-402).

101 Ten states currently prohibit the use of electronic devices to record or eavesdrop on communications without the consent of all parties: California (Cal. Penal Code Sec. 632) (statute prohibits only eavesdropping on or recording a conversation that a person would reasonably expect to be confined to the parties present); Florida (Fla. Stat. Sec. 934.03); Illinois (720 Ill. Comp. Stat. 5/14-1 to 2); Maryland (Md. Code Ann., Md. Cts. & Jud. Proc. Sec. 10-402) (state courts have interpreted the statute to prohibit eavesdropping only when the parties have a reasonable expectation of privacy, *Malpas v. Maryland*, 695 A.2d 588 (Md. Ct. Spec. App. 1997); Massachusetts (Mass. Gen. Laws ch. 272, Sec. 99); Montana (Mont. Code Ann. Sec. 45-8-213); New Hampshire (N.H. Rev. Stat. Ann. Sec. 570-A:2); Oregon (Or. Rev. Stat. Sec. 165.535, 165.540); Pennsylvania (18 Pa. Cons. Stat. Secs. 5702-5704) (consent is required in oral communications only where the person speaking has a reasonable expectation of privacy in the communication); Washington (Wash. Rev. Code Sec. 9.73.030).

102 *See, e.g.,* Wis. Stat. Sec. 968.31.

103 *Desnick v. American Broad. Co.*, 44 F.3d 1345 (7th Cir. 1995).

104 *Willis/Kids on Broadway, Inc. v. Griffin Television*, LLC, Case No. 91, 812 (Okla. Civ. App. March 5, 1999).

105 *See, e.g.*, *Branzburg v. Hayes*, 408 U.S. 665 (1972).

106 *See, e.g.*, VA. CODE ANN. Sec. 4.1-305. It is illegal in 37 states and Washington, D.C., for people under 21 to attempt to purchase alcohol. Nine additional states make it a crime for people under 21 to actually purchase alcohol. *See* "State Profiles of Underage Drinking Laws," Nat'l Inst. on Alcohol Abuse & Alcoholism, Alcohol Policy Info. Sys., *available at* http://alcoholpolicy.niaaa.nih.gov/State_Profiles_of_Underage_Drinking_Laws.html (last visited Sept. 1, 2013).

107 *Glik v. Cunniffe*, 655 F.3d 78 (1st Cir. 2011); *ACLU v. Alvarez*, 679 F. 3rd 583 (7th Cir. 2012).

108 *See, e.g.*, *Chavez v. Oakland*, 37 Media L. Rep. 1905 (N.D. Cal. 2009) (holding that a police officer did not violate a journalist's First Amendment rights when he arrested a photojournalist who exited his vehicle on the freeway and stood in the freeway to take pictures); *State v. Lashinsky*, 404 A.2d 1121 (N.J. 1979) (upholding the conviction of a press photographer for disorderly conduct when the photographer took pictures of an accident scene on a highway, ignored a police officer's repeated requests to leave the scene, and argued with the officer).

109 David W. Dunlap, "You Can Photograph That Federal Building," *The New York Times*, Oct. 18, 2010, *available at* http://lens.blogs.nytimes.com/2010/10/18/you-can-photograph-that-federal-building/ (last visited Sept. 1, 2013).

110 *See, e.g.*, *Food Lion, Inc. v. Capital Cities/ABC, Inc.*, 194 F.3d 505 (4th Cir. 1999); *Desnick v. Am. Broad. Cos.*, 44 F.3d 1345 (7th Cir. 1995); *In re King World Prods., Inc.*, 898 F.2d 56 (6th Cir. 1990).

111 *See* George Freeman et al., "'60 Minutes' and the Law: Can Journalists Be Liable for Tortious Interference With Contract?" 68 N.Y. ST. B. J. 24, 28 (1997).

112 *See Food Lion, Inc. v. Capital Cities/ABC, Inc.*, 194 F.3d 505 (4th Cir. 1999).

113 *Id.* at 510.

114 *Id.* at 511.

115 *Food Lion, Inc. v. Capital Cities/ABC, Inc.*, 887 F. Supp. 811, 816 (M.D.N.C. 1995).

116 *See Food Lion,* 194 F.3d at 511. In post-trial proceedings the district court ruled that the punitive damages award was excessive, reducing it to $315,000. *Id.*

117 *Id.* at 521.

118 *See Restatement (Second) of Torts*, Sec. 652C.

119 Such consent is unlikely in the case of student athletes given the prohibitions regarding endorsements commonly placed upon them by scholastic athletic associations.

120 *See, e.g.*, CAL. CIV. CODE SEC. 3344; FLA. STAT. Sec. 743.08(1)(b); N.Y. CLS Civ.R. Sec. 50. Note that the requirement that a parent provide consent is unique to misappropriation invasion of privacy claims.

121 *Wallace v. Weiss*, 372 N.Y.S.2d 416 (Monroe Cty. Sup. Ct. 1975).

122 *See, e.g.*, *Namath v. Sports Illustrated*, 371 N.Y.S.2d 10 (N.Y. Supp. Ct. 1975), *aff'd*, 386 N.Y.S.2d 397, 352 N.E.2d 584 (N.Y. 1976); *Learman v. Flynt Distrib.*, 789 F.2d 164 (2d Cir. 1986), *cert. denied*, 479 U.S. 932 (1986); *Booth v. Curtis Publ'g Co.*, 223 N.Y.S.2d 737 (N.Y. App. Div. 1962), *aff'd.*, 28 N.Y.S.2d 468 (N.Y. 1962) (actress' right of publicity not violated by the publication of her photograph from an earlier edition of magazine in a later edition advertising the periodical). *See also Montana v. San Jose Mercury News, Inc.*, 40 Cal. Rptr. 2d 639 (Cal. App. Ct. 1995) (reproduction and sale of front page of newspaper that featured professional football team in poster form did not constitute misappropriation.) *But see Mendonsa v. Time, Inc.*, 678 F. Supp. 967 (D.R.I. 1988) (Life Magazine's sale of famous photo of sailor kissing nurse on V-J to readers for $1,600 a copy stated cause of action under "purposes of trade" provision of Rhode Island law), compare to *ETW Corp. v. Jireh Publ'g, Inc.* 99 F. Supp. 2d 829 (N.D. Ohio 2000), *aff'd*, 332 F.3d 915 (6th Cir. 2003) (artist's painting of golfer Tiger Woods' victory at golf tournament, prints of which were offered for sale as part of a "limited edition," was "sufficiently transformative" of golfer's image to warrant First Amendment protection and defeat right of publicity claim).

123 *Hanlon v. Berger*, 526 U.S. 808 (1999); *Wilson v. Layne*, 526 U.S. 603 (1999). *But see Brunette v. Humane Society of Ventura County*, 294 F.3d 1205 (9th Cir. 2002) (finding no liability where a reporter was solely an observer to a government search and not a "willful participant").

124 *See Berger v. Hanlon*, 188 F.3d 1155 (9th Cir. 1999) (holding that although the law enforcement defendants were entitled to qualified immunity because the law governing the issue of whether the Fourth Amendment prohibited officers from allowing news media to accompany them on searches was not clearly established when the search warrant was executed, members of the news media were liable because they were not entitled to assert a qualified immunity defense).

125 *But see Shields v. Gross*, 7 Med. L. Rptr. 2349 (N.Y. Sup. Ct. 1981), *modified*, 451 N.Y.S. 419, (N.Y. App. Div. 1982), *aff'd as modified*, 58 N.Y.2d 338 (N.Y. 1983), *rehearing denied*, 59 N.Y.2d 762 (N.Y. 1983) (TABLE, NO. 396) (mother's written consent allowing photographer to take non-pornographic nude photos of her then 10-year-old daughter, actress Brooke Shields, held irrevocable notwithstanding actress's disaffirmance of the consent when she was 17 years old); *Learo v. Auburn Publishers, Inc.*, 27 Med. L. Rptr. 1062 (N.Y. Sup. Ct. 1998) (mother's consent to have child photographed was binding even though mother herself was a minor).

126 *Le Mistral Inc. v. CBS*, 402 N.Y.S.2d 815 (N.Y. App. Div. 1978).

127 *See* discussion of Family Educational Rights and Privacy Act at page 231.

128 *Restatement* (Second) of Torts, Sec. 892A.

129 *Id.*, Comment on subsection (2).

130 *See Lane v. MRA Holdings*, 242 F. Supp. 2d 1205 (M.D.Fla. 2002) (17-year-old who allowed herself to be videotaped exposing her breasts in public places was legally capable of authorizing and consenting to publication of her image in "Girls Gone Wild" video where no contract for compensation was involved); *Howell v. Tribune Entm't Co.*, 106 F.3d 215 (7th Cir. 1997) (holding that *The Charles Perez Show* did not invade the privacy of a 16-year-old minor by airing her stepmother's reading of the minor's police record in response to the minor's verbal attacks on her stepmother during the same broadcast). The *Howell* court based its holding on a finding that the minor appeared on the show's tape to be sufficiently

mature and capable of realizing that by verbally attacking her stepmother on national television she would be exposing skeletons in her own closet to public airing. The court concluded: "We need not decide at what age a child is sufficiently mature to waive her right of privacy, but 16 is old enough when no circumstances of deception or overreaching or limited competence are shown." *Id.* at 221.

131 *See Parker v. Multimedia KSDK, Inc.*, 27 Med. L. Rptr. 2305 (Mo. Cir. Ct. 1999) (finding that consent of minors or adults is not necessary to publish information about newsworthy event); *Anonsen v. Donahue*, 857 S.W.2d 700 (Tex. Ct. App. 1993), *cert. denied*, 511 U.S. 1128 (1994). In *Anonsen*, the court found that a grandmother's revelation on the *Phil Donahue* TV talk show that her former husband had raped her then-11-year-old daughter who had given birth did not support invasion of privacy claim by her 16-year-old grandson/ adopted son. The court found that the grandmother's account was newsworthy and held that a person has a First Amendment right to reveal her identity and accurately tell her own life story even where others may be identified against their wishes. *See also Weber v. Multimedia Entm't Co.*, 2000 WL 526726 (S.D.N.Y. May 2, 2000) (finding that it is not necessary to gain the consent of a featured minor or the minor's parents when the published piece is sufficiently "newsworthy"). In *Weber*, the court held that *The Sally Jesse Raphael Show* did not defame or invade the privacy of a 15-year-old girl who represented herself as a prostitute on the show. The court found that because the show about teenage prostitution fell within the definition of "newsworthy," it was not necessary to obtain consent of the minor or her parents to broadcast the story. *Id.* The court also found that because the girl consented to the presentation of herself as a teenage prostitute that she could not then turn around and later win on a defamation claim. *Id.*; *See also McWhir v. Krementz*, 15 Med. L. Rptr. 1367 (N.Y. Sup. Ct. 1988) (finding use of infant's photo in nursery book to be of public interest and not for purposes of trade even where parental consent was refused); *Prescott v. Newsday*, 541 N.Y.S.2d 501 (N.Y. App. Div. 1989) (finding that neither newspaper nor high school officials had a legal duty to obtain parental permission before 17-year-old student was interviewed at school about his participation in alternative education program); *Heath v. Playboy Enter. Inc.*, 732 F. Supp. 1145 (S.D. Fla. 1990) (photograph of minor child — the grandson of former talk show host Johnny Carson — taken while in arms of his mother on courthouse steps after widely publicized paternity hearing did not give rise to "private facts" case against adult magazine that published photo despite lack of consent to photo by child).

132 In *KOVR-TV, Inc. v. Superior Court*, the court held that a reporter intentionally and negligently inflicted emotional distress upon three girls, ages 11, 7 and 5, by coming to their home uninvited and announcing the murder of two next-door-neighbor playmates. 31 Cal. App. 4th 1023 (Cal. App. Ct. 1995). The girls did not know of their playmates' violent death, and the reporter informed the children that their friends' mother had killed her children and then herself. *Id.* at 1027. Because the reporter told the children of the murders in such a manner as to cause them emotional distress that would be demonstrative to the TV audience, interrogated the girls about the murdered family on camera and intruded uninvited into the minors' home while fully aware that the children's parents were not home, the court found that the reporter acted with an "alarming absence of sensitivity and civility" and was therefore liable for intentional infliction of emotional distress. *Id.* at 1028.

133 *See, e.g., Leonhard v. United States*, 633 F.2d 599 (2d Cir. 1980), *cert. denied*, 451 U.S. 908 (1981) (children who consented to being taken into hiding with stepfather under the federal witness protection program could not later sue the government for abduction and false imprisonment); *Westbrook v. Hutchinson*, 10 S.E.2d 145 (S.C. 1940) (court implied that woman sued for false imprisonment by 11-year-old would have defense if she proved child stayed with her voluntarily).

134 *Gibbs v. State Farm Mut. Ins. Co.*, 544 F.2d 423 (9th Cir. 1976).

135 *Redman v. State*, 580 S.W.2d 945 (Ark. 1979).

136 *Gallegos v. Colorado*, 370 U.S. 49 (1962), reh'g denied, 370 U.S. 965 (1962).

137 *M.R.B. v. Puyallup School Dist.*, 282 P.3d 1124 (Wash. App. 2012).

138 *Hanlon v. Berger*, 526 U.S. 808 (1999); *Wilson v. Layne*, 526 U.S. 603 (1999).

139 *Anonsen* v. Donahue, 857 S.W.2d 700, 706 (Tex. App. Ct. 1993), *cert. denied*, 511 U.S. 1128 (1994).

140 *Edwards v. Paddock Publ'g*, 763 N.E.2d 328 (Ill. App. Ct. 2001), *appeal denied*, 775 N.E.2d 1 (Ill. 2002) (TABLE, NO. 93379).

141 '*Bartnicki* v. Vopper, 532 U.S. 514 (2001), but compare *Boehner v. McDermott*, 484 F.3d 573 (D.C. Cir. 2007) (Congressman McDermott liable for intentionally disclosing an illegally intercepted cellular telephone call, even though he took no part in the illegal recording). For an analysis of *Bartnicki* and *Boehner*, *see* Joseph A. Tomain, "Congressman Liable for Disclosure of Intercepted Cellular Call Involving Matter of Public Concern," *Client Advisory: First Amendment, Media & Advertising* (May 2007), *available at* http://www.frostbrowntodd.com/media/publication/432_Media_20Online_205-07.pdf (last viewed May 5, 2013).

142 *See Florida Star v. B.J.F.*, 491 U.S. 524 (1989).

143 *See Chiquita Brands Int'l, Inc. v. Gallagher*, No. C-1-98-467 (S.D. Ohio 1998) (unpublished); "Reporter sentenced over Chiquita voice-mail theft," *News Media Update* (Reporters Committee for Freedom of the Press), (July 26, 1999)

CHAPTER 14

Obscenity and Indecency

The cases below all involve an understanding of the issue of obscenity. Identifying legally obscene material is important because the Supreme Court has ruled that obscene content does not enjoy First Amendment protection. True obscenity, therefore, may be censored and could be subject to criminal prosecution.

But defining obscenity is easier said than done. Indeed, if calls to the Student Press Law Center are an indication, obscenity is one of the least understood legal issues faced by the student press. Expression is often casually labeled "obscene" as a justification for censoring materials deemed objectionable or "in poor taste." Obscenity, however, is a legal term, and simply calling something "obscene" does not make it so.

DEFINING OBSCENITY: "I KNOW IT WHEN I SEE IT"

Courts have had a tough — some would say a wholly unsuccessful — time coming up with a legal definition of obscenity. In fact, the Supreme Court has struggled to establish a precise and workable definition of obscenity since 1957.[1] Frustration with inadequate definitions of obscenity led Supreme Court Justice Potter Stewart to remark in 1964 that obscenity "may be indefinable." "But," he continued, "I know it when I see it...."[2] In the 1973 case *Miller v. California*,[3] the Supreme Court announced a three-part test for determining whether something would be considered obscene and thus beyond the protection of the First Amendment. Under *Miller*, a court considers:

1. whether "a reasonable person applying contemporary community standards" would find that the work, taken as a whole, appeals to a prurient (lustful) interest;[4]
2. whether the work depicts or describes, in a patently offensive way, sexual conduct specifically defined as obscene by the applicable state law; and
3. whether the work, taken as a whole, lacks serious literary, artistic, political or scientific value.

For something to be classified legally obscene, *all* three parts of this test must be met.

The *Miller* test — as inexact as it is — has nevertheless been the standard for defining obscenity for more than 40 years. Essentially, only "hard-core," explicit descriptions of sexual activity that arouse sexual feelings are obscene under Miller. Profanity, nudity and offensive material are not in themselves obscene if they do not arouse sexual feelings or depict "hard core" sexual situations or if they occur in a serious literary, artistic, political or scientific context. Adult magazines like *Playboy* and *Penthouse*, while offensive to some, are not obscene. Words alone will seldom support a criminal obscenity charge.

Student journalists rarely approach the bounds of *Miller* and, to date, there are no

> True obscenity does not enjoy First Amendment protection. But identifying obscenity is easier said than done.

> Profanity, nudity and offensive material are not in themselves obscene if they do not arouse sexual feelings or depict "hard core" sexual situations or if they occur in a serious literary, artistic, political or scientific context.

reported rulings of a successful obscenity prosecution against the high school or college student media. Free press advocate and journalism professor Louis Inglehart, in his 1993 book on student publications, said "alleged obscenity in college student publications is only a fearful reaction to poor taste."[5]

The leading court decision at the college level where obscenity was raised as a justification for censorship is *Papish v. Board of Curators of University of Missouri*,[6] decided the same year as *Miller*. The U.S. Supreme Court found that the university wrongly expelled graduate student Barbara Papish for the content of a newspaper she distributed on campus. The newspaper included a political cartoon depicting policemen raping the Statue of Liberty and the Goddess of Justice, as well as a lead story titled "Motherfucker Acquitted." The cartoon and headline were not obscene, the Court found, even if they were offensive.[7] *Papish* suggests that college student media are subject to the same obscenity standards applicable to the adult public at large. As a result, it is virtually impossible for college and university officials to validly punish student media or censor for "obscenity" when their charge is based solely on foul language or mildly explicit images.

"Obscene as to Minors"

Material that would not be considered obscene as to adults could be considered obscene as to minors.

The value of *Miller* and *Papish* to high school media is limited. Prior to *Miller*, the Supreme Court in 1968 decided *Ginsberg v. New York*.[8] In *Ginsberg*, the Court found that a state legislature could legitimately distinguish between minors and adults in limiting the sale of obscene material. The *Ginsberg* Court applied a three-part test similar to what later appeared in *Miller*. The Court defined "obscenity as to minors" as any description or representation of nudity or sexual conduct which: (1) predominantly appeals to the prurient, shameful or morbid interest of minors; (2) is patently offensive to prevailing standards in the adult community as a whole with respect to what is suitable material for minors; and (3) is utterly without redeeming social importance for minors.

As with the *Miller*, all three parts of the test must be satisfied.

In recent years, the "obscenity as to minors" standard has been seemingly diluted by a number of states that have passed laws making it a crime to distribute or make available to young people material deemed "harmful to minors,"[9] a standard similar to but arguably broader and more restrictive of speech than "obscene as to minors."[10] The precise effect *Miller* had on *Ginsberg* is not clear — and there exists little case law to help define what constitutes "obscene as to minors" or "harmful to minors" or how these standards differ from regular obscenity.[11] Nevertheless, it is safe to say that material that would not be considered obscene for adults can lose its constitutional protection when minors are involved.[12] It is also safe to say that some advocacy groups and lawmakers have, with mixed success, taken advantage of the lower standards applicable to minors to drive through restrictions on speech that would be unconstitutional if applied solely to adults. As some courts and commentators have noted, the effect of such laws would often be to reduce adults to reading or publishing only what is fit for the very youngest readers or Internet users among us.[13]

REGULATION OF "INDECENT" SPEECH IN HIGH SCHOOL: BETHEL V. FRASER

As mentioned above, school officials frequently label material obscene that would more accurately be categorized as vulgar or indecent. Profanities are not by themselves legally obscene. But court decisions indicate that even vulgar language may sometimes be censored in the high school context. In 1986, the Supreme Court affirmed the permissibility of such a distinction in the case *Bethel School District v. Fraser*.[14] Matthew Fraser, a high school debate team champion, gave a speech in support of a student government candidate before a voluntary high school assembly audience of 600 students. Part of Fraser's speech contained the following:

> "I know a man who is firm — he's firm in his pants, he's firm in his shirt, his character is firm — but most...of all, his belief in you, the students of Bethel. Jeff Kuhlman is a man who takes his point and pounds it in. If necessary, he'll take an issue and nail it to the wall. He doesn't attack things in spurts — he drives hard, pushing, pushing and pushing until finally — he succeeds. Jeff is a man who will go to the very end — even the climax, for each and every one of you. So vote for Jeff for A.S.B. vice-president — he'll never come between you and the best our high school can be."[15]

Fraser sued after school officials suspended him for three days and removed his name from the list of possible graduation speakers. The Supreme Court eventually upheld Fraser's suspension as a permissible sanction of student expression, even though the speech fell far short of obscenity under *Miller*. The Court indicated it believed that Fraser's speech was materially disruptive under the *Tinker* standard.[16] But it also suggested the appropriateness of a dual standard for First Amendment protection. Writing for the majority, Chief Justice Burger said, "It does not follow . . . that simply because the use of an offensive form of expression may not be prohibited to adults making what the speaker considers a political point, the same latitude must be permitted to children in a public school."[17] The Court concluded that schools have a responsibility to teach the "'habits and manners of civility' essential to a democratic society."[18] That, the Court reasoned, meant that schools could restrict vulgar and lewd speech. Many believe that the *Fraser* ruling set the stage for the Court's *Hazelwood* decision two years later.

But *Fraser* was not necessarily a broad holding giving high school administrators the last word in defining indecency as to minors. Two facts, in particular, make it an unusual case. First, Fraser gave his speech during a school-sponsored assembly to an audience of students who had to choose between the election-speech assembly and study hall. Testimony indicated that students and staff present had no practical means of leaving the gymnasium during Fraser's brief talk if they were offended.[19] Thus the students at the assembly were literally a "captive audience" at an official school program.[20] If the audience had not been captive or if the forum had not been an official school-sponsored activity, the Court might not have held that administrators could punish speech that was merely indecent and not obscene.[21] Second, the Court emphasized that Fraser's punishment had nothing to do with the political content of his message and whether a particular student was competent for student government office.[22] Thus, *Fraser* should not reach a scenario in which a school tried to censor a student's opinion conveyed with vulgar words if the school was censoring because it disagreed with the opinion.

Even where it is determined the *Fraser* standard should apply, students, administrators — and courts themselves — must still try to figure out how to identify speech that is "vulgar," "indecent," "profane," "lewd," or "plainly offensive" — or one of the many other terms that have been used by various courts and school officials. The problem is that these terms are different from "obscenity": for the most part, they are adjectives, not legal standards.

If courts have had a tough time coming up with a clear and workable definition of "obscenity," which has a substantial body of case law behind it, they have had even less success with the even less precise and legally undefined terms generated by the *Fraser* decision. Unfortunately, with few exceptions, judges have done little to help clarify the situation. Instead, courts have generally either labeled (or not labeled) speech "indecent" or "vulgar" without providing an explanation or a legal test for how they reached their conclusions, or they have essentially thrown up their hands and left the decision to school officials.[23]

Still, there are several cases that high school students can point to in urging a narrow interpretation of *Fraser*. For example, the Seventh Circuit issued one of the key pre-*Fraser* decisions that addressed language and a subject matter that today might be targeted by critics as "indecent" or "offensive."[24] In *Scoville v. Board of Education of Joliet Township High School District 204*, the Court of Appeals reversed the expulsions of two students whose unofficial newspaper included the line, "ORAL SEX MAY PREVENT TOOTH DECAY."[25] The court applied the *Tinker* standard to determine whether the publication could have reasonably been foreseen as a cause of material disruption of school activities. The court wrote, "Today's students in high school are not insulated from the shocking but legally accepted language used by demonstrators and protesters in streets and on campuses and by authors of best-selling modern literature."[26]

The Seventh Circuit went further in *Jacobs v. Board of School Commissioners*,[27] holding "that the occasional presence" of "a few earthy words relating to bodily functions and sexual intercourse" in an independent high school student publication did not threaten to disrupt school activities or "impair the accomplishment of educational objectives."[28] Though the court recognized "a difference in maturity and sophistication between students at a university and at a high school," it found that *Papish* nonetheless applied to nonobscene profanity at the high-school level.[29] Among the factors that weighed in favor of the students in *Jacobs* was that the offensive material comprised only "a very small part" of the 8- or 12-page tabloid, and the language used was neither erotic nor sexually explicit.

Most recently and most significantly, the federal Third Circuit sharply limited the applicability of the *Fraser* "lewdness" standard in a case that involved two Pennsylvania middle-school students disciplined for wearing breast-cancer awareness bracelets.[30] The school district attempted to rely on the *Fraser* case to say that the message on the rubber bracelets – "I [Heart] Boobies" – could be banned as lewd speech. But the *en banc* Third Circuit decided that the bracelets were constitutionally protected speech, and in doing so, narrowed the type of speech that falls within *Fraser*. Schools may not ban or punish speech that (like the bracelets) is "ambiguously lewd," the court decided, if the message even arguably might be understood as addressing an issue of social or political concern.[31] This limited understanding of *Fraser* should be highly protective of journalistic or artistic expression, at least in the states covered by the Third Circuit (Pennsylvania, New Jersey, Delaware).

One federal appeals court, however, interpreted *Fraser*'s holding much more broadly. In *Bystrom v. Fridley High School*, the Eighth Circuit Court of Appeals cited *Fraser* in upholding a school policy prohibiting "'pervasively indecent or vulgar' material." Still, the court said it understood the students' concern that an "indecency"-based standard was vague and overbroad: "The concepts of indecency contain large elements of subjectivity... and is a question on which reasonable people might well differ....'Courts have a First Amendment responsibility to insure that robust rhetoric in student publications is not suppressed by prudish failures to distinguish the vigorous from the vulgar.'"[32] The District Court of Minnesota, on remand from the Eighth Circuit, upheld the suspension of three students for distribution of an unofficial campus newspaper.[33] In determining whether the punishment was justified, the lower court made three separate inquiries: (1) Did the underground newspaper create a material disruption of school activities? (2) Did the newspaper advocate violence against teachers? and (3) Were the suspensions justified because of the publication's use of vulgar and indecent language?[34] On the count of vulgar and indecent language, the lower court cited *Fraser* and upheld the suspensions.[35]

The Ninth Circuit Court of Appeals has addressed the issue of vulgar and indecent student speech in at least two cases. In *Chandler v. McMinnville School District*, the court found that buttons worn by students on their clothing during a teacher's strike that included the word "scab" could not be considered "per se vulgar, lewd, obscene, or plainly offensive within the meaning of *Fraser*."[36] Like most such rulings, however, the court provided no real guidance for how it arrived at such a conclusion. In a 2002 case, the Ninth Circuit held that sexual content was the key to whether student speech could be proscribed as indecent. In *LaVine v. Blaine School District*, the court found that a poem written by high school student that was filled with imagery of violent death, suicide and the shooting of fellow students was not vulgar, lewd, obscene or plainly offensive because the speech was "not 'an elaborate, graphic, and explicit sexual metaphor' as was the student's speech in *Fraser* . . . ." [37]

In a case involving a narrative in a student literary magazine, the federal court for the Eastern District of New York, acknowledging a dual standard for obscenity as to adults and minors, concluded nevertheless that a story employing "four-letter words" and describing a movie scene in which "a couple 'fell into bed'" was not obscene as to minors, nor did it create a "substantial disruption" under *Tinker*.[38] The court praised the literary value of the work and emphasized that the story was not "a predominant appeal to prurient interest," but rather contained dialogue young people ordinarily hear on a city street.[39]

The federal court for the Southern District of Texas ruled in *Sullivan v. Houston Independent School District*[40] that an underground high school newspaper that included the phrase "High Skool is Fucked" (sic) was neither obscene nor disruptive. The court noted that school officials had little justification for objecting to that language when they had placed a number of books and periodicals in the school libraries that contained "similar vulgarisms."[41]

On the other hand, two California state courts upheld the authority of high school officials to censor or punish a student for using profanity, even though the state has a strong student free expression law. The Superior Court of Marin County upheld the suspension of a student who wore a button to school that read "Fuck the Draft."[42] The U.S. Supreme Court held in *Cohen v. California* that the same phrase on a man's jacket in a courthouse was merely a profanity and not obscene, and thus not punishable.[43] Noting both *Cohen* and *Tinker*, the California court nevertheless found that the *Ginsberg* standard controlled, and regulation of profanity was permissible as to minors as long as the regulation was not "'arbitrary, capricious or patently unreasonable.'"[44]

More recently, another California court found that several profanities and the words "ass" and "tit" in a video drama about teenage pregnancy did not meet "professional standards of English and journalism" that California law required schools to teach.[45] (Ironically, the video won an award for "Best High School Drama" in California.) The court determined that all of the censored language was profane,[46] and that the intent of the statute was to prohibit "four-letter words" and words that would not be used in professional community newspapers.

In another state with a student free expression law on the books, Massachusetts, a court struck down a high school's decision to ban shirts with the slogans "Coed Naked Band: Do It To the Rhythm" and "See Dick Drink. See Dick Drive. See Dick Die. Don't be a Dick."[47] Citing the state law, the court said that students have a right to engage in nonschool-sponsored expression that may reasonably be considered vulgar provided it causes no "disruption or disorder within the school."[48]

A federal appellate court hearing an appeal from Vermont rejected an attempt to broaden the scope of *Fraser* to encompass speech deemed "inappropriate" by school officials.[49] The district court had ruled that a T-shirt criticizing President Bush as the "Chicken Hawk-in-Chief," and using pictures of alcohol and drugs in order to mock Bush's alleged history of drug and alcohol abuse, could be prohibited because "the images of drugs and alcohol are offensive or inappropriate for the middle school environment."[50] The appellate court reversed, stating that *Tinker* and not *Fraser* should be the controlling standard because the language was not "plainly offensive" in the way intended by

Vulgar or indecent language alone does not legally justify censoring a student publication under the *Tinker* standard.

Fraser. As the opinion explained, "courts that address *Fraser* appear to treat 'plainly offensive' synonymously with and as part and parcel of speech that is lewd, vulgar, and indecent — meaning speech that is something less than obscene but related to that concept, that is to say, speech containing sexual innuendo and profanity."[51]

The non-school-sponsored nature of students' speech was also a significant factor for two federal district court judges in Pennsylvania who found that the First Amendment limited the ability of school officials to punish students who engaged in lewd and vulgar speech online when off-campus.[52] In one case that recognized the ability of school officials to prohibit "lewd, vulgar or profane language on school property," the court ruled that school officials could not punish a student who published "lewd, abusive, and derogatory" comments about the school athletic director on his personal website.[53] The judge wrote that "the First Amendment protection of freedom of expression may not be made a casualty of the effort to force-feed good manners to the ruffians among us."[54] In the other case, involving a parody MySpace profile mocking the school principal, the court concluded the content was "lewd, profane and sexually inappropriate," but held that the school lacked the authority to discipline the speech without a "nexus" to the school that makes the speech school-related, such as a material disruption of the school day.[55]

After an Oregon trial court dismissed a student's claim against a school district that had him expelled for circulating an underground magazine, a dissenting appeals court judge in Oregon came to a similar conclusion when reviewing the language contained in the publication.[56] The judge noted that the language in the magazine was "vulgar and threatening," but that — as non-school-sponsored speech — it could not be censored on those grounds.[57] The majority, however, took a different approach to the question. It found that the magazine was unprotected because it was disruptive. It went on to say, however, that the publication could also have been banned simply on a finding that it was vulgar: "It is untenable to argue that the use of vulgar or threatening language not resulting in actual disruption is not subject to discipline."[58]

First Amendment advocates have argued that the *Fraser* legal standard makes sense only in a setting where, as at Matthew Fraser's speech, the speech is forced onto a "captive" listening audience at an official school function. That interpretation would spare student publications from regulation under *Fraser*, since publications must be sought out by the reader. Nonetheless, at least one federal appeals court has applied *Fraser* even to media that students independently produce and try to distribute to a willing campus audience.

In *R.O. v. Ithaca City School District*,[59] student editors challenged a New York high school's order forbidding publication of a student-drawn cartoon mocking the school's sex-education programs. Their principal first ordered the cartoon removed from the official school-funded newspaper, *The Tattler,* and then also refused to allow distribution of an independently produced "underground" newspaper that carried the same drawing. Describing the stick-figure cartoon as "unquestionably lewd," the Second Circuit U.S. Court of Appeals decided that both the school-sponsored and the independently funded newspaper could lawfully be censored under the authority of *Fraser.*[60]

REGULATION OF "INDECENT SPEECH" IN BROADCASTING

High schools are not the only place that regulation of "indecent" speech (as opposed to obscenity, which is always unprotected) has been allowed. The Federal Communications Commission (FCC) regulates indecent programming on television and in radio broadcasts.[61] In 1978, in a famous case involving the broadcast of comedian George Carlin's "Filthy Words" monologue, the Supreme Court upheld the FCC's discretion in defining and regulating indecency, noting "the pervasive presence of broadcast speech in the lives of all Americans" and that "broadcasting is uniquely accessible to children."[62]

In language that has remained largely unchanged for nearly 30 years, the FCC defines indecency as "language or material that, in context, depicts or describes, in terms patently offensive as measured by contemporary community standards for the broadcast medium, sexual or excretory activities or organs."[63]

It is important to note that the FCC has jurisdiction only over programming broadcast over the public airwaves. It does not, for example, regulate programming distributed exclusively via cable, satellite, closed circuit systems or the Internet (for example, "streamed" Internet-only radio). Also, the FCC does not independently monitor broadcast programming. Rather, it responds to specific listener or viewer complaints and determines whether a particular program is indecent.

The FCC's authority to regulate indecent broadcast speech is limited in other ways as well. Before a particular regulation is allowed, the agency must identify a compelling government interest that warrants regulation and explain how its regulation is narrowly tailored to further those interests.

One long-recognized "compelling government interest" has been the welfare of children — however broadly that notion may be defined. The Supreme Court has ruled that an indecent broadcast may be regulated despite its literary, artistic or scientific value if there is reasonable risk that children are in the audience.[64] Toward that end, in 1995, the FCC implemented its so-called "safe harbor" rules that limit the broadcast of indecent speech to the hours of 10 p.m. to 6 a.m., a period when most children are presumably asleep.[65] Programming that occurs outside of those hours is subject to indecency regulation.

Not surprisingly, the FCC's indecency rules have always been controversial. They have also often been confusing. In an attempt "to provide guidance to the broadcast industry regarding our case law interpreting the indecency statute and our enforcement policies with respect to broadcast indecency," the FCC in 2001 issued a Policy Statement describing the Commission's process for making indecency determinations.[66] The agency listed three "principal factors" that it said have proven significant in its determination that a particular song or other type of broadcast speech was "indecent." They are:

> (1) the *explicitness or graphic nature* of the description or depiction of sexual or excretory organs or activities;
> (2) whether the material *dwells on or repeats at length* descriptions of sexual or excretory organs or activities;
> (3) *whether the material appears to pander or is used to titillate, or whether the material appears to have been presented for its shock value.* (Emphasis in original).

The FCC noted, "in assessing all of the factors, and particularly the third factor, the overall context of the broadcast in which the disputed material appeared is critical."

For example, the FCC ruled that it was *not* "indecent" when the National Public Radio program *All Things Considered* broadcast a news story that included an excerpt from the wiretap of a telephone conversation during which the organized crime figure John Gotti used the "f-word" ten times in seven sentences. The FCC found that the broadcast of the tape containing the explicit language, which was submitted as evidence in a widely reported trial, was an "integral part of a bona fide news story concerning organized crime."[67] The FCC said that it did "not find the use of such coarse words in a legitimate news report to have been gratuitous, pandering, titillating or otherwise 'patently offensive' as that term is used in our indecency definition."[68] On the other hand, the FCC has stated that "even relatively fleeting references may be found indecent where other factors contribute to a finding of patent offensiveness."[69]

Precisely what the FCC intended in its 2001 regulations became the central question in a pair of recent court cases. In one of the cases, the FCC concluded that a single use of profanity ("fucking brilliant") during the 2003 Golden Globe Awards telecast was indecent.[70] While acknowledging that the profanity was not intended to describe a sexual act, the FCC ruled that any use of the word in question "invariably invokes a coarse sexual image."[71] In rejecting the broadcasters' additional claim that the word was an example of the type of fleeting reference that had not been punished in years past, the Commission reversed its prior rulings permitting such uses.[72] On appeal, the U.S. Court of Appeals for the Second Circuit reversed the FCC's decision, holding by a 2-1 majority that the FCC's change in policy was arbitrary and capricious.[73]

The other recently decided case derives from the broadcast of the 2004 Super Bowl halftime show, the scene of singer Janet Jackson's infamous "wardrobe malfunction," which resulted in a less-than-one-second flash of the singer's breast on a live nationwide telecast. The FCC concluded that the broadcast was indecent and fined CBS Broadcasting. But CBS successfully appealed the fine, which was thrown out by the Third Circuit U.S. Court of Appeals in 2011.[74] That ruling was based on the FCC's failure to explain why it suddenly decided to start fining broadcasters for "fleeting" nudity when other instances had gone unpunished.[75]

The Supreme Court accepted the FCC's petition to hear the Fox case during its 2011-12 term. Advocates for the broadcast industry argued that the basis for giving the FCC so much power to regulate the content of speech — the "scarcity" of broadcasting channels — no longer made sense with the explosion of outlets available through cable, satellite and the Internet. Hopes were high for a strong message from the Supreme Court finally clarifying when (if ever) the FCC could issue fines for profanity or nudity. But those hopes were deflated when, at the end of its 2012 term, the Court basically punted the difficult First Amendment questions.[76] The Court unanimously threw out the fines against Fox on the grounds that the station's FIfth Amendment due process rights were violated by imposing fines without fair notice.[77] But the Court did not decide the bigger-picture issue of exactly when over-the-air speech becomes punishable. (Having "decided not to decide," the Court unsurprisingly turned down a petition to review the CBS case,[78] letting the Third Circuit's decision stand.)

In the months following the Supreme Court's non-decision, the FCC appeared reluctant to spend more resources fighting over indecency. The Commission began closing old indecency cases without imposing penalties, stating its intent to focus only on "egregious" cases. In April 2013, the Commission issued a notice that it was reconsidering the "fleeting expletive" policy,[79] again raising hopes that broadcasters might (finally) feel confident where the line of "indecency" exists.

Fortunately, indecency claims against student broadcast media are rare.[80] In one student-broadcast case from the early 1990s, the FCC fined WSUC-FM, a station at the State University of New York in Cortland, $23,750 for playing a sexually graphic song about "yodeling in the valley," a euphemism for oral sex.[81] The FCC said the broadcast, which contained significant profanity, was actionable because the station aired the song during mid-afternoon, when there was a reasonable risk that children were listening. The school claimed the broadcast violated station policy and that a rogue student employee, who had had several serious run-ins with the station, had likely played the song.

After receiving testimony from SUNY-Cortland's student government that the fine exceeded the radio station's entire annual budget — and noting the immediate steps taken by SUNY officials to remedy the situation and prevent future occurrences — the FCC eventually reduced the fine to $4,200.[82]

From the moment it became clear the Internet was more than just a playground for computer "geeks" — that it was going to change how the world communicated — a fierce ideological battle broke out. The clash was between those — led largely by civil-rights groups and Internet pioneers — who envisioned cyberspace as a tolerant, government-free speech zone, where a website devoted to Michelangelo could peacefully coexist a mouse click away from MikesHotBikerBabes.com, and those — aided by lawmakers in Congress — who wanted an Internet that more resembled broadcast television, potentially full of useful information, but with strict laws and regulations that kept more offensive material out.

The first major battle occurred in 1997 when the U.S. Supreme Court, in a landmark decision, struck down an indecency standard for the Internet.[83] Part of the federal Communications Decency Act of 1996 (CDA) made it a crime for any person to post material on the Internet that would be considered either obscene or indecent.[84] In striking down the indecency provision, the Court held that the use of the term "indecent," without definition, to describe prohibited content was too vague to withstand constitutional scrutiny.[85]

The Court explicitly rejected the government's argument that cyberspace should be subject to the same complex regulatory scheme and indecency rules imposed on broadcast speech and made it clear that Internet speech was entitled to the same protections as print-based counterparts: "Although the Government has an interest in protecting children from potentially harmful materials... the CDA pursues that interest by suppressing a large amount of speech that adults have a constitutional right to send and receive.... Its breadth is wholly unprecedented."[86]

Such a sweeping pronouncement, however, has not stopped determined lawmakers from continuing to try to crack down on Internet speech they find distasteful. A year after the Supreme Court struck part of the CDA, Congress once again attempted to police pornography and other objectionable material on the Internet by passing the Child Online Protection Act (COPA).[87] Using the Supreme Court's CDA decision as their blueprint, the framers of COPA narrowed the sources of speech subject to prosecution and substituted a "harmful to minors" standard for the indecency language in the CDA.[88] In 2003, a federal appeals court upheld an injunction against COPA's enforcement, finding COPA was likely unconstitutional, and the Supreme Court upheld the decision.[89] The injunction became permanent, effectively wiping COPA off the books, when the federal Third Circuit found the act to be unconstitutionally vague and overbroad, and the Supreme Court refused to take up the government's appeal.[90]

The Supreme Court has also struck down a federal law that criminalized drawings or images that "appear to depict minors" or visual depictions that "convey the impression" that a minor is engaging in sex acts, whether an actual minor was involved or not.[91] State lawmakers, too, have tried to restrict online speech, frequently patterning their laws after the CDA and COPA. Once challenged in court, the laws have generally met the same fate as their federal counterparts. While it is possible to penalize one-to-one communications where it is clear that the sender targeted harmful material to a child, courts have refused to hold speakers responsible for "harmful" content in widely available films, magazines or websites that children happen to view.[92]

While most laws restricting Internet-based speech have fallen in the face of constitutional challenges, courts have allowed lawmakers — enacting a variety of other acronymic statutes — to tinker around the edges, particularly in cases regarding access to the Internet (rather than Internet content) where the stated goal is the "protection of children."

For example, in 2003, the Supreme Court upheld the Children's Internet Protection Act (CIPA), a law that conditions a public school or library's receipt of federal funding for Internet access on its use of Internet blocking software that prevents user access to obscenity, child pornography and material deemed harmful to minors.[93] The law allows the blocking software to be turned off at the request of an adult user. Several states have also enacted or proposed similar laws that require Internet blocking software or some other method for restricting minors' access to online material some consider harmful.[94]

Another federal law enacted with the stated purpose of protecting kids while online is the Children's Online Privacy Protection Act (COPPA). Among other things, COPPA requires commercial websites directed at children under the age of thirteen to obtain parental permission before collecting personal information from child users.[95]

Finally, teachers may also find that their right to access certain material on the Internet is limited. For example, in 2001 a federal court of appeals upheld a Virginia law that restricted public employee access to sexually explicit materials on state computers.[96] Several university professors had challenged the law claiming it limited their right of academic freedom to conduct Internet-based research.

While the Internet today remains by and large the borderless, unfettered free speech zone its builders envisioned, the Battle for Cyberspace appears to be far from over.

DEVELOPING A POLICY ON PROFANITY AND "OFFENSIVE" LANGUAGE

Many reputable publications, including *The New York Times*, *Newsweek* and *Time* magazine, avoid the use of four-letter profanities. When editors believe the potentially offensive words are crucial to a story, many use a first letter and dashes or underlines (for example, f---) in their place. On the other hand, many important works of literature and historical texts commonly found in school libraries contain words and phrases some might find vulgar. Examples include the King James Version of the Bible, the Nixon White House tapes, and the works of William Shakespeare, Geoffrey Chaucer, Ernest Hemingway, Lord Byron, Robert Burns, Samuel Beckett, D.H. Lawrence and Jonathan Swift. Some reputable commercial publications, especially those directed at a younger or less traditional audience, do not restrict the use of four-letter words because they know that their readers are not offended by them.

Students should carefully weigh the benefits and costs of publishing language that any segment of their readers might find offensive. Among the issues to consider: (1) Is the language necessary to communicate the message of a story or to give a quote authenticity? Or will it divert attention from the article's primary focus? (2) Is the author simply using certain words for shock value without a journalistic or literary justification? (3) Is there less offensive language that would communicate the same idea? (4) Is a fight over profanity or sexually graphic images the free speech battle you want to wage? High school students especially might want to consider whether the use of profane language warrants a possible confrontation with readers or school administrators, including possible long-term effects on the publication's credibility and editorial autonomy.

SUMMARY

Obscenity is frequently misunderstood and almost never seen in traditional student media. More often the term is mistakenly thrown about by school officials or others upset over material they find offensive. True obscenity, however, is not merely "offensive" or "lewd" or "vulgar" or "inappropriate" or "indecent." Obscenity is a legal term that defines a crime and is accurately applied only to extreme, hard-core, sexually explicit (typically pictorial) material. Moderate profanity or mild nudity is not obscene. For most college student print and online media, where readers are older, the bar is sufficiently high to pose virtually no legal problem; decisions regarding whether to publish can generally be made based on editorial and ethical considerations. College broadcasters — like all broadcasters — must adhere to FCC indecency regulations.

It is a different story for high school student media, where courts have increasingly allowed school officials to censor and/or punish for material brought on campus that falls far short of being legally obscene. While the standard is hard — or even impossible — to clearly define, high school students should generally avoid "indecent" or vulgar speech, including most profanity and pictorial nudity, where the publication or Web site will be distributed or purposefully made available on school grounds.

CASE STUDY

The Student Times staff really wanted to shake things up in its annual April Fools' Day issue. In addition to other jokes and parodies, the college paper — specially labeled *The Stupid Times* — published a spoof sex-advice column that contained "How-to Advice for Budding Rapists," including a sexually explicit "checklist to ensure a productive experience for all parties involved." The issue also contained a half-page "ad" featuring profanity (including a number of sexual terms) in giant block letters, "because we are allowed to print it," it said, and a bogus news story on the return of the streaking fad to America's college campuses. The latter included a full frontal photo of a man and a woman running in front of a prominent campus building clad only in tennis shoes.

Not surprisingly, the paper caused a quite a stir. Women's groups on campus were outraged by the sex column, which they claimed was "obscene" and demeaning to women. Community members were angry at KNUT, the college radio station, whose "shock jocks" read some of the more graphic passages from *The Student Times* on their mid-morning show. The station also aired a couple of examples of the profanity as part of a story about the brewing controversy during its evening newscast. Alumni from across the country called the school to complain about the posting of the streaking photo on the newspaper's website.

Unfortunately, the ripple effects from the paper continued to be felt a week later when the student editor of a nearby high school newspaper was suspended for a week for publishing a story on *The Student Times* controversy that included a scanned copy of the profanity-filled ad.

You are Dr. Triplexx, a widely acclaimed expert on obscenity. You've been asked by the college and high school to help them sort through the entire mess. They particularly want to know if any of the students broke the law.

ANSWER:
As you count them, there are six potential trouble spots:

(1) Publication of the sex advice column in *The Stupid Times*.
As an expert on obscenity, you know from experience that most of what people label "obscenity" — isn't. That's the case here. While the sex advice column is offensive, disgusting and in poor taste, it does not meet the legal definition of obscenity under the U.S. Supreme Court's *Miller* test. Specifically, it would be difficult to show that the column is devoid of any serious literary or artistic value, as required by *Miller*'s third prong. Obviously, the editors thought the column was funny when they wrote it, and while they may be in the minority, there are likely to be readers who feel the same. The Supreme Court has said that the First Amendment requires that expression, including misfired attempts at humor, be given breathing space.

(2) Publication of the profanity-filled ad in *The Stupid Times*.
Words alone rarely rise to the level of obscenity. A list of profanity, published in a college newspaper distributed to adult-aged students, that makes no attempt to describe sexual conduct or arouse sexual feelings is not legally obscene.

(3) Publication of the streaking photo in *The Stupid Times*.
Nude photos, drawings or other pictorial images are not automatically obscene. Whether a photo crosses the obscenity line generally depends on what the bare-skinned people in the photo are doing. Images of naked adults that are not engaged in sexual conduct or that do not arouse sexual

feelings are not obscene. That would seem to be the case here, where the photo simply captures two people running on campus without clothes.

(4) Posting of the streaking photo on *The Stupid Times* Web site.

If the photo is not obscene in the print version of the paper, as you've determined, it does not become obscene or otherwise illegal simply because it is posted online. At least for now, there is no separate legal standard for "offensive" material on the Internet.

(5) KNUT "shock jocks'" reading from The Student Times.

While it's your belief that there is nothing obscene in *The Stupid Times*, a more restrictive "indecency" standard applies to material when it is broadcast over public airwaves. Applying the FCC's indecency definition, and being mindful of how the FCC has interpreted that definition in previous cases, it looks like KNUT and its disc jockeys might have a legal problem. First, the program was broadcast during mid-morning, outside of the "safe harbor" time period of 10 p.m. to 6 a.m. when indecent programming can safely be aired. Second, the sex advice column is described as "sexually explicit." Assuming that it explicitly or graphically describes the physical acts of a sexual assault, it likely meets the FCC definition. Finally, assuming the "shock jocks" simply read the profanity-filled ad word-for-word it's likely that the FCC might interpret that as presenting the material simply for its shock value, which is one of the factors the Commission uses to determine indecency.

(6) KNUT newscast about *The Stupid Times* controversy.

Unlike the shock jocks' morning program, it is much less likely that accurately reporting some of the contents of *The Stupid Times* as part of a bona fide newscast would create an indecency problem. *The Stupid Times* controversy is news and providing accurate information about the specific words that sparked the controversy, in context, is less likely to be viewed as gratuitous, pandering, titillating or otherwise "patently offensive," as required by the FCC's indecency standard. Of course, reading the entire profanity-laden ad might cross the line, but in this case you understand the newscast used only "a couple examples." Still, most news organizations would probably think long and hard about repeating profanity on the air if they felt the story could reasonably be told by describing the newspaper in more general terms.

(7) High school student editor's republication of the ad from *The Stupid Times*.

While it's unlikely that the high school editor broke any laws in republishing the ad, he *may* be hard-pressed to argue that school officials acted unlawfully in punishing him for his decision. Unless there exists a state law, policy or practice that provides extra legal protection, a growing number of courts have held that high school students have no First Amendment right to publish or engage in indecent, vulgar, lewd or profane speech while on school grounds — even, as here, where such speech is part of a legitimate and newsworthy story. If the editor wanted to cover the story, he would have been better served by simply describing the issue in general terms (for example, "*The Stupid Times* included a half page ad featuring profanity in giant block letters") and, if he felt an image from the paper was necessary, scanning the full page of the newspaper at a size that made the specific language in the spoof ad impossible to read.

ENDNOTES

1   *See Roth v. United States*, 354 U.S. 476 (1957), *reh'g denied*, 355 U.S. 852 (1957) (ruling that obscenity is not protected by the First Amendment).
2   *Jacobellis v. Ohio*, 378 U.S. 184, 197 (Stewart, J., concurring).
3   Miller v. California, 413 U.S. 15 (1973), *reh'g denied*, 414 U.S. 881 (1973).
4   The test was changed from "an average person" to "a reasonable person" by the Court's decision in *Pope v. Illinois*, 481 U.S. 497, 500-01 (1987).
5   LOUIS E. INGLEHART, STUDENT PUBLICATIONS: LEGALITIES, GOVERNANCE, AND OPERATION, 104 (Iowa State University Press 1993).
6   *Papish v. Bd. of Curators*, 410 U.S. 667 (1973), *reh'g denied*, 411 U.S. 960 (1973).
7   *Id.* at 670.
8   *Ginsberg v. New York*, 390 U.S. 629 (1968), *reh'g denied*, 391 U.S. 971 (1968).
9   *See, e.g.*, MASS. GEN. LAWS ANN. ch. 272, Sec. 28 (West 2008) (prohibiting dissemination to a minor

of "any matter harmful to minors"). *See also Crawford v. Lungren*, 96 F.3d 380, 389 (9th Cir. 1996) (upholding a California law that banned the sale of "harmful matter" from unsupervised sidewalk vending machines because it was "narrowly tailored to protect children without depriving adults" of access to the publications); *State v. Evenson*, 33 P.3d 780 (Ariz. Ct. App. 2001), review dismissed, 65 P.3d 433 (Ariz. 2003), cert. denied, 540 U.S. 874 (2003) (upholding the constitutionality of an Arizona law that prohibited the sale or display of any vending machine material "harmful to minors").

10 See *ACLU v. Ashcroft*, 322 F.3d 240, 253 (3d Cir. 2003) (finding that "harmful to minors" standard contained in federal Children's Online Protection Act "endangers a wide range of communications, exhibits, and speakers whose messages do not comport with the type of harmful materials legitimately targeted under COPA, i.e., material that is obscene as to minors"), *aff'd and remanded*, 542 U.S. 656 (2004) ("Attaching criminal sanctions to a mistaken judgment about the contours of the novel and nebulous category of 'harmful to minors' speech clearly imposes a heavy burden on the exercise of First Amendment freedoms.") (Stevens, J., concurring).

11 See, e.g., *Commonwealth v. Sullivan*, 774 N.E.2d 679, 682-83, (Mass. App. Ct. 2002), review denied, 777 N.E.2d 1263 (Mass. 2002) (table op.) (finding that a prosecutor was not required to provide testimony — and acknowledging that there was no case law on the subject — about what constituted material that was "harmful to minors" under state law; rather it was up to judge to draw from her "own knowledge of normative views" in her community). *Compare Entertainment Software Ass'n v. Blagojevich*, 404 F. Supp. 2d 1051, 1076 (N.D. Ill. 2005) (noting that "Ginsberg does not provide the state with general authority to regulate speech that is deemed harmful to minors; rather it concerned obscene material, which is not entitled to First Amendment protection.").

12 See, e.g., *People v. Maupin*, No. F034753, 2002 WL 337427 (Cal. Ct. App., 5th Dist., Feb. 25, 2002), *habeas corpus denied, Maupin v. Garcia*, No. CVF03-6051, 2005 WL 1875651 (E.D. Cal. Aug. 4, 2005) (finding that the jury could determine that movies shown to minors violated state's harmful to minor statute where victims described the movies as "nasty" and "dirty" and as portraying people doing "[s]ick stuff"); *Lewis v. State*, 726 N.E.2d 836, 841 (Ind. Ct. App. 2000) (finding that a videotape that depicted a naked man on a bed kissing a clothed woman fell within statutory definition of matter harmful to minors).

13 See, e.g., *Cyberspace Communications, Inc. v. Engler*, 55 F. Supp. 2d 737, 747 (E.D. Mich. 1999), aff'd, 238 F.3d 420 (6th Cir. 2000) (table op.) (granting an injunction against the enforcement of a Michigan law that criminalized the use of computers to disseminate sexually explicit materials to minors, noting that to comply with the law, one "must speak only in language suitable for children"). *Compare Simmons v. State*, 944 So. 2d 317, 327 (Fla. 2006) (upholding a Florida statute that defined "harmful to minors" using the three-pronged test associated with obscenity as to minors). For a comprehensive look at the history and growing trend toward restricting speech in the name of protecting children, see MARJORIE HEINS, NOT IN FRONT OF THE CHILDREN: "INDECENCY," CENSORSHIP, AND THE INNOCENCE OF YOUTH (2001).

14 *Bethel Sch. Dist. No. 403 v. Fraser*, 478 U.S. 675 (1986).

15 *Id.* at 687.

16 *Id.* at 680. *See also id.* at 688-89 (Brennan, J., concurring).

17 *Id.* at 682.

18 *Id.* at 681.

19 Brief of Petitioners at 22, *Bethel Sch. Dist. No. 403 v. Fraser*, 1984 WL 565918 (9th Cir. Nov. 27, 1984).

20 See MELVILLE B. NIMMER, NIMMER ON FREEDOM OF SPEECH: A TREATISE ON THE THEORY OF THE FIRST AMENDMENT Sec. 3.04, p. 3-30 (Cumulative Supp. 1992).

21 *But see Chandler v. McMinnville Sch. Dist.*, 978 F.2d 524, 529 (9th Cir. 1992) ("[S]chool officials may suppress speech that is vulgar, lewd, obscene, or plainly offensive without a showing that such speech occurred during a school-sponsored event or threatened to 'substantially interfere with [the school's] work.'"). Some of the difficulty in determining the limitations of *Fraser* have been caused by later courts stating the facts of the case differently or changing the definition of what constitutes a "school event." *See, e.g., Muller v. Jefferson Lighthouse Sch.*, 98 F.3d 1530, 1538 (7th Cir. 1996) (describing the assembly in *Fraser* as a "voluntary school assembly") and *Morse v. Frederick*, 127 S. Ct. 2618 (2007), remanded, 499 F.3d 926 (9th Cir. 2007) (finding that a student standing on a public sidewalk outside a high school during the passing of the Olympic torch was "in school" for purposes of determining his speech rights, even though students were permitted to leave the school to watch the event).

22 *Fraser*, 478 U.S. at 685.

23 See, e.g., *J.S. ex rel. H.S. v. Bethlehem Area Sch. Dist.*, 807 A.2d 847 (Pa. 2002). The Supreme Court of Pennsylvania found that statements made on a website created by a junior high school student and which were viewed on school grounds were lewd, vulgar or plainly offensive. The statements included a joke that the principal was having sex with another principal, an image of a math teacher morphing into Hitler, and a fictitious appeal for money to hire a hit man to kill a teacher. The court held that "[i]t is for school districts to determine what is vulgar, lewd or plainly offensive, at least in the first instance. Great deference should be given to their determination, as courts must not become embroiled in micromanaging school officials' administration of the institution's daily affairs." *Id.* at 868 n.13. *Compare Layshock v. Hermitage Sch. Dist.*, 496 F. Supp. 2d 587, 599 (W.D. Pa. 2007) ("This Court has no difficulty concluding, and will assume arguendo, that Justin's profile is lewd, profane and sexually inappropriate. Nevertheless, *Fraser* does not give the school district authority to punish him for creating it."). In *Layshock*, the federal district court held that a parody MySpace profile mocking a school principal was not on-campus conduct subject to *Fraser*. In both *J.S.* and *Layshock*, the courts opined that the students' words fell within the range of vulgar and lewd speech proscribable under *Fraser*, but the two courts reached differing outcomes on other bases.

24 *Scoville v. Bd. of Educ.*, 425 F.2d 10 (7th Cir. 1970), cert. denied, 400 U.S. 826 (1970).

25 *Id.* at 14 (capitalization in original).

26 *Id.*
27 *Jacobs v. Bd. of Sch. Commissioners*, 490 F.2d 601 (7th Cir. 1973), *vacated as moot*, 420 U.S. 128 (1975).
28 *Id.* at 610.
29 *See id.* The Fourth Circuit Court of Appeals in *Baughman v. Freienmuth*, 478 F.2d 1345 (4th Cir. 1973), followed the lead of the Seventh Circuit. The *Baughman* court found that the undefined term "obscene" in a school policy was too vague to be adequate criteria for censorship. In its holding, the court admonished school officials not to use "such vague labels" to "choke off criticism, either of themselves, or of school policies, which they find disrespectful, tasteless, or offensive." Id. at 1351 (citing *Scoville v. Bd. of Educ.*, 425 F.2d 10, 14 (7th Cir. 1970)).
30 *B.H. v. Easton Area Sch. Dist.*, __ F.3d __, No. 11-2067, 2013 WL 3970093 (3d Cir. Aug. 5, 2013) (en banc).
31 *Id.* at *16.
32 *Bystrom v. Fridley High Sch., Indep. Sch. Dist. No. 14* (Bystrom I), 822 F.2d 747, 752-753 (8th Cir. 1987) (citing, in part, language in *Fraser* quoting *Thomas v. Bd. of Educ., Granville Cent. Sch. Dist.*, 607 F. 2d Cir. 1979)).
33 *Bystrom v. Fridley High Sch., Indep. Sch. Dist. No. 14* (Bystrom II), 686 F. Supp. 1387 (D. Minn. 1987), aff'd, 855 F.2d 855 (8th Cir. 1988).
34 *Brystrom II*, 686 F. Supp. at 1392.
35 *Id.* at 1393. The only example of offensive language quoted by the court was the use of "damn" as an adverbial modifier. See *id.* at 1390.
36 *Chandler v. McMinnville Sch. Dist.*, 978 F.2d 524, 530 (9th Cir. 1992).
37 *LaVine v. Blaine Sch. Dist.*, 257 F.3d 981, 989 (9th Cir. 2001), *reconsideration en banc denied*, 279 F.3d 719 (9th Cir. 2002), *cert. denied*, 536 U.S. 959 (2002).
38 *Koppell v. Levine*, 347 F. Supp. 456, 458-60 (E.D.N.Y. 1972). The magazine was printed using school funds, and submissions — although selected by student editors — were approved by the magazine's faculty adviser and the chairman of the English department. *Id.* at 458. Nevertheless, the court noted that "[t]he name of the school did not appear on the publication" and the magazine "had the character of a private creation by the student editors." *Id.* at 460.
39 *Id.* at 459.
40 *Sullivan v. Houston Indep. Sch. Dist.*, 333 F. Supp. 1149 (S.D. Tex. 1971), *vacated on other grounds*, 475 F.2d 1071 (5th Cir. 1973), *reh'g denied*, 475 F.2d 1404 (5th Cir. 1973), *cert. denied*, 414 U.S. 1032 (1973).
41 *Id.* at 1165. *A Separate Peace* by John Knowles, *The Catcher in the Rye* by J.D. Salinger and *The Confessions of Nat Turner* by William Styron were among the library materials mentioned by the court. *Id.* n.19.
42 *Hinze v. Superior Court of Marin County*, 174 Cal. Rptr. 403 (Cal. Ct. App. 1981) (unpublished opinion).
43 *Cohen v. California*, 403 U.S. 15, 20, *reh'g denied*, 404 U.S. 876 (1971) (finding that, in order to be obscene, "expression must be, in some significant way, erotic").
44 *Hinze*, 174 Cal. Rptr. at 404 (quoting *Sternoff v. State Bd. of Equalization*, 103 Cal. Rptr. 3d 828 (1980)).
45 *Lopez v. Tulare Joint Union High Sch. Dist.*, 34 Cal. App. 4th 1302, 1322 (Cal. Ct. App. 1995).
46 *Id.* at 1329.
47 *Pyle v. Sch. Committee of South Hadley*, 667 N.E.2d 869 (Mass. 1996).
48 *Id.* at 872.
49 *Guiles v. Marineau*, 461 F.3d 320 (2d Cir. 2006), *aff'g in part, vacating in part* 349 F. Supp. 2d 871 (D. Vt. 2004), *cert. denied*, 127 S. Ct. 3054 (2007).
50 *Guiles*, 349 F. Supp. 2d at 881.
51 *Guiles*, 461 F.3d at 328.
52 *Killion v. Franklin Reg'l Sch. Dist.*, 136 F. Supp. 2d 446 (W.D. Pa. 2001); *Layshock v. Hermitage Sch. Dist.*, 496 F. Supp. 2d 587 (W.D. Pa. 2007).
53 *Killion*, 136 F. Supp. 2d at 453, 457. The court found the following remark, along with other comments posted on the student's Web site, to be lewd, abusive and derogatory: "Because of his extensive gut factor, the 'man' hasn't seen his own penis in over a decade." *Id.* at 457.
54 *Id.* at 457.
55 *Layshock*, 496 F. Supp. 2d at 599.
56 *Pangle v. Bend-LaPine Sch. Dist.*, 10 P.3d 275, 277 (Or. Ct. App. 2000), *review denied*, 34 P.3d 1176 (Or. 2001).
57 *Id.* at 290 (Or. Ct. App. 2000) (Armstrong, J., concurring in part and dissenting in part).
58 *Id.* at 286.
59 645 F.3d 533 (2d Cir. 2011).
60 *Id.* at 541.
61 18 U.S.C. Sec. 1464.
62 *FCC v. Pacifica Foundation*, 438 U.S. 726, 748-49, *reh'g denied*, 439 U.S. 883 (1978).
63 *See, e.g., Action for Children's Television v. FCC*, 58 F.3d 654, 657 (D.C. Cir. 1995), *cert. denied*, 516 U.S. 1043 (1996) ("ACT III").
64 *Pacifica*, 438 U.S. at 732 n.5.
65 Broadcast Indecency, 60 Fed. Reg. 44439-01, 1995 WL 504837 (August 28, 1995) (*codified in* 47 C.F.R. Sec. 73.3999 (2008)).
66 In the Matter of Industry Guidance on the Commission's Case Law Interpreting 18 U.S.C. Sec. 146 and Enforcement Policies Regarding Broadcast Indecency, 16 F.C.C.R. 7999 (April 6, 2001) [hereinafter *FCC Indecency Policy Statement*].
67 Letter from the Federal Communications Commission to Mr. Peter Branton, 6 F.C.C.R. 610 (Jan. 24,

1991).

68   *Id.*

69   *FCC Indecency Policy Statement* at 8009. According to the FCC, such factors include broadcasting references to sexual activities with children or airing material that, although fleeting, is graphic or explicit. *See, e.g.,* Letter to Tempe Radio, Inc., Licensee, KUPD-FM, 12 F.C.C.R. 21828 (Dec. 17, 1997) (finding that a radio announcer's two-sentence joke about having sex with an 8-year-old was indecent, though the joke did not contain profanity); Letter to LBJS Broadcasting Company, L.P., Licensee, KLBJ(FM), 13 F.C.C.R. 20956, 20958 (Oct. 26, 1998) (finding that a six-word sentence containing two words of "explicit" profanity was indecent).

70   In the Matter of Complaints Against Various Broadcast Licensees Regarding Their Airing of the "Golden Globe Awards" Program, 19 F.C.C.R. 4975 (Mar. 18, 2004).

71   *Id.* at 4979.

72   *Id.* at 4980.

73   *Fox Television Stations, Inc. v. FCC*, 489 F.3d 444 (2d Cir. 2007), *cert. granted*, 128 S. Ct. 1647 (2008).

74   *CBS Corp. v. FCC*, 663 F.3d 122 (3d Cir. 2011)

75   *Id.* at 151-52.

76   *FCC v. Fox Television Stations, Inc.*, 132 S.Ct. 2307 (2012).

77   *Id.* at 2320.

78   *FCC v. CBS Corp.*, 132 S.Ct. 2677 (2012).

79   Federal Communications Commission, "FCC Reduces Backlog of Broadcast Indecency Complaints by 70% (More Than One Million Complaints); Seeks Comments on Adopting Egregious Cases Policy," 78 Fed. Reg. 23563-02, Docket No. 13-86 (Apr. 19, 2013).

80   For a discussion of indecency issues at college broadcast stations see "Dirty Words," Student Press Law Center *Report*, Fall 2008, p. 31.

81   Letter re. Notice of Apparent Liability for a Forfeiture to Licensee, WSUC-FM, SUNY-Cortland, 8 F.C.C.R. 456, 456-57 (Jan. 7, 1993).

82   In the Matter of State University of New York, 13 F.C.C.R. 23,810, 23,812 (Aug. 6, 1998).

83   *Reno v. ACLU*, 521 U.S. 844 (1997). *See also Nitke v. Ashcroft*, 253 F. Supp. 2d 587 (S.D.N.Y. 2003), and *Nitke v. Gonzales*, 413 F. Supp. 2d 262 (S.D.N.Y. 2005), aff'd, 547 U.S. 1015 (2006) (challenging provisions of the CDA that rely on local community standards to define obscenity).

84   Pub. L. 108-21 Sec. 603(2), 117 Stat. 650, 686 (West 2003) (detailing changes to 47 U.S.C. Sec. 223(a)(1)(B)(ii)). The Court also struck down a provision in the law that made it a crime to depict "sexual or excretory activities or organs" in a "patently offensive" way. See *Id.* (detailing changes to 47 U.S.C. Sec. 223(d)).

85   *Reno*, 521 U.S. at 871.

86   *Id.* at 846 (citations omitted).

87   47 U.S.C. Sec. 231. COPA made it illegal to knowingly post any material on the World Wide Web (excluding e-mail, newsgroups, etc.) that is harmful to minors, for commercial purposes, and accessible to persons under the age of 17. It primarily targeted businesses seeking to make a profit from posting such materials. Like the CDA, COPA allowed businesses to avoid prosecution through (1) the use of a credit card or other age verification system, and (2) any good-faith effort to restrict access by minors.

88   Whether material published on the World Wide Web is "harmful to minors" was governed by a three-part test, every prong of which must be satisfied before one can be found liable under COPA: (a) the average person, applying contemporary community standards, would find, taking the material as a whole and with respect to minors, that the material is designed to appeal to, or is designed to pander to, the prurient interest; (b) the material depicts, describes, or represents, in a manner patently offensive with respect to minors, an actual or simulated sexual act or sexual contact, an actual or simulated normal or perverted sexual act, or a lewd exhibition of the genitals or post-pubescent female breast; and (c) taken as a whole, the material lacks serious literary, artistic, political, or scientific value for minors. 47 U.S.C. Sec. 231(e)(6).

89   *ACLU v. Ashcroft*, 322 F.3d 240 (3d Cir. 2003), *aff'd and remanded,* 542 U.S. 656 (2004), on remand, 478 F. Supp. 2d 775 (E.D. Pa. 2007), aff'd, 534 F. 3d 181 (3d Cir. 3008).

90   *ACLU v. Mukasey*, 534 F. 3d 181 (3d Cir. 2008), cert denied, Mukasey v. ACLU, 555 U.S. 1137 (2009).

91   *Ashcroft v. The Free Speech Coalition*, 535 U.S. 234, 239, 257 (2002) (striking down the Child Pornography Prevention Act of 1996 (CPPA)).

92   *See, e.g., American Booksellers Foundation for Free Expression v. Sullvan*, 799 F.Supp.2d 1078 (D. Alaska 2011) (halting enforcement of Alaska statute that criminalized "knowingly distributing" sexually indecent material to minors, which failed to require knowledge or intent that the material reach viewers under 18); *American Booksellers Foundation for Free Expression v. Coakley*, No. 10-11165–RWZ, 2010 WL 4273802 (D. Mass. Oct. 26, 2010) (invalidating Massachusetts law against electronic distribution of material "harmful to minors," because law applied to publicly viewable websites where publishers could not determine age of viewers); *American Booksellers Foundation v. Dean*, 342 F.3d 96 (2d Cir. 2003) (striking down a Vermont law prohibiting distribution to minors of any material that is sexually explicit and harmful to minors); *Bookfriends, Inc. v. Taft*, 223 F. Supp. 2d 932, 935 (S.D. Ohio 2002) (enjoining enforcement of an Ohio bill that prohibited "the dissemination, etc., of materials to juveniles which come within the definition of 'harmful to juveniles'" and finding the standard set out by the legislature was overbroad); *PSINet Inc. v. Chapman*, 167 F. Supp. 2d 878 (W.D. Va. 2001), aff'd , 362 F.3d 227 (4th Cir. 2004) (striking down a Virginia law that criminalized the commercial distribution of an "electronic file or message" to minors if it contained certain sexual images or words); *American Library Ass'n v. Pataki*, 969 F. Supp. 160 (S.D.N.Y. 1997) (striking down a New York statute that made it a crime to use a computer to disseminate material to children

where the material was deemed "harmful to minors"); *ACLU v. Johnson*, 4 F. Supp. 2d 1029 (D.N.M. 1998), aff'd, 194 F.3d 1149 (10th Cir. 1999) (striking down a New Mexico statute that criminalized the dissemination by computer of materials harmful to minors); *Cyberspace Communications, Inc. v. Engler*, 55 F. Supp. 2d 737 (E.D. Mich. 1999), aff'd, 238 F.3d 420 (6th Cir. 2000) (unpublished table op.), subsequent proceedings, 142 F. Supp. 2d 827 (E.D. Mich. 2001) (granting an injunction against enforcement of a Michigan law that criminalized the use of computers to disseminate sexually explicit materials to minors).

93 *United States v. American Library Ass'n, Inc.*, 539 U.S. 194 (2003) (upholding CIPA provisions as applied to public libraries; the law as applied to public schools was not challenged). *Compare Mainstream Loudoun v. Bd. of Trustees of the Loudoun County Library*, 24 F. Supp. 2d 552, 556 (E.D. Va. 1998) (striking down a library policy that required that "all library computers... be equipped with site-blocking software to block all sites displaying: (a) child pornography and obscenity; and (b) material deemed harmful to juveniles" where the sites contained no opt-out provision for adults).

94 *See* National Conference of State Legislatures, *Children and the Internet: Laws Relating to Filtering, Blocking, and Usage Policies in Schools and Libraries* (last updated Dec. 17, 2007), http://www.ncsl.org/programs/lis/cip/filterlaws.htm (last visited Sept. 11, 2013).

95 15 U.S.C. Sec. 6501 (2000). Because few college and high school student online media would be considered commercial and directed at students younger than thirteen, it is unlikely COPPA will cause most student Web sites to change how they operate. Moreover, the law does not affect sites that do not collect otherwise-private information from visitors. For more information on COPPA, see the Federal Trade Commission's Web site at: http://www.ftc.gov/privacy/ (last visited Sept. 11, 2013).

96 *Urofsky v. Gilmore*, 216 F.3d 401 (4th Cir. 2000), *cert. denied*, 531 U.S. 1070 (2001).

CHAPTER 15

Copyright

A college magazine regularly published the satirical work of a popular student cartoonist. In one issue, the cartoonist took on the topic of youth pregnancy. To do so, he used characters from a popular national comic strip involving a group of children, duplicating them detail-by-detail but with one notable difference. In his cartoon, a girl character was pregnant, one of the boys was the father and their pet beagle was the local abortionist.

A few weeks after the magazine was distributed, the magazine's editor received a letter from lawyers representing the distributor of the "Peanuts" comic strip. They claimed the cartoon had infringed the copyright of the characters, and threatened a lawsuit. They demanded that the editors destroy all remaining copies of that issue of the publication, publish a letter of apology and promise in writing that they would not use the characters again in the future. After consulting with her own lawyers, the editor did what the lawyers requested.

Student journalists in both the print and electronic media confront issues relating to copyright law every day. With the advent of technologies that allow student journalists to easily reproduce cartoon characters, photos, song lyrics, or news stories with only a few keystrokes — and the recent media attention to copyright enforcement actions by the recording industry and other large copyright owners against colleges and students — student journalists today are more likely to be aware that copyright law exists, but are also likely to be more confused than ever about how it applies to their daily actions.

Copyright law can be both a friend and a foe of the student media. On one hand, it protects student journalists against the unauthorized use of their stories, drawings or photographs. On the other hand it limits their ability to reproduce the works of others. Unfortunately, the consequences of ignorance can be expensive. This chapter explains the basics of copyright law and should help student journalists navigate the sometimes murky and changing waters between the rights of copyright ownership and journalistic free speech and fair use.

WHAT IS COPYRIGHT?

Copyright is a set of federal laws granting those who create "works of authorship" a bundle of exclusive rights to control the use of those creations. Although the copyright clause in the Constitution is not as well known as the First Amendment, the federal statutes that govern copyright were written based on constitutional authority, so copyright interests are typically considered on the same plane as First Amendment interests. The purpose of copyright law, as stated in the Constitution, is "to Promote the progress of Science and the Useful Arts."[1] The idea is to encourage people to contribute their creativity to society by letting them control how the works they create are copied and distributed. If, for example, members of the public (or a movie studio) could freely copy John Grisham's latest novel without obtaining his permission, he and other authors would likely be unwilling to invest the time, energy and resources to create books in the first place. At the same time, were Grisham and other "creators" allowed total control over their work — including limiting any discussion or study of it — society's progress would similarly be thwarted.

Copyright protects the owner of an original work of authorship against unauthorized use of his work.

The basics of copyright are fairly straightforward. Copyright gives authors control over their intellectual property. A person owns a copyright in much the same way he owns a car. Just as it is against the law to use or borrow someone's car without the owner's permission, it is generally against the law to use someone's copyrighted work without first obtaining her consent. Additionally, just as no one but the automobile owner can legally sell, give away or change the appearance of a car, no one but the copyright owner, with a few exceptions, may legally transfer or alter a copyrighted work.

Journalists — who both create their own work and are also committed to sharing or reporting the creations of others — have a complicated love-hate relationship with copyright. On the one hand, copyright serves the interests of free expression. By granting authors and designers, including journalists and media organizations, the right to benefit exclusively from their works, copyright encourages the production of more works. But copyright and the First Amendment are also inherently in tension. One person's exclusive dominion over some expression necessarily deprives others of the right to freely use that same expression. Many journalists incorrectly believe that the "fair use" exception to exclusive copyrights give them free rein to make copies for the purposes of news reporting or commentary. While the fair use rule does allow reasonable copying for those purposes, the analysis is more subtle. In fact, the Supreme Court has in the past held that copying by a news magazine was not fair use at all, even taking into account First Amendment concerns.

The Supreme Court faced a First Amendment-copyright conflict in the case *Harper & Row, Publishers v. Nation Enterprises*.[2] *The Nation* magazine, without permission, printed about 300 words from a then-forthcoming 200,000 word (approximately 600 pages) autobiography by former President Gerald Ford that was being published by Harper & Row. *The Nation* claimed that because there was a substantial public interest in wide access to quotes in the memoirs, First Amendment protection should overcome the publisher's copyright. The Court rejected that argument, finding that allowing the unauthorized, prepublication use of the Ford memoirs would not be in the public interest as it could discourage other potential political biographers who might fear the practice would limit their sales, and because the small fraction actually constituted the "heart of the work" – in other words, a substantial portion of the value of the book.[3]

WHAT CAN BE COPYRIGHT PROTECTED?

Original works are copyrighted automatically as soon as they are created, which is when they are "fixed" in their medium of expression.

From the moment an "original work of authorship" is "fixed in a tangible medium of expression," it is protected by copyright law. Copyright protection extends to literary works (like books, articles, poems, and other written works), to music (including both the composition and a particular sound recording), to "pictorial, graphic, and sculptural works" (including photographs, drawings, paintings, and most other 2-D and 3-D artwork), to dramatic works and motion pictures, to architectural works, and even to computer programs.[4] In the context of student publications, this includes news stories, photographs, artwork, graphics, fiction or poetry. Original works retain their copyright protections when they are used in compilations or collections such as newspapers and when they are modified to produce "derivative works."[5]

Copyright does not protect titles, short phrases, slogans, ideas, procedures or facts.

There are two important limitations in the definition of what is protected by copyright. First, the work must be original.[6] This means the author must have shown at least a small spark of creativity when she made the work. For example, courts have said that simply arranging listings in a telephone book alphabetically according to the last name of the phone service subscriber lacks the creativity necessary to qualify for copyright protection.[7] Second, the work must be "fixed in a tangible medium of expression."[8] Only works preserved in a tangible form, such as on paper, in a book, a newspaper, a video, a website or on a computer disk are protected by copyright. There is no protection for something existing entirely in the author's mind, or even spoken out loud but not recorded in any way.

Copyright does not extend to some forms of expression, even though they are arguably original and fixed. Copyright does not protect titles, short phrases or slogans, lists of ingredients, and familiar symbols or designs because such items lack the necessary originality and creativity to distinguish them from the ideas they represent.[9] For example, the bare words in the NFL broadcast's title "Monday Night Football" cannot be protected by copyright and therefore could be used as a headline or tag to illustrate a photo collage of school athletes in a high school yearbook. The full logo (words in special typeface with the NFL logo) probably cannot be used — barring permission or a "fair use" argument — because unlike the three "bare" words, the design of the title is sufficiently creative and can be copyrighted. Note, too, that the words "Monday Night Football" are trademarked and could not be used in a non-NFL advertisement.

Most importantly, copyright does not protect ideas, procedures or facts.[10] Thus while a news story may be copyrighted, the events the story describes cannot be. The copyright protects the way the reporter tells the story, the words and organization, but not the news event the reporter covered. So while *Time* magazine will have a copyright in the exact words and arrangement of an article on teen drug use, the facts discovered in *Time's* reporting belong to no one and can therefore be used as a source for other reporters. Likewise, two editorial writers may express the same opinion without running afoul of the copyright laws, as long as the editorials are not substantially similar in their word choice and organization as a result of copying.

WHAT ABOUT PLAGIARISM?

Plagiarism is not a legal term; it is a term for the academic crime of claiming the words, ideas or methods of someone else as your own. Just because copyright law allows you to use the ideas in someone else's work without fear of infringing their copyright does not mean you should use those ideas without giving credit to the original author. And even if a particular expression is not protected by copyright, that does not mean it is fair game. For example, a person could plagiarize Shakespeare's works by not giving the Bard proper credit. He would not, however, be guilty of copyright infringement because all of Shakespeare's works are hundreds of years old and are in the public domain. You may not be guilty of copyright infringement if you steal someone else's ideas or otherwise plagiarize someone else's work, but you might be subject to censure by your publication staff, and perhaps your school. And you certainly should be embarrassed.[11]

WHO OWNS THE COPYRIGHT?

Generally, the creator of a work owns the copyright.[12] However, under the "work made for hire" exception, employers own the copyright of works created by their employees while working in the scope of their employment.[13] Even outside of the employer-employee relationship, for certain kinds of works (including contributions to collective works such as publications) a work made for hire can come into existence by a written agreement between parties.[14] The work made for hire exception raises interesting, sometimes complicated, questions for student media who must determine whether works produced by reporters, artists and photographers belong to them or to the publication for which they work. If the student journalist is considered an "employee," then the reporter or photographer's contribution is owned by the publication, and the publication controls the future use of the work, including reprints and other uses. In such case, a publication could legally prevent a photographer from making additional copies of the photo for her own employment portfolio or for personal use, for example. But if the publication is not an "employer" and the student is acting as an "independent contractor," then the student author owns the copyright and can control future uses of the work, including preventing the publication from granting reprint permissions.[15] The issue of who is an employee is particularly significant for the student media where a traditional employee-employer relationship often does not exist.

> Generally, the person who owns the copyright to a work is the person who created it. But an employer can claim the copyright to works created by an employee when they are "works for hire."

While there are no reported cases involving student journalists, the U.S. Supreme Court in Community for *Creative Non-Violence v. Reid*[16] provided a list of factors to be considered in determining whether someone is an employee or an independent contractor, including:

- *The amount of skill required to perform the work.* Students whose contributions require special skills, such as graphic designers, are more likely to be considered independent contractors.

- *The source of supplies and tools.* A photographer who uses his own gear is more likely to be considered an independent contractor than one who uses school equipment.
- *The location where the work is performed.* Students who work in their own homes or studios are more likely to be considered independent contractors than those who work in school facilities.
- *The duration of the relationship.* A student artist who contributes a single illustration to a school newspaper is likely to be considered an independent contractor.
- *The hiring party's ability to assign additional projects to the creator.* If student writers, artists and photographers can select their own projects and are free to turn down projects, they are likely to be considered independent contractors.
- *The creator's discretion regarding when and how long to work.* A student who sets her own schedule is more likely to be considered an independent contractor.
- *The tax treatment of the creator.* When a student is paid for his work, if the publication does not withhold Social Security or income taxes, the student is likely to be considered an independent contractor.

None of these factors (or the other factors listed in *Reid*) alone is determinative in deciding whether a publication contributor is an employee or an independent contractor.[17] Nevertheless, taken as a whole, they would seem to require a fairly formal and traditional employer-employee relationship, something that likely does not exist in most student media situations, where students often volunteer their time and services or are paid a token stipend that bears no reasonable relationship to actual work performed.[18] Even when students are paid, it is often on a per photo or story or issue basis, much like a freelancer, which would suggest treatment as an independent contractor.[19] In fact, the Court noted in *Reid* that "in using the term 'employee,' [...] Congress meant to refer to a hired party in a conventional employment relationship."[20]

The best way to avoid a copyright dispute between a student publication and a reporter, artist or photographer is to deal with the issue in advance. Before starting work, both parties should establish the nature of their relationship and put the agreement in writing. A written agreement would determine the outcome of most potential controversies without having to rely on the *CCNV v. Reid* factors. For example, such an agreement could give a publication the ownership of the copyright in photographs but give the photographer a license to display them in exhibits and portfolios. Or, the agreement could provide that the photographer owns the copyright, but the publication may print it both in its initial publication and on its website. Both the student and a representative of the publication should sign and date the agreement and keep a copy. Such an agreement does not have to be complex; it should simply spell out who has what rights to the work the student creates, and if a work for hire is intended, explicitly say so.

WHAT KIND OF AGREEMENT?

If we assume that most student contributors to student media would be considered independent contractors (and therefore the owners of the copyright in the works they contribute to student publications), the question remains what uses the publication can make of the contribution in the future. This is no idle question. A group of freelance authors successfully took their case all the way to the Supreme Court to stop *The New York Times* and other publications from including their articles in electronic databases without their permission. On the other hand, a freelance photographer unsuccessfully sued *National Geographic* magazine to stop it from including his famous magazine cover images in CD-ROM collections of the magazine without his permission.[21] In both cases, neither party envisioned that there might be new ways to exploit the work later on. Ultimately, the courts held that while the individual works could not be separated and exploited without permission of the authors, the Copyright Act permits publishers — who own the copyright in their "collective works" — to republish those "collective works" in new media and collections of the original editions.[22]

There are two ways student media can handle this issue. Either the student publication can require transfer of copyright as a condition of publishing the work, or the parties can have a written license spelling out what the publication can do with the work without further permission from the author. Since most student reporters, artists, and photographers are working for no or very little money, it is probably unfair to ask them to give up their copyright entirely. If the publication does so, it should at least include in the agreement a written license back to the author, allowing the author to make copies for her own personal use and public display. It may make more sense, and is probably more in keeping with the spirit with which student media work and student authors contribute to those publications, for the student author to keep the copyright but spell out the uses allowed by the student publication.

For example, it is pretty obvious that the parties would intend for a photo to be used in the initial printing of the student newspaper in which the article it accompanies appears. Does that mean permission is also granted to use the photo on the publication's website? May it also be used as a stock photo in future editions? How about in the school yearbook? What if the school district or university likes the photo so much it wants to use it in its annual report? These are the kinds of scenarios student media should keep in mind when drafting agreements for contributors. A simple agreement might look something like this:

> Any individual work contributed to [publication] by [author] is not considered a work made for hire and is the sole property of author. By contributing the works to publication, author grants a nonexclusive license to publication to reproduce, display and distribute copies of the work in the publication for which the work was initially submitted, in future or commemorative issues of [publication], on the [publication's] website or other Internet-based medium and in other noncommercial, editorial uses directly controlled by [publication]. Any future use of the work by publication that would result in payment to [publication] (beyond normal subscription and reprint fees, if any) requires an additional license from [author]. If, after diligent efforts to contact the author to obtain such permission, the author cannot be found, such additional permission may be presumed to be granted. All publications of the work must include credit to [author].

_____   _____
Author   Date

_____   _____
Publication   Date

For a longer agreement, which might be better suited to larger publications, visit the SPLC Web site at www.splc.org/copyrightagreement.

WHAT RIGHTS DOES COPYRIGHT PROVIDE?

A copyright gives its owner five basic exclusive rights: reproduction, adaptation, distribution, public performance, and public display.[23] A copyright owner can give away some or all of these rights, or can keep the rights for herself but grant licenses to others to use them in various ways. For example, photographer Annie Leibovitz has taken many portraits of famous people. She can grant _Vanity Fair_ permission to reproduce a portrait on its cover, then later grant a poster company a license to adapt that same photo into a poster for sale and distribution to the public, and then grant a museum permission to publicly display the photo to its visitors, and also grant the museum permission to include the image in a book that memorializes the exhibit.

Moreover, there can be more than one copyright embodied in a single material object, such as a CD or a magazine. In fact, there are at least two separate copyrights in every musical recording — a copyright for the song itself, and a copyright for the recorded performance.[24] The song itself is called a "musical work," and the copyright in the musical work covers the notes and lyrics that make up the underlying composition. It can be helpful to think of the musical work as the sheet music that the artists used when singing the song. The recorded performance is called a "sound recording," and the copyright in the sound recording covers the interpretive efforts of the singer, the musicians, the backup vocalists, and even the recording engineer who helps bring it all together. So on one CD, there can be literally dozens of separate copyrights. For instance, take The Ataris' 2003 album, *So Long Astoria*. The band scored a hit with their rendition of the song "The Boys of Summer." The group (or, more likely, their record company) owns the rights to the sound recording, but Don Henley, former member of The Eagles, wrote the song and he (or more likely his publishing company) owns the rights to the musical work. The Ataris had to pay Don Henley for the right to perform the song he wrote.[25] And every time someone listens to that sound recording streamed over the Internet, both The Ataris and Don Henley are owed a royalty. There are separate sound recording and musical works copyrights for each of the 15 tracks on the album. There is also a separate copyright for the art used to illustrate the package of the CD, and the artist (or, more likely, the record company) controls that copyright, including the right to reproduce or display that art. Similarly, an issue of *Newsweek* might have some photos and articles created as works made for hire by employees, and others created by freelancers as independent contractors. *Newsweek* would own the copyright in the magazine as a whole, but the individual stories, photos, and illustrations might all be separately owned.

HOW IS A WORK PROTECTED BY COPYRIGHT?

Nowadays, you do not need to do anything special to protect your work. Original works are protected by copyright the moment they are "fixed" in a tangible medium of expression.[26] This was not always the case. For works created before January 1, 1978, copyright notice on published works was mandatory to ensure copyright protection. Notice was also mandatory, with few exceptions, for published works created between January 1, 1978 and March 1, 1989. Where notice is required, it should appear on all copies of the work.

KNOW YOUR LINGO!

Remember, copyright is not a verb — you do not take any action to "copyright" your work. Copyright subsists in the work from the moment it is fixed. You may register your copyright to take advantage of the extra protections registration provides, but registration is not "copyrighting." Prior to enactment of the Copyright Act of 1976, authors did have to take positive steps to copyright their work, so it was proper then to speak of "copyrighting" a work. But that usage is now about 30 years out of date!

Placing copyright notice on a work is no longer legally required, but it can be beneficial. Notice has three parts:
The symbol ©
The year of first publication
The name of the copyright owner.

Even though copyright notice is not required for works created today, it is a good practice to include a copyright notice on all published works.[27] The notice has three parts: (1) the letter C in a circle — "©" — (or the letter P in a circle for phonorecords of sound recordings) or the word "copyright" or abbreviation "copr."; (2) the year of first publication of the work; and (3) the name of the copyright owner.[28] For example, this book bears a copyright notice that says "© 2013 Student Press Law Center, Inc." No permission or registration is required to publish a copyright notice on your original work. Notice should appear in a place that gives "reasonable notice" of the claim of copyright — usually in the masthead or on the contents page for publications. Although notice is not required, it is recommended for several reasons. First, it makes it a lot easier for users to contact the copyright owner to ask for permission to use the work. Second, it makes it almost impossible for someone later accused of copyright infringement to argue that they did not know about the copyright.[29]

After creation of a work, the owner of the copyright must deposit two complete copies of the work with the Copyright Office of the Library of Congress within three months of creation.[30] These deposits help form the collection of the Library of Congress in Washington, D.C. While copyright law mandates deposit, failure to send in the required copies of your work will not in any way affect the validity of your copyright.[31] If you plan to register your copyright later, you can request a receipt for your deposit so you do not have to include more copies of your work with your registration application.

Registration of copyrighted works with the Copyright Office in Washington, D.C., is purely voluntary. Registration and the deposit requirement may be satisfied simultaneously if the registrant sends the material together.[32] In fact, for unpublished works, you can both file the registration electronically and upload copies of the work, submitting all the materials without even standing up from your desk.[33] Registration is not required, but it does confer extra benefits on the copyright holder. First, registration is the key to the courthouse door — registration is required before a lawsuit may be filed for copyright infringement.[34] Second, while you have a right to register your copyright at any time, you get extra benefits if you register within a certain amount of time after the work is published. If you register your work within five years of publication, a court must presume that you are the owner of a valid copyright if you are involved in a copyright infringement action.[35] Most importantly, certain damages and the ability to ask for reimbursement of your attorney's fees if you have to sue for copyright infringement are available only if you register the work within three months of its initial publication.[36]

Registration is easy, and does not require the help of an attorney. It entails completing a fairly straightforward form, paying a small fee (generally $35), and including the required number of copies of your work along with the forms and fees.[37] Serials such as magazines or newspapers can sometimes be registered in groups for a reduced fee.[38] Because of the hassle and expense, many student publications forego the benefits of registration. It takes the Copyright Office several months to process copyright registrations and issue the official registration certificate, but once complete, registration is effective from the date the registration was received by the Copyright Office. It is best to send the registration either by registered mail, return receipt requested, or via commercial courier such as Federal Express or UPS, to ensure that you have proof of when you sent your registration.

WHICH FORMS?

The U.S. Copyright Office's website — found at www.copyright.gov — provides all of the information you need to register copyrights. Registration requires filling out different forms depending on the type of item you want to register. Simple registration applications can be filed using an electronic form called eCO or its paper equivalent, form CO; other works require a paper form. All of the forms and the instructions for completing the forms are available as PDFs at http://www.copyright.gov/forms/. The Copyright Office's circulars and brochures explain in detail the procedures for registration and just about anything else you might need to know about copyright law, and are found at http://www.copyright.gov/circs/. In brief:

If you are registering ...	Use form ...
A single newspaper or magazine article in the name of the author.	eCO, CO, TX or short form TX
A poem or other literary work.	eCO, CO, TX or short form TX
A single photograph or illustration in the name of the author.	eCO, CO, VA or short form VA
Multiple photographs by the same author published in the same year.	eCO, CO, VA plus GR/PPh/CON
A single issue of a newspaper, newsletter, magazine, annual, or journal that generally bears volume numbering or chronological designations.	SE or short form SE
Multiple issues of a newspaper, newsletter, magazine, annual, or journal that generally bears volume numbering or chronological designations published within a 90-day period.	SE/Group
A month's worth of issues of a daily newspaper or newsletter	G/DN

The Copyright Office has copyright information specialists available to answer questions by telephone about any aspect of copyright registration or deposit. Copyright information specialists can be reached at (202) 707-5959.

Electronic Filing

In mid-2008, the U.S. Copyright Office started to simplify the registration process by creating a new form called "CO." Form CO can be used to register any single work (e.g., a newspaper story, an image, a song, a movie, etc.) or a single issue of a serial work, if all the works being claimed are owned by the same claimant (e.g., the content of a single issue of the student paper, as a "collective work" owned by the publication). For most applicants, form CO will be the only form they ever need to use — though if you want the older forms, the Copyright Office will mail them to you, and will accept applications using those forms.

The introduction of CO was followed by its online equivalent, eCO. With eCO, you can fill out the form, submit it, and pay for the registration online; if the works you are submitting are unpublished, you can even upload them to fulfill the deposit requirement. If the works have already been published, you will still have to mail them in, but the processing time will be much faster, as the new forms use two-dimensional barcodes (like the ones used by United Parcel Service) to allow for machines to process the paperwork.

If you register using eCO, you will get an e-mail notice that your application has been received. The date of the e-mail is the date of your effective registration, once it has been accepted.

HOW LONG DOES A COPYRIGHT LAST?

Calculating the duration of copyright protection can be a complicated task. It can also be very important, because once copyright expires the work becomes part of the public domain and can be used freely without permission from the former copyright owner.[39] For example, film producers in Hollywood are free to create a script and movie of Nathaniel Hawthorne's book *The Scarlet Letter* with no legal liability for copyright infringement because the novel is in the public domain. In 2003, the U.S. Supreme Court upheld the Sonny Bono Copyright Extension Act,[40] which lengthened the duration of existing and future copyrights by 20 years, and therefore kept many works created in the early-to-mid 1900s out of the public domain for several more years.[41]

For works created after January 1, 1978, copyright generally will last for the life of the creator plus 70 years, regardless of whether or when the work is published. The copyright for works made for hire extends for either 95 years from publication or 120 years from creation, whichever comes sooner.[42] The math is a little more complicated if the work was created before January 1, 1978, and depends in part on when (or if) the work was published subsequent to its creation. If the work was created prior to January 1, 1978, but not registered or published until after that date, the work's copyright duration is calculated the same way duration is calculated for new works, life-plus-70, or 95/120 for works made for hire.[43] (Older works that were in danger of copyright expiration got some additional protection from Congress, which set a minimum expiration date of December 31, 2047, for any work created before 1978 and registered or published before 2002.)

The math gets even trickier if the work was created and published with notice, or registered, prior to 1978. If the work was copyrighted between January 1, 1964 and December 31, 1977, the term is 28 years plus an automatic renewal of 67 years, for a total of 95 years protection. Works copyrighted before December 31, 1963 had a term of 28 years, and could be extended for a renewal term (recently enlarged to 67 years) only if the copyright owner formally filed a renewal application with the Copyright Office before the end of the 28-year term. For works copyrighted before January 1, 1950, and renewed before 1978, the renewal term was automatically extended to 67 years as well.

For all works in their renewal term when the Copyright Term Extension Act became effective on October 27, 1998, the copyright term was extended to a total of 95 years.[44] Thus, works created as far back as 1923 (i.e., works that had not yet run the course of their original plus extension terms as of the date of the 1998 Act) may still be protected by copyright until at least 2018 if they were properly renewed. No matter when the work was created, copyright always expires on December 31 of the applicable year.[45]

STILL CONFUSED?

For more help in determining the duration of a copyright, use the SPLC's Copyright Duration Calculator at: http://www.splc.org/copyrightcalculator

---

WHAT REMEDIES ARE AVAILABLE TO COPYRIGHT OWNERS?

Copyright owners may sue for copyright infringement if someone has exercised one of the copyright owner's exclusive rights without permission or in a manner that would not be considered fair use.[46] If the copyright owner prevails in the action, the court may award her actual damages, as well as injunctive relief and impoundment of the infringing material.[47] The court may also award attorney's fees or statutory damages if registration was timely.[48] Actual damages are the measure of the actual amount of money lost by the copyright owner due to the unauthorized use plus any revenues made by the infringer that are not included in the actual damages.[49] For example, if someone sold 30 unauthorized photocopies of a book at $10 per copy, actual damages would be at least $300.

Statutory damages range from $200 to $150,000 per infringement, depending in part on whether the infringement was "innocent" or "willful."[50] The actual amount awarded is in the sole discretion of the jury, or a judge if there is not a jury trial.[51]

Attorney's fees and costs can cost infringers several thousands of dollars beyond the damages awarded. Injunctive relief, which is normally a court order to stop violating a copyright, and impoundment, which is the court-ordered confiscation of infringing material and the machinery or tools used to create it, are also common remedies.

THE DIGITAL MILLENNIUM COPYRIGHT ACT: WHAT YOU NEED TO KNOW

In 1998, Congress passed the biggest revision to the Copyright Act since the entire statute was rewritten in 1976. The Digital Millennium Copyright Act,[52] or DMCA, was Congress' attempt to anticipate some of the ways the growing use of the Internet and other digital media would affect the rights of copyright owners. Congress recognized that the growing ease of making perfect digital copies might make infringement easier and selling licensed copies of a work more difficult.

The DMCA included several provisions that might be of interest to students in general, and one section that is relevant to student media outlets that maintain websites. The DMCA made it illegal to circumvent technological measures that copyright owners put in place to protect their works. This provision has been applied to prevent journalists from even reporting circumvention techniques that were created by others. So, for example, a federal court has held that a hacker publication violated the DMCA when it published a program called deCSS that would enable users to get around the content scramble system that cryptically encodes the information on DVDs.[53] The court rejected the publication's argument that the First Amendment should allow it to report the deCSS program, and even ordered the magazine's website not to link to other websites that published the deCSS program. The law here is still unsettled, however, as a California court recently overturned a similar injunction on First Amendment grounds.[54]

The second part of the DMCA that is of interest to students in general, and student publications specifically, are the provisions that provide "safe harbors" for online service providers. Congress decided that the law of contributory liability — that is, the idea that someone could be responsible for merely providing the means by which another person commits copyright infringement — should not hold service providers like AOL and MSN responsible for infringement by their subscribers that is outside of their control. (For example, Congress deemed it unfair to hold AOL liable for copyright infringement simply because one of its millions of subscribers posted copyrighted photos of the latest teen idol on a personal website without permission.) At the same time, Congress wanted copyright owners to have a way to protect their works when Internet users post illegal copies.

The DMCA addressed this problem by setting up a complicated "notice-and-takedown" system that provides a safe harbor for service providers who cut off access to allegedly infringing materials upon notice from a copyright holder. If the service provider promptly cuts off access after getting a notice, it cannot be held liable for contributory copyright infringement.

The definition of a "service provider" is so broad that it may be applicable not only to the AOLs and Googles of the world, but also to the owner of any website that allows outside people to upload and post information on the site.[55] So if you allow users to participate in discussion groups, or post files or comments on your publication's website, you open yourself to the possibility that the users might post infringing materials for which your publication could be held liable. But you can take advantage of the safe harbor only if you have registered with the Copyright Office in advance and clearly posted information on your website about where a copyright owner can contact you to complain about possible infringement.

The Copyright Office has information about how to register an agent on its website.[56] But remember, the safe harbors cannot protect you if you publish infringing materials. It only provides protection if people outside of your control post copyrighted material on your website (for example, in a "reader feedback" section), and you follow the procedures to remove the allegedly infringing material as soon as you know about it.

USING COPYRIGHTED WORK: OBTAINING PERMISSION

The surest way to use a copyrighted work legitimately is to get permission from the copyright holder. Simply giving copyright owners credit for their work — without first seeking their okay — is not enough. Explicit permission is required. Sometimes that is not difficult. For example, a daily commercial newspaper would probably agree to allow a nearby high school student yearbook to reprint a photo of a local news event, as long as the students gave credit to the original source. On the other hand, getting permission can sometimes pose a challenge. Many organizations have strict policies regulating use of their copyrighted work, that range from barring permission altogether, to requiring time-consuming procedures by which permission must be secured, to charging expensive licensing fees.

Video yearbooks and other multimedia often find obtaining permission to use popular music or films to be an especially trying experience. Just as CDs and magazines can have multiple copyrighted works in them, movies also usually have multiple copyrighted works incorporated in them, including musical works, sound recordings, audiovisual works, or pictorial, graphic, and sculptural works. In addition, each of the copyrights described above are protected by several separate rights (for example, reproduction, distribution, performance, and display), each of which must be licensed separately and may well be owned by separate entities. The types of licenses required vary depending on what you are trying to do. Adding your entire prom theme song to your video yearbook, for example, requires a license both for the song itself (the musical work) and for the performance (the sound recording) — and remember, there are probably separate owners for each of those copyrights. Getting a local band to perform the song for your video yearbook would eliminate the need to get permission to use the popular sound recording, but you would still need a license to record the musical work. In music industry lingo, the license to record the musical work is called a "mechanical license" (because you are making a mechanical reproduction of the musical work when you burn it onto a CD or video) while the license to line up a sound recording with video is called a "synchronization license" or "synch license" (because you are synchronizing the sound recording with your video to create an audiovisual work).

Because of the complexities involved, you may want to limit your use of these items to what would be considered a "fair use," (for example, to accompany your official survey of the five most popular music videos at your high school, you could probably run a very short clip of each) or — if you have the budget — you may want to contact a company that specializes in obtaining copyright permission, either to produce your video completely, or to help you obtain permissions for particular songs. There are some licensing clearinghouse organizations that administer licenses on behalf of many copyright owners. A group called the Harry Fox Agency (www.harryfox.com), for example, can — for a fee — probably arrange permission for you to get a mechanical license for the ever-popular "We Are Family" (popularly performed by Sister Sledge) or a number of other well-known songs on your CD or other audio-only project. If you want to use the Sister Sledge version of the song rather than a version you record yourself, or you want to synch the version you record to video, you further need to get permission from the individual record company that owns the sound recording.[57] A group called SoundExchange administers the right of public performance by means of a digital audio transmission for most sound recordings. While it cannot grant permission to reproduce a sound recording, it provides on its website a helpful list of permissions offices for the major record labels.[58]

Simply giving the copyright owner credit when you use their work is not enough. Copyright law requires explicit permission be obtained.

If you think it will be necessary to obtain copyright permission, start early. While the time required varies, you should allow yourself months, rather than days or even weeks, to secure copyright permission.

The first step is to locate the copyright holder, either by using the copyright notice (for example, © 2013 Time Magazine, Inc.) or by contacting the Copyright Office in Washington, D.C. You can search their copyright registration records yourself on the Internet, or you can pay them to do the search for you.[59] Remember that neither registration nor copyright notice is required for a work to be protected, so the work may be protected even if it does not have a notice or a listing at the Copyright Office.

Once you know who owns the copyright, you need to ask that person or company for permission. While it is probably worth an initial telephone call, particularly at a smaller or less formal organization, most copyright holders require a written request. Your request should include:

- Your name, address and telephone number, the name and expected date of publication, the number of copies you intend to produce and the price, if any, you will charge. If you are a non-profit student publication, be sure to make that absolutely clear.
- A precise description of what you want to use and, if possible, a photocopy of your layout or sketch of your plans.
- A (polite) statement regarding your deadline for getting a response.
- While student media are frequently successful in obtaining copyright permission, that is certainly not always the case. You should have a back-up plan in place should your request be denied, ignored or should the owner demand a payment for use of the copyrighted material that is beyond your budget. In the end, for example, you may find it much easier — and almost always cheaper — to use so-called "production music," which, though less "famous" than its Top-40 cousins, is specifically intended for use in multimedia projects.[60] Similarly, photos or stories can be purchased and downloaded fairly easily — and in some cases, very reasonably — from a variety of online wire and photo services.[61]

You may have heard of ASCAP, BMI, and SESAC. Together, these three groups administer the rights of public performance for most musical works. While most student media (except for student-run radio stations, TV stations or webcasts) will not need to worry about public performance rights, these performing rights societies have helpful databases accessible through their websites for determining who is the copyright owner for a particular song. They allow you to type in the name of the song, or the name of the artist who performs the song, and find out who actually owns the musical work. Composers can only be a member of one of the three societies so it is important not to stop at one database if you fail to get a hit. The websites can be found, respectively, at:

http://www.ascap.com
http://www.bmi.com
http://www.sesac.com

USING COPYRIGHT WORK: FAIR USE

Fair use is a very important exception to the general rule that copyrighted material cannot be used without consent, and a defense to a claim of copyright infringement. It is particularly significant to the news media, which in the business of conveying information, some of it based on copyrighted work.

Federal copyright law states than an individual other than the copyright owner can use a copyrighted work without permission if the use would be considered a "fair use."[62] The Fair Use Doctrine is, in effect, a compromise. It represents a balance by lawmakers and courts of the need to encourage scientific and cultural progress by making sure creators get credit for what they do against society's need for readily accessible information. Recognizing the inherent conflict in these two goals, fair use strives to find a reasonable middle ground.

Whether the use of a copyrighted work by a non-owner would be considered a "fair use" is not always an easy call. There is no black-and-white rule; each case must be examined on its own. Indeed, it is this lack of a rigid standard that has led some to label fair use "the metaphysics of law." Nevertheless, as one of the country's leading experts on copyright law once said: "Ninety-nine times out of a hundred a scholar who wants to quote a reasonable portion of a copyrighted work can do so without obtaining permission as long as the quotation does not constitute a substitute for the original."[63] The same holds true for student journalists.

Fair use can include uses for such purposes as "criticism, comment, news reporting, teaching... scholarship, or research...."[64] Even if the use is for purposes of commentary or news reporting, courts will not automatically find that the use is fair. Courts look at four factors to determine whether the use of the copyrighted work is fair:

- *The purpose and character of the use.* Non-commercial uses for purposes like news reporting, teaching, criticism and commentary are much more likely to be fair than commercial uses. If there is a profit motive behind the use, it is less likely to be considered fair, but even a non-commercial use can be found to be an infringement depending upon the balance of the remaining factors.[65] A use is more likely to be deemed fair if it in some way "transforms" the original work by changing its purpose, character, meaning, or message.[66] To put it another way, a "transformative use" occurs when you are using the work in a way that adds new meaning and value to it, rather than a way that takes the existing meaning and value. For example, it would probably be a transformative use to take a racy picture from a beauty pageant winner's modeling portfolio to use in a story that is critical of the pageant giving the crown to someone with such work in their history.[67]

- *The nature of the copyrighted work.* Uses of works containing mostly factual material like maps or biographies are more likely to be fair than uses of highly creative and original works like novels and cartoons.

- *The amount and substantiality of the portion used in relation to the copyrighted work as a whole.* No more of the work than is necessary may be used. The test is both quantitative (how many words of a 200,000-word book are reproduced?) and qualitative (using the "core" or "heart" of a work — no matter how small — is less likely to be fair use).

- *The effect of the use upon the potential market for or value of the copyrighted work.*[68] This is the most important factor.[69] If consumers are willing to buy the substitute use instead of the original, it probably will not qualify as a fair use. If students might be willing to buy a video yearbook for its compilation of current music rather than purchase the same songs on CD from a music store, then the work in question is less likely a fair use.

It is important to keep in mind that the fair use analysis is a balancing test. Ultimately, only a court can say for sure if a given use is fair, and even a slight variation in the facts from a prior case that found fair use might be enough to tip the balance away from fair use. For this reason, most book publishers and movie studios, for example, get permission for each and every use of another work, even if that use would arguably be found to be a fair use.

Educational Uses as Fair Use

When the Copyright Act was first revised in 1976, Congress was particularly concerned with balancing the rights of copyright owners against the needs of educators and students to share and use copyrighted works. At Congress' urging, organizations representing copyright owners and educational organizations together drafted guidelines to illustrate the type of copying of books, periodicals and other print materials for educational purposes that would be considered fair use in a classroom setting. The guidelines are not an official part of the Copyright Act, but they are intended to help educators understand what Congress intended as fair use. One of the limitations the guidelines impose on fair use is that under most circumstances, educators may not use more than 10 percent of a work.[70] The guidelines include a spontaneity requirement. The idea is that the guidelines provide for copying "at the instance and inspiration of the individual teacher."[71] Where a teacher intends to use the copyrighted material as a regular and ongoing part of her classroom instruction, however, the guidelines suggest that permission be obtained. In fact, courts have found that copying of course packets was not fair use where the materials were planned in advance and no attempt was made to obtain permission.[72]

In 1996, a similar group of copyright owners and educators created Fair Use Guidelines for Educational Multimedia.[73] The multimedia guidelines carry no official sanction by Congress, but the Copyright Office, various copyright owner organizations and many educational institutions have endorsed or adopted them. The guidelines generally allow students and teachers making multimedia presentations for *classroom purposes* to reproduce the lesser of 3 minutes or 10 percent of an audio-visual work, and the lesser of 30 seconds or 10 percent of a musical work, the lyrics thereof, or a sound recording.

The educational guidelines are not precisely applicable to uses by student media since student publications are usually distributed outside of the traditional classroom setting. However, if non-profit student media — particularly those that are produced as part of a curriculum-based journalism program and whose circulations are limited primarily to the school community — keep their copying within the parameters set by the guidelines, a reasonable argument can be made that the copying should be considered fair. This would be particularly true when there is not enough time to obtain permissions.

Parody as Fair Use

Fortunately for the student media, copyright law gives parodies and spoofs a fair share of breathing room. But what is a parody? The Supreme Court has said that a parody is a work "that imitates the characteristic style of an author or a work for comic effect or ridicule."[74] The key is that parody must mimic the original to make its point. For example, it is probably not parody (and not fair use) to change the words of a Lady Gaga song so that it comments on the members of your senior class — no matter how funny the end result. On the other hand, it probably would be considered parody (and therefore fair use) to change the lyrics to make fun of Gaga herself.

It is much more difficult to prove fair use if you just borrow from a popular song or cartoon character as a gimmick for satirically attacking something other than the original work.[75] In one famous case, for example, Walt Disney Productions sued a counter-cultural magazine for copyright infringement, and won.[76] The magazine had portrayed Disney characters, including Mickey Mouse and Donald Duck, as promiscuous drug users.[77] The key legal problem with the parody, according to the court, was that the Disney characters were used only for their value as popular icons. More recently, a court held that a book about the O.J. Simpson murder trial written in the style of Dr. Seuss and illustrated with drawings of O.J. Simpson wearing a "Cat in the Hat" striped stovepipe hat was not fair use.[78] A valid cartoon parody must make use of the original work not merely for recognition value, but to make a point by playing on qualities unique to the original. Just like any other fair use question, the decision as to whether a parody is fair use depends on a court's analysis of the four statutory factors. However, the U.S. Supreme Court — in a case involving a rap song by 2 Live Crew that crudely made fun of Roy Orbison's song "Pretty Woman" — applied the factors in the specific context of parody and established several basic requirements.[79] First, the Court required that the parody be obvious.[80] The audience must reasonably perceive that the use is a criticism or commentary of the original. A disclaimer or notice that clearly alerts the readers of the parody may prove useful. Second, the Court held that an artist who wants to parody an original must not use more of the original work than is necessary to "conjure-up," or evoke thoughts of the original in the viewer's mind.[81] If only a mannerism, a classic line of dialogue or a physical attribute of a character is necessary to make the parody succeed, then only that element may be used. Courts have noticed that a caricature of a popular work often makes a parody as effective (if not more so) than an exact duplicate, and the caricature poses far less a risk of copyright infringement. Finally, the parody must not directly threaten the market value of the original work.[82] If the public will buy the parody version instead of buying the original (or instead of buying a parody of the original created by the copyright owner), then the use is probably not fair.

Be aware that parody is distinct from satire. Parody is borrowing a work to ridicule or make a point about the work being borrowed; satire is borrowing a work to make a point about something else. Because criticism of a work requires some use of the work, true parody is more likely to be a fair use than satire.[83]

Fair Use FAQ's for Student Media

As Congress recognized when it passed the fair use statute, "the endless variety of situations and combinations of circumstances that can arise in particular cases precludes the formulation of exact rules...."[84] In other words, unless a prior court case is factually identical, it can be extremely difficult — sometimes impossible — to conclude whether a particular use is legal. For student media faced daily with specific fair-use questions that demand a clear-cut answer ("Is this fair use?"), the law's "grayness" can be quite frustrating. Still, there are some general principles that are important to keep in mind. For example, fair use is most likely to be found when a use is for purposes of "criticism, comment, news reporting, teaching... scholarship, or research."[85] Fair use is more likely to be found if your publication is not-for-profit rather than for-profit. Fair use is more likely to be found if the publication is produced in the context of a classroom for purposes of teaching, rather than independent of the school or as an extracurricular activity. Limited uses of an original are favored over liberal uses. And — perhaps most importantly — a use whose negative impact on the market value of the original is negligible is much more likely to be found a fair use than one that harms its value. The following examples are intended to give you an idea of how to perform a fair use analysis. But remember, new cases are decided every day, and these examples cannot substitute for legal advice based upon your unique circumstances.

Can I scan the cover art of a CD at 50 percent size to illustrate a music CD review in my student newspaper?
Probably. A quick application of the four-part fair use test reveals the following: First, the purpose of the use here would be to aid in criticism and commentary of the CD, while allowing readers to quickly identify the CD being discussed on sight. However, the *nature* of the work is artistic, and the *amount* of the artwork taken would be the entire amount, and so the second and third factors would weigh against fair use. Still, the *effect on the market* for the original would probably not be negative. In fact, the use would be more likely to encourage sales of the CD itself, and it is not likely that there is a market for selling such images to reviewers. Shrinking the size of the image and reproducing it in black-and-white instead of color can help reduce any alleged impact on the market value of the original. (Note that if you've actually received a review copy of the CD from the record company along with art for the purpose of illustrating your review, it would be better to use the provided artwork in accordance with the terms stated in the press packet.) While no court has addressed this issue specifically, at least one court has held that using a smaller, lower-resolution version of a photograph for purposes of telling people where to find the real thing is fair use.[86]

> For a parody to pass as a fair use, a publication must not use more of the original work than is necessary to evoke thought of the original in the viewer's mind.

Can I use 30 seconds of a song to illustrate a review of a new CD on a student cable radio show?
Probably. In the first place, your radio station most likely already has a blanket license for the public performance of music from the performing rights societies, and so fair use would not even be an issue. But assuming there is no license in place, the *purpose* of the use here would be to aid in criticism and commentary of the CD, while providing listeners with some context for the review. The *nature* of the work is artistic, which would weigh against fair use, but the *amount* of the song taken would be small (and is, for example, within the amount set out by the Multimedia Guidelines discussed above). Using less than 30 seconds would make it even more likely that a court would find fair use. The *effect on the market* for the original would probably not be negative; even a bad review publicizes the CD. And there probably is not a "market" to sell the rights to play a short review clip to student media.

Can I take one or two still images from a movie's official website to illustrate a movie review in a student newspaper?
Probably. The *purpose* of the use here would be to aid in criticism and commentary of the movie, which could weigh in favor of fair use. The *amount* taken of the work — a few frames from a full length film — would probably weigh in favor of fair use, but a court might consider the photo a separate copyrighted work and decide that taking the entire photo weighs against fair use. The *effect on the market* would probably weigh in favor of a finding of fair use, as movie studios routinely provide such photos for free for the very purpose of illustrating reviews. If you do make such a use, be sure to give credit to the movie studio for the photo.

Can I use candid photos of a movie star taken from *People Magazine* to illustrate a movie review?
Probably not. Unlike photos from the movie itself, a candid photo of someone who just happens to be in the movie is not being used for the *purpose* of commenting or criticizing the photo itself. Moreover, there is a rich and vibrant market for the photos that appear in the likes of *People*. The magazine often pays photographers and their agents top dollar for photos of sought-after celebrities. It might be arguable that a less sophisticated publication (such as a high school monthly) would not be affecting the

market because there is no real market to sell such photos to those kinds of publications, but a more sophisticated student publication (such as a college daily that subscribes to the Associated Press) would have a hard time convincing a court of this. Since the *nature* of the photo would be very artistic and the *amount* of the photo would be the entire work or close to it (and, even if cropped, certainly the "heart" of the work) the use probably would not be considered fair.

Can I use a photo of a major athletic event scanned from *Sports Illustrated* magazine to illustrate our student newspaper's story about the event?
Maybe — but only in very limited circumstances. In this example, the publication is at least back to one of the core *purposes* of fair use: news reporting. Courts have tended to find fair use when a particular video or photograph is itself the news and its use is necessary to tell a very timely news story, with no time to get permission. For example, a Puerto Rican newspaper that published partially nude professional photographs of a beauty queen as part of a story about the scandal surrounding the photos was exonerated based on a fair use defense.[87] Also, CNN and other news organizations successfully defended against a claim of copyright infringement for airing, without permission of the video photographer, the tape of the Los Angeles police beating of Rodney King that sparked widespread rioting.[88] A fair use of another news organization's photos might also be found if the story is about news media coverage of a particular topic or event. For example, to illustrate a feature story on America's obsession with weight loss, it would probably be fair use to include thumbnail images of the covers of *Time*, *Newsweek* and other publications whose issues were devoted to the latest dieting fad. In all cases, be sure to give credit to the source of the photograph. For most routine news coverage, permission must be obtained from a photo source before including their images in your publication or on your website.

Can I reprint an infographic published in USA Today, giving credit to USA Today as the source?
Probably not. Taking the entirety of an illustration from another publication, even when giving that publication credit, is probably not fair use. Copyright does not protect facts, and you certainly can reprint the facts in the graphic (although you should still give credit to your source). But you really should have your own artists create a graphic for your publication.

Can I use a popular cartoon character as the main image on the cover of my yearbook without permission?
No. Even if the *purpose* of the use might be non-commercial in the sense that you are not making a profit from the yearbook, the *character* of the use would be neither strictly educational nor news reporting. The artistic *nature* of the work and the fact that you would be taking a large *amount* of the character would weigh against fair use. And most importantly, the owners of cartoon characters make much of their money by licensing their works for various uses. Because there is a market for such licenses, this factor weighs against a finding of fair use. For example, Bill Watterson, the creator of the "Calvin and Hobbes" comic strips, has chosen not to license the characters for T-shirts, stuffed animals and other such items, and is very vigilant about trying to stop people from using the characters in unauthorized ways. Bottom line: If you want Bart Simpson or SpongeBob SquarePants to star on your cover, you will need to get permission.

Can I call my yearbook *The Central High School Inquirer* and design the cover to look like the cover of a supermarket tabloid, similar to *National Enquirer*?
Probably — but put plenty of creative effort into it. This would probably be an acceptable parody. There is no copyright in the look and feel of the *National Enquirer*, or in the name, so the question would be more of a trademark analysis. The more creative you are and the more you do to transform your cover into something that is unique to your school and artistically distinguishes it from a *National Enquirer* cover the better. For example, be sure to write your own "screaming" headlines and use your own "shocking" (but legal and hopefully humorous) photos.

Note that the more creative or unique the spoofed work, the less likely its use would be allowed. While designing a yearbook cover that has a "supermarket tabloid" feel to it is okay (after all, the *National Enquirer* is just one of a number of similar "gossip" publications), a *Cat in the Hat*-themed yearbook, with clear references to that very unique book, probably would not be acceptable.[89]

Can I allow a parent to buy an ad in our yearbook that includes two stanzas (about 50 words) from Dr. Seuss' poem "Oh, the Places You'll Go!"
Maybe — but get permission anyway. The *purpose* of the use is arguably commercial, since the ad would be helping to finance your yearbook. The *nature* of the work, a poem in book form, is highly creative, and this would also weigh against a finding of fair use. The *amount* taken would be fairly short, and whether it would be the heart of the work would depend on which stanzas are taken (it arguably would be the "heart" or it would not be an effective excerpt). The *effect on the market* factor is the most difficult to pin down in this situation, because it would depend in part on how the court defines the market. On the one hand, the use certainly would not substitute for buying a complete copy of the Dr. Seuss book. On the other hand, it is likely that there is a viable market for Dr. Seuss excerpts (for example, greeting cards, posters, etc.) that your use might affect. A long publication lead time counsels that you should probably seek permission, and Dr. Seuss' publisher does regularly field requests for reprints. If you do this without getting advance permission, at least limit the amount used as much as possible, and be sure the ad gives credit to Dr. Seuss.

REPRODUCING MONEY AND POSTAGE STAMPS

Student publications often run into uncertainty when they want to reproduce money or stamps to illustrate a story. Federal statutes specifically cover the reproduction of money and stamps, and copyright laws apply to stamps as well.

The United States in 1864 passed a law governing the reproduction of money.[90] The law was meant to counter a surge in counterfeiting during the Civil War. In the century that followed, the U.S. Department of Treasury developed a practice to grant permission for the reproduction of money pursuant to requests. Congress codified that practice in 1958.[91] The 1958 law allowed the printing of money and postage stamps only "for philatelic, numismatic, educational, historical, or newsworthy purposes" subject to three restrictions: (1) the likeness must be in black and white, (2) the likeness must be less then three-fourths or more than one and one-half times the size of the original, and (3) the negative and plates used to create the likeness must be destroyed after their use.[92] In *Regan v. Time, Inc.*, *Time* magazine objected to government complaints about the magazine's graphic depictions of money.[93] The Supreme Court found the content restrictions on the reproduction of money — for philatelic, etc., purposes — unconstitutional.[94] But the Court upheld the color, size and plate restrictions as constitutionally permissible to further the end of combating counterfeiting.[95] Subsequently, the Department of the Treasury has used its rulemaking authority to authorize one-sided color reproductions that follow the size and plate limitations.[96]

Congress amended the 1958 law to allow more flexibility in the reproduction of postage stamps. Depictions of postage stamps may now be in color if they follow the size restriction.[97] Also, black-and-white reproductions of color stamps and reproductions of canceled color stamps may be depicted at full size.[98]

Since 1976, the U.S. Postal Service has been claiming copyright protection for the artwork on all postage stamps.[99] So in addition to the statutory restrictions on reproducing stamps, journalists wanting to depict stamps must follow copyright requirements. If the use of the stamp is a fair use under the copyright law, and such would likely be the case if the stamp were the primary subject of a news story, then the permission of the Postal Service is not required. A request for permission must be in writing and include all the details of the intended use, including when and where the reproductions will take place and be distributed, how many images will be produced, and the purpose of the use, emphasizing any educational or nonprofit nature of the use. [100]

TRADEMARK AND PATENT LAW

Copyright law is different from its close relatives, trademark and patent law. All three are areas of "intellectual property" law, meaning copyrights, trademarks and patents may be owned, bought and sold by individuals and businesses much like land and personal property. Like copyrights, patent protection is drawn from the Constitution. While copyrights protect non-functional expressions of information in fixed media, patents protect functional processes, methods and machines.[101] Copyright fosters the work of authors, and patent fosters the work of inventors. Both guarantee exclusive rights to creations for a limited period of time. Student media generally do not have to worry about running afoul of the patent laws.

A trademark is the word, phrase, or symbol that a business uses to get its customers to recognize the source of its goods or services. For example, Coca-Cola® is the trademark that tells you that the carbonated beverage in that two-liter bottle is manufactured and distributed by the Coca-Cola Company. When customers see the Coca-Cola® trademark, and the distinctive script logo, they expect the beverage in the bottle will have a certain level of quality and a certain taste that is associated with the company. Similarly, the swoosh logo on a pair of sneakers tells the purchaser that Nike is the source of those sneakers. Trademarks can simply be the name or logo of the company, or can be another indication of the source of a product, such as the packaging, likeness or even scent.[102] Even the names of publications can be trademarks. For example, *National Geographic* is a trademark for a monthly magazine about science, nature and travel.

Unlike copyrights and patents, trademarks do not expire after a limited time. Trademarks get stronger the longer they are used to identify goods or services, and the more goodwill a trademark creates, the more valuable it is to its owner. In fact, a trademark owner's biggest fear is that the trademark will become so singularly identified with the product it identifies that the trademark becomes generic. Not many people realize, for example, that Aspirin used to be a trademark for a particular brand of pain reliever put out by the Bayer Company. If trademark owners do not actively try to stop people from using their trademarks in generic ways, they could lose their trademarks forever. That is why the owners of products such as Kleenex® tissues, and Xerox® photocopiers sometimes write to student media when they perceive that publications are misusing their trademarks. Companies that send such letters are not trying to pick on student publications, but if they do not enforce their trademarks, they can lose them. This does not mean you cannot use a trademark like Coke®, it just means that you should use it only when you are actually referring to the product made by the Coca-Cola Company, and not as a shorthand for any carbonated beverage. (For example, you do not just drink a coke. You drink Coke® — or some other cola beverage.)

> Patent law protects the rights of inventors to their functional processes and machines.

The use-it-or-lose-it nature of trademarks also explains why trademark owners often write "cease and desist" letters to student media at the first whiff of the use of a trademark that is at all similar to theirs. Trademarks are infringed if the complained-of use causes either actual confusion regarding the source of the item, or a likelihood of confusion.

The Internet has increased sensitivity on the part of many companies — including media companies — where publications that are geographically thousands of miles apart exist only a few keystrokes away in cyberspace. Some larger newspapers, for example, have tried to enforce their names as trademarks against student publications. For instance, *The Village Voice* newspaper in New York sent a cease-and-desist letter to *The Voice*, the Bloomsburg University student newspaper, claiming the Pennsylvania college's student newspaper was likely to confuse readers. (For the record, *The Voice* is still *The Voice*.) The more generic the major publication's name is, the less likely it is to be protected by trademark. Just calling a student paper *The Times* probably would not be a problem, but a New York student publication that called itself *The New York*

Times (or even *The New York Student Times*) would almost certainly raise eyebrows at that famous newspaper's offices.

Trademark and patent can conflict with the First Amendment just like copyright, and courts have created similar approaches in those areas to balance the competing interests of free expression with the protection of intellectual property. It is legal, for example, to use a trademarked name in a news story to describe the goods and services to which the trademark applies. For example, McDonald's owns a trademark in its name, but the company cannot prevent a student reporter from using the company name in a news story or review of the restaurant.

Trademark law protects the goodwill between a company and its customers created by the customer's recognition of the company.

Trademarks may also sometimes be parodied. The question in trademark law is whether the parody is likely to cause confusion with the original, as well as whether it disparages or tarnishes the original trademark. For example, courts have found that parodies that associate the original with illegal drugs or pornography were not fair use.[103] The parody must be obvious enough that it does not trick people into thinking that the owner of the trademark is the source of the parody. It does not matter that no one has been actually confused — if a likelihood of confusion exists, or if the use could make the public think less of the mark, the owner of a famous trademark can sue to prohibit the use.[104] In the context of student media, for example, this means that an underground paper cannot use the name and masthead of the official student newspaper to trick readers into thinking the official newspaper is the source of the parody articles.

DOMAIN NAMES

Although we may not think of them as being trademarks in the same way a company's logo is a trademark, a domain name is also a trademark; it inherently identifies the origin of goods or services and is the first thing you know about a company when you find it through a search engine. Accordingly, companies are as protective of their domain names as they are of their other trademarks, and often are more protective.

For a comprehensive list of other common trademarks and their generic terms, see the International Trademark Association's Trademark Checklist: http://www.inta.org

The legal mechanisms used to resolve disputes over domain name ownership do take into account Fair Use arguments. However, the fair use argument has to apply to the domain name itself, and not just to the content of the Web site.

Most trademark owners who dispute the ownership of a domain name do it through an arbitration process mandated by the Internet Corporation of Assigned Names and Numbers, the group in charge of administering top-level domain names like .com, .net and .org. All domain name registrars agree to require customers to consent to the group's Uniform Dispute Resolution Policy (UDRP) when a name is registered.[105] That policy protects "legitimate noncommercial and fair use" of a trademark, provided there is no intent to confuse web users with the name.[106] That means that the fair use must be clear from the domain name *itself*, because a consumer will have already been confused by the domain name if the fair use is clear only on the site.

For example, a student who hates XYZ University's sports team, the "Fighting Alphabet," could register AlphabetSucks.com, because it is clear from the domain name alone that the student is making a use of the Alphabet trademark for purposes of criticism. On the other hand, he could not register FightingAlphabet.com, as people looking for the official Fighting Alphabet site would be diverted to his criticism instead.

U.S. law offers similar protection to trademark owners — and a similar fair-use right to domain name registrants.107 The law generally is less used than the UDRP, however, because the cost of bringing a lawsuit is much greater than the cost of the arbitration.

SUMMARY

Copyright is one of many areas of law in which different public interests collide. The Constitution itself created a contradiction when it ordered Congress to "make no law" restricting free expression, yet explicitly gave Congress the power to protect the creations of authors and inventors from unauthorized use. New communications technologies have only further intensified the conflict, as modern methods of duplication blur the boundary between original and copy. Student media find themselves directly in the middle of the conflict as they are both protected and hindered by copyright. They are protected like all authors, photographers or other "creators" from having their work stolen and used by others without permission. They are also, however, limited in their ability to use the copyrighted work of others in their reporting. The fair use exception is especially important for student journalists and allows them to walk the fine line between legal and illegal usage of copyrighted material. Unfortunately, the rules of fair use are somewhat murky, and — like the whole of copyright law itself — evolving with new technology.

CASE STUDY

Jay Dee, editor of Central High School's student yearbook, has some decisions to make.

The yearbook staff has voted that the book's theme be based on popular daytime soap operas. "The Days of Our Lives" was suggested as the yearbook title. The various section headers will also use the name of a soap opera ("The Young and the Restless" for student activities, the "Bold and the Beautiful" for the prom section, etc.). In addition, the staff wants to pepper the book with references to soap operas, including cast photos and dialogue excerpts.

For the current events section, his writers are putting together a "Year in Review" piece. They read through *People* and summarized some of the magazine's leading stories as "news briefs" to include in their list of the year's top ten news stories. In addition, they have scanned the photos accompanying the stories and want to use them to illustrate the news briefs. His staff has assured Jay that they will include a credit line ("Photo courtesy of *People* magazine") under each image they use.

His entertainment section editor is a cartoon nut and would like to do a mock interview with various cartoon characters commenting on life at Central High School. The interview will include hand-copied images of the characters drawn by a student staff member.

Finally, the sports editor would like to do a profile of Peter "Paddles" Pierce, a recent graduate of Central that has hit it big on the international pingpong circuit. She found a bunch of great photos of "Paddles" in action on two "unofficial" fan websites. Luckily, she told Jay, none of the photos had a copyright notice. To be doubly certain, though, she e-mailed the operators of both websites to make sure it was okay to use the photos. So far, the editor has heard back from just one of the website operators, who told her to use any of the photos she wanted.

With so many decisions to make, Jay Dee's head is spinning. He's come to you — the Copyright Law Guru — for guidance. What, if anything, should he be concerned about?

Soap opera theme

The U.S. Copyright Office has determined that certain categories of material cannot be copyrighted because they lack the necessary creativity. Among them: names, titles, short phrases, expressions or catchwords, slogans and mottoes. NBC cannot, for example, copyright the bare, unadorned words, "days of our lives," and Jay is free to use them as a yearbook title, a section header or anyplace else without obtaining NBC's permission. However, NBC does own the rights to the popular daytime soap opera, "Days of Our Lives," and if the yearbook staff wants to spice up the look of the yearbook by using other material from the show, such as photos of cast members, scripts, dialogue or the show's hourglass logo — all of which are copyrighted — Jay will need to obtain permission from NBC.

"Year in Review" section

There is no problem in reviewing and summarizing news stories reported by other news sources. *People* does not "own" the facts they uncover and report. As long as you use their stories only as a source for factual information and write your own summary of the news event in your own words, there is no copyright problem. Unless the facts have been widely reported by numerous sources and are generally known, good journalism demands that the source be properly attributed (for example, "*People* reported in March that…."). Jay probably cannot use another news source's photos to accompany the news briefs without permission. Unlike the "facts," *People* (or someone) likely does own the copyright on the photos that appear in its magazine. Since you are using the photos simply to illustrate the news event and not to comment on the artistic quality of the photos themselves or on *People*'s coverage — uses where you might be able to argue "fair use" — you will need to seek permission or try to find an alternative source for the images, such as the Associated Press or another commercial service. Other "news" photos may be available from U.S. government sources, for which copyright permission is generally not required. Note that simply giving credit to *People* — without first getting permission — is insufficient.

Cartoon characters' mock interview

Creating a "mock interview" with famous cartoon characters might be considered an acceptable parody. However, it will be important for the interviews to use the cartoon characters not merely for their recognition value, but to comment or poke fun at them by playing on their unique qualities and characteristics. In other words, while there is *some* wiggle room, the focus of a successful parody involving Bart Simpson would be the character himself, not Central High School. In addition, successful parodies add creative elements to an original work; they should not simply be a substitute for the real thing. For example, tracing an exact copy of the characters to include alongside the interview is really no better than photocopying or scanning the images directly. To qualify as a fair use, the words or images used by the yearbook should include no more of a copyrighted work than is necessary to "conjure up" the original. Jay wants his readers to recognize the cartoon characters, but he should instruct his writers and artists to add enough of their own creative effort so that the work stands on its own and is not simply a duplicate of the original.

Peter "Paddles" Pierce profile

Unfortunately, you tell Jay, he might have a problem using the "Paddles" photos. First, you remind him that the lack of a copyright notice (for example, "© 2013 Paddles, Inc.") on the photos means nothing. The law no longer requires such notices. The photos were copyrighted the moment they were taken. Also, it would probably be a stretch to use the photos based on fair use. Using someone else's photos of a news event will usually not constitute fair use unless the photos themselves (rather than the event they show) are the subject of the news reporting or commentary. That said, if part of your story focuses on the fame that has come to the former Central High School student, you probably could use a single, reduced-size screen shot of the fan website, which may include one of Paddles' photos, to show how famous he has become. While the sports section editor has appropriately sought and received permission to use Paddles' photos from one of the website operators, such permission is valid only if the website operator had the authority to give it. In other words, unless the operator was the owner of the photos (or had worked out some sort of deal with the owner), his permission is worthless since he is probably using the photos illegally as well.

ENDNOTES

1   U.S. Const. Art. I, Sec. 8.
2   *Harper & Row, Publishers, Inc. v. Nation Enter.*, 471 U.S. 539 (1985). Congress subsequently amended statutory fair use, 17 U.S.C. Sec. 107, to clarify that the fact of a work being unpublished should not outweigh a finding of fair use made under that provision.
3   *Id.* at 557.
4   17 U.S.C. Sec. 102.
5   *Id.* at Sec. 103.
6   *Id.* at Sec. 102(a).
7   *Feist Publications, Inc. v. Rural Telephone Serv.*, 499 U.S. 340 (1991).
8   17 U.S.C. Sec. 102(a).
9   Copyright Office, Library of Congress, Circular 1, *Copyright Basics* p. 3 (2008) (hereinafter Circular 1).
10   17 U.S.C. Sec. 102(b).

11 For more information on plagiarism, see Mike Hiestand, *Special Report: Plagiarism, in* CSPA Stylebook (Columbia Scholastic Press Association 1996).

12 17 U.S.C. Sec. 102.

13 17 U.S.C.S. Sec. 101 (1977 & Supp. 1992).

14 *Id.* The work must fall into one of nine categories specified by the law and specifically and clearly state the intent to create a work for hire.

15 *New York Times Co., Inc. v. Tasini*, 533 U.S. 483 (2001) (independent contractors can prevent publications from placing works in electronic databases without their permission).

16 *Community for Creative Non-Violence v. Reid*, 490 U.S. 730 (1989).

17 *Id.* at 751-52.

18 *See, e.g., O'Connor v. Davis*, 126 F.3d 112, 115-16 (2d Cir. 1997) (where there is no payment to a student for her work, there is no "hire" and therefore no need to even undertake the employee versus independent contractor analysis; "[w]here no financial benefit is obtained by the purported employee from the employer, no 'plausible' employment relationship of any sort can be said to exist because although 'compensation by the putative employer to the putative employee in exchange for his services is not a sufficient condition, … it is an essential condition to the existence of an employer-employee relationship.'"). *O'Connor* was not a copyright case, but it applied the analysis of *CCNV v. Reid* and determined that a student volunteer at a hospital was not an employee, even though she received work-study monies for her work, because she was not paid by the hospital

19 *See, e.g., Marco v. Accent Publ'g Co., Inc.*, 969 F.2d 1547 (3d Cir. 1992) (freelance photographer for magazine classified as independent contractor where evidence showed he used his own equipment, paid his own taxes, supplied his own studio, did not receive employee benefits and was paid by the job); *Schiller & Schmidt, Inc. v. Nordisco Corp.*, 969 F.2d 410, 412 (7th Cir. 1992) ("no one could suppose…that [freelance photographer] was an employee" where specific statement to that effect was not signed prior to work being performed").

20 *Reid*, 490 U.S. at 743.

21 Compare *New York Times Co., Inc. v. Tasini*, 533 U.S. 483 (2001) with *Greenberg v. National Geographic Society*, No. 05-16964, 2008 WL 2571333 (11th Cir. June 30, 2008) (en banc).

22 *See* 17 U.S.C. Sec. 201(c).

23 17 U.S.C. Sec. 106.

24 Where the music and lyrics have different authors, those copyrights can be separate as well.

25 Under certain circumstances, the law grants what is called a "compulsory license" to make copies, which means you do not have to get explicit permission to use someone else's work so long as you pay them in accordance with the statute. So, for example, once a song has been recorded, others may make their own recording of it without permission as long as they pay a royalty. 17 U.S.C. Sec. 115. Student media outlets should *never* assume they have a compulsory license, however.

26 17 U.S.C. Sec. 102. *See also* Circular 1, supra note 9, at 3.

27 17 U.S.C. Sec. 401-402. *See also* Copyright Office, Library of Congress, Circular 3, Copyright Notice at 2 (2004).

28 *Id.* at 2-3.

29 *Id.* at 2.

30 17 U.S.C. Sec. 407. *See also* Copyright Office, Library of Congress, Circular 7d, Mandatory Deposit of Copies or Phonorecords for the Library of Congress at 1 (2008). The address to which materials should be sent for deposit is: Register of Copyrights, Attn: 407 Deposits, Library of Congress, Washington, D.C. 20559-6000. The deposit requirement also applies to most Web content; for more information, see Copyright Office, Library of Congress, Circular 66, Copyright Registration for Online Works at 1 (2008). It is possible to request a waiver of the mandatory deposit requirement by writing to: Chief, Copyright Acquisitions Division, Copyright Office, Library of Congress, Washington, DC 20559-4130. Fax: (202) 707-4435.

31 17 U.S.C. Sec. 407(a)(2).

32 Circular 7d. Attempting to register a work without fulfilling the deposit requirement can result in a fine. *Id.* at (d).

33 *See* Library of Congress, *eCO Frequently Asked Questions*, at http://www.copyright.gov/eco/faq.html#eCO_ 1.4 (last visited June 21, 2013).

34 17 U.S.C. Sec. 411. Circular 1, supra note 9, at 7.

35 17 U.S.C. Sec. 410 (registration within five years prima facie evidence of copyright validity); *see also* Circular 1, supra note 9, at 7.

36 17 U.S.C. Sec. 412 (statutory damages and attorneys fees). *See also* Circular 1, supra note 9, at 7.

37 Copyright Office, Library of Congress, Circular 4, Copyright Office Fees at 6 (2008).

38 *Id.*

39 *See generally* Copyright Office, Library of Congress, Circular 15a, Duration of Copyright (2004).

40 Pub. L. No. 105-298, 112 Stat. 2827.

41 *Eldred v. Ashcroft*, 537 U.S. 186 (2003).

42 17 U.S.C. Sec. 302.

43 17 U.S.C. Sec. 303.

44 17 U.S.C. Sec. 304.

45 17 U.S.C. Sec. 305.

46 17 U.S.C. Sec. 501

47 17 U.S.C. Sec. 502-505 (remedies for infringement).

48 17 U.S.C. Sec. 504(c)(statutory damages); Sec. 505 (costs and attorney's fees); Sec. 412 (registration as a prerequisite for these remedies).

49 17 U.S.C. Sec. 504(b).

50 17 U.S.C Sec. 504(c).

51 *Feltner v. Columbia Pictures Television, Inc.*, 520 U.S. 340 (1998) (constitutional right to jury trial to

determine amount of statutory damages in copyright action).

52 Pub. L. No. 105-304, 112 Stat. 2860.

53 *Universal City Studios, Inc. v. Corley*, 273 F.3d 429 (2d Cir. 2001).

54 *DVD Copy Control Ass'n Inc. v. Bunner*, 116 Cal.App.4th 241 (Cal. Dist. Ct. App. 2004). *See also Pavlovich v. Superior Court*, 29 Cal.4th 262 (Cal. 2002) (holding that California courts did not have jurisdiction to hear case brought by California-based DVD association against Indiana college student who published DVD decryption software on the Internet).

55 17 U.S.C. Sec. 512(k) (definition); 17 U.S.C. Sec. 512(c) (safe harbor procedures).

56 http://www.copyright.gov/onlinesp (last visited Sept. 15, 2008).

57 *See* 17 U.S.C. Sec. 115(a)(1) (limiting availability of compulsory license to those with a "primary purpose" of making sound recordings to deliver to the public for private performance).

58 *See* http://www.soundexchange.com/service-provider/licensing-101/.

59 *See* http://www.copyright.gov/records. *See also* Copyright Office, Library of Congress, Circular 22: How to Investigate the Copyright Status of a Work (2004).

60 The Journalism Education Association's digital media website offers links to some copyright-free music resources at http://www.jeadigitalmedia.org/2012/07/06/royalty-free-music-for-video-production/ (last viewed June 21, 2013). Another good source for information on production music for student media is SchoolTV.com. *See* Keith Kyker and Christopher Curchy, "Music for Video Production," *Florida Media Quarterly* (http://www.schooltv.com/vidview21.htm) (last viewed June 21, 2013).

61 For example, photo/wire service companies commonly used by student media include: MCT Campus (http://www.mctcampus.com); Newscom (http://www.newscom.com), and iStockphoto (http://www.istockphoto.com). (All sites current as of June 21, 2013.) In addition, the Associated Press, through its AP Images division, has offered a student yearbook photo package.

62 17 U.S.C. Sec. 107.

63 L. Ray Patterson (Brock Professor of Law at the University of Georgia) cited by David W. Stowe, *Just Do It: How to Beat the Copyright Racke*t, Lingua Franca (Nov./Dec. 1995) at 38.

64 17 U.S.C. Sec. 107.

65 *Campbell v. Acuff-Rose Music, Inc.*, 510 U.S. 569, 584 (1994) ("the mere fact that a use is educational and not for profit does not insulate it from a finding of infringement").

66 *Id.* at 579.

67 These facts were derived from *Nuñez v. Caribbean Int'l News Corp.*, 235 F.3d 18, 23 (1st Cir. 2000) ("Rather, what is important here is that plaintiff's photographs were originally intended to appear in modeling portfolios, not in the newspaper; the former use, not the latter, motivated the creation of the work. Thus, by using the photographs in conjunction with editorial commentary, [the newspaper] did not merely supersede the objects of the original creations, but instead used the works for a further purpose, giving them a new meaning, or message. It is this transformation of the works into news—and not the mere newsworthiness of the works themselves—that weighs in favor of fair use...") (internal citations, quotes, and brackets omitted).

68 *Id.*

69 *Harper & Row, Publishers v. Nation Enter.*, 471 U.S. 539 (1985).

70 H.R. Rep. No. 94-1733, 94th Cong., 2d Sess., at 70 (Sept. 29, 1976) (citing to H.R. Rep. No. 94-1476, 94th Cong., 2d Sess., at 68-70 (Sept. 3, 1976)).

71 H.R Rep. No. 94-1476, 94th Cong., 2d Sess., at 68 (Sept. 3, 1976).

72 *See, e.g., Basic Books, Inc. v. Kinko's Graphics Corp.*, 758 F. Supp. 1522 (S.D.N.Y. 1991) (copying not fair use); *Princeton Univ. Press v. Michigan Document Serv., Inc.*, 99 F.3d 1381 (6th Cir. 1996) (same)

73 The guidelines were created as a part of the Conference on Fair Use (CONFU), a public-private project convened as part of the work of the federal government's Information Infrastructure Task Force (IITF). President Clinton created the IITF in 1993 to study, among other things, intellectual property policy. Exec. Order No. 12864, 3 C.F.R. 634 (1993). The guidelines were completed in 1996, and have been endorsed by many educators and copyright owners. The complete report can be found at http://www.uspto.gov/web/offices/dcom/olia/confu/report.htm (last viewed August 28, 2008).

74 *Campbell v. Acuff-Rose Music, Inc.*, 510 U.S. 569, 580 (1994).

75 *Id.* at 581.

76 *Walt Disney Productions v. Air Pirates*, 581 F.2d 751, 752 (9th Cir. 1978), cert. denied sub nom., *O'Neill v. Walt Disney Productions*, 439 U.S. 1132 (1979).

77 *Id.* at 753.

78 *Dr. Seuss Enter. L.P. v. Penguin Books USA, Inc.*, 109 F.3d 1394 (9th Cir. 1997).

79 Campbell, 510 U.S. at 569.

80 *Id.* at 582.

81 *Id.* at 588-89.

82 *Id.* at 590.

83 For a discussion of the seminal cases in this area, read *Elsmere Music v. NBC*, 482 F. Supp. 741 (S.D.N.Y. 1980), aff'd, 623 F.2d 252 (2d Cir. 1980). In *Elsmere*, the composer of the "I Love NY" advertising jingle sued NBC after "Saturday Night Live" ran a parody sketch where the Biblical city of Sodom decided to improve its image with an advertising campaign that involved cast members singing "I Love Sodom" to the same four-note melody as the composer's work. The case turned on whether "I Love Sodom" was a satire of New York City or a *parody* of the lyrics of the song. The court, finding that the NBC work used the "heart of the work," nevertheless found the song was a fair use, because the original jingle had been used to sell the city, thus making a parody of one a parody of the other.

84 H.R. Rep. No. 94-1476, 94th Cong., 2d Sess., at 68 (Sept. 3, 1976).

85 17 U.S.C. Sec. 107.

86 *See Kelly v. Arriba Soft Corp.*, 336 F.3d 811 (9th Cir. 2003) and *Perfect 10, Inc. v. Amazon.com, Inc.*, 487 F.3d 701 (9th Cir. 2007).

87 *Nuñez v. Caribbean Int'l News Corp.*, 235 F.3d 18 (1st Cir. 2000). A more recent case elaborated on the *Nuñez* ruling and its limits. In the case of *Monge v. Maya Magazines, Inc.*, 688 F.3d 1164 (9th Cir. 2012),

a federal appeals court refused to apply the "fair use" doctrine to a celebrity gossip magazine's publication of leaked photos documenting the undisclosed marriage of a popular Puerto Rican singer to her manager. The judges referenced the *Nuñez* ruling, but found it inapplicable, because the wedding photos in the Monge case were not themselves newsworthy or a source of controversy; they were merely evidence of the *secret* marriage, which was the subject of the article. As these comparable cases illustrate, there is a fine line between reproduction of photos that are themselves a news event (fair use) versus reproduction of photos that merely memorialize a news event (not fair use).

88 *See* Leslie Ann Reis, Comment, *The Rodney King Beating – Beyond Fair Use: A Broadcaster's Right To Air Copyrighted Videotape as Part of a Newscast*, 13 J. Marshall J. Computer & Info. L. 269 (1995) (recounting oral ruling in *Holliday v. CNN*, CV 92-3287 IH (C.D. Cal. June 11, 1993)).

89 *Dr. Seuss Enter. L.P. v. Penguin Books USA, Inc.*, 109 F.3d 1394 (9th Cir. 1997).

90 *Regan v. Time, Inc.*, 468 U.S. 641, 644 n.1 (1984) (citing 18 U.S.C. Sec. 474).

91 *Id.* (citing 18 U.S.C. Sec. 504).

92 18 U.S.C. Sec. 504.

93 *Regan*, 468 U.S. at 646.

94 *Id.* at 647.

95 *Id.*

96 31 C.F.R. Sec. 411 (1996). *See also* 18 U.S.C. Sec. 504(1)(iii) (rulemaking authority).

97 18 U.S.C. Sec. 504.

98 *Id.*

99 39 C.F.R. Sec. 602.1.

100 For uses that require permission, federal regulations state that you should contact the Office of Licensing, Philatelic and Retail Services Department, US Postal Service, 475 L'Enfant Plaza SW., Washington, DC 20260-6700. *See* 39 C.F.R. Sec. 602.3.

101 Edward D. Lanquist, Jr., "Patent, Copyright and Trademark Law for the General Practitioner: Answering the Questions and Dispelling the Myths," *Barrister*, Fall 1993, at 20.

102 *Id.*

103 *See, e.g., Coca-Cola Co. v. Gemini Rising, Inc.*, 346 F. Supp. 1183 (E.D.N.Y. 1972). (enjoining the use of poster featuring slogan "Enjoy Cocaine" in the distinctive Coca-Cola script); *Dallas Cowboys Cheerleaders, Inc. v. Pussycat Cinema, Ltd.*, 604 F.2d 200 (2d Cir. 1979) (porno film "Debbie Does Dallas," in which star appears clad – albeit partially – in what appears to be a Dallas Cowboys cheerleader uniform).

104 15 U.S.C. Sec. 1125(c). This section, amended by Congress in 2006, overruled a Supreme Court decision, *Mosley v. V Secret Catalogue, Inc.*, 537 U.S. 418 (2003), that had found actual confusion was required.

105 Uniform Domain Name Dispute Resolution Policy, October 29, 1999, at http://www.icann.org/en/help/dndr/udrp for more information go to http://archive.icann.org/en/dndr/udrp/ (last viewed July 14, 2013).

106 UDRP at Sec. 4(c)(3).

107 15 U.S.C. Sec. 1125(d).

CHAPTER 16

Liability for Student Media

"With great power comes great responsibility" isn't just a line from Spider-Man. It's an essential reminder for anyone who publishes, whether on a social-networking page or in the pages of a national newsmagazine. The American legal system recognizes that people who cause harm through their own lack of due care can be forced in a court of law to pay for the damage they inflict. A journalist who libels someone, invades his privacy or infringes copyrighted material can be sued and ordered to pay substantial money damages.

School administrators and their attorneys often incorrectly view student media as a minefield of legal risk. In fact, the law is highly protective in giving journalists leeway to publish, and that is doubly so of student journalists, who rarely are the target of lawsuits (despite the occasional "I'm suing you!" bluster) and even more rarely are on the losing end.

The rarity of liability suits should not, of course, cause any journalist to cut corners. Lawsuits do happen, and when they do, it typically is the result of a hasty decision to distribute information without adequate verification (and even when hasty errors do not produce lawsuits, they do cause embarrassment and loss of reputation). The ease and immediacy of online platforms may make publishing seem more casual, but they should never make journalists casual about accuracy.

Many clashes between administrators and student media result from "urban legends" about liability risks that are fictitious or are so remote as to be practically impossible (for instance, the unsubstantiated "tall tale" that publishing photos of minors leads to child abductions for which schools can be sued). Running a successful student media program requires being able to separate myth from reality — and, where liability risks genuinely do exist, knowing the best professional practices to minimize them.

The general principle behind legal liability is that any person who could and should have prevented an injury from occurring can be held responsible for it. The same reasoning applies to students, even minors.

WHO CAN BE HELD LIABLE?

The general principle behind legal liability is that any person who should and reasonably could have prevented an injury from occurring can be held responsible for it. Thus in the context of a libel claim against a newspaper based on a news story, the reporter who wrote the story[1] and any editors or other staff members who had significant responsibility for overseeing its inclusion in the paper[2] could be required to pay for the damage to reputation the story caused. In the words of one court, "Everyone who takes a responsible part in the publication is liable for the defamation."[3]

That same reasoning applies to student journalists, even those who are minors.[4] A 16- year-old high school student reporter who libels a teacher will not be shielded from responsibility by her youth. More than one high school journalist has called the Student Press Law Center when threatened with a libel lawsuit and been surprised to learn that she can be sued and ordered to pay damages. Practically, few libel plaintiffs are inclined to sue high school students individually because of the appearance that they are "picking on a kid who made a mistake" and because they know that they are not likely to collect much of a damage award from a cash-poor student. But if they choose to make such a claim against a minor, the law will not keep them from doing so.

On the other hand, those who have borne no significant role in publishing a defamatory or other unlawful statement can generally escape liability, regardless of their age. For example, a business manager or other non-editorial employee of a student publication will not be liable for a defamatory statement where he had no direct participation or knowledge of its production.[5] Similarly, the author of an originally non-defamatory statement is not liable for editing changes, made without her knowledge, that convert the statement from innocent to actionable.[6]

Student media advisers often ask the Student Press Law Center if they can be held liable for the student publications they advise. The short answer is that they are legally in the same position as the school itself. If they dictate content decisions to student editors, they likely will be liable. Where they leave content control to students, even if they do offer advice and suggestions on particular stories but make clear (ideally by a written policy) that they are leaving the final decision to the editors, they can avoid liability.[7]

ARE MOM AND DAD LIABLE FOR WHAT JOHNNY WRITES?

Parents normally are not responsible for the speech of their children. As of 2013, there were no published court decisions holding parents civilly liable for the unlawful speech of their child. But according to legal scholars, parents can be held responsible for the harm caused by their minor children in certain circumstances and some states have established this responsibility by statute.[8] The circumstances where parental liability exists, however, will be rare. Only when parents are aware of their child's unlawful expression and fail to act reasonably to control it will they be held responsible for what their child publishes.

Of course, if parents play an independent and active role in the publishing process — for example, by editing their daughter's article before it is published in an underground paper or contributing their own column to their son's website — they can be held responsible for their own work.

At a public college or university, a school that does not censor or otherwise control the content of a school-sponsored student publication should be protected from liability for what students publish.

SCHOOL LIABILITY: PUBLIC COLLEGES PROTECTED

While libel, invasion of privacy and other content-based lawsuits against college publications are relatively rare, college administrators still may be concerned about their potential liability for what their students publish. For a person suing, a college or university is often the most desirable defendant because it can afford to pay a greater amount of money damages than an asset-poor student newspaper or student staff members. They are frequently described as having the "deep pockets."

The good news for anxious administrators is that courts have said that public colleges and universities will not be held financially liable for what their student media publish as long as the school is not censoring or exercising some other form of content control. Thus, schools that exercise a "hands-off" editorial policy are in a better position to avoid liability for student media mistakes than those that carefully screen and approve content prior to publication.

Plaintiffs trying to reach the "deep pockets" of a university have attempted to argue various legal theories. Some have tried to claim that the school should be held liable for its student media because it functions as the publisher. For commercial media, publishers are generally liable for everything published under their name.[9] However, in the student media context, comparable positions may not exist. Most student publications do not have a named "publisher," and those that do typically do not allow them to interfere with content decisions of student editors. The private publisher of *The Los Angeles Times* is different from the president of California State University. As one federal appeals court noted, a public "university is clearly an arm of the state and this single fact will always distinguish it from the purely private publisher…"[10]

In one of the first cases to reject such a "publisher" theory, a Louisiana state court refused to impose liability on Southern Louisiana University of New Orleans for a libel claim brought against that school's student newspaper. In *Milliner v. Turner*,[11] members of the faculty sued for libel after the student newspaper called them "racists" and "proven fools." The Louisiana Court of Appeals held that the university could not be held liable because it did not have the authority to control the content of newspaper. The court found:

> "The relationship between a university and its student newspaper is anomalous and cannot be compared with a publisher and its newspaper. The latter may exercise censorship to the fullest, as it deems commercially proper to do so, but the former is almost completely barred from censoring its student paper since that would be prior restraint and would impede the free flow and expression of ideas....We find the First Amendment of the United States Constitution would bar [the university] from exercising anything but advisory control over the paper, therefore, exempting the university from liability or responsibility."[12]

Those suing student media have also tried to claim that colleges are responsible for the acts of their student media staffs because the students act as "agents" of the university. The "agency" legal theory is often asserted by those hoping to hold "deep pocketed" employers responsible for the actions of their employees while on the job. To make such a claim, however, it is necessary to show, among other things, that the employer has the right to control his employees in the performance of their duties. Financial sponsorship alone does not create an agency relationship.[13] Applying this "agency" theory to the relationship between a public college and its student media simply does not work; a consistent body of case law makes clear that public colleges are constitutionally prohibited from exercising practical control over the day-to-day editorial operations of student media.

The "agency" theory was first rejected by a New York court after the student newspaper at the State University of New York's Binghamton campus published a letter to the editor that described two students at the school as members of the "gay community." The students filed a libel suit in which they named the university as a defendant. The court ruled in *Mazart v. State*[14] that the university could not be held liable because it did not have the right to control the content of the newspaper; therefore, no agency relationship could be established. The court rejected the students' agency claim even though it noted that the newspaper was funded in part by student activity fees, that the university provided office space, desks and janitorial services at no cost and that students working on the publication could receive English credit for their efforts.

These factors were insufficient, however, "to overcome the university's lack of control over the newspaper.... Such accoutrements are nothing more than a form of financial aid to the newspaper which cannot be traded off in return for editorial control."[15]

The reasoning of *Mazart* was reaffirmed in a case against Clemson University in South Carolina.[16] In that case, the university was held not responsible for an alleged defamatory article printed in its student newspaper because the paper was not subject to prior review by university officials.

The court found "[t]here is overwhelming authority across the country in support of the position that a public university which does not censor or otherwise control the content of a school-sponsored newspaper is not liable for what is published by the students in the student-run newspaper."[17]

A New York court similarly rejected the agency theory of liability in *McEvaddy v. City University of New York*.[18] As in earlier cases, the court found it irrelevant that the university provided the paper with a faculty adviser and funding. The key, the court said, was that the university was legally prohibited from exercising — and, in fact, did not exercise — control over the content of the newspaper that would justify the imposition of liability.

The issue of vicarious liability was most recently confronted by a Minnesota state appellate court when a professor sued St. Cloud University for an allegedly defamatory article published in the student newspaper.[19] The court acknowledged the "plethora of connections"[20] between the student newspaper and the university, which the professor pointed out, but rejected his claim that the university could be held liable based on either a "university as publisher" or agency theory. Of particular relevance to the Minnesota court in shielding the university from liability was a university system policy that prohibited school officials from exercising any control over student-funded publications.[21]

Another possible theory for university liability is negligence. To prevail, the person bringing suit would have to establish that the university had a legal responsibility to protect others from harm — for example, by providing student staff with editing guidelines and procedures for avoiding the publication of libelous material — but failed to do so. Such a theory was rejected in the *Mazart* case, discussed above.[22] The court noted that college students are legally adults, not children; therefore, the university had no duty to provide or enforce editing guidelines because as adults college student journalists were presumed to already know how to perform their editing responsibilities.

As the cases above indicate, school officials seeking to avoid liability for their student publications are best served by simply keeping their distance. This is legally consistent with the restraints imposed on public colleges by the First Amendment; it also comports with common sense. As one legal scholar has said, "There is simply no justification for imposing liability on a state university that is powerless to prevent the alleged harm."[23]

On the other hand, these cases also indicate that where a public college, including its administrators or student media advisers, interfere with the content decisions of students (despite the First Amendment prohibitions against such action), the school can be held legally liable for that publication's content. In such cases the school would not only be setting itself up to be sued for First Amendment infringement by students, it would also be exposing itself to liability for any content-based mistakes its students make. For public colleges and universities under the jurisdiction of the federal Seventh Circuit Court of Appeals and its decision in *Hosty v. Carter* (discussed in detail in Chapter 6), the incentive for enacting policies designating student media as public forums would seem to be even stronger because of that case's implication that the school could be held responsible if it was reserving the right to censor.

If a private school adopts a written policy that gives content control over student publications to student editors, such a policy could protect the school from liability.

LIABILITY AT PRIVATE SCHOOLS

The situation may be different at private universities and high schools. While a school policy, state constitution or state law may offer some free speech protection, the First Amendment does not prohibit private schools from censoring or regulating the content of their student publications.

Because of the lack of a First Amendment bar to censorship, an agency theory of liability may be more successful where school officials fail to set up clear boundaries prohibiting administrative censorship. For example, in *Wallace v. Weiss* a student sued the University of Rochester for libel based on material published in a student publication.[24] The court refused to dismiss the case against the university, saying that a private school is not limited by the First Amendment in its ability to censor as a public school would be. "The University ... may well be responsible for the acts of the organization, at least insofar as the University has the power to exercise control," the court said.[25] The court said it would be up to the university to show at a full trial that it did not have the power to exercise control. (The case ultimately was settled out of court so there was no final ruling on the issue.)

Although the decision in *Wallace* suggests that private schools could be held liable for what their student publications publish,[26] the ruling certainly did not settle the issue. The decision suggests that if a private school adopts a written policy that gives content control over student publications to student editors, the legally binding restrictions such a policy may place on the school could protect it from liability.[27] As a matter of deference, a court may hesitate to second-guess a private school's judgment that allowing student publications to operate without prior review or controls is the better educational practice.

In fact, at least one court did find that a private university was protected from liability for material published by the student newspaper at the school. In that case, a New Jersey appellate court ruled that Princeton University was not liable for alleged defamatory statements made in *The Daily Princetonian*.[28] *The Daily Princetonian* is the primary student newspaper operating on campus and is separately incorporated. The court made no mention of that fact, other than noting that the publication was "independent." "[D] efamatory statements that appeared in the independent University publications are not attributable to Princeton and its administrators," the court concluded.[29]

Just as in public schools, it appears the best way for a private school to protect itself from liability is to prohibit school officials from interfering with content decisions made by student editors. A clear, strong written policy affirming the right of student editors to make all editorial decisions in exchange for students assuming all responsibility for content would present the strongest basis for protecting the school from liability.[30] If faced with a lawsuit, the school could argue that the policy is a legally enforceable contract that creates an independent contractor relationship with the students and prevents the school from exercising control over the students' activities as they would with university employees. A similar argument could be made at schools where state constitutional provisions protect student press freedom (and in California, where the state legislature has given private school students free press protections[31]).

Other precautions that can be taken to limit university exposure include: (1) printing a disclaimer in every edition (and/or on the website or broadcast) emphasizing the medium's separate operation from the school and stating that all views expressed are not necessarily those of the school; (2) administering funds apart from those of the university in a separate account; or (3) becoming an independent legal entity, for example, by incorporating.

PROTECTION FOR ONLINE SPEECH: SECTION 230

Despite the fears of many school officials — some of whom more tightly regulate online speech than speech in print — schools are probably less at risk for what their students publish in an online version of their publication than they are for what appears in the traditional print version of the same newspaper. That is because a federal law — Section 230 of the Communications Decency Act — limits the liability of users or providers of "interactive computer services " (which specifically includes systems operated by "educational institutions"[32]) for material created or provided by someone else.[33] In other words, where school employees have played no editorial role in creating content in an online student newspaper, Congress has said the school will not be held responsible even where the offending material is housed on the school's computers.

Section 230 also provides some protection to student media staff. In addition to shielding its school host, Section 230 would also likely protect student media from liability for libelous or other unlawful material posted on their website by a third party. For example, Section 230 probably limits a student newspaper's liability for reader comments or statements posted to a message board or reader-response forum on the newspaper's website. (In a rare test of this immunity, a Louisiana circuit judge ruled in 2009 that the student-run *Daily Reveille* at Louisiana State University could not be held responsible for reader-posted insults questioning the mental health of a student who was named in a police-beat story.[34])

Note that the law provides a shield from liability only for content created or provided by an outside party. A student publication remains completely responsible for anything the staff itself produces and posts online. Section 230 does include a so-called "good samaritan" provision that allows an online student publication to screen and delete material, including any unlawful or other "inappropriate" material, posted to its website by outsiders without incurring liability. In other words, the staff does not become the "creator" of reader comments simply by exercising a gatekeeping function. However, were a staff member to substantially rewrite or add words to a letter to the editor or a comment posted by a reader, the newspaper risks crossing the line between merely allowing for distribution of the material (and being protected by Section 230) and "creating" the work, thereby assuming responsibility for it. The law also does not provide protection from violations of federal criminal statutes or infringements of others' copyrights.[35]

Another word of caution: while Section 230 of the Communications Decency Act inarguably provides significant protection for online speech, the law — like the Internet itself — is relatively new and some key questions remain unanswered. For example, while it is clear that large Internet service providers (AOL, Comcast) and search engines (Google, Yahoo!) are protected from liability, the Supreme Court has yet to say that website operators or newsgroup hosts are covered, although an overwhelming number of lower courts have indicated that they are.[36] Online publishers should be aware of and understand the protections available under Section 230. They must also understand that the scope of those protections is still evolving.

PUBLIC HIGH SCHOOL LIABILITY

The SPLC has yet to turn up a single published court decision in which a public high school has ever been held legally liable for something in a student publication anywhere, anytime.

As a result of the *Hazelwood* ruling, public high school officials have greater authority to control some school-sponsored publications, as discussed fully in Chapter 5. It is reasonable to expect, however, that officials choosing to exercise such editorial control will also bear greater financial responsibility for mistakes that student media staffs might make and administrators fail to catch. Where a principal insists on mandatory prior review and approval of a student newspaper she is, in effect, giving the publication the school's official "seal of approval" for which the school district can probably be held at least partially accountable. On the other hand, if a public secondary school establishes a policy that gives students press freedom and limits administrative interference, a strong argument can be made that — like a public college — it should be shielded from liability if damaging content is published.

Many of the state laws and school district policies that establish free press protections for high school students have recognized this. Like public college administrators, officials at these schools are legally prohibited from interfering with editorial content except in narrow circumstances specified by law. In such cases — again, just like at a public college — it will be more difficult to show that student journalists act as "agents" for the school so as to justify imposing institutional liability.[37] The issue is even clearer in Colorado, Iowa, Kansas and Massachusetts, where student free expression statutes explicitly limit the liability of school officials for material in student publications unless they have interfered with the content decisions of student editors.[38]

Schools that exercise prior review of underground publications dramatically increase their potential liability for the contents of those publications.

Unfortunately, high school administrators frequently attempt to use the potential for liability as an excuse to control editorial content. In fact, the risk is extremely low. To date, the Student Press Law Center has found no published court decision anywhere in the country where a high school was held financially liable for the content of its student media. Liability for student media, while a concern, ought not to overrule sound educational policy and a commitment to journalistic excellence.

Some questions remain for courts to answer. In the meantime, public high school officials may best be able to protect themselves from liability by allowing their student media to operate independently and ensuring their students have the resources and support — specifically including competent, trained journalism advisers — to succeed.

INDEPENDENT PUBLICATIONS

Barring unusual circumstances, a school bears no legal responsibility for the content of an independent or "underground" student publication (even where it is distributed on school grounds) or a private, off-campus website created by students.[39] The situation is somewhat akin to the liability a bookstore would have for material in a magazine it sells to the public. Neither the school nor the periodical vendor has in any way determined the content of those materials being distributed and thus should bear no responsibility for them. However, outside the school setting, courts have indicated that a distributor can be held responsible if he knows the contents of a publication are libelous or reasonably should have known.[40] Thus schools exercising prior review of underground publications or assuming some responsibility for private websites dramatically increase their potential liability for the contents of those publications. Again, the best way a school can protect itself from liability is to distance itself from the content of a publication.

In recent years, parents of children victimized by online bullying have tried to hold schools legally responsible for what students publish on off-campus websites. The first wave of lawsuits has been largely unsuccessful, as courts are hesitant to impose a legal duty on schools to patrol Facebook, Twitter and other non-school websites.[41] State legislatures have invited these lawsuits by enacting "cyberbullying" statutes that give schools unprecedented power to regulate off-campus speech.[42] To the extent that schools have any legally enforceable duty to police speech on websites not owned by the school, however, that duty should apply only in the most extreme cases (such as "burn" websites devoted solely to personal gossip about specific victims[43]) and not to journalistic publications.

LIBEL INSURANCE

To buy, or not to buy: that is the question. For student media, the question is not always an easy one to answer. Some college student publications — particularly those with a large circulation and substantial assets — have accepted libel insurance, like newsprint and keyboards, as a routine cost of doing business. But libel insurance can be expensive, prohibitively so for many student media operations. Also, some have argued that for most student media, which are generally small, asset-poor operations, insurance may actually provide an incentive to sue that might not otherwise exist. Proponents, on the other hand, argue that libel insurance provides peace of mind — for both student media and anxious school administrators. It can also buy editorial freedom. Where school officials, fearing lawsuits, are reluctant to turn over the reins of editorial control to students, libel insurance may provide the boost of confidence they need to finally let go.

Rates for insurance vary considerably. Probably the biggest factors affecting the cost of an insurance policy are circulation and location. Insurance costs for a daily college newspaper with a circulation of 25,000 in a major metropolitan city will understandably be much higher than a policy issued to a weekly student newspaper in a more rural setting with a circulation of under 1,000.

Most media insurance policies cover such claims as libel, invasion of privacy and copyright infringement. "Errors and omissions" coverage for printer's errors is almost always an additional charge.

If a student publication decides to purchase insurance, it is important to shop carefully. For example, one of the key questions to ask is who gets to decide whether a story is retracted or corrected. Many editors believe that the newspaper, not the insurance company's lawyer, should decide whether to publish a retraction and what should be in it.

Other factors to consider include whether there are discounts for publishing without incidents for a set period of time, whether the policy covers intentional or malicious acts, whether the insurance company will pay attorneys' fees in addition to the policy limit on judgment costs and whether the policy covers punitive damages.

If you are interested in exploring the possibility of libel insurance for your publication, contact a local insurance agent. The Student Press Law Center also maintains a list of companies that have offered libel insurance to student media.[44]

SUMMARY

Despite some high-profile libel and privacy lawsuits against the commercial news media in past years, lawsuits based on material published in student publications remain exceedingly rare. In any given year, the Student Press Law Center rarely learns of more than two lawsuits that are filed against high school and college student media anywhere in the country. Most of those cases eventually are dropped or are settled out of court. The risk is especially low for high school student media.

To be sure, the notion of being faced with a lawsuit is disturbing. But the rarity of such claims suggests that school officials, advisers and even students who allow fear of liability to drive their management of a student publication are doing themselves, their publication staffs and their readers a grave disservice. If the potential for liability were the most important criteria for determining the value of a student activity, then extracurricular sports, which prompt far more lawsuits than student media, should have been disbanded long ago.

There are a range of legally sound and educationally legitimate responses to fear of liability, but "more school control" is not one of those options. Putting the fingerprints of school employees all over editorial decisions that legally belong to the students will maximize, not minimize, the likelihood of liability for the institution. It is professionally irresponsible for attorneys to advise schools otherwise.

The reality is — as with most of life's endeavors — the specter of legal liability can never be completely erased from student journalism. It is, therefore, important that student staff be made aware of the individual responsibility a free press brings with it. Ensuring that a publication staff has a basic knowledge of the law — and their responsibilities under it — is your best assurance that liability is an issue you will rarely have to confront.

ENDNOTES

1   *See, e.g., Havalunch, Inc. v. Mazza*, 170 W.Va. 268, 294 S.E.2d 70 (W.Va. 1981) (student staff writer of college newspaper sued for writing tongue-in-cheek, humorous review of local restaurant that included comment, "Bring a can of Raid if you plan to eat here;" appeals court reversed jury's award of punitive damages).
2   *See, e.g., Faulkner v. Martin*, 45 A.2d 596 (N.J. 1946) (finding that managing editor of a newspaper is liable for the publication of a libelous article, whether or not he knows of the publication, since "it is his business to know, and mere want of knowledge constitutes no defense.").
3   *Lewis v. Time Inc.*, 83 F.R.D. 455, 463 (E.D. Calif. 1979), *aff'd*, 710 F.2d 549 (9th Cir. 1983).
4   *See* 42 Am. Jur. 2d, Infants Sec. 127 (2008) ("[M]inority is not a shield against tort liability....").
5   *Sakuma v. Zellerbach Paper Co.*, 77 P.2d 313 (Calif. App. Dist. 1938) (business manager not responsible for libel published in foreign language newspaper that he did not and could not read).
6   *Montandon v. Cox Broad. Corp.*, 45 Cal.App.3d 932, 936 (Calif. App. Dist. 1975).
7   *See, e.g., Lewis v. St. Cloud State Univ.*, 693 N.W.2d 466 (Minn. App. 2005), *review denied*, 2005 Minn. LEXIS 347; *McEvaddy v. City Univ. of New York*, 633 N.Y.S.2d 4 (N.Y. App. Div. 1995), *appeal denied*, 642 N.Y.S.2d 195 (N.Y. 1996); *Mazart v. State*, 441 N.Y.S.2d 600 (N.Y. Ct. Cl. 1981); *Yeo v. Town of Lexington*, 131 F. 3d 241 (1st Cir. 1997) (en banc), *cert. denied*, 118 S. Ct. 2060 (1998).
8   *See* Note, *The Development and Current Status of Parental Liability for the Torts of Minors*, 76 N. Dak. L. Rev. 89 (2000). *See also* Restatement (Second) of Torts Sec. 316 (1965), which discusses the duty of a parent to control the conduct of his child.
9   *See, e.g., Worrell-Payne v. Gannett Co.*, 49 Fed. Appx. 105 (9th Cir. 2002) (Virginia-based publishing company sued for statements published in The Idaho Statesman.)
10 *Bazaar v. Fortune*, 476 F.2d 570, 574, *aff'd en banc with modification*, 489 F.2d 225 (5th Cir. 1973) (per curiam), *cert. denied*, 416 U.S. 995 (1974).
11 *Milliner v. Turner*, 436 So. 2d 1300 (La. Ct. App. 1983).
12 *Id.* at 1302-03.
13 *Batzel v. Smith*, 333 F.3d 1018 (9th Cir. 2003) (finding that private company's financial sponsorship of Web site did not "support an inference that [company] possessed practical control of [Web site's]

editorial content," which is required to establish an agency relationship). *See also Matson v. Dvorak*, 46 Cal.Rptr.2d 880 (Cal. App. 1995) (holding that a party whose "only contribution to a political campaign is financial, and who is not involved in the preparation, review or publication of campaign literature, cannot be subjected to liability in a defamation action for statements contained in that literature").

14   *Mazart v. State*, 441 N.Y.S.2d 600 (N.Y. Ct. Cl. 1981).
15   *Id.* at 606. A similar sentiment was expressed by a federal court in Massachusetts, which found the fact that a school financially supports a publication fails to make the college president "ultimately responsible for what is printed." *Antonelli v. Hammond*, 308 F. Supp. 1329, 1336 (D. Mass. 1970).
16   *Lentz v. Clemson Univ.*, No. 95-CP-39-66 (S.C. Ct. of Common Pleas Dec. 20, 1995) (unpublished).
17   *Id.* at 6.
18   633 N.Y.S.2d 4 (N.Y. App. Div. 1995), *appeal denied*, 642 N.Y.S.2d 195 (N.Y. 1996) (TABLE).
19   *Lewis v. St. Cloud State Univ.*, 693 N.W.2d 466 (Minn. App. 2005), *review denied*, 2005 Minn. LEXIS 347.
20   The court noted: "[I]t is undisputed that SCSU plays a role in selection of the *Chronicle's* editor, business manager, and faculty advisor; provides start-up operating funds at the beginning of each year; requires the *Chronicle* to undergo a certification process each year; allows the use of SCSU's trademarked logo; provides equipment, services, and facilities free of charge; provides a full-time faculty advisor employed by SCSU whose role is to represent and protect the interests of SCSU; requires the *Chronicle* to have a constitution and bylaws, which state that it exists for the benefit of, and concerning, the students, faculty, staff, administration, and St. Cloud community; and requires the *Chronicle* to submit an annual recognition form listing officers and pledging its compliance with all SCSU policies and procedures in the code of conduct and student organization manual." *Id.* at 472, fn. 1
21   The policy read, in part: "[s]tudent-funded publications shall be free of censorship and advance approval of copy, and their editors and managers shall be free to develop their own editorial and news coverage policies." *Id.* at 469
22   *Mazart*, 441 N.Y.S.2d at 607.
23   Ruth Walden, *The University's Liability for Libel and Privacy Invasion by the Student Press*, Vol. 65 Journalism Quarterly No. 3, p. 702 (Fall 1988).
24   *Wallace. v. Weiss*, 372 N.Y.S.2d 416 (N.Y. Sup. Ct. 1975).
25   *Id.* at 422 ("A private university may be in a position to take precautions against the publication of libelous matter in its student publications. At least it may issue instructions and guidelines to those in charge of student publications so those persons are made aware of the dangers of libel and ways to safeguard against it.").
26   *Id.* ("By assisting the organization in its activities, it cannot avoid responsibility by refusing to exercise control or by delegating that control to another student organization.").
27   In addition to a binding legal agreement, a state constitution or statute might also provide a legal basis for protecting a private school from liability. For more information, *See* Chapter 6.
28   *Gallo v. Princeton Univ.*, 656 A.2d 1267 (N.J. Super. 1995).
29   *Id.* at 1275. *See also Dow v. New York Univ.*, 786 N.Y.S. 2d (N.Y. County Sup. Ct. 2004) (holding that "since [the newspaper] has its own First Amendment rights, over which NYU exercised no control," an order limiting NYU's speech did not apply to the student paper).
30   *See, e.g., Batzel v. Smith*, 333 F.3d 1018 (9th Cir. 2003) (finding that sponsorship agreement between private company and website that clearly prohibited company's right to control editorial content defeated "agency" claim and protected company from liability for alleged libelous statements published on Web site.).
31   Cal. Educ. Code sec. 48950 (high schools), sec. 94367 (colleges).
32   47 U.S.C. Sec. 230 (f)(2).
33   47 U.S.C. Sec. 230.
34   Lisa Waananen, "Judge dismisses former LSU student's lawsuit against campus newspaper," SPLC *News Flash*, April 2, 2009, *available at* http://www.splc.org/news/newsflash.asp?id=1893.
35   47 U.S.C. Sec. 230(e). A separate federal statute, the Online Copyright Infringement Liability Limitation Act (OCILLA), 17 U.S.C. Sec. 512 (a)-(k), provides limited insulation for operators of Web sites that innocently host third-party content that turns out to be pirated copyright material. The Act establishes a safe harbor that allows a Web site operator to escape liability for infringement by promptly removing infringing content. The OCILLA is explained in greater detail in Chapter 9, Online Media.
36   *Chicago Lawyers' Comm. v. Craigslist, Inc.*, 519 F.3d 666 (7th Cir. 2008); *Carafano v. Metrosplash.com Inc.*, 207 F. Supp. 2d 1055 (C.D. Cal. Mar 11, 2002), *aff'd on other grounds*, 339 F.3d 1119 (9th Cir. 2003) (finding website Matchmaker.com to be an "interactive computer service provider" for purposes of Section 230 immunity); *Schneider v. Amazon, Inc.*, 31 P.3d 37 (Wash. Ct. App. 2001) (online retailer Amazon.com not liable for negative book reviews posted by readers to its website under Section 230); *Braverman v. Yelp, Inc.*, No. 155629/12, 2013 NY Slip Op 31407 (NY Sup. Ct. June 28, 2013) (holding that consumer review website Yelp.com was immune from suit under Section 230 for reader's defamatory posts about dentist's services, even though Yelp filtered comments and rated some as "best"). In very extreme cases, a website's involvement in creating the defamatory portion of a reader's submission may cross the line of immunity and leave the website exposed to a defamation claim. *See, e.g., Jones v. Dirty World Ent'mt Recordings, Inc.*, 840 F.Supp.2d 1008 (E.D. Ky. 2012). In the *Jones* case, a federal district court said that a gossip website, TheDirty.com, became directly liable for creating the rumors submitted by readers because the webmaster not only chose which submissions to publish but also added his own approving editorial comments that suggested the website was vouching for the truthfulness of the statements.
37   *See, e.g., Yeo v. Town of Lexington*, 131 F. 3d 241 (1st Cir. 1997) (en banc), *cert. denied*, 524 U.S. 904 (1998) (finding that high school student journalists, unlike publication advisers and other school officials, were not "state actors" when they rejected advertisement submitted to student yearbook); *Owasso Indep. Sch. Dist. v. Falvo*, 534 U.S. 426 (2002) (finding that high school students do not "act for" teachers or other school officials when grading classmate's work).
38   Colo. Rev. Stat. Ann. sec. 22-1-120(7); Iowa Code Ann. sec. 280.22(6); Kans. Stat. Ann. sec. 72-1506(e)

(1993); Mass. Gen. Laws Ann. ch. 71, sec. 82.

39 In 2002, a Los Angeles teacher was awarded $4.35 million in a suit against the Los Angeles Unified School District, claiming that the district failed to take immediate corrective action against students that the teacher claimed sexually harassed her by publishing an underground newspaper that jokingly suggested she was a porn star. The teacher did not sue the students. However, the jury award was thrown out, and a new trial granted, in light of changes to a state sexual harassment liability law. In granting the school district's request for a new trial, a judge noted, "[P]ublic schools cannot, by reason of various and significant constitutional and due process limitations, exercise the level and nature of control over student conduct that private employers can exercise over adult employees." *Adams v. Los Angeles Unified Sch. Dist.*, No. BC-235667 (Super. Ct. Los Angeles, June 7, 2002) (unpublished). Later proceedings at 2004 WL 1834405 (Cal. Ct. App. Aug. 17, 2004); 2007 WL 68104 (Cal. Ct. App. Jan. 11, 2007).

40 *See, e.g., Hartmann v. American News Co.*, 171 F.2d 581 (7th Cir. 1948), *cert. denied*, 337 U.S. 907 (1949).

41 *See, e.g., Morrow v. Balaski*, 719 F.3d 160 (3d Cir. 2013) (en banc) (finding that high school had no constitutionally enforceable duty to protect students against bullying, which included both on-campus attacks as well as threatening messages sent by cellphone and by postings on MySpace social networking page). The reluctance to hold schools responsible even for bullying that they are aware of is rooted in the Supreme Court's decision in *DeShaney v. Winnebago Cnty. Dep't of Social Servs.*, 489 U.S. 189 (1989) that the state cannot be held liable for the wrongful acts of third parties unless the state actually created the danger, such as by stopping the victim from getting help.

42 Harvard Law School's Berkman Center published a thorough discussion of state online bullying laws in 2012. *See* Dena Sacco et al., "An Overview of State Anti-Bullying Legislation and Other Related Laws," Berkman Center for Internet & Society (Feb. 22, 2012), *available at* http://cyber.law.harvard.edu/publications/2012/state_anti_bullying_legislation_overview (last viewed Aug. 27, 2013).

43 *See* Associated Press, "Unanimous assembly OKs measure to expand schools' disciplinary power online," *San Jose Mercury News*, April 17, 2012 at 1B (describing phenomenon of online "burn books," popularized in the cult 2004 film comedy "Mean Girls," in which students settle scores by compiling journals of hateful observations about rival students).

44 For a list of insurance companies that have provided libel insurance to student media see the SPLC website at: http://www.splc.org/legalresearch.asp?id=28.

CHAPTER 17

Reporter's Privilege

FROM THE SPLC CASE FILES

In April 2010, the editor of *The Breeze*, the student newspaper at James Madison University, was awakened by a startling phone call: Ten armed, uniformed police officers were at the newsroom with a state prosecutor, demanding to see all of the newspaper's unpublished photographs from "Springfest," an annual street party in Harrisonburg, Va. Drunken rowdiness at Springfest had escalated into violence as revelers threw cans and bottles at each other, and then at police. Car windows were smashed out, and a trash bin was set on fire. Police used tear gas and pepper spray to disperse the estimated 8,000 partygoers; about 30 were arrested. *The Breeze* had photographers on-scene faster than other media outlets, and its computers contained hundreds of images beyond those editors had decided to publish. The question: Were the editors required to surrender the photos, or could they keep them confidential?

Each year journalists all over the country, both student and professional, find themselves in a potential ethical and legal quandary. They must decide whether they should comply with threats or a court order to reveal the identity of a source, to testify about something in their notes, or even to provide information about an already published or broadcast story. In some cases, journalists who refuse risk jail time or costly fines.

As the student media's role in their schools and communities increases, they become more susceptible to the perils that commercial journalists face. Fortunately, journalists have some protection against compelled disclosure in the form of state or federal constitutional provisions, state shield laws or common law. These bundles of laws are referred to as the reporter's privilege. (Note that although the standard term is "reporter's" privilege, the privilege can apply equally to other newsgatherers, such as photographers or videographers; for simplicity, this chapter will use the accepted term "reporter's" privilege to refer to any journalist.) Although privilege laws may appear to be about protecting reporters, they really are as much or more about protecting sources. It is the leaker, not the journalist, who is likely to face firing or even criminal prosecution if the journalist is forced to name names.[1]

It is important to note at the outset that reporter's privilege laws vary by state or federal jurisdiction. Some laws provide broad protection, shielding both published and unpublished information as well as confidential and non-confidential sources and materials from compelled disclosure. Others are much less protective. Also, as will be discussed, on rare occasions student journalists may be hard-pressed to take advantage of the legal protections available to the commercial media. For a state-by-state analysis of specific reporter's privilege laws and their application to student media see the *State-by-State Guide to the Reporter's Privilege for Student Media*, available on the Student Press Law Center website.[2]

> Journalists argue that the law should recognize a privilege that protects them from legal actions that threaten the integrity of their effort to gather and disseminate news. The subpoena is one legal action that poses such a threat.

WHAT IS A REPORTER'S PRIVILEGE?

Reporters who commonly use confidential sources in their stories or information from confidential sources are probably familiar with the concept of a reporter's privilege. A privilege in law is exactly what it sounds like, something that gives one person an advantage another does not have. Where applicable, a reporter's privilege allows journalists to avoid providing material evidence or testifying in judicial — and sometimes administrative — proceedings about something they filmed or wrote, information gathered from an interview or a source's identity. This is considered a privilege because it overrides the usual that citizens have a civic duty to cooperate in the interest of justice.

Journalists argue that, if they are subject to legal penalties for protecting the integrity of

---

their effort to gather and disseminate news, their jobs will be much more difficult and the public will ultimately lose out because less information will be available.

The most common such threat to the media is the subpoena. A subpoena is a court order commanding the recipient to appear at a certain time and place to give testimony under oath or provide specified materials such as notes, photos, negatives, data files or tapes. Courts can issue subpoenas on their own initiative, but usually they issue them at the request of attorneys in civil and criminal cases. Attorneys use subpoenas to gather information or to uncover the identity of a confidential source that they believe will prove helpful in preparing their cases. A person who fails to comply with a subpoena can be charged with contempt of court and fined or even sent to jail. In federal court, for example, a judge may jail someone who has been held in civil contempt until he provides the information requested or for the duration of the court proceeding or grand jury term (up to 18 months).[3] Such was the case when Judith Miller, a *New York Times* reporter, refused to appear before a grand jury in 2004 to testify about her receipt of leaked information unmasking CIA operative Valerie Plame. The Court of Appeals for the D.C. Circuit upheld the 18-month prison sentence in the summer of 2005. After spending 85 days in jail, she was released after Bush administration official I. Lewis "Scooter" Libby reaffirmed a release of confidentiality allowing her to testify about their conversations.

A 2008 national survey found that 55 percent of those polled oppose court orders that require journalists to reveal their sources.
Source: First Amendment Center, *State of the First Amendment 2008*

WHY IS A REPORTER'S PRIVILEGE IMPORTANT?

Student journalists who are not as familiar with using confidential sources may wonder why it is important to protect secret sources or information after a story is published. Journalists stay true to their word for many reasons, both ethical and legal. Sources are crucial to the newsgathering process. Confidential sources frequently come forward with information reporters and the public could never find by themselves. Some people would not talk to a reporter if they were not promised anonymity, leaving important stories untold. Confidential sources have been instrumental in bringing to light stories such as President Richard Nixon's culpability in the Watergate burglary cover-up and, more recently, in disclosing war crimes and other atrocities committed during the Bosnian war.[4]

Keeping promises to sources helps ensure that they will continue to trust you and your publication. This is important because sources not only talk to you but also to each other. News travels, and an untrustworthy reporter will find it hard to find future sources. Keeping promises of confidentiality also helps people to trust the profession of journalism. Student media are often a person's first direct exposure to the press. If your classmates' earliest perception of the media is that reporters cannot be trusted it is unlikely their views will change later.

Many journalists believe that by revealing confidential information you not only put your source in a position she was unwilling to put herself in voluntarily (for reasons of job security, personal relationships, etc.), you may also have breached your professional code of ethics as a journalist.[5] On the other hand, some reporters consider it their ethical duty as citizens to testify when called upon by the courts in certain circumstances, especially if someone's health or safety is at issue. These are considerations every journalist must weigh — hopefully before any promises are made to a source.

Another consideration when weighing the obligation to protect a source is legal liability. A journalist who reveals a source or information received based on a promise of confidentiality can be sued by the source for divulging the information.[6] A promise of confidentiality is, in essence, a contract between the source and the reporter. If it is broken, the reporter might have to pay for any damage caused. (See sidebar, "Keeping your promise of confidentiality: An ethical and legal obligation).

But it is not just when confidential sources or information are at issue that journalists feel compelled to maintain their independence. Many journalists are also concerned that by testifying for the government in any context about their work product they will appear as an arm of the state, in effect functioning as a "private investigator" for law enforcement officials, school administrators or other private parties.

Journalists, who generally strive to remain neutral and balanced in their reporting, fear being perceived as an advocate during a criminal or civil dispute if called to testify or provide evidence that will be used for or against a particular party. Journalists often have access to people or events to which police or other non-neutral parties would not be welcome. Such access gives the public a close-up look at news that would otherwise go unreported. If the press is viewed as an extension of government authorities — if journalists lose their status as independent, neutral observers — such access quickly ends, and the public loses.

Finally, responding to subpoenas can be extremely burdensome. Journalists argue that subpoenas allow private lawyers and government prosecutors to use the press as a cheap method for conducting their investigations. A sharp lawyer knows that it may be faster and easier to ask a news photographer to turn over her negatives of an accident scene than it would be to attempt to find and interview the other witnesses to the incident. Subpoenas can force a news organization to use precious staff hours and resources to do someone else's work.

Unfortunately, responding to subpoenas has become commonplace for news media organizations. In a 2001 survey conducted by the Reporters Committee for Freedom of the Press, 319 news organizations reported receiving 823 subpoenas during the year.[7] And subpoenas are not, by far, the only threat. Tech-savvy federal law enforcement agencies and national-security agencies have figured out ways to bypass issuing subpoenas to media organizations, which might be successfully resisted in court, by gathering information directly from the phone and Internet companies that journalists use.[8]

While journalists feel strongly that their independence should not be compromised, government officials and private attorneys who subpoena journalists to identify confidential sources or turn over information argue that the public interest in law enforcement and civil justice outweighs the public interest in an unfettered press.

Journalists can face legal consequences if they break promises to confidential sources.

Confronted with these opposing perspectives, legislatures and courts have generated a patchwork of protections for journalists that vary by jurisdiction. A small number recognize no reporter's privilege at all; others recognize a privilege that is virtually absolute. But it is fair to say that in most parts of the country reporters are seen as filling a special role in society that deserves some protection.

KEEPING YOUR PROMISE OF CONFIDENTIALITY: AN ETHICAL AND LEGAL OBLIGATION

Once a decision has been made to promise confidentiality, there is little question that the journalist's integrity demands that the promise be kept. A broken promise to one source dries up other sources and persuades sources and readers alike to doubt the journalist's and the profession's credibility.

In addition to ethical consequences, journalists can also face legal consequences if they break promises to confidential sources. In a 1991 case, *Cohen v. Cowles Media Co.,*[9] editors at two Minnesota newspapers thought they were making only an editorial decision when they decided to reveal that Dan Cohen, an employee of a political candidate, was the reporter's source for information on the candidate's opponent. Cohen sued the newspapers on grounds that a binding agreement had been formed between Cohen and the reporters when the promise was made. The Supreme Court ruled 5 to 4 for Cohen, finding that the First Amendment does not immunize journalists against liability for broken promises. In the wake of *Cohen*, other courts have allowed sources to sue reporters for revealing their identities,[10] while some have rejected such claims.[11]

The Supreme Court's *Branzburg* decision has been widely interpreted as recognizing that a reporters' privilege under the First Amendment does exist in some circumstances.

THE SUPREME COURT'S PERSPECTIVE

The Supreme Court has dealt directly with the issue of a journalist's privilege only once. In the 1972 case *Branzburg v. Hayes*,[12] a sharply divided Court decided that reporters had no First Amendment privilege to resist testifying before a grand jury about sources the reporters witnessed engaging in criminal activity. While the Court found that newsgathering does enjoy special First Amendment protection, Justice Byron White wrote for the Court that "the public interest in law enforcement" and "effective grand jury proceedings" outweighs the First Amendment interest in a reporter's privilege when thereporter has witnessed criminal activity.[13] The Court acknowledged that the absence of special protections might have a chilling effect on the media's sources, but decided that journalists nonetheless have the same duty as other citizens to participate in the criminal justice system at least when a grand jury proceeding is involved.

An adviser should never be privy to confidential information provided by a student reporter's source nor should they know a confidential source's identity.

However, the *Branzburg* decision has been widely interpreted by courts as recognizing that a reporter's privilege under the First Amendment does exist in some circumstances. First, the Court's majority opinion said that a subpoena of a journalist would be subject to a "good-faith" test.[14] Attorneys may not use subpoenas to disrupt a journalist's relationship with his sources. One of the five justices in the Court's majority, Justice Louis Powell, wrote a separate opinion stating more explicitly that a subpoena for a journalist would be subject to a balancing test of First Amendment interests and criminal justice interests.[15] This should, for example, protect a reporter's source when the connection between the investigation and the information sought is "remote and tenuous."[16] Second, the four dissenting justices all believed a privilege should exist. Thus five justices, a majority of the court, explicitly endorsed some notion of a reporter's privilege that involved a balancing of the competing interests.

The *Branzburg* decision also left room for the states to establish their own protections for reporters and for Congress to enact a federal shield statute. While Congress has failed to enact such a federal statute since the 1972 decision,[17] 49 states and the District of Columbia have recognized some form of a reporter's privilege. While state protections are valuable, the lack of a federal statute or a federal standard has bred some inconsistency and confusion. This can be especially true for student journalists where, as is discussed more fully below, differences in the law can sometimes limit — or even prevent — some student journalists from claiming legal protection.

ADVISERS: IGNORANCE IS BLISS

Although both student staff and a student media adviser may want to be involved in determining the newsroom's confidentiality policy, the adviser's role should end there. An adviser should never be privy to confidential information provided by a student reporter's source nor should she know a confidential source's identity. In the case of a story about unlawful or dangerous activity on school grounds, for example, the adviser —a school employee — may be legally bound to report what she knows. The adviser could then be faced with either revealing the confidential information — thus violating ethical and possibly legal obligations to the source and damaging the trust of her student staff — or keeping the secret and being subject to possible sanctions or punishment from the school. Obviously, neither of these is an attractive choice. Before promising a source confidentiality, advisers and their students should create a system that shields an adviser from protected information. While keeping an adviser in the dark is not an ideal solution, it can help student media avoid even bigger and more serious headaches.

SOURCES FOR REPORTER'S PRIVILEGE LAWS

Absent a federal statute, student journalists must rely on: (1) a state shield law or (2) a reporter's privilege recognized by the courts. A court-recognized privilege (CRP) is usually based on the First Amendment, a state constitution or common (judge-made) law. While CRP's are in many cases as effective as state shield laws, shield laws are more common. CRP's generally incorporate the *Branzburg* balancing test and typically protect as a "journalist" a person who gathered information to disseminate to the public. State shield laws, by contrast, sometimes focus on professional affiliation rather than the individual's function or intent in determining who is protected. This can be problematic for student journalists, especially those who are unpaid. For example, some state shield laws protect only those who earn a living as a journalist or work for a media organization that publishes or broadcasts at least once a week. These limitations on the privilege favor career journalists and commercial news media organizations that tend to publish or broadcast more regularly than typical student publications.

TYPES OF REPORTER'S PRIVILEGES

Reporter's privilege laws, while having a similar purpose, can vary significantly. In addition to tracing their source to either a state shield law or CRP (court-recognized privilege), reporter's privilege laws can also vary according to where they come from, the nature of the protection they provide, who they cover and what they cover. Before relying on a reporter's privilege law for protection, student journalists must be familiar with the strength and limitations of their particular privilege.

State or Federal Law

Most court orders to journalists arise from state rather than federal cases. In such situations, the reporter's choice of defense is usually clear: a state shield law (if available) and/or a state CRP. In addition, some state courts have held that the state's constitution or its common law gives journalists the protection of a privilege.

To date, thirty-six states and the District of Columbia have shield laws, and courts in thirteen states without shield laws have recognized some degree of a reporter's privilege. Only Wyoming has yet to recognize a reporter's privilege, although federal courts may offer protection to reporters in that state. The advantages conferred on journalists by shield laws and court-created privileges vary significantly by state. Some protect both sources and information, others only one or the other. In some states a promise of confidentiality must have been made before the protections will apply.

When a subpoena is issued in a federal case, things can get a bit more complicated. In such cases, the federal court can apply a federal CRP (generally based on the First Amendment), the law of the state in which the federal court sits, or sometimes — where the controversy crosses state lines — the law of another state. (Despite decades of work by advocates by the news media, Congress has yet to enact a federal statute that enables reporters to protect confidential information in federal court proceedings.)

The United States is divided into 12 federal circuits, each of which — like courts in each of the 50 states — can apply a different reporter's privilege standard. (See page 3 for a list of federal circuits and states.) A majority of the federal courts of appeal have held that the Supreme Court's *Branzburg* decision recognized a "qualified" privilege under the First Amendment. The privilege protects reporters from subpoenas, but it can be overcome in some circumstances. The First, Second, Third, Fourth, Fifth, Eighth, Ninth, Tenth, Eleventh and District of Columbia circuit courts of appeals all have recognized some form of a privilege.[18] In the Sixth Circuit, a limited privilege has been recognized in civil cases at the district court level.[19] The Seventh Circuit has suggested that a reporter's privilege does not exist — at least for cases involving non-confidential sources — and instead adopted a "reasonable in the circumstances" test for subpoenas directed to the media. The "reasonable in the circumstances" test may allow reporters to avoid testifying or providing evidentiary material in much the same way that a reporter's privilege does. The court, however, specifically rejected much of the rationale used by other circuits to justify a First Amendment-based reporter's privilege for non-confidential sources.[20]

Courts tend to give journalists less protection in criminal cases (particularly grand jury investigations), where the accused's constitutional right to a fair trial and the interest in effective law enforcement can come into play. For more information on federal CRP's (and using the reporter's privilege generally), see *The Reporter's Privilege Compendium*, an outstanding resource published by the Reporters Committee for Freedom of the Press and available free on their website.[21]

SHIELD LAW GUIDE

STATES WITH SHIELD LAWS OR RULES:
Alabama,[22] Alaska,[23] Arizona,[24] Arkansas,[25] California,[26] Colorado,[27] Connecticut,[28] Delaware,[29] Florida,[30] Georgia,[31] Hawaii,[32] Illinois,[33] Indiana,[34] Kentucky,[35] Louisiana,[36] Maine,[37] Maryland,[38] Michigan,[39] Minnesota,[40] Montana,[41] Nebraska,[42] Nevada,[43] New Jersey,[44] New Mexico,[45] New York,[46] North Carolina,[47] North Dakota,[48] Ohio,[49] Oklahoma,[50] Oregon,[51] Pennsylvania,[52] Rhode Island,[53] South Carolina,[54] Tennessee,[55] Utah,[56] Washington[57] West Virginia,[58] and the District of Columbia.[59]

STATES WITH COURT-RECOGNIZED REPORTER'S PRIVILEGES[60] (states with both a shield law and a court-recognized privilege are italicized):
Alabama, Alaska, Arizona, Arkansas, California, Connecticut, Delaware, Florida, Georgia, Idaho, *Illinois, Indiana,* Iowa, Kansas, *Louisiana, Maine, Maryland* (public policy), Massachusetts, *Michigan, Minnesota,* Mississippi, Missouri, New Hampshire, *New York, North Carolina, Ohio, Oklahoma, Pennsylvania,* South Dakota, Texas, *Utah,* Vermont, Virginia, *Washington,* West Virginia and Wisconsin.

STATES WITH NEITHER:
Wyoming.

A First Amendment privilege can be overcome when a court is persuaded that the information being sought from the journalist is:
• Highly material and relevant,
• Necessary or critical to the maintenance of the legal claim and
• Not obtainable from other available resources.

Absolute Privilege Versus Qualified Privilege

Reporter's privilege laws are generally classified as either absolute or qualified. An absolute privilege will always protect the reporter from disclosing any information protected by the privilege. These broad privileges are rare. A qualified privilege, on the other hand, can be outweighed by a competing interest presented in a given situation. Qualified privileges are much more common because states are concerned about the balance between the reporter's First Amendment rights and those of the party requesting the reporter to testify. Qualified privileges create a presumption that a reporter will not have to comply with a subpoena. In most cases, the privilege can be overcome only if the subpoenaing party can show that the information in the journalist's possession:

(1) is highly material and relevant to the matter before the court;
(2) is necessary or critical to the case; and
(3) cannot be obtained from an alternative, non-journalist source.

The first prong attempts to weed out claims for information that are frivolous or irrelevant. The second filters claims for information that is "merely useful" or cumulative to establishing a case. The final part of the test is typically the toughest to overcome for those seeking information from the press. Courts will generally require that obvious witnesses be contacted before a privilege is overcome, even if that means dozens of interviews or depositions have to be conducted.[61] As one court said, a party that "has not even worked up a sweat, much less exhausted itself" in tracking down alternative sources cannot defeat the privilege.[62]

Sources Versus Information

State shield laws and CRP's often treat information and sources differently. While information for a news story may come from a confidential source, it is more often obtained through research or other traditional newsgathering. Information, whether received from a confidential or non-confidential source or from some other type of newsgathering activity, is not always protected to the same degree as the source itself and may not be covered at all.

Confidential Versus Non-Confidential Sources

Depending on the state law, the reporter's privilege can also protect two different types of sources: confidential and non-confidential. Most state laws cover at least confidential sources. These are the sources that will talk to a reporter only after the reporter promises not to reveal their identity. Because a journalist's interest in protecting non-confidential sources is deemed to be of less importance, non-confidential sources generally receive less protection under reporter's privilege laws. While revealing the identity of a nonconfidential source may not present all of the ethical and legal dilemmas discussed above (for instance, a non-confidential source cannot sue you for revealing his name) a journalist still should consider whether it is ethically appropriate to get involved in a legal proceeding.

Published Versus Unpublished Information

Yet another distinction in shield laws is that of published versus unpublished materials. Published materials often receive little protection because the courts anticipate fewer First Amendment implications when ordering a reporter to talk about information or turn over information already in the public eye. However, most subpoenas seek unpublished material; if material were already published — especially now that so many publications are electronically archived online — there would be little need for a subpoena. Examples of unpublished materials are reporter notes, outtakes, tape recordings, drafts, photo negatives or image files and internal memos. These pieces of information are often protected under state laws for the same reasons that a confidential source would be protected. By keeping this information private, it encourages the free flow of information and the freedom of the press to gather and disseminate news.

The Reporters Committee for Freedom of the Press publishes a free guide to reporter's privilege at: **www.rcfp.org/ privilege.** The SPLC's *Student Media Guide to Protecting Sources and Information*, which looks at the applicability of state privileges to student media, can be found at: **www.splc.org/ reportersprivilege guide**

STUDENT JOURNALISTS: A SPECIAL CLASS?

Even where courts have recognized a reporter's privilege or in states that have enacted shield laws, it is not always clear whether those protections will apply to student journalists. While most states have not yet had the opportunity to consider whether their reporter's privilege law is applicable to student journalists, the overwhelming majority of those that have addressed the issue have extended the privilege to the student press, finding no reason to distinguish between student media and their commercial counterparts.[63] In fact, in many cases, a journalist's "student status" has been a non-issue, as courts have simply assumed a student news organization is entitled to seek the protection of a recognized reporter's privilege. A minority of courts denies college journalists the same level of protection that non-student professionals enjoy.[64] The lack of court decisions involving high school (as opposed to college) journalists makes their situation a bit less certain, but no court has suggested that high school journalists would be any less entitled to the protection of a reporter's privilege simply because they are high school students.[65]

Even in those states where privileges and shield laws apply, it is not always clear whether their protections cover student journalists.

A generation ago, it was relatively easy to identify the universe of "journalists." They were people with press passes who ran around with cameras, notepads and tape recorders collecting information on a daily basis for newspapers, broadcast stations and wire services. But technology has changed the game. Since there are no "journalist licenses" and anyone can work in the field, it is not always easy to draw a line between a "serious" journalist versus a hobbyist who occasionally writes a blog post or shares a photo.[66] Major media outlets regularly invite amateurs to submit videos that end up posted on sites like CNN's "iReport,"[67] blurring the line between journalist and audience member.

Shield laws in nine jurisdictions, however, seem to benefit only the "professional" media. For example, in Delaware, a journalist must gain his "principal livelihood" by reporting or spending 20 hours per week in the business to qualify for the statute's protection.[68] The Rhode Island shield law refers to publications with paid circulation, and the shield laws in Florida, Indiana, New Mexico, Nevada, Texas, Washington and the District of Columbia all refer to the "employment," "professional capacity" or "income" of the journalist.[69] Student journalists who are paid could have a better chance of qualifying under these statutes. Absent that, student media and "citizen journalists" in these states may have to rely on a CRP.

In one of the only cases to reject a reporter's privilege claim based solely on the journalist's "student status," a New York court, relying on language in its state shield law that covers only newspapers with a "paid circulation" and a second-class postage permit, held that the state's shield law did not apply to student reporters for the Hofstra University student newspaper.[70] The New York statute also says that a privileged journalist must be a "professional" working "for gain or livelihood."[71] Since that decision, however, at least two other courts in New York have recognized a qualified privilege under the First Amendment (a CRP) that excuses a student journalist from having to divulge confidential information.[72] As one of those courts concluded, the proper inquiry to determine whom a qualified privilege protects is not whether the person is a journalist by profession, but rather "how the person asserting the privilege intended to use the information gathered."[73] If the information gatherer sought the material with the original intent of disseminating information to the public, through whatever medium, then the information gatherer deserves a qualified privilege. Not all courts will necessarily interpret the law as broadly. For more information about how the courts in your state might rule when a student journalist is subpoenaed, see the Student Press Law Center's *State-by-State Guide to the Reporter's Privilege for Student Media*, which you can find on the SPLC website.[74]

FROM THE SPLC CASE FILES

As a graduate student at Northwestern University's Medill School of Journalism, Carolyn Nielsen began digging into the case of Thaddeus Jimenez, who was serving a 45-year sentence on a murder conviction. With her help and the help of other Northwestern researchers, Jimenez proved that his conviction was legally flawed, and in May 2009, he was freed after 16 years behind bars. Jimenez then filed a federal civil-rights lawsuit against the City of Chicago for wrongful imprisonment. By that time, Nielsen had moved to Washington state, where she was teaching college journalism and working on a book about the Jimenez case. To gather evidence for the lawsuit, the City of Chicago tried to compel Nielsen to give testimony about her conversations with Jimenez and turn over copies of letters she'd received from him. Although the case was in federal court, where no statutory reporter's privilege exists, the U.S. District Court recognized that the First Amendment offers journalists some protection for communications with sources — even student journalists, and even journalism instructors who intend to publish books:

> "All of the documents were created with journalistic intent from inception, and culminated or are intended to culminate in publicly-consumable publication. Given that other circuits have not differentiated professional journalists from students in this context, this Court finds no reason to deny her standing simply because she was a student when some of the documents were created. Nielsen is eligible for journalist's privilege."[75]

SHOULD STUDENT JOURNALISTS MAKE PROMISES OF CONFIDENTIALITY?

Promises of confidentiality should not be handed out lightly. In fact, some journalists flatly condemn the use of confidential sources. Most quote unnamed sources only as a last resort. If your newsroom permits the use of confidential sources there should be a policy in place to guide students faced with the decision of whether to offer this protection to a source. A clear policy can avoid problems. In most cases, a promise should not be made without the approval of an editor. Before making a promise of confidentiality, the Poynter Institute suggests reporters and editors ask themselves the following:

(1) Is the story of overwhelming public concern?

(2) Is there any other way to get the information on the record?

(3) Is the information from the confidential source verifiable?

(4) Are you willing to reveal to the public why the source cannot be named (without accidentally revealing the identity of the source) and what, if any, promises you made to get the information?

(5) How would your audience evaluate the same information if they knew the source's identity?[76]

The use of a masked informant where the information can be obtained through more open channels or with a little — or a lot — of thorough and competent reporting is simply bad journalism. When a reporter uses an unnamed source he has decided to make a trade-off. Because it is the business of the profession to reveal the truth, a reporter who pledges confidentiality has decided it is worth the price of concealing part of the truth — and risking some loss of credibility — in order to expose a greater or larger truth. Such a trade-off must always be judiciously entered into.

CAN SCHOOL OFFICIALS FORCE A STUDENT REPORTER TO REVEAL CONFIDENTIAL MATERIAL OR SOURCES?

School administrators pose a more common threat to student journalists trying to protect confidential sources and information than court-issued subpoenas. Sometimes reporters and editors are asked by school officials (instead of courts) to disclose information, usually in the course of a school investigation into misconduct.

No court has ever decided whether a student journalist may claim a reporter's privilege against inquiries by school administrators. A student's strongest argument against compelled disclosure to school officials is that school administrators — unless they seek the information through formal legal channels — simply lack the authority to force students to reveal confidential information. Without a court-issued subpoena ordering disclosure, students can argue that they are under no obligation to respond to the demands of school officials.

Students in public schools might also be able to claim a constitutional, statutory or evidentiary privilege against releasing information to school administrators, although courts — especially in the high school context — may balance students' rights against the public interest in maintaining order in the school. For example, a federal court in Pennsylvania granted a high school student's request to issue a protective order against school officials who demanded that he reveal the names of classmates who helped create, distribute or who received an e-mail containing a Top Ten list that poked fun at the school's athletic director.[77] Before issuing the order, the court considered — but dismissed — the school's claim that revealing the names was necessary to show that the Top Ten list created a disturbance at the school.

Private school students may stand on shakier ground than their public school counterparts. Traditionally, constitutional protections restrict only the actions of government actors or those performing governmental functions. Private educators have been repeatedly excluded from this group. Thus it is likely that students at private schools could be subject to discipline if they refuse to comply with administrators' demands. However, private school students can use the same arguments against forced disclosure as they use against censorship: policy arguments in favor of a reporter's privilege and contract claims based on promises their school may have made in student handbooks that guarantee student rights. (See Chapter 7 for a discussion of press freedom at private schools.) Moreover, where a private school coerces its student media to reveal confidential information, public pressure should be brought to bear that at least forces school officials to take the heat for their decision.

WHAT TO DO IF YOUR RECEIVE A SUBPOENA

If a lawyer or police officer asks that you turn over materials or reveal information you have gathered as a part of your work as a journalist, you should first insist on being given an opportunity to consult your editor in chief and/or a lawyer before deciding whether to comply. You can say, truthfully, that you have been told there are sometimes liability risks for journalists who compromise confidential information, and that you must first look out for your own interests and your family's to be sure you aren't inviting a lawsuit.

If you are pressed for a response, respond that your publication's policy is to deny all such requests unless the information has been published. Politely respond that you cannot comply with their request even for non-sensitive information without a subpoena and that if subpoenaed you will claim a reporter's privilege and ask that the subpoena be quashed. Many demands will end there, when the attorney or police officer realizes that you will not be intimidated into immediate submission and they will have to spend additional time and energy getting the information from you.

If a law enforcement official serves you with a subpoena, accept it and look to see when you are to appear and whether you are expected to bring any documents. Seek legal assistance immediately; it helps to be familiar with what the law in your state says about reporter's privilege and whether it extends to students. After receiving a subpoena (or even if you have only been told you will be receiving one), do not destroy notes or erase photos. Even if the law ultimately protects your materials, a court will look harshly on an attempt to destroy potential evidence.

Depending on the information sought and the degree of privilege you have, there are four possible courses of action from which you must choose after receiving a subpoena:

(1) Move to quash, or nullify, the subpoena. This will require filing a document with the court. Note that some states have elaborate procedures that must be followed to the letter for a valid subpoena to be issued. Thus you may be able to get a subpoena quashed because it is legally flawed, even if you are not covered by a shield law or privilege. If you choose to fight a subpoena and you lose, you will be faced with the decision of whether to comply with the order. Reporters who do not comply at this point can face fines, jail time and contempt of court charges. Some journalists, including students, have accepted these punishments rather than violate their ethical principles.

(2) Show up as the subpoena requires — with legal counsel if at all possible — and assert a reporter's privilege in refusing to respond to each inappropriate question or request. Consider how you will respond if threatened with contempt charges.

(3) Show up as the subpoena requires and offer to submit the material to the judge for her to review by herself behind closed doors (called "in camera review"). Based on this examination, the judge might be able to determine that the information is not necessary to the case and quash the subpoena on that basis. Again, however, if the judge believes the information is relevant or if she refuses to agree to the compromise of in camera review, you should be prepared to face contempt charges if you feel ethically that you cannot comply.

(4) Appear and testify fully or provide the information requested. Few journalists willingly choose this alternative if the request is for anything other than material that has already been published. Before you make your decision, be sure you have considered the ethical and legal implications of divulging confidential information.

NEWSROOM SEARCHES

Besides the subpoena, another type of document that can be brought to bear against journalists is the search warrant. A search warrant is like a subpoena in that it is a device to gather information. But while subpoenas apply to people and their possessions, search warrants apply to places, and allow law enforcement officials to collect the information themselves. Newsroom searches could be an effective tool for law enforcement officials to gather information, but allowing seizure of items in the newsroom poses a serious threat to newsgatherers' freedoms. Fortunately, newsroom searches are rare.[78]

The most important court case concerning newsroom searches involved a student newspaper. The Supreme Court found in *Zurcher v. Stanford Daily*[79] that officers' execution of a search warrant at the Stanford University student newspaper office to obtain photos of a campus demonstration did not violate the First Amendment. In response to *Zurcher*, Congress passed the Privacy Protection Act of 1980.[80] In 2010, student editors at James Madison University's *The Breeze* successfully asserted the Privacy Protection Act to get back hundreds of unpublished photos unlawfully seized from their newsroom by police during a surprise raid.[81]

> The federal Privacy Protection Act prohibits law enforcement officials from seizing work product materials or documents possessed by journalists or news organizations except in very limited situations.

FROM THE SPLC CASE FILES

For about 30 hours, a large group of student demonstrators had kept police at bay. They had taken over the administrative offices of a university hospital as part of a campus sit-in protesting the firing of a janitor. A photographer for the student newspaper was with a small group of reporters and bystanders nearby covering the demonstration.

After several futile attempts to persuade the demonstrators to leave peacefully, police used a battering ram to break through the offices' heavy glass doors. Some of the demonstrators responded by turning fire hoses on the police. Another group charged some of the police with sticks and clubs. One officer was knocked to the floor and struck repeatedly on the head; another suffered a broken shoulder. In all, twenty people — nine of them police officers — were injured. Furniture and partitions were destroyed, and telephones were ripped out of the walls. Police arrested more than 50 demonstrators who had caused about $100,000 in damages. Police, however, could conclusively identify only two of the students who assaulted their injured colleagues.

Two days later, the student newspaper published a special edition that included articles and photographs devoted to the hospital protest and the violent clash between demonstrators and police.

The next day, police showed up at the newspaper's offices armed with a search warrant. For about 15 minutes, police thoroughly searched the newspaper's photo lab, filing cabinets, desks and trashcans for additional evidence. On top of one of the desks were reporter's notes containing the name of a confidential source. In the end, police found only the photographs that had been previously published.

Privacy Protection Act of 1980

In a nutshell, the Privacy Protection Act provides members of the media protection from most newsroom searches and seizures by government officials engaged in a criminal investigation. The PPA divides materials into (1) "work product" materials and (2) "documentary" materials, and the law provides different protections and exceptions depending on the type of material involved.

It is important to note that the PPA applies only to searches and seizures by the government during a criminal investigation.[82] Requests for documents by a party in a civil lawsuit, for example, are not covered by the act. Note also, however, that the PPA applies to any "government officer or employee" not just law enforcement officials.[83] This is significant, especially for student media who not only have to worry about police, but also deans, principals, campus safety personnel (who might not technically be considered "law enforcement officials"), maintenance workers, building supervisors, teachers and a host of other government employees who might want to snoop around a student newsroom. The PPA should provide student media some protection from all of their prying eyes (and hands) as long as the search or seizure relates to a criminal investigation. Finally, while the PPA is often referred to as the "newsroom search law," its protection is not limited to the physical confines of a newsroom, but rather can protect reporters — wherever they are — from improper searches or confiscation of their working material.

Unfortunately, private school student media probably cannot rely on the PPA to protect them from searches by their school administrators (although they are still protected from searches by federal, state or local police and other government officials). The PPA applies only to searches and seizures conducted by government officials.

Work Product

The first section of the PPA protects a reporter's "work product" materials. As defined by the PPA, "work product" includes materials that are "prepared, produced, authored, or created" for the purpose of communicating such materials to the public.[84] For most student media and their staff the public dissemination element will be easily satisfied. The PPA's "work product" definition also protects a reporter's "mental impressions, conclusions, opinions or theories" concerning such material.[85] Work product materials, therefore, should normally include a reporter's notes, story drafts and internal memoranda. Indeed, as long as it could be understood by a reasonable person that that a reporter intended to disseminate the information in his possession to the general public, any form of the reporter's "work product" should be protected from search and seizure.[86]

The PPA's protections extend to any person intending to publish material in "a newspaper, book, broadcast or other similar form of public communication."[87] This suggests that reporters for a newspaper, yearbook, online publication, radio station or any other kind of medium could seek protection under the PPA.

This privilege, however, is not absolute, and the PPA lists several exceptions. The first exception — the "probable cause" exception — concerns criminal acts that may have been committed by the reporter himself. Under this exception, if "probable cause" exists that the person in possession of the "work product" material has committed or is in the process of committing a crime, then the government official may conduct the search.[88] To fit within the exception, the "work product" must relate to the crime in question.

For example, if a reporter actually purchases illegal drugs from a dealer instead of just interviewing him, the reporter could not use the PPA to shield himself from a police search of his newsroom desk or employee locker to look for the drugs if police had probable cause to believe he was hiding them there. Journalists have no special license to break the law and the PPA does not change that.

The government cannot use the "probable cause" exception to get around the PPA if the only "crime" a reporter is charged with consists of the receipt, possession or communication of the work product information itself.[89] Though there are a small number of very limited exceptions to this rule,[90] this would generally prevent a prosecutor, for example, from charging a reporter who has innocently obtained a copy of a stolen document with "receipt of stolen documents" simply so that she can use the "probable cause" exception to search the newsroom.

The second exception is more easily understood. When government officials have "reason to believe" that "work product" materials must be seized immediately to prevent someone's death or a serious bodily injury, they may seize the materials without violating the PPA.[91] This exemption will rarely come into play and government officials who abuse it can be held accountable.

Documentary Materials

The second section of the PPA protects a journalist's "documentary materials." The PPA defines "documentary materials" rather broadly as "materials upon which information is recorded."[92] These may include photographs, motion pictures, audiotapes and film negatives. Computer disks are also considered "documentary materials" along with any other "mechanically, magnetically or electronically recorded tape, card or disk."[93]

"Documentary materials" do not include items associated with a criminal act.[94] For example, a gun picked up by a reporter at the scene of a robbery, sheets of paper on which the robbers' plans are written, and any cash found at the scene would not be considered "documentary materials" protected by the PPA.

For the most part, the PPA treats "documentary materials" the same as "work product" materials and makes it unlawful for a government official to search and/or seize "documentary materials" during the course of a criminal investigation where the person subject to the search is connected with an attempt to disseminate the information to the general public.[95]

There are four exceptions for "documentary materials." The first two exceptions that allow government officials to get around the PPA are the same as for "work product" materials: (1) "probable cause" that the reporter has evidence linking him to a crime that he has committed and (2) a reason to believe that death or serious injury will result if a newsroom search is delayed.[96]

A third exception permits a search or seizure of documentary materials when there is a "reason to believe" that the materials sought by government officials would be destroyed, hidden or altered if the materials were requested through a subpoena.[97] Unless government officials can present evidence that a news organization has indicated an intent to damage the material or that this has been the organization's practice in the past, government officials should have little success invoking this exception. For this reason, student media are cautioned never to suggest that they will illegally impede an official investigation or destroy evidence.

The fourth and final exception applies when the person in possession of the "documentary materials" has not produced them in accordance with a court order, typically in the form of a subpoena.[98] For this exception to apply, the government must show one of two things. First, they can show that they tried to obtain the materials in court and that — even after all avenues for appeal had been exhausted — the reporter or news organization still refused to obey a final court order.[99] Alternatively, even if the government has not sought the materials in court — or if an appeal in court is still pending — the government can get around the PPA's protections if they show that any further delay would "threaten the interests of justice."[100] To prevent government officials from abusing this rather fuzzy exception, the PPA requires that the individual in possession of the materials must be given an opportunity to contest the government's claim prior to any materials actually being seized.

Remedies Under the PPA

To discourage illegal searches and seizures, the PPA allows those harmed to file a civil lawsuit if they believe the search and/or seizure was conducted in violation of the PPA. Where a reporter or media organization prevails they will be awarded a minimum of $1,000 in damages.[101] Moreover, those responsible for the illegal search or seizure may also be forced to pay the media organization's attorney fees and litigation costs, an amount that can easily reach into the tens of thousands of dollars.[102]

Application of the PPA to Student Media

Despite being sparked by a student media case, there are, to date, no published court decisions where the PPA has been used by the student media to punish a newsroom search or confiscation. While questions have occasionally been raised about whether the PPA provides student media the same protection as professional reporters, in most cases there should be little reason to worry.

As discussed above, the PPA applies to "government officials" conducting an investigation into criminal activity. The PPA does not specifically mention or distinguish between professional and student media and given the history and intent of lawmakers in enacting the PPA — namely, overturning a Supreme Court decision that allowed for the search of a student newspaper's newsroom — it is hard to imagine a court finding such a distinction.

The taking of a reporter's property without cause and without the procedural safeguards of the judicial system can lead to a charge of criminal theft or a civil conversion of property or trespass claim.

The law, however, does state that only those individuals engaged in the dissemination of information to the public who are "in or affecting interstate or foreign commerce" are protected.[103] This is a common legal phrase that appears in many federal laws, since Congress cannot regulate the affairs of purely local businesses that have zero impact outside of their local area.

While this requirement may exclude a small number of student media, most should be safe. One national survey estimated that 90 percent of all high school publications accept advertising.[104] For college student media, the number is probably even higher. Many of these ads are purchased by either local or national businesses who themselves are most certainly within the stream of interstate commerce. This should bring most student media within the friendly confines of the PPA.

In addition, many student media sell subscriptions to their publications. Often, the recipients are alumni who live outside of the state. This, too, should be enough to fit within the interstate commerce requirement. In such cases, a student publication would be in a position no different than a small-town commercial newspaper, which is presumably covered by the law. Finally, evidence that the student paper's online edition was regularly viewed by out-of-staters might also be helpful evidence. In short, the "interstate commerce" requirement is largely a formality and should be easily satisfied.

AN ALTERNATIVE TO THE PPA: STATE LAW PROTECTION

In addition to the PPA, at least seven states have their own laws governing newsroom search and seizures: California, Connecticut, Nebraska, New Jersey, Oregon, Texas and Washington.[105]

In some cases, these state laws may provide student media with greater protection than the PPA. For example, New Jersey's newsroom search law protects "any person ... engaged in [or] connected with..." gathering, editing or publishing news for the public.[106] Unlike the PPA, there is no requirement that the media affect interstate or foreign commerce. Such a broad definition of a newsperson would almost certainly cover New Jersey student journalists.

MAN THE FIREWALL!

Before simply plugging the newsroom's computers into the school's network or using a school's email system to contact a confidential source, student media need to carefully consider how this might impact the security of such information and the sensitive files they might possess. Where, for example, student reporters have promised a source anonymity, they have a duty to reasonably ensure his identity remains confidential and protected from prying eyes — both inside and outside of school. In addition to using passwords, firewalls and security software to block hackers and other unauthorized users, student media using school-owned equipment should obtain verifiable assurance from school officials that — regardless of what the school's policy is for other school computers — student media computers and data, including e-mail and Internet logs, will not be tampered with or examined without prior written authorization of a student editor. Where such assurances are not provided, student editors may need to consider other options for storing or accessing sensitive information and communicating with confidential sources.

Such practical steps are important because, while the First Amendment or statutes such as the Privacy Protection Act should shield public school student media from unauthorized intrusions, recent court rulings raise at least some concern about the legal protections available to students when using school-owned computers or technological resources. For example, in one case a judge found that privacy laws did not prohibit public college administrators or law enforcement officials from searching the university's data "recycle bin" to find files deleted by a student (not a student journalist) using a school-owned computer.[107] For students using school-owned computers or networks at private schools, the legal protections are even less clear.[108]

CONFISCATION OF PROPERTY

FROM THE SPLC CASE FILES

While on assignment covering an off-campus party for the student newspaper, a photographer was ordered by an undercover law enforcement officer to turn over his film. The officer, who was working on behalf of the university police, claimed the photograph could blow her cover. Two days later, after the student newspaper threatened to pursue legal action against the police under the federal Privacy Protection Act, police returned the undeveloped film and apologized.[109]

While newsroom searches are rare, the confiscation of material such as cameras, film, tape recorders and notes by school officials or other individuals (for example, police or private security guards and shopkeepers) with neither warrant nor subpoena is regrettably common. As discussed above, the Privacy Protection Act offers significant legal protection against not only newsroom searches, but also against unlawful confiscation of "work product" or "documentary materials," which would include notes, film, digital memory cards, or audio and videotape.

In addition to the defenses offered by the Privacy Protection Act, or where the law may not be applicable, the taking of a reporter's property without cause and without the procedural safeguards of the judicial system can lead to a charge of criminal theft (and possibly criminal battery) or a civil conversion of property or trespass claim. If the person is a government official, which includes most public school employees and law enforcement officials, a First Amendment claim may also be available.

For example, in 1996 a California jury awarded a former high school student photographer $450,600 after it found the city of Los Angeles negligent for not returning photographs confiscated by the police "at gunpoint" that the former student claimed captured the 1968 assassination of Robert F. Kennedy at a downtown hotel.[110]

A journalist should protest confiscation at the time the official asks for the material, but if the official insists, the best course is to hand the material over, then immediately pursue complaints and appeals. A first step would be to file a written police report. Of course, if a confiscating official exposes undeveloped film or destroys notes, complaints and criminal charges will not bring the material back. But at least a complaint and charges might bring disciplinary action, fines or other legal penalties and will send the message that journalists will not tolerate such unauthorized confiscations.

Knock! Knock! A Student Journalist's Practical Guide to Combating Searches and Seizures

First, don't panic. While police officers, FBI agents or school administrators can be intimidating, their authority is not unlimited and, as you have read above, the law provides the press with significant legal rights and protections that government officials must observe. It is important that you maintain a professional demeanor. Be firm but courteous in explaining your position. It will do you no good to get into a shouting match. Chances are good that those demanding to search your newsroom or confiscate your property have never even heard of the Privacy Protection Act and may not understand why journalists would be reluctant to cooperate. Your job is to educate them — and that requires a clear, cool head.

Attempt to delay the search. Ask to see the search warrant. Take time to read the whole thing. Also, ask to see the official's identification. Obtain copies of all documents, if possible. Politely ask the officials what they are looking for and why they want it. You should not unreasonably interfere or attempt to physically prevent their search, but inform them in no uncertain terms that you object to any intrusion into your newsroom or confiscation of your property and believe it is unlawful. If you consent to the search or confiscation — either explicitly or implicitly (for example, by opening a file cabinet without objection) — you may lose your right to contest their actions later on.

Refer to the law. Have a copy of the Privacy Protection Act available in the newsroom to present to officials. One college newsroom has gone so far as to hang a framed copy of the law inscribed with the words "Break glass in case of emergency" on their newsroom wall. It's funny — but it is also an effective reminder for the newspaper's staff. You can find a copy of the PPA on the Student Press Law Center's website.[111] If you live in one of the seven states that has a state newsroom search law, be sure you obtain a copy of that as well.

Get help. Ask that officers give you an opportunity to call your attorney or the SPLC. Suggest that they may also want to consult with their own lawyers before proceeding. Inform them that you may be forced to sue if they go forward with the search or confiscation and that the penalties for violating the law are significant.

Document the scene. If, despite your best efforts, your property is seized or the search proceeds, carefully monitor and document the officers' actions. Note what they are looking through and record any material seized or copied. Write down the names of everyone present. Where possible, quietly and unobtrusively videotape and photograph the search. Photos can be important not just as evidence in a subsequent legal challenge but also for your press coverage of what is a serious and legitimate news event.

Launch a legal challenge. Once the search is over or after officers have confiscated your photos or notes, move into high gear. If you have not already contacted an attorney, do so. You will need legal representation to take your case before a judge. If material was illegally seized, it is important to move quickly to obtain a court order to have it returned before it is altered or destroyed. You should also alert local media, your state press organization — and, of course, the Student Press Law Center.

Be prepared. Finally, the time to prepare for a confrontation over the confiscation of newsgathering materials or a newsroom search is before it happens. Be sure that new staff members are given instructions about what to do in the event of a threatened confiscation of materials or newsroom search. Make sure they understand the danger of consenting to such actions. Show them where you keep the newsroom's copy of the PPA. Prominently display contact information for the publication's editors, adviser and attorney.

SUMMARY

Reporter's privilege has long been a gray area in media law. Supreme Court rulings such as *Branzburg* v. Hayes muddied the waters with conflicting statements asserting the importance of First Amendment interests on the one hand and limiting the application of a reporter's privilege on the other. Efforts by state courts and legislatures to create a reporter's privilege and to make it consistent with their notions of press freedom have created a patchwork of standards. But today, most jurisdictions provide for some mechanism by which a journalist's claim of privilege can be balanced against the need for disclosure. In addition, the federal Privacy Protection Act and some state laws provide strong protections against newsroom searches and confiscation of a reporter's property or working materials.

While most journalists detest the idea of compelled disclosure and do their best to combat such intrusions, reporters probably do themselves a favor when they limit the situations in which the issue arises. As a general rule, student journalists are advised to be miserly in offering promises of confidentiality to obtain information. Indeed, the use of a "masked informant" where the information could be obtained through more open channels with thorough and competent reporting is usually just lazy journalism.

Where the decision is made to use a confidential source, however, journalists must be prepared — and willing — to fight in the event a subpoena follows. For every time a court or other governmental body is successful in compelling a journalist to supply information, be it scribbled notes taken at a rowdy pep rally or videotape of student demonstrations on campus, a precedent is laid whereby the next effort to force disclosure will be just that much easier.

CASE STUDY

A fight broke out at a football game between fans of the opposing teams. Two people were seriously injured and about a dozen arrests were made. The game was suspended for nearly an hour while order was restored in the packed 20,000-seat stadium. You're the editor of *The Student Times*. One of your photographers, Shawna Shutter, was on the field covering the game for the newspaper. When she heard the commotion in the stands, she turned and snapped a number of photos of the fight and the resulting arrests. The next day, the newspaper published a front-page story about the brawl along with one of Shutter's photos that showed one of those arrested, Barry Knuckles, struggling with police as he was being led away in handcuffs. The story, written by *Student Times* reporter Scoop Jackson, included comments by "a top school official who asked not to be identified" criticizing the campus police chief — who was responsible for stadium security — for failing to be better prepared to control such disturbances.

That afternoon, the sheriff called the newspaper. He was investigating the incident and said he wanted to see any other photos Shutter had taken.

The next day, Knuckles' lawyer showed up at *The Student Times* newsroom with a subpoena. She says Knuckles claims he was simply defending himself and is innocent of assault charges. The subpoena demands that Shutter appear at a deposition the following week to answer questions and turn over copies of all of her photos to assist in Knuckles' defense.

That night, as you're working late in your office trying to figure out what to do, you hear noise coming from the "empty" newsroom. You open your office door to see Gigi Byte, the head of the school's technical support department, seated at a computer terminal where she has plugged in a portable flash drive. When you confront her, the startled techie nervously admits that she's here by order of the campus police chief. She says the chief is ticked about the comments made about him and wants her to dig around to uncover the identity of Jackson's anonymous source.

Clearly, this thing has gotten out of hand. How will you respond?

Sheriff's telephone call

This is an easy one. Until the sheriff actually serves you with a subpoena, you're under no legal obligation to do anything. However, it pays to be courteous. You should probably return his phone call and politely explain that — to avoid the appearance of bias — it is newspaper policy not to provide unpublished work to anyone and to contest any subpoena that is issued. Hopefully, that will be enough to convince him to conduct his own investigation before bothering you further.

Barry Knuckles' subpoena

Unlike the telephone call from the sheriff, you cannot safely ignore a subpoena (unless the attorney's hand-delivery to the newsroom was somehow procedurally defective under the rules of your state). Your options: (1) Shutter can testify and provide the photos, as ordered; (2) you can try to negotiate a compromise with Knuckles' attorney (for example, offering to provide copies of the negatives or files of the published photos that they can magnify and inspect), or (3) Shutter can contest the subpoena — either before or at the deposition — asserting a reporter's privilege not to testify.

After talking it over with Shutter, you decide on the third option. You feel strongly about not setting a precedent where *The Student Times* plays "private investigator" for individual parties or the state, potentially compromising its role as a neutral observer.

Once you have decided to contest the subpoena, you'll need to find out what sort of legal protection is available in your state. Unless Knuckles is also making some sort of civil-rights claim against the police, his case is probably going to be heard in a state court, which means you'll want to assert a state shield law or privilege. Whether your state has a shield law or court-recognized privilege — which you can find out by looking at the SPLC's *State-by-State Guide to the Reporter's Privilege for Student Media*[112] or the Reporter's Committee's *Reporter's Privilege Compendium*[113] — you'll want to read the law and/or court cases interpreting the law or privilege carefully to see whether there is any language that might exclude student media. In most cases, the law does not distinguish between student and commercial news media. You'll also want to note whether the law covers: (1) sources or information or both; (2) published or unpublished material or both, and (3) confidential or non-confidential sources/information or both. Shutter — who simply took photos of a news event as it happened — seeks to protect non-confidential, unpublished information.

Assuming that a shield law or qualified privilege is applicable, the next question is whether the privilege can be overcome. Under most shield laws and qualified privileges, courts employ a threepart test to weigh a journalist's rights against the rights of those seeking the information. Courts will ask whether the information possessed by the reporter: (1) is highly material and relevant to the underlying claim; (2) is necessary or critical to the maintenance of the claim, and (3) cannot be obtained from an alternative, non-journalist source. Shutter's photos of the fight likely are relevant to Knuckles' legal defense. It is less clear that Knuckles can overcome the second prong, but depending on what the photos show, they could prove critical to his defense (for example, if they clearly show Knuckles minding his own business until he is whacked from behind). The third part of the test, however, is likely to end Knuckles' quest. Shutter was not the only witness to the fight. In fact, there are 19,998 other potential witnesses. Since Shutter was down on the field, she may not even be the best witness to what happened up in the stands. Has Knuckles' lawyer tried to locate and contact any of the other fans at the game? You received the subpoena less than a week after the fight, so obviously she hasn't tried too hard. A court will probably require Knuckles' attorney to show that she has deposed or at least interviewed many of the fans or stadium personnel who might have seen the fight before she can turn to Shutter. It appears that Knuckles' lawyer is using Shutter as a shortcut to get information that she could obtain on her own with some effort. Depending on the specifics of the law in your jurisdiction, it is likely you can put a halt to her plans.

Gigi Byte's newsroom search

Clearly the most serious and troubling incident of the last few days is Gigi Byte's attempt to secretly tap into *The Student Times'* computers. It's not 100 percent clear if Byte's newsroom break-in violates the federal Privacy Protection Act since the PPA only protects against unauthorized newsroom searches or seizures of reporters' materials that are part of a criminal investigation. You can probably argue that Byte's intrusion is part of a broadly defined criminal investigation, particularly if campus police are involved in investigating the stadium fight. The fact that Byte is not a law enforcement official does not preclude such an argument. You will also want to look into the applicability of a state newsroom search law, some of which provide more protection than the PPA. Even if the federal or a state newsroom search law is inapplicable, Byte may have violated other criminal and civil laws, including criminal trespass, conversion of property and invasion of privacy. In addition, if you attend a public school, a First Amendment claim may be available.

Finally, whether you pursue legal action against the school or not, you will certainly want to let your readers know what has happened through both news articles and editorials.

ENDNOTES

1. *See* Jamie Goldberg, "House GOP may target journalists over security leaks," *Los Angeles Times*, July 12, 2012, at 12 (noting that, while leakers have been prosecuted for disclosing classified information, no journalist has ever been prosecuted under the Espionage Act).
2. http://www.splc.org/reportersprivilege.
3. 28 U.S.C.S. Sec. 1826. The Reporters Committee for Freedom of the Press keeps a running list of reporters jailed or fined for refusing to reveal confidential information or sources, *available at* http://www.rcfp.org/jail.html (last visited June 17, 2013). Joshua Wolf, a video journalist in California, was jailed for 226 days after refusing to comply with a subpoena requesting footage of a protest in San Francisco in 2005. Though at the time a student at San Francisco State University, he was not representing a school-sponsored media outlet.
4. In one of the first cases outside the United States to recognize a reporter's privilege, the United Nations International Criminal Tribunal decided in 2002 that a qualified reporter's privilege should be applied to protect war correspondents from being forced to provide evidence in prosecutions before the tribunal. The court noted: "If war correspondents were to be perceived as potential witnesses for the Prosecution, two consequences may follow: First, they may have difficulties in gathering significant information because the interviewed persons, particularly those committing human rights violations, may talk less freely with them and may deny them access to conflict zones. Second, war correspondents may shift from being observers of those committing human rights violations to being their targets, thereby putting their own lives at risk." *Prosecutor v. Radoslav Brdjanin* (Dec. 11, 2002). *See Tribune win may influence other courts*, The News Media & The Law (Winter 2003), at 40, *available at* http://www.rcfp.org/news/mag/27-1/con-tribunal.html (last visited Sept. 13, 2013).
5. *See* The Society of Professional Journalists, *Code of Ethics* (Revised 1996).
6. See, e.g., *Cohen v. Cowles Media Co.*, 501 U.S. 663 (1991), *on remand*, 479 N.W.2d 387 (Minn. 1992), *remanded and reh'g denied*, 481 N.W.2d 840 (Minn. 1992).
7. Dan Bischof, "Fewer media organizations face subpoenas," The News Media and the Law (Winter 2001) at 20, *available at* http://www.rcfp.org/browse-media-law-resources/news-media-law/news-media-and-law-winter-2001/fewer-media-organizations-f (last visited June 14, 2013).
8. *See* Bill Keller, "Secrets and Leaks," *The New York Times*, June 3, 2013, at A21 (describing how the CIA intercepted a Fox News reporter's emails and electronically tracked the location of his State Department security badge to track down source of leaked information about North Korea's nuclear program).
9. *Cohen*, 501 U.S. at 663.
10. *Ruzicka v. Conde Nast Publications*, 939 F.2d 578 (8th Cir. 1991), *on remand*, 794 F. Supp. 303 (D. Minn. 1992), *vacated*, 999 F.2d 1319 (8th Cir. 1993); *Anderson v. Strong Mem. Hosp.*, 573 N.Y.S.2d 828 (N.Y. Sup. Ct. 1991).
11. *Pierce v. Clarion Ledger*, 452 F. Supp. 2d 661 (S.D. Miss. 2006); *Steele v. Isikoff*, 130 F. Supp. 2d 23 (D.D.C. 2000); *Morgan v. Celender*, 780 F. Supp. 307 (W.D. Pa. 1992).
12. *Branzburg v. Hayes*, 408 U.S. 665 (1972).
13. *Id.* at 690, 707.
14. *Id.* at 707.
15. *Id.* at 710 (Powell, J., concurring).
16. *Id.*
17. For a brief history of the attempts to enact a federal shield law, *see Leggett's case revives talk about shield law*, News Media & the Law (Winter 2002), at 7, *available at* http://www.rcfp.org/news/mag/26-1/cov-leggetts.html (last visited July 15, 2008).
18. *Cusumano v. Microsoft Corp.*, 162 F.3d 708 (1st Cir. 1998); *United States v. Burke*, 700 F.2d 70 (2d Cir. 1983); *Coughlin v. Westinghouse Broad. & Cable, Inc.*, 780 F.2d 340 (3d Cir. 1985); *Titan Sports, Inc. v. Turner Broad. Sys.(In re Madden)*, 151 F.3d 125 (3d Cir. 1998); *Ashcraft v. Conoco, Inc.*, 218 F.3d 282 (4th Cir. 2000); *In re Selcraig*, 705 F.2d 789 (5th Cir. 1983); *Cervantes v. Time, Inc.*, 464 F.2d 986 (8th Cir. 1972), *cert. denied*, 409 U.S. 1125 (1973); *Wright v. FBI*, 241 Fed. Appx. 367 (9th Cir. 2007); *Silkwood v. Kerr-McGee Corp.*, 563 F.2d 433 (10th Cir. 1977); *Price v. Time, Inc.*, 416 F.3d 1327 (11th Cir. 2005); *Lee v. DOJ*, 413 F.3d 53 (D.C. Cir. 2005).
19. *Southwell v. Southern Poverty Law Ctr.*, 949 F. Supp. 1303 (W.D. Mich. 1996) (rejecting a public

figure's application to compel disclosure of a confidential source in a libel suit against the Southern Poverty Law Center, which asserted a First Amendment privilege not to name the source). *But see Hade v. City of Freemont*, 233 F. Supp. 2d 884 (N.D. Ohio 2002) (rejecting reporter's privilege for unpublished information from a non-confidential source and finding that, at most, a reporter is entitled to relief from a subpoena only when reporter is being harassed, the party seeking information is acting in bad faith or the subpoena is not sufficiently relevant to the suit). *See also Omokehinde v. Detroit Bd. of Educ.*, 36 Media L. Rep. 1302 (E.D. Mich. 2007).

20 *McKevitt v. Pallasch*, 339 F.3d 530 (7th Cir. 2003), *reh'g and reh'g en banc denied*, 2003 U.S. App. LEXIS 21057 (7th Cir. Oct. 14, 2003).
21 http://www.rcfp.org/privilege (last visited June 14, 2013).
22 Ala. Code Section 12-21-142 (2008).
23 Alaska Stat. Sections 09.25.300-.390 (2007).
24 Ariz. Rev. Stat. Ann. Section 12-2237 (2008) ("The Arizona Shield Law"); Ariz. Rev. Stat. Ann. Section 12-2214 (2008) ("The Arizona Media Subpoenas Law").
25 Ark. Code Ann. Section 16-85-510 (2008).
26 Cal. Evid. Code Section 1070 (2008); Cal. Const. Art. 1, section 2 (2008); Cal. Civ. Proc. Code Sec. 1986.1 (2008).
27 Col. Rev. Stat. Ann. Sections 13-90-119; 24-72.5-101 to 24-72.5-106 (2007).
28 Conn. Gen. Stat. Section 52-146 (2008).
29 Del. Code Ann. tit. 10, subchapter II, Sections 4320-4326 (2008).
30 Fla. Stat. Ann. Section 90.5015 (2008).
31 Ga. Code Ann. Section 24-9-30 (2008).
32 Hi. Rev. Stat. Section 4:33-621 (2008). Hawaii's shield statute, providing broad protection for amateur as well as professional journalists, was signed into law in 2008. The continued existence of the law is under a cloud, however, since legislators in their 2013 session were unable to agree on its renewal, triggering an automatic "sunset" repeal clause effective June 30, 2013.
33 735 ILCS 5/8-901 to 8-909 (2008).
34 Burns Ind. Code Section 34-46-4-1 to 34-46-4-2 (2008).
35 Ky. Rev. Stat. Ann. Section 421.100 (2008).
36 La. Rev. Stat. Ann. Sections 45:1451 to 1459 (2008).
37 16 MRSA Sec.61.
38 Md. Courts And Judicial Proceedings Code Ann. Section 9-112 (2008).
39 Mich. Comp. Laws Sections 767.5a and 767A.6 (2008).
40 Minn. Stat. Ann. Sections 595.021 to 595.025 (2007).
41 Mont. Code Ann. Sections 26-1-901 to 26-1-903 (2007); Mont. Code Ann. Sections 26-1-901 to 26-1-903 (2007).
42 Neb. Rev. Stat. Sections 20-144 to 20-147 (2008).
43 Nev. Rev. Stat. Ann. Section 49.275 (2008).
44 N.J. Stat. Ann. Sections 2A:84A-21 to 2A:84A-21.9, 2A:84A-29 (2008).
45 N.M. Stat. Ann. Section 38-6-7 (2008); N.M. R.E. 11-514 (2008).
46 N.Y. Civ. Rights Law Section 79-h (2008).
47 N.C. Gen. Stat. Section 8-53.11 (2008).
48 N.D. Cent. Code Section 31-01-06.2 (2008).
49 Ohio Rev. Code Ann. Sections 2739.04 and 2739.12 (2008).
50 Okla. Stat. Ann. Title 12, Ch. 40, Article V, Section 2506 (West, WESTLAW through end of 2002 Regular Session).
51 Or. Rev. Stat. Section 44.510-44.540 (2007).
52 42 PA. Cons. Stat. Ann. Section 5942(a) (2007).
53 R. I. Gen. Laws Sections 9-19.1-1 to 9-19.1-3 (2008).
54 S.C. Code Ann. Section 19-11-100 (2007).
55 Tenn. Code Ann. Section 24-1-208 (2008).
56 Utah Supreme Court Rule 509.
57 Rev. Code Wash. Section 5.68.010 (2008).
58 W. Va. Code Section 57-3-10 (2011).
59 D.C. Code Ann. Section 16-4701 to 16-4704 (2008).
60 *See The Reporter's Privilege Compendium, Reporter's Committee for Freedom of the Press* (Arlington, Va.) (2002), *available at* http://www.rcfp.org/reporters-privilege (last visited Sept. 13, 2013); Goodale, J., "Reporter's Privilege Cases," reported in Communications Law 2003, Vol. III (Practising Law Institute), pages 493-954.
61 *See, e.g., Tripp v. Dept. of Defense*, 284 F. Supp. 2d 50, 61 (D.D.C. 2003) (noting cases suggesting that taking 25-60 depositions would be a reasonable burden to impose prior to overcoming reporter's privilege).
62 *In re Pan Am Corp.*, 161 B.R. 577, 585 (S.D.N.Y. 1993).
63 *See, e.g., People v. McAndrew*, No. 2010CR04406 (Ill. Cir. Ct. June 21, 2011) (quashing attorney's subpoena to Loyola University's Phoenix newspaper on the grounds of Illinois' reporter shield law); *Persky v. Yeshiva Univ.*, No. 01 Civ. 5278, 2002 WL 31769704 (S.D.N.Y. Dec. 10, 2002) (finding First Amendment-based reporter's privilege protected New York private college student reporter from revealing confidential source); *In re Investigation of March 1999 Riots in East Lansing*, 617 N.W.2d 310 (Mich. 2000) (Michigan state shield law protected public university student newspaper from turning over unpublished photos of campus riot); *Tracy v. City of Missoula*, Missoula County Cause No. DV-00-849 (Mont. Dist. Ct. March 9, 2001) (state shield law protected University of Montana journalism student subpoenaed to turn over raw videotape of Hell's Angels gathering); *California v. Chavez*, Case No. 99M11384 (Calif. Super. Ct. Sacramento Cty. April 7, 2000) (California shield law protected editor of public college newspaper subpoenaed to turn over negatives and unpublished photos taken of an arrest

at a football game); *Behrens v. Rutgers Univ.*, Civ. No. 94-358 (D.N.J. Aug. 3, 1995) (finding First Amendment-based reporter's privilege protected New Jersey public college student reporter from turning over interview notes); *VanMilligan v. Ale-Ebrahim*, CIV No. 89-C-681 (Kan. Dist. Ct. Sedgwick County, June 20, 1990) (Kansas court extended qualified privilege to college student reporter subpoenaed to testify in a civil lawsuit about information he had gathered in covering dispute between residents of a fraternity house and neighboring property owners); *New Hampshire v. Siel*, 444 A.2d 499 (N.H. 1982) (New Hampshire Supreme Court affirmed extension of a qualified privilege to college student newspaper reporters). In a highly publicized recent case, *People v. McKinney*, a state court in Illinois ordered Northwestern University to turn over all notes, memos and other unpublished information gathered by student journalists investigating a potentially wrongful murder conviction as part of the Medill Innocence Project, an investigative reporting lab. The judge did not delve into whether being a student affected the journalists' right to claim privilege. Rather, the conclusive fact was that the students' materials were shared with investigators and lawyers for the inmate's legal defense team, thus waiving any entitlement to privilege. *See* Jason Meisner, "Judge rules Northwestern students must turn over emails in murder case," *Chicago Tribune*, Sept. 7, 2011.

64 *See New York v. Hennessey*, 13 Med. L. Rep. 1109 (N.Y. Dist. Ct. 1986) (finding that language in New York state shield law excluded unpaid student reporters working for private university student newspaper that did not have a second-class postage permit); *State v. Buchanan*, 436 P.2d 729 (Or. 1968), *cert. denied*, 392 U.S. 905 (1968) (in a pre-*Branzburg* decision believed to be the first reporter's privilege case involving a student journalist and decided before passage of the state's shield law, the Supreme Court of Oregon rejected a college newspaper reporter's First Amendment claim and ordered her to disclose the identities of her interviewees who claimed to be marijuana users). For more information on student reporters privilege, *See Student Media Guide to Protecting Sources and Information*, available on the SPLC website at http://www.splc.org/reportersprivilegeguide.

65 To date, the SPLC is aware of only two court cases addressing a reporter's privilege for high school student media. The first involved a New Jersey newspaper adviser subpoenaed after the student newspaper published an interview with an unnamed drug dealer. Because the case involved a now-repealed version of the state shield law, it has no ongoing legal significance to New Jersey student journalists. *See Close Encounter*, Student Press Law Center *Report*, Fall 1981, at 12. In Washington State, a high school editor refused prosecutors' demands to turn over photos of a fight in the school's parking lot. The fight was witnessed by as many as 150 other students. At no point did the court question the applicability of the state's First Amendment-based reporter's privilege to high school student media. However, the court noted that no promise of confidentiality was made and therefore it refused to grant the editor's request to quash the subpoena. Still, the editor never revealed the newspaper's photos and was never found in contempt. *See Editor's firm stand on principle earns victory for h.s. journalists*, Student Press Law Center *Report*, Fall 1996, at 37.

66 *See* Kelly Heyboer, "Are bloggers journalists?", *The Star-Ledger*, May 6, 2009, at 13 (reporting on libel suit against woman who claimed to be a "journalist" when pressed to identify her sources of information for a blog post she wrote on a consumer website criticizing a software company's products).

67 *See* http://ireport.cnn.com/ (last visited June 17, 2013).

68 Del. Code Ann. tit. 10, Secs. 4320-4326 (2008).

69 R. I. Gen. Laws Sections 9-19.1-1 (2008); Fla. Stat. Ann. Section 90.5015(1)(a) (2008); Burns Ind. Code Section 34-46-4-1 (2008); N.M. Stat. Ann. Section 38-6-7 (2008); N.M. R.E. 11-514 (2008); Nev. Rev. Stat. Ann. Section 49.275 (2008); Tex. Code Crim. Pro. Art. 38.11, Sec. 1(D)(2) (2009); Rev. Code Wash. Section 5.68.010 (2008); D.C. Code Ann. Section 16-4702 (2008).

70 *New York v. Hennessey*, 13 Med. L. Rptr. 1109 (N.Y. Dist. Ct. 1986).

71 N.Y. Civ. Rights Law Sec. 79-h (2008).

72 *Blum v. Schlegel*, 150 F.R.D. 42 (W.D.N.Y. 1993), aff'd, 18 F.3d 1005 (2d Cir. 1994); *Persky v. Yeshiva Univ.*, No. 01 Civ. 5278, 2002 WL 31769704 (S.D.N.Y. Dec. 10, 2002).

73 *Blum*, 150 F.R.D. at 45.

74 http://www.splc.org/reportersprivilegeguide.

75 *Jimenez v. City of Chicago*, 733 F.Supp.2d 1268, 1272 (W.D. Wash. 2010).

76 *See* Al Tompkins, *Guidelines for Interviewing Confidential Sources: Who, When, and Why?*, Aug. 13, 2002, *available at* http://www.poynter.org/content/content_view.asp?id=4361 (last visited Sept. 13, 2013). Student media considering the use of confidential sources are also urged to read the very thoughtful and comprehensive "Confidential News Sources," policy of *The New York Times* (published Feb. 24, 2004).

77 *Killion v. Franklin Reg'l Sch. Dist.*, 46 Fed. R.Serv.3d 856 (W.D. Pa. 2001).

78 Though not all-inclusive, respondents to the 2001 survey by the Reporters Committee for Freedom of the Press reported no newsroom searches. In their 1991 survey, five newsroom searches were reported. *See supra* note 7.

79 *Zurcher v. Stanford Daily*, 436 U.S. 547, reh'g denied, 439 U.S. 885 (1978).

80 42 U.S.C.S. Sec. 2000aa (2008).

81 *See* Sommer Ingram, "Agreement ends battle over seized Breeze photos," SPLC News Flash, June 1, 2010, *available at* http://www.splc.org/news/newsflash.asp?id=2099.

82 42 U.S.C.S. Sec.2000aa(a), (b).

83 *See id.*

84 42 U.S.C.S. Sec.2000aa-7(b).

85 42 U.S.C.S. Sec.2000aa-7(b)(3).

86 *Steve Jackson Games, Inc. v. United States Secret Serv.*, 816 F. Supp. 432, 441 (W.D. Tex. 1993) (government officials must conduct a reasonable investigation into the party to be searched to determine the party is not one who disseminates information to the public).

87 42 U.S.C.S. Sec.2000aa(a).

88 42 U.S.C.S. Sec.2000aa(a)(1).

89 42 U.S.C.S. Sec.2000aa(a)(1).

90 The PPA allows government officials to search newsrooms where a reporter receives, possesses or communicates certain information relating to national defense, classified or restricted information (*See* 42 USCS Sec. 2000aa(a)(1)) or if the offense relates to the possession or distribution of child pornography, sexual exploitation of children or child slavery. "Child Pornography Prevention Act," 18 U.S.C.S. Sec.2252(6).

91 42 U.S.C.S. Sec.2000aa(a)(2).

92 42 U.S.C.S. Sec.2000aa-7(a).

93 *Id.*

94 *Id.*

95 42 U.S.C.S. Sec.2000aa(b).

96 42 U.S.C.S. Sec.2000aa(b)(1),(2).

97 42 U.S.C.S. Sec.2000aa(b)(3).

98 42 U.S.C.S. Sec.2000aa(b)(4).

99 42 U.S.C.S. Sec.2000aa(b)(4)(A).

100 42 U.S.C.S. Sec.2000aa(b)(4)(B).

101 42 U.S.C.S. Sec.2000aa-6(f).

102 42 U.S.C.S. Sec.2000aa-6(f).

103 42 U.S.C.S. Sec.2000aa(a),(b).

104 Freedom Forum, *Death by Cheeseburger: High School Journalism in the 1990's and Beyond* (1994), p. 4.

105 CAL. PENAL CODE Sec. 1524(g) (2008); CAL. EVIDENCE CODE Sec. 1070 (2007); CONN. GEN. STAT. Sec. 54-33(j) (2008); NEB. REV. STAT. Sec. 29-813 (2008); N.J. STAT. Sec. 2A:84A-21.9 (2008); OR. REV. STAT. Sec. 44.520(2) (2007); TEX. CODE CRIM. PROC. art. 18.01(e) (2007); WASH. REV. CODE SEC. 10.79.015(3) (2008).

106 N.J. STAT. Sec. 2A:84A-21.9 (2001).

107 *United States v. Bunnell*, No. CRIM.02-13-B-S, 2002 WL 981457 (D. Me. May 10, 2002). *See also United States v. Butler,* 151 F. Supp. 2d 82 (D. Me. 2001) (student had no reasonable expectation of privacy in storing files on university-owned computers in public computer lab).

108 *See United States v. Simons*, 206 F.3d 392, 398-99 (4th Cir.2000) (finding no reasonable expectation of privacy in files downloaded from the Internet to hard drive of employee's office computer where private employer had express policy of monitoring Internet activities of employees).

109 "Editor secures return of confiscated film," Student Press Law Center *Report*, Fall 2001, at 14.

110 Though not disputing the legitimacy of the former student's claim, a state appeals court later overturned the judgment on the grounds of prejudicial juror misconduct. *Enyart v. City of L.A.*, 76 Cal. App. 4th 499 (Cal. App. 2d Dist. 1999); *Court Sides With City in Kennedy Photographs Case, L.A. Times*, Dec. 2, 1999, at B4.

111 http://www.splc.org/law_library.asp?id=19.

112 http://www.splc.org/reportersprivilege.

113 http://www.rcfp.org/privilege (last visited Sept. 13, 2013).

CHAPTER 18

Freedom of Information Law

"Knowledge will forever govern ignorance; and a people who mean to be their own governors, must arm themselves with the power which knowledge gives."
— James Madison

WHAT IS FREEDOM OF INFORMATION LAW?

In America, the government belongs to the people. Freedom of information law is simply one means by which citizens, the owners, have given themselves the ability to keep tabs on what their government and those who run it are doing. Freedom of information law is based on the belief that the people do not and should not give their public servants unchecked authority to decide what the public should know.

While the First Amendment guarantees citizens the right to be free from government interference when they distribute information, federal courts so far have not recognized a constitutional right of access to government documents.[1] Indeed, in a 2013 ruling, the Supreme Court rejected the idea that the Constitution entitles citizens to any particular level of responsiveness to requests for government records.[2] Because there is no clear constitutional right of access to government documents, citizens must rely on rights created by Congress and state legislatures. These rights are set forth in freedom-of-information statutes that exist in federal law and in the law of every U.S. state and territory. The effectiveness of these laws depends on the way exemptions are interpreted and applied, on the willingness of citizens (including the student media) to hold government agencies accountable for consistent compliance, and on the firmness of courts that are asked to decide whether particular records may or may not be withheld.

As our government has grown, so too has the compulsion on the part of government officials to hide information. The numbers speak for themselves. During fiscal year 2011, the U.S. government classified a staggering amount of information — more than 92 million documents and communications — as off-limits to the public on the basis of national security, according to the annual *Report to the President* issued by the Information Security Oversight Office.[3] For some government officials and agencies, the "Top Secret" stamp has become the rule rather than the exception, often to the point of absurdity. For example, the following records are among those that government officials have hidden from public view:

- A 1917 report held by the National Archives concerning troop movements in Europe during World War I.[4] It was finally released some 75 years later, and contained, according to one commentator, "fewer national security revelations... than one can find in a Tom Clancy novel."[5]
- A 1980 memo from military helicopter pilots reporting that milk packed in their lunch boxes spoiled in the desert heat. Pentagon officials kept this document secret for twelve years.[6]
- A CIA operations plan, drafted in 1962, detailing the agency's proposal to float thousands of small balloons over Cuba that would drop anti-Castro and anticommunism propaganda, including toy balloons and stickers for Cuban children. Only after a long and costly legal battle was this document released — 31 years later.[7]
- A foreign leader's date of birth, the names of book authors, newspaper articles and — in one amazing case — a joke in a 1974 CIA Intelligence Report, withheld from disclosure until 1999, about a possible terrorist attack on Santa Claus.[8]

As Robert Steele, openness advocate and former deputy director of the U.S. Marine

> Freedom of information law is based on the belief that the people do not and should not give their public servants an unfettered right to decide what the people should know.

> Did You Know? During fiscal year 2007, the U.S. government classified 23,102,257 national security secrets, or an average of about 63,294 per day.

Corps Intelligence Center, said before the Presidential Inter-Agency Task Force on National Security Information, "It has been my experience that employees of various intelligence organizations routinely classify *everything* they collect, everything they write. This is in part because there are severe penalties for under-classifying information and *there are no penalties for over-classification, even if over-classification is against the public interest.*"[9]

Fortunately, student journalists rarely will need access to documents implicating matters of national security. But that's not to say that access is any easier when dealing with agencies at the state and local level. As confirmed by decades of public-records "audits" by journalists and watchdog groups, government officials — whether because of poor training, indifference to public transparency or a deliberate motive to conceal — regularly withhold records to which the public has a clear legal right of access.[10] Colleges and schools are, regrettably, among the most flagrant open-government scofflaws. In a ground-breaking investigative series published in 2010, *The Columbus Dispatch* found that colleges routinely made frivolous claims of "student privacy" when asked for records such as the lists of VIP's given complementary football tickets; colleges in the same state, subject to the same public-records act, gave conflicting interpretations of those acts and produced wildly varying responses to the *Dispatch* survey.[11] In 2013, the Society of Professional Journalists "awarded" its most humiliating "honor" (the "Black Hole Award") to Oklahoma State University for concealing — even from its own police department — the fact that a student found to have committed four sexual assaults was still at large on the campus.[12]

The public filed nearly 22 million Freedom of Information requests with the federal government in 2007, only one in three was granted.
Source: *U.S. News & World Report*

Control of information is power. Dissemination of information, which is the necessary and proper role of journalists in our society, is a redistribution of that power. While most people recognize the need for some secrecy in government (for example, future battle plans or the identity of undercover law enforcement officials), freedom of information laws, or "sunshine laws" as they are often called, recognize that most of what the government does should be subject to public review and scrutiny, carried out in the sunshine even when government officials might prefer otherwise.

Too often, student journalists fail to take advantage of the extraordinary promise of freedom of information law. The university president refuses to answer a student reporter's question about his travel expenses. School board members bar a reporter from a budget meeting to discuss controversial school closings. The campus police chief locks up all records about an alleged sexual assault that took place in front of the school library. A principal refuses to answer questions about a rumor that she was arrested for shoplifting. For student journalists who know the basics of freedom of information law, "no comments" and locked doors are not dead ends — just temporary obstacles that can often be overcome.

Freedom of information laws fall into five categories: (1) the federal Freedom of Information Act, (2) state open record laws, (3) the federal open meetings law, (4) state open meetings laws and (5) miscellaneous state and federal freedom of information provisions, sometimes called "pocket FOI" laws because they are tucked away in the statute books somewhere other than the main freedom-of-information law. The federal laws are used to obtain access to the meetings of federal governmental bodies or records in the possession or control of a U.S. government agency; state laws are used to obtain access to the meetings or records of state or local government agencies. Each of the 50 states and the District of Columbia has an open records and open meeting law.[13] "Pocket" FOI laws occur at all levels of government, and fortunately for those covering private colleges, a few even apply to private as well as public institutions.

WHAT DO FREEDOM OF INFORMATION LAWS SAY?

Generally, freedom of information laws require that all records generated or meetings conducted by a public body or agency be open to the public unless the law specifically exempts them. Even when a specific exemption does exist, many laws still leave disclosure up to the government official agency. In other words, an official often can disclose exempt records or grant access to exempt meetings. Sunshine laws generally set the floor for the minimum disclosure required by law, not a ceiling for the maximum allowed by law; an official should seldom be allowed to get away with the excuse that disclosure of a document is "prohibited" by an open records law. Where legal disputes occur, they generally concern the scope of a particular exemption or question whether a specific entity is a "public body" subject to the law.[14] While private bodies (such as private schools) are generally not covered by freedom of information laws, some laws ensure compliance by private entities by threatening to withhold government funding if certain information is not disclosed.

When requesting access under federal law, the exemptions are uniform across the country. Under state law, however, the exemptions can vary. For example, while Connecticut's open records law makes arrest records available to the public,[15] Delaware's law apparently exempts that same information.[16]

Under most freedom of information laws, a public record or meeting is presumed to be open. This is important because it means that where a public official decides to deny access, it is up to the official to justify his decision legally. Further, if a requester feels a public official incorrectly denied her access, most freedom of information laws allow the decision to be appealed.

Every newsroom should have a copy of the state's open meetings and records law and the federal Freedom of Information Act available for consultation should questions arise. If your newsroom does not, your state press association, a local newspaper or attorney, or the Student Press Law Center can assist you in obtaining copies.

> Freedom of information laws fall into five basic categories: (1) the federal Freedom of Information Act, (2) state open record laws, (3) the federal open meetings law, (4) state open meetings laws and (5) miscellaneous state and federal freedom of information provisions.

WHAT WOULD YOU LIKE TO KNOW?

The amount your school president/principal was paid last year?
Public schools — state open records law
Private schools — IRS Form 990 (available from school upon request)

The number of sexual assaults that occurred on your campus last year?
All colleges — federal Clery Act[17]
Public schools — state open records law

Information about a particular sexual assault (or other crime) that was reported only to campus police?
Public schools — state open records law and/or federal Clery Act[18]
Private schools — state open campus crime log law (if available) and federal Clery Act[19]

Information about a particular crime that was reported to local (city or county) police?
All — state open records law

The graduation rate of all students at your school? Of student athletes?
All colleges — federal Student Right-to-Know Act[20]
Public schools — state open records law

How much money your school spent on its football program last year?
All colleges — Equity in Athletics Disclosure Act of 1994[21]
Public schools — state open records law

What is in your own school records?
All — federal Family Educational Rights and Privacy Act of 1974 (FERPA), also known as known as the Buckley Amendment[22]

Which public school board members voted themselves a pay raise at the last board meeting?
State open meetings law

Whether your school received a federal grant to research bovine flatulence?[23]
All - federal Freedom of Information Act[24]

Does the FBI have a file on me?
Federal Privacy Act[25] and Freedom of Information Act[26]

Has your school's cafeteria ever been cited for health code violations by the city or state health inspector?
All - state open records law request, submitted either to the public health agency (public and private schools) or the school itself (public schools only)

HOW DOES FREEDOM OF INFORMATION LAW WORK?

Fortunately, access to government meetings and records is often granted on an informal basis by public officials who recognize the importance of open government — or at least understand their legal obligation to do so. Therefore, before waving your copy of the law in front of a government employee and demanding compliance, you will usually find officials more receptive to your request by simply — and politely — asking for their assistance obtaining the information you seek. When the informal approach is unsuccessful, however, a freedom of information law may need to be invoked.

Open Meeting Laws

Using freedom of information law is simple. For meetings of governmental bodies, just show up. If the meeting is small or if your presence is questioned, you should identify yourself as a reporter and politely explain your interest in attending the meeting. Remember that you are not looking for a confrontation; you are looking to gather news. If you are told that the meeting is closed, ask why. This is also a good time to tactfully explain to the meeting's chair why you think you are entitled to attend, being sure to cite the relevant open meetings law. If the officials still tell you the meeting is closed, ask that your objection and their response be read into the minutes and then leave. Upon leaving, be sure to record the names and titles of everyone you talked to and carefully note what was said.

If, after leaving, you still feel that you were wrongly denied access, you may wish to consider an appeal. If you need help at this stage, consider contacting an attorney experienced in freedom of information law or the Student Press Law Center.

Open Record Laws

To request records, many state laws say that all you have to do is go to the person responsible for keeping the documents you are looking for and ask for them. Indeed, a quick telephone call or visit is often all it takes. To formally request records from a federal agency, or to request records from a state agency when you think they might not act on an verbal request, a written request is required. Again, the process is fairly straightforward. A sample freedom of information records request letter containing the basic information you should include in your request has been reproduced in the Appendix to assist you. You can also use the Student Press Law Center's automated freedom of information letter generator, available on the SPLC website.[27]

In writing your letter, be sure to cite the relevant freedom of information law and note the specifics relating to how much time the law gives an agency to respond to your request and any penalties associated with noncompliance. Also, make sure that you "reasonably describe" the material that you want. If you know for sure that you want only the police

Each of the 50 states and the District of Columbia has an open records and open meetings law.

If asked to leave a government meeting that you believe is covered by an open meetings law, ask that your objection be entered into the minutes before you leave.

incident reports relating to an assault committed in front of Memorial Library on June 4, 2013, say so. A letter that merely requests access to "all crime information" will probably only delay your obtaining access to the information you want. If your desired information is not so specifically focused, be wary of pinning yourself down too narrowly. A literal-minded bureaucrat may interpret your request for "all reports of crimes during September 2013" to exclude the double-homicide that took place at 11:45 p.m. on August 31.

You do not need to know a document's exact name or number, but your request should be specific enough that a public employee familiar with the subject area can locate the records with a reasonable amount of effort. Again, you will find that courtesy and professionalism are rewarded.

Two points are worth special note, because they are frequent sources of confusion. First, sunshine laws speak in terms of "public" access to meetings and records, not "press" access; a person need not be employed by or affiliated with a recognized news agency to take full advantage of sunshine laws. Second, with very rare exceptions, the purpose for which the requester intends to use government information is irrelevant to whether the request can be denied.[28] A government agency may not demand to know what you are writing about as a precondition to honoring your request. No greater justification is needed than simple human curiosity.

As with meetings, if you feel your request for access to records has been wrongly denied, you should consult your open records law to determine the procedure for appealing the decision. Usually, you will be required to write a formal letter of appeal to a higher authority. If your appeal is denied (or ignored), some states provide for administrative review; others require that you go to court. If you have questions, this might be the time to consider seeking professional guidance.

CHECK THIS OUT

SPLC Automated, Fill-in-the-Blanks
State Open Records Law Request Letter Generator
http://www.splc.org/foiletter.asp

Other Sources of Freedom of Information Law

While open meeting and open record laws are the primary tools of most journalists when trying to obtain information from and about their government, they are not the only source of law available. Scattered throughout various state and federal statutes are pockets of freedom of information law that, once you know where to find them and how to use them, can provide valuable information about how the government or your school conducts its business. For example, as part of a large body of law regulating federal financial aid for students, Congress also included a small section requiring that colleges and universities provide statistical information regarding campus graduation rates. Another law requires most colleges to compile and provide access to information about their athletic programs. And buried deep within the voluminous federal tax code is a provision that requires private colleges and other non-profit organizations to provide, upon request, some of the information about where their money comes from and how it is spent. The details of these and other freedom of information laws are provided below.

OF SPECIAL CONCERN: CAMPUS CRIME

Of all the public records and meetings that are available using freedom of information law, calls to the Student Press Law Center indicate that those of most interest to student journalists are the ones that relate to campus crime. Readers want and need to know

Citations to the open meeting laws of each of the 50 states and the District of Columbia are available at: **www.splc.org/ openmeetinglaws**

Citations to the open records laws of each of the 50 states and the District of Columbia are available at: **www.splc.org/ openrecordlaws**

If an open records law allows the government agency to withhold some information contained in a crime report, the agency usually must delete that information and release the remaining portion of the record.

about campus crime. Armed with accurate information, students, faculty and staff can avoid high-risk areas or activities, stay alert for previously reported problems or persons, and protect themselves from becoming the next campus crime victims.

Unfortunately, the battle for access to such information has been an uphill struggle. Some schools, convinced that high campus crime rates result in lower application rates, have gone out of their way to hide or manipulate reports on their school's crime problems. More concerned with their school's reputation as an idyllic setting for learning than with the safety of their students, these schools have done their best to deter student crime reporters from obtaining accurate and timely information about campus criminal activity. This has become particularly true with respect to access to internal campus court or disciplinary proceedings, where colleges and universities across the country continue to hear serious criminal charges, often to the exclusion of the public court system, with virtually no public oversight or accountability.

While the battle for access continues, there has been a marked trend toward openness, with advocates of more open and honest campus crime information winning significant legislative victories at both the federal and state level.[29] At the federal level, laws now require almost all colleges and universities (including private schools) to: (1) maintain and provide access to a daily campus police log, (2) compile an annual statistical report detailing the number of serious campus crimes, (3) provide public immediate warnings regarding ongoing threats to student safety and (4) adhere to a sexual assault victim's bill of rights, including a full disclosure to both the victim and accused of the outcome of any disciplinary hearing. At the state level, some lawmakers have enacted state versions of a crime statistics law; others have passed laws requiring all schools — both public and private — to maintain an open campus crime log. Additionally, campus police or safety departments at public schools must adhere to the same state open records law requirements that apply to any state or local government law enforcement agency. (These laws — and others — are discussed in the Freedom of Information Toolbox section, below.)

Much more information about covering campus crime is available in the comprehensive Student Press Law Center publication *Covering Campus Crime: A Handbook for Journalists*. Downloadable copies are available free on the SPLC website.[30]

THE BUCKLEY AMENDMENT

What was once one of the biggest obstacles to effective campus crime reporting has been cut down to size — though not yet eliminated. The Family Educational Rights and Privacy Act[31] (FERPA), commonly known as the Buckley Amendment, was enacted in 1974 in part to curb the indiscriminate release of student records by school officials. (A second part requires that schools provide students with access to their own records.) Under the law, schools that release a student's "education records" without permission can have their federal funding cut.

While the law appears reasonable on its face, the application of FERPA has resulted in considerable controversy, focusing largely on the question: what exactly is an "education record?" Many schools have used FERPA as a shield of convenience, interpreting the term to hide records that have nothing to do with a student's scholastic or academic performance when it suits their purposes.[32] For example, despite court rulings to the contrary, many schools at one time — with the blessing of the U.S. Department of Education — claimed that the definition of "education records" included campus police and security department reports. As a result, they denied such information to the student media and public. In 1992, Congress amended FERPA to specifically exclude campus law enforcement records from the "education records" definition, effectively eliminating the FERPA excuse.

Unfortunately, schools have continued to take advantage of FERPA's imprecision in other areas, forcing ongoing disagreements and legal battles between news media and schools — and occasionally legislative intervention. In 1998, for example, Congress once again amended FERPA to allow for the release of certain disciplinary — or campus court — records.[33]

Some states have passed laws that require all schools — both public and private — to maintain open police logs.

Schools may have a duty to warn students of foreseeable dangers from campus crime.

FERPA is, in many ways, a good law gone bad. The law, critics argue, was intended to protect test scores and transcripts, not criminal records and other documents relating to a student's nonacademic pursuits. Although access advocates have applauded some of the changes Congress has made, many believe lawmakers have not gone far enough and continue to call for FERPA's reform. (For more information on FERPA, see the discussion in the FOI Toolbox, below.)

SUMMARY

Whether for a report on campus crime or a list of next year's school district budget cuts, student journalists should take the time to learn how to use freedom of information law. For student journalists and all those interested in the nuts and bolts of government, a working knowledge of freedom of information law is essential. In addition to this introduction, the Student Press Law Center can recommend other sources that will provide additional, more detailed information on how to get the most out of freedom of information law. For example, these are just a few of the titles available in the SPLC's Access Series:

- *Access to Student Government Records and Meetings*
- *Access to College Accreditation Reports*
- *Access to College Athletic Program Information*
- *Access to Common High School Records*
- *Access to College Foundation Records*

More information about these and many other publications — including, in some cases, free downloadable versions — can be obtained on the SPLC website. Remember, freedom of information law can be a potent tool and ally — but first you have to use it.

THE FREEDOM OF INFORMATION LAW TOOLBOX

Freedom of Information Tool: Federal Freedom of Information Act (FOIA) [5 U.S.C. Sec. 552]

Type of Information Available: All records created, possessed or controlled by a federal agency or maintained for such an agency by an entity under government contract, unless those records fall within one of nine categories of exempt information that agencies are permitted (but not required) to withhold. The exemptions are: (1) national security, (2) internal agency rules, (3) information specifically exempted by other federal laws already on the books — the so-called "catch-all" exemption, (4) trade secrets, (5) internal agency memoranda, (6) personal privacy, (7) law enforcement records, (8) bank reports, (9) oil and gas well data. The exemptions, however, are not always as broad as the exemption headings might suggest. For example, the law enforcement exemption can be used only where an agency demonstrates that release of a document could reasonably be expected to jeopardize an ongoing civil or criminal investigation, deprive a person of a right to a fair trial, or cause harm to persons who assist law enforcement officials. Unfortunately, interpreting the federal FOIA has become increasingly complex and questions or record requests that seem fairly straightforward often are not. To clear through the brush on the national level, the Reporters Committee for Freedom of the Press publishes an excellent guide, *How To Use The Federal FOI Act*, which is available free on the RCFP website.[34] The National Freedom of Information Center website, based at the University of Missouri, also contains useful information.[35]

Who is Covered: Every "agency," "department," "regulatory commission," "government controlled corporation" and "other establishment" in the executive branch of the federal government. The FOIA does not apply to Congress, the federal courts, private corporations or federally funded state agencies. However, documents generated by these bodies and filed with a federal government agency become subject to the Act unless

The Family Educational Rights and Privacy Act (FERPA) was amended in 1992 to explicitly exclude campus law enforcement unit records. In 1998 it was again amended to allow disclosure of some campus court records.

Covering Campus Crime: A Handbook for Journalists, the SPLC's comprehensive guide to obtaining access to college crime information, can be downloaded for free at: **www.splc.org/ccc**

they fall within one of the exemptions. Also, records maintained for a covered agency by an entity under government contract are also subject to disclosure.

How to Use it: To save yourself some time and trouble, you may want to first try an informal verbal request to obtain the documents you are seeking. However, agencies frequently will require that requests be made in writing. Also, to preserve your rights under the Act, a formal request must be in writing. Filing a formal request is usually not difficult. You need only "reasonably describe" the records you want in a letter, which you then submit to the FOIA officer at the federal agency you believe has custody of those records (for example, the FBI or the Environmental Protection Agency). (You can use the Reporters Committee for Freedom of the Press automated federal freedom of information letter generator.[36]) If you are unsure which federal agency has the records you want, you can send the same request to several agencies. Likewise, if a federal agency has numerous branches or field offices and you believe the records might be held by one of them, send a copy of your request to that location as well. Mark the outside of the envelope "Freedom of Information Act Request," and send it registered mail, return receipt requested. The statute requires that agencies grant or deny your request within 20 working days unless an "unusual circumstance" specifically described in the statute occurs.

Penalties for Noncompliance: If your request is wholly or partially denied, the FOIA gives you the right to appeal. Your appeal can be a brief letter to the agency administrator asking that he review your request and explaining why you think the denial was improper. The Student Press Law Center can provide you with a sample FOIA appeal letter. If your appeal is denied you may file a FOIA lawsuit in the nearest federal district court. It is probably wise — although not necessary — to have legal help in filing your complaint. The Act provides for the payment of attorneys fees and court costs if you "substantially prevail" in your lawsuit.[37] The Act also provides that an "arbitrary" or "capricious" denial of properly requested information by an agency employee can subject that person to written reprimands, fines and/or removal.

Freedom of Information Tool: **State Open Record Laws** (a list of citations to all state open record laws is available on the SPLC website.[38]

Type of Information Available: Varies by state. However, the general idea is that all "public records" are available unless they fall under a specific exemption listed by the state law. For specific information on the law in your state, there is no better resource than the *Open Government Guide*, an exceptional 50-state compendium published for journalists by the Reporters Committee for Freedom of the Press and available free on their website.[39]

Who is Covered: Varies by state. Again, however, the general idea is that all "state agencies" or state "public officials" must provide access to their official records when requested to do so.'

How to Use it: Many state laws — unlike the federal Act — expressly provide that a simple verbal request to the person who maintains the records is sufficient. In these cases, the state official must provide reasonable and prompt access to the requester during normal business hours. If your verbal request is denied, it is important that you note the name, title and response of any official you deal with. In states where verbal requests are not recognized — and any time such a request has been denied — a formal written request should be submitted. (The sample freedom of information request letter on page 405, may be used as your model or you can use the SPLC's automated state freedom of information letter generator.[40])

As with a federal freedom of information request, your letter should reasonably describe the material you are seeking and be sent to the person(s) or agency(s) responsible for holding that information. Note that you need not direct the request to the very individual

— often a secretary or clerk — who has physical possession of the document you want; the request should go to the department head, the agency's FOI coordinator, or to a responsible agency official who has supervisory authority over the record-keeper.

Penalties for Noncompliance: Penalties vary by state. Almost all states provide for an eventual court order in which improperly concealed records are required to be opened. Some states require that a requester first appeal a denial through an established administrative process before going to court. About a third of the states have established a public-access agency or ombudsman who works out of the state attorney general's office or a state-organized freedom of information council or commission. Some ombudsman offices write legal opinions responding to public questions; a few are available to mediate freedom of information law disputes.[41] Such offices can provide a welcome alternative to court if an open records request is denied. Many states allow a prevailing requester to collect money for attorney fees and court costs. Additionally, many states also allow for the imposition of monetary fines (and some even prescribe jail sentences) against a state agency or officer who improperly denies an open records request.

CHECK THIS OUT

For specific information on your state's freedom of information laws, there is simply no better resource for journalists than the Open Government Guide. This outstanding 50-state compendium, published by the Reporters Committee for Freedom of the Press, should be a staple in every newsroom. It is available for free on the RCFP website at http://www.rcfp.org/ogg.

Freedom of Information Tool: Federal Government in the Sunshine Act (Federal Open Meetings Law) [5 U.S.C. Sec. 552b]

Type of Information Available: This freedom of information tool acts as a standing invitation for journalists and other members of the public to attend the business meetings of most federal government boards, commissions and agencies. It also requires that agencies covered by the law give at least one week's public notice of a meeting's topic, time and place. All meetings — including budget deliberations — must be open unless the agency demonstrates that the discussion would fall under one of ten exemptions. The first nine of these exemptions parallel the federal FOIA exemptions, discussed above. The tenth exemption provides for closure when an agency is involved in arbitration or adjudication of a case.

Who is Covered: The statute lists about 50 federal boards, commissions and agencies[42] that must comply with the federal open meetings law. Like FOIA, the Sunshine Act does not apply to Congress, the federal courts, private corporations or state agencies.

How to Use it: Simply show up at the time and place posted on the public notice. If there is a topic that you are particularly interested in, most agencies will put your name on a mailing or e-mail list to receive public notices of upcoming meetings. If you hear that a meeting is closed or if you are asked to leave once you have arrived to cover a meeting, ask that the meeting's chair provide you with a reason (preferably in writing) for the closure. If you believe that the meeting is being closed improperly, ask that your objection to the closure be read into the minutes of the meeting, being sure to cite to the federal open meetings law. Record the names and responses of all government officials you speak with — and then leave. Short of going to court, it is often helpful to submit a written letter of objection to both the meeting's chair and, if applicable, the chair's supervisor or other individual in a position to exert pressure on the chair to comply with the open meeting law's requirements. In the letter, you should briefly explain how you were denied access to the meeting and why you believe that action was wrong. Give the recipient a reasonable deadline for addressing your complaint and let him know that, if necessary, you are prepared to legally appeal the decision of the chair.

Penalties for Noncompliance: The Sunshine Act allows a court to dissolve an improperly noticed or closed meeting. Where such an injunction is issued, future improper notices or closings could result in a court finding the agency in contempt. This is why, if you are barred from a meeting you believe was closed unlawfully, you should contact a lawyer immediately; an attorney may even be able to obtain a telephonic order from a judge to halt an illegally closed meeting in progress.

Freedom of Information Tool: State Open Meetings Laws

Type of Information Available: Varies by state. Generally, a state's open meetings law guarantees the right of the public to attend meetings of a public body in which a quorum exists and during which official business will be discussed. The laws usually require agencies to give advance notice of the time, place and agenda of all meetings. The laws also usually require agencies to keep minutes of all meetings, even those that can be legally closed to the public. Every state allows agencies to discuss some matters in closed session. The kinds of meetings that can be closed vary by state, but most laws permit the following discussions to be in secret: personnel matters, litigation matters, negotiations and collective bargaining sessions, and discussions regarding the acquisition of real estate. Once again, the single best resource for journalists wanting to find specific information on the applicability and mechanics of their state open meetings law is the Reporters Committee for Freedom of the Press 50-state compendium, *Open Government Guide*, available free on their website.[43]

Who is Covered: Varies by state. Most states — but not all — require a meeting be open only when a sufficient number of the body's members are present to constitute a quorum. Chance social or informal gatherings of agency officials generally are not covered. However, officials cannot hide behind the pretext of a social or other "non-official" gathering (such as a "retreat" or "workshop") if the agency is meeting to discuss public issues and make decisions. Non-governmental groups (for example, a university foundation) may fall under an open meetings law where they are supported in whole or in part by public funds, are created by a government body, use public facilities or perform traditionally governmental functions.[44] Where student governments at a public school are responsible for allocating student activity fees or other public money — or where they have been delegated decision-making authority by the school — a state's sunshine law will often cover them. Unlike the federal open meetings law, some state laws also include certain legislative and judicial bodies, in addition to executive branch agencies, as among those required to conduct their business in public.

How to Use it: See discussion under the Federal Government in the Sunshine Act, above.

Penalties for Noncompliance: In some states, action taken at an improperly closed meeting can be declared null and void, requiring the agency to take the action again in an open meeting. In other states, government officials may be liable for criminal or civil fines. Also, attorney fees are often available to those who successfully contest a closed meeting.

Freedom of Information Tool: Jeanne Clery Disclosure of Campus Security Policy and Campus Crime Statistics Act, commonly known as the "Clery Act" (formerly the Campus Security Act) [20 U.S.C. Sec. 1092(f); *see also* 34 C.F.R. 668][45]

Type of Information Available: The Clery Act requires college to gather and report three different types of campus crime information:

Annual Campus Security Report (including campus crime statistics)
Colleges and universities are required to publish and distribute by October 1 of each year an annual security report containing: (1) campus security policies and procedures, including security and access to campus dorms and other buildings; (2) the law enforcement authority status of security personnel, including their working relationship

with state and local police agencies; (3) a description of crime prevention and drug and alcohol abuse programs available to the campus community; (4) a listing of any policies that encourage accurate and prompt reporting of crime to the appropriate police agencies; (5) a description of programs designed to inform students and employees about campus security and encourage them to be responsible for their own security; (6) campus policies regarding law enforcement relating to drug and alcohol use; (7) a policy statement about how local police monitor criminal activity at off-campus, institution-recognized student organizations; (8) notification of where individuals may obtain information about registered sex offenders, and (9) the school's campus crime statistics for the previous three years.

Statistics must be released for the following crimes and violations: murder, rape or other sex offense (both forcible and non-forcible), robbery, aggravated assault, burglary, motor vehicle theft, manslaughter, arson and certain hate crimes. Where an arrest or disciplinary referral is made, a school must also report statistics concerning: liquor law violations, drug law violations and weapons possession. In 2008, President Bush signed legislation adding four new criminal offenses to the hate crimes list: intimidation; larceny-theft; destruction, damage or vandalism of property; and simple assault.[46] Statistics must be compiled for incidents that occur "on campus, in or on a noncampus building or property and on public property...within the same reasonably contiguous geographic area of an institution." All occurrences that were reported to campus security authorities (which, by federal regulation, includes "any official of the institution that has significant responsibility for student and campus activities...but who do not have significant counseling responsibilities") and local police agencies must be included in the report. The school must distinguish criminal offenses that occur on campus, in or on an off-campus building or property, on public property, and in student dorms.

Daily Campus Police/Security Log
Under the Clery Act, any covered institution with a police or security department must "make, keep and maintain a daily log, written in a form that can be easily understood, recording all crimes reported" to that department. Unlike the statistical report, *all* crimes reported to the campus police or security department must be included in the daily log. There is no set list of crimes. Also, off-campus crimes that occur "within the patrol jurisdiction" of the campus security office are reportable. The information recorded must include the nature, date, time, general location of each crime and the disposition of the complaint, if such information is known. The crimes must be included on the daily public log within two days of the initial report, except where disclosure is prohibited by law or would jeopardize the confidentiality of the victim. The department must also update a log entry within two days after receiving new information about an incident in the log. However, if the release of such information clearly would jeopardize an ongoing criminal investigation or an individual's safety, cause a suspect to flee or lead to the destruction of evidence, the information may be withheld until the release of the information is no longer likely to lead to such consequences.

Timely Reports
In addition to the annual statistical report and daily log, the Clery Act imposes two directives that require campus officials to disseminate information about ongoing threats to students. First, the act requires that schools make "timely reports to the campus community on crimes from statistical crime list above considered to be a threat to other students and employees ... ."The statute does not define "timely reports" and the Department of Education has stated that the need for such reports much be decided on a case-by-case basis.

In the wake of recent campus shootings, an additional provision was added to the law in August 2008 requiring campuses to publish policies that include procedures to "immediately notify the campus community upon the confirmation of a significant emergency or dangerous situation" that threatens the health or safety of individuals on campus, "unless issuing a notification will compromise efforts to contain the emergency."

This new provision supplements, but does not replace, the "timely" reporting requirement.

Who is Covered: All institutions — public and private — receiving federal financial assistance (for example, federal work-study or grants and National Direct Student Loans).

How to Use it: The mechanics for obtaining the information depend on what you are looking for. Schools generally can comply with the reporting requirements by publishing the information on the Internet, provided that any individuals required or entitled to receive the information are notified of its online availability and given the exact Internet address where the reports can found. Paper copies must also be made available on request.

Annual Campus Security Report
The law requires that schools "prepare, publish and distribute" the annual security report to all current students and employees and to any school applicant who requests the information. The actual reports compiled by schools have taken many forms, from a no-frills mailing to a full-color, tabloid-sized brochure complete with poster-size maps and safety tips. Other schools are reportedly including the required information in existing campus publications, like school catalogues or student handbooks or via the Internet. Additionally, the *Chronicle of Higher Education* and the U.S. Department of Education[47] compile comprehensive lists of crime statistics that are publicly available.

Daily Campus Police/Security Log
While it is not necessary for schools to affirmatively distribute their daily crime log, logs for the most recent 60 days must be physically available on request for public inspection during the police or security department's normal business hours. Archived logs older than 60 days must be made available within two days of a request being made. The Department of Education has specified "crime logs must be kept for three years following the publication of the last annual security report to which they apply" (in effect, seven years).[48]

Timely Reports
Unfortunately — though debate continues on the issue[49] — as this book went to press neither the law nor the regulations provided much guidance as to what will or will not qualify as a timely report. However, the statute does state that a report must "be provided to students and employees in a manner that is timely and that will aid in the prevention of similar occurrences."[50] It is clear, therefore, that schools have an obligation to notify the campus community of a threat quickly and actively. It certainly can be argued that alerting campus news media would be a fundamental part of any reasonable notification process. Furthermore, as institutions are now required to create and disseminate a policy of "immediate" notification of emergencies and dangerous situations, a reporter could assert that any delay is a violation of that policy.

Penalties for Noncompliance: Schools that do not comply with the Clery Act — which would include providing inaccurate information — risk being fined up to $27,500 for each violation and could lose their eligibility for federal aid. The Department of Education has been charged with monitoring schools' compliance with the Clery Act and has taken action against a number of schools in recent years, including a record fine of $350,000 assessed against Eastern Michigan University in 2007.[51] Individuals who believe their school is not accurately providing the required information should file a written complaint with their Regional Office of the Department of Education. (It does not appear that the Act gives an individual who is denied crime information the right to go to court or appeal the denial administratively, although that right may exist under state open-records law.)

When bringing a complaint to the DOE, provide a summary of your situation and any evidence of the school's noncompliance. Follow your letter with a telephone call confirming that your complaint was received and asking if any further information is required. Carefully document all contact with the Department and ask to be notified of the agency's findings. Contact the Student Press Law Center and your members of Congress if you have any problems with the Department of Education's response. More information about the Clery Act is available in the Student Press Law Center's publication, *Covering Campus Crime: A Handbook for Journalists*, which can be downloaded free from the SPLC website.[52]

Freedom of Information Tool: State Campus Crime Statistics Law

Type of Information Available: These laws are the state versions of the federal Clery Act, discussed above, which require schools to compile and release statistical information regarding campus crime. The advantage to some of these laws is that they may require schools to report more information than required by the federal law (for example, more or different categories of crime, crimes from a broader geographic area, or more detailed descriptions of criminal incidents). As of the spring of 2013 at least sixteen states (California,[53] Connecticut,[54] Delaware,[55] Florida,[56] Kentucky,[57] Louisiana,[58] Massachusetts,[59] Nevada,[60] New York,[61] Pennsylvania,[62] Rhode Island,[63] Tennessee,[64] Texas,[65] Virginia,[66] Washington[67] and Wisconsin[68]) had some form of campus crime statistics statutes on the books.

Who is Covered: Varies by state. Some states clearly limit the reporting requirements to public schools; other laws either explicitly include private schools or contain language that would appear to do so (for example, "each institution of higher education").

How to Use it: Varies by state. Some laws require schools to actively distribute the information to students, faculty, etc. Other laws require only that the information be made available on request.

Penalties for Noncompliance: Varies by state. Some states have made failure to comply with the law a crime, punishable by fine. Other states have put little "bite" in their respective laws. Students in these states would probably be limited to obtaining a court order compelling a school to release the information.

Freedom of Information Tool: State Campus Police Log Laws

Type of Information Available: These laws are the state versions of the open campus crime log provision in the federal Clery Act, discussed above, but in some cases require more detailed or different information than the federal law. In general, these laws require — in unambiguous language — that campus police forces maintain and provide public access to their records. While most state open record laws would provide much of the same information at public schools, these laws head off any attempt by school officials to argue that they are exempt. Currently, California,[69] Georgia,[70] Kentucky,[71] Massachusetts,[72] Pennsylvania,[73] Tennessee,[74] Virginia[75] and West Virginia[76] have such laws on the books. North Carolina joined the club in 2013, enacting a statute that requires private college police to disclose the same information as any other law enforcement agency, including the circumstances surrounding any arrest.[77] Oklahoma passed a law that, while not explicitly requiring schools to open their crime logs, does classify both public and private school police forces as "public agencies,"[78] which could indicate they must comply with Oklahoma's Open Records Law.

Who is Covered: Varies by state. One of the key features of the laws passed so far is that they apply to both public and private schools. In California, schools with less than 1,000 students are exempt.

How to Use it: Varies by state. In Kentucky, Massachusetts, Pennsylvania, Tennessee and Virginia, a person need only show up at the campus police office during regular business hours and request access to the police log. Kentucky's law also requires that the information be available online. In West Virginia, school officials must make crime information available within 10 days of the crime being reported. In California, school officials must make crime information available to an individual within two business days of that person's request.

Penalties for Noncompliance: The Kentucky, Massachusetts, North Carolina, Pennsylvania, Tennessee, Virginia and West Virginia laws do not include provisions that penalize school officials for noncompliance. Those seeking to enforce the provisions in these states are presumably limited to obtaining a court injunction ordering disclosure. The California law allows an individual to sue an institution for up to $1,000 if it fails to provide the required information.

Freedom of Information Tool: Campus Sexual Assault Victims' Bill of Rights [20 U.S.C. Sec. 1092(f)(8)]

Type of Information Available: This freedom of information tool — a companion to the Clery Act, discussed above — may provide student journalists with a look at what goes on behind the closed doors of an on-campus disciplinary body in cases involving sexual assault. In such cases, this law requires that a school provide information regarding the outcome of an on-campus disciplinary action to both the accused and accuser. Furthermore, the annual campus crime report required by the Clery Act (discussed above) must include a statement outlining the school's programs to prevent and respond to sexual assaults. The statement must address the availability of educational programs intended to heighten awareness of rape and acquaintance rape, what students should do if a sex offense occurs, the on-campus disciplinary procedures involved and the possible penalties for committing a sex offense.

Who is Covered: All institutions receiving federal financial assistance (for example, federal work-study or grants and National Direct Student Loans), which will include many private institutions.

How to Use it: While the law does not require that the information be released directly to the public, journalists have the opportunity to contact an accused or accuser, if their identities are known, and ask if they will agree to have the information reported. In the past, journalists often found that their hands were tied for lack of information, even when an apparent victim of sexual assault wanted her story told. Further, because the law also requires schools to inform students of their option to report the incident to the local, off-campus police, it is likely that more information regarding sexual assault on campus may be available through normal police reporting channels.

Penalties for Noncompliance: Schools that do not comply risk losing their eligibility for federal aid. Violations should be reported to their Regional Office of the U.S. Department of Education.

Freedom of Information Tool: Campus Sex Crimes Prevention Act [42 U.S.C. Sec. 14071j; 20 U.S.C. Sec. 1092(f)(1)(I); 20 U.S.C. Sec. 1232g(b)(7)(A)]

Type of Information Available: This law, which amended the Violent Crime Control and Law Enforcement Act of 1994, calls for the tracking of convicted, registered sex offenders who are students at colleges and universities or working on campus. The legislation, which became effective in October 2002, requires registered sex offenders to provide notice to higher education institutions when they are enrolled or working on campus. Such notice must be reported to local law enforcement agencies. Additionally, the law partially amends the federal Clery Act and requires institutions of higher education to issue a statement (which can be accomplished by inserting it into the school's annual crime report) advising the campus community where residents can obtain information about sex offenders on campus. The law also amends the Family Educational Rights and Privacy Act (FERPA) to make clear that the statute does not prohibit release of data on registered sex offenders.

Who is Covered: All institutions receiving federal financial assistance (for example, federal work-study or grants and National Direct Student Loans).

How to Use it: Most schools probably will make information about campus sex offenders available in their campus police or security department office or post it online. Your annual campus security report — which the school must give to each student — will have more information about how to obtain records.

Penalties for Noncompliance: Schools that do not comply risk losing their eligibility for federal aid.

Freedom of Information Tool: Student Right-to-Know Act: Completion/Graduation Rates; Accreditation/ Academic Standards, Student Indebtedness [20 U.S.C. Sec. 1092(a)-(d); *see also* 34 CFR 668.41 and 668.45]

Type of Information Available: This law was passed in large part to combat the growing default rate on government-insured financial aid. It requires that colleges submit a report to the Secretary of Education that includes: (1) the identity of and procedures used by an institution's accrediting or licensing body; (2) academic standards adopted by a school; (3) student completion and/or graduation rates; (4) student financial aid deferment policies; (5) average indebtedness of students receiving federal aid, including average monthly payments; (6) the cost of attending the institution, including tuition, estimated room and board, fees, books, and estimated transportation costs; (7) the availability of financial aid and the methods of award and disbursal; and (8) students' responsibilities upon receiving financial aid.

Who is Covered: All institutions participating in federal financial aid programs (such as federal work-study and grants and National Direct Student Loans).

How to Use it: Colleges are required to give the information to students and prospective students, their parents, high school coaches and high school counselors upon request. Also, the national reports are made available by the Department of Education, which must compile various reports showing how schools rank nationally.

Penalties for Noncompliance: Colleges that do not comply risk losing their eligibility for federal aid.

Freedom of Information Tool: Student Right-to-Know Act: Completion/Graduation Rates for Student, Athletes, Athletic Scholarship Information [20 U.S.C. Sec. 1092(e). *See also* 34 CFR 668.41 and 668.48]

Type of Information Available: This section of the Student Right-to-Know Act was passed to remedy the perceived abuse surrounding athletic scholarships and other financial aid. It requires that colleges annually report the following information to the Secretary of Education: (1) the number of students receiving athletically related aid, broken down by race and sex, who participate in basketball, football, baseball, cross country/track, and all other sports combined; (2) total number of students at the school, broken down by race and sex; (3) completion or graduation rate of students receiving athletic aid, again broken down by race, sex and sport; (4) completion or graduation rates of all students, broken down by race and sex; (5) average completion or graduation rates for the four most recent classes of those receiving athletically related financial aid, broken down by race, sex and sport; and (6) average completion or graduation rate for the four most recent classes of all students, broken down by race and sex.

Who is Covered: All institutions participating in federal financial aid programs (such as federal work-study and grants, and National Direct Student Loans). Schools that already publish the required athletic scholarship information do not have to duplicate it.

How to Use it: The school must provide enrolled students, prospective student athletes, parents, guidance counselors and coaches with an annual report by July 1 of each year. The report must include the one-year period ending August 31 of the preceding year. If a school is a member of an athletic conference or association that already requires substantially similar reporting, that data may be substituted for the report to the Department of Education and should be readily available from the athletic conference or association. (For example, the National Collegiate Athletic Association requires that member schools make graduation rate data available to the public and compile that data into publicly available reports.) Also, once this information is submitted to the Department of Education, the Department must compile various reports showing how schools rank nationally.

Penalties for Noncompliance: Colleges that do not comply with the Student-Right-to-Know Act risk losing their eligibility for federal aid.

Freedom of Information Tool: Equity in Athletics Disclosure Act of 1994 [20 U.S.C. Sec. 1092(g); *see also* 34 C.F.R. 668.41 and 668.47; 60 Fed. Reg. 61,424 (Nov. 29, 1995), 64 Fed. Reg. 43,581 (Aug. 10, 1999), and 64 Fed. Reg. 59,060 (Nov. 1, 1999)]

Type of Information Available: This federal law requires schools to compile an annual report detailing revenues and expenditures that can be attributed to their athletic programs. "Revenues" specifically include gate receipts, payments for broadcast rights, concessions and advertising. Reportable expenses include, for example, grants-in-aid, salaries, travel, equipment and supplies. The school must also break down the ratio of male to female aid, spending on men's and women's teams, the average salaries paid to head and assistant coaches of men's teams and the average salaries paid to head and assistant coaches of women's teams. The report will also include the total revenues and expenditures for football, men's basketball, women's basketball, all other men's sports combined, and all other women's sports combined. Additionally, the information must detail the number of male and female full-time undergraduates at the school, the number of participants on each varsity team, a gender breakdown of head and assistant coaches of varsity teams and the amount spent on recruiting for men's and women's teams.

Who is Covered: All co-ed postsecondary schools that participate in a federal financial aid program (such as federal work-study and grants and National Direct Student Loans), have an intercollegiate athletic program and offer athletically related financial aid.

How to Use It: There is no regulation indicating where the report must be made available. The Department of Education suggested that if copies were left at the intercollegiate athletic offices, admissions offices, libraries or sent to each student by e-mail, this requirement would be satisfied. Students, prospective students, parents or coaches may not be charged for this information. Members of the public can be charged reasonable copy fees.

The Department recommends that notice of the reports' availability be given at least once annually in a widely circulated school publication, such as an institution bulletin or newsletter. Alternatively, the information can be found online at http://ope.ed.gov/athletics/, or it should be available by submitting a request under the federal Freedom of Information Act.

Penalties for Noncompliance: Schools that do not comply risk losing their eligibility for federal financial assistance.

Freedom of Information Tool: Disclosure of Foreign Gifts [20 U.S.C. Sec. 1011f]

Type of Information Available: This law requires colleges or universities to disclose information to the Department of Education about their relationship with certain "foreign sources," which includes foreign governments, businesses and individuals — or agents of any of the above. Where required, the disclosure report will indicate how much money came from contracts or gifts attributable to a particular country, a description of any conditions or restrictions placed on the gift or contract and, if applicable, the date on which the foreign source assumed ownership or control of the institution and any changes in program or structure resulting from the change in ownership or control.

Who is Covered: Any public or private postsecondary institution. The law requires a disclosure report from: (1) any institution owned or controlled by a foreign source or (2) any institution that receives a gift or enters into a contract with a foreign source, the value of which is $250,000 or more, considered alone or in combination with all other gifts from or contracts with that foreign source within a calendar year. Some states also have their own versions of the law. Connecticut,[79] Missouri,[80] New York,[81] Pennsylvania,[82] and Texas,[83] for example, have similar provisions, with some lowering the threshold amount for reporting to less than $250,000.

How to Use it: The law states that, once submitted, all disclosure reports become public record and are available for inspection and copying at the Department of Education during normal business hours. Alternatively, you may submit a written request to the Department.

Penalties for Noncompliance: The federal government can sue schools that fail to comply. If a violation is found, the school will be required to reimburse the government for all court costs, legal fees and all other costs associated with the government's investigation and enforcement action.

Freedom of Information Tool: Federal Non-Profit Tax Returns (Internal Revenue Service Form 990) [26 U.S.C. Secs. 6104, 6652(c), 6685; see also 26 CFR 301.6104(d)-1 through 301.6104(d)-3]

Type of Information Available: Private school student journalists, in particular, should know how to use this powerful freedom of information tool. The IRS Form 990 and the supporting schedules that go with it disclose a wealth of information about the inner workings of tax exempt bodies — information you probably cannot obtain elsewhere. The following examples of information reported on the Form 990 should pique your interest: (1) the amount of money the organization has taken in each year (including grants), with a breakdown indicating the general sources and amounts of that money; (2) a comprehensive listing of where the money was spent, how much was spent and for what; (3) a detailed balance sheet indicating both the assets and liabilities of the organization at the end of each fiscal year; (4) information on the sale or purchase of the organization's investments (such as stock portfolios, bonds, trusts and endowment funds) and how they have fared each year; (5) the identities and salaries of the top organization employees, consultants and professional service providers making more than $50,000 a year and (6) any legal fees paid by the organization.

Who is Covered: Tax-exempt organizations, such as private schools, college foundations, charities and non-profit corporations. Most religious organizations — including church-affiliated secondary schools — are not required to file a Form 990 (although most religiously affiliated colleges and universities do), nor are organizations whose gross receipts are less than $25,000 per year.

How to Use it: Changes to the law — and the Internet — have made obtaining a Form 990 easier than ever. By law, copies of a tax-exempt organization's Form 990 and supporting documents can be obtained through the Internal Revenue Service, inspected on the institution's premises or, increasingly, acquired online. Because of the time involved in obtaining a copy from the IRS (up to three months), it is suggested you first go to the organization itself or use the Internet. Federal law requires that the organization make both its application for recognition of tax-exempt status and its annual information returns (Form 990 and supporting documents) for at least the last three years available to the public upon request either in person or by mail.

To make an in-person request, contact the organization's business office during regular business hours. Ask to inspect the form or ask to be directed to the office where the form is kept. The organization must allow you to inspect the form and take notes. Unless the form can be easily obtained on the Internet, copies must be provided on request, although a reasonable photocopying fee may apply. Except in unusual circumstances, the law requires that you be allowed to inspect and obtain a copy of an organization's Form 900 on the same day you make your request. If you encounter reluctance, you should submit a written request, citing the law (including the penalties for noncompliance, discussed below) and stating that you will go to the IRS if denied access. You may also wish to send a copy of your request to the organization's attorney.

If your request is solely by mail (or e-mail), the organization has 30 days to mail you a copy of the form.

If you are searching online, a helpful website to consult is www.guidestar.org. After a free, quick registration process, GuideStar allows users to view copies of many schools' (or any other tax-exempt organization, such as a university foundation's) 990 forms and other information. Though GuideStar is not an official government site, it provides a way to obtain this information faster than through traditional channels. To obtain a copy of the form from the IRS, contact the IRS Service Center that serves your state. The Student Press Law Center guide, *IRS Form 990: A Public Record for the Private School Journalist*, describes the 990 form and its use in greater detail.

Penalties for Noncompliance: If you are refused access to all or part of the form by an organization, keep a careful written record of who turned you down and when and how it occurred. Organizations can be fined $20 per day (up to $10,000) for noncompliance.[84] Moreover, where the denial is "willful," the individual responsible may also be fined $5,000 for each document he or she refused to provide.[85] Official complaints — along with supporting documentation — should be sent to the district director of the IRS Key District Office in which the organization is located.

Freedom of Information Tool: Family Educational Rights and Privacy Act (FERPA), also known as the "Buckley Amendment" [20 U.S.C. Sec. 1232g; *see also* 34 CFR 99]

Type of Information Available: Most student journalists have encountered FERPA only as a roadblock to access. But the law has two sides. First, FERPA penalizes schools that release a student's "education records" to outsiders without that student's permission (or, if the student is a minor living at home, the student's parents) by withholding federal funds from educational institutions that routinely release such information. The other side of the law, however, requires that schools release a student's own "education records" to the student upon request. Further, students have a right to ask that the school correct or delete any information contained in their records that the student believes to be inaccurate, misleading or an invasion of privacy. For example, despite a vigorous protest from schools, FERPA was used by some students to gain access to their own admissions files, providing them with information on the selection criteria used by schools in granting or denying offers of admission.[86] (Note, however, that if a student voluntarily waives his right to see a record — such as a recommendation letter written by a faculty member — FERPA will not apply.)

Still, for the purposes of student media, FERPA will more often be an impediment to access and news-gathering. Schools and colleges have taken to aggressively classifying records as exempt from disclosure, even when they contain no educational information and even when their contents are already widely known. While journalists have had some successes in pushing back against the mischaracterization of documents as "confidential education records,"[87] those battles have required considerable waste of time and money.

As the misuse of FERPA to obstruct the public's right to know has become increasingly well-documented, calls on Congress to reform FERPA have heightened — including calls from the law's namesake sponsor, former senator James Buckley.[88]

Who is Covered: Faculty, administrators, employees or the "agents" of any educational agency or institution that receives any type of federal funding (including student work study grants). This includes all public colleges and high schools, virtually all private colleges and most private high schools.

How to Use it: To obtain your own education records, you may want to first try an informal verbal request in person. If an in-person request is not feasible (for example, because of distance) — and any time such a request has been denied — a formal written request should be submitted. (The sample freedom of information request letter in the Appendix may be used as your model). Be sure to include in your letter any information that would assist the record keeper in locating your records, such as your Social Security number, a special school I.D. number, the dates of attendance and any alternative name or names under which your records would be kept. Your request should reasonably describe the records you are seeking (although a request asking for the contents of your permanent academic file probably would be sufficient) and be sent to the person or department at your school responsible for keeping that information. While policies vary, elementary and secondary schools typically transfer education records to a central location after a few years. Therefore, it may be worth a telephone call to the school or district to determine where old files are kept. The law requires that schools provide access to the records within 45 days.

Penalties for Noncompliance: Schools that do not comply risk losing their eligibility for federal financial assistance.

ENDNOTES

1   *See, e.g., Cincinnati Enquirer v. Cincinnati Bd. of Educ.*, 249 F.Supp.2d 911 (S.D. Ohio 2003) (rejecting newspaper's contention that the First Amendment entitled journalists to obtain resumes of candidates considered for superintendent of Cincinnati Public Schools); *see also Houchins v. KQED, Inc.*, 438 U.S. 1, 16 (1978) (Stewart, J., concurring) ("The First and the Fourteenth Amendments do not guarantee the public a right of access to information generated or controlled by government, nor do they guarantee the press any basic right of access superior to that of the public generally. The Constitution does no more than assure the public and the press equal access once government has opened its doors.").
2   *McBurney v. Young*, 133 S.Ct. 1709, 1718 (2013) ("This Court has repeatedly made clear that there is no constitutional right to obtain all the information provided by FOIA laws.").
3   ISOO 2011 *Annual Report to the President* (May 18, 2012), *available* on the National Archives website at: http://www.archives.gov/isoo/reports/2011-annual-report.pdf (last visited June 2, 2013).
4   Steven Aftergood, "The Perils of Government Secrecy," *Issues in Science and Technology*, Vol. 8, No. 4, Summer 1992, p. 82.
5   Benjamin Wittes, "The Cold War Is Over, So Who Are We Keeping All Those Secrets From?" *Washington City Paper*, December 3, 1993, p. 23.
6   The National Security Archive (Washington, DC), *Document of the Month* memorandum, July 28, 1993.
7   The National Security Archive (Washington, DC), *Document of the Month* memorandum, August 27, 1993.
8   The Reporters Committee for Freedom of the Press, *Agents of Discovery: A Report on the Incidence of Subpoenas Served on the News Media in 2001* (2001) (Arlington, VA), *available at* http://www.rcfp.org/sites/default/files/agents-of-discovery.pdf (last visited Sept. 15, 2013).
9   *Wittes, supra*, at 25 (emphasis in original).
10 The National Freedom of Information Coalition maintains a list and summaries of the results from the various state FOI law audits/surveys at: http://www.nfoic.org/foi-audits (last visited June 2, 2013).
11 Jill Riepenhoff & Todd Jones, "Secrecy 101," *The Columbus Dispatch*, Dec. 17, 2010 at A1.
12 Society of Professional Journalists news release, "SPJ announces winner of 2013 Black Hole Award," March 22, 2013, *available at* http://www.spj.org/news.asp?REF=1158 (last visited June 2, 2013).
13 A list of citations for each of the state open record and open meeting laws is available on the SPLC website at: http://www.splc.org/openrecordlaws
14 Freedom of information laws typically include a fairly expansive definition of "public body" that encompasses most governmental agencies, particularly those in the executive branch. (The federal FOIA does not apply to judicial and legislative bodies. The same holds true under some state sunshine laws.) In an interesting case, the Texas Attorney General found that a public college student newspaper was not a "governmental body" under that state's open records law and thus was not required to disclose reporters' notes and recordings from an investigation into alleged misconduct by student government officials. Student government officials at the University of Texas at Tyler, upset with stories in *The*

Patriot student newspaper detailing alleged campus voting rule violations, had filed a formal freedom of information request for the information. Tex. A.G. OR2001-2594 (June 19, 2001).

15 Conn. Gen. Stat. Sec. 1-215.

16 29 Del. C. Sec. 10002(g)(4) (exempting "all criminal records and files," except for one's own, from public disclosure).

17 Jeanne Clery Disclosure of Campus Security Policy and Campus Crime Statistics Act, 20 U.S.C. Sec. 1092(f).

18 *Id.*

19 *Id.*

20 20 U.S.C. Sec. 1092(a)-(d).

21 20 U.S.C. Sec. 1092(g).

22 20 U.S.C. Sec. 1232g.

23 *The Washington Post* reported that the Environmental Protection Agency gave Utah State University an $800,000 grant to study the impact of bovine flatulence on global warming. *The Washington Post*, June 21, 1994, A15.

24 5 U.S.C. Sec. 552.

25 5 U.S.C. Sec. 552a.

26 5 U.S.C. Sec. 552.

27 http://www.splc.org/foiletter.

28 A few states have carved out exceptions to disclosure for motor vehicle accident records, because of concerns that the reports could be used by personal-injury lawyers and others to track down car-crash victims for marketing purposes. But even in those states, legitimate news reporters should be allowed access to accident reports. *See, e.g.*, Georgia Code Ann. Sec. 50-18-72(a)(4.1) (limiting access to motor vehicle accident reports to specified requesters, including representatives of news media organizations).

29 Among the most active and successful of these groups has been the Clery Center for Security on Campus (formerly Security on Campus Inc.), a group founded by Connie Clery and her late husband Howard after their daughter Jeanne was murdered in her dorm at Lehigh University in 1986. For more information, visit the Clery Center for Security on Campus website at: http://clerycenter.org (last visited August 25, 2013).

30 http://www.splc.org/ccc.

31 20 U.S.C. Sec. 1232(g).

32 *See, e.g.*, *Bd. of Trustees, Cut Bank Pub. Sch. v. Cut Bank Pioneer Press*, 337 Mont. 229, 160 P.3d 482 (Mont. 2007) (holding, in suit brought by Montana newspaper under state constitution's "right-to-know" provision, that FERPA did not allow school to ignore state-law disclosure requirements and ordering school to turn over records reflecting outcome of disciplinary proceedings, with student names redacted, as requested by newspaper).

33 20 U.S.C. Sec. 1232g(b)(6)(B) states that the outcomes of campus disciplinary proceedings involving crimes of violence or nonforcible sex offenses are not covered by FERPA when the accused is found guilty in that proceeding. Among other things, the law specifically allows for the release of the accused's name and his or her punishment.

34 http://www.rcfp.org/foiact (last visited August 25, 2013).

35 http://nfoic.org/foi-center/ (last visited August 25, 2013).

36 http://www.rcfp.org/foi_letter/generate.php (last visited Sept. 15, 2013).

37 In late 2007, Congress passed and President George W. Bush signed amendments to FOIA, which, among other things, should make it easier for journalists to obtain attorney fees if a federal agency inappropriately denies records requests. OPEN Government Act of 2007, Pub. L. No. 110-175, 121 Stat. 2524 (2007) (to be codified at 5 U.S.C. Sec. 552).

38 http://www.splc.org/openrecordlaws.

39 http://www.rcfp.org/ogg (last visited August 25, 2013).

40 http://www.splc.org/foiletter.

41 "Public records ombudsmen mediate disputes between government officials, public," *News Media & the Law* (Spring 2005), p. 12.

42 The law defines an "agency" covered by the law as "any executive department, military department, Government corporation, Government controlled corporation, or other establishment in the executive branch of the Government (including the Executive Office of the President), or any independent regulatory agency...." 5 U.S.C. Sec. 552e.

43 http://rcfp.org/ogg (last visited August 25, 2013).

44 *See, e.g.*, *Bd. of Regents of the Regency Univ. Sys. v. Reynard*, 686 N.E.2d 1222 (Ill. Ct. App. 1997) (Athletic Council of Illinois State University — comprised of faculty, administrators and students who advise athletic department on compliance with NCAA requirements — is public body subject to Illinois' openmeetings and open-records acts, even though its decisions are advisory only); *Jackson v. Eastern Michigan Univ. Foundation*, 544 N.W.2d 737 (Mich. App. 1996) (university foundation is public body covered by Michigan's open-meetings and open-records statutes, because it received more than half of its money from state university and was empowered by university board of regents to exercise authority over university's endowment fund).

45 The following resources are particularly useful to student media seeking additional information about campus crime reporting and the Clery Act: *Covering Campus Crime*, Student Press Law Center, *available at* http://www.splc.org/ccc; *The Handbook for Campus Crime Reporting* (2005), U.S. Department of Education, *available at* http://www.ed.gov/admins/lead/safety/handbook.pdf (last visited August 25, 2013). In addition, the nonprofit group Security on Campus maintains a website at http://www.securityoncampus.org that includes news and information regarding campus crime and safety.

46 Higher Education Opportunity Act, Pub. L. No. 110-315 (2008) (amending 20 U.S.C. Sec. 1092(f)(1) (F)(ii)).

47 The U.S. Department of Education's Office of Postsecondary Education maintains the Campus Security Data Analysis Cutting Tool, an online database that allows users to obtain customized campus crime data of campus crime statistics. It is available on the DOE website at: http://ope.ed.gov/security/ (last

visited August 25, 2013).

48 The Handbook for Campus Crime Reporting (2005), U.S. Department of Education, p. 71.
49 In February 2008, the U.S. House of Representatives passed a bill 354-58 that would have clarified the definition of "timely reports" and required colleges and universities to issue public warnings within 30 minutes of a threat or emergency. College Opportunity and Affordability Act, H.R. 4137, 110th Cong. Sec. 488(b)(4) (2007). The language was not present in the final version of the bill, signed into law in August 2008. Higher Education Opportunity Act, Pub. L. No. 110-315 (2008) (amending 20 U.S.C. Sec. 1092(f) et seq.).
50 20 U.S.C. Sec. 1092(f)(3).
51 "Eastern Mich. U agrees to largest-ever fine for violations of crime reporting law," Student Press Law Center News Flash, June 6, 2008, *available at* http://www.splc.org/newsflash.asp?id=1769.
52 http://www.splc.org/ccc.
53 CALIF. ED. CODE Secs. 67380-67382.
54 CONN. GEN. STAT. Ann. Secs. 10a-55 - 10a-55c.
55 DEL. CODE Ann. tit. 14, Sec. 9001-07.
56 FLA. STAT. Ann. Sec. 1006.67.
57 KY. REV. Stat. Ch. 164.948; 164.9481-9487.
58 LA. REV. STAT. Ann. Sec. 17:3351C.
59 MASS. ANN. LAWS ch. 6, Sec. 168c.
60 NEV. REV. STAT. Sec. 396.329.
61 N.Y. EDUC. LAW Sec. 6433.
62 18 PA. STAT. Ann. Sec. 20.303.
63 R.I. GEN. LAWS 1956, Sec. 42-28-46.
64 TENN. CODE ANN. Secs. 49-7-2203 - 49-7-2205.
65 TEXAS EDUCATION CODE Ann. Sec 51.216.
66 VA. CODE ANN. Sec. 23-9.1:1.
67 WASH. REV. CODE Ann. Sec. 28B.10.569.
68 WIS. STAT. ANN. Sec. 36.11(22).
69 CALIF. ED. CODE Sec. 67380 (most public colleges and universities); 94380 (private colleges with enrollments over 1,000).
70 GA. CODE ANN. Sec. 20-8-7. *See also* Ga. Code Ann. Sec. 20-8-6 (requiring reporting of criminal gang activity near campus) and Ga. Code Ann. Sec. 35-3-36(i) (requiring all state or local criminal justice agencies to separately identify any victim who is a student, along with the name of the student's school).
71 KY. REV. STAT. Ch. 164.9481–9487.
72 MASS. ANN. LAWS ch. 41, Sec 98F.
73 18 PA. STAT. Ann. Sec. 20.303.
74 TENN. CODE Ann. Sec 49-7-2206.
75 VA. CODE Ann. 23-232.2.
76 W. VA. CODE Sec. 18B-4-5a.
77 N.C. SESSION LAW 2013-97.
78 OKLA. STAT. Ann. tit. 74, Sec 360.17(D).
79 CONN. GEN. STAT. Ann. Sec. 10a-150b-c.
80 MO. STAT. Ann. Sec. 173.275.
81 N.Y. EDUC. LAW Sec. 207-a.
82 24 PA. STATS. SEC. 6302.
83 TEX. EDUC. CODE Sec. 51.571-575.
84 26 U.S.C. Sec. 6652(c)(1)(C)-(D).
85 26 U.S.C. Sec. 6685.
86 *Buckley opens college admission sheets*, Student Press Law Center *Report*, Spring 1992, at 15.
87 *See, e.g., News & Observer Publ'g Co. v. Baddour*, No. 10-CVS-1941 (N.C. Super. Ct. Apr. 19, 2011) (ruling that neither cellphone records of football coaching staff nor parking tickets issued to student-athletes were covered by FERPA); *Poway Unif. Sch. Dist. v. Superior Court* (Copley Press), 62 Cal. App.4th 1496, 73 Cal.Rptr.2d 777 (Cal. App. 1998) (ordering disclosure of family's lawsuit notice sent to school district, which school attempted to withhold on the basis of FERPA). *But see, e.g., State ex rel. ESPN v. Ohio State Univ.*, 132 Ohio St.3d 212, 970 N.E.2d 939 (Ohio 2012) (deferring to university's classification of various athletic-department records involving alleged misconduct by student-athletes as FERPA records and permitting university to redact identifying information before disclosure).
88 *See, e.g.*, Rob Silverblatt, Note, "Hiding Behind Ivory Towers: Penalizing Schools that Improperly Invoke Student Privacy to Suppress Open Records Requests," 101 GEO. L.J. 493 (2013) (calling for Congress to impose financial penalties on institutions that knowingly misclassify documents as FERPA records to evade compliance with open-records requests); Mary Margaret Penrose, "Tattoos, Tickets, and Other Tawdry Behavior: How Universities Use Federal Law To Hide Their Scandals," 33 CARDOZO L. REV. 1555 (2012) (questioning athletic departments' use of open-ended "education records" definition to conceal documents that might expose embarrassing misconduct by athletes); Jill Riepenhoff & Todd Jones, "Secrecy 101: College athletic departments use vague law to keep public records from being seen," *The Columbus Dispatch*, May 31, 2009, at A1 (documenting results of nationwide open-records study in which colleges invoked FERPA to withhold even non-educational records such as lists of recipients of complementary football tickets, and quoting FERPA sponsor Buckley urging Congress to narrow the law to comport with its original intent). The Student Press Law Center has catalogued some of the more outlandish misuses of FERPA at http://ferpafact. tumblr.com.

CHAPTER 19

Advertising and Business Concerns

An ad manager at a public college student newspaper received the following ad:

> "**GET RICH** and experience the **ADVENTURE OF A LIFETIME** working in beautiful **ALASKA** this summer!!! Earn up to $1000 A WEEK. Companies begin hiring soon so act quickly! For more information, send $20 to: Alaska Summer Jobs, P.O. Box 555, Anchorage, Alaska 95555."

The advertiser wanted to run the ad weekly and was willing to pay the full amount in advance. But something smelled fishy. Could the paper legally publish such an advertisement the ad manager wondered?

ANSWER:
Yes. While the ad may seem full of sound and fury, it actually promises very little. Certainly no job is guaranteed. In this case, the ad merely provides an address where readers can write to obtain a list of Alaskan companies that hire summer help. Of course, readers may be able to obtain the same information for free on the Internet or at the library with a little effort. While charging $20 for this information may be excessive, it is not unlawful or misleading and — unless the ad manager specifically knows that the company is engaged in fraudulent behavior (for example, no list of companies is ever provided) — the newspaper would face no legal problems if it chose to publish the ad. While many student publications might not accept such an advertisement, the decision is an editorial one, not one compelled by the law.

Advertising is a vital part of most student media. According to a 2007 survey, more than one-half of college student newspapers obtained 50 percent or more of their funding from advertising revenue.[1] For high schools, a 1993 survey showed that almost nine out of ten student newspapers depended on ad revenue to at least some degree.[2] Given these numbers it is no wonder that legal questions about advertising are high on many student journalists' lists.

Student media frequently ask questions about what ads they can and cannot accept, about advertising guidelines, about billing — and, more than any other topic, about restrictions on advertising by school officials and others. This chapter will attempt to address these issues, focusing on the constitutional protections afforded advertising in student publications.

COMMERCIAL SPEECH AND THE FIRST AMENDMENT

As a starting point, the following two principles should be kept in mind when discussing the constitutional protections afforded commercial speech: (1) commercial speech is protected by the First Amendment; (2) commercial speech is entitled to less First Amendment protection than other constitutionally protected expression.

The U.S. Supreme Court has defined commercial speech as expression that "does no more than propose a commercial transaction,"[3] and which is "related solely to the

Did You Know? According to a 2007 survey, more than one-half of college student newspapers obtained 50 percent or more of their funding from advertising revenue. For high schools, a 1993 survey showed that almost nine out of ten student newspapers generated ad revenue.

Commercial speech is entitled to less First Amendment protection than over forms of speech. But not all advertising is considered commercial speech.

economic interests of the speaker and its audience."[4] Thus, commercial speech does not include all advertising. This is important because even though the First Amendment protects commercial speech, that protection is less than that afforded noncommercial speech, such as a traditional news story or opinion column. For example, the civil rights advertisement that was the subject of the libel claim in the landmark *New York Times Co. v. Sullivan*[5] case is an example of a noncommercial editorial ad that would not be subject to the lesser commercial speech standard. Other examples of noncommercial advertisements that may be of interest to student media are those whose primary message is the promotion of responsible drinking or safe sex, those that offer medical, legal or similar information or those that advance political beliefs. If an advertisement's primary purpose is to convey information or "sell" an idea or belief — as opposed to a product or service — the ad should be accorded the higher standard of First Amendment protection.[6]

NOTE TO PRIVATE SCHOOL STUDENTS

The First Amendment limits censorship only by government officials, or by those acting as an arm or extension of the government. It does not shield private school student media from censorship or regulation of advertising by their private high school or college administrators, although other forms of legal protection may be available. Outside of the issue of censorship, however, most other information in this chapter applies to public and private schools alike. For more information about the rights of private school student media, see Chapter 7.

A BRIEF HISTORY

It may come as a surprise to many, but until the mid-1970s, courts treated commercial speech as a type of expression not worthy of any First Amendment protection at all.[7] Prior to that period, courts allowed the government to regulate almost any type of advertising that had as its purpose the promotion of goods or services for sale. The rationale was that such speech was nothing more than crass commercialism. The hawkers of goods and services were not trying to express political viewpoints or new ideas, courts reasoned; they were merely trying to make money, and that kind of activity was unworthy of constitutional protection.

But beginning in 1973, the U.S. Supreme Court handed down a number of decisions restricting the power of government to prohibit or regulate commercial speech.[8] The landmark decision was *Bigelow v. Virginia*,[9] in which the Court struck down a Virginia law making it a crime for a publication to encourage abortion. Editor Jeffrey Bigelow was convicted under the statute after his commercial newspaper published an advertisement for a New York abortion referral agency. The advertisement, published in Virginia and distributed primarily on the campus of the University of Virginia, stated that abortions were legal in New York (they were then illegal in Virginia), and were available to nonresidents. In reversing Bigelow's conviction, the Court held, "[S]peech is not stripped of First Amendment protection merely because it appears [in the form of paid commercial advertisements]."[10] In subsequent decisions, the Supreme Court struck down state laws or regulations prohibiting the advertising of prescription drug prices,[11] advertising or display of contraceptives[12] and advertising of attorneys' services.[13]

The *Central Hudson* Test

Having ruled that the government's power to censor commercial speech was constitutionally limited, the next question for the Court was to determine how and where to draw the line. In its 1980 decision in *Central Hudson Gas & Electric Corp. v. Public Service Commission*,[14] the Supreme Court developed the following four-part test for determining when a state or someone acting on the government's behalf could

---

constitutionally restrict commercial advertising:

(1) *Is the speech protected by the First Amendment?* To be protected, commercial speech must concern lawful activity and must not be misleading. Commercial speech that is unlawful, false or misleading is not protected by the First Amendment and the government is free to regulate or prohibit it. Obvious examples of advertisements that school officials could prohibit include ads for illegal drugs or weapons, prostitutes, child pornography, or clear and serious invitations to participate in illegal activity (for example, an offer to take an exam for another student). (For a discussion of other special categories of ads that may be subject to regulation, see discussion beginning on page 355).

Once it is determined that the commercial speech at issue is entitled to First Amendment protection, the government can regulate that speech only where it is able to answer "yes" to each of the following questions.

In the *Central Hudson* case, the Supreme Court announced a four-part test for determining when the government may restrict commercial advertising.

(2) *Is the governmental interest in regulating the speech substantial?* The First Amendment requires that courts carefully weigh all government restrictions on speech. Therefore, before the government is permitted to restrict speech of any kind, it must show that its reasons for doing so are important. Restrictions on speech for trivial or petty reasons will be struck down. Courts have consistently found, for example, that school administrators have a substantial interest in ensuring the orderly operation of schools and in preventing student expression that creates a material and substantial disruption of school activities. On the other hand, a school official's interest in regulating commercial speech for goods or services that compete with those offered by the school or in restricting advertising that school officials consider an "eyesore" would be less substantial.[15]

(3) *Does the regulation directly advance that governmental interest?* Taken together, parts three and four are basically a test for the "fit" between why the government says it needs to regulate — its "end," or goal — and the means government officials have chosen to achieve that end. For example, suppose that a school board's goal is to eliminate gang activity in its high schools. While the board clearly has a substantial interest in reducing such behavior, a court must ask whether a ban on all advertisements from stores that sell the type of shoes worn by gang members would directly achieve their goal. For colleges, a question that comes up occasionally is whether banning alcohol-related advertising actually reduces illegal or irresponsible drinking by students.

(4) *Does the regulation reach no farther than necessary to advance that governmental interest?* Government regulations on speech should be carefully tailored to limit only that speech deemed problematic. Restrictions on speech will be struck down if, as the saying goes, they throw the baby out with the bath water. For example, if school officials want to censor an advertisement in a student newspaper because they are concerned it will appear that the school itself condones or approves of the ad's message, a court should ask whether there is a less drastic alternative available. Would publishing a prominent disclaimer in the student newspaper stating that the views it expresses are those of students and not school officials solve the problem without having to engage in censorship? In the example of the shoe store ad ban mentioned above, it is clear that prohibiting all ads from all stores that happen to carry the particular brand of tennis shoe goes far beyond the school's goal of discouraging the wearing of gang attire.

Central Hudson to Present: A Legal Roller-Coaster Ride

When *Central Hudson* was decided in 1980, it seemed clear to most legal experts at the time that the test provided substantial First Amendment protection to commercial speech. They were right. Unfortunately, it took a majority of the Supreme Court over a decade to come to the same conclusion.

Shortly after *Central Hudson* was decided, the Supreme Court issued a series of decisions that began to water down the decision's four-part test. The Court first turned its attention to part two of *Central Hudson* and indicated that government officials should have considerable leeway to determine for themselves — without interference from courts — whether they had a substantial interest in regulating a particular type of commercial speech.[16] The next round of decisions said the third part of *Central Hudson* required only that there be a "reasonable fit" between that interest and the means or regulations chosen to achieve their goal.[17] Finally — in what would be the low point for the First Amendment protection of commercial speech — the Court backed off *Central Hudson*'s fourth requirement that a regulation be the least restrictive means available and instead required only that any regulation be "narrowly tailored" to meet its goal.[18]

The pendulum began to swing back, however, beginning with the Court's 1993 decision in *City of Cincinnati v. Discovery Network, Inc.*[19] In that case, Cincinnati had banned newsracks dispensing advertising fliers but allowed those that dispensed newspapers. Noting that the advertising newsracks were "no greater an eyesore" than the newsracks that remained, the Court struck down the city ordinance.[20] The decision narrowed the "reasonable fit" requirement to a standard more in line with the original *Central Hudson* requirement. Justice Stevens, writing for the majority, criticized city officials for suggesting there was little First Amendment value in advertising handbills: "In our view, the city's argument attaches more importance to the distinction between commercial and noncommercial speech than our cases warrant and seriously underestimates the value of commercial speech."[21]

Since then, the Court has issued a series of decisions reaffirming and strengthening the four-part *Central Hudson* test and expressing its commitment to strong commercial free speech protections.[22]

For example, in several cases involving the marketing and advertising of alcohol, gambling and tobacco, the Court rejected arguments that the Court should simply defer to government regulators' discretion in controlling commercial speech about allegedly harmful, but legal, "vice" products or activities.[23] It is not the government's business, the Court has said, to restrict truthful, nonmisleading commercial information in an attempt to keep members of the public from making bad choices.[24]

Similarly, the Court made clear that the government cannot simply assert its interest in "protecting children" as its sole justification for banning otherwise lawful commercial speech. In striking down Massachusetts' regulations that prohibited certain forms of tobacco advertising within 1,000 feet of a school, the Court explained:

> The State's interest in preventing underage tobacco use is substantial, and even compelling, but it is no less true that the sale and use of tobacco products by adults is a legal activity. We must consider that tobacco retailers and manufacturers have an interest in conveying truthful information about their products to adults, and adults have a corresponding interest in receiving truthful information about tobacco products. In a case involving indecent speech on the Internet we explained that "the governmental interest in protecting children from harmful materials ... does not justify an unnecessarily broad suppression of speech addressed to adults."[25]

Rather than simply accepting the government's claim that it has a substantial interest in regulating commercial speech, as it suggested was appropriate in earlier cases and which allowed regulations to easily clear the second part of *Central Hudson*, the Court indicated that it will now first examine both the "quality" of the asserted government interests and the type of information sought to be suppressed.[26] The Court also suggested that part three of *Central Hudson* (which requires that a regulation directly advance a government interest) calls for the government to do more than simply state — without substantial evidence or proof — that advertising increases the demand for a harmful product and that regulating or restricting advertising will therefore advance the government's goal by limiting demand.[27] The government's burden under *Central Hudson*, the Court has said, "is not satisfied by mere speculation or conjecture; rather, a governmental body seeking to sustain a restriction on commercial speech must demonstrate that the harms it recites are real and that its restriction will in fact alleviate them to a material degree."[28]

Even more promising for free-speech proponents may be the Court's clarification that a government regulation will fail the fourth prong of *Central Hudson* — which requires that a regulation reach no farther than necessary to advance the asserted governmental interest — if there are other ways to accomplish its goals that would impose less or no burden on speech. As the Court stated: "We have made clear that if the Government could achieve its interests in a manner that does not restrict speech, or that restricts less speech, the government must do so.... If the First Amendment means anything, it means that regulating speech must be a last — not first — resort."[29]

Even though the Court has reversed course on its earlier lackluster defense of commercial speech and finally used *Central Hudson* to tighten the reins on would-be government regulators, a number of the justices on the Court have nevertheless indicated that commercial speech may be entitled to even greater First Amendment protection than *Central Hudson* provides. At least four of the nine current Supreme Court justices have, at various times, suggested some degree of willingness to abandon *Central Hudson* in favor of a more protective constitutional standard for commercial speech.[30] So the roller coaster continues. Fortunately, however, it appears to be headed up — at least for now.

THE IMPACT OF *HAZELWOOD* ON ADVERTISING IN HIGH SCHOOL STUDENT MEDIA

Because of the U.S. Supreme Court's 1988 decision in *Hazelwood School District v. Kuhlmeier*,[31] public high school students working on school-sponsored, non-public forum student media may face an additional censorship hurdle. For even where an advertisement is protected by the First Amendment under the traditional commercial speech test, high school officials still may try to argue that they have a valid educational reason for censoring it.

For example, in one of the first post-*Hazelwood* cases, a federal appeals court upheld a school district's right to ban pregnancy-related advertisements submitted to various high school publications.[32] The case arose after Nevada school officials rejected an advertisement submitted by Planned Parenthood, a family planning organization. Planned Parenthood sued. No students were involved in the case and the issue of student First Amendment rights was not raised. Still, the case may provide some useful guidance.

Both the advertiser and the school district agreed that the ad was protected speech under the First Amendment.[33] Nevertheless, citing *Hazelwood*, the court ruled that the school district's justification for refusing to publish the ad was reasonable to: (1) avoid the perception of school sponsorship and endorsement of an ad that some might find controversial, (2) avoid being forced to open up school publications to organizations having competing views and (3) avoid any conflict with a state-prescribed sex education curriculum.[34]

Though this decision upheld school censorship of advertising, it does not stand for the principle that school officials have the ability to censor any advertisement that they happen to disagree with or dislike. The *Hazelwood* decision — where it applies (remember not all high school student media are covered by it) — still requires that school administrators provide a reasonable educational justification for their censorship.[35] It also probably requires that the censorship be viewpoint-neutral.[36] For example, if a principal allows a political advertisement urging the passage of a school

The *Hazelwood* decision may allow restrictions on advertising in some high school publications when school officials can show that they have a reasonable educational justification for their censorship and that their censorship was not directed at a particular viewpoint.

tax, her subsequent censorship of an advertisement opposing the levy would likely be unconstitutional; she would not be permitted to censor the ad simply because she disagreed with the viewpoint it presented.

An understanding of the constitutional protections afforded commercial speech is important. Unfortunately, for many high school student journalists, it may not be enough. For a complete discussion regarding the impact of the *Hazelwood* decision on high school student media, see Chapter 5.

ADVERTISING IN THE COLLEGE MEDIA

Only a handful of cases have dealt specifically with advertising in college student media. Those decisions suggest that the First Amendment provides important protection for commercial speech and that public college student media are entitled to essentially the same legal protections as commercial and other privately owned media organizations.[37] A 1990 Michigan college case is a good illustration. A federal district court judge ruled that a state college official acted illegally when he told the school's student newspaper editor she could no longer publish an advertisement for a Canadian nude dancing club.[38] The ad noted that the Canadian drinking age was 19. (Michigan's drinking age was 21, and at the time of the case, state law prohibited totally nude dancing.)[39] The school claimed that it banned the ad because it was degrading to women, promoted underage drinking, and conflicted with the school's educational mission and values.[40]

The court applied the *Central Hudson* test. First, it found that the ad concerned lawful activity (as long as it took place in Canada, as the ad stated) and was not misleading. Second, the court did not dispute the school's claim that it had a substantial interest in protecting women from degradation and students from underage drinking. Turning to the final two prongs of *Central Hudson*, however, the court ruled that the school's regulation of advertising was "not narrowly tailored" to serve those interests. The court found that the school's attempt to regulate advertising was "anything but 'carefully designed.'"[41] With no advertising guidelines in place, school officials subjected the student newspaper to "virtual unbridled regulatory authority," and made no effort to distinguish harmful speech from harmless speech.[42] This, the court concluded, violated the newspaper editor's free press rights.

More recently, a federal appeals court in Virginia ruled that the state could not lawfully enforce a decades-old regulation on alcoholic beverage ads in college newspapers at schools like Virginia Tech and the University of Virginia, where most audience members are of legal drinking age. [43] The court held that, while the state does have a substantial interest in curbing underage drinking, banning alcohol ads in student media is an unconstitutionally broad remedy, because it represents an attempt by government to deny information to consumers about a product that, for most of them, is legal to buy and use.

INDEPENDENT STUDENT MEDIA AND THE RIGHT TO DISTRIBUTE COMMERCIAL SPEECH

Like public college media, "underground," or independent student media — at both the college and high school level — are entitled to significant commercial speech protection. However, in addition to banning specific advertisements, First Amendment battles can also arise when public school officials seek to ban entirely non-school sponsored publications from school grounds because they contain ads or because they are sold rather than given away free. Officials claim that such publications are nothing more than "commercial activity," and deserve no special treatment. (Schools probably have the power to prohibit or limit purely commercial activity such as the on-campus sale of candy, sweatshirts or concert tickets.[44])

While some regulation of the time, place and manner of distribution has been allowed[45], courts have typically rejected absolute bans, permitting both high school and college students either to sell or freely distribute independently produced student publications containing lawful advertisements on school grounds.[46] And while it would seem to be obvious, at least one court has explicitly ruled that administrators cannot prohibit the publishers of a non-school-sponsored publication from canvassing the community to sell ads.[47] In all of these cases, the courts recognized that unlike other types of moneymaking products and services, commercial speech contains opinions, facts and ideas, and thus enjoys First Amendment protection.

Such reasoning was evident in a 1992 Texas case where a federal court of appeals ruled that Southwest Texas State University officials could not prohibit the *Hays County Guardian*, a small, off-campus publication that concentrated on environmental and social justice issues, from distributing on school grounds just because the newspaper contained advertising.[48] The school claimed that banning the *Guardian* would prevent litter, congestion and invasions of privacy resulting from individuals being offered the newspaper as they walked across campus. The school also claimed that its regulations were necessary to maintain the "academic environment," because "unlimited distribution of newspapers, coupons, flyers, and the like throughout campus would create a circus atmosphere, destroying the unique quality of the University campus."[49]

The fact that a publication contains advertising does not mean it can be considered commercial speech.

The court flatly rejected the school's arguments, calling them "speculative."[50] It also found that the burden imposed on speech by the ban far outweighed the school's asserted interests. Importantly, the court refused to accept the school's argument that the *Guardian*'s acceptance of advertising automatically subjected the newspaper to less First Amendment protection than commercial-free publications. "[T]he Guardian is not commercial speech," the court wrote. "It is speech about matters of highest public concern — political and economic reform and the local and international environment. The advertisements in the Guardian were included to finance the publication. Under such circumstances, commercial speech was inextricably linked to the newspaper's noncommercial speech, making the whole paper non-commercial."[51]

"SPECIAL CASE" ADVERTISING

While the First Amendment creates important limitations on the right to restrict commercial speech, its protection is not absolute, and lawmakers and government agencies have enacted (and, in some cases, courts have upheld) various state and federal laws or regulations that restrict specific categories or types of advertising. Often the restriction is directed to the person or group placing the ad; in a few cases — such as in the case of certain discriminatory housing ads — the restriction applies to the advertisement's publisher. The following types of advertisements are among those that may be of special interest to student media.

Adoption/Egg Donor/Surrogacy

Given the age of their readers, it is not surprising that student media are frequently asked to publish ads from individuals seeking to adopt children or hoping to find willing egg donors or surrogate mothers.

An April 2012 survey found that approximately 30 states had enacted statutes that in some way regulated adoption ads.

According to an April 2012 survey by the Child Welfare Information Gateway,[52] approximately 30 states had enacted statutes that in some way regulated adoption ads, which may be construed in some states as also applying to egg donor advertisements or surrogacy arrangements: Alabama,[53] California,[54] Connecticut,[55] Delaware,[56] Florida,[57] Georgia,[58] Idaho,[59] Illinois,[60] Indiana,[61] Kansas,[62] Kentucky,[63] Louisiana,[64] Maine,[65] Massachusetts,[66] Mississippi,[67] Montana,[68] Nebraska,[69] Nevada,[70] New Hampshire,[71] North Carolina,[72] North Dakota,[73] Ohio,[74] Oklahoma,[75] Oregon,[76] Tennessee,[77] Texas,[78] Utah,[79] Virginia,[80] Washington State[81] and Wisconsin.[82] The language in most of the statutes appears to affect only the advertisers who place such ads, but the laws of at least six of these states — Florida, Kentucky, Nevada, Oklahoma, Washington and Wisconsin — address their applicability (or in the case of Nevada, inapplicability) to media organizations that publish the ad. A typical statute prohibits any person or organization — other than state-licensed adoption agencies — from advertising that the person or organization will adopt children or offer children to be adopted. To date, the constitutionality of these laws — and particularly their applicability to media — has not been tested in a published court decision testing their constitutionality.[83] Before running such ads, it would be wise to consult the particular law of your state.

Alcohol

Where a state's drinking age is 21, high school officials can almost certainly prohibit alcohol ads in their student media. Such a ban is more difficult to defend at the college level, however, where many (and usually most) readers are over 21, although courts have reached differing results.[84] This would be particularly true where colleges single out student publications for such a ban but allow the college bookstore or newsracks on campus to continue to distribute non-student publications that carry alcohol-related advertising (for example, *Time, Cosmopolitan* and local newspapers).

In short, a prohibition of alcohol ads targeting college students — the majority of whom are legal consumers of alcohol — appears to run contrary to the First Amendment. The Supreme Court has shown an increasing reluctance to allow regulatory restrictions on truthful, non-misleading commercial speech of legal products or services, even where the products or services themselves are subject to significant government regulation.[85] In *44 Liquormart, Inc. v. Rhode Island*, for example, the Court struck down a state ban prohibiting the advertisement of all liquor prices, except on price tags.[86] The Court found that while alcohol regulation serves a substantial government interest, regulations on alcohol advertising must be narrowly tailored to serve that interest.[87] While limiting underage drinking is a valid governmental concern, the Court recognized in a 2001 tobacco advertising case that "the governmental interest in protecting children from harmful materials . . . does not justify an unnecessarily broad suppression of speech addressed to adults."[88]

Because of the apparent strong legal protections shielding alcohol advertising in college student media from government regulation, some lawmakers have attempted to restrict alcohol ads in more "creative" ways. For example, in 1997 Pennsylvania passed Act 199, which prohibited liquor licensees from placing alcohol advertisements in campus publications.[89] While the law pointedly did not prohibit student media from running such ads, the effect, of course, was the same. The staff of *The Pitt News*, a University of Pittsburgh student newspaper that lost approximately $17,000 in ad revenue after the law went into effect, launched a legal battle to lift the statewide ban.[90] In 2004, then-appellate court judge Samuel Alito, later confirmed to the U.S. Supreme Court, authored the circuit's opinion striking down Act 199 and ruling that the law's very structure rendered it "presumptively unconstitutional."[91]

Even though government and school regulations restricting alcohol advertising by college media are rare and probably unconstitutional, alcohol advertising in student media — at least by major companies — nevertheless appears to be on the wane. After the Federal Trade Commission identified alcohol ads placed in campus newspapers as a "source of concern," the alcohol industry — partly in an effort to head off government intervention — adopted self-regulatory codes that limit the placement of alcohol advertising in media where underage drinkers make up a significant part of the readers or audience.[92] For instance, the Beer Institute amended its code in 2003 to require that adults over 21 constitute at least 70 percent of the audience for its member companies' ads.[93] The Wine Institute and Distilled Spirits Council flatly prohibit their members from advertising in college and university newspapers.[94] Additionally, some student media have voluntarily decided to forgo some or all alcohol advertising.

Recent court decisions suggest a prohibition of alcohol ads targeting college students — the majority of whom are legal consumers of alcohol — is contrary to the First Amendment.

Birth Control Products and Services

States cannot ban truthful advertisements for birth control products, abortion clinics or other pregnancy-related medical or counseling services, though high school student media subject to the Supreme Court's *Hazelwood* decision may, as explained above, face additional censorship hurdles from school administrators.[95] While such ads may offend individual sensitivities, they do not offer illegal products or services, and are therefore constitutionally protected.

Credit Card, Insurance Policy and Travel Ads in Nonprofit Mailings

Postal regulations prohibit mailing most credit card or debit card ads and travel arrangement ads at third-class, nonprofit postal rates, which is a common way of sending student newspapers and magazines to mail subscribers.[96] Unfortunately, the regulations — and the applicable exceptions — are rather confusing and not uniformly enforced. In 2003, a federal appellate court struck down postal regulations that had similarly restricted the mailing of publications containing insurance policy ads.[97] Because of the continuing confusion, a student newspaper that carries advertising for credit cards, debit cards or travel services may be well-advised to consult legal counsel before sending copies to subscribers through third-class mail.

Drug Paraphernalia

Even though drug-related paraphernalia (bongs, pipes, rolling papers, etc.) can legally be used for tobacco and may not be illegal in a particular jurisdiction, some courts have nevertheless upheld advertising restrictions for such products and the stores that sell them ("head shops") on the theory that drug paraphernalia ads encourage drug use, which is illegal everywhere.[98] At least one court has upheld a total ban on such advertisements in publications directed at high-school aged students.[99] Moreover, the Supreme Court ruled in 2007 that public high school officials have the authority to punish students for engaging in speech in connection with school-sponsored activities that advocates illegal drug use, which likely would include advertisements for merchandise or services closely tied to unlawful drug use.[100] Before accepting such an ad, it would be a good idea to check the status of your state and local law.

False or Deceptive Ads

As discussed above, the First Amendment does not protect advertisements that are misleading. In addition to losing their constitutional protection, advertisers that run false, deceptive or unfair ads may also incur the wrath of the Federal Trade Commission (FTC). The Federal Trade Commission Act makes it unlawful to publish false and misleading advertising.[101] Nearly all states have similar laws on the books. Note, however, that historically only the company or individual that placed the ad — and in a few cases the advertising agency that created the ad[102] — have been held subject to FTC regulations. Publishers (for example, a student newspaper or yearbook) that have played no role in creating the misleading content for the ad and had no knowledge of the ad's false or deceptive content when they published it have not been subject to FTC or state-law regulation.[103]

Where the FTC, acting on a complaint, determines that an ad is deceptive or unfair, it has the authority to require that the company either substantiate its claims or stop running the ad. It can also impose fines and seek civil penalties. In recent years, the FTC has been particularly aggressive in going after advertisers who have falsely promoted easy weight loss remedies, herbal cures and dietary supplements. While student media organizations will generally incur no liability for publishing false or deceptive ads, they should be aware of the potential repercussion to their reputation. (For more information regarding publisher liability, see discussion below.)

Employment (Help Wanted) Ads

While federal statutes do not prohibit the media from publishing discriminatory "Help Wanted" ads,[104] many state and local laws do. Such laws or ordinances typically prohibit discrimination in employment on the basis of race, religion, national origin, disability, place of birth, or gender except in cases where the reasonable qualifications of a job require such discrimination (for example, a Baptist church seeking a minister can require that applicants be Baptist).[105] Even where the laws prohibit only employers and employment agencies from publishing such ads, state and local agencies have occasionally attempted to charge newspapers with "aiding or abetting" those employers who do violate the law.[106]

Legal Notices

While few student publications run legal or public notices (for example, "Notices to Creditors," official "Notices of Public Hearings," etc.), it is important for any that do to check their state laws to determine whether the newspaper must meet any eligibility requirements prior to accepting or publishing such ads.[107]

Online Gambling

The legality of online gambling sites is still an open question.

Student media are urged to proceed cautiously before accepting advertisements for Internet-based gambling websites. The legality of online gambling sites is still an open question. The U.S. Justice Department has said that it believes online gambling is illegal under existing federal law, and federal and state lawmakers have and continue to propose new legislation that would outlaw Internet gambling or commercial transactions involving such activity. A 2007 summary at Gambling Law US found that eight states — Illinois,[108] Indiana,[109] Louisiana,[110] Montana,[111] Nevada,[112] Oregon,[113] South Dakota,[114] Washington[115] and Wisconsin[116] — had passed legislation specifically relating to Internet gambling.[117] Other states, including New York and Montana, have all-encompassing prohibitions that make all gambling illegal unless authorized by the state.[118] Proponents of Internet gambling argue that existing laws do not extend to Internet gambling operations, particularly those based offshore. The legal status of online gambling is important for if the underlying activity is deemed illegal, the First Amendment would offer little protection were school officials to prohibit future Internet gambling ads.

The scope and intent of the state laws vary. In most cases, the laws apply only to the gambling businesses themselves; student media likely would not be subject to penalty for publishing online gambling ads. However, the law of at least one state — Illinois — not only prohibits Internet gambling but also specifically declares it unlawful to advertise any gambling activity not sanctioned by the state.[119] In Georgia, a statute prohibits the advertising of all gambling, presumably including online gambling.[120] Arguably, such laws would apply only to advertisers, not publishers, though zealous prosecutors might attempt to hold publishers liable for aiding and abetting advertisers. Significantly, the constitutionality of applying such laws to publishers has yet to be tested.

In 2006, Congress passed the Unlawful Internet Gambling Enforcement Act (UIGEA), citing concerns that "traditional law enforcement mechanisms are often inadequate for enforcing gambling prohibitions or regulations on the Internet ... ."[121] While a person who runs a gambling site may not knowingly accept fees from a user who is violating a gambling ban in the user's location, the Act does not restrict advertising on its face, nor target players.[122] However, it does create a daunting atmosphere for Internet gambling site owners and operators who accept U.S. customers, as the laws of an individual customer's state may render the sites liable for violating UIGEA.[123]

Real Estate/Housing

The Civil Rights Act of 1968,[124] as amended in 1988, makes it unlawful to "make, print, or publish ... any ... advertisement, with respect to the sale or rental of a dwelling that indicates any preference, limitation, or discrimination based on race, color, religion, sex, handicap, familial status, or national origin, or an intention to make any such preference, limitation, or discrimination." This section applies to media publishers.[125]

Given their frequency in student media, advertisements for rental property pose a particular risk. Staff should watch for language or photographs that suggest a landlord will be selective based on any of the criteria set out above. For example, an ad could legally include a preference for "no pets," but not for "no children." An ad stating, "Tenants sought for Christian Apartment Complex," or even a series of ads containing photos showing only single, white professionals as would-be neighbors could also spell trouble. Note, however, that some of these statutory prohibitions may not apply in the context of roommate, or rent-to-share, ads. At least two states have indicated that the Civil Rights Act does not prevent newspapers from publishing ads that designate whether a male or female roommate is sought.[126] Additionally, the U.S. Department of Justice has issued an informal statement indicating that it "will not take legal action where sexual [gender] preferences are stated in ads involving shared living facilities, but such ads cannot legally include a preference or limitation based on race, religion, or national origin."[127]

> Federal law makes it unlawful for publishers to print housing ads that indicate a discriminatory preference based on race, color, religion, sex, handicap, familial status, or national origin.

Sex-Related Products or Services

As a rule, the First Amendment protects the advertisement of lawful, sex-related products and services. Regulations or laws enacted by state or local governments (and in at least one case, a college) to prohibit or limit such advertising generally have been struck down. For example, courts have rejected attempts to limit ads for sex toys,[128] adult theaters and bookstores,[129] strip clubs[130] and adult escort and massage services[131] where the ads did not solicit illegal activity. The Supreme Court has suggested that the First Amendment does not allow for restrictions on otherwise lawful "vice" activities simply because they might be deemed harmful by the government.[132] Of course, high school student media must exercise good judgment in deciding whether any such ad could be appropriate for an under-18 audience, and must also contend with the censorship authority given to school officials under the *Hazelwood* standard, where applicable.

Term Papers

A number of states have enacted laws that prohibit the sale — and occasionally the advertising — of term papers where one knows or has reason to know the paper will be directly submitted for academic credit.[133] As a legal matter, such laws should pose little threat to student media that publish ads for term paper companies. Selling a "model" or "sample" term paper — used solely for research purposes — is not illegal, and that is what virtually all "term paper assistance companies" advertise. While such companies operate with something of a "wink," student media have no legal obligation to verify how readers actually use the papers. Most of these laws have yet to be challenged in court and there remain questions regarding their constitutionality.[134] While many student publications probably would choose not to accept such advertisements, the decision is an editorial one, not one compelled by the law. Where such ads are accepted, they should include a prominent disclaimer stating that the material is intended solely for research purposes.

On the other hand, many of these laws also prohibit individuals from taking or offering to take an exam on behalf of another student, a "service" that is clearly illegal and whose advertising almost certainly would not be protected.

Tobacco Ads

Federal law prohibits the advertising of tobacco products on radio, television and other electronic media regulated by the FTC.[135] Cigarette ads in print media must carry a health warning, per FTC regulations.[136] Because most states have laws that prohibit minors (usually defined as anyone under the age of 18) from purchasing or using tobacco products (including, in most cases, smokeless tobacco), high school officials would likely be able to ban such ads from their student media since their readers are predominantly minors. Otherwise, lawful tobacco advertising in college student publications — where most readers can lawfully purchase and use such products — should be protected.[137]

PUBLISHER LIABILITY FOR ADVERTISING: BUYER BEWARE

As a general rule, student media have no legal duty to investigate or verify the accuracy of commercial claims or promises made in the ads they publish, such as how well a product will work or whether a service is reliable.[138] Though the legal theories argued by those seeking to hold publishers responsible vary, the result has been the same: buyers beware. While many student publications reject ads whose claims seem far-fetched or whose offers, though legal, feel "shady," they are guided more by editorial or ethical concerns than the law, which generally absolves broadcasters and publishers from liability for physical or economic injury to readers or audience members who rely on false statements in the advertisements.

> As a general rule, student media have no legal duty to investigate or verify the accuracy of commercial claims or promises made in the ads they publish.

In one frequently cited case, for example, a federal appeals court held that mushroom enthusiasts could not recover damages from the publisher of *The Encyclopedia of Mushrooms*, when they required liver transplants after having collected and consumed wild, poisonous mushrooms that they said the book described as safe to eat.[139] In another case, a California court dismissed a magazine subscriber's claim against *Seventeen*, ruling that the publisher was not liable for failing to investigate the safety of a tampon advertised in the magazine, which the subscriber claimed induced her to purchase the product.[140] The tampons were found to contain an ingredient that resulted in Toxic Shock Syndrome. In rejecting the injured subscriber's claim, the court found that "*Seventeen* did not in any way sponsor or endorse products advertised in its pages. There was no representation of quality, no promotional effort, and no attempt to induce the public to buy Playtex tampons beyond merely printing the advertisement."[141]

While media publishers are generally not responsible for the claims of advertisers, a publisher or broadcaster may, as the *Seventeen Magazine* court suggested, assume some responsibility where it independently endorses or sponsors an advertised item. For instance, if a publisher asserts that it has verified a product's quality or a service's reliability — such as *Good Housekeeping Magazine* has done with its well-known Good Housekeeping Seal of Approval® — some courts have forced publishers to stand behind their endorsements.[142] This would be particularly true where an endorsement or sponsorship is shown to result in the publisher's own economic gain.

In addition to generally having no legal duty to investigate or verify the accuracy of an ad, publishers are also typically not responsible for how readers respond to an ad or how they use the information it provides, even if such information is inaccurate or dangerous. For example, the Florida Supreme Court found that the maker of a Mountain Dew® commercial that showed young people riding down a ramp and jumping their bikes into a lake (and finishing with a refreshing swig of the drink) was not liable for the injury suffered by a 14-year-old boy who, after watching the commercial, attempted the same stunt into a three-foot deep stream and broke his neck.[143] Similarly, the Boy Scouts of America organization, publisher of *Boy's Life* magazine, was found not liable for the death of a 12-year-old scout who accidentally killed himself while handling a rifle, which he apparently was inspired to do after reading an advertising supplement in the magazine.[144]

While such an outcome may seem harsh, courts have recognized that any other rule would

---

impose unreasonable, probably catastrophic, liability on media publishers, which society must avoid if it wants to reap the greater benefit of a productive and robust press.[145] As a practical matter, publishers simply have no ability under the current system to screen and certify all of the various claims made within each of the hundreds — or in some cases, thousands — of ads they receive.[146] As one commentator has said: "A society that rendered a newspaper, selling for fifty cents or a dollar, responsible for the results of every possible reliance on information in the publication would either have no newspapers, no newspapers selling for fifty cents or a dollar, or no newspapers containing information worth having."[147] Additionally, those who feel they have been harmed by an advertisement can usually pursue legal action against the advertiser (typically the product manufacturer or service provider), who, after all, bears the greatest responsibility for both the claims made in an ad and the harm caused by a particular product or service.

A rarely applicable exception to the general rule may exist where a publisher or broadcaster either knew or clearly should have known that the publication of an ad could result in serious, perhaps deadly, harm. For example, in one of the few cases on record upholding liability against a publisher, a federal district court in Alabama held (and a federal appeals court confirmed) that *Soldier of Fortune* magazine could be held responsible for the tragic results of the following classified ad: "GUN FOR HIRE: 37 year old professional mercenary desires jobs. Vietnam Veteran. Discrete and very private. Bodyguard, courier, and other special skills. All jobs considered."[148] The ad included daytime and nighttime telephone numbers and a mailing address. Court testimony showed that after seeing the ad, a man contacted the advertiser and arranged for the murder of his business partner. The court upheld a claim brought against the magazine by the victim's sons, finding that a reasonable publisher would have understood that the ad posed a "clearly identifiable unreasonable risk that the advertiser was available to commit serious violent crimes."[149]

In an earlier case against *Soldier of Fortune*, an Arkansas judge had refused to dismiss a similar claim against the magazine, ruling that a reasonable juror could find that the alleged consequences of the magazine's conduct in publishing "gun for hire" advertisements were foreseeable.[150] The publisher reportedly agreed to a settlement.

Such cases seem to be limited to the most egregious or shocking ads. These examples are obviously extreme and of little practical concern to student media, though they serve as a reminder that there likely exist limits to a court's tolerance for letting advertising publishers off the hook. For most student media, a concern for their own reputation and the well-being of their readers or audience will prevent most problems.

Finally, keep in mind that the general protections shielding publishers from liability for an advertiser's commercial claims or offers will not necessarily immunize them from other legal problems posed by ads. For example, a publisher remains responsible for libelous ads or those that invade another's legal right to privacy. A publisher likewise can be liable if the advertisement uses copyrighted material without permission. Additionally, all student media should have a procedure for verifying the source of advertising submissions. Bogus personal ads — submitted by pranksters — containing embarrassing (usually false) personal disclosures, have been a particular source of trouble. An indemnity clause in an advertising contract or rate card, which shifts financial responsibility for illegal ads to the advertiser, can help. (See discussion, page 363)

THE RIGHT TO REJECT ADVERTISING

Mention the First Amendment and most people think of the freedom to say, print or do something (such as establish a religion or petition the government). But the free-speech guarantees of the First Amendment are actually a two-way street. They not only protect the right to express oneself, they also protect the right to refuse to express oneself, to simply remain silent.[151]

For commercial, private school or independent student media, the law is clear: the right to reject advertising is virtually absolute.[152] The First Amendment does not require privately owned print or online media to carry any advertisement they do not wish to publish.

Similarly, publishers can (and should) reserve the right to edit advertising content as a condition of publication.[153] This is true of both editorial advertising and commercial advertising. While potential advertisers do have the First Amendment right to engage in commercial speech, neither the advertiser nor the government has the right to force a privately owned publication to carry particular ads.

For student media at a public school, the answer can sometimes be a bit more complicated. Because the First Amendment prohibits only government-sanctioned censorship, the right of students to reject advertising in the publications they produce is protected. As long as student staff — and not school officials (including a faculty adviser) — make the advertising decisions for a student publication, courts have said that public school student media generally have the same right to reject advertising as their privately owned counterparts because there is no "state action."[154]

For example, a federal court of appeals upheld the right of *The Daily Nebraskan*, the student newspaper at the University of Nebraska at Lincoln, to refuse ads that included the following lines:

(1) "Lesbian woman needs roommate to share large 4 bedroom house with fireplace."
(2) "Lesbian pet lover to share large 4 bedroom house with fireplace."
(3) "Gay male seeks roommate."[155]

At the time these ads were submitted, the newspaper's advertising policy prohibited discrimination in advertising based on "sexual orientation." The editor decided to reject the ads based on this policy.

The court, in rejecting the advertisers' First Amendment claim against the newspaper, found that "[t]here is no evidence that the University ... has attempted, through the Publications Committee or otherwise, to regulate or direct the content of *the Daily Nebraskan*."[156] Because of this, the court of appeals agreed with the lower court, finding that the *Daily Nebraskan* functioned like a private newspaper with respect to its content decision-making process. As the lower court judge had noted:

> The campus newspaper of a state supported university is entitled to the constitutional protections afforded the "press," including freedom of expression for the editors. Editors necessarily exercise subjective discretion in refusing or accepting proffered materials. The degree of discretion which editors utilize in rejecting advertisements is not distinguishable, under the First Amendment analysis, from that exercised over any other submitted matter.[157]

More recently, a six-judge panel of the United States Court of Appeals for the First Circuit unanimously ruled that public high school student journalists were similarly entitled to reject advertisements they did not want to include in their publication, provided the final decision was made solely by students.[158] In that case, student editors at a Massachusetts high school refused to print an ad submitted by a community activist that advocated sexual abstinence.

The ad read: "We know you can do it! ABSTINENCE: The Healthy Choice," and offered an address where students could obtain information about "abstinence, safer sex and condoms."[159]

Students on the yearbook and newspaper staff had an unwritten policy of not accepting political or advocacy advertisements and decided not to run the ad, though they did offer the advertiser an opportunity to present his message in a letter to the editor, which he refused.[160]

The court carefully reviewed the factual record and determined that student editors — not school officials or the student media adviser — had made the final decision to reject the ad.[161] The court also rejected the advertiser's claim that student journalists working on school-sponsored publications were themselves "state actors."[162] Because no state action was present, there was no First Amendment violation, the court ruled: "As a matter of law, we see no legal duty here on the part of school administrators to control the content of the editorial judgments of student editors or publications."[163]

As the cases above illustrate, the mere fact that a university provides financial support, operating space or an adviser to a student publication will typically not be enough to show the presence of state action.[164] It is only where advertisers have clearly shown that school officials had a role in rejecting their ad that they have prevailed.[165] Given the constitutional or statutory barriers that explicitly prohibit school officials from interfering with the content of most college student media and some high school student media, such an argument will often be difficult for advertisers to make.[166]

Finally, keep in mind that even though most student editors have the right to reject any ad they choose, this right probably only exists until a contract is formed. Once a publication agrees to run an ad, it generally must do so or risk paying contractual damages.[167]

ADVERTISING CONTRACTS/RATE CARDS

Rate cards and advertising contracts are commonly used by both student and commercial media, and can offer effective legal protection when soliciting or accepting advertising. The following issues are among those commonly (and wisely) addressed in such documents:

(1) Right to Edit or Reject Ads. As discussed above, student editors (or ad managers) have a virtually unlimited right to reject or edit ads prior to acceptance, and should explicitly say so in their rate cards and advertising contracts.

(2) Placement of Advertisements. While publishers usually try to accommodate an advertiser's request, they generally reserve the right to position an advertisement where layout demands require.

(3) Ownership of Advertising Copy. Where a student media's advertising staff has substantially contributed to the creation or production of an advertisement for an advertiser — and where such services are not separately paid for — the media organization will usually stipulate in its advertising agreement that it retains all copyrights to the advertisement. It will further require that the advertiser obtain written permission from the publisher before reproducing the ad, in whole or in part, for use in any other medium.

(4) Responsibility for Errors or Omissions. All advertising agreements should disclaim liability for both: (a) the incorrect publication (including typographical errors), insertion or omission of material within an advertisement and (b) any losses that result from such mistakes. Student media should contractually limit their liability to the cost of the advertisement.

(5) Cancellation Policies. It is generally a good idea to stipulate a policy and any penalties regarding the cancellation of ads by an advertiser.

(6) Refunds/Charges for Contracted Advertising Space. In return for a better rate, advertisers commonly agree in advance to purchase a certain amount of advertising (measured either by volume or cost) during a specified contractual term. Where an

Once a publication agrees to run an ad, it must do so or risk paying contractual damages.

Rate cards and advertising contracts commonly include an indemnification clause that shields the media organization from liability caused by an ad submitted by a third party.

advertiser falls short of or exceeds the amount agreed upon, an advertising agreement should explain how charges would be recalculated.

(7) Amount and Terms of Payment. In addition to setting forth specific advertising charges, taxes (if applicable) and payment due dates, advertising agreements also commonly include provisions that require an advertiser to reimburse the publisher for all expenses and costs (including court costs and attorneys' fees) associated with collecting unpaid bills.

Rate cards and advertising contracts also commonly include an indemnification clause that shields the media organization from liability caused by an ad submitted by a third party. An indemnification clause would kick in, for example, were an advertiser to submit an ad that contained an unauthorized celebrity endorsement. In such case, the indemnity clause (or hold harmless agreement) would permit the newspaper to seek reimbursement from the advertiser for any costs and expenses it incurs as a result of a claim or lawsuit brought by the celebrity endorser. (It does not immunize the newspaper from the lawsuit itself.)

The following is a typical indemnification clause:

> "The advertiser and advertising agency (if applicable) agree to assume liability, jointly and severally, for the content of any advertisement they have caused to be published in *The Student Times* and related media (for example, *The Student Times* Web site and commemorative reprint issues) and any claim arising from such publication, including, but not limited to, claims for libel, invasion of privacy, commercial appropriation of one's name or likeness, copyright infringement, trademark, trade name or patent infringement, commercial defamation, false advertising, or any other claim whether based in tort or contract, or on account of any state or federal statute, including state and federal deceptive trade practices acts. In addition, the advertiser and advertising agency agree, jointly and severally, to indemnify, defend and hold *The Student Times* harmless for all claims (whether valid or invalid), lawsuits, judgments, liabilities, damages, losses, costs and expenses of any nature (including the assessment of reasonable attorneys' fees) resulting from or caused by the publication of any advertisement placed by the advertiser or advertising agency."

Indemnification provisions generally have survived court challenge. It is doubtful, however, that student media would be indemnified for their own mistakes. For example, if a student advertising staff revises an ad created by a third party and includes unlawful or otherwise harmful material in the copy without the approval or direction of the advertiser, an indemnification clause probably won't help.

EXCLUSIVE YEARBOOK PHOTOGRAPHY AND ANTITRUST LAWS

It is common practice for schools to contract with a local, commercial photographer to provide individual portrait services to its student yearbook. Sometimes the contract provides for other services as well (for example, student identification photos or athletic program photos) and almost all permit photographers to offer students a portrait package for purchase. The photographer typically is selected through a bidding system. Oftentimes, to ensure consistency in photos, the yearbook staff will only accept for publication those portraits taken by the official photographer.

Over the years, photographers have occasionally threatened schools with state or federal antitrust lawsuits, charging that the exclusive contract arrangement unfairly prevents them from competing in the marketplace.[168] In a growing number of cases, courts have said that as long as certain rules are adhered to, these agreements do not violate antitrust laws.[169] A detailed analysis of the application of antitrust laws to yearbook photography contracts is beyond the scope of this book. However, several issues that courts will be particularly interested in are: (1) was the bidding system fair and impartial,[170] (2) was the contract devoid of anything that could be considered an illegal bribe or kickback[171] and (3) was there an effort to create a monopoly?[172] Antitrust law can be particularly complex and schools or yearbooks threatened with an actual lawsuit should probably consult an attorney before taking action.

In addition, at least one state education commissioner has said that students cannot be forced to use a designated photographer for the yearbook photos. The New York State Education Department commissioner has said that a school may use a designated photographer, but must still allow students to submit pictures from the photographers of their choice provided the photograph meets yearbook specifications.[173] The education commissioner also said school personnel cannot help the designated photographer take orders from students for personal photos.

Still, in most states it appears that exclusive contracts for yearbook photography are, in appropriate circumstances, legally permissible. In all states — at least where students exert editorial control — student yearbook staffs can establish and require adherence to reasonable photo specifications (whomever the photographer) to ensure editorial consistency.

ADVERTISING GUIDELINES AND CONTROVERSIAL ADS

One can hope that the most frequent question a student publication must address is not "Will school officials allow me to run this ad?" but "Should I accept the ad in the first place?" The legal answer to this question is often fairly easy. As long as the ad concerns lawful activity, is not false or misleading and is otherwise protected by the First Amendment (the material is not libelous, obscene, etc.) it can be accepted. The next — and sometimes more difficult — question is, should the ad be accepted. Are there editorial, ethical or other non-legal reasons for rejecting an advertisement?

FROM THE SPLC CASE FILES

In the spring of 2001, college student newspapers across the country received an advertisement titled, "Ten Reasons Why Reparations for Blacks is a Bad Idea for Blacks — and Racist, Too." The ad was written and paid for by conservative activist David Horowitz and explained why he felt the U.S. government should not pay for reparations to descendants of slaves. The ad was deemed racist by some and prompted protests — and the trashing of newspapers — at many of the colleges where it ran. Despite significant differences in the tone and content of the ads, such scenes were reminiscent of those that took place the decade before when dozens of college newspapers, and at least a few high school newspapers, received a full-page advertisement whose basic message was to argue that the extent of the Nazi Holocaust of Jews during World War II has been exaggerated. Neither ad contained any legal problems (for example, obscenity or libelous material). In both cases newspapers published the ads for a variety of reasons: some primarily for the money, others because they believed that a newspaper's role is to provide for a "marketplace of ideas," even those "ideas" that many would find upsetting. Readers, those newspapers believed, should be trusted and allowed to make up their own minds about the value of such speech. Other newspapers rejected the ads. Some did so because they knew the ads would offend many of their readers; a few feared the impact on their bottom line. Others rejected the ads because they felt it was wrong for a newspaper to publish something the editors disagreed with deeply. What would you do?

To answer this question, many student publications have found it useful to adopt — or at least discuss — advertising acceptance policies. Such policies allow a student media staff to consider complex editorial or ethical issues in a calm environment before actually being handed a potentially volatile ad and having to make a hasty decision.

Policies also help student editors deftly respond to the fire-storm of public criticism that frequently follows whatever decision they make. Whether the guidelines should be in the form of a formal written statement or more fluid verbal discussion is subject to debate. On the one hand, written guidelines can be inflexible, a particular problem for student media whose editorial staffs — and therefore advertising philosophies — are subject to frequent change. Moreover, deciding whether to accept a particular advertisement is not a science and some decisions may be more appropriately made on case-by-case basis. On the other hand, written guidelines can help ensure consistency in the ad acceptance policy. Potential advertisers may be more likely to understand a publication's decision to refuse their ad — or be more willing to accept specific content changes — if the publication can show that it is basing its decision on policy, not just on whim.

Written guidelines can range from a single sentence declaring that the publication prohibits advertising only of illegal products or services, to a multi-page document that spells out the publication's policy on hundreds of advertising categories ("*The Student Times* will accept 'responsible drinking' ads; it will not accept adoption ads; personal ads will be run only in the classified section and will be limited to 50 words," etc.). Guidelines are voluntary and exist primarily for the benefit of a publication's staff; therefore guidelines should include a statement notifying readers that the publication retains the right to refuse any ad for any reason. Like editorial policies, advertising policies reflect the philosophy of a publication; there is no single "best" policy.

There is no doubt that student media will continue to be targeted by those seeking publicity for their controversial ideas or concerns for one simple reason: it works. In many, if not most cases, such advertisers are more interested in the publicity generated by student reaction to their ad (or to the publication's refusal to run the ad) than the advertisement itself. For that reason alone, student media do themselves a favor — and reduce their exposure as unwitting pawns — by addressing the question of advertising acceptance before a publicity-seeking advertiser catches them off-guard.

SCAM ALERT: BOGUS ADVERTISERS

Sometimes they seem just too good to be true. "Dear Business Manager," the letter reads, "Enclosed please find a two column, two-inch advertisement regarding lucrative work-at-home opportunities. I would like it run in each issue of your newspaper this fall, starting immediately. Please bill me at the above address." If only all of your accounts were so easy: no cold calls, no follow-ups, no mock ads — no time or effort at all. Unfortunately, that good feeling quickly goes bad when the bill you send out six issues later comes back marked "Return to Sender: Address Unknown." Around the country, unscrupulous scam artists have tricked student media into publishing ads for free, harming not only the publication, but also readers who might have responded to the offers and found the product they received, if they received one at all, was worth much less than the money they paid for it. (While student media generally have no legal duty to investigate or verify the accuracy of advertisements, as discussed above, the desire to maintain credibility with readers prompts most publications to try and steer clear of illegitimate ads.)

In most cases, particularly where the account is small and the advertiser is out-of-state or out of business, the time, expense and effort necessary to collect on the account will outweigh the debt. For local accounts, phone calls, letters and personal contacts can be effective. If this approach is unsuccessful, an attorney can write a letter to the debtor demanding payment. As a last resort, the staff can consider filing a lawsuit. Most cities or counties have a special "small claims" court where persons can sue for limited amounts, typically capped at between $1500 and $7500, though a few states permit higher claims. These courts are relatively user-friendly (think "The People's Court" or "Judge Judy" TV shows) and most do not require — and some do not permit — representation by an attorney, which significantly reduces a party's expenses.

To avoid being taken in the first place, student publications should adopt a formal billing policy.

For new, unfamiliar — and particularly non-local — accounts this policy can require a signed contract to advertise and payment in advance. If checks are accepted, advertisers can be told that their ad will not run until their check has cleared the bank. If you have questions about the legitimacy of a particular ad prior to running it, a telephone call or visit to the website of the Better Business Bureau might be in order. If you believe that you have been the victim of an intentional scam, you may wish to contact your state attorney general's office. If the advertiser used the mail, you may also want to file a complaint with the fraud unit for the U.S. Postal Service. If the account is large, you may also wish to consult your own attorney.

SUMMARY

The First Amendment protects commercial advertising as long as it concerns lawful activity and is not false or misleading. Commercial speech does not, however, enjoy as much First Amendment protection as noncommercial, or so-called "pure" speech, and government officials (including public school administrators) are allowed more leeway in regulating it, though recent U.S. Supreme Court decisions have tended to limit such regulation. While the U.S. Supreme Court's *Hazelwood* decision might make it more difficult for some high school student publications to defeat attempts by school officials to censor commercial advertising, the First Amendment remains an important source of protection both for public college and for independent student publications.

In addition to protecting against censorship of particular ads, the First Amendment also forbids schools from banning publications simply because they contain advertising or because they are sold. The First Amendment also protects the right of student publications to reject advertising — as long as students, and not school officials, are the ones who make the decision.

Finally, student media will often find that they can avoid many potential advertising headaches if they use well-crafted advertising agreements and take the time to adopt (or at least thoroughly discuss) a clear, well-reasoned advertising policy that accurately reflects the editorial philosophy of the publication.

CASE STUDY

Patty Kakes, *The Student Times* ad manager, arrived at work to find the following ads waiting on her desk:

(1) For Sale: Civil War-era saber. Used by General Robert E. Lee at Battle of Gettysburg. Displayed in beautiful, glass-enclosed case. Excellent condition. $1,000.

(2) AIDS ALERT: My name is Janey Doe. I'm bisexual. I recently tested positive for the HIV (AIDS) virus. If you have had sexual contact with me, please contact me at Campus Box 1845 or contact the health department ASAP.

(3) Professional photographer seeking cute female models. All races, all body types. $35/hour. Very easy work.

(4) Same-sex marriage is wrong! Marriage is a sacred bond between a man and a woman. God instructed His people to go forth upon the earth and multiply. Homosexuals can't multiply. AIDS is God's revenge. Christians (and others) please join the Student Friends of God United campus rally Wednesday night at 7 p.m. at The Commons. Let God's Voice be Heard!!! Before it's too late.

(5) Roommate wanted. Female seeking female roommate for large 2-bedroom apartment in quiet building about two miles from campus. Parking available. Apartment is clean, nicely furnished

and decorated in all white and neutral tones. Utilities included. $500/month. Serious students only, please.

Advertising deadline is in two hours. What can and cannot be published?

ANSWER:
Patty should probably first separate the commercial advertisements — those whose primary purpose is buying/selling/trading a product or service — from noncommercial ads. Noncommercial ads are entitled to the same First Amendment protections available to other editorial content in *The Student Times*. Noncommercial content in public college student media is entitled to significant First Amendment protection, being limited in most cases only by whether the content is defamatory, obscene, invasive of privacy or in some other way unlawful. High school protections vary depending on the nature of the student media and where it is located. For example, school-sponsored student media subject to the Supreme Court's *Hazelwood* decision may face additional censorship hurdles, even if the ads themselves can lawfully be published.

Once she has identified the commercial advertisements, the first question Patty must ask herself is whether the ads are legally protected. Under the Supreme Court's *Central Hudson* test, the First Amendment protects ads that concern a lawful product or service and that are not misleading. Are there any local, state or federal laws or ordinances that may be relevant? How about school regulations?

Where there are laws or regulations, they must be constitutional. The First Amendment protects commercial speech; government (including public school) officials do not have unlimited authority to regulate advertising. To be constitutionally valid, government restrictions on truthful ads for lawful products or services must pass three additional hurdles: (1) the government has to have a very good — a "substantial" — reason for its restrictions, (2) the restrictions must make sense and actually help the government achieve its goal and (3) the government must show that the restrictions are a last — not first — resort.

Assuming the ads are for a lawful product or service, Patty must also screen the ads for any other legal problems. Specifically, are there any libel or privacy problems with the ads? Are there any copyright concerns?

With all of this in mind, Patty turns to each of the ads.

Ad #1: Civil War saber. Patty determines there is no legal problem in publishing the ad. When used (or displayed) appropriately, battle sabers are lawful products. While the advertiser's claim that General Lee used the saber sounds far-fetched, it may be true. Patty has no legal obligation to verify the claim. That's a matter between the advertiser and buyer. Once she has determined that the ad can be run without breaking any laws, however, the next question is should it be run? It is *The Student Times*' policy to refuse ads for guns and other weapons. But the ad policy exists for the benefit of *The Student Times* staff and can be "adapted" as the staff deems necessary. After talking it over with the editor, they decide to amend the policy to allow ads for "weapons" that are historical artifacts for display. The ad goes in.

Ad #2: AIDS ALERT. This is an example of a noncommercial ad (and believe it or not, is based on an ad actually published). As such, Patty's primary legal concern is whether the ad contains any unprotected speech — and her alarm bells are ringing. First, she wonders if the ad is legitimate. Does Janey Doe exist? If so, did she actually submit the ad? Patty knows that personal ads are a prime target of pranksters or those with more sinister motives. Unfortunately, the "prank" here could land everyone involved in deep legal trouble. If the ad is true, disclosing that Doe has AIDS without her consent would likely constitute an illegal invasion of her privacy. If the charge in the ad is false, it's probably defamatory. If Doe did submit the ad — and assuming that she is capable of understanding what she is doing and the consequences of making such a public disclosure — it is legal. Patty must again decide, however, whether *The Student Times* wants to be in the business of publishing such ads. In this case, grappling with such a difficult ethical question is unnecessary. When contacted by telephone, Doe flatly denies that she placed the ad. The ad is out.

Ad #3: Professional photographer seeking models. There is nothing overtly illegal about this ad. Commercial photography frequently involves models and — outside of child pornography — there is generally nothing illegal about the practice or advertising for it. Still, this is one of those ads that have a bit of a "cringe factor" to them. For that reason, *The Student Times* advertising policy requires that "model" ads include language specifying that the photographer seeks only adult models. The ad must also include the name of the photographer or the photography studio. When Patty calls the advertiser to tell him of the changes required, he yells at her and threatens to sue if his ad isn't published as written "down to the last period." Patty informs her editor, but isn't worried. Since both she and her editor are students and will be the only ones involved in rejecting the ad, there is no "state action" and thus no First Amendment problem. They have the right to reject or require edits to any ad for any reason. The ad is out.

Ad #4: Same sex marriage. As an issue-oriented ad, this is another example of a noncommercial advertisement. While its message will be offensive to many readers, Patty determines that there is nothing unlawful in the ad. No specific individuals are targeted; no unlawful activity is proposed. Patty also confirms that the Christian group listed in the ad actually submitted it. Newspaper policy requires that all issue-oriented ads be brought before a special advertising committee convened by the editor in chief. Patty and her assistant ad manager sit on the committee as do members of the student editorial board. The ad committee has established a list of criteria that they use to vote on whether *The Student Times* will publish a particular ad. For example, ads that contain accurate facts and information are more likely to be published than ads that simply point fingers or engage in mean-spirited name-calling. The committee has frequently worked with an advertiser to revise, add or delete material from an advertisement in an effort to publish something that is acceptable to both sides. In addition, all issue-oriented ads must include a prominent disclaimer making it clear that the ad does not necessarily reflect the view of *The Student Times* or the school.

Ad #5: Roommate wanted. Though she had to read it through a couple of times to make sure, Patty concludes that there are no legal problems with this ad. Patty knows from experience that housingrelated ads require extra attention. Federal (and in many cases, state) law prohibits publishers from running ads that contain specific types of discriminatory language (for example, religion, ethnicity, handicap). While this ad does contain a preference for a "female" roommate (gender discrimination), federal regulators and officials in at least a couple of states have said that they will allow such language in shared-housing type ads. (Were this a whole apartment for rent or a house for sale, an ad indicating a gender preference or restriction would be unlawful.) Patty also noticed the language stating that the apartment was decorated in "all white and neutral tones." It may seem silly in this case, but Patty knows that regulators have cracked down on advertisers who use "code words" or phrases to indicate illegal preferences. For example, phrases such as "traditional neighborhood," "near synagogue," "great for empty-nesters" can all connote an illegal preference. Patty satisfies herself that the words, as they appear on their face, simply describe the apartment's interior, which is legal. Finally, there is no legal problem specifying a preference for good students. The ad goes in.

ENDNOTES

1   Kopenhaver, L. and Spielberger, R., "Newspapers post salary gains, experience revenue slowdown," (June 2007). In addition, the survey found that 81.5 percent of college and university newspapers reported at least some advertising revenue.
2   Freedom Forum, *Death By Cheeseburger: High School Journalism in the 1990s and Beyond* (1994), p. 4. The 1993 survey indicated that 89.8 percent of high school student newspapers carried advertisements. *See also* Jack Nelson, *Captive Voices: High School Journalism in America* (1973), p. 217 (survey published in 1973 found that 83 percent of high school student newspapers carried advertisements).
3   *Va. State Bd. of Pharmacy v. Va. Citizens Consumer Council*, 425 U.S. 748, 776, 760 (1976).
4   *Central Hudson Gas & Elec. Corp. v. Pub. Serv. Comm'n*, 447 U.S. 557, 561 (1980), *on remand*, 413 N.E.2d 365 (N.Y. 1980).
5   *New York Times Co. v. Sullivan*, 376 U.S. 254 (1964).
6   *See, e.g.*, *Zucker v. Panitz*, 299 F. Supp. 102 (S.D.N.Y. 1969) (high school journalists ruled to have First Amendment right to publish ad opposing Vietnam war). *But see Kasky v. Nike, Inc.*, 45 P.3d 243 (Cal. 2002), *cert. denied*, 539 U.S. 654 (2003) (Supreme Court of California opinion finding shoe company's statements defending itself from attacks on its labor practices to be commercial speech and adopting a definition of "commercial speech" that would include almost any statement made by a company

concerning itself, or its products or services, that is heard by or repeated to potential customers).

7   *See Valentine v. Chrestensen*, 316 U.S. 52, 54 (1942). *See, e.g., May v. People*, 636 P.2d 672, 677 (Colo. 1981), for a quick summary of the Supreme Court's later rejection of this approach.

8   The first of these cases was *Pittsburgh Press v. Pittsburgh Comm'n on Human Relations*, 413 U.S. 376, 388 (1973), *reh'g denied*, 414 U.S. 881 (1973) (application of city ordinance to forbid newspapers from running "help wanted" ads under gender captions held constitutional).

9   *Bigelow v. Virginia*, 421 U.S. 809 (1975).

10 *Id.* at 818.

11 *Virginia State Bd. of Pharmacy v. Virginia Citizens Consumer Council*, 425 U.S. 748 (1976).

12 *Carey v. Population Services Int'l*, 431 U.S. 678 (1977).

13 *Bates v. State Bar of Ariz.*, 433 U.S. 350 (1977), *reh'g. denied*, 434 U.S 881 (1977).

14 447 U.S. 557 (1980), *on remand*, 413 N.E.2d 365 (N.Y. 1980).

15 See *City of Cincinnati v. Discovery Network, Inc.*, 507 U.S. 410, 425 (1993) (dismissing city's assertion that its interest in aesthetics allowed it to ban newsracks and finding that "publishers' newsracks are no greater an eyesore than the newsracks permitted to remain on Cincinnati's sidewalks"); *Hays County Guardian v. Supple*, 969 F.2d 111, 119 (5th Cir. 1992) (dismissing university's claim that desire to prevent litter justified its ban on on-campus distribution of free community newspaper), *reh'g denied*, 974 F.2d 169 (5th Cir. 1992) (en banc), *cert. denied*, 506 U.S. 1087 (1993).

16 *See Metromedia, Inc. v. City of San Diego*, 453 U.S. 490, 509 (1981) (deferring to the "common-sense judgment" of local lawmakers in deciding whether city's interest in regulating billboards was substantial), *on remand*, 649 P.2d 902 (Cal. 1982); *Renton v. Playtime Theaters, Inc.*, 475 U.S. 41, 54 (1986) (holding that a substantial governmental interest included the catch-all interest of "preserving the quality of life in the community at large"), *reh'g denied*, 475 U.S. 1132 (1986).

17 *Posadas de Puerto Rico Associates v. Tourism Co. of Puerto Rico*, 478 U.S. 328 (1986); *Bd. of Trustees of the State Univ. of New York v. Fox*, 492 U.S. 469, 480 (1989), *mot. denied*, 493 U.S. 887 (1989), later proceeding, 764 F. Supp. 747 (N.D.N.Y. 1991).

18 *Fox*, 492 U.S. at 478.

19 *City of Cincinnati v. Discovery Network, Inc.*, 507 U.S. 410 (1993).

20 *Id.* at 425.

21 *Id.* at 419.

22 *Rubin v. Coors Brewing Co.*, 514 U.S. 476 (1995) (striking down a ban on accurate alcohol-by-volume label disclosures for beer); *44 Liquormart, Inc. v. Rhode Island*, 517 U.S. 484 (1996) (striking down state ban on alcohol price advertising); *Greater New Orleans Broadcasting Ass'n v. United States*, 527 U.S. 173 (1999) (striking down FCC regulation prohibiting broadcast advertising of lawful private casino gambling); *Lorillard Tobacco Co. v. Reilly*, 533 U.S. 525 (2001) (striking down state regulations prohibiting certain forms of tobacco advertising within 1,000 feet of schools); *Thompson v. W. States Med. Ctr.*, 535 U.S. 357 (2002) (striking down federal regulations prohibiting truthful advertising about compounded drugs by pharmacies).

23 *Rubin*, 514 U.S. at 482 n.2; *44 Liquormart*, 517 U.S. at 509; *Greater New Orleans*, 527 U.S. at 182.

24 *See Thompson*, 533 U.S. at 374.

25 *Lorillard*, 533 U.S. at 564 (citing *Reno v. American Civil Liberties Union*, 521 U.S. 844, 875 (1997)) (striking down portions of the federal Communications Decency Act that prohibited transmission of indecent telecommunications to persons under 18). The *Lorillard* court also based its reasoning on *Bolger v. Youngs Drug Products Corp.*, 463 U.S. 60, 74 (1983) ("The level of discourse reaching a mailbox simply cannot be limited to that which would be suitable for a sandbox").

26 *Greater New Orleans*, 527 U.S. at 187.

27 *Id.* at 188-89.

28 *Id.* at 188 (quoting *Edenfield v. Fane*, 507 U.S. 761, 770-771 (1993)).

29 *Thompson*, 533 U.S. at 371, 373 (emphasis added).

30 *See id.* at 367-68 (noting that "several Members of the Court have expressed doubts about the *Central Hudson* analysis and whether it should apply in particular cases") (citing *Greater New Orleans Broadcasting Assn., Inc. v. United States*, 527 U.S. 173, 197 (Thomas, J., concurring in judgment)); *44 Liquormart, Inc. v. Rhode Island*, 517 U.S. 484, 501, 510-514 (1996) (opinion of Stevens, J., joined by Kennedy and Ginsburg, JJ.); *Id.* at 517 (Scalia, J., concurring in part and concurring in judgment); *Id.* at 518 (Thomas, J., concurring in part and concurring in judgment). Justice Samuel Alito, who joined the Court in 2006, may provide a fifth vote. *See, e.g., Pitt News v. Pappert*, 379 F.3d 96 (3d Cir. 2004) (opinion by then-Judge Alito striking down state law that restricted alcohol advertising in college student media as an impermissible restriction on commercial speech).

31 484 U.S. 260 (1988).

32 *Planned Parenthood of Southern Nevada v. Clark County Sch. Dist.*, 941 F.2d 817 (9th Cir. 1991) (en banc).

33 *Id.* at 821.

34 *Id.* at 829.

35 *See Hazelwood*, 484 U.S. at 273.

36 *See Id.* at 270, 272-73. The Court required censorship to be "reasonable," citing its prior decision in *Perry Educ. Ass'n v. Perry Local Educators' Ass'n*, 460 U.S. 37, 46 (1983), *on remand*, 705 F.2d 462 (7th Cir. 1983). *Id.* at 270 (noting that "school officials were entitled to regulate the contents of Spectrum in any reasonable manner"). To be "reasonable," the *Perry* Court held, the restriction on speech must not be "an effort to suppress expression merely because public officials oppose the speaker's view." *Perry Educ. Ass'n*, 460 U.S. at 37. *See also Planned Parenthood of Southern Nevada*, 941 F.2d at 829 (finding that the schools' refusal to publish family planning organization's ads was "viewpoint neutral," as the schools' intent was to "maintain a position of neutrality on the sensitive and controversial issue of family planning...."); *Searcey v. Harris*, 888 F.2d 1314, 1319 n. 7 (11th Cir. 1989) (rejecting school's claim that *Hazelwood* eliminated requirement of viewpoint neutrality). But

See, e.g., *Fleming v. Jefferson County Sch. Dist.*, 298 F.3d 918, 926-928 (10th Cir. 2002), cert denied, 537 U.S. 1110 (2003) (allowing viewpoint discrimination in censorship decision by public high school officials). *See also Busch v. Marple Newtown Sch. Dist.*, 2007 WL 1589507, *8 n. 15 (E.D.Pa. May 31, 2007) (discussing conflicts among circuits).

37 *See* discussion in Chapter 6.

38 *Lueth v. St. Clair County Community College*, 732 F. Supp. 1410 (E.D. Mich. 1990).

39 *Id.* at 1412.

40 *Id.* at 1415.

41 *Id.* at 1416.

42 *Id.*

43 *Educational Media Co. at Virginia Tech v. Insley*, ___ F.3d ___, No. 12-2183 (4th Cir. Sept. 25, 2013).

44 *See Board of Trustees of the State Univ. of N.Y v. Fox*, 492 U.S. 469 (1989), *mot. denied*, 493 U.S. 887 (1989), later proceeding, 764 F. Supp. 747 (N.D.N.Y. 1991).

45 Time, place and manner regulations are discussed in chapter 8.

46 *See, e.g., Hernandez v. Hanson*, 430 F. Supp. 1154, 1161 (D. Neb. 1977) (federal court struck down a high school rule banning the distribution of any "commercial literature" on school grounds; the court stated that before any such literature could be banned, school officials would have to prove that the publication would cause a "substantial disruption" to school activities); *Peterson v. Bd. of Educ.*, 370 F. Supp. 1208, 1214 (D. Neb. 1973) (high school administrators could not prove that a "counter-culture" newspaper created a "substantial disruption" justifying a ban on distributing it, rejecting the school's argument that the paper could be prohibited because it contained advertisements, contributions were sought from those receiving copies and the paper was published and distributed by non-students); *Jacobs v. Bd. Of Sch. Comm'rs*, 490 F.2d 601 (7th Cir. 1973), *vacated as moot*, 420 U.S. 128 (1975) (striking down an outright ban on the sale of literature on the grounds of a public high school; the Supreme Court vacated and remanded this case on procedural grounds); *Nitzberg v. Parks*, 525 F.2d 378, 383, n.4 (4th Cir. 1975) (in reviewing school board policy regulating non-school-sponsored student publications, court found "no constitutional basis for distinguishing between commercial literature (which, under the policy, was subject to prior review) and 'free' literature" (which was not subject to prior review)); *Burbridge v. Sampson*, 74 F. Supp. 2d 940 (C.D. Calif. 1999) (striking down community college policy that imposed greater restrictions on commercial speech than noncommericial speech). *See also Substitutes United for Better Schools v. Rohter*, 496 F. Supp. 1017 (N.D. Ill. 1980) (upholding right of teachers to sell newspapers on campus). But *see Katz v. McAulay*, 438 F.2d 1058, 1059 (2d Cir. 1971), *cert. denied*, 405 U.S. 933 (1972) (denying a request for preliminary injunction brought by students challenging enforcement of a school board policy that prohibited "soliciting funds from the pupils in the public schools;" the students had sought to distribute leaflets requesting money for legal defense fund); *Williams v. Spencer*, 622 F.2d 1200, 1205 (4th Cir. 1980) (upholding a ban on the distribution of an underground newspaper on the grounds of a high school because the paper carried an advertisement for a store that sold drug paraphernalia).

47 *Pliscou v. Holtville Unified Sch. Dist.*, 411 F. Supp. 842 (S.D. Cal. 1976). The editor of a California high school underground paper sued school officials after they denied her permission to sell advertisements to finance the publication. The court ordered the school officials to permit such solicitation, stating that "[s]chool officials cannot impinge upon the First Amendment rights of the [staff members] . . . by arbitrarily denying their activity request to solicit advertising." *Id.* at 848-49.

48 *Hays County Guardian v. Supple*, 969 F.2d 111 (5th Cir. 1992), *reh'g denied*, 974 F.2d 169 (5th Cir. 1992) (en banc), *cert. denied*, 506 U.S. 1087 (1993).

49 *Id.* at 120.

50 *Id.* at 119.

51 *Id.* at 120.

52 "Use of Advertising and Facilitators in Adoptive Placements," Child Welfare Information Gateway (2006), *available at* http://www.childwelfare.gov/systemwide/laws_policies/statutes/advertising.cfm) (last visited June 21, 2013).

53 Only licensed persons and organizations may place adoption ads in Alabama. Ala. Code Sec. 26-10A-36 (2007).

54 In California, no one may "cause [an ad for adoption] to be published." While courts have yet to address the issue, this might be construed as subjecting publishers to liability. Cal. Fam. Code Sec. 8609 (2007).

55 Connecticut allows "any birth parent" or "prospective adoptive parent" to advertise in any public media in the state. Conn. Ann. Stat. Sec. 45a-728d (2007).

56 Only licensed persons and organizations may place adoption ads in Delaware. Del. Code Ann. tit. 13, Sec. 930 (2007).

57 Only licensed persons and organizations may place adoption ads in Florida. Additionally, media may not publish ads without including the advertiser's license number. Fla. Stat. Sec. 63.212(1)(g) (2007).

58 Only licensed persons and organizations may place adoption ads in Georgia. Ga. Code Ann. Sec. 19-8-24(a)(1) (2007).

59 In Idaho, "[n]o person or entity shall cause to be published for circulation or broadcast" an adoption ad except for duly licensed persons and organizations. While courts have yet to address the issue, this might be construed as subjecting publishers to liability. Idaho Ann. Code Sec. 18-1512A(A) (2007).

60 Only birth parents, prospective adoptive parents, or licensed child welfare agencies may place an adoption ad. Ill. Stat. tit. 225, Sec. 10/12.

61 Only a licensed attorney or child placement agency may advertise adoption services. Ind. Ann. Code Sec. 35-46-1-21.

62 Only the state or licensed persons and organizations may place adoption ads in Kansas. Kan. Stat. Ann. Sec. 59-2123 (2007).

63 Kentucky prohibits the publication of all adoption ads. The statute appears to apply both to media publishers and advertisers. Ky. Rev. Stat. Ann. Sec. 199.590(1) (2007).

64 Only licensed persons and organizations may place adoption ads in Louisiana. La. Rev. Stat. Ann. Sec. 46:1425(A) (2008).

65 Only licensed persons and organizations may place adoption ads in Maine. Advertising is further regulated by the state's licensing body. Me. Rev. Stat. Ann. tit. 18-A Sec. 9-313 (2007).

66 No one may "cause" adoption ads to be published in Massachusetts unless placed by a licensed or approved placement agency or with written approval of the state. While courts have yet to address the issue, this might be construed as subjecting publishers to liability. Additionally, the law requires that all ads include the license or registration number of the advertiser. Violations are punishable by fine. Mass. Gen. Laws ch. 210, Sec. 11A (2007).

67 No child placement agency may place an ad seeking children or birth mothers for adoption placement without a valid state license. The statute does not address ads by birth mothers themselves. Miss. Ann. Code Sec. 43-15-117.

68 Only licensed persons and organizations may place adoption ads in Montana. Mont. Code Ann. Sec. 42-7- 105 (2007).

69 Only licensed persons and organizations may "place," "assist in placing" or "advertise a child for placement" in Nebraska. Neb. Rev. Stat. Sec. 43-701 (2007). While courts have yet to address the issue, this might be construed as subjecting publishers to liability.

70 Only licensed persons and organizations may place adoption ads in Nevada. Publishers are not liable for violations of the law. Nev. Rev. Stat. Sec. 127.310 (2007).

71 Only licensed or permitted persons and organizations may place adoption ads in New Hampshire. N.H. Rev. Stat. Sec. 170-E:39 (2007).

72 Only government social service agencies and licensed persons or organizations may place adoption ads in North Carolina. However, the law explicitly allows individuals to place an ad indicating their desire to adopt. N.C. Gen. Stat. Sec. 48-10-101 (2007).

73 North Dakota law restricts adoption-related advertising by hospitals, certain foster care facilities and maternity homes for unmarried mothers. N.D. Cen. Code Secs. 23-16-08; 50-11-06; 50-19-11 (2007).

74 Only certified private child placement agencies or government child services agencies may place adoption ads in Ohio. Moreover, persons may not "in any manner knowingly become a party to the separation of a child from the child's parents or guardians." While courts have yet to address this last provision, it could be construed as subjecting publishers to liability. Ohio Rev. Code Sec. 5103.17.

75 Only licensed "child-placing" agencies and Oklahoma attorneys may place adoption ads for living children. Other individuals are permitted to place ads soliciting pregnant women to consider an adoptive placement provided they provide written verification that they have "received a favorable preplacement home study recommendation" as proscribed by state law. Okla. Ann. Stat. tit. 21, Secs. 866(A)(1)(g)-(h) (2007). The law also explicitly prohibits media from publishing ads that do not comply with the law's requirements, with violations punishable by up to a $5000 fine. Id. at Sec. 866(B).

76 Only the State Department of Human Services and licensed agencies and persons who have completed the state-mandated home study course and received a favorable recommendation to be an adoptive parent (or their Oregon-licensed attorney) may place adoption ads in Oregon. Ore. Rev. Stat. Sec. 109.311(4).

77 A birth mother may not place an ad offering her child for adoption; only a licensed child placement agency, licensed clinical social worker, prospective adoptive parent or Tennessee-licensed attorney may advertise for child placement. Tenn. Ann. Code Sec. 36-1-108(a)(2).

78 Texas law prohibits any person or entity other than licensed child-placing agencies from advertising to place a child for adoption or to provide or obtain a child for adoption. Tex. Penal Code Sec. 25.09 (2007).

79 Utah law prohibits attorneys, physicians and other persons from advertising that they are available to provide child-placing assistance. Utah Ann. Code Sec. 62A-4a-602(2)(b) (2007).

80 Virginia prohibits any person from advertising to solicit or perform any activity prohibited by the state's adoption laws, the bulk of which relate to compensation for adoption-related services and activities. Virginia Ann. Code Secs. 63.2-1218; 63.2-1225 (2007).

81 Only licensed persons and organizations may place adoption ads in Washington. Media publishers are protected from liability if they accept ads "in good faith without knowledge of its violation" of the law. Wash. Rev. Code Sec. 26.33.400 (2007).

82 Wisconsin law prohibits anyone other than state agencies, licensed persons or organizations, individuals who have received favorable recommendations regarding their fitness to be an adoptive parent and parents seeking to place their child for adoption from placing adoption ads. Media publishers who obtain a copy of the advertiser's license to provide adoption services within the state may be entitled to protection from liability. Wisc. Ann. Stat. Sec. 48.825 (2007).

83 An earlier version of Alabama's adoption ad statute was determined to be unconstitutionally vague and was replaced with the current law. *State v. Gooden*, 570 So.2d 865 (Ala. Crim. App. 1990).

84 *Kernel Press, Inc. v. Alcoholic Beverage Control Bd.*, CIV No. 87611 (Franklin Cir. Ct., June 8, 1977) (State regulation prohibiting alcohol advertising in "any educational institution's newspaper" held unenforceable against University of Kentucky student newspaper because, among other reasons, 57 percent of the school's students were over 21. The court also noted that faculty and staff readers would push that number even higher.). More recently, however, a federal appeals court has rebuffed constitutional challenges to a state regulation against advertising alcoholic beverages in college student publications, finding the ban justified by the special concern for excessive "binge" drinking at colleges. *See Educational Media Co. at Virginia Tech v. Swecker*, 602 F.3d 583, 591 (4th Cir. 2010). (Subsequently, a federal district court also upheld the same regulation when asked the narrower question of whether it could be applied even to newspapers that primarily circulate to people 21 and over. *Educational Media Co. v. Insley*, No. 3:06cv396, Order on Summary Judgment (Sept. 7, 2012) (unpublished)). *But see Khademi v. South Orange Community College*, 194 F. Supp.2d 1011 (C.D. Calif. 2002) (upholding community college policy that banned advertising for illegal substances, but striking down ban insofar as it prohibited ads for legal substances including alcohol, tobacco and firearms.) Laws restricting alcohol ads in college student media remain on the books in both New Hampshire, N.H. Rev.

STAT. Ann. Sec. 179:31 (XI) (2003) and Utah, UTAH ADMIN. CODE Sec. R81-1-1796(iv) (2004). As of July 2013, neither statute had been challenged in court. According to a U.S. Census Bureau survey, nearly 57 percent of those enrolled in American colleges and universities during 2009 were 22 years of age or older. The full survey is *available at*: http://www.census.gov/compendia/statab/2012/tables/12s0283.pdf (last visited July 14, 2013). Of course, student publications are also read by college employees, faculty, alumni and outside community members, most of who are also of legal drinking age.

85   *Rubin v. Coors Brewing Co.*, 514 U.S. 476 (1995) (striking down a ban on accurate alcohol by volume label disclosures for beer); *44 Liquormart, Inc. v. Rhode Island*, 517 U.S. 484 (1996) (state's ban prohibiting all advertisement of liquor prices, except on signs and price tags, held unconstitutional); *Greater New Orleans Broad. Assoc. v. U.S.*, 527 U.S. 173 (1999) (FCC could not prohibit advertisements of lawful private casino gambling broadcast by radio or television stations located in Louisiana, where such gambling was legal); *Lorillard Tobacco Co. v. Reilly,* 533 U.S. 525 (2001) (holding unconstitutional Massachusetts' regulations prohibiting outdoor tobacco advertising within 1,000 feet of a school and mandating that tobacco advertising could not be placed lower than five feet from the floor of any retail establishment within 1,000 feet of a school). Lower federal courts have also weighed in. *See, e.g., Utah Licensed Beverage Ass'n v. Leavitt*, 256 F.3d 1061 (10th Cir. 2001) (state restrictions on wine and spirits advertising held unconstitutional).

86   *44 Liquormart, Inc.*, 517 U.S. at 516. *See also Rubin*, 514 U.S. at 476 (striking down a ban on accurate alcohol by volume label disclosures for beer).

87   *44 Liquormart, Inc.*, 517 U.S. at 505-07.

88   *Lorillard Tobacco Co.*, 533 U.S. 525 at 564 (quoting *Reno v. American Civil Liberties Union*, 521 U.S. 844, 875 (1997), which struck down portions of the Communications Decency Act prohibiting transmission of obscene or indecent telecommunications to persons under 18).

89   PA. STAT. Sec. 4-498(e)(5) (1997) ("No advertisement shall be permitted, either directly or indirectly, in any booklet, program book, yearbook, magazine, newspaper, periodical, brochure, circular or other similar publication published by, for or in behalf of any educational institution.") (This statute was held unconstitutional in *Pitt News v. Pappert*, 379 F.3d 96 (3d Cir. 2004)).

90   *Pitt News v. Fisher*, 215 F.3d 354 (3d Cir. 2000), *cert. denied*, 531 U.S. 1113 (2001). In this early challenge to the 1997 statute, the Third Circuit acknowledged that *The Pitt News* had standing to challenge the statute but concluded that the newspaper could not show that its First Amendment rights had been violated. *Id.* at 366.

91   *Pitt News*, 379 F.3d at 101, 111 (holding that the First Amendment precludes the enforcement of the Pennsylvania regulation against advertisers in *The Pitt News* and reversing the order of the district court denying a permanent injunction).

92   *See* Federal Trade Commission, *Alcohol Marketing and Advertising: A Report to Congress 18-19* (Sept. 2003), *Available at* http://www.ftc.gov/os/2003/09/alcohol08report.pdf (last visited July 14, 2013).

93   *Id.* at 13. *See also* Beer Institute, *Advertising and Marketing Code and Buying Guidelines 3* (Jan. 2006), http://www.beerinstitute.org/assets/uploads/BI-AdCode-5-2011.pdf (last visited July 14, 2013).

94   *Id.* at 18-19. *See also* Wine Institute, *Code of Advertising Standards*, http://www.wineinstitute.org/initiatives/issuesandpolicy/adcode/details (revised Sept. 2005) (last visited July 14, 2013); Distilled Spirits Council of the United States, *Code of Responsible Practices for Beverage Alcohol Advertising and Marketing*, http://www.discus.org/responsibility/code/ (updated May 26, 2011) (last visited July 14, 2013).

95   *Carey v. Population Services Int'l*, 431 U.S. 678 (1977); *Bigelow v. Virginia*, 421 U.S. 809 (1975); Meadowbrook Women's Clinic v. Minnesota, 557 F. Supp. 1172 (D. Minn. 1983). *But see Planned Parenthood v. Clark County Sch. Dist.*, 941 F.2d 817 (9th Cir. 1991) (en banc) (public high school officials can prohibit pregnancy-related ads in non-forum, school-sponsored publications after *Hazelwood*).

96   For more information, *See* United States Postal Service, *Publication 417: Nonprofit Standard Mail Eligibility 49* (Mar. 2006), *Available at* http://pe.usps.gov/text/pub417/welcome.htm (last visited July 14, 2013). Additional information can be obtained from the Alliance for Nonprofit Mailers, http://www.nonprofitmailers.org (registration required) (last visited July 14, 2013).

97   *Aid Ass'n for Lutherans v. U.S. Postal Service*, 321 F.3d 1166 (D.C. Cir. 2003).

98   *See, e.g., Village of Hoffman Estates v. Flipside, Hoffman Estates, Inc.*, 455 U.S. 489 (1982); *Camille Corp. v. Phares*, 705 F.2d 223 (7th Cir. 1983); *Gen. Stores, Inc. v. Bingaman*, 695 F.2d 502 (10th Cir. 1982); *Stoianoff v. Montana*, 695 F.2d 1214 (9th Cir. 1983).

99   *Williams v. Spencer*, 622 F.2d 1200 (4th Cir. 1980) (ban on distribution of underground newspaper on high school grounds because it carried advertisement for "head shop" upheld).

100 *Morse v. Frederick*, 127 S.Ct. 2618 (2007).

101 Federal Trade Commission Act Sec. 45, 15 U.S.C. Secs. 41-58 (2006).

102 *See, e.g., In re J. Walter Thompson USA, Inc., 120 F.T.C. 829* (1995) (FTC found advertising agency liable where agency knew or should have known that claims of diet program were false).

103 A full discussion of the applicability (and constitutionality) of the Federal Trade Commission Act and various state "Printers' Ink" laws to media publishers is beyond the scope of this book. Suffice it say, however, that FTC officials have only gone so far as to informally say that the Commission is "unlikely [to] include any media in a formal complaint unless the broadcast station or the publication was an active party to and stood to profit by the falsity or deception of the advertising." Paul Dixon, Chairman, Fed. Trade Comm'n, speech before the Arizona Broadcasters Association: Broadcast Media and the Federal Trade Commission (May 25, 1973). Recently, for example, the FTC vaguely hinted that it might consider holding media responsible for publishing deceptive weight loss claims. Following protests by the publishing industry, the threat appears to have faded. *See In the Matter of Advertising of Weight Loss Products Workshop, No. P024527*, Comments of the Newspaper Association of America (Oct. 29, 2002), *Available at* http:// ftc.gov/bcp/workshops/weightloss/comments/NAA.pdf (last visited July 14, 2013). For a more thorough discussion of the issue, *See* Steven G. Brody & Bruce E. H. Johnson, *Advertising and Commercial Speech: A First Amendment Guide 381-390* (Practicing Law Institute

2001).

104 *See* Equal Opportunity Employment Act, 42 U.S.C. Sec. 2000e-3(b) (2007), *available at* http://www.law. cornell.edu/uscode/42/2000e-3.html (last visited July 14, 2013); Age Discrimination in Employment Act, 29 U.S.C. Sec. 623(e) (2006), *Available at* http://www.law.cornell.edu/uscode/text/29/623 (last visited July 14, 2013). Both of these laws only prohibit employers from publishing discriminatory ads.

105 A number of state press associations provide information on their state's anti-discrimination laws regarding employment advertising. *See, e.g.*, New Jersey Press Association Legal Hotline (May 2006), *available at* http://www.njpa.org/njpa/legal_hotline/advertising.html (last visited July 14, 2013); Pennsylvania Newspaper Association Newspaper Handbook, *available at:* http://panewsmedia.org/legal/ publications/newspaperhandbook/advertising (last visited July 14, 2013).

106 *Pittsburgh Press Co. v. Pittsburgh Comm'n on Human Relations*, 287 A.2d 161 (1972), aff'd, 413 U.S. 376 (1973), *reh'g denied*, 414 U.S. 881 (1973); *Evening Sentinel v. Nat'l Organization for Women*, 357 A.2d 498 (1975).

107 *See, e.g.*, N.C. GEN. STAT. Secs. 1-596 to 1-600 (2006) (limiting rates that may be charged for legal notices and providing other specifications for publication of notices). For example, N.C. GEN. STAT. Sec. 1-156 requires that the newspaper file a sworn statement of its ad rates with the clerk of the superior court prior to accepting legal advertising. Your state press association may be a good source for information about eligibility requirements in your state.

108 720 ILL. COMP. STAT. Ann. 5/28-1(a)(12) (West 2007).

109 IND. CODE Sec. 35-45-5-3(b) (2007).

110 LA. REV. STAT. Ann. Sec. 14:90.3 (2007), *available at* http://www.legis.state.la.us/lss/lss.asp?doc=78701 (last visited May 2013).

111 MONT. CODE Ann. Sec. 23-5-112-17(e) (2007).

112 NEV. REV. STAT. Secs.465.091-.094 (2007), *available at* http://www.leg.state.nv.us/NRS/NRS-465.html (last visited July 14, 2013).

113 OR. REV. STAT. Sec. 167.109 (2007).

114 S.D. CODIFIED LAWS Sec. 22-25A-1 to -15 (2007), *available at* http://legis.state.sd.us/statutes/ DisplayStatute. aspx?Statute=22-25A&Type=Statute (last visited July 14, 2013).

115 WASH. REV. CODE Sec. 9.46.240 (2007).

116 WIS. STAT. SEC. 945.06 (2007) (mandating that public utilities and carriers discontinue access to users transmitting or receiving gambling information, when notified in writing by a federal, state, or local authority of the unlawful transmission).

117 Chuck Humphrey, State Gambling Law Summary (2007), *available at* http://www.gambling-law-us.com/ State-Law-Summary/ (last visited July 14, 2013).

118 N.Y. Const. art. I, Sec. 9, cl. 1; Mont. Const. art. III, Sec. 9.

119 720 ILL. COMP. STAT. Ann. 5/28-1(a)(10) (West 2007).

120 GA. CODE Ann. Sec. 16-12-26 (2007).

121 31 U.S.C. Sec. 5361 (2007). The body of the Act may be found at 31 U.S.C. Secs. 5361-5367.

122 31 U.S.C. Sec. 5363 (2007).

123 *See id.* Sec. 5362(10)(A) (2007) (defining Internet gambling as unlawful "where such bet or wager is unlawful under any applicable Federal or State law in the State . . . in which the bet or wager is initiated, received, or otherwise made").; Chuck Humphrey, *Internet Gambling Funding Ban*, Gambling Law US, Oct. 13, 2006, http://www.gambling-law-us.com/Federal-Laws/internet-gambling-ban.htm (last visited July 14, 2013).

124 42 U.S.C. Sec. 3604(c).

125 *United States v. Hunter*, 459 F.2d 205 (4th Cir. 1972), *cert. denied*, 409 U.S. 934 (1973), *reh'g denied*, 413 U.S. 923 (1973).

126 Wash. A.G.O. 1976 No. 17, *available at* http://www.atg.wa.gov/opinion.aspx?section=topic&id=7710 (in addition to gender preference, opinion also allows roommate ads to contain religious preference) (last visited July 14, 2013); Allan Wolper, *Classified Ad Controversy is Resolved*, Editor & Publisher, March 26, 1994, at 22 (report on Feb. 18, 1994, memorandum by Don Grove, executive director of Iowa Civil Rights Commission).

127 Schwartz, *Rent-To-Share Ads Can Discriminate by Sex*, Publisher's Auxiliary, Oct. 20, 1986, at 3.

128 *This That and the Other Gift and Tobacco, Inc. v. Cobb County*, 285 F.3d 1319 (11th Cir. 2002).

129 *Basiardanes v. City of Galveston*, 682 F.2d 1203 (5th Cir. 1982); *Wolff v. City of Monticello*, 803 F. Supp. 1568 (D. Minn. 1992).

130 *Lueth v. St. Clair County Community College*, 732 F. Supp. 1410 (E.D. Mich. 1990).

131 *Evenson v. Ortega*, 605 F. Supp. 1115 (D. Ariz. 1985) (at least indirectly recognizing legality of escort service ads in rejecting plaintiff newspaper publisher's motion to enjoin police department from placing bogus ads as part of sting operation). *See also Republic Entm't, Inc. v. Clark County Liquor & Gaming Licensing Bd.*, 672 P.2d 634 (Nev. 1983) (Nevada Supreme Court upheld a county code that permitted only licensed "sexually-oriented" escort services to place ads).

132 *See, e.g., Rubin v. Coors Brewing Co.*, 514 U.S. 476, 482 n.2 (1995); *44 Liquormart, Inc. v. Rhode Island*, 517 U.S. 484, 497 (1996).

133 *See, e.g.*, CAL. EDUC. CODE Sec. 66400 (West 2008); COLO. REV. STAT. Ann. Sec. 23-4-103 (West 2007); CONN. GEN. STAT. Sec. 53-392b (2007); FLA. STAT. Ann. Sec. 877.17 (West 2007) (prohibits "advertis[ing] for sale" of term papers); 110 ILL. COMP. STAT. Ann. Sec. 5/1 (West 2007) (allowing for court order prohibiting "advertising for sale" of term papers); 17-A MAINE REV. STAT. Ann. Sec. 705(1)(B)(1) (2007); MD. CODE Ann., Educ. Sec. 26-201 (West 2008); MASS. GEN. LAWS Ann. Ch. 271, Sec. 50 (West 2007); NEV. REV. STAT. Sec. 207.320 (West 2007); N.J. STAT. Ann. Sec. 18A:2-3 (West 2007); N.Y. EDUC. LAW Sec. 213-b (McKinney 2007); N.C. GEN. STAT. Ann. Sec. 14-118.2 (West 2007); OR. REV. STAT. Ann. Sec. 165.114 (West 2007); 18 PA. CONS. STAT. Ann. 7324 (West 2007); TEX. PENAL CODE Ann. Sec. 32.50 (Vernon 2007); VA. CODE Ann. Secs. 18.2-505-508 (West 2007); WASH. REV. CODE Sec. 28B.10.584 (West 2007).

134 *See Trustees of Boston Univ. v. ASM Communications*, 33 F. Supp. 2d 66 (D. Mass. 1998) (dismissing

lawsuit brought by Boston University against Internet-based term paper companies under federal RICO statute and Massachusetts state law). But *See People v. Magee*, 423 N.Y.S.2d 417, 419 (N.Y. Sup. Ct. 1979) (rejecting term paper company's First Amendment claim that New York law was unconstitutional and finding that term papers were "plainly designed to deceive and would have no other utility in the world of scholarship").

135 15 U.S.C. Sec. 1335 (2005).

136 15 U.S.C. Sec. 1333 (2005).

137 *See, e.g., Lorillard Tobacco Co. v. Reilly*, 533 U.S. 525, 554 (2001); *Khademi v. South Orange Community College*, 194 F. Supp.2d 1011 (C.D. Calif. 2002) (upholding community college policy that banned advertising for illegal substances, but striking down ban insofar as it prohibited ads for legal substances including alcohol, tobacco and firearms).

138 *See, e.g., Boyd v. Keyboard, Network Magazine*, No. C 99-04430,2000 WL 274204, at *2 (N.D. Cal. Mar. 1, 2000), *aff'd*, 246 F.3d 672 (9th Cir. 2000) (dismissing claim that publisher was liable to reader of magazine for failing to investigate the authenticity of an ad that reader alleged was a con game that cost him "thousands of dollars" and "destroyed" his credit); *Ginsburg v. Agora, Inc.*, 915 F. Supp. 733 (D. Md. 1995) (holding that the defendants were not liable for the investor's financial losses, which investor blamed on false information in the defendants' investment newsletter); *Barden v. HarperCollins Publishers, Inc.*, 863 F. Supp. 41 (D. Mass. 1994) (holding that the publisher was not liable to a person who hired a lawyer based on book's false information about the lawyer's qualifications); *Smith v. Linn*, 563 A.2d 123, (Pa. Super. Ct. 1989), aff'd, 587 A.2d 309 (N.J. App. Ct. 1991) (finding that publisher was not liable for a death that allegedly resulted from its "liquid protein" diet book); *Yuhas v. Mudge*, 322 A.2d 824 (N.J. Super. Ct. App. Div. 1974) (holding that the publisher was not liable for injuries that resulted from use of fireworks advertised in its magazine); *MacKown v. Illinois Publ'g Co.*, 6 N.E.2d 526 (Ill. Ct. App. 1937) (finding that a newspaper was not liable for an injury sustained by a reader who made and used an alcohol and mercury-based dandruff remedy published in the newspaper).

139 *Winter v. G.P. Putnam's Sons*, 938 F.2d 1033 (9th Cir. 1991).

140 *Walters v. Seventeen Magazine*, 195 Cal. App. 3d 1119 (Cal. Ct. App. 1987).

141 *Id.* at 1122.

142 *See Hanberry v. Hearst Corp.*, 276 Cal. App. 2d 680 (Cal. Ct. App. 1969) (holding the publisher of Good Housekeeping magazine liable for negligent misrepresentation stemming from an injury suffered as a result of a defective shoe that was awarded the magazine's *Good Housekeeping* Seal of Approval. The seal stated: "We satisfy ourselves that products advertised in *Good Housekeeping* are good ones and that the advertising claims made for them in our magazine are truthful." *Id.* at 682.).

143 *Sakon v. Pepsico, Inc.*, 553 So. 2d 163 (Fla. 1989).

144 *Way v. Boy Scouts of America*, 856 S.W.2d 230 (Tex. App. 1993). Compare *Walter v. Bauer*, 439 N.Y.S.2d 821 (N.Y. Sup. Ct. 1981), *modified by* 451 N.Y.S.2d 533 (N.Y. App. Div. 1982) (denying attempt to bring defective-product claim against a science textbook publisher on behalf of fourth-grade student who was injured while conducting an experiment described in the book that the suit alleged was dangerous and defective).

145 *See, e.g., Winter v. G.P. Putnam's Sons*, 938 F.2d 1033, 1035 (9th Cir. 1991) (finding "[t]he threat of liability without fault (financial responsibility for our words and ideas in the absence of fault or a special undertaking or responsibility) could seriously inhibit those who wish to share thoughts and theories.").

146 *See, e.g., In the Matter of Advertising of Weight Loss Products Workshop*, No. P024527, Comments of the Newspaper Association of America, Sec. III (Oct. 29, 2002), *available at* http://ftc.gov/bcp/workshops/weightloss/comments/NAA.pdf (last visited Sept. 18, 2013).

147 P. Cameron DeVore & Robert D. Sack, *Advertising and Commercial Speech: A First Amendment Guide* 10-5 (Steven G. Brody & Bruce E.H. Johnson, eds., Practising Law Institute 2003).

148 *Braun v. Soldier of Fortune Magazine*, 968 F.2d 1110, 1112 (11th Cir. 1992), *cert. denied*, 506 U.S. 1071 (1993). Compare *Eimann v. Soldier of Fortune Magazine, Inc.*, 680 F. Supp. 863 (S.D. Tex. 1988), rev'd., 880 F.2d 830 (5th Cir. 1989), *cert. denied*, 493 U.S. 1024 (1990), where a federal district court found *Soldier of Fortune* liable for running a similar ad, ruling that a publication must avoid unusually "dangerous" classified ads or suffer the legal consequences. A federal court of appeals later reversed the decision, finding insufficient evidence of illegal intent on behalf of the publisher. *Eimann*, 880 F.2d at 838.

149 *Braun*, 968 F.2d at 1119, 1120.

150 *Norwood v. Soldier of Fortune Magazine*, 651 F. Supp. 1397, 1402-03 (W.D. Ark. 1987). *See also Braun*, 968 F.2d 1110 at 1121 (upholding a finding of publisher liability for "gun-for-hire" advertisement where ad on its face "makes it apparent that there was a substantial danger that [the advertiser] was soliciting illegal jobs involving the use of a gun").

151 *See, e.g., Turner Broad. Sys. v. FCC*, 512 U.S. 622, 641 (1994) ("At the heart of the First Amendment lies the principle that each person should decide for him or herself the ideas and beliefs deserving of expression, consideration, and adherence."). *See also West Virginia State Bd. of Educ. v. Barnette*, 319 U.S. 624 (1943).

152 *See, e.g., Miami Herald Publ'g Co. v. Tornillo*, 418 U.S. 241 (1974); *Pacific Gas & Electric v. Public Utilities Comm'n*, 475 U.S. 1 (1986), *reh'g denied*, 475 U.S. 1133 (1986); *Wisconsin Ass'n of Nursing Homes, Inc. v. The Journal Co.*, 285 N.W.2d 891 (Wis. Ct. App. 1979); *Newspaper Printing Corp. v. Galbreath*, 580 S.W.2d 777 (Tenn. 1979), *cert. denied*, 444 U.S. 870 (1979). Only in the context of violations of antitrust laws, which would seldom be relevant to the student media, can the rejection of ads be legally limited.

153 *See, e.g., Newspaper Printing Corp. v. Galbreath*, 580 S.W.2d 777, 780 (Tenn. 1979) ("[S]ince it [the newspaper publisher] may refuse to publish [the ad] at all, it may require that advertisements submitted to it for publication comply with such rules and regulations as the publishers deem proper."), *cert. denied*, 444 U.S. 870 (1979).

154 *Mississippi Gay Alliance v. Goudelock*, 536 F.2d 1073 (5th Cir. 1976), *cert. denied*, 430 U.S. 982 (1977) (student newspaper's refusal to print a homosexual organization's ad did not violate the First

Amendment even though newspaper partially funded by student fees); *Owens v. Idaho Argonaut*, No. C-193 (Idaho Dist. Ct. 1987) (student newspaper at the University of Idaho had right to reject ad its editor believed was unsuitable for publication after judge determined no contract existed); *Yeo v. Town of Lexington*, 131 F.3d 241 (1st Cir. 1997) (en banc), *cert. denied*, 524 U.S. 904 (1988) (holding that the editors of high school student newspaper were not required to run an advertisement submitted by a community group urging sexual abstinence where no state action was involved in editor's rejection of the ad, and further noting that a Massachusetts state law protecting free expression rights of high school student journalists precluded school officials from playing a role in the ad's rejection); *Leeds v. Meltz*, 85 F.3d 51 (2d Cir. 1996) (dismissing First Amendment claim of advertiser where student editors of a public college newspaper are not "state actors" and their rejection of advertisement not state action). *See also Avins v. Rutgers*, 385 F.2d 151 (3d Cir. 1967), *cert. denied*, 390 U.S. 920 (1968) (upholding right of student editor of public university law review to reject articles submitted for publication).

155 *Sinn v. Daily Nebraskan*, 829 F.2d 662, 663 (8th Cir. 1987).

156 *Id.* at 663 (quoting 638 F. Supp 143, 148 (1986)).

157 *Sinn v. Daily Nebraskan*, 638 F. Supp. 143, 146 (D. Neb. 1986).

158 *Yeo v. Town of Lexington*, 131 F.3d 241 (1st Cir. 1997) (en banc), *cert. denied*, 524 U.S. 904 (1998).

159 *Id.* at 244.

160 *Id.* at 243, 246.

161 *Id.* at 252.

162 *Id.* (finding that "[t]he publishing of a newspaper or a yearbook is most emphatically not a traditional function nor an exclusive prerogative of the government in this country"). Compare *Owasso Indep. Sch. Dist. v. Falvo*, 534 U.S. 426 (2002) (finding that students that grade classmates' papers are not "acting for" school).

163 *Yeo*, 131 F.3d at 253.

164 *Sinn*, 829 F.2d at 664-665; *Yeo*, 131 F.3d at 254. *See also Rendell-Baker v. Kohn*, 457 U.S. 830 (1982).

165 *See Lee v. Bd. of Regents*, 306 F. Supp. 1097 (W.D. Wis. 1969), *aff'd*, 441 F.2d 1257 (7th Cir. 1971) (holding that a student newspaper's rejection of various editorial advertisements violated the First Amendment where the president of the state university had the power to enforce the newspaper's advertising policies); *Portland Women's Health Ctr. v. Portland Community College*, No. 80-558 (D. Or. Sept. 4, 1981) (ruling that public college student newspaper could not reject abortion-related advertisement where content decisions were made by publication's faculty adviser); *San Diego Committee Against Registration and the Draft v. Governing Bd. of Grossmont Union High Sch. Dist.*, 790 F.2d 1471 (9th Cir. 1986) (holding that a school board violated First Amendment by prohibiting student newspaper from running an advertisement from a committee against draft registration). *See also Rutgers 1000 Alumni Council v. Rutgers*, 803 A.2d 679 (N.J. Super. Ct. App. Div. 2002) (finding that public university violated First Amendment where it rejected issue-oriented advertisement submitted for publication in official university magazine edited and produced by university administrators).

166 *See Sinn*, 638 F. Supp. at 148-49 (finding that "[s]tate action is not present in the editorial decisionmaking of *the Daily Nebraskan* . . . [where it] functions like a private newspaper"); *Yeo*, 131 F.3d at 249 (finding that school administrators based their decision not to interfere with the student's editorial judgment in part on Massachusett's student free expression law).

167 *See Herald-Telephone v. Fatouros*, 431 N.E.2d 171 (Ind. Ct. App. 1982).

168 State antitrust laws vary. At the federal level, Section 1 of the Sherman Antitrust Act states in pertinent part, "[e]very contract...in restraint of trade commerce among the several [s]tates . . . is declared to be illegal." Section 2 reads: "[e]very person who shall monopolize, or attempt to monopolize...any part of trade or commerce among the several [s]tates...shall be deemed guilty of a felony..." 15 U.S.C. Sec. 1, 2 (2006). For a Section 1 violation, the U.S. Supreme Court has held that the restraint must be unreasonable. Standard Oil of New Jersey v. United States, 221 U.S. 1 (1911). The Robinson-Patman Act states, in pertinent part, that "[i]t shall be unlawful for any person engaged in commerce...to pay or grant, or to receive or accept, anything of value as a commission...or other compensation...except for services rendered in connection with the sale or purchase of goods...either to the other party to such [a] transaction or to an agent, representative, or other intermediary. . . ." Note, however, that the Robinson-Patman Act does not apply to purchases of supplies by a school for its own use. 15 U.S.C. Sec.13(c) (2006).

169 *Bridges v. MacLean-Stevens Studios, Inc.*, 201 F.3d 6 (1st Cir. 2000) (holding that agreement to offer portrait services to school did not restrain trade); *Foto USA, Inc. v. Board of Regents of the Univ. Sys. of Florida*, 141 F.3d 1032 (11th Cir. 1998) (holding that a university can enter into an exclusive contract with a photographer to take pictures of graduates as they receive their diplomas); *Burns v. Cover Studios, Inc.*, 818 F. Supp. 888 (W.D. Pa. 1993) (holding that an exclusivity contract was not a monopoly and did not violate antitrust laws); *Thaxton v. Medina City Bd. of Educ.*, 488 N.E.2d 136 (Ohio 1986) (holding that a school board that entered into contract for photography services was acting within its government capacity to provide for and manage extracurricular activities); *Burge v. Bryant Public Sch. Dist. of Saline County*, 658 F.2d 611 (8th Cir. 1981) (affirming a grant of summary judgment in favor of the defendant school district); *LaPorte v. Escanaba Area Pub. Sch.*, 214 N.W.2d 840 (Mich. Ct. App. 1974) (holding that a school district could enter into contract with photographer who planned to profit from the ancillary sales of photo packages).

170 *See LaPorte*, 214 N.W.2d at 843 ("The plaintiffs bid and lost. Absent proof of fraud in the bidding process, they are entitled to no more from this Court").

171 *See Burge*, 520 F. Supp at 332-333; *Bridges*, 201 F.3d at 9-12; *Stephen Jay Photography, Ltd. v. Olan Mills, Inc.*, 903 F.2d 988, 991-94 (4th Cir. 1990).

172 *See Bridges*, 201 F.3d at 14; *Burns*, 818 F. Supp. at 892; *Stephen Jay Photography*, 903 F.2d at 994-996.

173 *In the Matter of the Appeal of Tarolli*, Decision No. 13,982, 38 Ed. Dept. Rep. 60 (Aug. 7, 1998); *In the Matter of the Appeal of Puls*, Decision No. 9627, 17 Ed. Dept. Rep. 324 (Feb. 28, 1978).

APPENDIX

ACP MODEL CODE OF ETHICS FOR STUDENT MEDIA

Overview

To seek truth and to publish it is the two-step goal of a journalist. Though plainly stated, this process is not always simple or easy to achieve. To help journalists be true to this goal, print and online newspapers, magazines and yearbooks adopt rules and guidelines, which often include a code of ethics for their members to follow. The code contains standards of conduct and moral judgments. Some points are specific and ideally inflexible; others may be less rigid due to extenuating circumstances. Some are based on law. Once a code is adopted, it brings desirable uniformity to some degree to the news gathering process and in the group's search for truth. The code answers questions and reminds those who operate under it that standards of honesty and performance exist. A code of ethics is not a burden; rather, a code is a useful license to practice news gathering and publishing free of much uncertainty. The code can be used by individuals to measure their work. The code can also be used to evaluate the integrity of the publication as a whole. Readers should expect nothing less than the truth in all print and online news publications. Adoption of a code of ethics by those who publish news helps safeguard the public trust given to journalists.

ACP's model ethics code may be adopted without changes, but it is more likely that a staff may want to modify the code to fit any unique characteristics of the campus and the publication. Ideally, this model will be suitable for print and online newspapers, yearbooks and magazines published by students. However, some of the points may be more appropriate for one type of publication than another. Finally, the realities of budgets and staffing may make some points impractical or impossible to follow completely. If the complete model is unattainable, a staff will want to adopt those points that are important and attainable regardless of limitations caused by budgets and other factors.

A college student media staff should view a code of ethics as an evolving reference document. All staff members should have a copy; it should be discussed at a staff meeting at the start of a publishing term; all staff recruits, including volunteers and those who are paid, should be introduced to the code as a part of their orientation. It should be revised as needs change and it should be compared to other codes for completeness. Collegiate journalists who follow a code of ethics will find the transition to commercial or non-student media easier.

College and university media that adopt this code to their traditions and existing practices should take care to make certain that no staff member unilaterally imposes a standard of ethical conduct on the remainder of the staff. As ethics is more a process of decision making rather than a result, the ethical standards of a student media organization should be the product of discussion and debate among student journalists, guided by the standards that inform the practices of professional journalists in the United States. Adoption of and adherence to a journalism code of ethics will lead to greater credibility for the news media.

Index

01   Free Travel

To remain as free of influence or obligation to report a story, the journalist, in pursuit of a story, should not accept free travel, accommodations or meals related to travel. For convenience, sports reporters may travel on team charters, but the publication should pay the cost of the transportation and related expenses. The same pay-as-you-go policy should apply to non-sports reporting as well, including businesses and governments. Free travel and accommodations that are non-coverage related and provided by a vendor may be accepted if the primary purpose is for education or training and is related to the fulfillment of an agreement or contract.

02   Gifts

Gifts should not be accepted. Any gift should be returned to the sender or sent to a charity. If the gift is of de minimis (no significant) value, such as a desk trinket, small food item or pen, the staff member may retain the gift. As a guideline, if the value is under $10, the gift may be kept. More than one gift in one year, even if under $10, from the same giver, may not be accepted.

03   Free Tickets, Passes, Discounts

If money is available, staffers assigned to cover a sporting event, lecture, play, concert, movie or other entertainment event should pay for admission. Free tickets or passes may be accepted by staff members assigned to cover an event or by those attending for legitimate news purposes. Press facilities at these events may only be used by staff members who are assigned to cover the event. Free tickets or passes may be accepted by staff members for personal use only if tickets are available on the same complimentary basis to non-journalists.

04 Ownership of Books, Records, Other Products Given for Review

Any materials given to the publication for review become the property of the publication and not of any individual staff member. The editor reserves the right to disperse the property in an equitable way.

05 Other Employment

Other employment should not conflict with the staffer's first responsibilities to the publication. The staffer must report any other employment to the editor to avoid any conflicts of interest with assignments or other staff editorial or business responsibilities or influences.

06 Other Campus Media Work

To avoid a conflict of interest, a staffer should not hold similar positions on two or more campus news, public information or public relations media or organizations.

07 Online Media Work

Student journalists working with established student media may consider starting their own blog or digital-media sites to serve their campus communities. But care should be taken to keep in mind the potential consequences of their decision on the student newspaper, yearbook or other medium. Editors and managers should draft and enforce policies governing the work of student journalists in the online environment as that work impacts the ability of the student press to serve its mission in the campus community.

08 Other Off-campus or Free Lance Media Work

Approval of work for an off-campus news medium and free lance media work should be sought in advance of the commitment. It is permissible only in a non-competitive medium, on a staffer's own time and should not conflict with the staffer's obligations to the publication.

09 Membership in Campus Organizations

Staffers may not cover a campus organization they belong to, or participate in any editorial or business decisions regarding that organization. Staffers may provide story leads about the organizations to which they belong to other staffers. Staffers should report their memberships to their supervising editor. To maintain the role of the press as an independent watchdog of government, a staffer should not be an elected or appointed member of student government.

10 Outside Activities, Including Political

Political involvement, holding off-campus public office and service in community organizations should be considered carefully to avoid compromising professional integrity and that of the publication. The notion of the journalist as an independent observer and fact-finder is important to preserve. A staffer involved in specific political action, especially in a leadership role, should not be assigned to cover that involvement.

11 Relationships and Coverage

Staffers must declare conflicts and avoid involvement in stories dealing with members of their families. Staff members should not cover — in words, photographs or artwork — or make news judgments about family members or persons with whom they have financial, adversarial, romantic, sexual or closely personal relationships. Intra-staff dating is not recommended if one person assigns or evaluates the work of the other person or if one is in a position to promote the other to a higher staff position.

12   Use of Alcoholic Beverages While on Assignment

Even though a staffer may be able to drink legally, no or only light drinking in a social setting such as a dinner or reception is recommended to avoid any suspicion by a source or the public that the staffer's judgment, credibility or objectivity is impaired by alcohol. When covering an event where alcohol is served, staffers should not accept free drinks unless all drinks are free to everyone in attendance. Staffers should avoid the appearance that they are being "wined and dined" by any source or group.

13   Sexual Harassment

Sexual harassment is: (verbal) suggestive comments, sexual innuendo, threats, insults, jokes about sex-specific traits, sexual propositions; (nonverbal) vulgar gestures, whistling, leering, suggestive or insulting noises; (physical) touching, pinching, brushing the body, coercing sexual intercourse, assault. This conduct can be called job-related harassment when submission is made implicitly or explicitly a condition of employment, a condition of work-related assignments, compensation and other factors, or if such conduct interferes with the staffer's performance or creates a hostile, intimidating or offensive work environment. Sexual harassment is prohibited. A staff should establish a procedure to report any harassment claim. That procedure should include at least two alternate methods of reporting, information on how the claim will be investigated, and what will be done to correct the situation if it is real harassment. A staff meeting that includes a discussion of sexual harassment and working conditions is recommended at the start of each publishing term.

14   Plagiarism of Words, Art, Other

Plagiarism is prohibited and is illegal if the material is copyright protected. For the purposes of this code, plagiarism is defined as the word-for-word duplication of another person's writing or close summarization of the work of another source without giving the source proper credit. A comparable prohibition applies to the use of graphics. Information obtained from a published work must be independently verified before it can be reported as a new, original story. This policy also forbids lifting verbatim paragraphs from a wire service without attribution or pointing out that wire stories were used in compiling the story. Material that is published on the Internet should be treated in the same way as if it were published in more traditional broadcast media. Because plagiarism can significantly undermine the public trust of journalists and journalism, editors should be prepared to consider severe penalties for documented cases of plagiarism, including dismissal from the staff.

15   Fabrication of Any Kind

The use of composite characters or imaginary situations or characters will not be allowed in news or feature stories. A columnist may, occasionally, use such an approach in developing a piece, but it must be clear to the reader that the person or situation is fictional and that the column is commentary and not reporting. The growth of narrative story development (storytelling devices) means that reporters and editors should be especially careful to not mix fact and fiction, and not embellish fact with fictional details, regardless of their significance.

16   Electronically Altered Photos

Electronically altering the content of photos for news and general feature stories or as stand-alone news and feature photos is not allowed. Exceptions to this would be adjustments to contrast and similar technical enhancements that don't affect the truthfulness of the subject and context of the subject or the scene. Content may be altered for creative purposes as a special effect for a feature story if the caption or creditline includes that fact and if an average reader would not mistake the photo for reality. These photos are usually tagged as photo illustrations. In a news medium, readers expect photos and stories to be truthful.

17   Photo Illustration and Re-enactments
Set-ups or posed scenes may be used if the average reader will not be misled or if the caption or creditline tells readers that it is a photo illustration or a re-enactment or re-staging of an event, including award presentations. Recording the original action is always preferred.

18   Use of Photographs of Victims of Accidents, Fires, Natural Disasters
Photos have a tremendous impact on readers. The question of privacy versus the public's right to know should be considered. The line between good and bad taste and reality and sensationalism is not always easy to draw. Care should be taken to maintain the dignity of the subject as much as possible without undermining the truth of the event. In making a final decision on a photo of this type, an editor should consider: Do the readers need information from this photo that helps explain the event better than words or another photo? Who is hurt by the publication of this photo? How would I react if my photograph was taken at such a moment of tragedy and anguish?

19   Reporting Names, Addresses of Crime Victims
Staffers need to know the state laws that govern the publication of the names of crime victims. Customarily, the names of rape victims are not published; however, some news media have asked victims of sexual assault to identify themselves for publication. This may be negotiated between the victim and the publication. Victims of nonsexual crimes may be identified, but the publication has a responsibility to give some protection to the victims such as giving imprecise addresses. With the exception of major crimes, predetermined by the editor, an arrested person is not named until charges are filed. However, to avoid a subjective list of exceptions, it is acceptable to withhold all names, regardless of the crime, until charges are filed.

20   Cooperation with Law Enforcement, Government, College Administration
To be an effective watchdog on other agencies, a publication must remain independent. The publication should not take over any of the duties of any outside agency; cooperation or involvement in the work of these agencies should be restricted to what is required by law. Staffers should know any freedom of information, open meetings and shield laws that apply to their work. If a staffer thinks any public authority is interfering with the staffer's functions as a journalist, the incident should be reported to the editor. The editor should then seek advice from groups such as the Student Press Law Center, American Civil Liberties Union or an editor or media attorney for a nearby, non-student publication.

21   Scrutiny of a Public Person's Life
Conflicts exist between a person's desire for privacy and the public good or the public's right to know about a public person's life. Persons who freely choose to become public celebrities or public servants should expect a greater level of scrutiny of their life than a private person — even a private person who suddenly is involved in a public situation. Staffers should make judgments based on the real news value of the situation, common sense and decency. Reporters and photographers should not badger a person who has made it clear that he or she does not want to be interviewed or photographed. One exception is those who are involved in criminal activity or in court. Publishing intimate details of a person's life, such as their health or sexual activities, should be done with extreme care and only if the facts are important for the completeness of a story and reflect in a significant way upon the person's public life.

22   Profane, Vulgar Words, Explicit Sexual Language

The primary audience of a college publication is adults. Profane and vulgar words are a part of everyday conversation, but not generally used for scholarly or general audience writing. During the interview stage of news gathering, staffers will encounter interviewees who use words viewed as vulgar and profane. The staff may publish these words if the words are important to the reader's understanding of the situation — the reality of life — or if the words help establish the character of the interviewee. The staff may decide to limit references to prevent the vulgar or profane language from overshadowing the other, more important facts of the story. Profane and vulgar words are not acceptable for opinion writing — columns, editorials and other commentary. Though they may be vulgar or profane, individual words are not obscene. Explicit language — but not vulgar, street language — describing sexual activities and human body parts and functions should be used for accurate reporting of health stories and, in a more limited way, for sexual crime stories.

23   Sexist Language

Staffers should avoid sexist labels and descriptive language. Replace such language with neutral terms and descriptions.

24   Negative Stereotyping

Staffers should take care in writing to avoid applying commonly thought but usually erroneous group stereotypes to individuals who are a member of a particular group. Generalizations, often based upon stereotypes, can be misleading and inaccurate. In a broader sense, writers, photographers and artists should avoid more subtle stereotyping in their selection of interviewees and subjects of photographs or illustrations. Some examples of negative stereotypes: unmarried, black teen welfare mothers; unemployed, alcohol-using Native Americans; overweight, long-haired white biker outlaws; effeminate gays; inarticulate, "dumb" blonde women. It is also advisable to avoid sexual stereotyping in choice of subjects for stories, photographs and illustrations on sports or political or social issues such as equal rights.

25   Use of Racial, Ethnic, Religious, Sexual Orientation, Other
Group Identifiers

Identification of a person as a member of any population group should be limited to those cases when that membership is essential for the reader's complete understanding of the story; it should be done with great care so as not to perpetuate negative or positive group stereotyping. When identifiers are used, it is important that the correct one be used. Some examples of identifiers: Hispanic, Jew, lesbian, Italian, person with AIDS (PWA), physically challenged, deaf (or partially deaf). Please consult the style manual of the Associated Press or another news organization for guidance in properly and accurately identifying individuals on the basis of their membership in ethnic or religious groups or on the basis of their sexual orientation.

26   False Identity, Stolen Documents, Concealed Recording,
Eavesdropping

In the ordinary course of reporting, no staffers shall misrepresent themselves as anything other than representatives of the publication. In extraordinary circumstances, when an editor judges that the information cannot be gotten in any other way and the value of that information to the readers is important, the editor may authorize a misrepresentation. Staffers may not steal or knowingly receive stolen materials regardless of their importance to a story. Except in situations judged by an editor as extraordinary, a staffer shall not record an interview or meeting without the interviewee's permission or the obvious placement of a recording device (not hidden) at the start of the interview or meeting in which case the interviewee or newsmakers do not object and are aware of the presence of the recording device. Committing an illegal act to eavesdrop on a source is not allowed. State laws on the use of recording devices should be checked.

27   Granting and Preserving Confidentiality to Sources
A reporter should not promise confidentiality to a source without the permission of the editor. Confidentiality should only be given if there is a real danger that physical, emotional or financial harm will come to the source if his or her name were revealed. The editor should have all the facts and the source's name before the decision is made. The editor should know of any laws pertaining to confidentiality and disclosure before a decision is made. A reporter should make every attempt to get the same information from another source who agrees to be named since the goal is to attribute all information to a specific source for all stories.

28   Anonymous Sources
Generally, anonymous sources are not used in stories. Information that comes from an unnamed or unknown source should not be used unless it can be verified through another, known source. If two independent sources verify the information and both are unnamed, an editor may decide to publish the information with careful consideration of the need for immediacy and the news value of the information. The source may be identified generally as one associated with an agency to give some degree of credibility to the information. (See 27: Confidentiality.) The danger exists that the reader might not believe the information if sources are not given; the publication's credibility might suffer; information obtained later from a named source and verified might disprove the information given by the unnamed or unknown sources.

29   No Response from Subject
If the subject of a story does not respond to a reporter's inquiry, the reporter may use the failure to respond in the story. However, use the verb "refused" to respond cautiously because of its connotation. It is often better to use "declined" or "would not respond." If the subject cannot be reached, it is acceptable to say that the subject was not available for comment. The difference between not responding and not available for comment should be clear to the reader.

30   Sources on the Internet
Reporters who use the Internet and e-mail to interview sources should identify themselves as a reporter immediately, and should verify the source's identify with a follow-up telephone call. The source should be told that the information given is for a story. Information from Internet chat rooms and bulletin boards should not be used except as background or if it is used, it should be attributed as "from the Internet." Since some information on the Internet may not be accurate, verification of facts through another source is especially important. Raising particular concern among journalists is information from so-called "user-generated" sites such as Wikipedia, YouTube, blogs, Facebook and others. While not necessarily inaccurate, such sites allow users to post information and allegations without the benefit of editing or fact-checking.

31   Corrections
An inaccuracy is never knowingly published. If any error is found, the publication is obligated to correct the error as soon as possible, regardless of the source of the error. A consistent location for the publication of corrections is recommended. Such a location could be on the editorial or op-ed page of a newspaper. It should be clearly and prominently labeled as a correction. A magazine or yearbook published semi- or annually may want to publish a correction in the student newspaper, which is published more frequently. Clarifications may also be labeled and published in the same manner. For online publications, a corrections and clarifications link could be on the home page. Even in the age of the Internet, journalism is still regarded as 'the first rough draft of history.' As such, journalists should always keep

in mind the impacts their factual errors may have on the future record of a person or event. Editors should judge what policies they should develop to govern requests to modify or even delete information from their Web sites, which can continue to haunt journalists and their sources for years after publication.

32 Ownership of Work

Regardless of whether a staffer is paid or a volunteer, the publication "owns" the published and unpublished work done by staffers if the work was done as a staff assignment. Ownership of unpublished work may revert to the staffer at a certain time if the editor agrees with this arrangement. The publication has unlimited use of the work. The act of voluntarily joining a staff indicates approval of this policy. To clarify work-ownership issues, editors should have staff members sign an ownership agreement regarding their work. A model agreement created by the Student Press Law Center is available on the Web at nspa.studentpress. org/pdf/wheel_medialicense.pdf. As is practiced in professional media, readers of the student press should be made aware that ownership of reader submissions is taken by the student press at the time of submission. The publication may wish to develop a document transferring ownership to be signed by readers who submit materials for consideration.

33 Contests, Honors

The publication has a proprietary interest in the material it publishes. Thus, the publication as a voting group or top editors are entitled to determine which entries will represent it in contests. This will avoid the appearance of a conflict of interest that might occur if staffers were to win or accept awards from organizations they are assigned to cover. Awards presented to the staff as a whole or to the publication generally become the property of the publication. Individuals who win awards for work published in the staff publication may accept the award and retain ownership of it.

34 Separation of Reporting from Commentary

To help the reader separate fact-based reporting from commentary, in the form of personal columns, editorials, analysis and similar opinion writing, all commentary should be labled or somehow clearly and consistently identified as opinion, especially when it is outside the editorial or op-ed pages and mixed with fact-based reporting.

35 Influence of Advertisers

Editors should guard against attempts made by advertisers and others in the publication's business office to influence the editorial content of the print or online publication. The editorial staff reserves the right to make all decisions about any editorial coverage an advertiser may get in the publication, including advertising supplements. Readers should not perceive that an advertiser is getting favorable editorial mention simply because the advertiser has bought space in the publication.

36 Acceptance of Reader Feedback

Editors and reporters should invite reader feedback and participation in the publication. Reaction by readers to what has been published should be invited through all methods of communication: paper, e-mail, Web site, phone, fax and in-person visits. The publication should hold periodic open forums or open houses for readers. Reader opinions and suggestions on a range of issues can be solicited at these forums and can form the basis for future reporting or commentary.

37 Reporter's Checklist

Through all steps in the reporting process, from conceptualizing the story assignment, through information gathering and pre-writing, to writing, editing and final publication, a reporter must answer these questions:

1. Why am I reporting the story?
2. Is the story fair?
3. Have I attempted to report all angles?
4. Who will the story affect?
5. Can I defend my decision to report the story?

Often, a reporter consults with an editor regarding these questions, especially if the answers are troublesome.

38 Supplementary Reading

The Elements of Journalism, revised edition, Bill Kovach and Tom Rosenstiel, 2007, Three Rivers Press.

Media Ethics: Issues and Cases, Sixth Edition, Phillip Patterson and Lee Wilkins, 2007, McGraw-Hill.

Media Ethics: Cases and Moral Reasoning, Eighth Edition, Clifford G. Christians et al, 2008, Allyn & Bacon.

Media Ethics: A Philosophical Approach, Matthew Kieran, 1997, Praeger Publishers.

Speech, Media and Ethics: The Limits of Free Expression, Michael Cohen-Almagor, 2005, Palgrave Macmillan.

Media Ethics Goes to the Movies, Howard Good and Michael J. Dillon, 2002, Praeger Publishers.

Media Ethics and Social Change, Valerie Alia, 2004, Routledge.

Media Ethics and Accountability Systems, Claude-Jean Bertrand, 2000, Transaction Publishers.

Real-World Media Ethics, Phillipe Perebinossoff, 2008, Focal Press.

Contemporary Media Ethics: A Practical Guide for Students, Scholars and Professionals, Mitchell Land and Bill W. Hornaday, 2006, Marquette Books.

Media and Ethics: Principles for Moral Decisions, Elaine E. Englehardt and Ralph Barney, 2001, Wadsworth.

Issues in Journalism: A Discussion Guide for News Media Ethics, Maclyn McClary, 2005, BookSurge Publishing.

Online Journalism Ethics: Traditions and Transitions, Cecilia Friend and Jane B. Singer, 2007, M.E. Sharpe.

Journalism and Truth: Strange Bedfellows, Tom Goldstein and Howard Baker, 2007, Northwestern University Press,

American Carnival: Journalism Under Siege in an Age of New Media, Neil Henry, 2007, University of California Press.

We're All Journalists Now: The Transformation of the Press and Reshaping of the Law in the Internet Age, Scott Gant, 2007, Free Press.

Media Ethics: An Introduction and Overview, H. Ronning and F.P. Kasoma, 2004, Juta Academic.

Authors

The Model Code of Ethics was written for the Associated Collegiate Press by Albert DeLuca, a former assistant professor of journalism and adviser to the student newspaper at James Madison University in Harrisonburg, Va., and Tom Rolnicki, the former executive director of the National Scholastic Press Association and the Associated Collegiate Press in Minneapolis, Minn.

The fourth edition of the code was revised by Brian Steffen, Ph.D., associate professor of communication studies at Simpson College in Indianola, Iowa, where he is also adviser to the student newspaper. He is a former chairman of the Ethics Committee for College Media Association.

[Revised September 2008]

ASSOCIATION FOR EDUCATION IN JOURNALISM AND MASS COMMUNICATION RESOLUTION REGARDING THE 25TH ANNIVERSARY OF RULING IN *HAZELWOOD SCHOOL DISTRICT V. KUHLMEIER*

Reprinted with permission of the Association for Education in Journalism and Mass Communication.

Resolution

In recognition of society's increased reliance on student news-gatherers to fulfill basic community information needs, and the importance of unfiltered information about the performance of educational institutions,

In recognition of the well-documented misapplication of *Hazelwood* censorship authority to impede the teaching of professional journalistic values and practices, which include the willingness to question the performance of governance institutions,

In recognition that the primary concern of the Supreme Court in *Hazelwood* was to permit schools to restrict editorial content "unsuitable for immature audiences", a concern inapplicable at the postsecondary level.

In recognition of the combined 150 years' experience of states with statutory student free-press guarantees, demonstrating that the *Hazelwood* level of administrative control is unnecessary for the advancement of legitimate educational objectives,

Be it resolved that:
The Board of Directors of AEJMC declares that no legitimate pedagogical purpose is served by the censorship of student journalism even if it reflects unflatteringly on school policies and programs, candidly discusses sensitive social and political issues, or voices opinions challenging to majority views on matters of public concern. The censorship of such speech is detrimental to effective learning and teaching, and it cannot be justified by reference to "pedagogical concerns."

Be it further resolved that:
The AEJMC Board of Directors declares that the *Hazelwood* level of control over student journalistic and editorial expression is incompatible with the effective teaching of journalistic skills, values and practices at the collegiate level, and that institutions of postsecondary education should forswear reliance on Hazelwood as a legitimate source of authority for the governance of student and educator expression.

[Adopted 2013]

COLLEGE MEDIA ASSOCIATION CODE OF ETHICAL BEHAVIOR

Reprinted with permission of College Media Advisers Inc.

The adviser is a journalist, educator and manager who is, above all, a role model. Because of this, the adviser must be beyond reproach with regard to personal and professional ethical behavior; should encourage the student media advised to formulate, adhere to and publicize an organizational code of ethics; and ensure that neither the medium, its staff nor the adviser enter into the situations which would jeopardize the public's trust in and reliance on the medium as a fair and balanced source of news and analysis.

The Adviser's Professional Code

Freedom of expression and debate by means of a free and vigorous student media are essential to the effectiveness of an educational community in a democratic society. This implies the obligation of the student media to provide a forum for the expression of opinion – not only those opinions differing from established university or administrative policy, but those at odds with the media staff beliefs or opinions as well.

Student media must be free from all forms of external interference designed to regulate its content, including confiscation of its products or broadcasts; suspension of publication or transmission; academic personal or budgetary sanctions; arbitrary removal of staff members or faculty; or threats to the existence of student publications or broadcast outlets. In public institutions, the law is quite clear on guaranteeing broad freedom of expression to the students. In private institutions, media advisers should aid in developing governing documents and working with administrative guidelines which foster a free and open atmosphere for students involved in campus media work, if such freedoms do not currently exist.

Students should be made mindful of their obligation to avoid real and apparent conflicts of interest. They must be held to clear local policies in that regard.

Advisers, in addition to adhering to their code of ethics, should encourage the media they advise have established and published codes that apply to the student staffs and conform to nationally established and accepted journalistic norms regarding professional behavior, conflict of interest, acceptance of gifts and services, honesty and integrity.

Advisers, in these roles as professionals, must ensure that they have or gain the skills and education requisite to teach all aspects of the media they advise.

The Adviser's Personal Code

The ultimate goal of the student media adviser is to mold, preserve and protect an ethical and educational environment in which excellent communication skills and sound journalistic practice will be learned and practiced by students. There should never be an instance where an adviser maximizes quality by minimizing learning. Student media should always consist of student work.

Faculty, staff and other non-students who assume advisory roles with student media must remain aware of their obligation to defend and teach without censoring, editing, directing or producing. It should not be the media adviser's role to modify student writing or broadcasts, for it robs student journalists of educational opportunity and could severely damage their rights to free expression. Advisers to student media must demonstrate a firm dedication to accuracy, fairness, facts and honesty in all content of the medium.

Since there is no clear line between student media content and student media operations, ethical prohibitions against interference in content also apply to interference in student media operations in areas such as story assignments, decisions on inclusion or exclusion of content, staff selection, source selection, news and advertising acceptability standards, and most budgetary decisions. Using arbitrary policies, production guidelines or financial constraints to limit student decision making is no more ethical than rewriting or changing editorial content or influencing the physical appearance of media.

Advisers should be keenly aware of the potential for conflict of interest between their teaching/advising duties and their roles as university staff members and private citizens. It is vital that they avoid not only actual but apparent conflicts of interest. The publicity interests of the university and the news goals of the student media are often incompatible. Advisers should be aware of becoming the publicity focus of organizations to which they belong or for activities in which they are participating.

Advisers cannot expect student staff to respect their own ethical guidelines if advisers believe themselves exempt from strict ethical behavior. The requirements for ethical behavior extend to all operations for student media, not just the news or information function.

Perceptions of favoritism in the purchasing of services and equipment or granting of contracts can be just as damaging to credibility as perceived favoritism in news judgment. This is particularly true when offers of unrelated equipment or services are made in return for giving business to vendors. A clear policy that applies to all members of the student media operation should be communicated to all potential vendors.

The Adviser's Obligations

Membership in College Media Association signifies acceptance of this code and a willingness to abide by its tenets.

The organization will support those members who adhere to this code and thereby become victims of pressure or negative action from university administrators. This may involve formal censure of the offending institution of higher education.

[Valid as of September 2013]

NATIONAL COUNCIL OF TEACHERS OF ENGLISH RESOLUTION ON THE IMPORTANCE OF JOURNALISM COURSES AND PROGRAMS IN ENGLISH CURRICULA

Reprinted with permission.

Background

Many school districts have recently cut or eliminated journalism courses and student media. Budget cuts, emphasis on state curriculum standards, and remedial classes, as well as attempts to restrict students' speech and press rights, have contributed to the decline in the number and the quality of journalism programs.

Their loss is a blow to English curricula; journalism classes, including publications classes, are valuable courses.

According to *Applying NCTE/IRA Standards in Classroom Journalism Projects* (published by NCTE and JEA), "journalism courses and the often extracurricular media they produce [are] excellent ways to teach a vast range of high school, junior high/middle school, and even elementary school content" (Bowen and Tantillo). As school districts across the country become standards-based, it is imperative that journalism courses be recognized for their ability to meet the NCTE/IRA standards.

More than that, journalism helps "students become better thinkers, better communicators, and, as a result, better citizens" (Bowen and Tantillo).

The Journalism Education Association maintains its relationship with NCTE through the Assembly for Advisers of Student Publications. This assembly, which includes all members of the Journalism Education Association, serves advisers of student media by supporting free and responsible scholastic journalism; by providing resources and educational opportunities; by promoting professionalism; by encouraging and rewarding student excellence and teacher achievement; and by fostering an atmosphere that encompasses diversity yet builds unity.

Publication is an essential part of the writing process. Ensio and Boxeth comment on the enormous value of publishing to any writing program: "Not only does publication encourage students to write by creating purpose and vision, but it also serves to improve writing skills." Writing is vital to all publications, whether print, broadcast, or digital media.

In its *Writing Framework and Specification for the 1998 National Assessment of Educational Progress,* the National Assessment Governing Board recognizes the benefits of student publishing:

Developing student writers are expected to achieve an increasingly broad and deep knowledge and understanding of the value of writing in their lives, of their own individual writing processes, of the range of writing strategies available to them, and of the benefits of sharing and publishing their writing for a wider audience.

Furthermore, "Publications work is authentic assessment at its best: a synthesis of analysis and critical thinking, planning, and relating to an audience beyond the classroom, and performance-based outcomes. Student work leads naturally to a portfolio of specific completed tasks, and publications skills positively support school-to-career progress" (Graff).

It is important to note that a body of research provides data showing that students who participate in journalism programs do better on testing and college language arts courses. In *Journalism Kids Do Better* (Dvorak, Lain, Dickson), research shows students who take journalistic writing courses score higher on the Advanced Placement English Language and Composition exam than students who take only AP or honors English courses. They also score higher on college entrance exams such as the ACT. "We've done a number of research studies that show that high school journalism is equal to or exceeds standard English [courses], Dvorak said. "Journalism students' writing skills, their sensitivity to audience, their use of grammar, punctuation, spelling, their concern with accuracy, their use of sources -- all of these things tended to be significantly higher in their performances."

Related Information:
It has been twenty years since the NCTE passed a resolution on accepting journalism courses in English curricula. In the intervening years, journalism programs have responded to the changing nature of publishing and have diversified into a variety of media, including on-line, print, and broadcasting despite recent pressures seeking their extinction. Now is the time for the NCTE to recognize and promote journalism as a vital part of the discipline of English.

Works Cited:
Bowen, Candace Perkins, and Susan Hathaway Tantillo. *NCTE/IRA Standards in Classroom Journalism Projects.* (NCTE and JEA: Urbana, Ill.), 2002.

Dvorak, Jack, Larry Lain and Tom Dickson. *Journalism Kids Do Better: What Research Tells Us About High School Journalism.* (ERIC Clearinghouse on Reading, English, and Communication: Bloomington, Ind), 1994.

Ensio, Tobi C., and Krystal R. Boxeth. "The Effects of Publishing on Student Attitude toward Writing." (ERIC Research Report: University of Virginia), 2000.

Graff, Patricia. "Standards in the Journalism Classroom." *State of Scholastic Journalism: Principal's Guide to Scholastic Journalism.* (Quill and Scroll Foundation: University of Iowa), 2003.

Writing Framework and Specification for the 1998 National Assessment of Educational Progress. (National Assessment Governing Board: U.S. Department of Education), 1998.

Resolution
Be it therefore resolved, in light of recent cuts to journalism programs and challenges to the value of journalism and student media courses, that the National Council of Teachers of English develop a policy statement that reaffirms the value of journalism courses as part of the English language arts curriculum; supports maintaining, reinstating, or creating journalism programs and courses; and promotes the value of journalism programs that, under the guidance of a qualified journalism educator, give students a voice and allow them to exercise their constitutional right of free speech.

Be it further resolved, that NCTE working through the Assembly for Advisers of Student Publications, strengthen its relationship with the Journalism Education Association to provide leadership that supports journalism courses and programs at all levels of education; and highlight and support the professional contributions and continuing development of journalism educators through NCTE publications and other means.

[Adopted 2004]

JOURNALISM EDUCATION ASSOCIATION
ADVISER CODE OF ETHICS
Reprinted with permission of the Journalism Education Association.

Media advisers will:

Model standards of professional journalistic conduct to students, administrators and others.

Empower students to make decisions of style, structure and content by creating a learning atmosphere where students will actively practice critical thinking and decision-making.

Encourage students to seek out points of view and to explore a variety of information sources in their decision-making.

Ensure students have a free, robust and active forum for expression without prior review or restraint.

Emphasize the importance of accuracy, balance and clarity in all aspects of news gathering and reporting.

Show trust in students as they carry out their responsibilities by encouraging and supporting them in a caring learning environment.

Remain informed on press rights and responsibilities to provide students with sources of legal information.

Advise, not act as censors or decision makers.

Display professional and personal integrity in situations that might be construed as potential conflicts of interest.

Support free expression for others in local and larger communities.

Counsel students to avoid deceptive practices in all practices of publication work.

Model effective communications skills by continuously updating knowledge of media education.

[Valid as of September 2008]

JOURNALISM EDUCATION ASSOCIATION
POLICY ON PRIOR REVIEW
Reprinted with permission of the Journalism Education Association

The Journalism Education Association strongly opposes prior review of student expression.

Along with the Student Press Law Center, we believe no non-school sponsored or official publication, printed or electronic, should be reviewed by school administrators prior to distribution.

Prior review by administrators, school officials or teachers, other than publications advisers, is illogical, journalistically inappropriate and educationally unsound.

A journalism teacher working with students advises, counsels and supervises the editing process. Such internal discussions do not constitute prior review, so long a protected speech is not tampered with, and students make final content decisions.

In particular, prior review:

• violates the concept that it is the school's responsibility to teach and maintain, through example, the principles of democracy;

• gives school administrators, who are government officials, the power to decide in advance what people will read or know. Such officials are potential newsmakers, and their involvement with the news-making process can interfere with the public's right to know;

• contradicts every principle of sound journalism education and constitutes blatant but indirect censorship;

• negates the educational value of a trained, professionally active adviser and teacher working with students in a counseling, educational environment. Prior review simply makes the teacher an accessory, as if what is taught really doesn't matter;

• establishes the possibility of viewpoint discrimination, which destroys a free marketplace of ideas where a community can be fully informed and undermines all pretext of responsible journalism;

• leads toward self-censorship, the most chilling and pervasive form of censorship in schools. Fear like this can eliminate any change of critical thinking, decision making or respect for the opinions of others.

Instead we believe:

• a newspaper serves its readers only when it is editorially independent;

• good journalism occurs when a qualified faculty adviser, clear publications policies and professionally-oriented journalism curriculum exist;

• rights, not authority and discipline, prepare students for roles as citizens in a democracy;

• the potential for abuse is not sufficient reason to withhold a right or privilege;

• a student publication is a forum for ideas, and with ideas there is no clear right or wrong;

• a constructive criticism helps improve education;

• students become more aware of the country's values through a free press;

• students who make important decisions also strive to learn the history behind the country's principles and issues. Learning must be a dynamic process, one in which an adviser helps students adjust to change. Censorship interferes with this change and is the last resort of an educational system failing its present and future citizens.

Prior review is a weapon in the arsenal of censorship, and the Journalism Education Association opposes its use in America's schools.

[Adopted 1990]

JOURNALISM EDUCATION ASSOCIATION RESOLUTION REGARDING THE 25TH ANNIVERSARY OF RULING IN *HAZELWOOD SCHOOL DISTRICT V. KUHLMEIER*

Reprinted with permission of the Association for Education in Journalism and Mass Communication.

Resolution

This year marks 25 years since the Supreme Court significantly reduced the level of First Amendment protection afforded to students' journalistic speech in *Hazelwood School District v. Kuhlmeier.*

The Court's 5-3 majority concluded that schools could lawfully censor student expression in non-public-forum media for any "legitimate pedagogical purpose," and that among the recognized lawful purposes was the elimination of speech tending to "associate the school with any position other than neutrality on matters of political controversy."

In recognition of society's increased reliance on student news-gatherers to fulfill basic community information needs, and the importance of unfiltered information about the performance of educational institutions, In recognition of the well-documented misapplication of *Hazelwood* censorship authority to impede the teaching of professional journalistic values and practices, which include the willingness to question the performance of government institutions,

In recognition of the combined 150 years' experience of states with statutory student freepress guarantees, demonstrating that the *Hazelwood* level of administrative control is unnecessary for the advancement of legitimate educational objectives,

Be it resolved that:
The Journalism Education Association (JEA) joins with the Association of Education in Journalism and Mass Communication in stating that no legitimate pedagogical purpose is served by the censorship of student journalism on the grounds that it reflects unflatteringly on school policies and programs, that it candidly discusses sensitive social and political issues, or that it voices opinions challenging to majority views on matters of public concern. The censorship of such speech, or the punishment of media advisers based on that speech, is detrimental to effective learning and teaching, and it cannot be justified by reference to "pedagogical concerns."

Be it further resolved that:
JEA joins AEJMC in declaring that the *Hazelwood* level of control over student journalistic speech is clearly incompatible with the effective teaching of journalistic skills, values and practices, and that institutions of secondary and postsecondary education should forswear reliance on *Hazelwood* as a source of authority for the governance of student and educator expression.
[Adopted 2013]

SOCIETY OF PROFESSIONAL JOURNALISTS CODE OF ETHICS

Preamble

Members of the Society of Professional Journalists believe that public enlightenment is the forerunner of justice and the foundation of democracy. The duty of the journalist is to further those ends by seeking truth and providing a fair and comprehensive account of events and issues. Conscientious journalists from all media and specialties strive to serve the public with thoroughness and honesty. Professional integrity is the cornerstone of a journalist's credibility. Members of the Society share a dedication to ethical behavior and adopt this code to declare the Society's principles and standards of practice.

Seek Truth and Report It

Journalists should be honest, fair and courageous in gathering, reporting and interpreting information.

Journalists should:

– Test the accuracy of information from all sources and exercise care to avoid inadvertent error. Deliberate distortion is never permissible.

– Diligently seek out subjects of news stories to give them the opportunity to respond to allegations of wrongdoing.

– Identify sources whenever feasible. The public is entitled to as much information as possible on sources' reliability.

– Always question sources' motives before promising anonymity. Clarify conditions attached to any promise made in exchange for information. Keep promises.

– Make certain that headlines, news teases and promotional material, photos, video, audio, graphics, sound bites and quotations do not misrepresent. They should not oversimplify or highlight incidents out of context.

– Never distort the content of news photos or video. Image enhancement for technical clarity is always permissible. Label montages and photo illustrations.

– Avoid misleading re-enactments or staged news events. If re-enactment is necessary to tell a story, label it.

– Avoid undercover or other surreptitious methods of gathering information except when traditional open methods will not yield information vital to the public. Use of such methods should be explained as part of the story

– Never plagiarize.

– Tell the story of the diversity and magnitude of the human experience boldly, even when it is unpopular to do so.

– Examine their own cultural values and avoid imposing those values on others.

– Avoid stereotyping by race, gender, age, religion, ethnicity, geography, sexual orientation, disability, physical appearance or social status.

– Support the open exchange of views, even views they find repugnant.

– Give voice to the voiceless; official and unofficial sources of information can be equally valid.

– Distinguish between advocacy and news reporting. Analysis and commentary should be labeled and not misrepresent fact or context.

– Distinguish news from advertising and shun hybrids that blur the lines between the two.

– Recognize a special obligation to ensure that the public's business is conducted in the open and that government records are open to inspection.

Minimize Harm

Ethical journalists treat sources, subjects and colleagues as human beings deserving of respect.

Journalists should:
– Show compassion for those who may be affected adversely by news coverage. Use special sensitivity when dealing with children and inexperienced sources or subjects.

– Be sensitive when seeking or using interviews or photographs of those affected by tragedy or grief.

– Recognize that gathering and reporting information may cause harm or discomfort. Pursuit of the news is not a license for arrogance.

– Recognize that private people have a greater right to control information about themselves than do public officials and others who seek power, influence or attention. Only an overriding public need can justify intrusion into anyone's privacy.

– Show good taste. Avoid pandering to lurid curiosity.

– Be cautious about identifying juvenile suspects or victims of sex crimes.

– Be judicious about naming criminal suspects before the formal filing of charges.

– Balance a criminal suspect's fair trial rights with the public's right to be informed.

Act Independently

Journalists should be free of obligation to any interest other than the public's right to know.

Journalists should:

– Avoid conflicts of interest, real or perceived.

– Remain free of associations and activities that may compromise integrity or damage credibility.

– Refuse gifts, favors, fees, free travel and special treatment, and shun secondary employment, political involvement, public office and service in community organizations if they compromise journalistic integrity.

– Disclose unavoidable conflicts.

– Be vigilant and courageous about holding those with power accountable.

– Deny favored treatment to advertisers and special interests and resist their pressure to influence news coverage.

– Be wary of sources offering information for favors or money; avoid bidding for news.

Be accountable

Journalists are accountable to their readers, listeners, viewers and each other.

Journalists should:

– Clarify and explain news coverage and invite dialogue with the public over journalistic conduct.

– Encourage the public to voice grievances against the news media.

– Admit mistakes and correct them promptly.

– Expose unethical practices of journalists and the news media.

– Abide by the same high standards to which they hold others.

The SPJ Code of Ethics is voluntarily embraced by thousands of writers, editors and other news professionals. The present version of the code was adopted by the 1996 SPJ National Convention, after months of study and debate among the Society's members.

SOCIETY OF PROFESSIONAL JOURNALISTS
RESOLUTION ON HIGH SCHOOL PUBLICATIONS

Reprinted with permission of the Society of Professional Journalists.

WHEREAS, the Society of Professional Journalists is concerned about the First Amendment rights of all Americans, and

WHEREAS, the U.S. Supreme Court on January 13, 1988, ruled in *Hazelwood v. Kuhlmeier* that high school publications are subject to administrative control, and

WHEREAS, unnecessary restrictions on student expression inhibit understanding of the Bill of Rights among America's youth, and add to the general disregard for free speech guarantees in our democracy, and

WHEREAS, the Supreme Court previously guaranteed high school First Amendment rights to student speech that did not disrupt school activities and ensured that student journalists strive to achieve the ethical and legal responsibilities of professional journalists, and

WHEREAS, the *Hazelwood v. Kuhlmeier* decision has created a climate of self-censorship and caused many high school editors and publications' staff members to avoid sensitive issues for fear of punishment or academic reprisal, and

WHEREAS, *Hazelwood v. Kuhlmeier* does not require that school boards or principals exercise prior review or censor student publications,

THEREFORE it be resolved, that the 79th anniversary convention of the Society encourages state coordinating boards and local school boards to establish policies that encourage free expression in high school publications.

[Adopted 1988]

SOCIETY OF PROFESSIONAL JOURNALISTS
CAMPUS MEDIA STATEMENT

Reprinted with permission of the Society of Professional Journalists.

Student media are designated public forums, and free from censorship and advance approval of content. Because content and funding are unrelated, and because the role of adviser does not include advance review of content, student media are free to develop editorial policies and news coverage with the understanding that students and student organizations speak only for themselves. Administrators, faculty, staff or other agents shall not consider the student media's content when making decisions regarding the media's funding or faculty adviser.

[Adopted 2005]

STUDENT PRESS LAW CENTER
MODEL GUIDELINES FOR HIGH SCHOOL STUDENT MEDIA

© 2008-13 Student Press Law Center. Permission to reproduce with attribution for noncommericial purposes is granted.

Note: Model Guidelines for College Student Media are available at: www.splc.org/collegeguidelines

I. Statement of policy

Freedom of expression and press freedom are fundamental values in a democratic society. The mission of any institution committed to preparing productive citizens must include teaching students these values, both by lesson and by example.

As determined by the courts, student exercise of freedom of expression and press freedom is protected by both state and federal law, especially by the First Amendment to the United States Constitution. Accordingly, school officials are responsible for encouraging and ensuring freedom of expression and press freedom for all students.

It is the policy of the _____ Board of Education that (newspaper), (yearbook), (literary magazine) and (electronic or online media), the official, school-sponsored student media of _____ High School have been established as forums for student expression and as voices in the uninhibited, robust, free and open discussion of issues. Each medium should provide a full opportunity for students to inquire, question and exchange ideas. Content should reflect all areas of student interest, including topics about which there may be dissent or controversy.

It is the policy of the _____ Board of Education that student journalists shall have the right to determine the content of student media. Accordingly, the following guidelines relate only to establishing grounds for disciplinary actions subsequent to publication.

II. Official student media

A. Responsibilities of Student Journalists

Students who work on official, school-sponsored student publications or electronic media determine the content of their respective publications and are responsible for that content. These students should:

1. Determine the content of the student media;
2. Strive to produce media based upon professional standards of accuracy, objectivity and fairness;
3. Review material to improve sentence structure, grammar, spelling and punctuation;
4. Check and verify all facts and verify the accuracy of all quotations; and
5. In the case of editorials or letters to the editor concerning controversial issues, determine the need for rebuttal comments and opinions and provide space therefore if appropriate.

B. Unprotected Expression

The following types of student expression will not be protected:

1. Material that is "obscene as to minors." Obscene as to minors is defined as material that meets all three of the following requirements:
    (a) the average person, applying contemporary community standards, would find that the publication, taken as a whole, appeals to a minor's prurient interest in

sex; and

(b) the publication depicts or describes, in a patently offensive way, sexual conduct such as ultimate sexual acts (normal or perverted), masturbation and lewd exhibition of the genitals; and;

(c) the work, taken as a whole, lacks serious literary, artistic, political or scientific value.

Indecent or vulgar language is not obscene.

[Note: Most states have statutes defining what is "obscene as to minors." If such a statute is in force in your state, it should be substituted in place of section II(B)(1).]

2. Libelous material. Libelous statements are provably false and unprivileged statements of fact that do demonstrated injury to an individual's or business's reputation in the community. If the allegedly libeled party is a "public figure" or "public official" as defined below, then school officials must show that the false statement was published "with actual malice," i.e., that the student journalists knew that the statement was false or that they published it with reckless disregard for the truth — without trying to verify the truthfulness of the statement.

(a) A public official is a person who holds an elected or appointed public office and exercises a significant amount of governmental authority.

(b) A public figure is a person who either has sought the public's attention or is well known because of personal achievements or actions.

(c) School employees will be considered public officials or public figures in relationship to articles concerning their school-related activities.

(d) When an allegedly libelous statement concerns an individual who is not a public official or a public figure, school officials must show that the false statement was published willfully or negligently, i.e., the student journalist who wrote or published the statement has failed to exercise reasonably prudent care.

(e) Students are free to express opinions. Specifically, a student may criticize school policy or the performance of teachers, administrators, school officials and other school employees.

3. Material that will cause "a material and substantial disruption of school activities."

(a) Disruption is defined as student rioting, unlawful seizures of property, destruction of property, or substantial student participation in a school boycott, sit-in, walk-out or other related form of activity. Material such as racial, religious or ethnic slurs, however distasteful, is not in and of itself disruptive under these guidelines. Threats of violence are not materially disruptive without some act in furtherance of that threat or a reasonable belief and expectation that the author of the threat has the capability and intent of carrying through on that threat in a manner that does not allow acts other than suppression of speech to mitigate the threat in a timely manner. Material that stimulates heated discussion or debate does not constitute the type of disruption prohibited.

(b) For student media to be considered disruptive, specific facts must exist upon which one could reasonably forecast that a likelihood of immediate, substantial material disruption to normal school activity would occur if the material were further distributed or has occurred as a result of the material's distribution or dissemination. Mere undifferentiated fear or apprehension of disturbance is not enough; school administrators must be able affirmatively to show substantial facts that reasonably support a forecast of likely disruption.

(c) In determining whether student media is disruptive, consideration must be given to the context of the distribution as well as the content of the material. In this regard, consideration should be given to past experience in the school with similar material, past experience in the school in dealing with and supervising the students in the school, current events influencing student attitudes and behavior and whether there have been any instances of actual or threatened disruption prior to or contemporaneously with the dissemination of the student publication in question.

(d) School officials must protect advocates of unpopular viewpoints.

(e) "School activity" means educational student activity sponsored by the school and includes, by way of example and not by way of limitation, classroom work, official assemblies and other similar gatherings, school athletic contests, band concerts, school plays and scheduled in-school lunch periods.

C. Legal Advice

1. If, in the opinion of a student editor, student editorial staff or faculty adviser, material proposed for publication may be "obscene," "libelous" or would cause an "immediate, material and substantial disruption of school activities," the legal opinion of a practicing attorney should be sought. The services of the attorney for the local newspaper or the free assistance of the Student Press Law Center (703-807-1904) are recommended.

2. Any legal fees charged in connection with the consultation will be paid by the board of education.

3. The final decision of whether the material is to be published will be left to the student editor or student editorial staff.

D. Protected Speech

1. School officials cannot:
   a. Ban student expression solely because it is controversial, takes extreme, "fringe" or minority opinions, or is distasteful, unpopular or unpleasant;

   b. Ban the publication or distribution of material relating to sexual issues including, but not limited to, virginity, birth control and sexually-transmitted diseases (including AIDS);

   c. Censor or punish the occasional use of indecent, vulgar or so called "four-letter" words in student publications;

   d. Prohibit criticism of the policies, practices or performance of teachers, school officials, the school itself or of any public officials;

   e. Cut off funds to official student media because of disagreement over editorial policy;

   f. Ban student expression that merely advocates illegal conduct without proving that such speech is directed toward and will actually cause imminent unlawful action.

   g. Ban the publication or distribution by students of material written by non-students;

h. Prohibit the endorsement of candidates for student office or for public office at any level.

2. Commercial Speech

Advertising is constitutionally protected expression. Student media may accept advertising. Acceptance or rejection of advertising is within the purview of the publication staff, which may accept any ads except those for products or services that are illegal for all students. Ads for political candidates and ballot issues may be accepted; however publication staffs are encouraged to solicit ads from all sides on such issues.

E. Online Student Media and Use of Electronic Information Resources

1. Online Student Media.

Online media, including Internet-based Web sites, e-mail, listserves and discussion groups, may be used by students like any other communications media to reach both those within the school and those beyond it. All official, school-sponsored online student publications are entitled to the same protections and are subject to no greater limitations than other student media, as described in this policy.

2. Electronic Information Resources

Student journalists may use electronic information resources, including Internet-based Web sites, e-mail, listserves and discussion groups, to gather news and information, to communicate with other students and individuals and to ask questions of and consult with sources. School officials will apply the same criteria used in determining the suitability of other educational and information resources to attempts to remove or restrict student media access to online and electronic material. Just as the purchase, availability and use of media materials in a classroom or library does not indicate endorsement of their contents by school officials, neither does making electronic information available to students imply endorsement of that content.

Although faculty advisers to student media are encouraged to help students develop the intellectual skills needed to evaluate and appropriately use electronically available information to meet their newsgathering purposes, advisers are not responsible for approving the online resources used or created by their students.

3. Acceptable Use Policies

The Board recognizes that the technical and networking environment necessary for online communication may require that school officials define guidelines for student exploration and use of electronic information resources. The purpose of such guidelines will be to provide for the orderly, efficient and fair operation of the school's online resources. The guidelines may not be used to unreasonably restrict student use of or communication on the online media.

Such guidelines may address the following issues: file size limits, password management, system security, data downloading protocol, use of domain names, use of copyrighted software, access to computer facilities, computer hacking, computer etiquette and data privacy.

III. Adviser job security

The student media adviser is not a censor. No person who advises a student publication will be fired, transferred or removed from the advisership by reason of his or her refusal to exercise editorial control over student media or to otherwise suppress the protected free expression of student journalists.

IV. Non-school-sponsored media

A. Non-school-sponsored student media and the students who produce them are entitled to the protections provided in section II(D) of this policy. In addition, school officials may not ban the distribution of non-school-sponsored student media on school grounds. However, students who distribute material described in section II(B) of this policy may be subject to reasonable discipline after distribution at school has occurred.

   1. School officials may reasonably regulate the time, place and manner of distribution.
     (a) Non-school-sponsored media will have the same rights of distribution as official student media;
     (b) "Distribution" means dissemination of media to students at a time and place of normal school activity, or immediately prior or subsequent thereto, by means of handing out free copies, selling or offering copies for sale, accepting donations for copies of the media or displaying the media in areas of the school which are generally frequented by students.

   2. School officials cannot:
     (a) Prohibit the distribution of anonymous literature or other student media or require that it bear the name of the sponsoring organization or author;
     (b) Ban the distribution of student media because it contains advertising;
     (c) Ban the sale of student media; or
     (d) Create regulations that discriminate against non-school-sponsored media or interfere with the effective distribution of sponsored or non-sponsored media.

B. These regulations do not apply to media independently produced or obtained and distributed by students off school grounds and without school resources. Such material is fully protected by the First Amendment and is not subject to regulation by school authorities. Reference to or minimal contact with a school will not subject otherwise independent media, such as an independent, student-produced Web site, to school regulation.

V. Prior restraint

No student media, whether non-school-sponsored or official, will be reviewed by school administrators prior to distribution or withheld from distribution. The school assumes no liability for the content of any student publication, and urges all student journalists to recognize that with editorial control comes responsibility, including the responsibility to follow professional journalism standards each school year.

VI. Circulation

These guidelines will be included in the handbook on student rights and responsibilities and circulated to all students.

[Valid as of September 2013]

SAMPLE OPEN RECORDS REQUEST LETTER

Note: The highlighted portions should be changed to conform to your state's open records law and the specifics of your situation. An automated version of this form can be found at: www.splc.org/foiletter

A complete list of citations to state open records laws is available at: www.splc.org/openrecordlaws

September 1, 2013

Mr. Norman Mallard
Superintendent of Schools
Your School District
Your City, Anystate 00000

Dear **Mr. Mallard:**

Pursuant to the state open records law, **Anystate Rev. Stat. secs. 40.5 to 43.1,** I write to request access to and a copy of the **1994-95 school year budget** and other documents prepared or collected by your office relating to **the amount of money spent on male and female extra-curricular athletic programs this school year.**

I agree to pay any reasonable copying fee not more than **$3**. If the cost to me would be greater than that amount, please notify me.

As provided by the open records laws, I will expect your response within **ten (10) business days.**

If you choose to deny this request, please provide a written explanation for the denial including the specific statutory exemption for your action. Also, please provide any reasonably segregable portion of the records requested that are not exempt.

I request these records on behalf of **the student newspaper,** *Campus Voice.* Please be advised that we are prepared to pursue whatever legal remedy necessary to obtain our legal right of access to the requested records. I would note that willful violation of the open records law can result **in a fine of up to $500 and the award of court costs and attorneys fees.**

Thank you for your assistance.

Sincerely,

Ally Hiestand
Editor
Campus Voice
Your School
Your City, Anystate 00000

SAMPLE RELEASE FORM FOR MINORS

This is a sample release form for the non-commercial use of material provided by a minor to student media. Its primary purpose is to protect student media from claims of invasion of privacy or libel. It is assumed here that the minor is capable of providing informed consent. For very young children or other individuals incapable of fully understanding the nature and ramifications of their consent, the signature of a parent of legal guardian is required.

This form is meant to provide general guidance only and is neither intended nor represented as a substitute for obtaining case-specific advice from a licensed, local practicing attorney experienced in media law. The Student Press Law Center accepts no responsibility for liability that may result from the publication of unlawful material.

RELEASE

I hereby grant *The Student Times* permission to use any or all information obtained during the interview conducted on <u>March 14, 2008</u>, and in subsequent contacts, related to <u>my experiences as a teenage mother</u>. I also grant *The Student Times* permission to use any photograph or likeness of me taken by *The Student Times* photographers.

I understand that information from my interview and any photos may be used in a story to be published in *The Student Times*, the student newspaper at Central High School. I understand *The Student Times* is distributed both on school, throughout the community and nationally, for example, to paid mail subscribers and at student press conventions. I also understand that the story may be reproduced on *The Student Times* Web site, which can be read by anyone in the world with access to the Internet, and may be available for years to come. I have been advised by *The Student Times* staff that, as a minor, I may wish to discuss my decision to consent to such publication with my parents and others whose opinions I respect. I am providing permission to *The Student Times* to use my information and photographs of my own free will because I believe others may benefit from knowing of my experiences.

Specifically, my permission includes the following:

(1) The right to publish and republish, at any time, the above information or photos in *The Student Times*, on *The Student Times* Web site and in any subsequent medium for any noncommercial purpose, including promotion of *The Student Times*;

(2) The right of *The Student Times* or individual authors or photographers to copyright such information or photographs in their own name;

(3) The right of *The Student Times* to use my name in connection with such information or photos if it chooses.

I waive any right to inspect or approve the finished story or stories, photographs or other uses of my information that may be published.

In consideration of my participation, I understand that, at my request, *The Student Times* will provide me with up to ten copies of any issue that contains information or photographs related to me at no charge.

I hereby release and discharge *The Student Times*, its staff members, Central School District and its employees from any claims and demands arising out of or in connection with the use of the information or photographs described above, including any claims for libel or invasion of privacy.

I have read the above release prior to signing it and am fully familiar with its provisions.

Name (print full name):_____
Signature:_____
Date:_____
Address:_____
City, State, Zip:_____
Telephone:_____

[If a parent or guardian also signs, the following should be included:
I,_____[print full name]_____, am the parent/legal guardian of the individual named above. I have read this release and approve its terms.
Signature_____:
Date:_____]

Witness (print full name):_____
Signature:_____
Date:_____

STATE STUDENT FREE EXPRESSION LAWS

Arkansas Student Publications Act
Citation: Ark. Stat. Ann. Secs. 6-18-1201-1204

Section 6-18-1201. Title. This act shall be known and cited as the "Arkansas Student Publications Act."

Section 16-18-1202. Each school board shall adopt rules and regulations in the form of written student publications policy developed in conjunction with the student publication advisor(s) and the appropriate school administrator(s), consistent with the other provisions of this subchapter, which shall include reasonable provisions for the time, place, and manner of distributing student publications. Such policy shall be in place by January 1, 1996.

Section 6-18-1203. Student publications policies shall recognize that students may exercise their right of expression, within the framework outlined in Section 6-18-1202 of this act. This right includes expression in school-sponsored publications, whether such publications are supported financially by the school or by use of school facilities, or are produced in conjunction with a class, except as provided in Section 6-18-1204 of this act.

Section 6-18-1204. Student publications policies shall recognize that truth, fairness, accuracy, and responsibility are essential to the practice of journalism, and that the following types of publications by students are not authorized:
  (1) publications that are obscene as to minors, as defined by state law;

  (2) publications that are libelous or slanderous, as defined by state law;

  (3) publications that constitute an unwarranted invasion of privacy, as defined by state law; or

  (4) publications that so incite students as to create: (A) a clear and present danger of the commission of unlawful acts on school premises; (B) or the violations of lawful school regulations; (C) or the material and substantial disruption of the orderly operation of the school.

California Student Free Expression Law
Citation: Cal. Educ. Code Sec. 48907

Section 48907 - Student exercise of free expression. Students of the public schools shall have the right to exercise freedom of speech and of the press including, but not limited to, the use of bulletin boards, the distribution of printed materials or petitions, the wearing of buttons, badges, and other insignia, and the right of expression in official publications, whether or not such publications or other means of expression are supported financially by the school or by use of school facilities, except that expression shall be prohibited which is obscene, libelous, or slanderous. Also prohibited shall be material which so incites students as to create a clear and present danger of the commission of unlawful acts on school premises or the violation of lawful school regulations, or the substantial disruption of the orderly operation of the school.

Each governing board of a school district and each county board of education shall adopt rules and regulations in the form of a written publications code, which shall include reasonable provisions for the time, place, and manner of conducting such activities within its respective jurisdiction.

Student editors of official school publications shall be responsible for assigning and editing the news, editorial, and feature content of their publications subject to the limitations of this section. However, it shall be the responsibility of a journalism adviser or advisers of student publications within each school to supervise the production of the student staff, to maintain professional standards of English and journalism, and to maintain the provisions of this section.

There shall be no prior restraint of material prepared for official school publications except insofar as it violates this section. School officials shall have the burden of showing justification without undue delay prior to any limitation of student expression under this section.

"Official school publications" refers to materials produced by students in the journalism, newspaper, yearbook, or writing classes and distributed to the student body either free or for a fee.

Nothing in this section shall prohibit or prevent any governing board of a school district from adopting otherwise valid rules and regulations relating to oral communication by students upon the premises of each school.

Note: In addition to Section 48907, which protects the free press rights of public high school student journalists, California students are also covered by a number of other laws that protect their free expression rights, including:

Calif. Educ. Code Section 48950 (public and private high school students)
Calif. Educ. Code Section 66301 (public college student media)
Calif. Educ. Code Section 76120 (public community college students)
Calif. Educ. Code Section 94367 (private college students)
California Penal Code Section 490.7 (newspaper theft law)

The full-text of statutes are available in the SPLC Web site's Law Library (www.splc.org/law_library.asp).

Colorado Student Free Expression Law
Citation: Colo. Rev. Stat. Sec. 22-1-120

Section 22-1-120 — Rights of free expression for public school students
(1) The general assembly declares that students of the public schools shall have the right to exercise freedom of speech and of the press, and no expression contained in a student publication, whether or not such publication is school-sponsored, shall be subject to prior restraint except for the types of expression described in subsection (3) of this section. This section shall not prevent the advisor from encouraging expression which is consistent with high standards of English and journalism.

(2) If a publication written substantially by students is made generally available throughout a public school, it shall be a public forum for students of such school.

(3) Nothing in this section shall be interpreted to authorize the publication or distribution by students of the following:

(a) Expression that is obscene;

(b) Expression that is libelous, slanderous, or defamatory under state law;

(c) Expression that is false as to any person who is not a public figure or involved in a matter of public concern; or

(d) Expression that creates a clear and present danger of the commission of unlawful acts, the violation of lawful school regulations, or the material and substantial disruption of the orderly operation of the school or that violates the rights of others to privacy or that threatens violence to property or persons.

(4) The board of education of each school district shall adopt a written publications code, which shall be consistent with the terms of this section, and shall include reasonable provisions for the time, place, and manner of conducting free expression within the school district's jurisdiction. The publications code shall be distributed, posted, or otherwise made available to all students and teachers at the beginning of each school year.

(5)

(a) Student editors of school-sponsored student publications shall be responsible for determining the news, opinion, and advertising content of their publications subject to the limitations of this section. It shall be the responsibility of the publications advisor of school-sponsored student publications within each school to supervise the production of such publications and to teach and encourage free and responsible expression and professional standards for English and journalism.

(b) For the purposes of this section, "publications advisor" means a person whose duties include the supervision of school-sponsored student publications.

(6) If participation in a school-sponsored publication is part of a school class or activity for which grades or school credits are given, the provisions of this section shall not be interpreted to interfere with the authority of the publications advisor for such school-sponsored publications to establish or limit writing assignments for the students working with the publication and to otherwise direct and control the learning experience that the publication is intended to provide.

(7) No expression made by students in the exercise of freedom of speech or freedom of the press shall be deemed to be an expression of school policy, and no school district or employee, or parent, or legal guardian, or official of such school district shall be held liable in any civil or criminal action for any expression made or published by students.

(8) Nothing in this section shall be construed to limit the promulgation or enforcement of lawful school regulations designed to control gangs. For the purposes, of this section, the definition of "gang" shall be the definition found in section 19-1-103 (52), C.R.S.

Note: Colorado students are also protected by the state's newspaper theft law, Colorado Rev. Stat. Sec. 18-4-419, the full text of which is available in the SPLC Web site's Law Library (www.splc.org/law_library.asp).

Illinois College Campus Press Act
Citation: 110 ILCS 13

Section 1. Short title. This Act may be cited as the College Campus Press Act.

Section 5. Definitions. For purposes of this Act:

"Campus media" means any matter that is prepared, substantially written, published, or broadcast by students at State-sponsored institutions of higher learning, that is distributed or generally made available, either free of charge or for a fee, to members of the student body, and that is prepared under the direction of a student media adviser. "Campus media" does not include media that is intended for distribution or transmission solely in the classrooms in which it is produced.

"Campus policy" means the views and positions of State-sponsored institutions of higher learning promulgated by administrators, officials, or other agents of these institutions.

"Collegiate media adviser" means a person who is employed, appointed, or designated by the State-sponsored institution of higher learning to supervise or provide instruction relating to campus media.

"Collegiate student editor" means a student at a State-sponsored institution of higher learning who edits information prepared by collegiate student journalists for dissemination in campus media.

"Collegiate student journalist" means a student at a State-sponsored institution of higher learning who gathers, compiles, writes, photographs, records, or prepares information for dissemination in campus media.

"Prevailing party" includes any party who obtains some of his or her requested relief through judicial judgment in his or her favor, who obtains some of his or her requested relief through a settlement agreement approved by the court, or whose pursuit of a non-frivolous claim was a catalyst for a unilateral change in position by the opposing party relative to the relief sought.

"State-sponsored institution of higher learning" means the University of Illinois, Southern Illinois University, Chicago State University, Eastern Illinois University, Governors State University, Illinois State University, Northeastern Illinois University, Northern Illinois University, Western Illinois University, and public community colleges subject to the Public Community College Act.

Section 10. Public forum. All campus media produced primarily by students at a State-sponsored institution of higher learning is a public forum for expression by the student journalists and editors at the particular institution. Campus media, whether campus-sponsored or noncampus-sponsored, is not subject to prior review by public officials of a State-sponsored institution of higher learning.

Section 15. Grammar and journalism standards. Collegiate student editors of campus media are responsible for determining the news, opinions, feature content, and advertising content of campus media. This Section does not prevent a collegiate media adviser from teaching professional standards of grammar and journalism to collegiate student journalists. A collegiate media adviser must not be terminated, transferred, removed, otherwise disciplined, or retaliated against for refusing to suppress protected free expression rights of collegiate student journalists and of collegiate student editors.

Section 20. Injunction and declaratory relief. A collegiate student enrolled in a State-sponsored institution of higher learning or a collegiate media advisor of a State-sponsored institution of higher learning may commence a civil action to obtain appropriate injunctive and declaratory relief as determined by a court for violation of Section 10 of this Act by such State-sponsored institution of higher learning. Upon motion, a court may award attorney's fees to a prevailing party in a civil action brought under this Section.

Section 25. Campus policy and speech distinguished. Expression made by a collegiate student journalist, collegiate student editor, or other contributor in campus media is neither an expression of campus policy nor speech attributable to a State-sponsored institution of higher learning.

Section 30. Discipline; unprotected speech. Nothing in this Act prohibits the imposition of discipline for harassment, threats, or intimidation, unless constitutionally protected, or for speech that is not constitutionally protected, including obscenity or incitement.

Section 35. Immunity. A State-sponsored institution of higher learning shall be immune from any lawsuit arising from expression actually made in campus media, with the exception of the institution's own expression.

Section 97. Severability. The provisions of this Act are severable under Section 1.31 of the Statute on Statutes.

Iowa Student Free Expression Law
Citation: Iowa Code Sec. 280.22

Section 280.22 - Student exercise of free expression

1. Except as limited by this section, students of the public schools have the right to exercise freedom of speech, including the right of expression in official school publications.

2. Students shall not express, publish, or distribute any of the following:
   a. Materials which are obscene.

   b. Materials which are libelous or slanderous under chapter 659.

   c. Materials which encourage students to do any of the following:
      (1) Commit unlawful acts.
      (2) Violate lawful school regulations.
      (3) Cause the material and substantial disruption of the orderly operation of the school.

3. There shall be no prior restraint of material prepared for official school publications except when the material violates this section.

4. Each board of directors of a public school shall adopt rules in the form of a written publications code, which shall include reasonable provisions for the time, place, and manner of conducting such activities within its jurisdiction. The board shall make the code available to the students and their parents.

5. Student editors of official school publications shall assign and edit the news, editorial, and feature content of their publications subject to the limitations of this section. Journalism advisers of students producing official school publications shall supervise the production of the student staff, to maintain professional standards of English and journalism, and to comply with this section.

6. Any expression made by students in the exercise of free speech, including student expression in official school publications, shall not be deemed to be an expression of school policy, and the public school district and school employees or officials shall not be liable in any civil or criminal action for any student expression made or published by students, unless the school employees or officials have interfered with or altered the content of the student speech or expression, and then only to the extent of the interference or alteration of the speech or expression.

7. "Official school publications" means material produced by students in the journalism, newspaper, yearbook, or writing classes and distributed to the student body either free or for a fee.

8. This section does not prohibit a board of directors of a public school from adopting otherwise valid rules relating to oral communications by students upon the premises of each school.

Kansas Student Publications Act

Citation: Kan. Stat. Ann. Sections 72.1504 - 72.150

72-1504. Citation of act. This act shall be known and may be cited as the student publications act.

72-1505. Definitions. As used in this act:

(a) "School district" means any public school district organized and operating under the laws of this state.

(b) "Student publication" means any matter which is prepared, substantially written, or published by students, which is distributed or generally made available, either free of charge or for a fee, to members of the student body, and which is prepared under the direction of a certified employee.

72-1506. Liberty of press protected; regulation authorized; review of material not restraint on publication; material not protected; responsibilities of editor and advisers; liability, immunity and limitations.

(a) The liberty of the press in student publications shall be protected. School employees may regulate the number, length, frequency, distribution and format of student publications. Material shall not be suppressed solely because it involves political or controversial subject matter.

(b) Review of material prepared for student publications and encouragement of the expression of such material in a manner that is consistent with high standards of English and journalism shall not be deemed to be or construed as a restraint on publication of the material or an abridgment of the right to freedom of expression in student publications.

(c) Publication or other expression that is libelous, slanderous or obscene or matter that commands, requests, induces, encourages, commends or promotes conduct that is defined by law as a crime or conduct that constitutes a ground or grounds for the suspension or expulsion of students as enumerated in K.S.A. 72-8901, and amendments thereto, or which creates material or substantial disruption of the normal school activity is not protected by this act.

(d) Subject to the limitations imposed by this section, student editors of student publications are responsible for determining the news, opinion, and advertising content of such publications. Student publication advisers and other certified employees who supervise or direct the preparation of material for expression in student publications are responsible for teaching and encouraging free and responsible expression of material and high standards of English and journalism. No such adviser or employee shall be terminated from employment, transferred, or relieved of duties imposed under this subsection for refusal to abridge or infringe upon the right to freedom of expression conferred by this act.

(e) No publication or other expression of matter by students in the exercise of rights under this act shall be deemed to be an expression of school district policy. No school district, member of the board of education or employee thereof, shall be held responsible in any civil or criminal action for any publication or other expression of matter by students in the exercise of rights under this act. Student editors and other students of a school district, if such student editors and other students have attained the age of majority, shall be held liable in any civil or criminal action for matter expressed in student publications to the extent of any such student editor's or other student's responsibility for and involvement in the preparation and publication of such matter.

Massachusetts Student Free Expression Law
Citation: Mass. Gen. Laws Ann. ch. 71, Section 82

Section 82 - The right of students to freedom of expression in the public schools of the commonwealth shall not be abridged, provided that such right shall not cause any disruption or disorder within the school. Freedom of expression shall include without limitation, the rights and responsibilities of students, collectively and individually, (a) to express their views through speech and symbols, (b) to write, publish, and disseminate their views, (c) to assemble peaceably on school property for the purpose of expressing their opinions. Any assembly planned by students during regularly scheduled school hours shall be held only at a time and place approved in advance by the school principal or his designee.

No expression made by students in the exercise of such rights shall be deemed to be an expression of school policy and no school officials shall be held responsible in any civil or criminal action for any expression made or published by the students.

For the purposes of this section and sections eighty-three to eighty-five, inclusive, the word student shall mean any person attending a public secondary school in the commonwealth. The word school official shall mean any member or employee of the local school committee.

Oregon Student Free Expression Law
Citation: Ore. Rev. Stat. sec. 351.649

351.649 Student journalists; student expression; civil action.

(1) For the purposes of this section:

(a) "Public institution of higher education" means: (A) A community college;(B) A state institution of higher education listed in ORS 352.002; and (C) The Oregon Health and Science University.

(b) "School-sponsored media" means materials that are prepared, substantially written, published or broadcast by student journalists, that are distributed or generally made available, either free of charge or for a fee, to members of the student body and that are prepared under the direction of a student media adviser. "School-sponsored media" does not include media intended for distribution or transmission solely in the classrooms in which they are produced.

(c) "Student journalist" means a student who gathers, compiles, writes, edits, photographs, records or prepares information for dissemination in school-sponsored media.

(d) "Student media adviser" means a person who is employed, appointed or designated by a public institution of higher education to supervise, or provide instruction relating to, school-sponsored media.

(2) Student journalists are responsible for determining the news, opinion, feature and advertising content of school-sponsored media. This subsection does not prevent a student media adviser from teaching professional standards of English and journalism to the student journalists.

(3) Nothing in this section may be interpreted to authorize expression by students that:

(a) Is libelous or slanderous;

(b) Constitutes an unwarranted invasion of privacy;

(c) Violates federal or state statutes, rules or regulations or state common law; or

(d) So incites students as to create a clear and present danger of: (A) The commission of unlawful acts on or off school premises; (B) The violation of school policies; or (C) The material and substantial disruption of the orderly operation of the school. A school official must base a forecast of material and substantial disruption on specific facts, including past experience in the school and current events influencing student behavior, and not on undifferentiated fear or apprehension.

(4) Any student enrolled in a public institution of higher education may commence a civil action to obtain damages under this subsection and appropriate injunctive or declaratory relief as determined by a court for a violation of subsection (2) of this section, the First Amendment to the United States Constitution or section 8, Article I of the Oregon Constitution. Upon a motion, a court may award $100 in damages and injunctive and declaratory relief to a prevailing plaintiff in a civil action brought under this subsection.

Pennsylvania Administrative Code:
Student Rights and Responsibilities
Citation: 22 Pa. Code Section 12.9

Section 12.9. Freedom of expression.

(a) The right of public school students to freedom of speech is guaranteed by the Constitution of the United states and the Constitution of the Commonwealth.

(b) Students shall have the right to express themselves unless the expression materially and substantially interferes with the educational process, threatens serious harm to the school or community, encourages unlawful activity or interferes with another individual's rights.

(c) Students may use publications, handbills, announcements, assemblies, group meetings, buttons, armbands and any other means of common communication, provided that the use of public school communications facilities shall be in accordance with the regulations of the authority in charge of those facilities.

(1) Students have the responsibility to obey laws governing libel and obscenity and to be aware of the full meaning of their expression.

(2) Students have the responsibility to be aware of the feelings and opinions of others and to give others a fair opportunity to express their views.

(d) Identification of the individual student or at least one responsible person in a student group may be required on posted or distributed materials.

(e) School officials may require students to submit for prior approval a copy of materials to be displayed, posted or distributed on school property.

(f) Bulletin boards must conform to the following:

(1) School authorities may restrict the use of certain bulletin boards.

(2) Bulletin board space should be provided for the use of students and student organizations.

(3) School officials may require that notices or other communications be officially dated before posting, and that the materials be removed after a prescribed reasonable time to assure full access to the bulletin boards.

(g) School newspapers and publications must conform to the following:

(1) Students have a right and are as free as editors of other newspapers to report the news and to editorialize within the provisions in paragraphs (4) and (5).

(2) School officials shall supervise student newspapers published with school equipment, remove obscene or libelous material and edit other material that would cause a substantial disruption or interference with school activities.

(3) School officials may not censor or restrict material simply because it is critical of the school or its administration.

(4) Prior approval procedures regarding copy for school newspapers must identify the individual to whom the material is to be submitted and establish a limitation on the time required to make a decision. If the prescribed time for approval elapses without a decision, the material shall be considered authorized for distribution.

(5) Students who are not members of the newspaper staff shall have access to its pages. Written criteria for submission of material by nonstaff members shall be developed and distributed to all students.

(h) The wearing of buttons, badges or armbands shall be permitted as another form of expression within the restrictions listed in subsection (c).

(i) School officials may set forth the time and place of distribution of materials so that distribution would not materially or substantially interfere with the requirements of appropriate discipline in the operation of the school.

(1) A proper time and place set for distribution is one that would give the students the opportunity to reach fellow students.

(2) The place of the activity may be restricted to permit the normal flow of traffic within the school and at exterior doors.

Washington Administrative Code: Student Rights
Citation: WAC 392-40-215

In addition to other rights established by law, each student served by or in behalf of a common school district shall possess the following substantive rights, and no school district shall limit these rights except for good and sufficient cause:

(1) No student shall be unlawfully denied an equal educational opportunity or be unlawfully

discriminated against because of national origin, race, religion, economic status, sex, pregnancy, marital status, previous arrest, previous incarceration, or a physical, mental or sensory handicap.

(2) All students possess the constitutional right to freedom of speech and press, the constitutional right to peaceably assemble and to petition the government and its representatives for a redress of grievances, the constitutional right to the free exercise of religion and to have their schools free from sectarian control or influence, subject to reasonable limitations upon the time, place, and manner of exercising such right.

(3) All students possess the constitutional right to be secure in their persons, papers, and effects against unreasonable searches and seizures.

(4) All students shall have the right to be free from unlawful interference in their pursuit of an education while in the custody of a common school district.

(5) No student shall be deprived of the right to an equal educational opportunity in whole or in part by a school district without due process of law.

The foregoing enumeration of rights shall not be construed to deny or disparage other rights set forth in the constitution and the laws of the state of Washington or the rights retained by the people.

Washington, D.C. Municipal Regulations: Student Bill of Rights
Citation: DCMR 5-E2401

2401.1 Each student has the right to a meaningful public education, the maintenance of high educational standards, and a system of public education that adequately and equitably seeks to meet the need of the individual student.

2401.2 Each student has the right to access to a meaningful curriculum and the right to voice his or her opinions and provide input into the development of the public school curriculum.

2401.3 Each student has the right to express his or her views in matters that affect the quality and content of the education that is provided, including but not limited to, the right to participate individually or through elected representatives in the development of the rules and regulations to which the student is subject.

2401.4 Each student has the right to adequate and timely notice of all rules, regulations, policies and sanctions to which the student is subject. All rules and regulations shall be available in writing and be accessible to all students. A copy of the rules of the Board of Education shall be maintained in the library, guidance office, or other appropriate place in each public school in the District of Columbia. A copy of § 2401 (Student Bill of Rights) shall be provided to each student upon registration at a public school in the District of Columbia

2401.5 Each student has the right to physical safety and the protection of personal property, including the right to safe and sanitary school buildings and facilities.

2401.6 Each student has the right to adequate consultation with teachers, counselors, administrators, and other school personnel.

2401.7 Each student has the right to free election of peers in student organizations, as well as the right to seek and hold office.

2401.8 Each student and the student's parents or authorized representatives have the right to inspect and review the official records of the school system that relate directly to the individual student, as provided in § 2601. A student or the student's parent or guardian shall be notified if adverse comments are placed in his or her official records.

2401.9 Students have the right to participate in school activities without being subject to unlawful discrimination because of race, color, religion, national origin, sex, age, marital status, personal appearance, sexual orientation, family responsibilities, political affiliation, handicapping condition, or any other basis of unlawful discrimination under the laws of the District of Columbia.

2401.10   Where access to participation in programs or activities is on a competitive basis, each student has the right to an opportunity to compete on an equal basis.

2401.11   A student has the right to refuse to participate in school activities which are contrary to the student's moral, religious, or political beliefs.

2401.12   Each student shall have the right to respect from teachers, other students, administrators, and other school personnel, and shall not be subject to ridicule, harassment, or any punishment that is demeaning or derogatory. No student shall be subject to corporal punishment.

2401.13   Principals, assistant principals, school security personnel and other designated individuals may conduct, or cause to be conducted, such searches of students as are reasonable to maintain the security, discipline and educational atmosphere of a school building, event or program, in accordance with the provisions § 2404.

2401.14   Each student shall have the right to use reasonable physical means to defend himself or herself from assault or physical abuse, and shall not be subject to suspension for using limited, reasonable, physical means to restrain another person from physically assaulting or harming a third person.

2401.15   Each student has the right to present petitions, complaints, or grievances to school authorities and the right to receive prompt, authoritative replies from school officials regarding the disposition of the student's petitions, complaints, or grievances. The procedure for presenting complaints and grievances is set forth in § 2405.4 of this Chapter. The alternative procedure for presenting complaints alleging incidents of harassment and sexual harassment is set forth in § 2405.5 of this Chapter.

2401.16   Where a student is entitled to a hearing pursuant to this title, the hearing shall be impartial, and the student shall be afforded all other rights set forth in the hearing procedures.

2401.17   Each student shall have the right to exercise his or her constitutional rights of free speech, assembly, and expression without prior restraint, so long as the exercise of these rights does not substantially interfere with the rights of others.

2401.18   The exercise of the constitutional rights of free speech, assembly, and expression by students shall include, but is not necessarily limited to, the following:

(a)   Wearing political buttons, armbands, or other badges of symbolic expression;

(b)   Organizing and participating in political and social organizations;

(c)   Use of student bulletin boards without prior censorship, but not school bulletin boards without approval of the use which shall be reasonably provided by the schools;

(d)   Repealed.

(e)   Preparation and distribution of posters, newspapers, or other printed matter, on or off school grounds, and the reasonable use of the school public address system subject to standards adopted by the student government organization in cooperation with school officials; provided, that such distribution or use shall be limited to reasonable times before, during, and after school hours in order to prevent undue interference with classroom activities and the rights of others; and

(f)   Free expression and defense of views and opinions without having that expression affect the student's examinations, grades, academic achievement, or participation in extra-curricular activities.Additional Resources Available on the SPLC Web site

Automated Open Records Request Letter Generator
www.splc.org/foiletter

State Open Record Law Citations
www.splc.org/openrecordlaws

State Open Meeting Law Citations
www.splc.org/openmeetinglaws

Sample Press Release for Students Facing Censorship
www.splc.org/samplepr

SPLC Media Law Classroom Presentations
www.splc.org/presentations

SPLC Model Guidelines for College Student Media
www.splc.org/collegeguidelines

SPLC Model Student Free Expression Legislation
www.splc.org/modelfreepresslaws

State Student Free Expression Laws/Regulations
(As of September 2008, state free expression laws or regulations had been enacted in Arkansas, California, Colorado, Illinois, Iowa, Kansas, Massachusetts, Oregon, Pennsylvania and Washington. Legislation was pending in other states and will be added as they are enacted, so it is worth checking for updates.)

www.splc.org/studentfreepresslaws

SPLC Virtual Lawyer
http://www.splc.org/virtual_lawyer